ASIA PACIFIC FINANCIAL MARKETS IN COMPARATIVE PERSPECTIVE: ISSUES AND IMPLICATIONS FOR THE 21ST CENTURY

CONTEMPORARY STUDIES IN ECONOMICS AND FINANCIAL ANALYSIS

Series Editors: R.J. Thornton and J.R. Aronson

CONTEMPORARY STUDIES IN ECONOMICS AND
FINANCIAL ANALYSIS   VOLUME 86

ASIA PACIFIC FINANCIAL MARKETS IN COMPARATIVE PERSPECTIVE: ISSUES AND IMPLICATIONS FOR THE 21ST CENTURY

EDITED BY

THOMAS A. FETHERSTON

School of Business, University of Alabama at Birmingham, USA

JONATHAN A. BATTEN

Graduate School of Management, Macquarie University, Australia

*HG
187
A2A853
2005
web*

ELSEVIER

JAI

Amsterdam – Boston – Heidelberg – London – New York – Oxford
Paris – San Diego – San Francisco – Singapore – Sydney – Tokyo

AL

ELSEVIER B.V.	ELSEVIER Inc.	ELSEVIER Ltd	ELSEVIER Ltd
Radarweg 29	525 B Street, Suite 1900	The Boulevard, Langford	84 Theobalds Road
P.O. Box 211	San Diego	Lane, Kidlington	London
1000 AE Amsterdam,	CA 92101-4495	Oxford OX5 1GB	WC1X 8RR
The Netherlands	USA	UK	UK

First edition 2005

British Library Cataloguing in Publication Data
A catalogue record is available from the British Library.

ISBN-10: 0-7623-1258-0
ISBN-13: 978-0-7623-1258-0
ISSN: 1569-3759 (Series)

Transferred to digital printing 2007

CONTENTS

INVESTMENT PERFORMANCE

LIST OF CONTRIBUTORS

Zaleha Abdul Shukor	School of Accounting, Faculty of Economics and Business, Universiti Kebangsaan Malaysia, Bangi, Malaysia
Jonathan A. Batten	Macquarie Graduate School of Management, Macquarie University, Sydney, Australia
Bonnie Buchanan	Department of Finance, University of Melbourne, Victoria, Australia
Tyrone M. Carlin	Macquarie Graduate School of Management, Macquarie University, Sydney, Australia
Jianguo Chen	Department of Finance, Banking and Property, College of Business, Massey University, New Zealand
Wen-Kuei Chen	Graduate School of Management, I-Shou University, Taiwan
Jing Chi	Department of Finance, Banking and Property, Massey University, Palmerston North, New Zealand
Kevin James Daly	School of Economics & Finance, College of Law and Business, University of Western Sydney, Australia
Craig Alan Ellis	University of Western Sydney, Australia
Thomas A. Fetherston	School of Business, University of Alabama at Birmingham, AL, USA
Guy Ford	Macquarie Graduate School of Management, Macquarie University, Sydney, Australia

Abeyratna Gunasekarage   Department of Finance, Waikato
                              Management School, University of Waikato,
                              Hamilton, New Zealand

Pongsak Hoontrakul   Sasin Graduate Institute of Business
                              Administration, Chulalongkorn University,
                              Bangkok, Thailand

Muhd Kamil Ibrahim   Universiti Teknologi MARA, Shah Alam,
                              Malaysia

Justin W. Iu   School of Accounting, Economics
                              and Finance, Deakin University,
                              Australia

Bang Nam Jeon   Bennett S. LeBow College of Business, Drexel
                              University, PA, USA

Akiko Kamesaka   School of Business Administration, Aoyama
                              Gakuin University, Tokyo, Japan

Jagjit Kaur   Universiti Teknologi MARA, Shah Alam,
                              Malaysia

Colm Kearney   School of Business Studies, Institute for
                              International Integration Studies, Trinity
                              College Dublin, Ireland

Shu-Ling Lin   Department of International Trade and
                              Finance, Fu-Jen Catholic University, Taipei,
                              Taiwan

Ben R. Marshall   Department of Finance, Banking and
                              Property, College of Business, Massey
                              University, New Zealand

John McDermott   ANZ-National Bank, Wellington, New
                              Zealand

Hamezah Md Nor   School of Accounting, Faculty of Economics
                              and Business, Universiti Kebangsaan
                              Malaysia, Bangi, Malaysia

Cal Muckley

School of Business Studies, Trinity College Dublin, Ireland

Mukund Narayanamurti

School of Accounting, Economics and Finance, Deakin University, Australia

David Ng

Department of Accounting and Finance, Macquarie University, Sydney, Australia

Ben Petro

ANZ-National Bank, Wellington, New Zealand

David M. Power

Department of Accountancy and Business Finance, University of Dundee, Scotland, UK

Mehdi Sadeghi

Department of Accounting and Finance, Macquarie University, Sydney, Australia

Peter G. Szilagyi

Department of Finance, Tilburg University, Tilburg, The Netherlands

David Tripe

Massey University, Palmerston North, New Zealand

Yao-Chun Tsao

Cheng-Shiu University, I-Shou University, Taiwan

Xuan Vinh Vo

School of Economics & Finance, College of Law and Business, University of Western Sydney, Australia

Yun Wang

Performance Group, Commerce Commission, Wellington, New Zealand

Martin Young

Department of Finance, Banking and Property, Massey University, Palmerston North, New Zealand

Yang Zhang

Department of Finance, Banking and Property, College of Business, Massey University, New Zealand

ASIA PACIFIC FINANCIAL MARKETS IN COMPARATIVE PERSPECTIVE: ISSUES AND IMPLICATIONS FOR THE 21ST CENTURY

Jonathan A. Batten and Thomas A. Fetherston

OVERVIEW

The Asia Pacific region is a geographical appellation that many still feel with justification will be the dynamic economic arena for this century. Accepting this premise and acknowledging the importance of the role of finance in that development brings with it the imperative to gain a greater understanding of the unique financial characteristics of the region. This chapter has two major pursuits. The first goal is to provide some background on the various markets of the region. An understanding of institutional detail (size and scope) of the relevant markets affords a view that lends or detracts from the credibility of intermarket comparisons. An exposure to institutional detail also supplies information that may bear on the statistical results of the empirical analysis. The vital roles played by stock markets of pricing capital, issuing new shares, providing a liquidity-creating secondary feature, serving as a

Asia Pacific Financial Markets in Comparative Perspective: Issues and Implications for the 21st Century
Contemporary Studies in Economics and Financial Analysis, Volume 86, 1–25
Copyright © 2005 by Elsevier Ltd.
All rights of reproduction in any form reserved
ISSN: 1569-3759/doi:10.1016/S1569-3759(05)86001-2

vehicle for asset transfer and providing a linkage to international capital markets are as important to emerging markets as to developed countries. However, fixed income markets are still not as well developed in emerging markets and therefore an even heavier capital sourcing burden is placed on emerging stock markets. The Asia Pacific region derivatives markets (futures and options) play their risk-transfer role in equity and fixed income areas and are integral to the scene. The second pursuit in this chapter is to provide a thumbnail sketch of each of the contributions. The summary will include the nature of the empirical work, the type of methodology or statistical technique applied, and the results. In addition the results will be viewed in light of any reinforcement or digression from a priori expectations drawn from other markets. This volume contains 19 original research papers from 36 authors who represent major academic and financial institutions around the globe.

Traditional foreign exchange trading in Asian currencies generally recorded much faster growth than the global total between 2001 and 2004 (Table 1). Growth rates exceeding 100% were common (China, India, Indonesia, Korea, New Zealand and Taiwanese currencies). Renminbi and rupiah turnover increased particularly strongly. The main exceptions in this broad picture were the currencies of Hong Kong, Singapore and Malaysia where activity expanded more slowly than that of the Euro and the USD. Trading in the Japanese yen also grew relatively slowly over the same period, even by the standards of the major currencies. The rapid expansion in the trading of Asian currencies indicates a secular deepening of financial markets in the region. Currency derivatives markets – Cross-currency swaps and options have not been extensively traded in a number of Asian currencies (Table 2) and their absence is likely to impede further financial market development. However, where such markets have been established, they can show stronger turnover growth from their low bases than do more developed derivatives markets. The currency derivatives markets of Australia, China, Hong Kong, Korea, New Zealand, Taiwan and Thailand all grew faster than that of the Euro and USD since 2001.

The vital roles played by stock markets of pricing capital, issuing new shares, providing a liquidity-creating secondary feature, serving as a vehicle for asset transfer and providing a linkage to international capital markets are as important to the Asia Pacific region as to developed countries. However, fixed income markets are still not as well developed in emerging markets and therefore an even heavier capital sourcing burden is placed on emerging stock markets. Although the percentage of all countries' new equity raising for the Asia Pacific region for 2004 was down from 2003 the

Table 1. Traditional Foreign Exchange Market Turnover in Asia
Pacific, April 2004.

	Spot	Forward	Swap	Total	Growth since 2001 in (%)
			Daily Averages, in Millions of US Dollars		
Australian dollar	28,539	9,788	58,796	97,123	96
Chinese renminbi	992	811	9	1,812	5,303
Hong Kong dollar	6,827	2,221	24,133	33,181	21
Indian rupee	2,877	1,531	1,658	6,066	114
Indonesian rupiah	760	267	1,025	2,051	283
Japanese yen	130,382	47,135	181,715	359,231	35
Korean won	10,510	6,048	4,592	21,151	117
Malaysian ringgit	351	237	399	987	7
New Zealand dollar	4,018	1,462	12,181	17,661	163
Philippine peso	345	232	188	765	52
Singapore dollar	5,177	1,242	10,591	17,010	32
New Taiwan dollar	3,607	2,798	856	7,261	129
Thai baht	1,333	490	1,669	3,492	88
US dollar	528,639	170,357	874,083	1,573,080	48
Euro	272,887	88,243	298,231	659,361	49
Pound sterling	82,839	31,338	185,241	299,417	93
Canadian dollar	23,696	8,947	41,930	74,573	43

Source: BIS Quarterly Review, March 2005.

underlying trend in equity market share is up for the period 2002–2004 (see Table 3). In 2004 the Asia Pacific region raised slightly less than 20 percent of the equity capital for all countries. The absolute amount of new equity raised for the Asia Pacific region has grown year-over-year for the period 2002–2004.

The fixed income markets for the Asia Pacific region have grown over the three year period, 2002–2004 (see Table 4). However, the importance of the region expressed as a percentage of all countries international debt securities actually declined for the three year period.

CURRENCY ANALYSIS

In this paper, Kearney and Muckley examine the role of the yen in exchange-rate management in North and Southeast Asia. By excluding any dynamic adjustment in their models, previous researchers have assumed that

Table 2.   Turnover of Foreign Exchange Derivatives in Asia Pacific,
April 2004.

	Daily Averages, in Millions of US Dollars		Growth since 2001 (in %)	
	Cross-currency swaps	Options	Cross-currency swaps	Options
Australian dollar	1,573	8,543	208	150
Chinese renminbi	4	136	–	272,355
Hong Kong dollar	293	365	3	385
Indian rupee	97	100	10,162	–
Indonesian rupiah	24	7	93	–
Japanese yen	3,354	37,430	70	58
Korean won	342	579	645	265
Malaysian ringgit	11	1	–	–
New Zealand dollar	80	811	–21	1,397
Philippine peso	4	5	77	–
Singapore dollar	54	272	199	69
New Taiwan dollar	102	718	369	398
Thai baht	246	125	2,121	2,858
US dollar	17,605	92,276	196	94
Euro	9,732	51,085	344	95
Pound sterling	4,835	11,645	301	126
Canadian dollar	521	5,884	44	98

Source: BIS Quarterly Review, March 2005.

Table 3.   Equity Issues by Country and Region (Billions USD).

	2002	Percentage	2003	Percentage	2004	Percentage
All Countries	103	100(%)	120	100(%)	214.5	100(%)
Asia & Pacific	12	11.65	23.1	19.25	34.2	15.94
Australia	3.9	3.79	5.1	4.25	6.3	2.94
China	5.4	5.24	8.9	7.42	18.1	8.44
India	0.3	0.29	1.3	1.08	4.6	2.14
Indonesia	0.3	0.29	1.1	0.92	0.6	0.28
Malaysia	1.2	1.17	0.6	0.50	0.9	0.42
New Zealand	0.9	0.87	–	0.00	0.2	0.09
Papua New Guinea	0.1	0.10	0.2	0.17	–	0.00
Philippines	–	0.00	0.1	0.08	0.1	0.05
South Korea	1.6	1.55	1.2	1.00	5.4	2.52
Taiwan, China	3.1	3.01	8.3	6.92	3.4	1.59
Thailand	0.1	0.10	1.5	1.25	1	0.47

Source: BIS Quarterly Review, March 2005.

Table 4. International Debt Securities by Nationality of Issuer (In billions of US dollars).

	Amounts Outstanding		
	2002	2003	2004
All	9,189.60	11,661.80	13,928.00
Australia	137.5	189.3	257.1
Japan	248	269.6	298.3
United States	2,716.80	3,073.40	3,358.80
China	17.2	19.9	24.6
India	3.5	3.5	7
Indonesia	9	9	10
Malaysia	23.4	23.4	28.7
Philippines s	20.9	25.2	27
South Korea	54.6	63.9	74.5
Taiwan, China	12.4	19.7	24.5
Thailand	10.9	10	10.1
Asia & Pacific	537.4	633.5	761.8
Region as (%)	5.85	5.43	5.47

Source: BIS Quarterly Review, March 2005.

the monetary authorities adjust their exchange rates instantly to their preferred levels in relation to the world's main currencies. This is questionable, especially in studies that use either daily or weekly data to estimate their models. Central bankers throughout the world tend to meet at discrete intervals of at least a week to discuss and implement their foreign exchange policies. They like to have smooth exchange-rate movements, and they tend to adjust their exchange rates gradually. By failing to differentiate between short- and long-run multipliers, previously reported studies are mis-specified with possibly non-spherical errors. They overcome this by specifying a set of dynamic models that differentiate between the short- and long-run equilibrium responses of the monetary authorities. They consider long-run equilibrium responses only in this study. They model 9 Asian currencies (the Chinese yuan, the Hong Kong dollar, the Indonesian rupiah, the Korean won, the Malaysian ringgit, the Philippine peso, the Singapore dollar, the Taiwan dollar and the Thai baht) in response to the German mark, the Japanese yen, the UK pound and the US dollar. All their exchange rates are expressed in terms of the Swiss franc. They estimate their models using a general-to-specific estimation strategy (see Hendry & Krolzig (2001)) with Newey–West heteroscedastic- and autocorrelation-consistent significance tests (see Newey & West (1987)). They use a time-varying methodology. These models are estimated on a moving window of approximately 18 months in length over the period from November 1976 to December 2003.

They find that there has been a noticeable and significant rise in the influence of the US dollar on some of the region's currencies, combined with a decline in its influence on others since the Asian financial crisis of the late 1990s. This finding is at odds with McKinnon (2000) who describes a reversion to the pre-crisis regime after the Asian crisis. *Second*, they find that the Japanese yen was not a very influential regional currency during the decade prior to the Asian financial crisis. This contrasts with the findings of Frankel and Wei (1994), Kwan (1996), Zhou (1998) and Bowman (2004) among others who noted an emerging and significant yen influence as early as the late 1980s. Subsequent to the Asian crisis, however, the yen has gained influence on some of the region's currencies, with the notable exceptions of the Chinese yuan, the Hong Kong dollar and the Malaysian ringgit. This corroborates the findings of Gan (2000), Hernandez and Montiel (2002) and Bowman (2004), but is at odds with those of McKinnon (2000). *Third*, they find that the influence of the German mark on the region's currencies has grown significantly over time, which is not surprising in light of the growing trade linkages between Asia and Europe, while the influence of the UK sterling has diminished to almost zero from a low base. Overall, therefore, they find that the region continues to behave more like a US dollar block than a yen block, but that the declining influence of the US dollar since the late 1990s has been replaced by a growing influence of the German mark and the Japanese yen.

Numerous empirical studies suggest that foreign currency returns may not be independent (Xu & Gencay, 2003; Byers & Peel, 2001; Van De Gucht, Dekimpe, & Kwok, 1996; Muller et al., 1990) nor conform to a stable probability distribution (Nekhili, Altay-Salih and Gencay, 2002; Tucker & Scott, 1987; Wasserfallen & Zimmermann, 1985). In light of these findings a key empirical question concerns the effect that scaling the volatility of dependent processes will have on the pricing of related assets. The Ellis study provides an insight into this issue by investigating the long-term return properties of the spot USD/AUD. Several tests are first conducted for evidence of a scaling law in intraday USD/AUD returns. The economic implications of dependence in the returns series and the non-normality of the distribution of returns are then considered using the Garman and Kohlhagen-modified Black–Scholes model for valuing foreign currency options. The results suggest that the USD/AUD does not conform to a stable distribution and that as a result of differential scaling laws, Garman and

Kohlhagen option values using implied annual volatility will be consistently too high or too low.

The data examined comprise daily spot prices for the USD/AUD exchange rate for the period 01/01/1985 to 30/06/2004, a total of 4,724 observations. (For the method followed see Batten, Ellis, & Fetherston, 2000). Having formally defined the concept of linear rescaling and examined the origins of the '$T^{1/2}$ rule' for annualizing short-horizon volatility, three formal tests for scaling laws in the USD/AUD returns are applied. The results of these tests show that the long-term volatility of USD/AUD interday returns scales at approximately the square root of time. However in the shorter-term, weak evidence of a multi-fractal process in USD/AUD returns is provided. The economic implications for derivative asset pricing are then considered. Using the Garman and Kohlhagen modified Black–Scholes model for valuing foreign currency options, linearly rescaled volatility estimates are shown to misprice option values by as much as 1,905 basis points (12.5%) for at-the-money contracts. Further these results are shown to be highly sensitive to differences in the moneyness of the option. The findings are important since they demonstrate that even small violations of the assumption that foreign exchange rates follow a Brownian motion process can result in economic benefits or costs. However a word of caution should be made in interpreting dollar versus percentage differences in option values, since the latter have been seen to be exaggerated by very low values for out-of-the-money option contracts. Nonetheless, the results highlight the need for investors to consider the underlying distribution and independence of returns when using short-horizon returns to estimate long-horizon risk.

REGIONAL INTEGRATION

The Vo and Daly paper examines the long- and short-run relationships between Asian equity markets and a selection of advanced market economies covering a 10-year timeframe pre- and post- the 1997 Asian financial crisis. They attempt to provide insight to the question of the existence of the expected diversification benefits from investing in Asian equity markets that have changed since the Asian financial crisis of 1997. Given that significant changes have occurred across Asian capital markets since the crash, have the so-called benefits of international portfolio diversification across Asian equity markets changed with the reforms taking place across Asian capital markets? This paper is an extension of Daly (2003), which documents a significant increase in correlations and volatility transmission between equity markets during and after the 1997 stock market crash.

All data are daily closing prices from Datastream. The precise indices used are the Australia All Ordinaries Index, the French CAC 40 Price Index, the Germany DAX 30 Price Index, the Hong Kong Hang Seng Price Index, the Indonesia Jakarta SE Composite Price Index, the Japan Nikkei All Stock Price Index, the Korea SE Composite Price Index, the Malaysian Kuala Lumpur Composite Price Index, the Philippines SE Composite Price Index, the Singapore Straits Times Price Index, the Taiwan SE Composite Price Index, the Thailand Bangkok S.E.T. Price Index, the UK FTSE 100 Price Index and the United States S&P 500. The paper employs correlation, causality and cointegration techniques to describe the behavior of the above stock market indices. Vo and Daly's empirical results indicate that between 1993 and 1997, a period prior to the Asian Financial Crash, there is mixed evidence of cointegration ties between US equity market and Asian markets. Furthermore over the period covering 1998–2003, there appears to be no evidence of cointegration between Asian markets, the US and Australian markets. Finally, bivariate Granger causality tests revealed significant causality running from the US to all the Asian markets in both the pre- and post-Asian Financial crash.

The results have important implications for long-run diversification returns for a US or Australian investor contemplating investing in Asian financial markets. First, the Asian markets do not share a common stochastic trend with either the US or Australian equity market this indicating diversification benefits for long-term investors, this effect is particularly strong over the period covering the post-Asian financial crisis. Second, the ever-increasing pace of global financial integration indicates that equity return correlations will keep increasing and that would suggest that they be considered an important factor in asset allocation decisions in the future.

The Jeon paper investigates the East Asian economic/financial crisis, which broke out around July 1997, plunged the most rapidly growing and successful economies into financial chaos and deep economic depression. A remarkable feature of the Asian crisis was the degree to which it spread from Thailand to other countries in the region, including Indonesia, Malaysia, the Philippines and Korea, very quickly, in the span of a few months. There have been different explanations and proposals for why and how contagion spread so quickly in the region: macroeconomic similarities, trade links across countries, and cross-country financial links. The swift and global-scale contagion of the recent crises seem to support financial links, rather than trade links, as the key channel of contagion (Taylor, 1999). The major indicators of financial crises and contagion include volatile movements in the exchange rate, the depletion of international reserves, sharply rising short-term interest rates and falling stock market prices. During the major financial crises of the 1990s, these financial variables moved significantly in many of the affected countries. These indicators, therefore, may identify other countries affected by contagion. This paper aims at identifying channels of financial contagion that originated in Thailand and spread to its neighboring countries and Korea, by examining changes in the linkages of the financial variables and financial markets around the eruption of the 1997 Asian crises.

To examine the contagion effect of financial variables from Thailand to its neighboring countries and Korea, Jeon set up the (G)ARCH model following Bollerslev, Chou, and Kroner (1992). The results provided evidence of financial linkages across countries as a channel of contagion of currency crises in the case of the 1997 Asian crisis. Stock markets in the region were found to play an important role in transmitting initial and local shocks beyond its country of origin to other emerging economies during the 1997 crisis. Stock market linkages seem to have contributed importantly to the quick and wide-scale contagion of the ensuing exchange-rate crisis across countries in the 1997 Asian crisis episode. Contagion between stock markets is believed to have generated contagion of the exchange rate crisis during the crisis period in Asia. The first channel of spreading crises via stock market contagion will be the erosion of confidence by investors. A decline in confidence caused by currency crisis in the crisis-origin country will result in falling stock prices with greater volatility. The spillover effects of falling stock prices to another country will further reduce the investors' confidence in the other country and lead to a sharp decline in the value of its currency, causing a currency crisis in that country.

Stock market linkages provide an effective path for the spread of eroded confidence across countries. Speculative attack and self-fulfilling pessimism, which created the initial currency crisis in the origin country, are repeated in stock markets in other vulnerable emerging economies. Stock market linkages also work as an indirect channel of contagion through the role of foreign investors. When international investors are increasingly concerned about the prospect of crisis-stricken emerging economies, they try to withdraw from the emerging market economies and rebalance their portfolio positions. Liquidity difficulties facing international investors as a result of currency crises also force the investors to liquidate their positions in other national markets, consequently spreading the crises.

In this study, Shukor, Nor, Ibrahim and Kaur investigate the information content of tangible and intangible NCA (non-current assets) to determine whether relevant current accounting standards provide sufficient information for better decision making by financial analysts. An earlier study by Zaleha et al. (2004) found that intangible NCA has information content for financial analysts during economic crisis periods, but with higher uncertainty. Analysts' earnings forecasts error was found to be significantly associated with intangible NCA but the error was higher during the crisis period of 1997–1998 compared to during non-crisis periods. This finding suggests that intangibles provide relevant information to the capital market even though intangibles are by nature highly uncertain for predicting future cash flows. Barth and Clinch (1998) in a study of Australian firms found that in arriving at a firms' valuation, financial analysts utilized tangible NCA information more than intangible NCA, when they are at cost, and utilized both tangible and intangible NCA information as if they contain the same amount of useful information (to predict expected future cash flows). In this study, the definition of information content is based on a significant association between NCA and analysts forecasts accuracy (Bryan, 1997) during any economic period.

This study provides further evidence on the usefulness of balance sheet data for earnings forecasting activities during economic crisis, and specifically within the Malaysian capital market. This study also contributes to the literature of analysts forecasting activities by providing further evidence on the relative usefulness of tangible versus intangible NCA accounting information during economic crisis period. Empirical results from their sample data suggest that there is a tendency that the information content and usefulness of tangible NCA is higher than intangible NCA during economic crisis period to forecasts firms earnings or alternatively to predict firms' expected future cash flows. However, during non-crisis periods, there is a tendency that the information content or usefulness of intangible NCA is the same or even higher than tangible NCA to forecast firms' future earnings. Findings from this study will be further investigated by comparing profitable and non-profitable firms, as well as comparing large and small firms, among others, in our future analysis.

The Wang, Gunasekarage and Power paper investigates the integration among international capital markets and the mechanism whereby information is transmitted. Early investigations like Hilliard (1979) found that most intra-continental prices move simultaneously. More recently, Eun and Shim (1989) applied a vector autoregression (VAR) method and discovered a substantial amount of multi-lateral interaction among markets. Joen and von Furstenberg (1990) arrived at a similar view. Becker, Finnerty, and Gupta (1990) concluded that the information from the US market could be used to trade profitably in the Japanese market. Koch and Koch (1991) discovered a growing level of market interdependence within the same geographical region over time. Another branch of research concentrates on the transmission of international equity movements by studying the spillover of return and volatility across markets (Hamao, Masulis, & Ng (1990); Theodossiou & Lee (1993)). More recently, Scheicher (2001) reported that although the equity returns were affected by both regional and global factors, the volatilities were impacted by only regional influences. Fratzscher (2002) and Baele (2002) arrived at a similar conclusion.

This study contributes to that literature by focusing on the US and Japanese markets in an attempt to analyze the impacts of both regional and world shocks on South Asian equities. Second, they recognize that volatility transmission may be asymmetric in character – i.e. the negative innovations in one market may produce higher volatility spillovers in another market, than the positive innovations of equal magnitude. Finally, they address the possible effect of the Asian financial crisis on the transmission mechanism by disaggregating the data into three sample periods: (i) pre-crisis, (ii) in-crisis and (iii) post-crisis. This study examines return and volatility spillovers from the US and Japanese stock markets to three South Asian capital markets – (i) the Bombay Stock Exchange, (ii) the Karachi Stock Exchange and (iii) the Colombo Stock Exchange. The authors apply a univariate Exponential Generalised Autoregression Conditional Heteroskedasticity (EGARCH) spillover model, which allows the unexpected return of any particular South Asian market to be driven by a local shock, a regional shock from Japan, and a global shock from the USA. The study discovers return spillovers in all three markets and volatility spillovers from the US to the Indian and Sri Lankan markets, and from the Japanese to the Pakistani market. Regional factors seem to exert an influence on these three markets before the Asian financial crisis but the global factor becomes more important in the post-crisis period.

The objective of Batten, Fetherston and Hoontrakul's paper is to apply simple empirical techniques to investigate the relationships between sovereign bonds issued within the Asia Pacific region and the underlying US Treasury benchmark bonds with a maturity of 2, 5, 10 and 30 years. Such an analysis is essential to pricing and managing the risks of sovereign debt in international markets, while also providing an insight into the equilibrium relationship between different maturity classes of sovereign bonds and US Government benchmark bonds. Historically studies investigating long-term equilibrium relationships have been restricted to securities of developed countries (for example see Hiraki, Shiraishi, & Takezawa, 1996). These issues are investigated using empirical models based on Batten, Hogan, and Pynnonen (2000) for the equilibrium of relationships. Daily bond data were obtained from the Reuters Fixed Income Database for the period from the 30 December 1999 to the 28 November 2002 (749 daily observations). All bonds were fixed rate, semi-annual coupons priced on a 30/360-day basis. The yield to maturity (YTM) was calculated as the International Securities Markets Association (ISMA) yield to maturity, with indicative daily bids provided by market practitioners at the close of trading. To overcome potential distortions in yield due to illiquidity and the time path effects due to the bond approaching maturity, only liquid bonds and those with a modified duration of greater than 1 year were included in the final group of bonds. Only nine bonds issued by the governments of China (3 bonds), Korea (1 bond), Malaysia (1 bond), Philippines (3 bonds) and Thailand (1 bond) passed these simple tests and also had a complete set of price data. Table 1 reports this information as well as the information on the issue date of each bond and its maturity. The price and yield to maturity of the bond at the end of the sample period (28 November 2002) are also reported. The correlations between the bond pairs are generally low and are below 0.5. The highest correlation was between the US30 and US10 with a value of 0.473. The correlations between the nearest maturity Asian international bonds are higher than between bonds of differing maturity.

INVESTMENT PERFORMANCE

The Chen, Zhang and Marshall paper investigates the degree that the rapidly growing economic integration in Asia Pacific is also reflected in the relative importance of country and industry factors in Asia Pacific stocks return. Previous studies have indicated that greater integration among developed markets implies stronger co-movement between markets. That is an important concern for investors, given that international diversification works best when there is little co-movement between markets. The worldwide impact of the stock market crash in October 1987 highlighted how integrated markets have become. The great challenge for international fund managers is that the market correlations seem to increase when the volatility of markets increase. This is troublesome for global fund mangers or investors because the increased correlations occur at the same time when increased volatility is making diversification less effective. Against this background, they make two contributions in this paper. First, a cross-region analysis provides a comparison of the extent to which difference of country and sector effects occur between the Asia Pacific and developed markets. Second, an observation period selected from July 1994 through January 2002 was selected. The advantage of starting in 1994 is that data include the 1997 Asian Financial Crisis as an important benchmark. Thus, they divide a time series analysis into three parts, namely, 'pre-crisis, crisis, post-crisis', that enables them to assess how country and sector effects have changed over time. Following Heston and Rouwenhorst (1994), extended by Griffin and Karolyi (1998), they define that a stock return depends on four components: (1) a region effect; (2) sector effect; (3) country effect and (4) a firm-specific disturbance.

Given the evidence of stronger segmentation among Asia Pacific markets, they conclude that the country factor is the dominant influence in stock return, and thus country diversification is the most useful tool for managing Asia Pacific stock portfolio risk. Their study also confirms the increasing importance of the sectors-effect and the declining but stable and continuing contribution of the country factor.

The Kamesaka paper investigates aggregate buying and selling by foreign investors, subdivided into US, European and Asian investors, in the Japanese stock market over the period 1981–2004. The Tokyo Stock Exchange collects information on the yen value of client purchases and sales from securities firms each month. All client orders are categorized into trading by securities companies, banks, insurance companies, investment trusts, non-financial corporations, individuals, foreigners, etc. Foreigner trading is further categorized into US, European, South-East Asian (hereafter, abbreviated as Asian) and other foreign investors. Kamesaka, Nofsinger, and Kawakita (2003) found that foreign investors and securities companies trade with good market timing, while domestic individual investors and nonfinancial companies performed relatively poorly. However, the trades of foreign investors across different regions have never been analyzed statistically. In this paper, Kamesaka focuses on the behavior of four types of foreign investors in Japan: US, European, Asian and other foreigners. The sample period is from January 1981 to June 2004. It covers the bubble period of the latter half of the 1980s, followed by the crash in the early 1990s, and the Internet bubble period around 1999. Kamesaka analyze foreign investor behavior before, during and after the crash by dividing the data into three subperiods: from January 1981 to December 1989 (before the crash or bubble period), from January 1990 to December 1998 (during the crash), and from January 1999 to June 2004 (after the crash). The results before, during and after the crash indicate that all foreign investors increased their purchases, sales and net purchases (purchases less sales) at the same time. They increased their purchases and net purchases while stock prices were increasing, however, no relation was found between sales and stock returns. Therefore, an asymmetry exists between purchases, sales and stock price returns, and this asymmetry continues to exist regardless of the changes in the Japanese stock market. Foreign investors of each region tended to increase their net purchases after each investor's own net purchases of the previous month and after a few months' stock price fall before and during the crash period. However, these tended to disappear after the crash period. The stock prices tended to increase after European and Asian investors' net purchases during the 1980s; however, the relation disappears in the 1990s and thereafter.

By evaluating the 1-month following return, Kamesaka also observes positive stock returns following each foreign investor's net purchases, and negative stock returns after net sales. US investors performed extremely well by net purchasing during the Internet bubble around 1999. The overall performance of net sales did not differ among US, European and Asian investors. However, the results suggest that European investors sold after the stock price appreciation from the mid-1980s, and it is likely that they gained from investing in Japan by selling stocks they bought in the 1970s.

In this paper, Carlin and Ford examine one little researched aspect of the options debate, the question of options holding concentration, and present empirical evidence on whether holding concentration appears to be associated with the types of problems evident from the literature discussed below. Debates about the use of options as a component of employee compensation have burgeoned in the past few years. Much of the heat in this debate has surrounded the contentious issue of how best to account for and report on the financial consequences of using options as an element of remuneration (Core & Guay, 2001; Hall & Murphy, 2002). It is this element in particular, of the wider debate which has attracted a considerable degree of attention from the business press, thus bringing the argument into public domain. However, concern about the use of options plans has by no means been limited to issues of financial reporting and disclosure. A considerable body of literature has now developed in which the key thematic element relates to the incentive compatibility consequences of the adoption of options plans as a component of employee remuneration. The accumulation of knowledge embodied in this stream of literature is now giving rise to concern that, contrary to the agency theory-derived expectations of the value of options as tools for mitigating principal agency problems and thus generating improved shareholder value creation outcomes (Jensen & Meckling, 1976; Jensen & Murphy, 1990), a range of perverse, value-destroying incentives may be introduced as a result of the implementation of options-based compensation plans. Examples of problems identified in the literature thus far include evidence of opportunistically timed disclosures to capital markets (Aboody & Kasnik, 2000), questionably motivated share buyback programs (Yermack, 2001; Aboody & Kasnik, 2001), material changes to dividend policy (Lambert, Lanen, & Larker, 1989) and changes to the risk profile of projects undertaken by firms (Chen, 2002).

The Ng and Sadeghi piece explores an area of financial study emanating from Prospect theory, which focuses on the individual's behavior when faced with various scenarios. The innovation of Kahneman and Tversky (1979), found through experimental evidence, is that a risk-adverse individual would prefer a risk-adverse behavior when facing pure gain prospects, but would prefer a risk-seeking behavior when facing pure loss prospects, called 'a reflection of risk' behavior. Barberis, Huang, and Santos (2001) incorporate the ideal of the additional disutility from a loss in equity value in a lifetime utility maximization asset-pricing model. This additional disutility is experimentally concluded to follow a general process of editing and evaluation of the prospect, a process replicated by Barberis et al. (2001). The additional application of mental accounting and narrow framing theory considered by Kahneman and Tversky (1984) resulted in a relative match of estimated equity premium using simulation evidence in Barberis and Huang (2001).

This study focuses on the application of individual framing loss aversion asset pricing with prior gains and losses on empirical data from five countries, Australia, the United States, Hong Kong, Japan and Singapore. While Barberis and Huang (2001) estimate returns that are capable of matching average returns and volatility, they use a simulation of 500 stocks for 10,000 time periods to calculate their average means and variances. The use of empirical data allow the pairing of estimated returns and market values, providing a more rigorous test of the asset-pricing model and a greater analysis of its predictive powers. The use of empirical estimations also allows the analysis of its comparative abilities against the capital-asset-pricing model (CAPM) to test the differences from a rational and irrational asset-pricing model. Finally, the use of five Pacific-Basin countries allows the impact of each individual country's culture, its economic development as well as its financial markets development to impact on the estimated results. A mixture of these rational and irrational behaviors in each country will lead to an interesting comparison of the CAPM and the loss aversion model. The results, while not conclusive, are revealing. The analysis of sensitivity test provides an indication of the relative importance of stock market values and the additional diutility of losses. The results suggest that there is a much higher sensitivity when comparing Asian countries than when comparing western influenced countries. With this information, asset pricing within the Asian countries should take greater consideration of individual behaviors and irrationalities within their theoretical models and estimations.

The Tsao and Chen piece focuses on the Taiwanese market. It investigates firms whose trading was stopped temporarily or even de-listed by the authorities because of the firms' financial distress. Many of these firms transfer to the 'managed stock market' for trading again. The study of the 'managed stock' market includes 13 firms as follows: Tong Lung (code 8705), Victor (code 8707), Tah Chung (code 8708), YiShin (code 8710), CAC (Chinese Automobile Company, code 8712), TIDC (Taiwan Industrial Development Corporation, code 8718), Hung Fu (code 8719), Ensure (code 8720) and Sun Home (code 8721), TaTeh code 8722), Taiyu (code 8723), Lee Tah (code 8724) and Sun Splendor (code 8725). The study focuses on whether the firms 'managed stock' classification signals worse financial status. Moreover, do they improve financial status after transferring as 'managed stock' and how well does the stock price perform. In addition, do 'managed stocks' get valuation commensurate with TSE or OTC markets?

The authors conclude with some concrete suggestions from three different focuses. General investors should pay more attention to 'managed stock' market. In effect, there might be many profitable opportunities. In the case of investors who have already bought into the 'managed stock' market, they should be careful of the risk as well as the return attributes of 'managed stocks', and take notice of any fundamental changes in reference when adjusting their portfolios. In terms of the fundamental performance and stock price status of 'managed stocks', comparisons with the TSE and OTC market should be undertaken. The authors suggest that investors may well have a subjective perception of the 'managed stock' market as an inferior market. As for the authorities, it is noticeable that the stock price of an individual stock in the 'managed stock' market is much lower than its intrinsic value. From an institutional investors' viewpoint, the 'managed stock' category is dangerously illiquid and thus should be avoided by institutions.

INSTITUTIONS, MARKETS AND POLICY

The Lin study focuses upon and explores the causes, processes and institutional reforms, which have taken place in the 10 countries of Eastern Asia.

It further compares their differences and effectiveness. Additionally, through the fluctuation rate of GDP, stock indexes, exchange rates, currency inflation, unemployment rates and other macro-variables found in the 10 countries of Eastern Asia during the period 1993–2002. He utilizes Mann-Whitney U Test and Intervention Analysis to compare the differences for pre- and post-financial crisis in Asia. This is also used in further analyzing the concrete effectiveness of the financial reforms of 10 countries of Eastern Asia. From the results of the Mann-Whitney U Test, he finds that there was a significant difference in the fluctuation rate of GDP in Hong Kong for pre- and post-Asian financial crisis. The fluctuation rate of GDP for the other 9 countries did not show a significant difference. Regarding the stock index, other than Taiwan and China not indicating a significant difference in the average stock index for pre- or post-Asian financial crisis, the stock index of the others (Japan, Hong Kong, Thailand, Indonesia, Malaysia, Singapore, Korea and The Philippines) all showed a significant difference. Additionally, all 10 Eastern Asian countries showed a significant difference in the exchange rate standards and consumer price indexes for pre- and post-Asian financial crisis. Conversely, the fluctuation rate in the unemployment rate for all 10 Eastern Asian countries did not show significant difference. From the analysis and results of Intervention Analysis, he finds that the fluctuation rate of GDP for Taiwan was higher for post-Asian financial crisis. Conversely, the fluctuation rate of GDP for The Philippines was lower for post-Asian financial crisis. With regard to the stock index, the stock indexes of The Philippines and Korea were higher post Asian financial crisis. Conversely, the stock index for Malaysia was lower post-Asian financial crisis. The exchange rates in Malaysia, Thailand, The Philippines, Singapore and Korea all devaluated with regard to the Asian financial crisis. Moreover, the consumer price indexes (CPI) in Thailand and Singapore were higher for post Asian financial crisis. None of the 10 Eastern Asian countries reached level of significance for the fluctuation rates for the unemployment rate showing that the unemployment rate is not affected by Asian financial crises. Generally speaking, other than the fluctuation rate of GDP, the analysis and results of Mann-Whitney U Test and Intervention Analysis proved to be unanimous. Even so, a relationship does not exist between the financial reform variables (legal effectiveness, overdue loan ratio (NPL) in the banking industry, capital adequacy ratio, financial innovation, number of individuals employed in the finance industry, and mergers and numbers of financial departments) and macro-economic variables (fluctuation rate of GDP, stock index, exchange rate, CPI and fluctuation rate of the unemployment rate) for the 10 Eastern Asian countries.

China the largest emerging economy abandoned its financial derivatives market after some unregulated and illegal derivatives trading in the mid-1990s. The Chi and Young paper focuses on the way forward for the re-development of an official financial derivatives market in China, and the major issues surrounding this redevelopment. Consideration is also given to China's over-the-counter derivatives market. This research is aimed to assist policy makers, in particular, to move forward with the credible development of an official financial derivatives market in China. A summary of their recommendations is as follows: Developing a credible financial derivatives market is an essential part of the whole process of financial market development in China. This development should take place within a reasonably short time frame. The European model of having the derivative market attached to the physical market should be adopted, particularly given the fact that stock based derivative products are the ones most likely to be developed first. It is their view that the Shanghai financial derivatives market should be developed first as part of the Shanghai Stock Exchange operation. The trading system used by the exchanges should be an internationally recognized one to help ensure an international acceptance of these new exchanges. In particular they recommend that consideration be given to adopting the LIFFE-Connect[TM] trading system used by the Euronext exchanges. Settlement and risk management systems should also be internationally recognized ones. In relation to products traded, individual stock and stock index futures and options should be traded in the first instance. Exchange traded currency and interest rate futures and options should wait for exchange rate and interest rate deregulation in China. They consider that both the Shanghai and Shenzhen Stock Exchanges should develop indices based on the 100 top stocks on which to base the stock index contracts. As part of the development of these markets, controlled short selling and stock lending systems should be developed. The regulatory system has been a major concern and challenge for the development of the financial derivatives market in China. There are three main kinds of risks involved in a financial derivatives market, i.e. explicit risks, implicit risks and estimation risks. Among these, in the Chinese financial market, credit risk, accounting and disclosure risk, systematic risk and moral risk are our major focuses. Risks are analyzed in the Chinese context and suggestions are provided to improve the regulatory system to manage these major risks. The OTC market should continue to develop within the structure laid down recently within China. Although the regulatory system in the OTC market in most western countries is not a major concern for the government, due to the moral risk involved in the Chinese derivatives market, certain measures may be needed, such as the possible implementation of a Derivatives Product Company. Equity based-derivatives such as Contracts for Difference, could be traded in this market in the near future along with currency derivatives. They believe that, with due care, exchange-based financial derivatives trading can successfully return to China in the near future, along with further expansion of the OTC market, based on the structures suggested above.

The Narayanamurti and Batten paper extends the post-1997 panic-stricken triggered policy efforts to develop multiple avenues of intermediation (Shirai, 2001; Sharma, 2001). While these efforts have been impressive their focus has been anachronistic, by failing to appreciate that in an environment with increasingly borderless economies, financial and real sector linkages need to be established. Policy efforts have principally failed to appreciate that financial and real sector reform, due to their nexus need to be conducted simultaneously. This paper aims to bridge the gap by exploring the linkages between financial system design and the real sector in Asia. A multi-pillar paragon is constructed revolving around the previously considered mutually exclusive concepts of banking, financial markets, the law and functional reform. By doing so the major queries gripping crisis management and resolution in the region are addressed.

Asia imposes a special policy challenge, due to the extensive degree of deviation evident from the features of its financial systems and the predictions of standard theoretical models. Asian banks for instance failed to serve as efficient monitors and solvers of information asymmetries. The excessive lending by the banking sector to fund the acquisition of non-tradeables such as property, suggests a failure to effectively screen borrowers. The resultant effect was a maturity mismatch, triggering in turn a large volume of NPLs.

Market reform in Asia has been found to be impeded due to the absence of institutional investors, poor demand and supply of quality government and corporate bond issues, lack of a benchmark infrastructure and poorly developed derivative markets. Markets promote efficiency in the banking sector, through the provision of market-determined interest rates, which portrays the true cost of funds. Besides, the potentialities for growth in domestic bond markets are large given the region's high savings rate. For high growth outcomes to be reached in Asia, the development of multiple avenues of intermediation is important so as to help reduce the effect of future crisis in a particular avenue. Legal and functional reform must be undertaken simultaneously to facilitate banking and market reform. Therefore, while banks and markets may be viewed as supportive pillars to an effective growth paradigm, the legal system and ultimate financial services provided are complementary pillars. In Asia the legal system, through the quality of investor protection provided is seen to affect the corporate financing patterns of firms, by influencing the development of the region's equity and debt markets. Moreover attempts made to stimulate the banking sector and the capital markets of the region through capital and financial liberalization must involve a non-leapfrog approach. The results of the analysis undertaken suggest that, capital flight, asset bubbles, contagion and currency collapses in Asia were natural outcomes of failing to appreciate the linkage between liberalization and fragility. By portraying the causes of the crisis and impediments to reform, the paper has essentially highlighted that for high growth outcomes to be reached post-crisis, reform must involve the adoption of a multi-dimensional approach. In particular through the linkages established between the four pillars the paper shows that reform packages that espouse a restricted policy focus are unlikely to succeed.

The Szilagyi piece is in the vein of the academic research of the past decade advocating proposals on how Japan should reform, redesign and administer its bank-based financial system (Schinasi & Smith, 1998; Kuratani & Endo, 2000; Hattori, Koyama, & Yonetani, 2001; Rhee, 2001; Baba & Hisada, 2002; Batten & Szilagyi, 2003). Until the late 1980s, this unique regime, involving banks having cross-ownership with industry, was a driving force behind Japan's post-war economic miracle. However, the burst of the asset bubble, and the subsequent prolonged ailing of both the banking sector and the economy as a whole suggests that during the bubble period, the monitoring effectiveness of banks was compromised by a lack of independence from industry and the absence of external discipline. This banking crisis ultimately impaired the corporate sector's fund-raising ability, while trapping excess liquidity in the financial system through a lack of attractive investment choice afforded to risk-averse Japanese investors.

Japanese policymakers have made concerted efforts to resolve these problems and focused on capital market deregulation and liberalization. But, a key element of the reform agenda, the development of the corporate bond market has received perhaps unduly modest attention. Since the 1980s, extensive changes in the financial environment have helped the Japanese market become second only to its US counterpart. Today, the market's key role in the financing of Japanese firms is highlighted by the fact that it represents 17.1% of GDP, comparable to 22% in the US, as of June 2004. On the other hand, the spectacular growth of Japan's corporate bond market conceals the fact that it continues to lag behind the US and UK markets in most key aspects of development, effectiveness and diversity. At the same time, and as a result, it continues to struggle to attract borrowers with yen needs from the Euroyen market.

This paper advocates that the development of the corporate bond market is instrumental in ensuring the medium-term recovery of Japan's financial system. An improved market, providing a platform where excess liquidity is channelled to domestic and international borrowers, would help resolve the extreme waste of financial resources that is currently seen.

Buchanan presents a clinical examination of the impact of money laundering and off-shore financial centers on Asia Pacific financial markets. She describes the money laundering cycle, tools and techniques utilized in the Asia Pacific region as well as the anti-money laundering measures and regulations.

Money laundering remains a global phenomenon. International efforts continue to be made to address the problem of money laundering, particularly in the Asia Pacific region. The proposed new Basel Capital Accord identifies credit, market, interest rate and operational risk as four types of risk that banks closely need to monitor. Operational risk refers to "... the risk of direct or indirect loss resulting from inadequate or failed internal processes, people and systems or from external events." In a money-laundering context, operation risk is the most important. Banks still remain a very vulnerable part of the money-laundering process. Thus, to cover this risk, regulators need to make sure that banks have adequate measures in place to minimize the abuse of their services by money launderers. Added to that is the additional difficulty of monitoring possible in money laundering via e-commerce transactions. Ways to combat money laundering through e-commerce could include the reinforcement of current customer identification requirements, stronger 'know your customer' rules, prohibiting unlicensed financial institutions from offering their services and improving technological capabilities to detect suspicious online transactions. Buchanan asserts resolving the problems associated with money laundering will require co-operative links among regulatory, law enforcement agencies and the public and private sector both within and across borders. A coordinated response will be required for detection and investigation of this transnational activity.

A noticeable feature of the 1997–1998 Asian Financial Crisis (hereafter 'the Crisis') was that it exhibited a distinctly regional character. That is, countries within East Asia experienced the most immediate and extensive distress. This being the case, it becomes pertinent to discuss the development of a regionally based, rapid response mechanism capable of dealing with the occurrence of future financial crises. A proposal to develop a response mechanism is the task taken up by Iu. At the height of the Crisis the Japanese Government proposed the creation of a regionally based monetary institution known as the Asian Monetary Fund (AMF). The proposal to create the AMF came as a direct response to the diminishing faith of East

Asian governments in the ability of international policy makers to prescribe solutions to the incidence of financial crises. The proposal was an attempt to pool in the foreign currency reserves of members in order for the AMF to act as a regional lender of last resort providing liquidity in the event of a crisis (Sakakibuara, 2000). The AMF was intended to provide a quick distribution of funds, with low conditionality, to defend Asian countries against speculative attacks and balance of payment problems. Supporters of the AMF suggested that by being based within the region, more appropriate and culturally sensitive policy responses could be formulated to prevent prolonged and severe periods of economic turmoil. Importantly, the AMF was to redress criticisms in International Monetary Fund (IMF) prescriptions (below). Indeed, the AMF was mooted as an alternative to the existing international financial institutions, such as the IMF, as a means of protecting East Asian states against the vagaries of volatile capital flows.

The notion underlying the creation of the AMF – that benefits can be gained from familiarity with the specific needs of countries – was sound. However, obtaining the consensus required for effective regional cooperation is fraught with difficulties. Political and cultural imperatives often have a greater role in determining the success of multilateral cooperation than economic linkages (that already exist within the region). East Asia is a dynamic region with many and varied cultural traits. Such diversity and competing national interests have caused significant conflicts and tensions throughout the region's history. In this context, the primary purpose of this paper is to reconsider the challenges in achieving the integration of East Asian monetary policy as imagined under the AMF and advocate that collective action in East Asia is crucial to prevent and manage future financial crises. Moreover, the paper will determine the validity of the initial rejection of the idea, because the benefits of regionalism and a regional institution can contribute to the stability of international markets. This is a critical aspect that needs attention within the reform of international financial architecture.

REFERENCES

Aboody, D., & Kasnik, R. (2000). CEO stock option awards and the timing of corporate voluntary disclosures. *Journal of Accounting and Economics, 29*, 73–100.

Aboody, D., & Kasnik, R. (2001). *Executive stock option compensation and corporate cash payout policy.* Working Paper, Graduate School of Business, Stanford University.

Baba, N., & Hisada, T. (2002). *Japan's financial system: Its perspective and the authorities' roles in redesigning and administering the system.* IMES Discussion Paper 2002-E-1, Bank of Japan, Institute for Monetary and Economic Studies (IMES).

Baele, L. (2002). *Volatility spillover effects in European equity markets: Evidence from a regime switching model.* Working Paper, Ghent University.

Barberis, N., & Huang, M. (2001). Mental accounting, loss aversion and individual stock returns. *The Journal of Finance, LVI*(4), 1247–1295.

Barberis, N., Huang, M., & Santos, T. (2001). Prospect theory and asset prices. *Quarterly Journal of Economics, 116*, 1–53.

Barth, M. E., & Clinch, G. (1998). Revalued financial, tangible, and intangible assets: Associations with share prices and non-market-based value estimates. *Journal of Accounting Research, 36*(Supp), 199–233.

Batten, J., Ellis, C., & Fetherston, T. (2000). Are long-term return anomalies illusions? Evidence from the spot yen. *Japan and the World Economy, 12*, 337–349.

Batten, J., Hogan, W., & Pynnönen, S. (2000). The dynamics of Australian dollar bonds with different credit qualities. *International Review of Financial Analysis, 9*, 389–404.

Batten, J. A., & Szilagyi, P. G. (2003). Why Japan needs to develop its corporate bond market. *International Journal of the Economics of Business, 10*(1), 85–110.

Becker, K. G., Finnerty, J. E., & Gupta, M. (1990). The international relation between the US and Japanese stock markets. *Journal of Finance, 45*, 1297–1306.

Bollerslev, T., Chou, R. Y., & Kroner, K. F. (1992). ARCH modeling in finance: A review of the theory and empirical evidence. *Journal of Econometrics, 52*, 5–59.

Bowman, C. (2004). Yen block or Koala block? Currency relationships after the East Asian crisis. *Japan and the World Economy*, forthcoming.

Bryan, S. H. (1997). Incremental information content of required disclosures contained in management discussion and analysis. *The Accounting Review, 72*(2), 285–301.

Byers, J., & Peel, D. (2001). Volatility persistence in asset markets: Long memory in high/low prices. *Applied Financial Economics, 11*(3), 253–260.

Chen, Y. (2002). *Executive stock options and managerial risk taking.* Working Paper, University of Houston.

Core, J., & Guay, W. (2001). Stock option plans for non-executive employees. *Journal of Financial Economics, 61*(2), 253–287.

Daly, K. J. (2003). Southeast Asian stock market linkages, evidence from pre-and postOctober 1997. *ASEAN Economic Bulletin, 20*(1), 73–85.

Eun, C., & Shim, S. (1989). International transmission of stock market movements. *Journal of Financial and Quantitative Analysis, 24*, 241–256.

Frankel, J., & Wei, S. (1994). Yen block or dollar block? Exchange rate policies of the East Asian economies. In: T. Ito & A. O. Krueger (Eds), *Macroeconomic linkages: savings, exchange rates and capital flows* (pp. 295–329). Chicago: University of Chicago Press.

Fratzscher, M. (2002). Financial market integration in Europe: On the effects of EMU on stock markets. *International Journal of Finance and Economics, 7*, 165–193.

Gan, W. B. (2000). Exchange-rate policy in East Asia after the fall: How much have things changed? *Journal of Asian Economics, 11*(4), 403–430.

Griffin, J. M., & Karolyi, G. A. (1998). Another look at the role of industrial structure of markets for international diversification. *Journal of Financial Economics, 50*, 351–373.

Hall, B., & Murphy, K. (2002). Stock options for undiversified executives. *Journal of Accounting and Economics, 33*, 3–42.

Hamao, Y., Masulis, R., & Ng, V. (1990). Correlations in price changes and volatility across international stock markets. *Review of Financial Studies, 3*, 281–307.

Hernandez, L., & Montiel, P. (2002). *Post-crisis exchange rate policy in five Asian countries: Filling in the 'hollow middle'?* IMF Working Paper, code: WP/01/170.

Hattori, M., Koyama, K., & Yonetani, T. (2001). *Analysis of credit spread in Japan's corporate bond market.* BIS Papers No. 5., Bank for International Settlements.

Hendry, D., & Krolzig, H. (2001). Computer automation of general-to-specific model selection procedures. *Journal of Economic Dynamics and Control, 25*, 831–866.

Heston, S. L., & Rouwenhorst, K. G. (1994). Does industry structure explain the benefits of international diversification. *Journal of Financial Economics, 36*, 3–27.

Hilliard, J. (1979). The relationship between equity indices on world exchanges. *Journal of Finance, 34*, 103–114.

Hiraki, T., Shiraishi, N., & Takezawa, N. (1996). Cointegration, common factors, and the term structure of Yen offshore interest rates. *Journal of Fixed Income, 6*(3), 69–75.

Jensen, M., & Meckling, W. (1976). Theory of the firm: Managerial behaviour, agency costs and ownership structure. *Journal of Financial Economics, 3*, 305–360.

Jensen, M., & Murphy, K. (1990). CEO incentives: It's not how much you pay but how. *Harvard Business Review, 68*(May-June), 138–153.

Joen, B. N., & von Furstenberg, G. M. (1990). Growing international co-movement in stock price indexes. *Quarterly Review of Economics and Business, 30*, 15–30.

Kahneman, D., & Tversky, A. (1979). Prospect theory: An analysis of decision under risk. *Econometrica, 47*, 263–291.

Kahneman, D., & Tversky, A. (1984). Choices, values, and frames. *American Psychologist, XXXIX*, 341–350.

Kamesaka, A., Nofsinger, J., & Kawakita, H. (2003). Investment patterns and performance of investor groups in Japan. *Pacific Basin Finance Journal*, 1–22.

Koch, P. D., & Koch, T. W. (1991). Evaluation in dynamic linkages across daily national stock indexes. *Journal of International Money and Finance, 10*, 231–251.

Kuratani, M., & Endo, Y. (2000). *Establishing new financial markets in Japan.* NRI Papers No. 6, Nomura Research Institute.

Kwan, C. H. (1996). A yen block in Asia: An integrative approach. *Journal of the Asia Pacific Economy, 1*, 1–21.

Lambert, R., Lanen, W., & Larker, D. (1989). Executive stock option plans and corporate dividend policies. *Journal of Financial and Quantitative Analysis, 24*, 409–425.

Mckinnon, R. I. (2000). The East Asian Dollar standard. *Life after death? Economic Notes, 29*(1), 31–82.

Muller, U. A., Dacorogna, M. M., Olsen, R. B., Pictet, O. V., Schwarz, M., & Morgenegg, C. (1990). Statistical study of foreign exchange rates, empirical evidence of a price change scaling law, and intraday analysis. *Journal of Banking and Finance, 14*, 1189–1208.

Nekhili, R., Altay-Salih, A., & Gencay, R. (2002). Exploring exchange rates at different time horizons. *Physica A, 313*, 671–682.

Newey, W. K., & West, K. D. (1987). A simple, positive semi-definite, heteroscedasticity and autocorrelation consistent covariance matrix. *Econometrica, 55*(3), 703–708.

Rhee, S. G. (2001). Further reforms of the JGB market for the promotion of regional bond markets. Bond Market Development in Asia: 217–236. Organization for Economic Co-Operation and Development (OECD), Paris.

Sakakibuara, E. (2000). East Asian Crisis – two years later. *Proceedings of the conference on Development Economics*, 12th Annual Bank Conference on Development Economics, Washington, April 18–20.

Scheicher, M. (2001). The comovements of stock markets in Hungary, Poland, and the Czech Republic. *International Journal of Finance and Economics, 6*, 27–39.

Schinasi, G. J., & Smith, T. R. (1998). *Fixed income markets in the United States, Europe and Japan: Some lessons for emerging markets.* IMF Working Paper No. 98 (12): 1–70. International Monetary Fund, Washington, DC.

Sharma, K. (2001). The underlying constraints on corporate bond market development in South East Asia. *World Development, 29*(8), 1405–1419.

Shirai, S. (2001). *Overview of financial market structures in Asia – cases of the Republic of Korea, Malaysia, Thailand and Indonesia.* Asian Development Bank Institute Research Paper, 25.

Taylor, M. P. (1999). *Asset price bubbles, risky lending and the East Asian Crisis*, Center for Financial Studies, Warwick Business School, University of Warwick, Working Paper, November.

Theodossiou, P., & Lee, U. (1993). Mean and volatility spillovers across major national stock markets: Further empirical evidence. *Journal of Financial Research, 16*, 337–350.

Tucker, A. L., & Scott, E. (1987). A study of diffusion processes for foreign exchange rates. *Journal of International Money and Finance, 6*, 465–478.

Van De Gucht, L. M., Dekimpe, M. G., & Kwok, C. Y. (1996). Persistence in foreign exchange rates. *Journal of International Money and Finance, 15*(2), 191–220.

Wasserfallen, W., & Zimmermann, H. (1985). The behavior of intra-daily exchange rates. *Journal of Banking and Finance, 9*, 55–72.

Xu, Z., & Gencay, R. (2003). Scaling, self-similarity and multifractality in FX markets. *Physica A, 323*, 578–590.

Yermack, D. (2001). *Executive stock options: Puzzles, problems and mysteries.* Working Paper, Stern School of Business.

Zaleha, A. S., Hamezah, M. N., Muhd-Kamil, I., & Kaur, J. (2004). *Effect of economic crisis period on the information content of intangible non-current assets in Malaysia.* Working Paper. Universiti Kebangsaan Malaysia, Universiti Teknologi MARA.

Zhou, S. (1998). Exchange rate systems and linkages in the Pacific Basin. *Atlantic Economics Journal, 26*(1), 66–84.

CURRENCY ANALYSIS

THE ROLE OF THE JAPANESE YEN IN ASIAN EXCHANGE RATE DETERMINATION

Colm Kearney and Cal Muckley

ABSTRACT

We study up to 27 years of weekly data on nine currencies to examine the importance of the Japanese yen in exchange rate determination in North and Southeast Asia. We combine a time-varying methodology alongside a focus on long-run equilibrium. Our findings suggest that the Japanese yen had virtually no influence on Asian exchange rates in the 10-year period prior to the Asian financial crisis in the late 1990s. Since the crisis, the yen and the German mark in particular have exerted a significant influence over the region's exchange rates except for the Chinese yuan, the Hong Kong dollar and the Malaysian ringgit, which continue to be closely related to the US dollar.

1. INTRODUCTION

The economies of North and Southeast Asia progressed markedly over the last three decades of the 1900s. China, Indonesia, Japan, Malaysia and Thailand grew at annual average rates of between 3 and 5 per cent, while

Asia Pacific Financial Markets in Comparative Perspective: Issues and Implications for the 21st Century
Contemporary Studies in Economics and Financial Analysis, Volume 86, 29–51
ISSN: 1569-3759/doi:10.1016/S1569-3759(05)86002-4

Hong Kong SAR, Singapore, South Korea and Taiwan each achieved annual average growth rates in excess of 6 per cent. This remarkable performance over a sustained period without significant interruption attracted attention from economists and policymakers. The fastest growing countries in the region became known as the 'Asian tigers'. They delivered unprecedented rises in income per head with virtually continual full employment. They spawned a renewed interest in growth economics throughout the world as analysts endeavoured to understand the underlying principles behind 'the Asian growth model' with a view to emulating it in their own economies. With the benefit of hindsight gained from witnessing the collapse in performance of these economies following the Asian crisis during the late 1990s, many questions have since been raised about the appropriateness of the exchange rate systems operated by these countries, and about whether some form of coordinated regional exchange rate system could have prevented or mitigated its ill effects.

The real economies of Hong Kong SAR, Indonesia, Malaysia, the Philippines, Singapore, South Korea and Thailand collectively collapsed from an average growth rate of 6.8 per cent in 1996 to a contraction of 4.4 per cent in 1998 (see IMF, 1998). The financial turmoil that was initially confined to Asia spread across the world's financial markets in late 1997. The United States *Dow Jones* index suffered a 7 per cent decline on 27 October 1997 that forced the suspension of trading. In Russia, the authorities implemented a unilateral default on domestic debt, devalued the rouble and imposed severe capital controls. The Malaysian authorities also imposed capital controls following a series of public statements by Prime Minister Mahathir condemning the role of speculators in generating the financial turmoil. These events caused international investors and lenders to become increasingly risk averse. They reassessed other potentially vulnerable emerging markets and turned their attention to Brazil and Latin America more generally. The Russian default along with its spillover to Latin America caused large losses for some western banks and leveraged hedge funds. The highly publicized Long Term Capital Management Ltd episode showed how Western financial institutions could be vulnerable, and it also drew attention to analysts' lack of knowledge about the extent of derivative risk that exists in today's domestic and global financial markets.

A voluminous literature has sprung up which attempts to explain what caused the Asian financial crisis, and there are two broad explanations (see for example, Johnson, 1998; Krugman, 1998; Hutson & Kearney, 1999). The first asserts that it resulted mainly from international financial market failures such as informational asymmetries and moral hazard. The second points to fundamental weaknesses in the Asian economies themselves, including crony capitalism, poor corporate governance, inadequate financial regulation and inappropriate exchange rate policies. It is likely that the truth of the matter embodies some degree of each explanation. The region's foreign exchange markets, however, were central to the instigation and contagion of the crisis. When it commenced in May 1997 with the first speculative attack on the Thai baht, the crisis spread throughout the region with alarming speed. The Philippine peso was attacked in June and the Indonesian rupiah along with the Hong Kong SAR dollar and the Malaysian ringgit were attacked in July of the same year. The foreign exchange market turmoil spread to the stock markets in these countries and continued throughout the following three months. By October 1997, the International Monetary Fund (IMF) had been called in by Indonesia, the Philippines and Thailand, and the contagion reached Hong Kong SAR where the *Hang Seng* stock index lost a third of its value in 7 days. In November, Japan and South Korea's currency and stock markets came under attack, and the IMF was called in by South Korea in December.

The devastating impact of the crisis on the US dollar and Japanese yen exchange rates of the worst affected countries during 1997 and 1998 is presented in Table 1. Looking first at the top part of the table, the countries can be grouped into four sets. The Indonesian rupiah stands alone as having depreciated against the US dollar by 340 per cent by the end of 1998. The Malaysian ringgit, the Philippine peso, the South Korean won and the Thai baht depreciated by an average of 65 per cent, the Japanese yen, the Singapore dollar and the Taiwan dollar depreciated by an average of 20 per cent and the Chinese yuan along with the Hong Kong SAR dollar remained steady. The bottom part of the table shows, as expected, that the depreciations against the Japanese yen were less than against the dollar. As before, the Indonesian rupiah stands alone as having depreciated against the Japanese yen by over 260 per cent by the end of 1998. The Malaysian ringgit, the Philippine peso, the South Korean won and the Thai baht depreciated by an average of 38 per cent, the Singapore dollar and the Taiwan dollar remained steady on average, and the Chinese yuan along with the Hong Kong SAR dollar appreciated by an average of 14 per cent.

In this paper, we examine the role of the yen in exchange rate management in North and Southeast Asia. By excluding any dynamic adjustment in their models, previous researchers have assumed that the monetary authorities adjust their exchange rates instantly to their preferred levels in relation to the world's main currencies. This is questionable, especially in studies that use either daily or weekly data to estimate their models. Central bankers

Table 1.   Currency Movements During the Asian Crisis.

Currency	Domestic Currency per unit of Foreign Currency	1996 = 100	
	1996	1997	1998
US dollar exchange rates			
Chinese yuan	8.31	99.71	99.58
Hong Kong SAR dollar	7.73	100.11	100.16
Indonesian rupiah	2328	123.47	440.14
Japanese yen	108.69	111.31	120.29
Korean won	804.64	118.02	174.00
Malaysian ringgit	2.51	111.81	166.81
Philippine peso	23.61	113.06	156.17
Singapore dollar	1.41	105.37	118.17
Taiwan dollar	27.45	104.50	121.87
Thai baht	25.35	123.45	162.79
Japanese yen exchange rates			
Chinese yuan	0.08	89.75	89.21
Hong Kong SAR dollar	0.07	90.11	83.69
Indonesian rupiah	21.40	110.54	363.68
Korean won	7.39	105.86	145.42
Malaysian ringgit	0.02	100.31	140.09
Philippine peso	0.24	101.51	130.38
Singapore dollar	0.01	94.74	98.91
Taiwan dollar	0.25	93.96	101.69
Thai baht	0.23	110.71	135.78

Note: The data source is *Datastream International Ltd.* The first column of data gives the raw annual average exchange rates for 1996. The next two columns give the exchange rate indices for 1997 and 1998 with 1996 = 100.

throughout the world tend to meet at discrete intervals of at least a week to discuss and implement their foreign exchange policies. They like to have smooth exchange rate movements, and they tend to adjust their exchange rates gradually. By failing to differentiate between short- and long-run multipliers, previously reported studies are mis-specified with possibly non-spherical errors. We overcome this by specifying a set of dynamic models that differentiate between the short- and long-run equilibrium responses of the monetary authorities. We consider long-run equilibrium responses only in this study. We model nine Asian currencies (the Chinese yuan, the Hong Kong dollar, the Indonesian rupiah, the Korean won, the Malaysian ringgit, the Philippine peso, the Singapore dollar, the Taiwan dollar and the Thai baht) in response to the German mark, the Japanese yen, the UK pound and the US dollar. All our exchange rates are expressed in terms of the Swiss franc. We estimate our models using a general-to-specific estimation strategy (see Hendry & Krolzig, 2001) with Newey–West heteroscedastic- and autocorrelation-consistent significance tests (see Newey & West, 1987). We use a time-varying methodology. Our models are estimated on a moving window of approximately 18 months in length over the period from November 1976 to December 2003.

We find that there has been a noticeable and significant rise in the influence of the US dollar on some of the region's currencies, combined with a decline in its influence on others since the Asian financial crisis of the late 1990s. This finding is at odds with McKinnon (2000) who describes a reversion to the pre-crisis regime after the Asian crisis. Second, we find that the Japanese yen was not a very influential regional currency during the decade prior to the Asian financial crisis. This contrasts with the findings of Frankel and Wei (1994), Kwan (1996), Zhou (1998) and Bowman (2004) among others who noted an emerging and significant yen influence as early as the late 1980s. Subsequent to the Asian crisis, however, the yen has gained influence on some of the region's currencies, with the notable exceptions of the Chinese yuan, the Hong Kong dollar and the Malaysian ringgit. This corroborates the findings of Gan (2000), Hernandez and Montiel (2002) and Bowman (2004), but is at odds with those of McKinnon (2000). Third, we find that the influence of the German mark on the region's currencies has grown significantly over time, which is not surprising in light of the growing trade linkages between Asia and Europe, while the influence of the UK sterling has diminished to almost zero from a low base. Overall, therefore, we find that the region continues to behave more like a US dollar block than a yen block, but that the declining influence of the US dollar since the late 1990s has been replaced by a growing influence of the German mark and the Japanese yen.

Our chapter is structured as follows. In Section 2 we consider the nature and likelihood of an emerging yen block in North and Southeast Asia and we review the literature on the role of the yen in Asian exchange rate determination. Section 3 discusses emerging trade linkages in the region and performs a preliminary analysis of exchange rate correlations. In Section 4 we describe the model specification and the data and undertake a timevarying investigation of the role of the Japanese yen on exchange rate determination in the region. Section 5 concludes.

2. PREVIOUS RELATED RESEARCH

The issue of what constitutes a yen block has received three main interpretations, ranging from the general notion of regional interdependence in trade and investment flows, to the more specific idea of the yen acting as an important regional invoicing currency for trade and financial transactions, to the stricter definition whereby regional exchange rates may be determined largely by movements in the yen. This latter view is the focus of our study. It incorporates the possibility of the emergence of a regional exchange rate mechanism with the yen as its central currency, in an analogous fashion to the role played by the German mark in the EMS. This analogy is worthy of investigation because the European Monetary System (EMS) has been very successful in reducing intraEuropean exchange rate volatility. The likelihood of the emergence of a yen block in the region, however, is dependent upon a number of factors. The most important of these include: first, the growth in regional trade and investment linkages; second, the extent to which the region's economic and financial structure is tending towards an optimum currency area; third, the degree of confidence in the value of the yen due to Japan's macroeconomic performance and political stability; fourth, low and stable inflation rates in Japan; fifth, a well established set of active primary and secondary financial markets in which a wide array of yen-denominated instruments can be traded at low transaction costs without excessive regulation; and finally, a willingness by the Japanese authorities to allow and encourage the yen to become more globalised.

In evaluating these factors, the regional and global importance of the yen together with Japan's historically low inflation is accepted internationally, although the economy's recent sluggish performance together with its vulnerable banking sector and enhanced political uncertainty during the past decade has curtailed the growth of its influence. The failure by the Japanese authorities to unwind historically excessive regulation has impeded the development of yen-denominated financial instruments and markets, and this has also impeded the growth of the yen's regional and global influence. The Japanese authorities have been historically reluctant to internationalise the yen, but Das (1993) describes how this has changed over time. Although the yen does not perform a dominant role in the world or in the Asia-Pacific region as an invoicing currency, this is slowly changing. Japan itself invoices about one-third of its exports and one-sixth of its imports in US dollars, due largely to the fact that the US is a major market for Japanese exports, and Japanese firms invoice in foreign currency as a natural hedge against the consequences of trend appreciation. The yen is, on most measures, the third most important currency in the world behind the US dollar and the German mark. For example, approximately 50 per cent of international bank assets are denominated in US dollars, with the corresponding figures for the mark and the yen being 14 per cent and 12 per cent respectively. The US dollar accounts for approximately 60 per cent of the world's reserve currencies, with the corresponding figures for the mark and the yen being 19 per cent and 8 per cent respectively. The US dollar continues to occupy its pivotal roles as the dominant international unit of account, medium of exchange and store of value. It remains the most internationally used currency, central banks still hold the largest proportion of their official international reserves in US dollar denominated assets, and they continue to use the US dollar as the chief vehicle of their exchange rate intervention policies. Indeed, many countries in the region continue to manage their exchange rates by focusing on the US dollar value of their currencies to a greater or lesser extent. Although this constitutes strong evidence against the importance of the yen as a dominant regional currency, it does not imply that the influence of the yen is not rising over time in a manner consistent with an emerging yen block.

Previous research on the role of the yen in Asian exchange rate determination includes the work of Frankel (1993), Frankel and Wei (1994), Aggarwal and Mougoue (1996), Kwan (1996), Gan (2000), McKinnon (2000), Hernandez and Montiel (2002) and Bowman (2004). These studies employ standard least-squares regression and cointegration techniques alongside a variety of model specifications to determine the extent to which the region's currencies tend to follow the yen rather than other global currencies such as the euro (or the German mark prior to the euro), the UK pound sterling and the US dollar. The researchers have included in their datasets an extensive list of countries over different time periods, varying degrees of time aggregation (including daily, weekly, monthly and quarterly data), and different numeraires to overcome the '$n-1$' problem in exchange rate modelling (including the inverse of the consumer price index, the European currency unit (ECU), the Swiss franc and the US dollar). The more recent studies have also compared the post- and pre-crisis periods to examine whether there has been any discernible shift in exchange rate setting practices in the region. Overall, the literature suggests that although the yen is a significant currency in the region, the US dollar continues to be the most influential currency and there is limited evidence of an emerging yen block over time.

Frankel (1993) examines the influence of the yen in Asia-Pacific foreign exchange markets. He estimates the weights given to the British pound, the French franc, the mark, the yen and the US dollar by Asia-Pacific monetary authorities in their exchange rate management policies. Using monthly data from 1974 to 1990, he breaks the dataset into 7 sub-periods of 36 months each and reports inter alia the following findings. For the Hong Kong dollar, the US dollar weight is highly significant and close to unity, with a significant weight on the yen during 1979–1981. For Malaysia, the US dollar weight is also significant, but not the yen. For Singapore, the dollar weight diminishes and the yen weight increases until 1985, with only the dollar being significant from 1986 to 1990. For Thailand, the dollar weight is the highest, but diminishes slowly, with the yen and British pound showing significant weights from 1986. The Korean won is dollar-dominated from 1980 to 1988, and yen-dominated after this time.

Frankel and Wei (1994) also examine the influence of the US dollar, the yen and the mark on the exchange rates of smaller economies. Using monthly data from 1979 to 1990 broken into three sub-samples, they report that the Asian countries in their sample (China, Singapore, South Korea and Thailand) place no special weight on the yen, which was statistically significant only in Singapore and occasionally in the other countries. The US dollar, on the other hand, was highly significant for all countries in all sub-periods. Weak links between the yen and the Malaysian, Singapore and Thai currencies are found in the final 2 years of the study. In contrast to previous research, this paper reported heteroscedastic-consistent standard errors. Kwan (1996) examines the same issue using data from the 1995 period. The results suggest considerable increases in the weightings of the yen across the East Asian currencies during this period. Another approach to the possibility of a yen block is to examine whether a long-run relationship exists between currencies. Using daily data from 1988 to 1992, Aggarwal and Mougoue (1996) found that both the yen and the ASEANs (Malaysian, Philippine, Thai and Singapore currencies) and the yen and the 'Tigers' (Hong Kong dollar, South Korea, Singapore and Taiwan) are co-integrated, implying the existence of a long-run relationship between the currencies that prevents any one from getting too far out of line for an extended period of time. Although this does not imply the existence of a regional yen block, it constitutes evidence consistent with it.

Regarding the post-crisis exchange rate patterns Gan (2000) finds evidence of substantial re-weighting in the East Asian currencies' currency baskets. Particularly, the study suggests an increased weighting upon the Japanese yen in the East Asian region excluding Malaysia. In contrast, McKinnon (2000) finds that both the crisis and non-crisis East Asian countries have returned to a de facto policy of dollar pegging that is indistinguishable to what they were doing before the crisis. Hernandez and Montiel (2002) corroborates the Gan (2000) findings by suggesting that the crisis countries (Indonesia, Korea, Malaysia, the Philippines and Thailand) are floating more that they did prior to the crisis, except for Malaysia, which imposed capital controls and adopted a hard peg. Finally, Bowman (2004) notes the emerging importance of the yen to the region and investigates whether the Australian dollar might also be growing in importance. She carefully uses a variety of the methodologies found in the literature and finds that the US dollar is declining in importance in the post-crisis period and that the Australian dollar and the yen are emerging as important currencies in the region.

In summary, therefore, although previous related research provides good insight into the regional influences of the world's major currencies, it neglects to consider the equilibrium responses of the Asian rate returns to innovations in the important world currencies. The model specification procedures used in the received literature are ad hoc, concentrating exclusively on contemporaneous interactions. Also, the received literature is replete with single-period studies where it is implicitly assumed that the estimated dependencies are constant over time. Our study seeks to fill these gaps. We consider the equilibrium interdependencies in a time-varying framework. Overall, the literature suggests significant and strengthening trade, investment and financial linkages throughout North and Southeast Asia, and while the yen is not as dominant as the US dollar in Asia's financial markets, it may be gaining influence over time.

3. GROWING TRADE LINKAGES AND EXCHANGE RATE CORRELATIONS

The degree of regional trade integration amongst the countries included in this study over the past two decades is presented in Table 2, which is drawn from the IMF's *Direction of Trade Statistics*. The table shows each country's trade (measured as the sum of its exports to, and its imports from the other country as a percentage of its total exports and imports) with each other country in the region. The 'country' denoted 'NSA' stands for 'North and Southeast Asia minus Japan', i.e., it includes China, Hong Kong, Indonesia, Korea, Malaysia, the Philippines, Singapore and Thailand. This shows how much trade is done between the countries in the region excluding Japan, which obviously dominates the region's trade. The column figures for NSA are totals, and the row figures for NSA are averages. The table also shows the proportions of trade that the region and its countries conduct with Germany, the UK and the US. This comparison is useful insofar as it casts light on the trade linkages between the region and the world's other major

Table 2.   Direction of Trade Statistics for North and Southeast Asia.

	Ch	HK	In	Ja	Ko	Ma	Ph	Si	Th	NSA	Ge	UK	US
Panel A: Data for 1981													
China		15.1	0.3	25.4	NA	0.7	0.9	1.8	0.9	19.6	5.0	1.5	14.4
Hong Kong	15.5		2.0	14.6	2.7	0.8	1.2	6.0	1.2	29.5	4.2	5.7	18.6
Indonesia	0.7	0.6		43.4	2.2	0.3	1.9	10.0	0.5	16.3	3.3	1.9	17.3
Japan	3.5	2.0	5.9		3.1	1.8	1.2	2.2	1.1	20.8	2.8	2.5	21.8
Korea	NA	2.9	1.6	15.1		1.7	0.8	1.0	0.6	8.6	3.1	2.3	24.8
Malaysia	1.6	1.7	0.5	22.8	2.5		1.2	18.0	2.5	28.0	3.7	3.7	13.8
Philippines	2.0	3.2	2.6	20.3	2.2	2.0		1.7	0.4	14.1	4.1	2.6	26.2
Singapore	2.0	4.8	NA	15.1	1.2	13.8	0.8		2.8	25.4	2.7	2.7	12.9
Thailand	3.0	2.5	0.9	20.1	1.7	3.5	0.2	7.3		19.2	3.8	2.2	13.0
NSA	4.0	4.1	2.0	22.1	2.2	3.1	1.0	6.0	1.3	20.1	3.6	2.8	18.1
Germany	0.5	0.6	0.4	2.3	0.4	0.3	0.2	0.3	0.2	3.0		7.0	7.1
UK	0.3	1.5	0.2	2.8	0.5	0.4	0.2	0.6	0.1	3.7	11.2		12.1
US	1.1	1.7	1.5	12.2	2.1	0.8	0.8	1.0	0.4	9.4	4.4	5.1	
Panel B: Data for 1981													
China		11.8	1.6	18.3	7.6	1.8	0.7	2.4	1.5	27.3	4.3	2.2	16.4
Hong Kong	39.0		0.6	8.9	3.4	1.6	1.0	3.5	1.3	50.4	2.9	2.9	14.9
Indonesia	5.0	2.0		20.7	6.7	3.2	1.0	10.8	2.2	31.0	2.8	2.2	12.4
Japan	10.0	3.4	2.8		6.0	3.3	2.0	3.2	2.8	33.4	3.8	2.5	25.2
Korea	9.4	3.6	2.6	15.7		2.5	1.6	2.8	1.1	23.6	2.9	2.4	20.2
Malaysia	3.5	3.7	2.2	16.7	3.8		2.1	16.5	3.7	35.5	2.7	2.6	18.8
Philippines	1.9	4.2	1.2	15.8	4.8	3.4		7.1	2.8	25.5	2.8	2.5	22.7
Singapore	4.6	5.3	NA	12.3	3.6	17.6	2.5		4.3	37.8	3.1	2.3	16.2
Thailand	8.9	4.8	1.9	19.1	2.6	4.7	1.6	9.2		33.6	2.6	2.5	16.3
NSA	10.3	5.1	1.7	15.9	4.6	5.0	1.5	7.5	2.4	33.1	3.0	2.4	17.2
Germany	2.4	0.6	0.3	3.5	0.9	0.5	0.2	0.7	0.4	6.1		7.7	9.5
UK	1.6	2.2	0.4	3.5	1.2	0.8	0.4	1.0	0.5	8.0	12.3		14.6
US	6.0	1.3	0.7	10.5	3.3	1.8	1.1	1.8	1.2	17.2	4.4	4.2	

Note: The source is IMF Direction of Trade Statistics. Reading across the rows gives the sum of each country's exports and imports with each country named at the top of the column, as a percentage of its total exports and imports. NSA denotes 'North and Southeast Asia minus Japan', i.e., China, Hong Kong, Indonesia, Korea, Malaysia, the Philippines, Singapore and Thailand. The column figures for NSA are totals, and the row figures are averages. Taiwan is not recognized by the IMF as an independent country.

currencies in addition to the yen, which are the focus of the econometric analysis presented after this subsection. Panel A of the table shows the trading patterns in 1981, and Panel B shows the same data in 2000. Inspection of the table reveals a number of salient features of the region's trading patterns.

First, looking down the column labelled NSA in Panel B of the table, we can see that five countries are *highly* integrated within the region. Using the data for 2000, between a half and a third of all their trade is with NSA countries – i.e. countries in the region excluding Japan. These are Hong Kong (50.4 per cent), Japan (33.4 per cent), Malaysia (35.5 per cent), Singapore (37.8 per cent) and Thailand (33.6 per cent). The remaining four countries are *moderately* integrated within the region. Using the data for 2000, between a fifth and a third of all their trade is with NSA countries. These are China (27.3 per cent), Korea (23.6 per cent), Indonesia (31 per cent) and the Philippines (25.5 per cent).

Second, when trade with Japan is included in our measure of regional trade integration (which can be seen by adding the 'Ja' column and the NSA column in Panel B of the table), the degree of trade integration is almost 40 per cent or higher in all of the region's countries (excluding Japan). These are, in order of integration, Hong Kong (59.3 per cent), Thailand (52.7 per cent), Malaysia (52.2 per cent), Indonesia (51.7 per cent), Singapore (50.1 per cent), China (45.6 per cent), the Philippines (41.3 per cent) and Korea (39.3 per cent). The average figure for these eight countries is 49.04 per cent.

Third, looking at how the degree of trade integration has changed over the 20 years from 1981 to 2000 by comparing the figures from Panel B with those from Panel A of the table, reveals that the degree of regional trade integration has risen over time while the ordering has remained somewhat similar. When trade with Japan is included, the same eight countries mentioned in the previous point which together averaged 49.04 per cent of their trade within the region in 2000, averaged 42.18 per cent in 1981. It follows that trade integration amongst these countries within the region has risen by 16 per cent over the last two decades of the 1900s.

Fourth, the region's trade integration with Japan has declined by 28 per cent from 22.1 per cent in 1981 to 15.9 per cent in 2000. In contrast, Japan's trade integration with the region has risen from a fifth (20.8 per cent) in 1981 to over a third (33.4 per cent) in 2000. This is a 60 per cent increase in its degree of regional trade integration. It has done this while also increasing its integration with the United States by almost 16 per cent, increasing its integration with Germany from a low base, and maintaining its low degree of integration with the United Kingdom. By contrast, almost all countries in the region (the exception being Korea) have reduced their proportions of trade with Japan – by more than 30 per cent, from an average of 20 per cent to 14 per cent. Although the importance of the Japanese economy to the other countries in the region has declined, it remains a very important trading partner nonetheless. Looking across the rows of Panel B of the table shows that the most important trade dependencies in the region are Hong Kong on China (39 per cent), Indonesia on Japan (20.7 per cent), Thailand on Japan (19.1 per cent), China on Japan (18.3 per cent), Singapore on Malaysia (17.6 per cent), Malaysia on Japan (16.7 per cent), Malaysia on Singapore (16.5 per cent), the Philippines on Japan (15.8 per cent) and Korea on Japan (15.7 per cent). Although there are some obvious dependencies that do not include Japan, it remains by far the most dominant country in the region.

Fifth, trade between the region (excluding Japan) and Germany, the UK and the US has remained broadly stable over time, from 3.7 per cent, 2.8 per cent and 17.6 per cent, respectively in 1981 to 3.0 per cent, 2.4 per cent and 17.2 per cent in 2000. The dominant position of the United States economy in the region in addition to that of Japan is beyond question, with the relative importance of both Germany and the United Kingdom being minor in comparison to these.

Overall, therefore, the direction of trade statistics reveal that most countries in the region (China, Indonesia, Malaysia, the Philippines and Thailand) are heavily dependent on the Japanese economy with respect to international trade. Although two countries in the region are less directly dependent on the Japanese economy (Hong Kong and Singapore), they are closely integrated with other countries that are themselves heavily dependent on Japan. For example, although Hong Kong conducts less than 9 per cent of its total trade with Japan, it conducts almost 40 per cent of its trade with China, which in turn conducts over 18 per cent of its trade with Japan. Similar relationships exist between Singapore, Malaysia and Japan. The trade data also reveals that the United States economy is important to the region, and that Germany and the United Kingdom are of lesser importance to the economic welfare of North and Southeast Asia.

Having investigated the growth of regional trade integration in Asia, it is interesting to examine how the correlations between the region's exchange rates have behaved over time. Table 3 presents the correlations for the first half of the sample in Panel A, and for the whole sample in Panel B. At the bottom of each Panel, the mean correlation of each country's bilateral yen exchange rate with the other countries is provided. Overall, the average correlation coefficient for the first half of the sample is 0.57, and this falls to 0.54 during the full sample period. This indicates some tendency for the yen bilateral rates to move increasingly independently over time. Within this, however, a number of observations also suggest themselves. In the first half of the sample, seven countries (Hong Kong, Korea, Malaysia, the Philippines, Singapore, Taiwan and Thailand) have mean yen bilateral exchange

Table 3. Correlations of Yen Bilateral Exchange Rates.

Exchange rate	Ch	HK	In	Ko	Ma	Ph	Si	Ta	Th
Panel A: First sample, November 1976–June 1990									
China	1.00								
Hong Kong	0.30	1.00							
Indonesia	0.49	0.38	1.00						
Korea	0.46	0.60	0.42	1.00					
Malaysia	0.38	0.92	0.44	0.63	1.00				
Philippines	0.44	0.54	0.48	0.64	0.55	1.00			
Singapore	0.33	0.94	0.39	0.60	0.92	0.54	1.00		
Taiwan	0.49	0.63	0.54	0.73	0.63	0.76	0.64	1.00	
Thailand	0.53	0.51	0.55	0.64	0.57	0.67	0.55	0.64	1.00
Mean	0.43	0.60	0.46	0.59	0.63	0.58	0.61	0.61	0.58
Panel B: Full sample, November 1976–December 2003									
China	1.00								
Hong Kong	0.51	1.00							
Indonesia	0.26	0.30	1.00						
Korea	0.39	0.57	0.49	1.00					
Malaysia	0.31	0.61	0.43	0.61	1.00				
Philippines	0.45	0.64	0.45	0.60	0.47	1.00			
Singapore	0.47	0.89	0.44	0.61	0.67	0.64	1.00		
Taiwan	0.52	0.79	0.26	0.61	0.52	0.73	0.76	1.00	
Thailand	0.45	0.61	0.50	0.59	0.53	0.68	0.60	0.70	1.00
Mean	0.42	0.62	0.39	0.56	0.52	0.58	0.64	0.58	0.58

Note: The data source is *Datastream International Ltd.* It is the correlations of nominal yen bilateral exchange rates for the various countries. The average correlation during the first period is 0.57 and during the full period is 0.54.

rate correlations with all the other countries greater than 0.50 and four countries (Hong Kong, Malaysia, Taiwan and Singapore) have a mean correlation greater than 0.60. The countries with the lowest correlations are China and Indonesia, which together have an average correlation of 0.44. In the full sample, only two countries (Hong Kong and Singapore) have mean yen bilateral exchange rate correlations with all the other countries greater than 0.60 and five countries (Korea, Malaysia, the Philippines, Taiwan and Thailand) have mean correlations greater than 0.50. The countries with the lowest correlations in the full sample are the same as those for the first period, namely, China and Indonesia with an average correlation of 0.41. These two countries seem to operate their exchange rates less in relation to the other countries in an overall sense. Some country pairs (Hong Kong–Malaysia, Korea–Taiwan and Malaysia–Singapore) have experienced

significant declines in their yen exchange rate correlations, and these probably reflect tendencies towards greater dispersion in their trading relations
over time. Overall, therefore, the correlation analysis suggests that the yen
bilateral exchange rates in the region are tending to diverge somewhat over
time. This is not surprising, particularly in light of the trade data analysis
presented above, and it suggests interest in our econometric analysis of the
role of the yen.

4. ECONOMETRIC ESTIMATES OF THE YEN'S ROLE IN THE REGION

Our North and Southeast Asian currencies include the Chinese yuan, the
Hong Kong dollar, the Indonesian rupiah, the Korean won, the Malaysian
ringgit, the Philippine peso, the Singapore dollar, the Taiwan dollar and the
Thai baht. Our world currencies comprise the German mark (the euro since
1 January 1999), the Japanese yen, the UK pound sterling and the US
dollar. All data are obtained from *Datastream International Ltd*, and all
exchange rates are expressed as units of domestic currency in 1 Swiss franc.
The data are sampled at the close of trading on the last trading day of the
week. The full sample period is 19 November 1976 to 26 December 2003.
The Taiwan dollar and the Chinese yuan commenced on the 4th and 11th
January 1985, respectively. Figs. 1 and 2 depict the evolution of the Asian
and world exchange rates over the whole sample period.

Our econometric model is described below.

$$S_t^i = \alpha_0 + \sum_{j=1}^{N} \alpha_j S_{t-j}^i + \sum_{j=0}^{N} \beta_j S_{t-j}^{DM} + \sum_{j=0}^{N} \gamma_j S_{t-j}^{YEN}$$
$$+ \sum_{j=0}^{N} \delta_j S_{t-j}^{UK} + \sum_{j=0}^{N} \zeta_J S_{t-j}^{US} + \sum_{j=0}^{N} D_{j,t}^i + \varepsilon_t^i \qquad (1)$$

Here, S^i denotes the log change in the bilateral Swiss franc exchange rates of
the nine currencies included in the sample. S^{DM}, S^{YEN}, S^{UK} and S^{US} denote the log changes in the exogenous German mark, Japanese yen, UK
pound sterling and US dollar bilateral Swiss franc rates respectively. Since 1
January 1999, the German mark has been irrevocably tied to the euro. The
$D_{j,t}^i$ variables denote the *jth* currency-specific dummy variable for currency
i at time *t*, and they capture episodes of periodic interventions by the relevant monetary authorities that might have caused influential outliers or

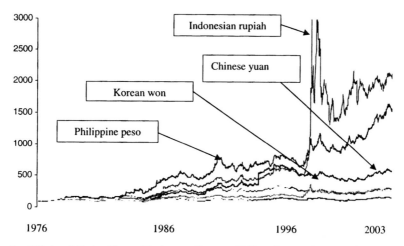

Fig. 1. Bilateral Swiss Franc Exchange Rates of Nine Currencies. Weekly, January 1985–December 2003.

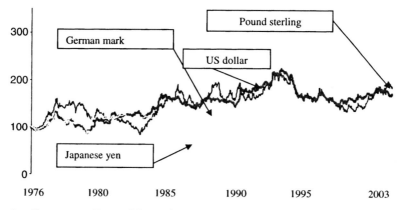

Fig. 2. Exogenous Rates, November 1976–December 2003. The US Dollar, the German Deutschemark and the Pound Sterling Swiss Franc Bilateral Rates.

structural breaks in the series. The Plaza dummy variable takes account of the Plaza Accord on the 4th October 1985 aimed at halting the rise of the US dollar. The Louvre dummy variable takes account of the Louvre Accord on the 6th March 1987 aimed at stabilising the foreign exchange value of the US dollar. Other included dummy variables are those found to be statistically significant in the parsimoniously derived models.[1]

Our specification is an improvement on the specifications of Frankel (1993) and Frankel and Wei (1994), which assume instantaneous interaction between the regional currencies and the important exogenous exchange rates. The models are couched in logarithmic difference form which is suitable for exchange rates (see Enders, 1995), and because this induces stationarity. The legitimacy of doing this was verified using the augmented Dickey Fuller (ADF) and Phillips Perron (PP) tests, and as reported in Kearney and Muckley (2005), the log change exchange rates are all without trend. The models have consequently been estimated in logarithmic first difference form using the general-to-specific dynamic estimation strategy (see Hendry & Krolzig, 2001). We initially include up to four lags of each variable in the models, and sequentially test then using Newey–West derived t-statistics until parsimonious specifications are obtained. The procedure is repeated for each Asian exchange rate for partially overlapping 52-week periods.

The resulting dynamic models are solved to obtain the long-run multipliers for the effects of variations in the mark, the yen, the pound sterling and the US dollar on the regional currencies. The long-run multipliers are obtained from the estimated versions of Eq. (1) as follows:

$$LRM_k^{s^i} = \frac{\sum_{j=0}^{N} \psi_j}{\sum_{j=1}^{N} \alpha_j} \qquad (2)$$

where $k =$ DM, YEN, UK and US, and $\psi = \beta, \gamma, \delta,$ and ζ in Eq. (1). Eq. (2) tells us the equilibrium responses of each regional exchange rate to variations in the exogenous rates.

We estimate the sequence of German mark, Japanese yen, UK pound and US dollar multipliers for each of the bilateral rates over a moving window of 52 weeks commencing on the 19th November 1976 and ending on the 26th December 2003. The windows are overlapping in the sense that each consecutive window drops the first observation in the preceding window and includes the incremental observation. Table 4 summarises the pre- and post-Asian crisis mean of the long-run multipliers for each currency, and Fig. 3 plots the long-run multipliers throughout the entire data period.

The pre- and post-crisis periods described in Table 4 are defined following Hernandez and Montiel (2002) such that the period of the crisis does not distort the long-run multiplier estimates. The sub-periods are approximately 5 years in length. The period from July 1997 to January 1999 is thought to span the crisis and it is removed from the analysis. This deleted sub-sample lies between the pre- and post-crisis periods. Overall, the results suggest that

Table 4.   Long-Run Multipliers Pre- and Post-Asian Crisis.

	German mark	Japanese yen	UK sterling	US dollar
Panel A: Long-run multiplier pre-Asian crisis				
Chinese yuan	−0.32	0.02	0.08	0.90
Hong Kong dollar	−0.11	−0.01	0.00	0.99
Indonesian rupiah	0.14	−0.03	0.05	0.95
Korean won	0.04	0.09	0.06	0.89
Malaysian ringgit	0.34	0.07	−0.11	0.90
Philippine peso	−0.09	0.06	0.18	0.85
Singapore dollar	0.03	0.08	−0.03	0.83
Taiwan dollar	−0.22	0.14	−0.06	0.92
Thai baht	0.07	0.10	0.05	0.82
Panel B: Long-run multiplier post-Asian crisis				
Chinese yuan	−0.89	0.00	0.00	1.00
Hong Kong dollar	−0.13	0.00	0.00	0.99
Indonesian rupiah	1.23	0.18	−0.25	0.68
Korean won	0.19	0.34	−0.01	0.63
Malaysian ringgit	0.19	0.00	0.00	0.99
Philippine peso	0.48	0.07	−0.09	0.88
Singapore dollar	0.45	0.22	0.03	0.60
Taiwan dollar	0.28	0.11	−0.05	0.79
Thai baht	0.46	0.24	−0.03	0.62

Note: The pre-Asian crisis period is from 10 July 1992 to 27 June 1997 and the post-Asian crisis is from 1 January 1999 to 26 December 2003. All models are estimated on moving windows of 12 months using Eq. (1), and the long-run multipliers are as derived in Eq. (2). The results presented in this table are arithmetic averages of the long-run multipliers over the pre- and post-Asian crisis periods.

the influence of the US dollar is in decline, that of the UK pound is immaterial in both sub-periods and that the influence of the German mark and the Japanese yen (particularly the former) has increased significantly. Specifically, the arithmetic mean of the US dollar multipliers has declined from approximately 90 per cent to approximately 80 per cent over the two sub-periods. The UK pound mean multiplier has changed from about 2 per cent to about −4 per cent while those of the German mark, and the UK pound have risen from approximately 1 and 5 per cent to approximately 25 and 12 per cent respectively. The mean statistics are calculated over all nine currencies considered in this chapter and as such they disguise a number of cases of interest regarding particular currencies. We consider these instances as they arise in our discussion of the evolution of the importance of the German mark, the Japanese yen, the UK pound and the US dollar to exchange rate determination in the region.

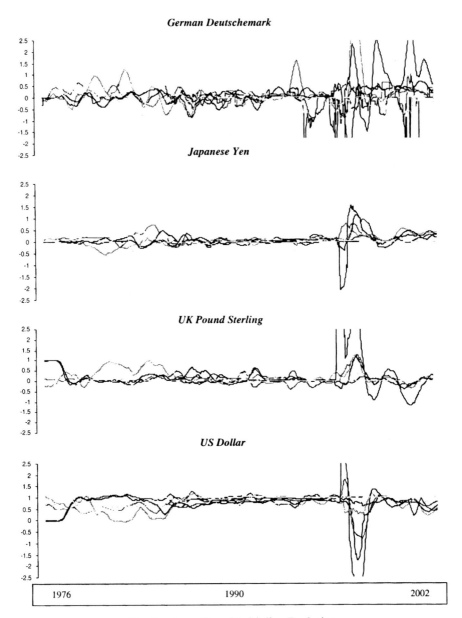

Fig. 3. Long-Run Multiplier Evolution.

There is a tendency for the German mark long-run multipliers to oscillate more and more closely to zero until the mid-1990s. Thereafter, they exhibit periods of turbulence initially with respect to the Chinese yuan and the Malaysian ringgit and then in the late 1990s with respect to the Indonesian rupiah, the Korean won, the Singapore dollar and the Thai baht. Since this latter turbulence (i.e., during the post-crisis period), it is apparent that the German mark has significantly increased in importance with respect to the Indonesian rupiah, the Korean won, the Philippine peso, the Singapore and the Taiwan dollars and the Thai baht. Its influence on the Thai baht specifically is approximately 0.46 throughout the post-crisis period. On average with respect to these six currencies, the influence of the mark multipliers has increased from 10 per cent in the pre-crisis period to 52 per cent in the post-crisis period (ignoring the negative signs on the Philippine and Taiwan multipliers in the first sub-period). Although all the multipliers increase significantly, it is the Indonesian rupiah's mark multiplier, which rises from 14 per cent prior to the crisis to 123 per cent after the crisis that is largely responsible for the size of the increase in the average mark influence on this sub-set of currencies.

During the 1986–1997 period, the Japanese yen long-run multipliers appear to oscillate tightly about zero for all nine of the regional rates. Prior to and immediately succeeding this tranquil period there are short periods of relative volatility. The multipliers demonstrate a marked tendency to increase since the Asian crisis particularly in reference to the Indonesian rupiah and the Korean won, although to a lesser extent with respect to the Singapore dollar and the Thai baht. The Taiwan dollar shows a stable but small yen influence in both sub-periods. The arithmetic mean of the yen multipliers on these five currencies rises from 8 per cent in the pre-crisis period to 22 per cent in the post-crisis period.

The UK pound multipliers for the regional rates form a distinct strand at approximately zero notwithstanding material discrepancies from zero in the early- to mid-1980s with respect to the Korean won and another period of extraordinary volatility in the late 1990s in reference to the Indonesian rupiah and to a lesser extent to the Korean won and Thai baht. In the late 1970s, prior to the convergence to zero, it appears that the Indonesian rupiah, the Philippine peso and the Thai baht shared an approximate 1:1 relationship with the UK pound (using the sample considered in this study).

The US dollar multipliers constitute a single tightly knit strand for the period of the late 1980s to the period of the Asian crisis in the late 1990s that exceeds 0.9 with the exceptions of the Thai baht, the Philippine peso and the

Singapore dollar multipliers, which nevertheless exceed 0.5 during this period. Prior to this confluence there are a variety of patterns of sensitivity to the US dollar displayed by the regional rates. During the late 1990s, there is extraordinary instability in the relationships – particularly concerning the Indonesian rupiah, the Thai baht, the Malaysian ringgit and to a lesser extent the Singapore dollar rate. The turbulence tapers off during the 20002001 period but the single strand of multipliers that prevailed prior to the Asian crisis does not reappear. Specifically, the Indonesian rupiah, the Korean won, the Singapore and Taiwan dollars and the Thai baht multipliers stray for prolonged periods from the preceding regime. The importance of the US dollar multipliers on these five currencies declines from 88 per cent prior to the crisis to 66 per cent in the post-crisis period. The decline in the influence of the US dollar is convincing in every instance. With respect to the Chinese yuan, the Hong Kong dollar, the Malaysian ringgit and the Philippine peso the US dollar's influence is strengthened or maintained in the post-crisis period.

In summary, the trade data shows that an important part of Japan's international trade occurs within the North and Southeast Asia region and that this part is increasing over time. Indeed, most countries in the region appear to be heavily dependent on the Japanese economy with respect to international trade. It follows that Japan may have a vested interest in stabilising the Asian exchange rate value of the Japanese yen, particularly with its primary trading partners in the region. Moreover, it is apparent from the preceding econometric analysis that the Japanese yen has, since the Asian financial crisis in the late 1990s, been allocated a significant weighting in the currency baskets of a number of Asian currencies, including those with which it enjoys significant and improving trade linkages, for example, the Korean won and the Thai baht currencies. Overall, these analyses suggest that the Japanese yen is determining many North and Southeast Asian exchange rates to a discernible extent and that it is well positioned to build on this role should it wish to do so. There is also a notable and growing German mark influence on the region's exchange rates. In contrast, the UK pound demonstrates no capacity to systematically influence the regions exchange rates since the late 1970s. The US dollar remains the most important currency in the region with respect to exchange rate determination; however, this importance appears to be in decline since the Asian crisis in the late 1990s. Overall, the evidence points to an emerging basket-of-currencies currency block with the German mark and the Japanese yen playing significant but minor roles, and the US dollar is remaining the predominant exchange rate determinant in the region.

5. SUMMARY AND CONCLUSIONS

The economies of North and Southeast Asia performed very well in the three decades prior to the Asian crisis of the late 1990s. The fastest growing countries became known as the 'Asian tigers'. Since the Asian crisis, however, questions have been asked about the exchange rate systems operated by these countries, and about whether some form of coordinated regional exchange rate system could have prevented or mitigated its ill effects. In this chapter, we review prior work on the extent to which there is evidence of an emerging yen influence that might be exploited in designing a more appropriate regional exchange rate system for Asia. We supplement this by carefully examining the extent of regional trade integration, and we demonstrate that there is a significant movement towards greater trade relations in the region particularly with respect to Japanese trade integration. Our analysis of yen regional exchange rate correlations shows a tendency towards declining correlations over time, which further motivates our study of exchange rate determinants in the region.

Our econometric modeling is based on up to 27 years of weekly data on nine bilateral Swiss franc exchange rates vis-à-vis the Hong Kong dollar, the Indonesian rupiah, the Malaysian ringgit, the Philippine peso, the Singapore dollar, the Thai baht, the Chinese yuan, the Korean won and the Taiwan dollar. We model the time series behaviour of these exchange rates within a time-varying framework, and we focus exclusively on dynamic effects to determine whether the Swiss franc exchange rates follow the yen in response to external shocks, as would be the case in a yen-dominated system. To this end, we estimate the German mark, the Japanese yen, the UK pound sterling and the US dollar long-run multiplier evolutions for each of the bilateral Swiss Franc rates.

The results suggest that the influence of the Japanese yen on exchange rate behaviour in the region largely stems from the aftermath of the Asian financial crisis in the late 1990s, as does that of the German mark. In contrast, the US dollar is found to decline in importance with respect to exchange rate determination in the region during this latter period. It ought to be emphasised, however, that the US dollar remains the primary currency with respect to influence in the region. Notwithstanding a brief period in the late 1970s the UK pound shows no systematic capacity to act as an exchange rate determinant. Our analysis of the IMF direction of trade statistics bears out the importance of Japan to the region's international trade and also its potential to play an increasingly important role with respect to exchange rate determination in the region of North and Southeast Asia.

NOTES

1. The following dummy variables are statistically significant at the 5per cent level: China (05/03/85, 07/18/86, 12/22/89 and 01/07/94), Hong Kong SAR (09/23/83, 05/12/95 and 09/22/95), Indonesia (04/08/83, 09/19/86, 01/30/98, 01/23/98 and 01/09/98), Korea (02/01/80, 03/29/85 and 08/02/85), Malaysia (02/20/81, 10/10/97, 01/09/98, 01/23/98, 01/30/98 and 10/30/98), the Philippines (01/12/79, 10/14/83, 06/15/84, 02/28/86 and 07/11/97), Singapore (02/20/81 and 06/19/98), Taiwan (05/03/85, 09/13/85, 09/27/85, 04/28/89, 05/12/95 and 11/07/97) and Thailand (11/09/84, 09/27/85, 10/04/85, 10/31/97, 01/09/98 and 03/13/98).

REFERENCES

Aggarwal, R., & Mougoue, M. (1996). Cointegration among Asian currencies: Evidence of the increasing influence of the Japanese yen. *Japan and the World Economy, 8*, 291–308.

Bowman, C. (2004). Yen block or Koala block? Currency relationships after the East Asian crisis. *Japan and the World Economy*, forthcoming.

Das, D. K. (1993). The internationalisation of the yen. In: D. K. Das (Ed.), *International finance: Contemporary issues* (pp. 580–591). London: Routledge.

Enders, W. (1995). *Applied econometric time-series* (pp. 157–229). Wiley: John Wiley & Sons.

Frankel, J. A. (1993). Is Japan creating a yen bloc in East Asia and the Pacific. In: J. Frankel & M. Kahler (Eds), *Regionalism and rivalry: Japan and the US in Pacific Asia* (pp. 53–85). Chicago: University of Chicago Press.

Frankel, J., & Wei, S. (1994). Yen block or dollar block? Exchange rate policies of the East Asian economies. In: T. Ito & A. O. Krueger (Eds), *Macroeconomic linkages: Savings, exchange rates and capital flows* (pp. 295–329). Chicago: University of Chicago Press.

Gan, W. B. (2000). Exchange-rate policy in East Asia after the fall: How much have things changed? *Journal of Asian Economics, 11*(4), 403–430.

Hendry, D., & Krolzig, H. (2001). Computer automation of general-to-specific model selection procedures. *Journal of Economic Dynamics and Control, 25*, 831–866.

Hernandez, L., & Montiel, P. (2002). *Post-crisis exchange rate policy in five Asian countries: Filling in the 'hollow middle'?* IMF Working Paper, code: WP/01/170.

Hutson, E., & Kearney, C. (1999). The Asian financial crisis and the IMF: A survey. *Journal of the Asia Pacific Economy, 4*, 393–412.

International Monetary Fund. (IMF). (1998). *World economic outlook* (various issues). Washington: IMF.

Johnson, C. (1998). Economic crisis in East Asia: The clash of capitalisms. *Cambridge Journal of Economics, 22*, 653–661.

Kearney, C., & Muckley, C. (2005). Reassessing the evidence of an emerging yen block in Southeast Asia. *International Review of Economics and Finance* (forthcoming).

Krugman, P. (1998). *What happened to Asia? Mimeographed.* Cambridge, MA: Department of Economics Massachusetts Institute of Technology.

Kwan, C. H. (1996). A yen block in Asia: An integrative approach. *Journal of the Asia Pacific Economy, 1*, 1–21.

McKinnon, R. I. (2000). The East Asian dollar standard: Life after death? *Economic Notes, 29*(1), 31–82.

Newey, W. K., & West, K. D. (1987). A simple, positive semi-definite, heteroscedasticity and autocorrelation consistent covariance matrix. *Econometrica, 55*(3), 703–708.

Zhou, S. (1998). Exchange rate systems and linkages in the Pacific Basin. *Atlantic Economics Journal, 26*(1), 66–84.

DOES STATISTICAL DEPENDENCE MATTER? EVIDENCE FROM THE USD/AUD

Craig A. Ellis

ABSTRACT

This study investigates the effect of volatility scaling on valuing financial assets by examining the long-term return properties of the spot USD/AUD. Tests are conducted for evidence of a scaling law in USD/AUD returns. The economic implications of dependence and non-normality of the distribution of returns are explored using the Garman and Kohlhagen modified Black–Scholes model for valuing foreign currency options. The results suggest that the USD/AUD does not conform to a stable distribution and that as a result of differential scaling laws, Garman and Kohlhagen option values using implied annual volatility will be consistently too high or too low.

1. INTRODUCTION

A defining characteristic of Gaussian random processes is the relationship between the increments of the time series at different intervals. When

Asia Pacific Financial Markets in Comparative Perspective: Issues and Implications for the 21st Century
Contemporary Studies in Economics and Financial Analysis, Volume 86, 53–72
ISSN: 1569-3759/doi:10.1016/S1569-3759(05)86003-6

returns are normally distributed, the risk of an asset over a long return interval can be precisely calculated by scaling the risk from shorter return intervals. Numerous empirical studies, however, suggest that foreign currency returns may not be independent (Xu & Gencay, 2003; Byers & Peel, 2001; Van De Gucht, Dekimpe, & Kwok, 1996; Muller et al., 1990) or conform to a stable probability distribution (Nekhili, Altay-Salih, & Gencay, 2002; Tucker & Scott, 1987; Wasserfallen & Zimmermann, 1985). In light of these findings, a key empirical question concerns the effect that scaling the volatility of dependent processes will have on the pricing of related assets.

This study provides an insight into this issue by investigating the long-term return properties of the spot USD/AUD. Several tests are first conducted for evidence of a scaling law in interday USD/AUD returns. The economic implications of dependence in the returns series and the non-normality of the distribution of returns is then considered using the Garman and Kohlhagen modified Black–Scholes model for valuing foreign currency options. The results suggest that the USD/AUD does not conform to a stable distribution and that as a result of differential scaling laws, Garman and Kohlhagen option values using implied annual volatility will be consistently too high or too low.

Following from Garman and Kohlhagen (1983), the valuation of foreign currency options in the Black–Scholes framework is mathematically equivalent to the procedure derived by Merton (1973) for valuing European call options on dividend-paying stock. Rather than receiving a known dividend yield q, the holder of a long position in currency earns the equivalent of the risk-free rate in the foreign currency, r_f. The risk-free rate in the Black–Scholes model is similarly the equivalent of the domestic risk-free interest rate r, in the Garman and Kohlhagen model. When the value of r_f is zero, the Garman and Kohlhagen model reduces to the Black and Scholes (1973) model. As is the case for stocks in the Black–Scholes model, foreign exchange rates are assumed to follow a Brownian motion (random walk) process with constant μ and σ (Hull, 1989, p. 270). The two implications of this assumption that are examined in this paper are that historic volatilities can be used to proxy future volatility and that there is zero dependence between successive price changes. Since volatility in the Black–Scholes model cannot be directly observed, this must be either backed-out as implied volatility or proxied by historic volatility. The Garman and Kohlhagen modified Black–Scholes model is given as follows:

$$C = Se^{-r_f t}N(d_1) - Xe^{-rt}N(d_2)$$
$$P = Xe^{-rt}N(-d_2) - Se^{-r_f t}N(-d_1)$$
$$d_1 = \frac{\ln(S/X) + \left(r - r_f + \frac{1}{2}\sigma^2\right)t}{\sigma\sqrt{t}} \tag{1}$$
$$d_2 = d_1 - \sigma\sqrt{t}$$

Early research by Goodman, Ross, and Schmidt (1985) on the pricing of foreign currency options using the Garman and Kohlhagen (1983) and Black and Scholes (1973) models found using daily and monthly volatility produced theoretical option values that were too high when compared to their actual value on the Philadelphia Stock Exchange (PHLX). The apparent overpricing is surmised by Goodman, Ross and Schmidt as being due to price makers using unrealistically high volatilities to value currency options, or to the (then) illiquidity of the foreign currency option market. While much focus has been given to the question of underlying biases in the modified Black–Scholes model in general (see Sarwar & Krebhiel, 2000; Melino & Turnbull, 1991; Bodurtha & Courtadon, 1987; Shastri & Tandon, 1986), and to the implementation of implied volatility specifically (see Hentschel, 2003; Kagenishi & Shinohara, 2001; Butler & Schachter, 1986) issues arising from the practice of annualising historic volatility for option valuation have received less attention.

2. LINEAR RESCALING AND THE "$T^{1/2}$ RULE"

Linear rescaling is the term used to describe the process by which the moments of a distribution, when measured over a short time interval (e.g. daily) can be scaled to replicate the equivalent moments for a long time interval (e.g. annual).

Consider a function S, comprising the points $X(t) = [X(t_0), X(t_1), \ldots, X(t_n)]$ in time t. The probability of incremental movement of $X(t)$ is restricted with respect to the direction of the movement to allow only forward changes in time, but is otherwise unrestricted. Changing the time scale of the function (horizontal axis measure) by a ratio $r < 1$, the required change in amplitude scale (vertical axis measure) is r^H.

Given the function S conforms to a Brownian process the distance from $X(t_0)$ to a point $X(t_0 + t)$ is shown by Mandelbrot (1982) to be a random multiple of $\sqrt{t}$. Setting $t_0 = 0$ it follows for $t > t_0$ that

$$X(t_0 + t) - X(t_0) \approx \varepsilon|(t_0 + t) - t_0|^{0.5} \approx \varepsilon_t^{0.5} \tag{2}$$

where ε is a random variable with zero mean and unit variance. Properly rescaled in time by r, and in amplitude by $\sqrt{r}$, the increments of the linearly rescaled function $(rS)/\sqrt{r}$ are given by

$$\frac{X(t_0 + rt) - X(t_0)}{\sqrt{r}} \tag{3}$$

When properly rescaled, the original and rescaled functions are statistically indistinguishable and the moments of the distribution therefore identical. The scaling factor $\sqrt{r} = r^H$ gives rise to what is commonly known as the "$T^{1/2}$ rule", using which the volatility of short-horizon returns can be rescaled by the square root of time $\sqrt{t}$, to construct the volatility of equivalent long-horizon returns. Allowing for any $0 \leq H \leq 1$; $H \neq 0.5$ it follows that Eq. (2) can be generalised by

$$X(t_0 + t) - X(t_0) \approx \varepsilon|(t_0 + t) - t_0|^H \approx \varepsilon_t^H \tag{4}$$

and Eq. (3) similarly generalised by

$$\frac{X(t_0 + rt) - X(t_0)}{r^H} \tag{5}$$

Functions in time that satisfy both of Eqs. (4) and (5) are described as being "self-affine". While this definition of self-affinity requires that every mathematical and statistical characteristic of the time series function and its self-affine rescaled function be examined, proof of self-affine behaviour can in practice, be "inferred from a single test that is only concerned with one facet of sameness" (Mandelbrot, 1982, p. 254). To this end, three separate tests are conducted in this paper to determine the existence of a scaling law in the volatility of interday USD/AUD returns.

The first test conducted is the relation described by the power law function

$$y \propto x^H \tag{6}$$

for the standard deviation of returns over return intervals $k = 1, 2, \ldots, 252$ days. Derived from the premise that amplitude and time do not vary independently, but instead are dependent, Eq. (6) states that the y-axis measure is proportional to time x, raised to a scale exponent H. The scale exponent is initially estimated by the coefficient γ_1 in the regression

$$\log(\sigma_k) = \gamma_0 + \gamma_1 \log(k) \tag{7}$$

where k is the length of the return interval and σ_k the standard deviation of k interval returns. The technique is similar to that employed by Muller et al. (1990) for intraday foreign exchange rates. Under the null hypothesis that interday USD/AUD returns conform to an independent Gaussian distribution, the expected value of the scale exponent is $H = 0.5$. Continuously, compounded returns for the USD/AUD are measured using $X_k = \ln(S_t/S_{t-k})$ for each of the above nominated values of k. The volatility of returns is estimated by the second moment of the distribution for each sample.

The self-affine relation described by Eqs. (4) and (5) is then tested by

$$[\sigma^2(S_t - S_{t-k})]^{0.5} = (k/n)^{0.5}[\sigma^2(S_t - S_{t-n})]^{0.5} \tag{8}$$

where k and n are pairs of return intervals $\infty \geq k \geq n \geq 1$, and S_t and S_{t-k} the natural logarithms of the daily spot exchange rates. This second test describes scaling relations between the volatility of returns measured over the discrete time intervals k, $n = 1, 5, 21$ and 252 days. The chosen values of k and n correspond to the daily (1), weekly (5), monthly (21), and annual (252) return intervals. The basis of this test is the $T^{1/2}$ rule, which provides that the volatility of returns at any time interval can be estimated from the volatility at any other interval.

2.1. The Classical Rescaled Adjusted Range

The third test conducted is for the level of dependence in interday USD/AUD returns. Proposed by Hurst (1951), the classical rescaled adjusted range statistic $(R/\sigma)_n$ is calculated by

$$(R/\sigma)_n = (1/\sigma_n)\left[\begin{array}{c}Max\\1 \leq k \leq n\end{array}\sum_{j=1}^{k}(X_j - \overline{X_n}) - \begin{array}{c}Min\\1 \leq k \leq n\end{array}\sum_{j=1}^{k}(X_j - \overline{X_n})\right] \tag{9}$$

where $\bar{X}_n$ is the sample mean $(1/n)\sum_j X_j$ and σ_n the series standard deviation

$$\sigma_n = \left[1/n\sum_{j=1}^{n}(X_j - \overline{X_n})^2\right]^{0.5} \tag{10}$$

The statistic is calculated using a number of steps. Firstly, the series N is divided into d times sub-series n, whose length is $n \leq N$. Eqs. (9) and (10) are then calculated for each of the d times sub-series. The statistic's Hurst exponent H, is finally estimated by the following OLS regression:

$$\log\left(R/\sigma\right)_n = \alpha + H\log(n) + e \tag{11}$$

Under the null hypothesis of no long-term dependence, the value of the Hurst exponent is $H = 0.5$. For series exhibiting positive long-term dependence, or persistence, the value of the exponent H will be $H > 0.5$. Antipersistent series are alternatively characterised by exponent values $H > 0.5$. Series characterised by $H = 0.5$ should be expected to exactly obey the $T^{1/2}$ rule. Alternatively, series characterised by $H > 0.5$ ($H < 0.5$) should be expected to scale faster (slower) than the square root of time. Using this interpretation of the Hurst exponent, it is seen that the exponent H in Eq. (11) is the equivalent of the scale exponent in for a self-affine function in Eqs. (4) and (5). Being non-parametric in nature, one advantage of the classical rescaled adjusted range is that the statistic is robustness to time series with significant third and fourth moments (Mandelbrot & Wallis, 1969) and to stochastic processes with infinite variance (Mandelbrot, 1972). The statistic may be biased, however, by structured short-term dependence and non-stationarity in the underlying series.

Since the classical rescaled adjusted range is a convergent statistic, estimated values for the statistic should be compared to their expected value $E(R/\sigma)_n$ when the series length is short. Utilising the gamma distribution, the expected value of the classical rescaled adjusted range for a Gaussian series is correctly modelled by Anis and Lloyd (1976) as

$$E\left(R/\sigma\right)_n = \frac{\Gamma(0.5(n-1))}{\pi^{0.5}\Gamma(0.5n)}\sum_{r=1}^{n-1}\left[(n-r)/r\right]^{0.5} \tag{12}$$

Estimated values of the classical rescaled adjusted range that exceed their expected value should be indicative of long-term dependence in the underlying series, again implying the series' innovations should be expected to scale faster (slower) than the square root of time.

3. DATA AND SAMPLE

Data examined comprises daily spot prices for the USD/AUD exchange rate for the period 01/01/1985–30/06/2004, a total of 4,724 observations. The BIS (2002) triennial survey of foreign exchange market activity estimates that the USD/AUD accounted for 4.2% of total daily turnover in the spot foreign exchange markets in 2001, making the currency the eighth most traded during that period. In the over-the-counter foreign exchange derivatives market, AUD denominated foreign currency options comprised 3.8% of the total notional amount outstanding and 5.7% of total gross market values at end-December 2003.[1] Indicative of a strong secondary market, average daily standardised open interest for USD/AUD currency options on the PHLX comprised approximately 50% of the total daily standardised open interest in June 2004.[2] To test the robustness of findings attributable to the three tests described above to changes in the sample period, the sample is divided in two sub-samples; 01/01/1985–30/12/1994 and 02/01/1995–30/06/2004. Tests for a scaling law consistent with long-term dependence and the examination of the implications thereof for option pricing are conducted for the whole sample and for each sub-sample.

Following from market convention for pricing and quoting foreign currency options, "American" terms are used herein for all exchange rate quotes. Using American terms, foreign exchange rates are quoted as the U.S. dollar price of one unit of foreign (Australian) currency (Moffett, Stonehill, & Eiteman, 2003, p. 125).

3.1. Descriptive Statistics of USD/AUD Returns

The time series properties of the natural logarithm of interday returns $\ln(S_t/S_{t-1})$, for the USD/AUD from 01/01/1985 to 30/06/2004 are presented in Tables 1–3. Results for the whole sample and each sub-sample are discussed in turn.

Table 1 provides information on the moments of the time series over the whole sample period, and each sub-sample. The sample means are slightly negative for all series, but not significantly different to zero. However, the sum of the daily ln returns shows the impact of the devaluation of the AUD. The USD/AUD began the sample period (01/01/1985) at 1AUD = 0.8255USD and ended the period (30/06/2004) at 0.6959USD, a loss of 0.1295USD. As confirmed by the sum of ln returns, the majority of the loss occurred during the second half of the sample period. The sum of ln returns for a white noise process should be approximately zero since gains would tend to equal losses. To determine the degree of randomness in the daily ln returns a non-parametric runs test is also conducted. The runs test p-value determines for α levels above the critical value if there is sufficient evidence to conclude that the interday returns are not random. This test rejects randomness at the 95% level of confidence for both the whole sample and second sub-sample (02/01/1995–30/06/2004), but not the first sub-sample (01/01/1985–30/12/1994). Taken together these results imply technical

Table 1.   Descriptive Statistics of the Spot USD/AUD Interday Returns.

USD/AUD Start: Finish:	01/01/1985 30/06/2004	01/01/1985 30/12/1994	02/01/1995 30/06/2004
Count	4724	2424	2300
Mean	−3.614E−05	−2.552E−05	−4.733E−05
Standard deviation	6.794E−03	6.751E−03	6.840E−03
Skewness	−0.6474	−1.1334	−0.1551
Excess kurtosis	7.6268	12.3453	2.9285
Sum of ln returns	−0.1707	−0.0619	−0.1089
USD/AUD			
Start of period	0.8255	0.8255	0.7760
Finish of period	0.6959	0.7760	0.6959
Gain/loss	−0.1295	−0.0495	−0.0800
Runs test (p-value)	0.0084	0.1309	0.0410
Anderson-Darling	38.674	36.507	8.311
p-value	0.000	0.000	0.000
Ryan-Joiner	0.9705	0.9516	0.9858
p-value	<0.01	<0.01	<0.01

trading strategies that exploited the long-term depreciation of the AUD would be expected to show positive returns over the sample period. Consistent with Fama (1998) and Batten, Ellis, and Fetherston (2000), these findings however also imply that where one starts and ends the series will have an impact on any potential trading gains.

All three samples are non-Gaussian, due more so to their leptokurtic nature than due to skewness, with both the Anderson–Darling and Ryan–Joiner p-values rejecting the null hypothesis of normality. This result is not surprising since leptokurtic, non-normal distributions are common in financial time series (Pagan, 1996). An important implication of this result is that even slight deviations from normality may impact on pricing and risk management practice due to the higher probability of observations being away from the mean return when the series displays leptokurtosis.

Each sample is then tested for the presence of autocorrelation up to 252 lags, with the results for lags 1, 2, 5, 21, 100 and 252 presented in Table 2. The results suggest slight autocorrelations in lags 1 and 2 returns for the whole sample and the first sub-sample. Observances of significant autocorrelation for these two samples, however quickly dissipate. The significance of the autocorrelations is tested using t-statistics and Ljung-Box Q statistics (reported as LBQ in Table 2). The t-statistics are high ($t > 1.25$) for the

Table 2. Autocorrelation of Spot USD/AUD Interday Returns.

Lag	1	2	5	21	100	252
01/01/1985 to 30/06/2004						
Autocorrelation	0.0366	−0.0478	0.0100	−0.0055	0.0069	−0.0128
t-statistic	2.5188	−3.2803	0.6811	−0.3756	0.4602	−0.8411
LBQ	6.3484	17.1470	21.2220	61.8180	119.4370	247.8620
p-value	0.0117	0.0002	0.0007	0.0000	0.0900	0.5618
01/01/1985 to 30/12/1994						
Autocorrelation	0.0618	−0.0583	0.0159	−0.0582	0.0040	−0.0198
t-statistic	3.0419	−2.8588	0.7772	−2.7944	0.1872	−0.8920
LBQ	9.2647	17.5130	21.5150	69.2440	131.6800	252.8980
p-value	0.0023	0.0002	0.0006	0.0000	0.0185	0.4722
02/01/1995 to 30/06/2004						
Autocorrelation	0.0108	−0.0372	0.0038	0.0482	0.0112	0.0006
t-statistic	0.5175	−1.7819	0.1821	2.2838	0.5144	0.0279
LBQ	0.2681	3.4500	4.2140	31.8410	98.2960	248.4370
p-value	0.6046	0.1782	0.5190	0.0608	0.5295	0.5516

whole sample and first sub-sample at lag 1 and for all three samples at lag 2 but not thereafter. This result is confirmed by the LBQ *p*-value at the 95% level for both the whole sample and first sub-sample. Over longer lags, the whole sample shows evidence of significant autocorrelation at the 95% level up to lag 21 (*p*-value = 0.000), and the first sub-sample up to lag 100 (*p*-value = 0.0185). There is no significant evidence of autocorrelation in the second sub-sample at any lag.

The next table, Table 3, reports tests for mean stationarity in the ln returns and for the AR(1) and MA(1) filtered returns for each sample.[3] The significantly high negative values for the Dicky-Fuller (DF), Augmented Dicky-Fuller (ADF), and Phillips-Perron (PP) tests indicate that the ln returns series are unit-root stationary over the whole sample period, and during each sub-sample. Both the AR(1) and MA(1) filtered returns are also unit-root stationary for all three samples. Critical values for the DF and ADF tests at the 1 and 5% levels are –3.96 and –3.41, respectively.

Overall, though the three samples show some evidence of being non-Gaussian with a slight autocorrelation structure, results provided in the first three tables provide no compelling evidence that the appropriate scale exponent should be other than $H = 0.5$. The results implies that linearly

Table 3. Stationarity Tests of Spot USD/AUD Interday Returns.

	ln Returns	AR(1) Residuals	MA(1) Residuals
01/01/1985 to 30/06/2004			
DF (0)	−66.246	−68.597	−68.849
ADF(10)	−20.246	−20.343	−20.347
ADF(31)	−12.682	−12.684	−12.684
PP(10)	−66.210	−68.690	−68.951
PP(31)	−66.206	−68.621	−68.877
01/01/1985 to 30/12/1994			
DF (0)	−46.282	−49.049	−49.422
ADF(8)	−15.805	−15.969	−15.968
ADF(26)	−9.419	−9.427	−9.424
PP(8)	−46.196	−49.149	−49.537
PP(26)	−46.206	−49.090	−49.471
02/01/1995 to 30/06/2004			
DF (0)	−47.439	−47.934	−47.974
ADF(8)	−16.445	−16.462	−16.463
ADF(26)	−8.739	−8.748	−8.749
PP(8)	−47.465	−47.983	−48.025
PP(26)	−47.455	−47.970	−48.012

rescaling short-horizon volatility should produce accurate estimates of annual standard deviations (volatility) and that option valuations derived from the implied annual volatilities should not be significantly different to those using observed annual volatility.

3.2. Scaling Properties of USD/AUD returns

The scaling properties of interday USD/AUD ln returns are studied using three tests. The first test is an investigation of the existence of a power law for the standard deviation of returns over the return intervals $k = 1, 2, 3, \ldots, 252$. The second test conducted is an examination of imputed scale exponents for standard deviations between the following discrete return intervals: $k = 1, 5, 21$ and 252. The final is the classical rescaled adjusted range. The economic significance of findings attributable to these tests is then considered by estimating the Garman and Kohlhagen modified Black–Scholes model using observed and implied annual volatilities of interday USD/AUD returns.

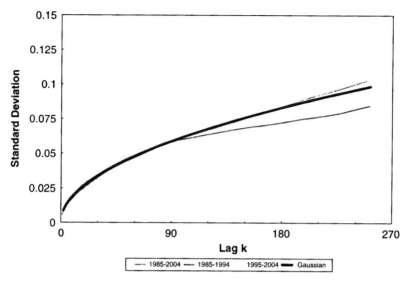

Fig. 1. Standard Deviation Versus Return Interval (Lag) k.

Standard deviations of k interval returns for each of the three samples and a Gaussian process are depicted in Fig. 1. The Gaussian process in the figure shows how standard deviations would appear under the assumption that risk scales according to the square root of time ($\sqrt{T}$).

Results in Fig. 1 indicate that the standard deviation of returns for the whole sample period (1985–2004) scale at a rate approximately equal to $\sqrt{T}$, yet scale slower than $\sqrt{T}$ for the first sub-sample (1985–1994), and faster than $\sqrt{T}$ over the second sub-sample (1995–2004). Furthermore it may be seen that the divergence between the observed and Gaussian k interval standard deviations for the two sub-samples increases as the return interval increases. This suggests that implied annual standard deviations will be higher than the equivalent observed annual standard deviations over the first sub-sample and lower than the observed annual value for the second sub-sample.

Regression scale exponents for each sample are presented in Table 4. Calculated using Eq. (7), the regression scale exponent γ_1 is the rate of change in the observed k interval standard deviation for the intervals $k = 1 - 252$. Values in Table 4 confirm that the standard deviations of daily USD/AUD returns scale at a variable rate slower/faster than the square root of time. That the scale exponent is lower (higher) during the first (second) sub-sample provides weak evidence of a multi-fractal process in USD/AUD

Table 4. Regression Scale Exponents for k Interval Standard
Deviations, $k = 1$ to 252.

	01/01/1985 to 30/06/2004	01/01/1985 to 30/12/1994	02/01/1995 to 30/06/2004
Regression scale exponent, γ_1	0.5084	0.4669	0.5425
Standard error	0.0011	0.0029	0.0031

Table 5. Imputed Scale Exponents for the Estimation of k Interval
Volatility from the Volatility of n Interval Returns.

	Observed Volatility $k =$	Implied Annual Volatility $H = 0.5$	Interval Length $k =$	Imputed Scale Exponent $\hat{H}$		
				$n = 1$	$n = 5$	$n = 21$
01/01/1985 to 30/06/2004	0.0062	0.0985	1			
	0.0137	0.0975	5	0.4934		
	0.0279	0.0967	21	0.4937	0.4941	
	0.1037	0.1037	252	0.5092	0.5157	0.5281
01/01/1985 to 30/12/1994	0.0058	0.0917	1			
	0.0129	0.0918	5	0.5010		
	0.0266	0.0920	21	0.5012	0.5016	
	0.0848	0.0848	252	0.4858	0.4796	0.4669
02/01/1995 to 30/06/2004	0.0067	0.1071	1			
	0.0148	0.1048	5	0.4868		
	0.0301	0.1042	21	0.4912	0.4962	
	0.1247	0.1247	252	0.5275	0.5443	0.5720

returns. A further implication for asset pricing is that USD/AUD currency
option values based on implied annual standard deviations should be expected to be higher than those based on observed annual standard deviations over the first sub-period, and lower than options values calculated
from the observed annual standard deviations over the second sub-period.[4]

The scaling properties of standard deviations of k and n interval returns
$(k, n = 1, 5, 21, 252; k \geq n \geq 1)$ for each sample are presented in Table 5.
Using observed values of the standard deviation of k and n interval returns,

the imputed scale exponent $\hat{H}$ is the value of H for which linearly rescaled values of the standard deviation of n interval returns exactly equal the standard deviation of k interval returns. The value of the scale exponent should be $H = 0.5$ for a Gaussian process. Additionally, the value of the scale exponent should be expected to remain approximately constant for all pairs of n and k if the distribution of returns is stable.

Consistent with results already presented in Fig. 1 and Table 4, imputed values of the scale exponent for the wholes sample data tend towards $H \approx 0.5$ as $k \to 252$ and $n \to 1$, yet tend towards $H < 0.5$ for the first sub-sample and to $H > 0.5$ for the second sub-sample. The finding is significant in that it provides further support for the proposition that the distributions of currency returns are not stable for different return intervals. The result is consistent with Xu and Gencay (2003) and Muller et al. (1990) both of whom also suggest that the distributions of foreign exchange returns are unstable.

Values for the classical rescaled adjusted range $(R/\sigma)_n$ for each sample, their expected values, and their respective bootstrap means and standard deviations are provided in Table 6. Relative to their expected values

Table 6. Rescaled Range Statistics for Spot USD/AUD Interday Returns.

	01/01/1985 to 30/06/2004	01/01/1985 to 30/12/1994	02/01/1995 to 30/06/2004
ln Returns			
$(R/\sigma)_n$	0.5514	0.5409	0.5775
$E(R/\sigma)_n$	0.5231	0.5260	0.5268
Bootstrap			
Mean	0.5237	0.5228	0.5241
Std dev	0.0448	0.0547	0.0565
AR(1) Residuals			
$(R/\sigma)_n$	0.5488	0.5361	0.5768
$E(R/\sigma)_n$	0.5231	0.5260	0.5268
Bootstrap			
Mean	0.5208	0.5203	0.5243
Std dev	0.0439	0.0447	0.0552
MA(1) Residuals			
$(R/\sigma)_n$	0.5487	0.5359	0.5767
$E(R/\sigma)_n$	0.5231	0.5260	0.5268
Bootstrap			
Mean	0.5248	0.5240	0.5242
Std dev	0.0554	0.0572	0.0557

$E(R/\sigma)_n$, values for the classical rescaled adjusted range for each sample are higher, indicating some degree of dependence in the samples. Consistent with prior evidence the result also suggests the existence of a scaling law other than $T^{1/2}$. The bootstrap methodology provides an alternative test of the significance of the estimated values in the table. Under the null of no long-term dependence, values for the classical rescaled adjusted range are expected to be within 1.645 standard deviations of their mean value at the 0.10 level of significance, and within 1.96 standard deviations of the mean at the 0.05 level. Compared to their mean value, the null is accepted for all ln return samples at the 0.10 and 0.05 levels.

One deficiency of the classical rescaled adjusted range methodology in empirical applications is its failure to accommodate structured short-term dependence. To test the robustness of the initial findings to the presence of short-term dependence, each of the samples are filtered for AR(1) and MA(1) dependencies.[5] Consistent with findings for the ln returns, results for the filtered data in Table 6 reject the null of long-term dependence when expected values $E(R/\sigma)_n$, are used but accept the null at the 0.10 and 0.05 levels when compared to the bootstrap means. Overall these results do not provide sufficient evidence that the series are random. In combination with results provided in Table 1, results attributable to the classical rescaled adjusted range do provide evidence of at least positive short-term dependence in each currency series.

4. VALUING USD/AUD CURRENCY OPTIONS

Option values using the Garman and Kohlhagen modified Black–Scholes model are calculated for a series of in-the-money, at-the-money, and out-of-the-money European call and put currency options. Option values in Table 7 are calculated for the following values for the variable parameters S, X, r_f, r, σ and t: The underlying asset value S, is the daily spot USD/AUD exchange rate at the end of each period (30/12/1994 and 30/06/2004). Strike prices X, are initially set at $+/-$ 20% the underlying asset value. Six-month Euro-rates for the USD and AUD as at 30/12/1994 and 30/06/2004 are used to proxy the foreign and domestic risk-free interest rates r_f and r, and the time to maturity t, is 180-days based on a 365-day year. Using the standard adopted by the PHLX, all USD/AUD currency option values are based on a contact size of 50, 000AUD per.

Historic volatilities for intervals of $n = 1, 5$ and 21 lags are calculated for the whole sample period and the two sub-sample periods, using which,

Table 7. Foreign Currency Option Values Calculated Using Implied Annual Standard Deviations (thousands of US Dollars)[a].

	Exchange Rate	Option Exercise	1(a)	5(b)	21(c)	252(d)
(A) In-the-money						
Call Options						
01/01/1985 to 30/06/2004	0.6959	0.5568	6.2851	6.2850	6.2849	6.2858
01/01/1985 to 30/12/1994	0.7760	0.6208	7.0946	7.0946	7.0946	7.0944
02/01/1995 to 30/06/2004	0.6959	0.5568	6.2864	6.2860	6.2859	6.2928
Put Options						
01/01/1985 to 30/06/2004	0.6959	0.8351	7.5036	7.5035	7.5033	7.5046
01/01/1985 to 30/12/1994	0.7760	0.9312	7.8997	7.8997	7.8997	7.8990
02/01/1995 to 30/06/2004	0.6959	0.8351	7.5056	7.5049	7.5048	7.5147
(B) At-the-money						
Call Options						
01/01/1985 to 30/06/2004	0.6959	0.6959	0.6693	0.6597	0.6521	0.7169
01/01/1985 to 30/12/1994	0.7760	0.7760	0.7699	0.7714	0.7735	0.6987
02/01/1999 to 30/06/2004	0.6959	0.6959	0.7487	0.7277	0.7224	0.9129
Put Options						
01/01/1985 to 30/06/2004	0.6959	0.6959	1.2783	1.2687	1.2611	1.3259
01/01/1985 to 30/12/1994	0.7760	0.7760	1.1721	1.1735	1.1757	1.1009
02/01/1995 to 30/06/2004	0.6959	0.6959	1.3577	1.3367	1.3314	1.5219
(C) Out-of-the-money						
Call Options						
01/01/1985 to 30/06/2004	0.6959	0.8351	0.0015	0.0013	0.0012	0.0025
01/01/1985 to 30/12/1994	0.7760	0.9312	0.0010	0.0011	0.0011	0.0004
02/01/1995 to 30/06/2004	0.6959	0.8351	0.0034	0.0028	0.0026	0.0125
Put Options						
01/01/1985 to 30/06/2004	0.6959	0.5568	0.0009	0.0008	0.0007	0.0016
01/01/1985 to 30/12/1994	0.7760	0.6208	0.0003	0.0003	0.0003	0.0001
02/01/1995 to 30/06/2004	0.6959	0.5568	0.0022	0.0018	0.0017	0.0086

[a]Provides four sets of call and put option values: (a) option value using an implied annual standard deviation from the standard deviation of daily returns; (b) option value using an implied annual standard deviation from the standard deviation of weekly returns; (c) option value using an implied annual standard deviation from the standard deviation of monthly returns; (d) option value using observed standard deviation of annual returns.

implied annual standard deviations $\hat{\sigma}$, are estimated. Option values using the implied annual standard deviations are then compared to values using the observed annual standard deviation, σ, for each period. Implied annual standard deviations are estimated using Eq. (8) under which the assumption that USD/AUD returns conform to a Brownian motion process with constant μ and σ, provides that option values derived using implied annual standard deviations $(k/n)^{0.5}[\sigma^2(S_t - S_{t-n})]^{0.5}$ should be equal to option values using observed annual standard deviations $[\sigma^2(S_t - S_{t-k})]^{0.5}$. The percentage error in valuation using implied annual volatility over n lags versus the observed annual volatility $(X_n - X_{252})/X_{252}$, is shown in the following Table 8.

Consistent with already discussed results for the whole sample period (refer Fig. 1, Tables 4 and 5) in-the-money call option values estimated using implied annual volatilities are within 10 basis points (bp) of their value using the observed annual volatility. In-the-money put option values are slightly more undervalued, but remain within 15bp of their value using the observed annual volatility. At-the-money call and put values for implied annual volatilities are likewise undervalued relative to values using observed annual volatilities, but more so than equivalent in-the-money calls and puts. Out-of-the-money call and put values, while under priced by no more than 10bp relative to their using observed annual volatilities (refer Table 7, panel C), exhibit the highest percentage degree of under pricing (41.4–54.0%) in Table 8. As for in-the-money calls and puts, out-of-the-money puts are slightly more undervalued. By contrast, the percentage degree of under pricing of at-the-money puts is nearly half that of equivalent at-the-money call values. Overall, results for the whole sample period provide evidence consistent of dollar vegas being highest for at-the-money options, while percentage changes in price are highest for deep out-of-the-money options, and approximately zero for deep in-the-money options.[6]

Option values for the first and second sub-samples exhibit the same general properties as for the whole sample period with respect to dollar versus percentage mispricing; at-the-money calls and puts exhibit the greatest dollar mispricing and out-of-the-money calls and puts the greatest percentage mispricing. Relative to each other, call and put option values calculated using implied annual volatility are overpriced during the first sample period, but underpriced during the second sample period. Considered in relation to results presented in Fig. 1, this result should not be unexpected. Specifically with respect to the relative overpricing of out-of-the-money call and put options during the first sub-period, the apparent asymmetry in overpricing (out-of-the-money calls are overpriced by 175.6% at most and puts by 227.0%) may be explained by the fact that the percentage degree of mispricing approaches the limit as the dollar option value tends to zero. Out-of-the-money put dollar values are less than one-third those of equivalent out-of-the-money calls for the first sub-sample.

Table 8. Percentage Valuation Error $(X_n - X_{252})/X_{252}$[a].

	$n = 1$ (a)	$n = 5$ (b)	$n = 21$ (c)
(A) In-the-money			
Call Options (%)			
01/01/1985 to 30/06/2004	−0.0110	−0.0120	−0.0140
01/01/1985 to 30/12/1994	0.0030	0.0030	0.0030
02/01/1995 to 30/06/2004	−0.1010	−0.1080	−0.1100
Put Options (%)			
01/01/1985 to 30/06/2004	−0.0140	−0.0160	−0.0170
01/01/1985 to 30/12/1994	0.0080	0.0080	0.0080
02/01/1995 to 30/06/2004	−0.1210	−0.1300	−0.1320
(B) At-the-money			
Call Options (%)			
01/01/1985 to 30/06/2004	−6.6380	−7.9720	−9.0360
01/01/1985 to 30/12/1994	10.1860	10.3950	10.6990
02/01/1995 to 30/06/2004	−17.9940	−20.2890	−20.8730
Put Options (%)			
01/01/1985 to 30/06/2004	−3.5890	−4.3100	−4.8850
01/01/1985 to 30/12/1994	6.4650	6.5980	6.7910
02/01/1995 to 30/06/2004	−10.7930%	−12.1710	−12.5210
(C) Out-of-the-money			
Call Options (%)			
01/01/1985 to 30/06/2004	−41.4170	−47.8610	−52.5980
01/01/1985 to 30/12/1994	163.7920	168.5580	175.6090
02/01/1995 to 30/06/2004	−72.9690	−78.0480	−79.2180
Put Options (%)			
01/01/1985 to 30/06/2004	−42.6840	−49.2330	−54.0280
01/01/1985 to 30/12/1994	210.7270	217.2870	227.0250
02/01/1995 to 30/06/2004	−74.3110	−79.3120	−80.4580

[a]Percentage valuation errors in this table represent the percentage difference in option value for four sets of call and put options: (a) option values using observed annual volatility versus option values using an implied annual volatility from the volatility of daily returns; (b) option values using observed annual volatility versus option values using an implied annual volatility from the volatility of weekly returns; (c) option values using observed annual volatility versus option values using an implied annual volatility from the volatility of monthly returns.

5. SUMMARY AND CONCLUSIONS

This paper examines some implications of statistical dependence in daily spot returns for the USD/AUD exchange rate. Having formally defined the concept of linear rescaling and examined the origins of the "$T^{1/2}$ rule" for annualising short-horizon volatility, three formal tests for scaling laws in the USD/AUD returns are applied. The results of these tests show that the long-term volatility of USD/AUD interday returns scales at approximately the square root of time. However, in the shorter term, weak evidence of a multi-fractal process in USD/AUD returns is provided. The economic implications for derivative asset pricing are then considered. Using the Garman and Kohlhagen modified Black–Scholes model for valuing foreign currency options, linearly rescaled volatility estimates are shown to misprice option values by as much as 1905 basis points (12.5%) for at-the-money contracts. Further these results are shown to be highly sensitive to differences in the moneyness of the option. The findings are important since they demonstrate that even small violations of the assumption that foreign exchange rates follow a Brownian motion process can result in economic benefits or costs. However, a word of caution should be made in interpreting dollar versus percentage differences in option values, since the latter have been seen to be exaggerated by very low values for out-of-the-money option contracts. Nonetheless, the results highlight the need for investors to consider the underlying distribution and independence of returns when using short-horizon returns to estimate long-horizon risk.

NOTES

1. Bank for International Settlements (BIS). Detailed data on over-the-counter (OTC) derivatives markets. June 2004.

2. Total daily standardised open interest is calculated as the sum of standardised daily open interest for Australian Dollar, British Pound, Canadian Dollar, Euro, Japanese Yen and Swiss Franc, and includes currency options with both European and American style exercises.

3. As will be discussed, the use of AR(1) and MA(1) filtered returns is necessary to consider the impact of structured dependence on the classical rescaled adjusted range.

4. It will be recalled that volatility and option value are directly related in the Black–Scholes model.

5. Tests are also conducted for AR and MA(1,1) filtered data for each sample but are not significantly different to those for either of the AR(1), or MA(1) filtered returns.

6. Vega is the rate of change in the value of an option with respect to volatility and may be approximated by the first derivative of the Garman and Kohlhagen modified Black–Scholes model with respect to volatility, ∂_f / ∂ where f is the option value and σ the volatility of the underlying asset (exchange rate).

REFERENCES

Anis, A. A., & Lloyd, E. H. (1976). The expected value of the adjusted rescaled hurst range of independent normal summands. *Biometrika, 63*(1), 111–116.

Bank for International Settlements (BIS). (2002). Triennial central bank survey of foreign exchange and derivatives market activity in 2001, Basle. March.

Batten, J., Ellis, C., & Fetherston, T. (2000). Are long-term return anomalies illusions? Evidence from the spot yen. *Japan and the World Economy, 12*, 337–349.

Black, F., & Scholes, M. (1973). The pricing of options and corporate liabilities. *Journal of Political Economy, 81*, 637–659.

Bodurtha, J. N., & Courtadon, G. R. (1987). Tests of an American option pricing model on the foreign currency options market. *Journal of Financial and Quantitative Analysis, 22*(2), 153–168.

Butler, J. S., & Schachter, B. (1986). Unbiased estimation of the Black/Scholes formula. *Journal of Financial Economics, 15*(3), 341–357.

Byers, J., & Peel, D. (2001). Volatility persistence in asset markets: Long memory in high/low prices. *Applied Financial Economics, 11*(3), 253–260.

Fama, E. F. (1998). Market efficiency, long-term returns, and behavioral finance. *Journal of Financial Economics, 49*, 283–306.

Garman, M. B., & Kohlhagen, S. W. (1983). Foreign currency option values. *Journal of International Money and Finance, 2*, 231–237.

Goodman, L. S., Ross, S., & Schmidt, F. (1985). Are foreign currency options overvalued? The early experience of the Philadelphia Stock Exchange. *Journal of Futures Markets, 5*(3), 349–359.

Hentschel, L. (2003). Errors in implied volatility estimation. *Journal of Financial and Quantitative Analysis, 38*(4), 779–810.

Hull, J. C. (1989). *Options, futures and other derivatives* (3rd ed.). Englewood Cliffs, NJ: Prentice-Hall.

Hurst, H. E. (1951). Long term storage capacity of reservoirs. *Transactions of the American Society of Civil Engineers, 116*, 770–799.

Kagenishi, Y., & Shinohara, Y. (2001). A note on computation of implied volatility. *Asia-Pacific Financial Markets, 8*(4), 361–386.

Mandelbrot, B. B. (1972). Statistical methodology for nonperiodic cycles: From the covariance to R/S analysis. *Annals of Economic and Social Measurement, 1*, 259–290.

Mandelbrot, B. B. (1982). *The fractal geometry of nature.* New York: W.H. Freeman and Company.

Mandelbrot, B. B., & Wallis, J. R. (1969). Robustness of the rescaled range R/S in the measurement of noncyclic long-run statistical dependence. *Water Resources Research, 5*, 967–988.

Melino, A., & Turnbull, S. M. (1991). The pricing of foreign currency options. *Canadian Journal of Economics, 24*(2), 251–281.

Merton, R. C. (1973). Theory of rational option pricing. *Bell Journal of Economics and Management Science, 4*(1), 141–183.

Moffett, M. H., Stonehill, A. I., & Eiteman, D. K. (2003). *Fundamentals of multinational finance.* Boston: Addison-Wesley.

Muller, U. A., Dacorogna, M. M., Olsen, R. B., Pictet, O. V., Schwarz, M., & Morgenegg, C. (1990). Statistical study of foreign exchange rates, empirical evidence of a price change scaling law, and intraday analysis. *Journal of Banking and Finance, 14,* 1189–1208.

Nekhili, R., Altay-Salih, A., & Gencay, R. (2002). Exploring exchange rates at different time horizons. *Physica A, 313,* 671–682.

Pagan, A. (1996). The econometrics of financial markets. *Journal of Empirical Finance, 3*(1), 15–102.

Sarwar, G., & Krebhiel, T. (2000). Empirical performance of alternative pricing models of currency options. *Journal of Futures Markets, 20*(2), 265–291.

Shastri, K., & Tandon, K. (1986). Valuation of foreign currency options: Some empirical tests. *Journal of Financial and Quantitative Analysis, 21*(2), 145–160.

Tucker, A. L., & Scott, E. (1987). A study of diffusion processes for foreign exchange rates. *Journal of International Money and Finance, 6,* 465–478.

Van De Gucht, L. M., Dekimpe, M. G., & Kwok, C. Y. (1996). Persistence in foreign exchange rates. *Journal of International Money and Finance, 15*(2), 191–220.

Wasserfallen, W., & Zimmermann, H. (1985). The behavior of intra-daily exchange rates. *Journal of Banking and Finance, 9,* 55–72.

Xu, Z., & Gencay, R. (2003). Scaling, self-similarity and multifractality in FX markets. *Physica A, 323,* 578–590.

REGIONAL INTEGRATION

INTERNATIONAL FINANCIAL INTEGRATION: AN EMPIRICAL INVESTIGATION INTO ASIAN EQUITY MARKETS PRE- AND POST-1997 ASIAN FINANCIAL CRISIS

Xuan Vinh Vo and Kevin James Daly

ABSTRACT

The study investigates the interdependence of the stock markets between the following countries Hong Kong, Japan, Korea, Taiwan, Indonesia, Malaysia, Philippines, Singapore, Thailand and the advanced stock markets of Australia, Germany, United Kingdom and the United States. Using data from 1994 to 2003 the paper employs both correlation, causality and cointegration analysis to describe the behaviour of the above stock market indices over the period pre and post the 1997 Asian Financial Crises. The paper investigates both the short- and long-run relationships between the Asian markets and the markets of selected advanced industrial countries.

Asia Pacific Financial Markets in Comparative Perspective: Issues and Implications for the 21st Century
Contemporary Studies in Economics and Financial Analysis, Volume 86, 75–100
Copyright © 2005 by Elsevier Ltd.
All rights of reproduction in any form reserved
ISSN: 1569-3759/doi:10.1016/S1569-3759(05)86004-8

1. INTRODUCTION

This paper examines the long- and short-run relationships between Asian equity markets and a selection of advanced market economies covering a 10-year timeframe pre and post the 1997 Asian financial crisis. International portfolio diversification produces economic gains because stock markets in different countries display relatively low correlations, based on the notion that most economic disturbances are country specific. International portfolio diversification aims to substantially reduce portfolio risk and increase expected returns. Previous studies have demonstrated the advantages of international diversification, the most recent of which are those by Meric and Meric (1989), Divecha et al. (1992) Michaud et al. (1996), and De Fusco et al. (1996). The common theme underlying these studies is that low correlations provide advantages to the holders of international diversified portfolios. The reasons for low-international correlations are barriers to international trade and investment, inadequate information on foreign securities or simply home investor bias. In contrast, another group of studies including Roll (1992), Lau and McInish (1993), Koutmos and Booth (1995), Campbell et al. (2001) and Daly (2003) document a significant increase in correlation and volatility transmission between equity markets during and after the 1997 stock market crash. In the latter studies, analysts have pointed to increased financial integration brought about by liberalisation and deregulation of capital markets as the main reason for increased correlations among global equity markets.

An interesting question arising from the prospective of foreign investors in Asian equity markets is whether the expected benefits from investing in Asian equity markets have changed since the Asian financial crisis of 1997? Given that significant changes have occurred across Asian capital markets since the crash, have the so-called benefits of international portfolio diversification across Asian equity markets changed with the reforms taking place across Asian capital markets. In other words, has the economic convergence between Asian countries produced a co-movement in their capital markets that has increased correlations amongequity markets that subsequently reduce the benefits for investors in Asian markets?

This paper examines equity market integrations during the 1990s and early into the new millennium by focussing on the following issues. Firstly, has the short-run relationship between the Asian equity markets changed since 1997? Secondly, what does the dynamic relationship between markets over the period suggest? Thirdly, has the return and volatility transmission process between advanced markets and emerging markets changed over the period of the study?

2. BACKGROUND

Researchers have developed a straightforward approach to measuring financial market integration across equity markets. They compare the correlation (or covariance) between two stock markets during a relatively stable period (generally measured as a historic average) to that during a period of turmoil (directly after a shock occurs). Market integration is defined as a significant increase in the cross-market correlation during the period of turmoil. If two markets are moderately correlated during periods of stability and one market sustains a shock, which has ripple effects leading to a significant increase in market co-movements, this would constitute market integration. Alternately, if correlations between stock market indices do not increase significantly, then any high level of market co-movement suggests strong real linkages exists between the economies. Based on this approach, financial market integration implies that the cross-market linkages are fundamentally different after a shock, while interdependence implies no significant change in cross-market relationships.

Evaluating if equity markets are integrated is important for several reasons. Firstly, a critical tenet of investment strategy is that most economic disturbances are country specific, such that correlations between stock market indices display relatively low correlations. International diversification would therefore, substantially reduce portfolio risk and increase expected returns. If contagion occurs after a negative shock, however, then market correlations would increase in bad states, which would undermine much of the rationale for international diversification. Secondly, many models of investor behaviour are based on the assumption that investors react differently after a large negative shock. Understanding how individual behaviour changes in good and bad states is a key to understanding how shocks are transmitted across markets. Third, many international institutions and policy makers worry that a negative shock to one country can have a negative impact on financial flows to another country even if the fundamentals of the second country are sound.

2.1. Market integration and international equity markets

The evidence on stock market integration is mixed and conflicting with many of the studies not directly comparable in so far as the studies are conducted on different stock market indices over various sample periods and often employ varying frequency of returns including daily, weekly and monthly returns. Forbes and Rigobon (1998) test for stock market co-movement during the

1997 East Asian crises, the 1994 Mexican peso crisis and the 1987 US stock market crisis. Their tests suggest that the high market co-movement during these periods were a continuation of strong cross-market linkages. In other words, during these three crises there was no increased financial integration, only interdependence. However, a serious concern with the latter study is the extremely short-time series allowed by the authors to conduct meaningful cointegration tests in relation to the stock markets of Southeast Asia.

Studies, which specifically focus on long-run relationships between stock markets after a shock, test for changes in the cointegrating relationships between stock markets. Arshanapalli and Doukas (1993) employ cointegration techniques to examine the linkages and dynamic interactions among stock price indices across the major world exchanges over a period pre- and post-October 1987. Their evidence indicates that the degree of international co-movements between stock market indices has changed significantly since the October 1987 crash. In particular, they note that over the post-1987 crash period, three European markets (France, Germany and the UK) were strongly linked (cointegrated) with the US stock market, which is in direct contrast to the pre-1987 period results. Allen and MacDonald (1995) investigated the benefits available from international stock market portfolio diversification to Australian investors by conducting bivariate cointegration tests between Australia and other national stock market indices. Employing both Engle and Granger (1987) and Johansen (1988) estimation techniques, the overall evidence from the above study points to only slight support for cointegration among the stock market indices considered.

More recently, Chen, Firth, and Rui (2002) investigated the interdependence of the major stock markets in Latin America over 1995 to 2000 employing cointegration analysis. Their results suggest that the potential for diversifying risk by investing in different Latin American markets is limited. Finally, Nieh (2003) investigated the effect of the Asian crisis on the interrelationships between exchange rate volatility, exports, imports and productivity for several East Asian economies. Cointegration tests show no change in the long-run relationships among theses variables throughout the crisis. Finally, Daly (2003) documents a significant increase in correlations and volatility transmission between equity markets during and after the 1997 stock market crash.

3. METHODOLOGY

The main aim of the paper is to examine the linkages in returns and volatility of Asian equity markets and those of the US and Australian equity markets. Equity market relationships can be examined using the following framework in prices:

$$\ln(P_{\text{Asia,t}}) = \beta_0 + \beta \ln(P_{\text{Adv,t}}) + e_t$$

where P_{Asia} is used to represent the Asian stock index (Thailand, Indonesia, Malaysia, Philippines, Singapore, etc.) and P_{Adv} represent the stock index of the Western developed countries, for example, the S&P500 index is used to represent the US equity market while the All Ordinaries Index (AOI) represents Australia's equity market. Within this type of equation, a number of relationships between equity markets can be analysed utilising a number of modelling techniques. These techniques provide a solution for describing the extent of the relationships between equity markets. Capital markets in general have been characterised by increased integration. Within this the extent and speed of these interactions have also increased. Harmonisation of regulatory and market structures, and the removal of capital control barriers are found to be driving forces in these increased market interactions.

Financial market integration reflecting interdependencies among national stock market indices has been the focus of several studies on the efficiency of international capital markets, especially equity markets. Market integration implies that assets of similar risk in different countries provide the same expected returns; this issue has been addressed through a variety of tests and procedures. On the other hand, equities in segmented stock markets are priced according to factors particular to that market. Using data from 1994 to 2003 the paper employs both correlation, causality and cointegration analysis to describe the behaviour of the above stock market indices over the period pre and post the 1997 Asian Financial Crises.

4. DATA DESCRIPTION

All data are daily closing prices from Datastream. The precise indices used are the Australia AOI, the French CAC 40 Price Index, the Germany DAX 30 Price Index, the Hong Kong Hang Seng Price Index, the Indonesia Jakarta SE Composite Price Index, the Japan Nikkei All Stock Price Index, the Korea SE Composite Price Index, the Malaysian Kuala Lumpur Composite Price Index, the Philippines SE Composite Price Index, the Singapore Straits Times Price Index, the Taiwan SE Composite Price Index, the Thailand Bangkok S.E.T. Price Index, the UK FTSE 100 Price Index and the United States S&P 500. To investigate stock market integration using cointegration tests, stock market returns series were calculated, all data were converted to US dollars and all series were normalised to a common base. The sample was divided into two time periods (the pre-crash period beginning in 4 April 1994 and ending in 1 September 1997, while the post-crash period starts in 1 November 1997 and ends in 5 October 2003). The timing of these sub-periods was influenced by trends in key economic variables.

The paper employs correlation, causality and cointegration techniques to describe the behaviour of the above stock market indices over. The time difference between trading times in the US market (New York time) and the Asian markets ranges from Korean and Japan time 14 h ahead of New York time, Singapore, Malaysia, Taiwan, Philippines and Hong Kong 13 h ahead, Indonesia and Thailand 12 h ahead, UK 5 h ahead, France and Germany 6 h ahead and Australia Sydney time 15/16 h ahead of New York time.

Given that the US closing stock price of a day (t-1) before Asian stock market opening price, what follows is that if Asian stock prices are sensitive to the US stock price changes and the market is efficient, all US, UK, France and Germany stock price information in the day t-1 should be reflected in the beginning price in day t of the Asian stocks. If the Asian stock market is partly efficient, only part of the information will be reflected in the Asian opening price of day t, with the remaining changes spilling over during the course of the day.

5. EMPIRICAL RESULTS

We begin our investigation into stock market integration by examining the summary statistics of country stock market returns over both the pre-and post-October 1997 crisis period. Fig. 1 presents time-series plots of the returns for all national stock market used in the study. Of particular note is the high volatility of the market returns series associated with the October 1997 Asian financial crisis. The stock markets of Southeast Asia do appear to have sustained a higher relative increase in volatility over this time compared to the five developed stock markets of Australia, France, Germany, United Kingdom and the United States.

In Tables 1(b) and (c) we compare the volatility of daily stock market returns over the pre- and post-1997 financial crisis. For the five developed country stock markets the average daily stock return were approximately 0.06 per cent over the pre-crash period. For the post-crash period these stocks yielded an average daily return of 0.01 per cent. The standard deviations for these markets over the pre-crash data were moderate at just over 0.8 per cent per day while the post-crash was almost twice that at 1.4. By

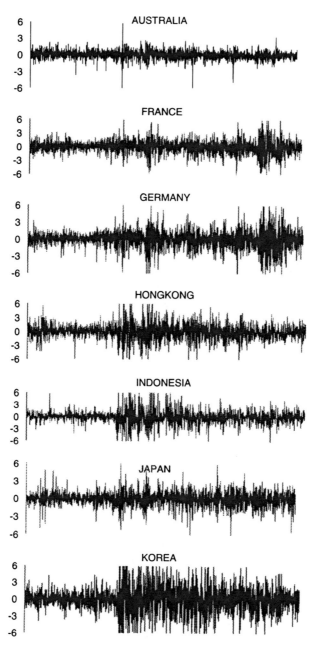

Fig. 1. Daily Returns of Indices.

Table 1.   The Characteristics of the Stock Market Returns.

	Mean	Maximum	Minimum	Std. Dev.	Skewness	Kurtosis
			For the whole period			
(a) Return descriptive statistics						
RAUS	0.02	5.74	−7.00	0.80	−0.49	8.96
RFRA	0.02	7.00	−7.68	1.47	−0.06	5.26
RGER	0.02	7.55	−9.16	1.62	−0.22	5.78
RHK	0.01	17.25	−14.73	1.74	0.13	13.38
RINDO	0.02	13.13	−12.73	1.70	0.12	11.58
RJAP	−0.02	6.34	−6.51	1.21	−0.05	5.41
RKOR	−0.01	10.02	−12.80	2.15	−0.06	6.29
RMAL	−0.01	20.82	−24.15	1.76	0.58	40.77
RPHI	−0.03	16.18	−9.74	1.53	0.86	15.99
RSING	0.00	14.87	−9.67	1.43	0.36	13.22
RTAI	−0.01	8.29	−9.87	1.70	−0.06	5.32
RTHA	−0.03	11.35	−10.03	1.80	0.54	7.32
RUK	0.01	6.72	−5.63	1.12	0.01	5.76
RUS	0.03	5.57	−7.11	1.15	−0.11	6.21
(b) Pre-crisis return summary statistics						
RAUS	0.03	2.35	−3.64	0.71	−0.19	4.50
RFRA	0.05	4.03	−3.99	1.04	−0.03	3.74
RGER	0.07	4.06	−4.14	0.95	−0.44	4.91
RHK	0.05	6.88	−7.59	1.25	−0.33	7.28
RINDO	0.02	10.69	−7.11	1.11	0.55	19.44
RJAP	−0.02	4.89	−5.00	0.92	0.13	7.16
RKOR	−0.04	4.38	−4.20	1.18	0.12	3.92
RMAL	−0.03	11.67	−5.82	1.21	1.20	16.17
RPHI	−0.04	7.29	−9.74	1.26	−0.42	10.04
RSING	0.00	3.92	−5.02	0.92	−0.37	6.38
RTAI	0.03	5.83	−8.03	1.46	−0.46	6.12
RTHA	−0.11	8.29	−6.18	1.54	0.45	6.43
RUK	0.06	3.06	−3.18	0.70	−0.20	4.55
RUS	0.09	3.08	−3.13	0.72	−0.23	5.06
(c) Post-crisis return summary statistics						
RAUS	0.02	3.39	−5.85	0.80	−0.42	6.40
RFRA	0.02	7.00	−7.68	1.64	−0.07	4.71
RGER	−0.01	7.55	−9.16	1.85	−0.11	4.60
RHK	0.01	13.40	−9.29	1.81	0.21	7.46
RINDO	0.02	13.13	−12.73	1.92	0.11	9.43
RJAP	−0.01	6.34	−6.51	1.33	−0.08	4.73
RKOR	0.03	10.02	−12.80	2.49	−0.07	5.13
RMAL	0.01	20.82	−24.15	1.97	0.49	38.08

Table 1. (*Continued*)

	Mean	Maximum	Minimum	Std. Dev.	Skewness	Kurtosis
			For the whole period			
RPHI	−0.02	16.18	−8.69	1.64	1.21	16.59
RSING	0.01	14.87	−9.10	1.61	0.52	11.33
RTAI	−0.01	8.29	−9.87	1.80	0.07	4.96
RTHA	0.03	11.35	−10.03	1.92	0.55	7.19
RUK	−0.01	6.72	−5.63	1.27	0.07	4.84
RUS	0.01	5.57	−7.04	1.30	0.01	4.83

comparison, the average daily returns over the pre-crisis period for the combined developing market countries of Hong Kong, Indonesia, Japan, Korea, Malaysia, Philippines, Singapore, Taiwan and Thailand was 0.02 per cent while the post-crash daily returns on these stocks was 0.07 per cent. Over the pre-crash period the standard deviation for the above markets were on average 1.2 per cent, while over the post-crash period the standard deviation was 1.37 per cent. Across both pre- and post-crash episodes none of the markets exhibited significant skewness with the exception of Malaysia and the Philippines.

The characteristics of the stock market returns as described above, provide a general comparison for both Asian and developed country stock markets. However inference on the integration of stock markets is restricted to examining whether distributional features are similar. These measures are therefore, not an adequate measure of stock market integration.

One simple test to investigate integration between stock markets is to consider the correlation coefficients across daily returns of the stock market indices. By comparing pre- and post-crash periods, one can determine whether the stock markets have become increasingly integrated. The correlation matrices for the pre- and post-crash sub-periods are reported in Table 2. The top diagonal Table 2(a); displays the correlations between the pre-crisis market indices while the lower diagonal displays the corresponding correlations for the post-crisis period. A comparison of the average (mean) correlation coefficients across the pre- and post-crash periods reveals (with the exception of Germany and Indonesia) an increase in correlations between all stock markets over the post-crash period relative to the pre-crash period. In particular, the table shows that the average correlation coefficient between Australia's stock market index and the combined market indices (developed and emerging country market indices) increased from 0.17 in the pre-crash period to 0.28 over the post-crash period. The US

Table 2. Return Correlation.

(a) Pre-crises

	AUS	FRA	GER	HK	IND	JAP	KOR	MAL	PHI	SIN	TAI	THI	UK	US
AUS	1													
FRA	0.15	1												
GER	-0.1	0.24	1											
HK	0.38	0.16	-0	1										
IND	0.3	0.1	0	0.4	1									
JAP	0.22	0.13	-0	0.26	0.15	1								
KOr	0.06	0.01	-0	0.1	0.03	-0	1							
MAL	0.19	0.08	0	0.4	0.4	0.14	0.04	1						
PHI	0.23	0.06	-0	0.31	0.42	0.14	0.05	0.31	1					
SIN	0.33	0.13	-0	0.57	0.48	0.24	0.07	0.56	0.4	1				
TAI	0.1	0	0	0.2	0.1	0.1	0	0.1	0.1	0.1	1			
THI	0.15	0.08	0	0.27	0.31	0.12	0.04	0.28	0.16	0.32	0.01	1		
UK	0.2	0.6	0.2	0.2	0.2	0.1	0.1	0.1	0.1	0.2	0	0.1	1	
US	0.09	0.3	0.51	0.11	0.07	0.02	0.05	0.06	0.07	0.09	-0	0.03	0.32	1

(b) Post-crises

	AUS	FRA	GER	HK	IND	JAP	KOR	MAL	PHI	SIN	TAI	THI	UK	US
AUS	1													
FRA	0.24	1												
GER	-0	0.03	1											
HK	0.49	0.31	0	1										
IND	0.2	0.1	0	0.3	1									
JAP	0.46	0.22	-0	0.42	0.21	1								
KOR	0.35	0.2	-0	0.38	0.2	0.34	1							
MAL	0.26	0.09	-0	0.32	0.24	0.21	0.21	1						
PHI	0.28	0.07	0	0.32	0.28	0.2	0.22	0.18	1					
SIN	0.44	0.28	-0	0.64	0.38	0.37	0.37	0.35	0.37	1				
TAI	0.3	0.1	0	0.3	0.2	0.2	0.3	0.2	0.1	0.3	1			
THI	0.29	0.16	-0	0.41	0.34	0.23	0.32	0.33	0.34	0.47	0.2	1		
UK	0.3	0.8	0	0.4	0.1	0.3	0.2	0.1	0.1	0.3	0.1	0.2	1	
US	0.1	0.48	0.19	0.14	0.02	0.11	0.1	-0	0.06	0.16	0.08	0.07	0.42	1

DJIA index also recorded a significant rise in its correlation with the combined indices over the post-crash period, increasing (from 0.13 to 0.15). Thailand's stock market index increased from (0.16 to 0.28), while Indonesia's stock market showed a slight fall in correlations with all markets over the post-crash episode. Australia experienced an increase in correlations with the US and the UK, and Japan but a fall with Germany. Overall, these results indicate that the majority of stock markets in the study have become more integrated since the crash. However, a drawback of this test is that it is a static test measuring only short-run stock market integration.

The characteristics of the stock market returns as described above provide a general comparison for both the Asian stock markets and a selected number of major developed country stock markets. However, in the above analysis inference on the integration of stock markets is restricted to examining whether distributional features are similar. In Section 5.1, we employ cointegration techniques to test for the effects of the 1997 crisis on the long-term relationship between the stock market indices.

5.1. Cointegration

A long-run relationship between two stock market indices, j and k, can be represented by where the stock market integration in the long run implies a linear relationship between the natural logarithms of the portfolio price indices, $Ln(P^j)$ and $Ln(P^k)$. This is a test of the cointegration of two variable series. If $Ln(P^j)$ and $Ln(P^k)$ are cointegrated, the error term e_t in the above equation is stationary and there exists a long-run equilibrium relationship between the two series.

If, as is typical for financial time series, $ln(P_j)$ and $ln(P_k)$ are both non-stationary and their first differences $ln(R_j)$ and $ln(R_k)$ are stationary, they are integrated of the order one, $I(1)$. When each price index is $I(1)$ and there is a linear combination of market indices that are stationary, the indices are said to be cointegrated and hence, there exists a form of long-run stock market integration. In order to gain more insight into the integration of the above markets, we apply cointegration techniques to determine the presence of any long-run relationships, which may have existed over the pre- and post-crisis. The existence of highly correlated long-run relationships between markets indicates that there exist little gains from diversifying among these markets. Below, we describe both bivariate and multivariate tests for cointegration between the stock market indices of a number of Asian economies at the centre of the 1997 financial crisis. Johansen cointegration tests

are performed over the entire sample period from 1994 to 2003 and two sub-
periods a pre-crisis period from 1994 to 1997 and a post-crisis period from
November 1997 to November 2003. Changes to the underlying relationships
between these stock markets arising from the stock market crash of October
1997 would provide useful information to both stock market investors and
international agencies concerned with the long-term effects of the crisis on
equity markets in the region. Further tests are performed on the implications of the crash for the long-term relationships between three major developed stock markets and the Asian stock markets at the centre of the 1997
financial crisis.

The first step in cointegration is to test whether the variables in question
are stationary or moving with time. If a variable is non-stationary in time
then it is said to have a unit root. The standard tests for stationarity or the
existence of a unit root are the Dicky and Fuller (1979) and augmented
Dicky–Fuller (ADF) tests. In Table 3, the results indicate the existence of
unit roots in the levels of all the indices (i.e. the null hypothesis cannot be
rejected). Furthermore, there is no evidence to support the presence of a unit
root in first differences of the stock price indices. These results are broadly
consistent with the hypothesis that national stock index series are individually integrated of order one, I (1).

5.1.1. Bivariate Cointegration Test Results

The purpose of this paper is to explore the issue of possible diversification
benefits, from the perspective of US (Australian) investors, who invest in the
Asian markets. Cointegration tests will reveal whether long-term common
stochastic trends exist between the US (Australia) and the nine Asian equity
markets. Evidence of such long-term co-movement would suggest overstat-
ed benefits for US (Australian) investors with longer-range investment horizons who seek diversification in these markets.

In order to gain an insight into the nature of the relationship between the
above stock markets, bivariate cointegration tests were carried out between
the US (Australia) stock markets and the developing Asian economy stock
markets (Hong Kong, Indonesia, Japan, Korea, Malaysia, Philippines, Singapore, Taiwan and Thailand). Further tests were performed to determine if
any long-run relationships exists between the stock markets of developed
country (Australia, Germany, France, Japan and the US) and between the
developing country stock markets of South East Asian. These tests inform
us about whether pairs of markets are cointegrated before we examine
whether multivariate cointegrating relationships exist. The results of the
pairwise tests are presented below in Table 4. The second stage in the

Table 3. Unit Root Test for the log of the index (The First Difference is the Return) (Trend & Intercept, Automatic Schwartz Info Criterion) Test Critical Value: 1% level − 3.961798, 5% level − 3.411646, 10% level − 3.127696.

Country	Whole Period		First Sub-Period		Second Sub-Period	
	Level ADF statistic	First difference ADF statistic	Level ADF statistic	First difference ADF statistic	Level ADF statistic	First difference ADF statistic
Australia	−2.632141	−49.16670	−2.885688	−28.18654	−2.474454	−39.86655
France	−0.865628	−48.63002	−1.907924	−28.43152	−1.816737	−39.20287
Germany	−0.979921	−49.76467	−1.337173	−28.65938	−2.101049	−40.01584
Hong Kong	−2.040507	−47.78340	−2.938030	−26.74585	−1.624737	−37.69065
Indonesia	−2.203113	−41.25719	−1.581485	−16.61270	−1.839177	−34.54198
Japan	−2.129318	−46.36694	−1.633372	−27.40648	−1.723978	−36.89171
Korea	−1.984937	−46.44756	−3.095419	−25.27494	−1.903734	−38.26895
Malaysia	−1.656970	−44.07142	−0.984369	−23.93829	−2.214349	−25.33372
Philippine	−2.444682	−40.98890	−0.945241	−23.24300	−2.250811	−33.61364
Singapore	−2.153061	−43.71324	−2.828916	−23.54139	−1.623262	−35.58703
Taiwan	−2.112191	−49.95920	−1.744925	−30.77432	−1.888568	−39.45686
Thailand	−0.178381	−42.67187	−1.984670	−24.33622	−0.731220	−36.16100
UK	−1.087310	−31.94110	−1.531390	−26.64004	−2.624081	−26.37065
US	−1.265243	−50.03362	−2.222390	−27.34058	−2.316179	−40.36823

cointegration analysis is to decide on the order of the underlying VAR model. The order of the VAR is determined by an inspection of either the Akaike (1974)-information criterion (AIC) or alternately the Schwarz (1978) Bayesian criterion (SBC). We selected the order of the VAR, by choosing in each case on the basis of the AIC and SBC coefficients as suggested by Johansen and Juselius (1990). However, as they give the same results, we report only the results based on the AIC.

Table 4 displays the Johansen (1988) maximum eigenvalue tests and trace tests for bivariate cointegration over the whole sample period (04-04-1994 to 10-11-2003), a pre-1997 Asian crisis period (04-04-1994) to (01-09-1997) and a post-crisis period (1-11-97) to (10-09-2003). The tables are used to determine (r) the number of cointegrating vectors for each pair of stock market indices, in other words the results inform us whether there exists a long-run equilibrium relationship between the two stock market indices. By comparing two sub-periods, one can determine whether the two stock markets have become increasingly integrated over time. For each test we compare

Table 4.   Bi-variate Cointegration Test Result.

Hypothesized number of CE(s)	Whole Period		First Sub-Period		Second Sub-Period	
	None	At most 1	None	At most 1	None	At most 1
Australia–US						
Eigenvalue	0.002751	0.001239	0.021801	0.001193	0.007020	0.001087
Trace Statistic	9.751746	3.026896	19.10027*	0.981509	12.93940	1.730931
Max-Eigen Statistic	6.724850		18.11876*		11.20847	
Australia–UK						
Eigenvalue	0.002639	0.000656	0.025321	0.002673	0.007489	0.000621
Trace Statistic	8.050737	1.600783	23.28257**	2.200258	12.94853	0.989006
Max-Eigen Statistic	6.449954		21.08232**		11.95952	
Australia–Germany						
Eigenvalue	0.001398	0.000197	0.016458	0.001092	0.004639	0.000151
Trace Statistic	3.896296	0.481581	14.53956	0.898456	7.638285	0.240957
Max-Eigen Statistic	3.414715		13.64110		7.397327	
Australia–Japan						
Eigenvalue	0.001698	0.000585	0.006530	1.80E−05	0.003463	0.000963
Trace Statistic	5.575774	1.427341	5.399959	0.014829	7.051684	1.533244
Max-Eigen Statistic	4.148433		5.385131		5.518440	
Australia–Indonesia						
Eigenvalue	0.001926	0.000733	0.004237	0.000983	0.003396	0.001822
Trace Statistic	6.495954	1.789006	4.298877	0.808721	8.312863	2.900785
Max-Eigen Statistic	4.706948		3.490156		5.412079	
Australia–Philippines						
Eigenvalue	0.003739	0.000447	0.006838	0.001962	0.004312	0.001657
Trace Statistic	10.23513	1.091393	7.254688	1.614643	9.512982	2.637898
Max-Eigen Statistic	9.143741		5.640046		6.875084	
Australia–Hong Kong						
Eigenvalue	0.002297	0.000729	0.023722	0.000190	0.003870	0.002453
Trace Statistic	7.393862	1.780912	19.89024*	0.156138	10.07620	3.907031
Max-Eigen Statistic	5.612949		19.73410**		6.169168	
Australia–Korea						
Eigenvalue	0.001921	0.000883	0.010764	4.89E−05	0.003461	0.001959
Trace Statistic	6.850923	2.156222	8.936144	0.040201	8.637011	3.120546

Table 4. (Continued)

Hypothesized number of CE(s)	Whole Period		First Sub-Period		Second Sub-Period	
	None	At most 1	None	At most 1	None	At most 1
Max-Eigen Statistic	4.694702		8.895943		5.516466	
Australia–Malaysia						
Eigenvalue	0.001845	0.000801	0.003930	0.002284	0.005681	0.001888
Trace Statistic	6.463001	1.955510	5.115696	1.879271	12.07179	3.007176
Max-Eigen Statistic	4.50749		3.236425		9.064616	
Australia–Singapore						
Eigenvalue	0.002065	0.000652	0.011993	4.68E−05	0.003795	0.001888
Trace Statistic	6.639084	1.592376	9.956644	0.038444	9.056326	3.007022
Max-Eigen Statistic	5.046708		9.918200		6.049304	
US–UK						
Eigenvalue	0.002643	0.000994	0.023813	0.002261	0.004527	0.000779
Trace Statistic	8.887053	2.428024	21.67171*	1.860892	8.458235	1.239489
Max-Eigen Statistic	6.459029		19.81081**		7.218746	
US–Germany						
Eigenvalue	0.001622	0.001560	0.010966	0.000597	0.004176	0.001370
Trace Statistic	7.773570	3.810023*	9.554926	0.491118	8.839191	2.180927
Max-Eigen Statistic	3.963547		9.063808		6.658264	
US–Japan						
Eigenvalue	0.001841	0.001061	0.004216	0.000968	0.007717	0.000952
Trace Statistic	7.090937	2.592185	4.269482	0.796256	13.84111	1.515367
Max-Eigen Statistic	4.498752		3.473226		12.32575	
US–Thailand						
Eigenvalue	0.002390	0.002007	0.009095	0.001959	0.002395	0.000667
Trace Statistic	10.74558	4.904988	9.122394	1.611695	4.876037	1.061567
Max-Eigen Statistic	5.840587		7.510699		3.814470	
US–Philippines						
Eigenvalue	0.001956	0.001255	0.004069	0.002679	0.004399	0.001526
Trace Statistic	7.844840	3.066374	5.557094	2.205149	9.444537	2.430515
Max-Eigen Statistic	4.778466		3.351945		7.014022	

Table 4. (*Continued*)

Hypothesized number of CE(s)	Whole Period		First Sub-Period		Second Sub-Period	
	None	At most 1	None	At most 1	None	At most 1
US–Singapore						
Eigenvalue	0.002085	0.001441	0.007951	0.001279	0.003420	0.001943
Trace Statistic	8.614508	3.519749	7.613893	1.051929	8.545590	3.094552
Max-Eigen Statistic	5.094759		6.561964		5.451038	
US–Indonesia						
Eigenvalue	0.002023	0.001257	0.005097	0.000434	0.001818	0.001681
Trace Statistic	8.012733	3.070643	4.557133	0.356913	5.572304	2.676895
Max-Eigen Statistic	4.942090		4.200220		2.895410	
Thailand–Indonesia						
Eigenvalue	0.003841	0.001741	0.006585	0.000619	0.008288	0.000555
Trace Statistic	13.64850	4.253703	5.939584	0.508766	14.12436	0.883838
Max-Eigen Statistic	9.394802		5.430818		13.24052	
Thailand–Japan						
Eigenvalue	0.003680	0.000828	0.003777	5.11E−06	0.003891	0.002347
Trace Statistic	11.02006	2.021720	3.114460	0.004197	9.941401	3.738767
Max-Eigen Statistic	8.998338		3.110263		6.202634	
Thailand–Singapore						
Eigenvalue	0.003054	0.001346	0.007203	7.41E−06	0.002180	0.000224
Trace Statistic	10.75370	3.287944	5.948543	0.006092	3.828242	0.356234
Max-Eigen Statistic	7.465753		5.942450		3.472009	
Thailand–Malaysia						
Eigenvalue	0.004287	0.001653	0.002587	0.002398	0.004736	0.000975
Trace Statistic	14.52409	4.037264*	4.102264	1.973252	9.104439	1.551755
Max-Eigen Statistic	10.48682		2.129012		7.552684	
Indonesia–Malaysia						
Eigenvalue	0.002890	0.001153	0.008606	0.004414	0.007327	0.001972
Trace Statistic	9.881112	2.816067	10.74119	3.636451	14.84206	3.141236
Max-Eigen Statistic	7.065045		7.104739		11.70082	
Indonesia–Philippines						
Eigenvalue	0.003386	0.000663	0.003556	0.001716	0.003499	0.001193
Trace Statistic	9.898244	1.618975	4.339686	1.411452	7.475774	1.899726

Table 4. (Continued)

Hypothesized number of CE(s)	Whole Period		First Sub-Period		Second Sub-Period	
	None	At most 1	None	At most 1	None	At most 1
Max-Eigen Statistic	8.279269		2.928234		5.576049	
Malaysia–Philippines						
Eigenvalue	0.001697	0.000809	0.020074	0.000998	0.003410	0.001270
Trace Statistic	6.121562	1.974701	17.48903*	0.820595	7.455847	2.021317
Max-Eigen Statistic	4.146860		16.66843*		5.434530	

*,** Denotes rejection of the hypothesis at the 5%(1%) level.
5% (1%): Trace critical Value for None Hypothesized No. of CE(s): 15.41 (20.04).
5% (1%): Trace critical Value for At most 1 Hypothesized No. of CE(s): 3.76 (6.65).
5% (1%): Critical Value for None Hypothesized No. of CE(s): 14.07 (18.63).
5% (1%): Max-Eigen critical Value for At most 1 Hypothesized No. of CE(s): 3.76 (6.65).

the null hypothesis of no cointegration against the alternative of cointegration. Critical values for both the Trace and Max-Eigen are provided at the 5% and 1%, respectively for 24 pairwise country cointegration equations. From the findings in Table 4, there appears to be overwhelming evidence of no bivariate cointegration in either the pre- or post-crisis periods for the majority of pairwise cointegration tests. These results are evidenced by the fact that the tests statistics (both trace and maximal eigenvalue forms of the test) are less than the corresponding critical values at the 5% (3.76) and 1% (6.65) indicating that the null hypothesis of no cointegration (i.e. at least 1 CE) cannot be rejected. Only in the case of Australia and Hong Kong, over the post-crisis period does the Johansen test statistics indicate a rejection of the null hypothesis of no cointegration under the trace statistic for at most 1 (one) cointegrating equation, where the trace test of 3.90 exceed the critical value of 3.76 at the 5 per cent level of significance. The results of the Gregory and Hansen (1996) cointegration method are not reported but are available on request. Generally, the results of the ADF_t^* and Z_t^* test statistics show that the null hypothesis of no cointegration against the alternative hypothesis of cointegration in the presence of a possible regime shift are not rejected at 5 per cent level. In addition the Z_t^* test statistic that tests the null hypothesis of the model C/T is not rejected at 5 per cent level. Therefore, the results are inconclusive. On the whole, the results of the Gregory and Hansen (1996) cointegration method show the same conclusion as the Johansen cointegration method.

Although, there is little or no evidence of cointegration on a bilateral basis between the developed stock markets and the emerging stock markets over the post-crisis period, it may be possible that country markets as a group are cointegrated. Table 5 contains multivariate cointegration test results from combining several country markets. There appears to be some country groupings, which display cointegrating relationships; for example country groupings (consisting of the advanced economies of Australia, France, Germany, UK and US) indicate strong evidence for at least one cointegrating vector over the pre-crisis period for both the trace and maximal eigenvalue forms of the test, however, no such evidence is present for the post-crisis period. In contrast, country groupings consisting of (Australia, Thailand, Singapore and Japan) provide no evidence of cointegrating relationships over either the pre- or post-crisis timeframes. Overall, the interpretation of these findings shows there to be a clear lack of any long-run relationships among the developed and emerging country equity markets.

5.2. Granger causality tests

Results from the cointegration tests suggest that there is no consistent evidence of a long-run relationship between Australia and the Asian equity markets and the US and Asian markets. However, this still leaves the possibility for the existence of short-run relationships. In this section we employ Granger causality tests to determine how much of a current variable, Y, can be explained by past values of y and whether adding lagged values of another variable, X, can improve the explanation. In this case, Y is said to be 'Granger-caused' by X if X helps explain to predict Y, what one is looking for is the coefficients on the lagged Xs to see if they are statistically significant based on an F-test.

The Granger-causality tests were applied to the first differences of each emerging Asian equity market with the Australian market across the two sub-periods. The results in Table 6 suggest Granger-causality running from the France, Germany, UK and USA to Australia with no feedback from Australia over both pre- and post-crisis. It is clear that the US market affects all markets without any evidence of feedbacks in any sub-period.

What can one conclude then, from the cointegration and Granger-causality results regarding the diversification benefits for an US or Australian investor wishing to invest in the Asian equity markets? First, the issue of cointegration continues to be debated, with some suggestions that absence of cointegration may be due to either structural breaks in the series or to invalid restrictions on the cointegration relationship. Nonetheless, in this

Table 5.   Multivariate Cointegration Result.

Unrestricted cointegration rank test

Hypothesized number of CE(s)	Eigen value	Trace statistic	5 per cent critical value	1 per cent critical value
Pre-Crisis (Australia, France, Germany, UK and US)				
None**	0.043217	89.69415	68.52	76.07
At most 1*	0.032655	53.37893	47.21	54.46
At most 2	0.019524	26.08854	29.68	35.65
At most 3	0.010269	9.881130	15.41	20.04
At most 4	0.001697	1.396219	3.76	6.65

Hypothesized number of CE(s)	Eigen value	Max-Eigen statistic	5 per cent critical value	1 per cent critical value
None*	0.043217	36.31522	33.46	38.77
At most 1*	0.032655	27.29039	27.07	32.24
At most 2	0.019524	16.20741	20.97	25.52
At most 3	0.010269	8.484910	14.07	18.63
At most 4	0.001697	1.396219	3.76	6.65

*,** denotes rejection of the hypothesis at the 5%(1%) level.
Trace test indicates 2 cointegrating equation (s) at the 5% level.
Trace test indicates 1 cointegrating equation (s) at the 1% level.
Max-eigenvalue test indicates 2 cointegrating equation (s) at the 5% level.
Max-eigenvalue test indicates no cointegration at the 1% level.

Post-Crisis (Australia, France, Germany, UK and US)

Unrestricted cointegration rank test

Hypothesized number of CE(s)	Eigen value	Trace statistic	5 per cent critical value	1 per cent critical value
None	0.020082	65.32038	68.52	76.07
At most 1	0.009260	33.04518	47.21	54.46

Table 5. (Continued)

Post-Crisis (Australia, France, Germany, UK and US)

Unrestricted cointegration rank test

Hypothesized number of CE(s)	Eigen value	Trace statistic	5 per cent critical value	1 per cent critical value
At most 2	0.006479	18.24324	29.68	35.65
At most 3	0.004075	7.901782	15.41	20.04
At most 4	0.000883	1.405740	3.76	6.65
Hypothesized number of CE(s)	Eigen value	Max-Eigen statistic	5 per cent critical value	1 per cent critical value
None	0.020082	32.27520	33.46	38.77
At most 1	0.009260	14.80194	27.07	32.24
At most 2	0.006479	10.34146	20.97	25.52
At most 3	0.004075	6.496042	14.07	18.63
At most 4	0.000883	1.405740	3.76	6.65

*,** Denotes rejection of the hypothesis at the 5%(1%) level.
Trace test indicates no cointegration at both 5% and 1% levels.
Max-eigenvalue test indicates no cointegration at both 5% and 1% levels.

Pre-Crisis Period (Australia, Thailand, Singapore and Japan)

Unrestricted cointegration rank test

Hypothesized number of CE(s)	Eigen value	Trace statistic	5 per cent critical value	1 per cent critical value
None	0.016841	28.52540	47.21	54.46
At most 1	0.011721	14.56441	29.68	35.65
At most 2	0.005600	4.872884	15.41	20.04
At most 3	0.000312	0.256896	3.76	6.65
Hypothesized number of CE(s)	Eigen value	Max-Eigen statistic	5 per cent critical value	1 per cent critical value

	Eigen value	Trace statistic	5 per cent critical value	1 per cent critical value
None	0.016841	13.96098	27.07	32.24
At most 1	0.011721	9.691529	20.97	25.52
At most 2	0.005600	4.615988	14.07	18.63
At most 3	0.000312	0.256896	3.76	6.65

*** Denotes rejection of the hypothesis at the 5%(1%) level.
Trace test indicates no cointegration at both 5% and 1% levels.
Max-eigenvalue test indicates no cointegration at both 5% and 1% levels.

Post-Crisis Period (Australia, Thailand, Singapore and Japan)

Unrestricted cointegration rank test

Hypothesized number of CE(s)	Eigen value	Trace statistic	5 per cent critical value	1 per cent critical value
None	0.010577	34.62936	47.21	54.46
At most 1	0.007295	17.71235	29.68	35.65
At most 2	0.002297	6.063735	15.41	20.04
At most 3	0.001510	2.404545	3.76	6.65
Hypothesized number of CE(s)	Eigen value	Max-Eigen statistic	5 per cent critical value	1 per cent critical value
None	0.010577	16.91701	27.07	32.24
At most 1	0.007295	11.64862	20.97	25.52
At most 2	0.002297	3.659190	14.07	18.63
At most 3	0.001510	2.404545	3.76	6.65

*** Denotes rejection of the hypothesis at the 5%(1%) level.
Trace test indicates no cointegration at both 5% and 1% levels.
Max-eigenvalue test indicates no cointegration at both 5% and 1% levels.

Table 6. Granger-Causality Tests.

Null Hypothesis:	Whole Period		Pre-crisis		Post-crisis	
	F-Statistic	Probability	F-Statistic	Probability	F-Statistic	Probability
Australia does not Granger cause France	3.40318	0.03343	3.46115	0.03185	5.1221	0.00606
France does not Granger cause Australia	193.899*	0	19.7612	4.20E−09	158.467*	0
Australia does not Granger cause Germany	0.64056	0.52709	3.39872	0.03389	2.35865	0.09488
Germany does not Granger cause Australia	93.2644*	0	79.0471*	0	44.3917*	0
Australia does not Granger cause Indonesia	0.09142	0.91264	2.76752	0.0634	0.23924	0.78725
Indonesia does not Granger cause Australia	0.53061	0.58831	1.38553	0.25078	0.33153	0.71787
Australia does not Granger cause Japan	0.66963	0.51199	0.12519	0.88235	1.15394	0.31566
Japan does not Granger cause Australia	0.48677	0.61467	1.48855	0.22631	0.19615	0.82191
Australia does not Granger cause Korea	0.3651	0.69416	0.88662	0.41244	0.32682	0.72126
Korea does not Granger cause Australia	2.02497	0.13222	3.86101	0.02143	0.76715	0.46451
Australia does not Granger cause Malaysia	0.3276	0.72068	0.37835	0.68511	1.65932	0.1906
Malaysia does not Granger cause Australia	1.3051	0.27134	2.26163	0.10483	0.05718	0.94442
Australia does not Granger cause Philippine	4.56719	0.01048	1.06111	0.34655	4.21154	0.01499
Philippine does not Granger cause Australia	1.96507	0.14037	2.66888	0.06993	1.33256	0.2641
Australia does not Granger cause Singapore	0.85621	0.4249	3.40019	0.03384	0.06619	0.93596
Singapore does not Granger cause Australia	3.45377	0.03178	3.58196	0.02826	4.77463	0.00856
Australia does not Granger cause Taiwan	9.28409	9.60E−05	2.8477	0.05855	4.22691	0.01476
Taiwan does not Granger cause Australia	0.09037	0.91359	0.25053	0.77845	0.21923	0.80316
Australia does not Granger cause Thailand	1.407	0.24508	0.05485	0.94663	2.56972	0.07688
Thailand does not Granger cause Australia	4.74035	0.00882	6.78135	0.0012	1.68369	0.18602
Australia does not Granger cause UK	5.06434	0.00638	0.98605	0.37349	5.93545	0.0027
UK does not Granger cause Australia	170.368*	0	25.4043	2.00E−11	140.279*	0
Australia does not Granger cause US	1.30445	0.27151	0.56045	0.57117	3.37314	0.03453
US does not Granger cause Australia	459.66*	0	132.025*	0	305.621*	0
Indonesia does not Granger cause US	0.23422	0.79121	2.67833	0.06928	0.02429	0.976
US does not Granger cause Indonesia	46.9838*	0	35.8769	1.20E−15	24.4506	3.50E−11

Japan does not Granger cause US	0.33582	0.71478	0.43798	0.64549	1.50053	0.22333
US does not Granger cause Japan	154.5T*	0	23.0468	1.80E−10	119.726*	0
Philippine does not Granger cause US	0.00821	0.99182	2.59351	0.07537	1.35728	0.25766
US does not Granger cause Philippine	52.7457*	0	17.8087	2.70E−08	42.1901*	0
Singapore does not Granger cause US	2.54413	0.07875	1.9497	0.14298	1.67122	0.18835
US does not Granger cause Singapore	159.362*	0	47.727*	0	107.151*	0
Thailand does not Granger cause US	1.45837	0.23282	3.84817	0.0217	0.44706	0.63959
US does not Granger cause Thailand	21.6458	4.80E−10	9.29571	0.0001	25.9476	8.20E−12
UK does not Granger cause US	1.53872	0.21486	2.01615	0.13383	2.09429	0.1235
US does not Granger cause UK	160.704*	0	43.3075*	0	101.009*	0

*Reject at 5% level of significance.

** Reject both at 1% and 5% level of significance.

paper the case for cointegration among the developed markets of the US and Australia and the emerging markets of South East Asia has not been demonstrated over six years since the Asian financial crisis of October 1997.

6. CONCLUSION

In this paper, we presented an analysis of cointegration between the US (Australia) and several South East Asian equity markets. The empirical results indicate that between (1993–1997), a period prior to the Asian Financial Crash there is mixed evidence of cointegration ties between US equity market and Asian markets. Furthermore, over the period covering (1998–2003), there appears to be no evidence of cointegration between Asian markets, the US and Australian markets. Finally, bivariate Granger causality tests revealed significant causality running from the US to all the Asian markets in both the pre- and post-Asian Financial crash.

The results have important implications for long-run diversification returns for a US or Australian investor contemplating investing in Asian financial markets. Firstly, the Asian markets do not share a common stochastic trend with either the US or Australian equity market this indicating diversification benefits for long-term investors, this effect is particularly strong over the period covering the post-Asian financial crisis. Secondly, the ever increasing pace of global financial integration indicates that equity return correlations will keep increasing and that would suggest that they be considered an important factor in asset allocation decisions in the future.

The relaxation of restrictions on foreign exchange and capital flows may not be sufficient to attract foreign investors and further strengthen international capital market linkages. Other factors such as poor accounting standards, information dissemination and political risks may influence the movement toward a universal Asian capital market. These reasons do provide significant justifications as to why Asian equity markets have not shown long-term co-movement with each other suggesting that potential diversification benefits within these Asian markets still exists for both US and Australian investors.

ACKNOWLEDGEMENT

The authors are grateful to the participants at the *Emerging Financial Markets & Services Asia-Pacific Conference*, Sydney (2004), *ASBBS 7th*

International Conference, James Cook University, Australia & American Society of Business and Behavioral Sciences, Cairns, Australia (2004) for critical comments and useful suggestions. We also acknowledge the generous financial support from University of Western Sydney to perform this research. Any remaining errors or shortcomings in this paper are of course our own responsibility.

REFERENCES

Akaike, H. (1974). *A new look at the statistics model identification.* IEEE *Transactions on Automatic Control* AC-19.

Allen, D. E., & MacDonald, G. (1995). The long run gains from international diversification: Australian evidence from cointegration tests. *Applied Financial Economics, 5*, 33–42.

Arshanapalli, B., & Doukas, J. (1993). International stock linkages: Evidence from the pre- and post-October 1987 period. *Journal of Banking and Finance, 17*, 193–208.

Campbell, J. Y., Lettau, M., Malkiel, B. G., & Xu, Y. (2001). Have individual stocks become more volatile? An empirical exploration of idiosyncratic risk. *The Journal of Finance, 6*(1), 1–43.

Chen, G. M., Firth, M., & Rui, O. M. (2002). Stock market linkages: Evidence from Latin America. *Journal of Banking and Finance, 26*(6), 1113–1141.

Daly, K. J. (2003). Southeast Asian stock market linkages, evidence from pre-and post October 1997. *ASEAN Economic Bulletin, 20*(1), 73–85.

De Fusco, R. A., Geppert, J. M., & Tsetsekos, G. P. (1996). Long-run diversification potential in emerging stock markets. *The Financial Review, 31*(2), 343–363.

Dickey, D. A., & Fuller, W. A. (1979). Distribution of the estimators for time series regressions with a unit root. *Journal of the American Business Association, 74*, 427–432.

Divecha, A. B., Drach, J., & Stefek, D. (1992). Emerging markets: A quantitative perspective. *Journal of Portfolio Management, 19*, 41–50.

Engle, R. F., & Granger, C. W. J. (1987). Cointegration and error-correction: Representation, estimation, and testing. *Econometrica, 55*, 251–276.

Forbes, K., & Rigobon, R. (1998). *No contagion, only interdependence: measuring stock market co-movements.* M.I.T.-Sloan School of Management Working Paper.

Gregory, A. W., & Hansen, B. E. (1996). Residual-based tests for cointegration in models with regime shifts. *Journal of Econometrics, 70*(1), 99–126.

Johansen, S. (1988). Statistical analysis of cointegration vectors. *Journal of Economic Dynamics and Control, 12*, 231–254.

Johansen, S., & Juselius, K. (1990). Maximum likelihood estimation and inferences on cointegration – with applications to the demand for money. *Oxford Bulletin of Economics and Statistics, 52*, 169–210.

Koutmos, G., & Booth, G. G. (1995). Asymmetric volatility transmission in international markets. *Journal of International Money and Finance, 14*(6), 747–762.

Lau, S. T., & McInish, T. H. (1993). Co-movements of international equity returns: A comparison of the pre-and post-October 19, 1987 periods. *Global Finance Journal, 1*(4), 1–19.

Meric, I., & Meric, G. (1989). Potential gains from international portfolio diversification and intertemporal stability and seasonality in international stock market relationships. *Journal of Banking and Finance, 13*, 627–640.

Michaud, R. O., Bergstrom, G. L., Frashure, R. D., & Wolahan, B. K. (1996). Twenty years of international equity investing. *Journal of Portfolio Management, 23*(1), 9–24.

Nieh, C. C. (2003). The effect of the Asian financial crisis on the relationships among open macroeconomic factors for Asian countries. *Journal of Applied Economics, 34*(4), 491–502.

Roll, R. (1992). Industrial structure and the competitive behaviour of international stock market indices. *Journal of Finance, 47*, 3–42.

FINANCIAL LINKS AND CONTAGION IN THE 1997 ASIAN CURRENCY CRISIS: AN EMPIRICAL EXAMINATION

Bang Nam Jeon

ABSTRACT

This paper provides evidence of financial linkages across countries as a channel of contagion of currency crises in the case of the 1997 Asian crisis using high-frequency data, focusing on the hardest hit countries in the region: Thailand, Indonesia, Malaysia, and Korea. Stock markets in the region were found to play an important role in transmitting initial and local shocks beyond its country of origin to other emerging economies during the 1997 crisis. Stock market linkages seem to have contributed importantly to the quick and wide-scale contagion of the ensuing exchange rate crisis across countries in the 1997 Asian crisis episode.

1. INTRODUCTION

The East Asian economic/financial crisis, which broke out around July 1997, plunged the most rapidly growing and successful economies into

Asia Pacific Financial Markets in Comparative Perspective: Issues and Implications for the 21ˢᵗ Century
Contemporary Studies in Economics and Financial Analysis, Volume 86, 101–114
ISSN: 1569-3759/doi:10.1016/S1569-3759(05)86005-X

financial chaos and deep economic depression. A remarkable feature of the Asian crisis was the degree to which it spread from Thailand to other countries in the region, including Indonesia, Malaysia, the Philippines, and Korea, very quickly, in the span of a few months.

There have been different explanations and proposals for why and how contagion spread so quickly in the region: macroeconomic similarities, trade links across countries, and cross-country financial links. Careful examination of macroeconomic indicators around the outbreak of the currency crises in the crisis-stricken nations reveals the relative irrelevance of macroeconomic fundamentals with the eruption and contagion of the 1997 Asian crisis (Radelet & Sachs, 1998; Chang & Velasco, 1998) The swift and global-scale contagion of the recent crises seem to support financial links, rather than trade links, as the key channel of contagion[1] (Taylor, 1999; Pritsker, 2001). Although these different explanations are not mutually exclusive, I propose that the ultimate determination of the relative roles of the different channels of contagion in the case of the Asian crises is an empirical question.

Relevant issues to financial links may include the existence of a common lender for emerging economies, market imperfections with information asymmetries, and portfolio diversification and leverage adjustment for financial asset liquidity. Studies by Frankel and Schmukler (1998) and Kaminsky, Lyons and Schmukler (2000) examined the role of mutual funds and closed-end country funds in spreading volatility and crisis in emerging economies. Krugman (2001) recently argued that the next generation of crises may affect not currencies but asset prices more generally. He proposed that the mechanisms for speculative attack and self-fulfilling pessimism identified in the currency-crisis models apply to stock markets as well (IMF, 2001).

The major indicators of financial crises and contagion include volatile movements in the exchange rate, the depletion of international reserves, sharply rising short-term interest rates and falling stock market prices. During the major financial crises of the 1990s, these financial variables moved significantly in many of the affected countries. These indicators, therefore, may identify other countries affected by contagion. This paper aims at identifying channels of financial contagion that originated in Thailand and spread to its neighboring countries and Korea, by examining changes in the linkages of the financial variables and financial markets around the eruption of the 1997 Asian crises.

This paper is structured as follows. Section 2 provides a brief review of literature on the identification of contagion channels. Section 3 reports evidence of increase in cross-market linkages in national stock markets after the 1997 crises in crisis-stricken Asian countries. Section 4 concludes this paper.

2. CONTAGION CHANNELS: LITERATURE REVIEW

The 1997–1998 Asian crises have shifted the focus of analysis of the underlying cause of the crises from a deterioration in macroeconomic fundamentals, as in "first-generation" models, to self-fulfilling speculative attacks caused by financial sector weaknesses and the globalization of financial markets in increasing an economy's vulnerability to sudden capital outflows, as in "second-generation" models of speculative attacks (IMF, 1999). In the second-generation model, a speculative attack can be triggered by a sudden and unpredictable shift in market expectations about the viability of a fixed exchange rate. These two different models present different views on the underlying reasons for spillover and contagion of crises from the country of origin to its neighboring countries (Eichengreen *et al.*, 1996). The first-generation model explains that common shocks and domestic fundamentals in the neighboring countries and trade spillovers in trade-partner countries are the main reasons for contagion effects. To the contrary, the second-generation model claims that financial linkages can be an important channel for spillover and contagion effects. The occurrence of a crisis in one country may induce global investors to rebalance their portfolios for various reasons. In the world of financially linked nations, shifts in investor sentiment or increased risk aversion can play an important role in the spread of crises.

The research on financial contagion, based on the second-generation model concept, has identified several channels through which shocks are transmitted due to different behavior in financial markets (Pritsker, 2001; Chiang, Cho, Jeon, & Li, 2004). The first channel is the correlated information channel. It argues that if two countries have real links, such as trade-investment linkages or industry linkages, then adverse information in one country will lead to the sale of financial assets, causing a downward pressure on asset prices in the other country's market, which is often amplified by information asymmetry (von Furstenberg, & Jeon, 1989; King & Wadhwani, 1990; Connolly & Wang, 2003). The wake-up call hypothesis, however, does not assume any real linkages between countries (Sachs, Tornell, & Velasco, 1995; Wolf, 1999). It argues that if one country has certain financial weaknesses, such as a weak-banking sector, then investors will reassess the risks of other countries with similar fundamentals, even if these investors have not changes their risk tolerance. This information inference transmits the shocks across markets.

The second channel is the liquidity channel. Since international investors hold portfolio positions in different markets when they have a capital loss in one market, they have to sell assets in other markets not directly related to the crisis country to meet certain requirements, such as margin calls (Forbes, 2000; Claessens, Dornbusch, & Park, 2001). The third channel is the cross-market hedging channel. It states that even if two countries have no common macroeconomic risks, their asset returns may still show strong co-movement due to asymmetric information from different types of investors (Calvo & Mendoza, 2000; Kodres & Pritsker, 2002). The fourth channel is the wealth-effect channel. For example, Kyle and Xiong (2001) modeled the wealth effect to explain the panic of hedge funds, banks, and securities firms after the fall of the hedge fund, long-term capital management. When erratic noise traders mismanage their assets that cause an unfavorable shock to asset prices, the wealth of short-term convergence traders decreases and they become more risk averse. As a result, they liquidate a large amount of risky positions across their entire portfolio, leading to price volatility and correlation across different national markets.

To conduct a direct test for identifying these channels of financial contagion is not an easy task due to the lack of microstructure data regarding investors.[2] Thus, most of the empirical efforts analyzing contagion effects turn to the investigation of asset-return comovements via correlation analysis (Baig & Goldfajn, 1998; Bordo & Murshid, 2001; Basu, 2002; Forbes & Rigobon, 2002; Corsetti, Pericoli, & Sbracia, 2002; Arestis, Caporale, & Cipollini, 2003; Billio & Pelizzon, 2003; Chiang, Jeon, & Li, 2006). This paper investigates the changing pattern of spillover and contagion effects in various financial markets across countries in Asia with the emphasis on the 1997 Asian crisis.

3. EMPIRICAL EVIDENCE

To examine the contagion effect of financial variables from Thailand to its neighboring countries and Korea, I set up the (G)ARCH model a la Bollerslev, Chou and Kroner (1992), which is appropriate to examine the interaction between the national financial markets in the region using volatile, high-frequency financial data, such as stock prices, exchange rates, and short-term money market rates, which often show heteroskedasticity and non-normality.

The GARCH model of orders p and q, i.e., GARCH(p, q), for changes in financial variables in the four hard-hit Asian countries – Thailand, Indonesia, Malaysia, and Korea – $R_{i,t}$ for country i, can be constructed as:

$$R_{i,t}|X_{i,t-1} \sim F(r_{i,t}, h_{i,t})$$

$$r_{i,t} = u_0 + \sum_{j=1, i \neq j}^{4} u_j r_{j,t}$$

for $i, j = 1$ (Thailand), 2 (Malaysia), 3 (Indonesia), and 4 (Korea), and

$$h_{i,t} = a_0 + \sum_{m=1}^{q} a_m e_{t-m}^2 + \sum_{n=1}^{p} b_n h_{t-n} \text{ and } e_{i,t} = R_{i,t} - r_{i,t}$$

where $F(r_t, h_t)$ is the conditional distribution of R_t, with conditional mean of r_t and variance h_t; X_{t-1} is the set of all information available up to time $t - 1$; and $a_0 > 0, a_m > 0$, and $b_n > 0$ as the non-negativity constraints associated with the parameters in the h_t equation are necessary to satisfy regularity conditions associated with the GARCH model. For country identifications, $i, j = 1$ (Thailand), 2 (Malaysia), 3 (Indonesia), and 4 (Korea).

I use the high-frequency data of the currency and financial markets in Thailand, Indonesia, Malaysia, and Korea. The data set includes foreign exchange rates, short-term money market rates, and national stock market indices, all on the daily basis. The data series will cover the period of January 1996–December 1999, which will be appropriate for the comparative analysis of the financial contagion effect during the pre- and the post-crisis period (Jeon & Seo, 2003). Main data sources include, among others, IMF *financial statistics* tape, *DataStream*, and central banks in the region.

First of all, the estimation results reported in Table 1 suggest that the stock market linkages in the four countries can be fitted by the GARCH specification model. The (G)ARCH effects become more conspicuous after the Thai crisis. Table 1 shows that there were "mean contagion effects" from South-East Asian countries to Korea during the post-crisis period. The largest stock market contagion to Korea came from Thailand with the positive and statistically significant coefficient, followed by Indonesia and Malaysia in this descending order. As reported in Table 2, there was no evidence of "volatility contagion" from South East Asian countries to Korea. With two different measures of volatility, GARCH variances and absolute returns, none of the coefficients of East Asian countries in the GARCH variance equation were statistically significant.

Table 1. The Contagion Effects of Stock Prices in Korea from stock Prices in the South-East Asian Countries, Thailand, Malaysia, and Indonesia during the Period of January 1996 through May 1999: Before and After the Thai Currency Crisis started on July 2, 1997.

	Before the Thai Crisis				After the Thai Crisis			
	1	2	3	4	5	6	7	8
Independent variable								
Constant	-0.068	-0.067	-0.046	-0.051	-0.097	-0.041	-0.056	-0.022
	(1.01)	(1.03)	(0.70)	(0.75)	(0.83)	(0.44)	(0.63)	(0.20)
Thailand	-0.022			-0.006	0.201			0.177
	(0.55)			(0.14)	(6.55)			(4.49)
Malaysia		0.001		0.067		0.156		0.096
		(0.02)		(0.88)		(4.68)		(2.48)
Indonesia			-0.158	-0.183			0.172	0.103
			(2.25)	(2.29)			(4.17)	(2.44)
GARCH effects								
Constant	0.483	0.517	0.431	0.445	0.347	0.102	0.109	0.120
	(3.49)	(3.12)	(3.18)	(2.96)	(2.85)	(3.06)	(3.23)	(1.54)
e_{t-1}^2	0.098	0.093	0.107	0.106	0.084	0.053	0.059	0.054
	(1.82)	(1.61)	(1.96)	(1.85)	(2.81)	(3.51)	(3.70)	(2.21)
$h(t-1)$	0.612	0.590	0.632	0.623	0.877	0.937	0.932	0.933
	(5.90)	(4.70)	(6.26)	(5.42)	(27.08)	(63.60)	(61.45)	(36.01)
Log-likelihood	-288.42	-288.79	-286.13	-285.71	-744.52	-741.06	-741.21	-730.05
Number of observation	390	390	390	390	492	492	492	492

Notes: Numbers in parentheses are *t*-statistics.
(1) The log-likelihood ratio test for H: A coefficient of Thailand, Malaysia, Indonesia, or those of all three is 0 in each estimation equation. The statistic is distributed as a chi-square with one (or three for regression equations 4 and 8) degrees of freedom. The 95 percent and 99 percent quantiles in the distribution of the test statistic, v^2 (1), are 3.84 and 6.63, respectively.
(2) The log-likelihood ratio test for H: A coefficient of Thailand, Malaysia, Indonesia or those of all three is 0, and there are no ARCH effects in each estimation equation. The statistic is distributed as a chi-square with four degrees of freedom. The 95 percent and 99 percent quantiles in the distribution of the test statistic, v^2 (4) are 9.49 and 13.28, respectively.

Table 2. The Contagion Effects of Stock Prices and Volatility in Korea from Stock Prices in the South East Asian Countries, Thailand, Malaysia, and Indonesia during the Period of July 2, 1997–May 21, 1999: After the Thai Currency Crisis Started on July 2, 1997.

	Volatility: GARCH Variances				Volatility: Absolute Returns			
	1	2	3	4	5	6	7	8
Independent variable								
Mean equation								
Constant	−0.085	0.001	−0.014	−0.036	−0.072	−0.020	−0.014	−0.049
	(0.76)	(0.01)	(0.16)	(0.33)	(0.65)	(0.21)	(0.16)	(0.45)
Thailand	0.213			0.186	0.221			0.186
	(6.16)			(4.10)	(6.04)			(4.18)
Malaysia		0.154		0.099		0.157		0.104
		(4.05)		(2.49)		(4.81)		(2.63)
Indonesia			0.182	0.097			0.183	0.087
			(4.13)	(2.07)			(4.19)	(1.83)
GARCH effects/GARCH variance equation								
Constant	0.173	0.107	0.153	0.187	0.061	0.121	0.142	0.199
	(0.92)	(1.32)	(1.16)	(1.04)	(0.66)	(3.13)	(2.82)	(2.62)
e_{t-1}^2	0.059	0.054	0.061	0.057	0.057	0.052	0.061	0.051
	(3.41)	(3.38)	(3.51)	(2.82)	(3.73)	(3.98)	(3.59)	(2.75)
$h(t-1)$	0.927	0.933	0.927	0.921	0.933	0.934	0.929	0.925
	(53.26)	(60.68)	(54.56)	(41.04)	(60.90)	(70.76)	(53.91)	(41.54)
Thailand	−0.004			−0.012	0.027			−0.032
	(0.20)			(2.21)	(0.84)			(3.09)
Malaysia		0.003		−0.001		0.006		−0.006
		(0.34)		(0.08)		(0.25)		(0.18)
Indonesia			−0.003	0.012			−0.012	0.039
			(0.16)	(0.46)			(0.35)	(0.68)
Log-likelihood	−733.88	−743.04	−742.97	−728.82	−733.52	−743.89	−742.93	−734.43

Note: Numbers in parentheses are *t*-statistics.

The estimation results for spot exchange rates and short-term interest rates are reported in Table 3. There is evidence of the "mean contagion" effects of the exchange rate from Thailand to Korea, neither from Malaysia or Indonesia to Korea. The contagion effect of short-term interest rates from Thailand and Malaysia to Korea during the post-crisis period was found. A lack of interest-rate contagion from Indonesia to Korea is consistent with the very volatile and abnormally high level of interest rates during the post-crisis period in Indonesia. Overall, stock prices among various financial variables seem to have played the most important role in financial contagion during the post-crisis period in the region.

To further investigate the dynamic pattern and speed of stock market contagion from South-East Asian countries to Korea, we set up the

Table 3. The Contagion Effects of Spot Exchange Rates and Short-term Interest Rates from the South East Asian Countries, Thailand, Malaysia, and Indonesia to Korea during the Period of Post-Thai Currency Crisis: July 2, 1997–July 28, 1999 (Exchange Rates) and through June 8, 1999 (Interest Rates).

	Spot Exchange Rates				Short-Term Interest Rates			
	1	2	3	4	5	6	7	8
Independent Variable								
Constant	-0.001	-0.006	0.015	-0.005	-0.748	-0.041	14.570	0.973
	(0.05)	(0.19)	(0.71)	(0.22)	(1.68)	(0.44)	(38.9)	(1.37)
Thailand	0.315			0.057	1.390			1.448
	(18.23)			(3.77)	(29.30)			(10.72)
Malaysia		-0.001		-0.017		0.125		-0.097
		(0.02)		(0.88)		(1.06)		(0.43)
Indonesia			0.005	-0.001			-0.081	-0.028
			(0.67)	(0.65)			(8.02)	(2.49)
GARCH effects								
Constant	0.001	0.001	0.006	0.011	1.456	0.381	0.168	1.918
	(6.10)	(5.78)	(5.75)	(4.12)	(5.77)	(0.78)	(0.09)	(2.86)
e_{t-1}^2	0.166	0.154	0.210	0.321	0.288	0.158	0.458	0.423
	(13.32)	(12.86)	(16.82)	(10.42)	(11.30)	(6.86)	(1.42)	(9.49)
$h(t-1)$	0.848	0.842	0.805	0.739	0.466	0.688	0.374	0.399
	(98.15)	(96.58)	(75.75)	(35.83)	(8.87)	(7.56)	(1.35)	(3.57)
Log-likelihood	-285.15	-172.19	-198.23	-158.20	-734.83	-779.84	-903.10	-746.11
Number of observation	540	540	540	540	504	504	504	504

Notes:
(1) Numbers in parentheses are *t*-statistics.
(2) Spot exchange rates are units of local currencies per U.S. dollar: Thai, Baht, Malay Ringgit, Indonesian Rupiah, and Korean Won.
(3) Short-term interest rates are NCD 91 days-received yield (Korea), time deposit 12 month-middle rate (Thailand), Deposit 1 month-middle rate (Indonesia), and Deposit 1 month-middle rate (Malaysia), respectively.

4-variable vector autoregression (VAR) system, which includes the series of close-to-close rates of stock price change in the Thailand, Malaysia, Indonesian, and Korean markets. Each variable is thus treated as endogenous and is regressed on lagged values of all variables in the system.

The 4-variable VAR system is:

$$\mathbf{RS} = \beta_0 + \sum_{j=1}^{m} \beta_j \mathbf{RS}_{t-j} + \varepsilon_t$$

where $\mathbf{RS} = \{RS_i\}_{4\times1}$ is a vector of differences in the log stock price index in each of the four Asian markets, $i = 1$ (Thailand), 2 (Malaysia), 3 (Indonesia), and 4 (Korea), for the 4-variable VAR system, and j identifies lagged variables upto m

$\beta_0 = \{\beta_{i,0}\}_{4\times1}$ is a vector of constants,

$\beta_j = \{\beta_{i,j}\}_{4\times4}$ is a matrix of regression coefficients,

m = the lag length,

$\varepsilon_t = \{\varepsilon_t\}_{4\times1}$ is the stochastic error process, which is assumed to satisfy the orthogonal conditions

$$E[\varepsilon_t \mathbf{RS}_{t-k}] = 0, \quad k = 1, \ldots, m$$

At most, one or two lags should appear in the VAR estimation for efficient markets, where stock prices adjust quickly to all relevant information. The log-likelihood ratio tests for the choice of the lag length confirmed that both the first lag and the second lag were significant in the tests, while there was no indication of statistical significance for a third lag and beyond.

Although contemporaneous values of all the variables do not appear on the right-hand side of the VAR model, contemporaneous correlations between the variables in the system are captured in the covariance matrix of disturbance terms. However, the contemporaneous correlation matrix without decomposition makes economic interpretation of the VAR very difficult. One device to deal with this difficulty is the triangular orthogonalization of the innovation matrix. To this end, we applied the Choleski factorization. Analysis of the pattern of innovations and responses in different markets were performed using the impulse response function (IRF) analysis available in the VAR model. The IRFs show the current and subsequent effects of innovation in a given variable on all variables in the system. The (orthogonal) impulses in this study are equal to one standard deviation of the variable that is shocked.

Several implications can be derived from the IRF analysis. The impulse-response relations have increased drastically after the 1997 crisis in all the four countries. Furthermore, there is strong evidence of stock market contagion during the post-crisis period, which is worthwhile noting. During the post-crisis period, as reported in Table 4, an average of 33.7 percent (0.85/2.52) of initial impulse from Thailand was transmitted to Korea, within a 24-h period, compared to none during the pre-crisis period. This spillover effect seems to last rather persistently for at least three days, during which a total of 60.7 percent (1.53/2.52) of initial impulse was spread to Korea.

A relatively weaker contagion effect was detected from Malaysia to Korea, with a 12.6 percent (0.37/2.94) of initial impulse transmitted during the post-crisis period, compared to 6.3 percent (0.05/0.79) during the pre-crisis period. Evidence of little contagion was found from Indonesia to Korea, although the nation generated contagion effect to its neighboring countries, with an average of 12–17 percent transmission of its initial impulse within a 24-h period and up to an average of 20–34 percent of initial innovation transmissions during the first 3-day period, respectively. The magnitude of transmission of initial innovations from Korea to the other Asian countries also increased from almost none during the pre-crisis period to 4–19 percent within 24 h during the post-crisis period. A total of 14–26 percent of initial innovations of stock return was found to be transmitted from Korea to the other Asian countries within a 3-day period.

4. CONCLUSION AND POLICY IMPLICATIONS

A currency crisis that hits one country may be expected to spread to its trading partners. However, the quick and massive nature of contagion in the region seem to suggest that financial market linkages were the prime channel of contagion in the case of the 1997–1999 East Asian crisis. In particular, the moral hazard view of the East Asian crisis suggests that asset prices, such as stock prices played an important role for contagion.

This paper provided evidence of financial linkages across countries as a channel of contagion of currency crises in the case of the 1997 Asian crisis using high-frequency data, focusing on the hardest hit countries in the region: Thailand, Indonesia, Malaysia, and Korea. Stock markets in the region were found to play an important role in transmitting initial and local shocks beyond its country of origin to other emerging economies during the 1997 crisis. Stock market linkages seem to have contributed importantly to the quick and wide-scale contagion of the ensuing exchange rate crisis across countries in the 1997 Asian crisis episode.

Table 4. Impulse Response Analysis: Dynamic Responses to the Triangularly Orthogonalized Innovations in the VAR System for the Asian Stock Markets (1/1/1996–5/21/1999).

	Period[a]	Horizon	(Response)			
			Thailand	Malaysia	Indonesia	Korea
Origin						
TH		1	1.44	0.13	0.12	0.01
	1	2	0.18	0.03	0.13	−0.07
		3	0.14	0.03	0.07	0.02
		1–3[b]	1.76	0.19	0.32	−0.04
		1	2.52	1.04	1.00	0.85
	2	2	0.36	0.15	0.60	0.54
		3	0.10	0.39	0.14	0.14
		1–3	2.98	1.58	1.74	1.53
MA		1	0.00	0.79	0.29	0.05
	1	2	0.01	0.06	0.10	0.03
		3	0.02	0.05	0.03	−0.19
		1–3	0.03	0.90	0.42	−0.11
		1	0.00	2.94	0.39	0.37
	2	2	0.11	−0.16	0.01	0.03
		3	0.10	0.06	−0.08	−0.01
		1–3	0.21	2.84	0.23	0.39
IN		1	0.00	0.00	0.76	−0.08
	1	2	−0.05	0.01	0.17	−0.05
		3	0.10	0.11	0.03	0.08
		1–3	0.06	0.12	0.96	−0.05
		1	0.00	0.00	2.35	−0.01
	2	2	0.30	0.40	0.39	−0.02
		3	0.17	0.41	0.16	0.05
		1–3	0.47	0.81	2.90	0.02
KR		1	0.00	0.00	0.00	1.22
	1	2	−0.09	−0.01	0.01	0.20
		3	0.06	0.01	0.06	−0.02
		1–3	−0.03	0.00	0.07	1.40
		1	0.00	0.00	0.00	2.78
	2	2	0.38	0.10	0.52	0.22
		3	0.34	0.30	0.16	−0.02
		1–3	0.72	0.40	0.68	2.98
Sizes of impulses	(1) pre-crisis period		1.44	0.79	0.76	1.22
	(2) post-crisis period		2.52	2.94	2.35	2.78

[a]Period 1 denotes the pre-July 1997 crisis period; period 2 denotes the post-crisis period.
[b]Cumulative responses after four days were not significantly different from this result when the sequence of the markets is reordered and redated.

Contagion between stock markets is believed to have generated contagion of the exchange rate crisis during the crisis period in Asia. The first channel of spreading crises via stock market contagion will be the erosion of confidence by investors. A decline in confidence caused by currency crisis in the crisis-origin country will result in falling stock prices with greater volatility. The spillover effects of falling stock prices to another country will further reduce the investors' confidence in the other country and lead to a sharp decline in the value of its currency, causing a currency crisis in that country.

Stock market linkages provide an effective path for the spread of eroded confidence across countries. Speculative attack and self-fulfilling pessimism, which created the initial currency crisis in the origin country, are repeated in stock markets in other vulnerable emerging economies. Stock market linkages also work as an indirect channel of contagion through the role of foreign investors (Froot, O'Connell, & Seasholes, 2001). When international investors are increasingly concerned about the prospect of crisis-stricken emerging economies, they try to withdraw from the emerging market economies and rebalance their portfolio positions. Liquidity difficulties facing international investors as a result of currency crises also force the investors to liquidate their positions in other national markets, consequently spreading the crises.

NOTES

1. Glick and Rose (1999) acknowledged the importance of financial links as a channel of contagion. However, they claimed that the limited availability of data precluded testing the role of financial market links.

2. Chiang, Cho, Jeon, and, Li (2004) looks at how sovereign credit rating changes affected the stock markets in the crisis countries. Sovereign credit rating changes in one country was shown to trigger stock market decline in another country, especially during the turbulent period. This is consistent with the wake-up call hypothesis and cross-market hedging hypothesis.

REFERENCES

Arestis, P., Caporale, G. M., & Cipollini, A. (2003). *Testing for financial contagion between developed and emerging markets during the 1997 East Asian crisis.* Working Paper no. 370. The Levy Economics Institute of Bard College.

Baig, T., & Goldfajn, I. (1998). *Financial market contagion in the Asian crisis.* IMF Working Paper no. 98/155.

Basu, R. (2002). *Financial contagion and investor 'learning': An empirical investigation*. IMF Working Paper no. 02/218.

Billio, M., & Pelizzon, L. (2003). Contagion and interdependence in stock markets: Have they been misdiagnosed? *Journal of Economics and Business, 55*, 405–426.

Bollerslev, T., Chou, R. Y., & Kroner, K. F. (1992). ARCH modeling in finance: A review of the theory and empirical evidence. *Journal of Econometrics, 52*, 5–59.

Bordo, M. D., & Murshid, A. P. (2001). Are financial crises becoming more contagious? What is the historical evidence on contagion? In: S. Claessens & K. Forbes (Eds), *International financial contagion*. Kluwer Academic Publishers.

Calvo, G., & Mendoza, E. (2000). Rational contagion and the globalization of securities market. *Journal of International Economics, 51*, 79–113.

Chang, R., & Velasco, A. (1998). *The Asian liquidity crisis*. NBER Working Paper Series no. W6796, November.

Chiang, T., Cho, S. Y., Jeon, B., & Li, H. (2004). *Sovereign credit rating changes, stock markets, and the 1997 Asian crisis*. Working Paper. Drexel University, Pheladelphia, PA.

Chiang, T., Jeon, B., & Li, H. (2006). Dynamic correlation analysis of financial contagion: Evidence from Asian markets. *Journal of International Money and Finance*, (forthcoming).

Claessens, S., Dornbusch, R., & Park, Y. C. (2001). Contagion: Why crises spread and how this can be stopped. In: S. Claessens & K. Forbes (Eds), *International financial contagion*. Kluwer Academic Publishers.

Connolly, R. A., & Wang, F. A. (2003). International equity market comovements: Economic fundamentals or contagion? *Pacific-Basin Finance Journal, 11*, 23–43.

Corsetti, G., Pericoli, M., & Sbracia, M. (2002). *Some contagion, some interdependence: More pitfalls in tests of financial contagion*. CEPR Working Paper no. 3310.

Eichengreen, B., Rose, A., & Wyplosz, C. (1996). Speculative attacks on pegged exchange rates: An empirical exploration with special reference to the European monetary system. In: M. Canzoneri, W. Ethier & V. Grilli (Eds), *The new transatlantic economy*. Cambridge University Press.

Forbes, K. (2000). *The Asian flu and Russian virus: Firm-level evidence on how crises are transmitted internationally*. NBER Working Paper no. W7808, July.

Forbes, K., & Rigobon, R. (2002). No contagion only interdependence: Measuring stock market comovements. *The Journal of Finance, LVII*(5), 2223–2261.

Frankel, J., & Schmukler, S. (1998). Crisis, contagion, and country funds: Effects on East Asia and Latin America. In: R. Glick (Ed.), *Managing capital flows and exchange rates*. Cambridge University Press.

Froot, K., O'Connell, P., & Seasholes, M. (2001). The portfolio flows of international investors I. *Journal of Financial Economics, 59*(2), 151–193.

Glick, R., & Rose, A. K. (1999). Contagion and trade: Why are currency crises regional? In: P. R. Agenor, M. Miller, D. Vines & A. Weber (Eds), *The Asian financial crisis: Causes, contagion, and consequences* (pp. 284–311). Cambridge, UK: Cambridge University Press.

International Monetary Fund (1999). *World Economic Outlook*, Washington, DC, May.

International Monetary Fund (2001). *IMF Survey*, January 22.

Jeon, B. N., & Seo, B. (2003). The impact of the Asian financial crisis on foreign exchange market efficiency: The cast of East Asian countries. *Pacific-Basin Finance Journal, 11*, 509–525.

Kaminsky, G., Lyons, R. K., & Schmukler, S. L. (2000). *Managers, investors, and crises: Mutual fund strategies in emerging markets.* World Bank Policy Research Working Paper no. 2399, July.

King, M., & Wadhwani, S. (1990). Transmission of volatility between stock markets. *The Review of Financial Studies, 3,* 5–33.

Kodres, L. E., & Pritsker, M. (2002). A rational expectations model of financial contagion. *The Journal of Finance, LVII*(2), 769–799.

Krugman, P. (2001). *Crisis: The next generation.* Paper presented at the conference in honor of Assaf Razin, Tel Aviv, Israel, March 25–26.

Kyle, A., & Xiong, W. (2001). Contagion as a wealth effect. *The Journal of Finance, LVI*(4), 1401–1440.

Pritsker, M. (2001). The channels for financial contagion. In: S. Claessens & K. Forbes (Eds), *International financial contagion.* Kluwer Academic Publishers.

Radelet, S., & Sachs, J. (1998). *The onset of the East Asian financial crisis.* NBER Working Paper no. 6680, August. Cambridge, MA.

Sachs, J., Tornell, A., & Velasco, A. (1995). *Financial crises in emerging markets: The lessons from 1995.* NBER Working Paper no. 5576.

Taylor, M. P. (1999). *Asset price bubbles, risky lending and the East Asian crisis.* Working Paper, November. Center for Financial Studies, Warwick Business School, University of Warwick.

von Furstenberg, G., & Jeon, B. N. (1989). International stock price movements: Links and messages. *Brookings Papers on Economic Activity, 1,* 125–167.

Wolf, H. (1999). International asset price and capital flow comovements during crisis: The role of contagion, demonstration effects and fundamentals. Prepared for Capital Flows, Financial Crisis, and Policies Conference, April 15–16.

TANGIBLE AND INTANGIBLE NON-CURRENT ASSETS: EVIDENCE OF INFORMATION CONTENT DURING ECONOMIC CRISIS PERIOD

Zaleha Abdul Shukor, Hamezah Md Nor, Muhd Kamil Ibrahim and Jagjit Kaur

ABSTRACT

In this paper, we investigate the information content of non-current assets (NCA) among firms listed on the main board of Bursa Malaysia. Specifically, we investigate the information content of tangible and intangible NCA during the economic crisis period of 1997–1998. Our empirical analysis uses time-varying and fixed effects models for the period 1995–1999. We measure information content based on the association of analysts' earnings forecasts errors (AFE) with both capitalized tangible and intangible NCA. We find evidence of higher information content in tangible NCA compared to intangible NCA during the Asian economic crisis period of 1997–1998. Our evidence is consistent with the assumption that

Asia Pacific Financial Markets in Comparative Perspective: Issues and Implications for the 21st Century
Contemporary Studies in Economics and Financial Analysis, Volume 86, 115–137
ISSN: 1569-3759/doi:10.1016/S1569-3759(05)86006-1

*tangible assets are more reliable compared to intangible assets for pre-
diction of expected cash flows during economic crisis periods.*

1. INTRODUCTION

The usefulness of non-current assets (NCA) information reported in the
financial statements of firms depends on their association with expected
future cash flows to the firms. Given that these NCA has significant associations with firms' expected future cash flows, we thus suggest that they
have information content. Hence, these NCAs provide useful information
towards users of financial statements, in making their relevant decisions,
such as earnings forecasting and setting market prices. In this study, we
focused on the decision-making of financial analysts, being professional
users of financial statements (Schipper, 1991; Beaver, 2002).

During the 1997 Asian economic crisis, the Malaysian capital market was
among the worst affected in Asia (Ang & Ma, 2001). As such, investigating
the Malaysian capital market reaction towards the usefulness of accounting
information is very pertinent and relevant not only to the accounting research community but also the accounting profession per se. The question is
whether accounting information has significant impact towards the decision
making activities of market participants during that period. Findings would
provide further evidence on the usefulness of accounting information, especially during non-normal periods.

In this study, we investigate the information content of tangible and intangible NCA to determine whether relevant current accounting standards
provide sufficient information for better decision making by financial analysts. In Malaysia, specific applicable accounting standard dealing with
intangible NCA is not yet available as of the date of this study. At the
international level, the International Accounting Standards Board (IASB) in
1998 issued IAS 38, *Intangible Assets*, on the accounting of intangible assets,
but it is not applicable in Malaysia. In Malaysia, intangibles are dealt with
under the Malaysian Accounting Standards Board (MASB) 4, *Research and
Development Costs* (MASB, 1999), and purchased goodwill under MASB
21, *Business Combinations* (MASB, 2001). Due to the lack of accounting
standards on intangible NCA, we implicitly assume that accounting for
intangible NCA in Malaysia will depend more on management discretion
rather than guided accounting practice. Intuitively, this poses the question
of the usefulness of intangible NCA accounting information compared to

tangible NCA especially during economic crisis periods. This is particularly important because in the year 1997, intangible NCA was found to comprise as much as 22% of firms' total assets, among listed firms on Bursa Malaysia (Corporate Handbook, 2000; Zaleha et al., 2000).

An earlier study by Zaleha, Hamezah, Muhd-Kamil, and Kaur (2004) found that intangible NCA has information content for financial analysts during economic crisis periods, but with higher uncertainty. Analysts' earnings forecasts error was found to be significantly associated with intangible NCA but the error was higher during the crisis period of 1997–1998 compared to during non-crisis periods. This finding suggests that intangibles provide relevant information to the capital market even though intangibles are by nature highly uncertain for predicting future cash flows. Barth and Clinch (1998) in a study of Australian firms found that in arriving at firms' valuation, financial analysts utilized tangible NCA information more than intangible NCA, when they are at cost, and utilized both tangible and intangible NCA information as if they contain the same amount of useful information (to predict expected future cash flows) when they had been revalued.

The next section provides literature and theoretical framework of intangible and tangible NCA information content. Section 3 presents research methods and sample data. Section 4 discusses findings of the study and finally Section 5 concludes.

2. LITERATURE REVIEW

The underlying framework in this study is based on the concept of fundamental information analysis undertaken by financial analysts (Lev & Thiagarajan, 1993). Fundamental information analysis examines the information content of accounting fundamental information towards prediction of firms' future cash flows. One of the main items is capital investment or capital expenditures. Changes in firms' capital expenditures signal news to the capital market (Dowen, 2001) and may happen for many reasons. It not only signals changes in the expenditures itself but also may be due to revaluation activities (Barth & Clinch, 1998), impairment of assets (Alciatore, Easton, & Spear, 2000), depreciation (Herrmann & Inoue, 1996), and asset sales (Herrmann, Inoue, & Thomas, 2001). At the same time, capital investment provides information on firms' operating assets which is important for firms' valuation (Ohlson, 1995).

We extend the issue of usefulness of capital expenditures further by breaking down the capital expenditures (that we define mainly as NCA) into four major components: fixed assets, intangible assets, investment property, and investments. We then examine the information content of tangible and intangible components of the capital expenditures separately in a multiple regression setting. In this study, we categorize fixed assets, investment property, and investments as tangible NCA, and all others as intangible NCA. We utilize these components because our aim is to investigate whether there is any difference in the information content of the various nature of capital expenditures towards financial analysts' earnings forecasts. Accounting standards on NCA normally require firms to report separately the components of capital expenditures. Hence, there is a need to investigate the usefulness of these components in separation.

2.1. Information Content of Tangible NCA

Kim, Joo, and Choi (1996) suggested that productivity measures can provide information about firms' performance just as useful as traditional earnings numbers. We employ the same argument in this study, but focus on reported NCA since we are interested in investigating the most transparent accounting information to users of financial statements apart from earnings numbers. Tangible NCA normally represent major portions of firms' net book value of equity and also normally represent the main portion of firms' capital expenditures (Deesomsak, Paudyal, & Pescetto, 2004; Singh & Nejadmalayeri, 2004; Corporate Handbook, 2000).

Abarbanell and Bushee (1997) found that even though capital expenditures represent important fundamental information used by market participants to predict future earnings (Penman, 1992), increase in capital expenditures does not necessarily mean good news. Abarbanell and Bushee (1997) found that increase in capital expenditures above industry average signal bad news for short-term future earnings. Changes in capital expenditures are conceptually associated better with long-term future earnings (Tan, 2000).

In another context, prior literature found that issues on movement in NCA are also always value relevant to the capital market. For example, impairment of tangible assets were found significant towards valuing firms in the petroleum industry in the US (Alciatore, Easton, & Spear, 2000), while revaluations of tangible NCA were found value relevant to both investors and analysts in Australia (Easton, Eddey, & Harris, 1993; Barth & Clinch, 1998; among others).

2.2. Information Content of Intangible NCA

Kohlbeck (2004) found that almost all components of the intangible assets of US publicly traded banks, whether recorded or not are value relevant and reliable towards firms' valuation. Hirschey and Richardson (2002) found that when the intangible portion of firms' value is impaired (such as in the write-off of goodwill), firms' share prices also drops. They suggest that the capital market reacts as such due to existence of useful information in firms' intangibles relevant towards investors' decision making. In this case, the information might be signalling firms' future growth opportunities. While Henning, Lewis, and Shaw (2000) found that overall, all components of goodwill from acquisitions, representing intangible portion of firms' value provide relevant information to the capital market. Jennings, LeClere, and Thompson (2001) also found evidence on the usefulness of reported intangibles amortization towards firms' valuation by the capital market.

In a more direct study on the usefulness of intangible assets, Aboody and Lev (1998) found that US firms' software capitalization has information content. The intangible is positively associated with firms' share returns and share prices. The intangible is also positively associated with one- and two-year ahead operating income and net income of the firms. Muhd-Kamil, Marzita, Radziah, and Zaleha (2003) using Malaysian data also found similar findings on the value relevant of reported goodwill information.

2.3. Effect of Economic Crisis Periods

Most prior studies on the usefulness of intangibles, especially in the US, use R&D expenditures to represent intangible assets (Lev & Sougiannis, 1996; Aboody & Lev, 1998; among others). While studies on tangible assets did not specifically investigate the actual reported tangible assets within the financial statements (among the exceptions are Barth & Clinch, 1998). Most studies focused on capital expenditures overall (for example, see Kerstein & Kim, 1995; among others).

Lev and Zarowin (1999) suggested that the usefulness of accounting information decreased during an era of rapid business changes because accounting information lagged behind in capturing firms' real value changes compared to capital market reaction. The 1990s in Malaysia can be associated with increasing business and innovation changes (for example, the establishment of the multimedia super corridor in the year 1998). However, Lev and Zarowin (1999) also found that rapid business changes can be represented by changes in R&D or intangibles spending. As such, in cases of stable intangible expenditures, it is expected that usefulness of accounting information will not reduce.

The nature of investments, though more likely to be a tangible asset, is however probably as unpredictable as intangibles especially during economic crisis. Investments could become uncertain in terms of its association with expected future cash flows during economic crisis (Green, 2004). Nevertheless, Joyce and Read (2002) found that UK firms were not misled by changes in announcements on inflation rates in determining firms' financial assets prices. This finding suggested that the capital market is still efficient even during economic crisis period. We therefore argue that this would also suggest that findings from our study would provide reliable evidence in terms of comparing the usefulness between tangible and intangible assets information.

During economic crisis periods, we expect that book value of net assets become more useful compared to earnings based on the abandonment option hypothesis (Hayn, 1995). Economic crisis period usually result in uncertainty towards firms' financial position. Especially when more firms liquidate or went for bankruptcy chapter, other firms might also be affected economically. The most practical solution in the short term would be to sell as much available assets to cover costs and pay debts. However, in the presence of economic crisis, it would not be easy to sell assets with uncertain nature, especially the intangibles. Goodwill, for example, could not be sold individually to obtain fast cash. With unpredictable future economy, investments would also not be in demand. Finally, only tangible fixed assets would be more likely able to become a source of cash in the short run.

Dowen (2001) found that the level of economic growth has an impact on the usefulness of capital expenditures information to market participants. The higher the difference between firms' capital expenditures compared to industry level, the higher the forecasts error. Hence, during normal economic growth period, prediction of firms' future cash flows is perceived as good news for firms with capital expenditures changes at the same level as industry average, but not otherwise. Conceptually, this is the same conclusion as Abarbanell and Bushee (1997) where increase in capital expenditures is not significant to forecast short-term earnings. Therefore, in general, NCA is more relevant for long-term usefulness investigation. However, during economic crisis, investors might not necessarily continue to focus on long-term usefulness of firms' assets when the future is actually unpredictable.

Ely and Waymire (1999) investigated the value-relevance of intangibles reported in the year 1927 among US listed firms, that is, before the US Securities Commission (SEC) era. Currently, US firms are not allowed to capitalize any intangible assets, except for particular computer software items. Ely and Waymire (1999) found that, in general, the significance of tangible book value were always higher than intangible book value. This suggests that tangible assets are expected to be more useful than intangible assets, even during normal economic periods.

3. RESEARCH METHODS, MODEL, AND SAMPLE DATA

In this study, our definition of information content is based on a significant association between NCA and analysts forecasts accuracy (Bryan, 1997) during any economic period. We argue that if all the components of NCA have information content towards financial analysts in making their earnings forecasts, all the components should be positively associated with analysts' forecasts accuracy. Alternatively, all the components should be negatively associated with analysts' forecasts error. These relationships would suggest that NCA provide useful information associated with firms' earnings, hence analysts do use the information to forecast more accurate earnings. However, during economic crisis, the information content of tangible NCA for prediction of future cash flows might not be the same compared to intangible NCA, especially due to the nature of each separate components of NCA.

With regard to the significant association between NCA and analysts' earnings forecasts error (AFE), a negative significant association would suggest that usefulness of NCA information has higher certainty in predicting expected future cash flows. Whereas, a positive significant association with AFE would suggest that usefulness of NCA information has higher uncertainty in predicting expected future cash flows.

In this study, we decompose NCA into four major components, mainly the fixed assets (FNCA), investment property (IPNCA), investments (IVNCA), and intangible assets (INCA). FNCA, IPNCA, and IVNCA represent tangible portions of NCA, while the latter represent intangible

NCA. In all the models we utilized in this study, we refer *NCA to represent all four major components, unless stated otherwise.

3.1. Main Model

The main objective of this study is to examine the information content and value-relevance of *NCA during economic crisis period. In order to examine this objective, we estimate the effect of reported *NCA on analysts' forecast accuracy using our main model, the following multiple cross-sectional regression for each of the years 1995–1999 (time-varying model) and for the pooled data (fixed effect model):

$$AFE_{it} = a_0 + a_1^* NCA_{CHANGEit} + a_2 \Delta^* NCA_{it} + a_3^* NCA_{PREVi(t-1)} + a_4 MV_{i(t-1)}$$
$$+ a_5 EARNS_{i(t-1)} + a_6 EARNV_{i(t-1)} + a_7 RTRNS_{it} + a_8 HRZON_{i(t-1)}$$
$$+ a_9 LOSS_{it} + e_{it}$$

where:

AFE_{it}	is absolute mean analyst forecast error for firm i at time t.
$^*NCA_{CHANGEit}$	is mean of the change between a difference in prior year *NCA with a difference in current year *NCA for firm i at time t.
Δ^*NCA_{it}	is the difference between beginning of year *NCA per share, with end of year *NCA per share, for firm i at time t.
$^*NCA_{PREVi(t-1)}$	is the reported year-end *NCA per share for firm i at time $t-1$.
$MV_{i(t-1)}$	is the log of market value of equity, based on the log of share market price multiply by number of shares, for firm i at time $t-1$.
$EARNS_{i(t-1)}$	is earnings skewness before extraordinary items based on the last five years earnings for firm i up to time $t-1$.
$EARNV_{i(t-1)}$	is earnings volatility measured by standard deviation of return on assets for the previous five-year period for firm i up to time $t-1$.
$RTRNS_{it}$	is share market returns for firm i during time t.

$HRZON_{i(t-1)}$ is forecast horizon measured by number of months before the end of firm fiscal year or number of months before actual EPS for firm i.

$LOSS_{it}$ is dummy 1 for firm i at time t having negative EPS, 0 otherwise.

e_{it} is error term.

As mentioned earlier, in the actual regression, each *NCA variables are separated into the four major components of NCA as follows:

$^*NCA_{CHANGEit}$	becomes	$FNCA_{CHANGEit}$, $IPNCA_{CHANGEit}$, $IVNCA_{CHANGEit}$, $INCA_{CHANGEit}$
Δ^*NCA_{it}	becomes	$\Delta FNCA_{it}$, $\Delta IPNCA_{it}$, $\Delta IVNCA_{it}$, $\Delta INCA_{it}$
$^*NCA_{PREVi(t-1)}$	becomes	$FNCA_{PREVi(t-1)}$, $IPNCA_{PREVi(t-1)}$, $IVNCA_{PREVi(t-1)}$, $INCA_{PREVi(t-1)}$

3.2. Measurement of Dependent and Independent Variables of Interest

To test on the information content of accounting information based on AFE, reference is made to the model specified in Chaney, Hogan, and Jeter (1999). Mathematically, AFE is the difference between analyst forecast and actual earnings reported by the firms, which reflects analysts' forecast accuracy. Based on prior studies (see, for example, Chang, Khanna, & Palepu, 2000; Duru & Reeb, 2002), we calculated AFE as follows:

$$AFE_{it} = \left|(AFC_{i(t-1)} - EARN_{it})/EARN_{it}\right|$$

where:

AFE_{it} is absolute mean analyst forecast error for firm i at time t.

$AFC_{i(t-1)}$ is mean analyst forecast of earnings per share at time t for firm i, made at time $(t-1)$.

$EARN_{it}$ is actual reported earnings per share for firm i at
                        time t.

In estimating our main model, we partition each of the components of
*NCA information affecting AFE into three main variables: $*NCA_{CHANGE}$,
$\Delta*NCA$, and $*NCA_{PREVIOUS}$. We calculate $*NCA_{CHANGE}$ based on the
following formulae (in the spirit of Bublitz & Ettredge, 1989):

$$*NCA_{CHANGEit} = (\Delta*NCA_{it} - \Delta*NCA_{i(t-1)})/P_{i(t-1)}$$

where:

$*NCA_{CHANGEit}$ is mean of the change between a difference in prior year
                  $\Delta*NCA_{(t-1)}$ with a difference in current year $\Delta*NCA_t$
                  for firm i at time t.
$\Delta*NCA_{it}$ is current change in *NCA, which is the difference between
                  beginning of year *NCA per share with end of year
                  *NCA per share for firm i at time t.
$\Delta*NCA_{i(t-1)}$ is the difference between beginning of year *NCA per
                  share, with end of year *NCA per share, for firm i at
                  time $t-1$.
$P_{i(t-1)}$ is year-end share price of firm i at time $t-1$.

The variable $*NCA_{CHANGE}$ is our proxy for firms' new information. It is
used under the assumption that analysts already incorporate previous
*NCA information ($*NCA_{t-1}$ and $\Delta*NCA_{t-1}$) as well as current internal
firms' information into their earnings' forecasts (Williams, 1996). As such,
information on $\Delta*NCA$ alone might not be significant to investigate information content of *NCA based on AFE. New information related to *NCA
($*NCA_{CHANGE}$) would be more appropriate to examine on the properties of
AFE. However, $*NCA_{CHANGE}$ might not be the only new information not
incorporated by analysts. Following the spirit of prior literature (such as
Bublitz & Ettredge, 1989), we also analyze the data using $\Delta*NCA$ to represent another proxy for new information on *NCA to measure information
content.

   We calculate current change in *NCA ($*NCA_t$) based on the following
formulae:

$$\Delta*NCA_{it} = (*NCA_{it} - *NCA_{i(t-1)}/P_{i(t-1)}).$$

We also analyze the data using $*NCA_{PREVi(t-1)}$ to represent expected future $*NCA$ information, based on the assumption of a random walk model for earnings forecasts (Bublitz & Ettredge, 1989). The expected $*NCA$ ($*NCA_{PREVi(t-1)}$) based on a random walk model is the reported year-end $*NCA$ per share, for firm i at time t-1 (as explained by Barron, Byard, Kile, & Riedl, 2002).

Six variables namely, RTRNS, MV, EARNS, EARNV, HRZON, and LOSS are used as control variables. RTRNS is share market returns to control for the influence of share returns (Chaney et al., 1999). Analysts' earnings forecasts should not have any significant association with RTRNS if the forecasts are efficient because any information from past returns concerning expected future earnings should have been incorporated into the forecasts (Chaney et al., 1999). MV is year-end market value of equity to control for size effect (Dowen, 2001). Analysts can forecast earnings better for larger firms due to higher availability of information (Gu & Wang, 2003). In order to control for the stability of earnings, we introduced two variables, EARNS which is earning skewness based on the last five years firm's earnings and EARNV which is earnings volatility measured by standard deviation of return on assets for the previous five-year period. We include HRZON to control the timing of the forecast measured by number of months before the end of firm fiscal year or number of months before the actual reported earnings per share (EPS). We also include LOSS to control for forecasts optimism (positive earnings forecast) by analysts in forecasting earnings for losing firms (Duru & Reeb, 2002).

3.3. Hypotheses Development

3.3.1. Variable $*NCA_{CHANGE}$

Our focus in this study is to investigate the information content of tangible and intangible NCA during economic crisis period. Nevertheless, we will start our discussion based on conditions during normal economic periods. If $*NCA$ has information content towards the capital market, with regard to predicting firms' future earnings, a surprise component of $*NCA$ (regardless of whether it is tangible or intangible) should make analysts forecasts less accurate (that is, associated with higher errors). Therefore, variable $*NCA_{CHANGE}$ is expected to result in a positive association (with respect to both tangible and intangible components) with AFE. This is based on the assumption that analysts will not refer to this variable but will refer to $\Delta *NCA_{i(t-1)}$ (change on $*NCA$ in prior year) as well as internal information (from management or otherwise) with regard to current and future capital expenditures to predict for current earnings. Therefore, the higher the change in $^*NCA_{CHANGE}$ variable with the assumption that it has information content, and the change is not expected by analysts, the higher will be AFE. During economic crisis period, when uncertainty in all sectors of the economy is heightened (Graham & King, 2000), the effect will become more significant. Hence, our first hypothesis is stated as follows:

H1. '$^*NCA_{CHANGE}$, is expected to be positively associated with AFE and higher during economic crisis period compared to during non-crisis period'.

3.3.2. Variable $\Delta*NCA$

In the case of variable Δ^*NCA, prior literature suggests possibility of different effect between tangible and intangible NCA towards AFE because this variable might not be a surprise component to analysts, but rather an idiosyncratic information (such as private information obtained from firms' management). Prior studies (such as Ely & Waymire, 1999; Barron et al., 2002; Gu & Wang, 2003; among others) generally found that intangibles are positively associated with AFE because of its uncertainty nature, even if the intangible information is an idiosyncratic information.

At the same time, prior studies also generally suggest that tangible NCA is less uncertain compared to intangible NCA in terms of their usefulness (Lev & Thiagarajan, 1993; Ely & Waymire, 1999). A positive change in tangible NCA would involve items such as new tangible investments, which are more certainly associated with expected future cash flows. Whereas a positive change in intangible NCA would involve research expenditures which is still uncertain in terms of its' expected future cash flows (MASB, 1999). Therefore, we expect more accurate forecasts from tangible NCA information compared to intangible NCA. Based on the above arguments, we separate our second hypotheses between tangible NCA association with AFE and intangible NCA association with AFE, and stated them as follows:

H2a. 'Δ^*NCA being a tangible component of NCA information is expected to be negatively associated with AFE during economic crisis period'.

H2b. 'Δ^*NCA being an intangible component of NCA information is expected to be positively associated with AFE during economic crisis period'.

3.3.3. Variable *NCA$_{PREV}$

For variable *NCA$_{PREV}$, it is already public information when the latest forecasts are made by analysts. Based on the argument that *NCA association with analysts' earnings forecasts is a random walk model (Bublitz & Ettredge, 1989), therefore, prior year *NCA information should have been incorporated by analysts into firms' earnings forecasts since they are expected to have information content towards the analysts. Therefore, we expect variable *NCA$_{PREV}$ to be associated with more accurate analysts' earnings forecasts (that is, associated with lower errors), specifically for the tangible portions of NCA.

For the intangible portions of NCA, if *NCA reflect uncertain information about future cash flows of the firm as suggested by prior studies (Gu & Wang, 2003; Barron et al., 2002), *NCA$_{PREV}$ could still be associated with higher forecasts errors even though previous intangible NCA information association with analysts' forecasts is based on the random walk model, that is already known and used by analysts for earnings forecasts. Based on the above arguments, we also separate our third hypotheses between tangible NCA association with AFE and intangible NCA association with AFE, and stated them as follows:

H3a. '*NCA$_{PREV}$ being a tangible component of NCA information is expected to be negatively associated with AFE during economic crisis period'.

H3b. '*NCA$_{PREV}$ being an intangible component of NCA information is expected to be positively associated with AFE during economic crisis period'.

3.4. Data and Sample Selection

This study used the sample of all firms in all industries listed on the main board of Bursa Malaysia, formerly known as the Kuala Lumpur Stock Exchange (KLSE). We examine the financial statements data and analysts' earnings forecasts data from the Corporate Handbook published by Thompson Information (S.E. Asia) in a five-year period. Sample period covers from the year 1995 until year 1999, inclusive. Into the valuation model we incorporate earning skewness and earning volatility over a longer period; i.e. 10 years from 1991 through 1999. Table 1 provides descriptive statistics of the sample data collected. Five years data were available for analysis on analysts' earnings forecasts errors, that is, from 1995 until 1999. Years 1997 and 1998, the established period of financial crisis in Asia (Ang

Table 1. Descriptive Statistics of Variables in Sample Data.

Variables	Mean	Median	S D	N
AFE	44.57	21.84	51.29	762
FNCA$_{CHANGE}$	−0.02	0.00	0.54	728
△FNCA	0.02	0.01	0.27	745
FNCA$_{PREV}$	1.81	1.17	3.31	753
IPNCA$_{CHANGE}$	−0.02	0.00	0.23	734
△IPNCA	0.00	0.00	0.16	742
IPNCA$_{PREV}$	0.14	0.00	0.60	754
IVNCA$_{CHANGE}$	−0.01	0.00	0.55	734
△IVNCA	0.03	0.00	0.29	742
IVNCA$_{PREV}$	1.26	0.34	3.54	754
INCA$_{CHANGE}$	−0.01	0.00	0.29	728
△INCA	−0.01	0.00	0.18	745
INCA$_{PREV}$	0.19	0.00	0.59	757
MV (log)	8.99	8.96	0.51	742
EARNS	0.13	0.23	1.06	676
EARNV	3.13	1.92	4.58	678
RTRNS	−0.02	−0.03	0.52	745
HRZON	7.43	6.00	5.80	763
LOSS	0.14	0.00	0.34	761

& Ma, 2001) are our years of interest. We take years 1995 and 1996 to become our economic non-crisis periods.

3.5. Descriptive Statistics

Table 1 provides descriptive statistics of each variable investigated in the study for the full sample. Most of the distributions of the variables in the current sample are not highly skewed except for AFE. AFE variable has mean and median much further from each other compared to the other variables.

Table 2 reports pair-wise parametric correlations between AFE and each independent variables, as well as among each pair of the independent variables. Prior investments (IVNCA$_{PREV}$), market value of equity (MV), share returns (RTRNS), change in fixed assets (FNCA$_{CHANGE}$), HRZON, and LOSS are all significantly correlated to AFE and mostly in the predicted directions. As expected, many of the variables are highly correlated with each other due to the original sources of the variables. Interestingly, the LOSS variable is significantly correlated with prior INCA and prior IVNCA, representing more probably components of uncertain or intangible

Table 2. Parametric Correlation among all Variables ($n = 728$).

	FNCAC	ΔFNCA	FNCAP	IPNCAC	ΔIPNCA	IPNCAP	IVNCAC	ΔIVNCA	IVNCAP
AFE	-0.11***	-0.03	-0.03	-0.06*	-0.01	-0.01	-0.05	-0.02	0.10***
ªFNCAC		0.56***	-0.22***	0.16***	0.22***	-0.04	0.14***	0.02	-0.01
ΔFNCA			0.02	0.27***	0.41***	-0.08**	0.04	-0.03	-0.02
ᵇFNCAP				0.01	-0.03	-0.05	-0.05	-0.02	0.03
IPNCAC					0.65***	-0.40***	-0.00	-0.00	0.03
ΔIPNCA						-0.13***	0.00	-0.01	0.00
IPNCAP							0.01	-0.02	-0.08**
IVNCAC								0.60***	-0.33***
ΔIVNCA									-0.02

	INCAC	ΔINCA	INCAP	MV	EARNS	EARNV	RTRNS	LOSS	HRZON
AFE	-0.08**	-0.09**	0.06*	-0.21***	-0.17***	0.06	-0.16***	0.43***	0.34***
FNCAC	0.06*	0.07*	0.03	0.14***	0.17***	0.12***	0.00	-0.08**	-0.06
ΔFNCA	0.02	0.06	0.08**	0.10***	0.08**	0.16***	0.04	-0.06	0.02
FNCAP	-0.00	-0.01	0.06	0.13***	-0.06	-0.01	-0.08**	0.06	-0.08**
IPNCAC	-0.01	-0.00	0.03	0.12***	0.08**	0.01	0.00	-0.11***	-0.05
ΔIPNCA	-0.01	0.00	0.00	0.04	0.07	0.01	0.04	-0.10***	0.02
IPNCAP	0.01	0.01	-0.06	-0.17***	0.03	-0.05	0.04	0.01	-0.11***
IVNCAC	0.29***	0.30***	-0.08**	0.08**	-0.01	0.04	0.04	-0.15***	-0.02
ΔIVNCA	0.19***	0.21***	-0.06	0.09***	-0.02	-0.07*	0.06	-0.16***	-0.01
IVNCAP	-0.09**	-0.08**	0.10***	0.08**	0.07*	-0.03	-0.06*	0.12***	0.02
INCAC		0.92***	-0.29***	0.05	0.09**	0.01	-0.04	-0.15***	-0.06
ΔINCA			-0.28***	0.08**	0.08**	0.00	-0.03	-0.16***	-0.05
INCAP				0.06*	-0.04	0.26***	0.01	0.17***	-0.04
MV					0.12***	0.02	-0.19***	-0.17***	-0.09**
EARNS						-0.09**	-0.07*	-0.24***	-0.05
EARNV							0.03	0.19***	-0.05
RTRNS								-0.10***	-0.04
LOSS									-0.17***

ªNCAC refers to NCACHANGE.
ᵇNCAP refers to NCAPREVIOUS.
*Significant at 10%.
**Significant at 5%.
***Significant at 1%.

NCA, but not with prior FNCA and prior IPNCA, representing more probably components of certain or tangible NCA. The assumption here is that firms with higher tangible NCA is less associated with cases of negative earnings compared to firms with higher intangible NCA. This might also provide suggestion that tangible NCA is more reliable in predicting expected future cash flows compared to intangible NCA.

We then investigate further using the multiple regression analysis to find the associations we expected from our hypotheses after incorporating relevant control and moderating variables. We proceed with our analysis on the data available, partitioning to yearly and full sample.

4. EMPIRICAL RESULTS

To test the value-relevance and information content of NCA, Table 3 provides estimates from our main model. In general, we focus on *all* a_1, a_2, and

Table 3. Mean Coefficient Estimates for Regressions of Analysts' Earnings Forecast Error on NCA (Time-Varying and Fixed Effect Models).

	Exp. Sign	1995	1996	1997	1998	1999	Overall
a_0		146.27	298.86	151.96	41.06	211.42	158.63
t = value		1.89*	3.51***	2.45**	0.59	2.60**	5.19***
a_{11} FNCA$_C$	+	−11.59	−23.90	4.27	−22.01	−11.86	−9.55
t = value		−0.20	−0.90	0.17	−2.51**	−1.81*	−2.18**
a_{21} △ FNCA	−	−0.75	54.69	−13.67	15.72	12.81	10.20
t = value		−0.09	1.50	−0.40	0.90	0.78	1.26
a_{31} FNCA$_P$	−	1.29	−0.72	0.97	−3.62	−1.39	−0.84
t = value		0.38	−0.29	0.60	−2.09**	−0.73	−1.03
a_{12} IPNCA$_C$	+	210.50	−68.11	45.82	20.08	−14.36	−7.10
t = value		0.69	−1.54	0.66	0.93	−0.42	−0.76
a_{22} △ IPNCA	−	−208.05	1.76	−18.53	−222.60	18.31	23.32
t = value		−0.67	0.02	−0.22	−2.06**	0.53	1.70
a_{32} IPNCA$_P$	−	27.40	−17.35	−0.78	−0.93	−3.38	0.15
t = value		0.56	−1.16	−0.14	−0.16	−0.60	0.05
a_{13} IVNCA$_C$	+	−36.04	−0.52	−39.75	−7.98	4.87	2.17
t = value		−1.81*	−0.02	−2.05**	−0.84	0.96	0.56
a_{23} △ IVNCA	−	7.28	26.77	5.82	11.93	−16.89	13.25
t = value		0.27	0.82	0.23	0.91	−0.84	1.94*
a_{33} IVNCA$_P$	−	−0.58	4.93	2.16	0.01	0.78	1.02
t = value		−0.19	1.67*	1.51	0.01	1.06	2.13**

Table 3. (*Continued*)

	Exp. Sign	1995	1996	1997	1998	1999	Overall
a_{14} INCA$_C$	+	39.88	203.24	80.00	35.80	−32.30	9.32
t = value		0.63	2.46**	1.82*	1.68*	−1.17	0.69
a_{24} △ INCA	+	10.41	−161.75	−16.50	−40.97	156.63	−18.32
t = value		0.08	−2.86***	−0.27	−1.16	1.01	−0.82
a_{34} INCA$_P$	+	12.57	3.23	−4.21	10.71	14.65	1.69
t = value		0.89	0.38	−0.97	1.47	1.04	0.61
a_4 MV	−	−16.31	−31.22	−14.82	−0.82	−22.13	−16.00
t = value		−1.85*	−3.32***	−2.16**	−0.11	−2.40**	−4.74***
a_5 EARNS	+	−0.53	−0.12	−3.54	−3.28	−5.80	−2.48
t = value		−0.13	−0.03	−1.11	−0.94	−1.27	−1.58
A_6 EARNV	+	0.57	1.87	0.28	−0.76	−1.41	0.13
t = value		0.47	1.31	0.39	−1.14	−0.83	0.34
A_7 RTRNS	?	−53.18	−32.18	−27.56	−10.41	1.99	−18.14
t = value		−3.79***	−2.27**	−3.07***	−1.21	0.32	−5.70***
A_8 HRZON	+	3.15	1.42	1.89	2.19	4.05	2.59
t = value		2.73***	1.99**	2.20**	3.51***	5.43***	9.36***
A_9 LOSS	+	185.74	72.48	70.38	75.97	17.05	64.04
t = value		3.93***	2.32**	6.33***	8.76***	1.59	12.75***
Adj. R^2		0.23	0.24	0.42	0.49	0.49	0.40
F-value		3.21***	3.53***	7.69***	9.12***	4.61***	25.62***
N		133	145	164	155	69	671

$AFE_{it} = a_0 + a_1 \, {}^*NCA_{CHANGEit} + a_2 \triangle {}^*NCA_{it} + a_3 \, {}^*NCA_{PREVi(t-1)} + a_4MV_{i(t-1)} + a_5EARNS_{(t-1)}$
$+ a_6EARNV_{i(t-1)} + a_7RTRNS_{it} + a_8HRZON_{i(t-1)} + a_9LOSS_{it} + e_{it}$

where: AFE_{it} = Absolute mean analyst forecast error for firm i at time t.

${}^*NCA_{CHANGEit}$ = Mean of the change between a difference in prior year ${}^*NCA$ with a difference in current year ${}^*NCA$ for firm i at time t.

$\triangle {}^*NCA_{it}$ = The differences between beginnings of year ${}^*NCA$ per share, with the end of year ${}^*NCA$ per share, for firm i at time t.

${}^*NCA_{PREVi(t-1)}$ = The reported year-end ${}^*NCA$ per share for firm i at time t–1.

$MV_{i(t-1)}$ = The year-end log of market value of equity, measured by market share price of total number of shares, for firm i at time t–1.

$EARNS_{i(t-1)}$ = Earnings skewness before extraordinary items based on the last five years earnings for firm i up to time t–1.

$EARNV_{i(t-1)}$ = Earnings volatility measured by standard deviation of return on assets for the previous five-year period for firm i up to time t–1.

$RTRNS_{it}$ = Share market returns for firm i during time t.

$HRZON_{i(t-1)}$ = Forecast horizon measured by number of months before end of firm fiscal year or number of months before actual EPS for firm i.

$LOSS_{it}$ = Dummy 1 for firms with negative earnings at time t, 0 otherwise.

e_{it} = Error term.

*Significant at 10%.
**Significant at 5%.
***Significant at 1%.

a_3, the slopes coefficient for *NCA (*NCA$_{CHANGE}$, Δ^*NCA, and *NCA$_{PREV,}$ respectively). Specifically, we focus on the slopes coefficient of the three parts (all a_1, a_2, and a_3, respectively) of each components of NCA: FNCA, IPNCA, IVNCA, and INCA. If analyst places value on the reported *NCA of a firm, then *NCA should be significantly associated with AFE. There are several prominent general findings associated with the results appearing in this table. The intercept term (a_0) is significantly non-zero for four years suggesting that the empirical intercept may be picking up part of the explanatory power of some omitted variables.

From Table 3, the year 1995 shows that almost all proxies for capitalized tangibles (t-statistics -0.20, -0.09, 0.38 for FNCA, t-statistics 0.69, -0.67, 0.56 for IPNCA, and t-statistics 0.27 and -0.19 for IVNCA) and intangibles (t-statistics 0.63, 0.08, 0.89 for INCA) were insignificant. Findings suggested that during 1995, a year of economic non-crisis period, capitalized *NCA information did not significantly influence analysts' earnings forecasts. While, all control variables that are significantly associated with AFE are in the expected directions.

For the year 1996, INCA$_{CHANGE}$ is positively associated with AFE at 5% level (t-statistic 2.46), supporting H1 in the case of intangible NCA. However, ΔINCA does not seem to increase analysts' uncertainty, it is negatively associated at 1% level. Year 1996 was the peak of non-crisis economic environment in Malaysia before the crisis. There might be a tendency that capitalized intangibles information was actually associated with future earnings consistent with the findings by Aboody and Lev (1998).

For the year 1997, findings were inconsistent throughout. INCA$_{CHANGE}$ mildly support our H1 for intangible NCA, positively associated with AFE at 10% level (t-statistic 1.82). However, even though IVNCA$_{CHANGE}$ was significantly associated with AFE, it did not support our H1. Year 1997 utilized information starting from year-end of 1996 until year-end of 1997, which does not provide much evidence on the economic crisis situations. Year 1997 was suggested to represent an uncertain economic time period due to starting of the Asian financial crisis in July that year (Ang & Ma, 2001). We argue that with uncertainty in almost all areas of economic development, analysts might be confused in trying to predict future events (Ang & Ma, 2001), hence the mixed insignificant results.

Year 1998 results highlight a better picture of the economic crisis period. There is a clearer tendency by analysts to move towards appreciating the usefulness of book value information rather than just earnings information. Expected future cash flows would be more certain in the existence of high book value of net assets when expectation on cash flows of earnings reduced

(Hayn, 1995). This means there is a change in the information content of capitalized NCA overall.

The trend of changes in the information content of tangible versus intangible NCA was also highlighted when comparing results of year 1996 to year 1998. Year 1996 was the year immediately before the actual Asian crisis period 1997. While the year 1998 results utilized information obtained from the actual crisis period. In the year 1998, $FNCA_{PREV}$ was negatively significant at the 5% level (*t*-statistic -2.09), while $INCA_{PREV}$ was positive but insignificantly associated (*t*-statistic 1.47). Variable $IPNCA_{PREV}$ has the expected sign. In the year 1999, the economic environment was in a recovering period, accounting information per se does not seem to be significantly associated with analysts forecasting activities.

Results for multiple regression analysis on overall sample data also shows some mild expected findings on tangible NCA compared to intangible NCA. The full sample could not produce significant results differentiating between tangible and intangible NCA most probably due to the event of financial crisis 1997 being a confounding factor. Overall findings suggested that INCA, especially $INCA_{PREV}$, provide uncertain information, which increases analysts' earnings forecast error. Whereas, $FNCA_{PREV}$ and $IPNCA_{PREV}$, which represent tangibles NCA information provide more certain information for prediction of firms' future cash flows, especially during economic crisis period.

Findings in this analysis correspond to arguments in prior literature. In terms of overall capitalization of NCA, Lie and Lie (2002) found analyst used book value of assets significantly in their forecasts of firms' value. However, they found that firms' valuation error (estimated value based on accounting information against market value) was much higher among firms with high intangibles value compared to firms with high tangible value. This suggests that during non-crisis period, market perceive firms with high intangibles to be more valuable investments compared to firms with less intangibles. Or it could also suggest that valuing firms with higher intangibles is much harder than valuing firms with low intangibles due to the uncertainty nature of intangibles.

The impact of economic crisis towards the usefulness of accounting fundamental information might not be the same from one country to another. In a country where the government has strong financial policies and economic fundamentals, such as Malaysia, we might expect non-typical results from our analysis. Even though the Asian financial crisis of 1997 affect mostly on East Asian countries (Ang & Ma, 2001), not all Malaysian economic variables show negative impact. For example, the inflation rate remained stable, around three percent throughout 1995 until 1999, especially Malaysian CPI (consumer price index) remained stable throughout 1995 until 1999, between a low 2.7 in the year 1997 and only highest of 5.3 in 1998 (BNM, 1999). Hence, the effect of economic crisis towards the usefulness of tangible versus intangible NCA in Malaysia might not be as clear cut as we would like to expect.

At the same time, firms' capital expenditures might also follow a certain trend familiar to financial analysts, under their fundamental analysis activities (Abarbanell & Bushee, 1997). Economic environment such as changes in the inflation rate, especially the consumer price index or the economic growth overall might change firms' capital expenditures trend which are followed closely by analysts, being part of the fundamental analysis. Industry specific issues might also provide certain trends in firms' capital expenditures spending, such as changes in technology affecting product sales and productions (Kim et al., 1996). This trend would have an impact towards $^*NCA_{CHANGE}$. If such a trend exists, the information in $^*NCA_{CHANGE}$ variable might not be a surprise to analysts. Nevertheless, since the trend is not easily captured or observable, and further this trend might be influenced by numerous exogenous variables, it might explain the reason for some of our results.

5. CONCLUSION

This study contributes to the accounting literature in terms of providing further evidence on the usefulness of balance sheet data for earnings forecasting activities during economic crisis, and specifically within Malaysia capital market. This study also contributes to the literature of analysts' forecasting activities by providing further evidence on the relative usefulness of tangible versus intangible NCA accounting information during economic crisis period. Empirical results from our sample data suggests that there is a tendency that the information content and usefulness of tangible NCA is higher than intangible NCA during economic crisis period to forecasts firms earnings or alternatively to predict firms' expected future cash flows. However, during non-crisis periods, there is a tendency that the information content or usefulness of intangible NCA is the same or even higher than tangible NCA to forecast firms' future earnings. Findings from this study will be further investigated by comparing between losing and profitable firms as well as comparing large and small firms, among others, in our future analysis.

ACKNOWLEDGMENTS

We appreciate comments from participants at the 2004 International Seminar on Economics and Business at Universitas Bengkulu, Indonesia. This study was made possible from the financial support of University Kebangsaan Malaysia under part of the fundamental research grant no. CC-035-2003.

REFERENCES

Abarbanell, J. S., & Bushee, B. J. (1997). Fundamental analysis, future earnings, and stock prices. *Journal of Accounting Research, 35*(1), 1–24.

Aboody, D., & Lev, B. (1998). The value relevance of intangibles: The case of software capitalization. *Journal of Accounting Research, 36*(Supplement), 161–191.

Alciatore, M., Easton, P., & Spear, N. (2000). Accounting for the impairment of long-lived assets: Evidence from the petroleum industry. *Journal of Accounting and Economics, 29*, 151–172.

Ang, J. S., & Ma, Y. (2001). The behavior of financial analysts during the Asian financial crisis in Indonesia, Korea, Malaysia, and Thailand. *Pacific-Basin Finance Journal, 9*, 233–263.

Bank Negara Malaysia (BNM). (1999). Annual Report 1999. Kuala Lumpur: BNM.

Barron, O. E., Byard, D., Kile, C., & Riedl, E. J. (2002). High-technology intangibles and analysts' forecasts. *Journal of Accounting Research, 40*(2), 289–312.

Barth, M. E., & Clinch, G. (1998). Revalued financial, tangible, and intangible assets: Associations with share prices and non-market-based value estimates. *Journal of Accounting Research, 36*(Supp), 199–233.

Beaver, W. H. (2002). Perspectives on recent capital market research. *The Accounting Review, 77*(2), 453–474.

Bryan, S. H. (1997). Incremental information content of required disclosures contained in Management Discussion and Analysis. *The Accounting Review, 72*(2), 285–301.

Bublitz, B., & Ettredge, M. (1989). The information in discretionary outlays: Advertising, research, and development. *The Accounting Review, 64*(1), 108–124.

Chaney, P. K., Hogan, C. E., & Jeter, D. C. (1999). The effect of reporting restructuring charges on analysts' forecast revisions and errors. *Journal of Accounting and Economics, 27*, 261–284.

Chang, J. J., Khanna, T., & Palepu, K. (2000). *Analyst activity around the world.* Working Paper. University of Pennsylvania and Harvard Business School.

Corporate Handbook – KLSE Main Board. (2000). Thomson Information, S.E. Asia.

Deesomsak, R., Paudyal, K., & Pescetto, G. (2004). The determinants of capital structure: Evidence from the Asia Pacific region. *Journal of Multinational Financial Management, 14*, 387–405.

Dowen, R. J. (2001). Fundamental information and monetary policy: The implications for earnings and earnings forecasts. *Journal of Business Finance & Accounting, 28*(3 & 4), 481–501.

Duru, A., & Reeb, D. M. (2002). International diversification and analysts' forecast accuracy and bias. *The Accounting Review, 77*(2), 415–433.

Easton, P. D., Eddey, P. H., & Harris, T. S. (1993). An investigation of revaluations of tangible long-lived assets. *Journal of Accounting Research, 31*(Suppl.), 1–38.

Ely, K., & Waymire, G. (1999). Intangible assets and stock prices in the Pre-SEC era. *Journal of Accounting Research, 37*(Suppl.), 17–44.

Graham, R. C., & King, R. D. (2000). Accounting practices and the market valuation of accounting numbers: Evidence from Indonesia, Korea, Malaysia, the Philippines, Taiwan, and Thailand. *The International Journal of Accounting, 35*(4), 445–470.

Green, D. J. (2004). Investment behavior and the economic crisis in Indonesia. *Journal of Asian Economics, 15*, 287–303.

Gu, F., & Wang, W. (2003). *Intangible assets and analyst's earnings forecasts.* Working Paper. Boston University and Tulane University.

Hayn, C. (1995). The information content of losses. *Journal of Accounting and Economics, 20*, 125–153.

Henning, S. L., Lewis, B. L., & Shaw, W. H. (2000). Valuation of the components of purchased goodwill. *Journal of Accounting Research, 38*(2), 375–386.

Herrmann, D., & Inoue, T. (1996). Income smoothing and incentives by operating condition: An empirical test using depreciation changes in Japan. *Journal of International Accounting, Auditing & Taxation, 5*(2), 161–177.

Herrmann, D., Inoue, T., & Thomas, W. B. (2001). *The sale of assets to manage earnings in Japan.* Working Paper. Oregon State University, Kwansei Gakuin University, University of Oklahoma.

Hirschey, M., & Richardson, V. J. (2002). Information content of accounting goodwill numbers. *Journal of Accounting and Public Policy, 21*, 173–191.

Jennings, R., LeClere, M., & Thompson II, R. B. (2001). Goodwill amortization and the usefulness of earnings. *Financial Analysts Journal, 57*(5), 20–28.

Joyce, M. A. S., & Read, V. (2002). Asset price reactions to RPI announcements. *Applied Financial Economics, 12*, 253–270.

Kerstein, J., & Kim, S. (1995). The incremental information content of capital expenditures. *The Accounting Review, 70*(3), 513–526.

Kim, J. H., Joo, I. K., & Choi, F. D. S. (1996). The information content of productivity measures: An international comparison. *Journal of International Financial Management and Accounting, 7*(3), 167–190.

Kohlbeck, M. (2004). Investor valuations and measuring bank intangible assets. *Journal of Accounting, Auditing & Finance, 19*(1), 29–60.

Lev, B., & Sougiannis, T. (1996). The capitalization, amortization, and value-relevance of R&D. *Journal of Accounting and Economics, 21*, 107–138.

Lev, B., & Thiagarajan, S. R. (1993). Fundamental information analysis. *Journal of Accounting Research, 31*(2), 190–215.

Lev, B., & Zarowin, P. (1999). The boundaries of financial reporting and how to extend them. *Journal of Accounting Research, 37*(2), 353–385.

Lie, E., & Lie, H. J. (2002). Multiples used to estimate corporate value. *Financial Analysts Journal, 58*(March/April), 44–54.

Malaysian Accounting Standards Board (MASB). (1999). MASB 4, Research and development costs. Kuala Lumpur: MASB.

Malaysian Accounting Standards Board (MASB). (2001). MASB 21, Business combinations. Kuala Lumpur: MASB.

Muhd-Kamil, I., Marzita, M. S., Radziah, A. L., & Zaleha, A. S. (2003). Value relevance of accounting numbers: An empirical investigation of purchased goodwill. *Malaysian Accounting Review, 2*(1), 106–123.

Ohlson, J. A. (1995). Earnings, book values, and dividends in equity valuation. *Contemporary Accounting Research, 11*(2), 661–687.

Penman, S. H. (1992). Return to fundamentals. *Journal of Accounting, Auditing and Finance, 7,* 465–482.

Schipper, K. (1991). Commentary on analysts' forecasts. *Accounting Horizons, 5*(December), 105–121.

Singh, M., & Nejadmalayeri, A. (2004). Internationalization, capital structure, and cost of capital: Evidence from French corporations. *Journal of Multinational Financial Management, 14,* 153–169.

Tan, L. T. (2000). *Finanacial accounting and reporting in Malaysia* (2nd ed.). Kuala Lumpur: PAAC.

Williams, P. (1996). The relation between a prior earnings forecast by management and analyst response to a current management forecast. *The Accounting Review, 71,* 103–115.

Zaleha, A. S., Hamezah, M. N., Muhd-Kamil, I., & Kaur, J. (2004). *Effect of economic crisis period on the information content of intangible non-current assets in Malaysia.* Working Paper. Universiti Kebangsaan Malaysia, Universiti Teknologi MARA.

Zaleha, A. S., Wan Madznah, W. I., Azimon, A. A., Noradiva, H., & Ruhanita, M. (2000). Presentation of intellectual property in Malaysia financial statements. Presented at the 12th Asian-Pacific Conference on International Accounting Issues, Beijing, China.

RETURN AND VOLATILITY SPILLOVERS FROM DEVELOPED TO EMERGING CAPITAL MARKETS: THE CASE OF SOUTH ASIA

Yun Wang, Abeyratna Gunasekarage and David M. Power

ABSTRACT

This study examines return and volatility spillovers from the US and Japanese stock markets to three South Asian capital markets – (i) the Bombay Stock Exchange, (ii) the Karachi Stock Exchange and (iii) the Colombo Stock Exchange. We construct a univariate EGARCH spillover model that allows the unexpected return of any particular South Asian market to be driven by a local shock, a regional shock from Japan and a global shock from the USA. The study discovers return spillovers in all three markets, and volatility spillovers from the US to the Indian and Sri Lankan markets, and from the Japanese to the Pakistani market. Regional factors seem to exert an influence on these three markets before

Asia Pacific Financial Markets in Comparative Perspective: Issues and Implications for the 21st Century
Contemporary Studies in Economics and Financial Analysis, Volume 86, 139–166
ISSN: 1569-3759/doi:10.1016/S1569-3759(05)86007-3

the Asian financial crisis but the global factor becomes more important in the post-crisis period.

1. INTRODUCTION

The theme of integration among international capital markets and the mechanism whereby information is transmitted among different stock exchanges has been extensively researched in the modern finance literature. This topic has attracted the attention of financial economists because the turmoils that occur in some capital markets have far-reaching consequences on security prices on their counterparts in other countries. For example, the October 1987 crash not only eliminated more than 20 per cent of the market value of US equities but also sent shock waves around the world. The Asian financial crisis had a similar impact on many other emerging markets in Latin America as well as in Eastern Europe. The liberalization of capital movements together with advances in computer technology and the improved worldwide processing of news have improved the possibilities for national financial markets to react rapidly to new information from international stock exchanges.

Early investigations in this area analysed the interrelatedness among developed capital markets using correlations of stock returns. For example, Hilliard (1979) examined indices for 10 international equity markets (Amsterdam, Frankfurt, London, Milan, New York, Paris, Sydney, Tokyo, Toronto and Zurich) during the worldwide financial crisis created by the OPEC embargo in the period 1973–1974 and found that most intra-continental prices move simultaneously. More recently, Eun and Shim (1989) applied vector autoregression (VAR) methodology to study daily index data for nine of the largest stock exchanges in the world (Australia, Canada, France, Germany, Hong Kong, Japan, Switzerland, the UK and the US) and discovered a substantial amount of multi-lateral interaction among these markets; the US stock market was the most influential and none of the other markets explained any movements in US returns. Joen and Von Furstenberg (1990) arrived at a similar view; they highlighted the evidence of growing international integration among the four major equity markets of Germany, Japan, the UK and the US in the 1980s. Becker, Finnerty, and Gupta (1990) concluded that the information from the US market could be used to trade profitably in the Japanese market, as there was a high correlation between the open-to-close returns of US shares in the previous trading day and the returns of Japanese equities in the current period. Koch and Koch (1991), who used a dynamic simultaneous equations model to investigate the contemporaneous and lead-lag relationships among eight national stock exchanges (Australia, Germany, Hong Kong, Japan, Singapore, Switzerland, the UK and the US), discovered a growing level of market interdependence within the same geographical regions over time; an increasing influence of the Japanese market at the expense of the US market was also detected.

Another branch of research concentrates on the transmission of international equity movements by studying the spillover of return and volatility across markets. For example, Hamao, Masulis, and Ng (1990), who studied three major stock markets (London, New York and Tokyo,) using univariate GARCH (generalized autoregressive conditional heteroskedasticity)-in-mean models, found volatility spillovers (i) from New York to Tokyo and London and (ii) from London to Tokyo. Theodossiou and Lee (1993) used multivariate GARCH-in-mean models to analyse the markets in Canada, Germany, Japan, the UK and the US; they discovered that the US market was the major exporter of volatility. More recently, Scheicher (2001) analysed three Eastern European markets (Czech Republic, Hungary and Poland) and reported that although the equity returns were affected by both regional and global factors, the volatilities were impacted by only regional influences. Fratzscher (2002) and Baele (2002) arrived at a similar conclusion; they documented evidence that shock transmissions from the aggregate European Union market to domestic European equities had become more pronounced in recent years.[1]

A number of researchers have addressed the question of whether the quantity of news (i.e. the size of an innovation) and the quality of the information (i.e. the sign of an innovation) are important determinants of the degree of volatility spillover across markets. This question has been motivated by findings of an 'asymmetric' or 'leverage' effect associated with equity returns; bad news has a different degree of predictability on future volatility compared to its good news counterpart.[2] This asymmetric effect has been examined in studies of volatility spillovers across markets. For example, Bae and Karolyi (1994), who examined the joint dynamics of overnight and daytime return volatility for the New York and Tokyo stock markets over the period 1988–1992, noted that the magnitude and persistence of shocks that originated in New York or Tokyo and was then transmitted to other markets, would be significantly understated if this asymmetric effect was ignored; bad news from domestic and foreign markets appear to have a much larger impact on subsequent return volatility than good news. Koutmos and Booth (1995) investigated the asymmetric impact of market advances and market declines (i.e. good and bad news, respectively) on volatility transmission across New York, Tokyo and London stock markets. Using daily open-to-close returns, they found unidirectional price spillovers (i) from New York to Tokyo, (ii) from New York to London and (iii) from Tokyo to London. They also uncovered bidirectional volatility spillovers among the three markets. In all instances, the volatility transmission mechanism was asymmetric – i.e. negative innovations in one market increased volatility in the other market considerably more than their positive counterparts. Booth, Martikainen, and Tse (1997) looked at the four Scandinavian markets and found significant and asymmetric volatility spillovers among Swedish, Danish, Norwegian and Finnish securities. Similar evidence has been reported for other European markets – London, Paris and Frankfurt – by Kanas (1998).

Only a minority of studies have focussed on the return and volatility spillovers from developed to emerging capital markets.[3] In particular, the evidence on market interactions and information transmissions in South Asian capital markets is hard to find. The Capital markets in South Asia have generated a considerable interest among local and foreign investors as a result of the increased economic activity in these countries arising from economic reforms and the liberalization of capital markets. In this research exercise, we investigate how information is transmitted from developed capital markets to three recently liberalized South Asian capital markets – the Bombay Stock Exchange (BSE) of India, the Karachi Stock Exchange (KSE) of Pakistan and the Colombo Stock Exchange (CSE) of Sri Lanka; return and volatility spillover models are tested on market index data. Our study differs from the previous research on this topic in three respects. First, unlike many existing studies that focus on how a single international market (often the US or a world market) influences other stock markets,[4] we consider the innovations from both the US and Japanese markets in an attempt to analyse the impacts of both regional and world shocks on South Asian equities. Second, we recognize that volatility transmission may be asymmetric in character – i.e. the negative innovations in one market may produce higher volatility spillovers in another market than the positive innovations of equal magnitude. Finally, we address the possible effect of the Asian financial crisis[5] on the transmission mechanism by disaggregating the data into three sample periods: (i) pre-crisis, (ii) in-crisis and (iii) post-crisis.

The remainder of this paper is organized as follows. Section 2 provides a brief overview of the South Asian stock markets. Section 3 describes the spillover models used to analyse the data in this study. Section 4 outlines the data employed in the study and presents the empirical results. The final section offers some conclusions.

2. AN OVERVIEW OF SOUTH ASIAN CAPITAL MARKETS

The South Asian region is notable for its large population (more than one-fifth of the world's total inhabitants) that is growing rapidly. India is by far the largest South Asian country, in terms of population, GDP and land area. Sri Lanka has the most open economy. Indian, Pakistan and Sri Lankan stock exchanges are also the three biggest markets in this region in terms of market capitalization. South Asia has experienced fast economic growth in recent years because of the economic reforms implemented by these countries' governments; it was the fastest growing region of the world in 1998. The emerging capital markets in this region have generated considerable interest among regional as well as global investors because of the rapid growth of these countries' economies and the concessions provided to foreign investors through radical liberalization processes.

The Bombay Stock Exchange is the oldest stock market in Asia – even older than the Tokyo Stock Exchange – and was established in 1875 as a voluntary non-profit making association. It is one of 25 stock markets throughout India. With over 20 million shareholders, India has the third largest investor base in the world after the US and Japan. India's market capitalization was the sixth highest among the emerging markets. Share trading on Colombo Stock Exchange dates back to the 19th century; in 1896 Colombo Brokers Association commenced the trading of shares in limited liability companies. By contrast, the stock market in Pakistan is relatively new. The Karachi Stock Exchange only came into existence in 1947. These capital markets exhibit a number of common features; they did not play a prominent role in the economic development of their countries until the respective governments started a programme of deregulation and economic liberalization. For example, India initiated financial reforms in conjunction with economic deregulation and permitted foreign companies to own a majority stake in quoted Indian firms from many different industries. The liberalization policies of the Pakistan government have led to rapid deregulation of the economy and the removal of impediments to private investment. The secondary stock market in Pakistan is now open to foreign investors; non-nationals are treated equally with local participants when trading shares. The Sri Lankan government took a number of steps including the opening of the banking sector to foreign owners, repealing the business acquisition act and privatizing government-owned business undertakings, in an attempt to create a well-functioning capital market in the country.

As a result of these changes, share markets in these three South Asian countries recorded a remarkable rate of growth in their trading activities. Table 1 reports some market statistics for the stock exchanges in these countries. According to this table, during the 10-year period ending by 2003, these markets have reported a phenomenal growth in market capitalization:

Table 1.   Growth in South Asian Stock Markets.

Market	Levels			Growth(%)	
	1993	1998	2003	93–98	93–03
Panel A: Market capitalization (billion)					
BSE	3,050	4,770	13,479	56.40	341.93
KSE	70	266	951	280	1,268.57
CSE	124	117	263	−5.65	112.10
Panel B: Market capitalization as % of GDP					
BSE	35.54	27.43	49.00	−22.82	37.87
KSE	5.22	16.20	18.62	210.35	256.71
CSE	24.85	11.46	15.73	−53.88	−36.70
Panel C: Annual turnover (billion)					
BSE	675	2,662	4,094	294.37	506.52
KSE	27	427	696	1,481.48	2,477.78
CSE	35	18	74	−48.57	111.43
Panel D: Number of listed companies					
BSE	3,263	5,860	5,644	79.59	72.97
KSE	630	773	701	22.70	11.27
CSE	201	240	244	19.40	21.39
Panel E: Value of the price index					
BSE	1,614	1,359	3,075	115.79	90.52
KSE	2,170	945	4,472	−56.45	106.08
CSE	979	597	1,062	−39.02	8.48

Note: Market statistics for the Bombay Stock Exchange (BSE), the Karachi Stock Exchange (KSE) and the Colombo Stock Exchange (CSE). Market capitalization and the annual value of turnover are in local currencies.*Source*: Emerging Stock Markets Factbook, www.bseindia.com, www.kse.com.pk.

BSE 341.93 per cent, KSE 1,268.57 per cent and CSE 112.10 per cent. Similar growth patterns can be observed with respect to market capitalization as a percentage of GDP, annual turnover, the number of listed companies and the market price index. The number of companies listed on the BSE at the end of December 1998 was 5,860. This was more than the aggregate total of companies listed in nine emerging markets (Malaysia, South Africa, Mexico, Taiwan, Korea, Philippines, Thailand, Brazil and Chile) at the same date. The number of listed companies was also larger than that in several developed markets: Japan, UK, Germany, France, Australia, Switzerland, Canada and Hong Kong. The KSE has also grown quickly, especially in recent years. It was declared the "best performing stock market of the World for the year 2002" by Business Week. The findings of this study will be interesting as little evidence appears in the finance literature on South Asian capital markets.

3. METHODOLOGY

EGARCH Model Estimation

GARCH models are generally used to explore the stochastic behaviour of several financial time series and, in particular, to explain the behaviour of volatility over time. However, such models do not work with negative data. The exponential GARCH (EGARCH) model developed by Nelson (1991)[6] overcomes this limitation and allows researchers to capture the leverage effect or asymmetric impact of shocks on volatilities. It therefore, avoids the imposition of non-negativity restrictions on the values of the GARCH parameters to be estimated. Specifically, time series of share returns are modeled in EGARCH (p, q) as follows:

$$R_t = \alpha_0 + \sum_{i=1}^{r} \alpha_i R_{t-i} + \varepsilon_t \tag{1}$$

$$\varepsilon_t | \Omega_{t-1} \sim N(0, \sigma_t^2) \tag{2}$$

$$\log(\sigma_t^2) = a_0 + \sum_{i-1}^{q} a_i f(z_{t-i}) + \sum_{i=1}^{p} b_i \log(\sigma_{t-i}^2) \tag{3}$$

$$f(z_{t-i}) = \theta\, z_{t-i} + [|z_{t-i}| - \mathrm{E}(|z_{t-i}|)] \tag{4}$$

$$E(|z_{t-i}|) \left[\frac{2}{\pi}\right]^{0.5} \tag{5}$$

where R_t is the return series in time t (i.e. continuously compounded returns generated taking the natural logarithm of the ratio of current price to the lagged price), ε_t is the stochastic error, Ω_{t-1} is the information set at time $t-1$, σ_t^2 is the conditional (time varying) variance and z_t is the standardized residual derived from ε_t/σ_t conditional on Ω_{t-1}. The term ε_t is assumed to be normally distributed with a zero mean and variance (σ_t^2). The term $[2/\pi]^{0.5}$ is a constant employed to make sure that the integral under the curve of the normal distribution of the residual from negative to positive infinity is equal to one.

Eq. (1) (the conditional mean equation) is modelled as an autoregressive process of order r [AR (r)], following Theodossiou and Lee (1993) and Karolyi (1995). To specify the lag length r for each return series, the autocorrelation function (ACF) and partial autocorrelation function (PACF) of each series are considered, and residuals from the mean equations are then tested for whiteness by using the Ljung–Box statistic. For the entire period (01/01/1993–31/12/2003), we use 1 lag for the US, Japanese and Indian return series and 2 lags for Pakistan and Sri Lankan series to yield uncorrelated residuals. For the sub-periods, whiteness in the residuals for each series is achieved using 1 lag except for the Pakistan series in the pre-crisis period and Indian series in the post-crisis period; in each of these two exceptions, 2 lags are needed.

Eq. (3) (the conditional variance equation) reflects the EGARCH (p, q) representation of the variance of ε_t. According to this EGARCH representation, the variance is conditional on its own past values as well as on past values of a function of z_t, or the standardized residuals (ε_t/σ_t). The persistence of volatility implied by Eq. (3) is measured by $\Sigma_{i=1}^{p} b_i$. The unconditional variance is finite if $\Sigma_{i=1}^{p} b_i < 1$ in absolute terms (see Nelson, 1991). If $\Sigma_{i=1}^{p} b_i = 1$, then the unconditional variance does not exist and the conditional variance follows an integrated process of order one. As noted by Hsieh (1989), the exponential specification is less likely to produce integrated variances. The smaller the, $\Sigma_{i=1}^{p} b_i$ the less persistent the volatility is after a shock.

In Eq. (4), asymmetry is present if θ is negative and statistically significant. Asymmetry in volatility transmission can be conveniently examined using its partial derivatives:

$$\frac{\partial f(z_t)}{\partial z_t} = \left\{ \begin{array}{l} 1 + \theta, \text{for } z_t > 0 \\ -1 + \theta, \text{for } z_t < 0 \end{array} \right\} \tag{6}$$

The term $[|z_t| - E(|z_t|)]$ measures the size effect of an innovation, whereas θz_t measures the corresponding sign effect. If θ is negative, a negative z_t tends to reinforce the size effect, whereas a positive z_t tends to partially offset it. If $\theta = 0$, a positive shock has the same effect as a negative shock of the same magnitude. If $-1 < \theta < 0$, a negative shock increases volatility more than a positive shock and, thus, θ measures the asymmetric effect of shocks on volatility. If $\theta < -1$, a negative (positive) shock increases (reduces) volatility. The relative importance of the asymmetry or the leverage effect can be measured by the ratio $|-1 + \theta|/(1 + \theta)$. Lag truncation lengths, p and q, are determined using likelihood ratio (LR) tests of alternative specifications.[7] Based on these tests, EGARCH (1,1) models were determined to be optimal.

The Univariate EGARCH Models of Price and Volatility Spillovers Estimation

In this study, the univariate EGARCH model is used to test for return and volatility spillovers from the two developed stock markets of the US and Japan to a third small stock market (India, Pakistan and Sri Lanka, respectively). We assume unidirectional return and volatility spillovers to be relevant because these small stock markets are not thought to have a substantial impact on the two developed markets considered. To test for spillovers from a foreign market to the domestic market, the approach adopted by Hamao et al. (1990) and Theodossiou and Lee (1993) is followed. According to this approach, the most recent squared residuals from the conditional mean–conditional variance formulation of the foreign market are introduced as an exogenous variable in the conditional variance equation of the domestic market. The univariate EGARCH (1,1) models of return and volatility spillovers for market j are specified as follows:

The conditional mean equation for India, Pakistan and Sri Lanka becomes:

$$R_{IND,t} = \alpha_{IND,0} + \alpha_{IND,1} R_{IND,t-1} + \beta_{IND,1} R_{US,t-1}$$
$$+ \beta_{IND,2} R_{JAP,t-1} + \varepsilon_{IND,t} \tag{7a}$$

$$R_{PAK,t} = \alpha_{PAK,0} + \alpha_{PAK,1} R_{PAK,t-1} + \alpha_{PAK,2} R_{PAK,t-2} + \beta_{PAK,1} R_{US,t-1}$$
$$+ \beta_{PAK,2} R_{JAP,t-1} + \varepsilon_{PAK,t} \tag{7b}$$

$$R_{SRI,t} = \alpha_{SRI,0} + \alpha_{SRI,1}R_{SRI,t-1} + \alpha_{SRI,2}R_{SRI,t-2} + \beta b_{SRI,1}R_{US,t-1}$$
$$+ \beta_{SRI,2}R_{JAP,t-1} + \varepsilon_{SRI,t} \qquad (7c)$$

The conditional variance equation for these three markets is:

$$\log\left(\sigma^2_{IND,t}\right) = a_{IND,0} + a_{IND,1}f(z_{IND,t-1}) + b_{IND,1}\log(\sigma^2_{IND,t-1})$$
$$+ c_{IND,1}\log(U_{US,t}) + c_{IND,2}\log(U_{JAP,t}) \qquad (8a)$$

$$\log\left(\sigma^2_{PAK,t}\right) = a_{PAK,0} + a_{PAK,1}f(z_{PAK,t-1}) + b_{PAK,1}\log(\sigma^2_{PAK,t})$$
$$+ c_{PAK,1}\log(U_{US,t}) + c_{PAK,2}\log(U_{JAP,t}) \qquad (8b)$$

$$\log\left(\sigma^2_{SRI,t}\right) = a_{SRI,0} + a_{SRI,1}f(z_{SRI,t-1}) + b_{SRI,1}\log(\sigma^2_{SRI,t})$$
$$+ c_{SRI,1}\log(U_{US,t}) + c_{SRI,2}\log(U_{JAP,t}) \qquad (8c)$$

where,

$$f(z_{IND,t-1}) = \theta_{IND}z_{IND,t-1} + \lfloor |z_{IND,t-1}| - E(|z_{IND,t-1}|)\rfloor \qquad (9a)$$

$$f(z_{PAK,t-1}) = \theta_{PAK}z_{PAK,t-1} + \lfloor |z_{PAK,t-1}| - E(|z_{PAK,t-1}|)\rfloor \qquad (9b)$$

$$f(z_{SRI,t-1}) = \theta_{SRI}z_{SRI,t-1} + \lfloor |z_{SRI,t-1}| - E(|z_{SRI,t-1}|)\rfloor \qquad (9c)$$

$U_{US,t}$ and $U_{JAP,t}$ are the contemporaneous squared residuals (from the AR (1) – EGARCH (1,1) models) for the US and Japanese returns, respectively, and z_{t-1} is the lagged standardized residuals.

Return spillovers occur when past information about the US and Japanese markets have persistent effects on small market returns, and volatility spillovers are related to the present information flows from the foreign markets. The univariate EGARCH model permits us to differentiate between the relative influence of the US and Japan on the three small markets. Existence of return spillovers is indicated by the statistical significance of β_1 (return spillovers from the US) and β_2 (return spillovers from Japan). Existence of volatility spillovers is indicated by the statistical significance of c_1 (volatility spillovers from the US) and c_2 (volatility spillovers from Japan). Statistical inference regarding c_1 and c_2 is based on robust standard errors derived by Bollerslev and Wooldridge (1992).[8] A significant c_1 (or c_2) coupled with a significantly negative θ implies that negative innovations in the US market (or Japanese market) have a higher impact on the volatility of market j than positive innovations, i.e. the volatility spillover mechanism is asymmetric.

Given a sample of T observations and conditional normality for the stock returns in each market, the log likelihood function for the univariate EG-ARCH can be written as:

$$L(\Theta) = (-T/2)\log(2\pi) - 0.5\sum_{t=1}^{T}\log(\sigma_t^2) \tag{10}$$

where Θ is the parameter vector $(\alpha_0 \ \alpha_1 \ \alpha_2 \ a_0 \ a_1 \ b_1 \ c_1 \ c_2 \ \theta)$ to be estimated.

4. EMPIRICAL FINDINGS

Data and Preliminary Statistics

The data used in the study consist of daily stock indices for five countries – the USA, Japan, India, Pakistan and Sri Lanka for the period 01/01/1993–31/12/1999; a total of 2,869 observations are employed for each market. The sample period is divided into three sub-periods – pre-crisis (01/01/1993–31/06/1997), in-crisis (01/07/1997–31/12/1999) and post-crisis (01/01/2000–31/12/2003). The index data are obtained from Datastream. The stock market indices used in this study are the S&P 500 (US), the Nikkei 500 (Japan), the BSE National Price Index (India), the Karachi 100 Price Index (Pakistan) and the Colombo All Share Price Index (Sri Lanka). In each market, we chose the most comprehensive and diversified stock index. The S&P 500 index consists of the 500 largest, publicly held companies representing approximately 76 per cent of total market capitalization. The Nikkei 500 index incorporates 500 Japanese companies listed in the First Section of the Tokyo Stock Exchange. The BSE National Index comprises 100 stocks listed at five major Indian stock exchanges (Mumbai, Calcutta, Delhi, Ahmedabad and Madras). The Karachi 100 includes the largest 100 companies in the exchange (27 companies representing 27 sectors and 73 companies representing the entire market) covering about 83 per cent of market capitalization of the exchange. The Colombo All Share Price Index consists of all the shares traded on the stock exchange.[9] With the exception of the Nikkei 500, all indices are calculated on a value-weighted basis. The Japanese index is a share price-weighted index that does not take dividend reinvestment into account. However, cash dividends paid on most Japanese stocks are relatively small, so this dividend omission is of little consequence.[10] The variable analysed in the study is the daily return that is calculated by taking the natural logarithm of the ratio of current price to the lagged price.[11]

Table 2 reports summary statistics for the daily returns of the five national stock markets. The mean returns are positive for four markets with the exception of Japan. The Pakistan market earned the highest mean return but with the largest risk as measured by the standard deviation. However, the sample means for all five markets are not statistically different from zero.

Table 2. Preliminary Statistics on Stock Market Returns.

Summary Statistics	US	JAP	IND	PAK	SRI
Panel A: Descriptive statistics for the daily returns					
Sample mean	0.0326	−0.0053	0.0332	0.0445	0.0196
	(1.6131)	(0.2325)	(1.1512)	(1.4199)	(0.9603)
Standard deviation	1.0826	1.2207	1.5449	1.6784	1.0931
Skewness	−0.1122***	−0.1383***	−0.1894***	−0.3319***	1.1984***
	(−2.4348)	(−3.0000)	(−4.1087)	(−7.2174)	(26.0652)
Kurtosis	3.7728***	2.8248***	3.1798***	7.0057***	44.1719***
	(41.5495)	(31.1209)	(35.0220)	(77.1429)	(486.2747)
Jarque–Bera statistics	1707.6	963.0	1225.8	5919.8	233930.8
	[0.0000]	[0.0000]	[0.0000]	[0.0000]	[0.0000]
LB(6)	10.34	35.67	57.66	26.31	302.07
	[0.1110]	[0.0000]	[0.0000]	[0.0000]	[0.0000]
LB(12)	20.61	41.58	72.75	49.81	328.63
	[0.0560]	[0.0000]	[0.0000]	[0.0000]	[0.0000]
$LB^2(6)$	475.46	275.94	430.33	496.85	220.04
	[0.0000]	[0.0000]	[0.0000]	[0.0000]	[0.0000]
$LB^2(12)$	779.11	375.62	574.03	656.46	265.32
	[0.0000]	[0.0000]	[0.0000]	[0.0000]	[0.0000]
ARCH(12) LM	298.57	198.53	263.62	321.87	218.70
statistics	[0.0000]	[0.0000]	[0.0000]	[0.0000]	[0.0000]
Panel B: Nonparametric Cross-correlations of Market Returns					
Countries	US	Japan	India	Pakistan	Sri Lanka
US	1	0.0880	0.0279	0.0071	0.0181
Japan		1	0.1232	0.0382	0.0393
India			1	0.0651	0.0501
Pakistan				1	0.0702
Sri Lanka					1

Note: The sample spans from 01 January 1993 to 31 December 2003 and includes 2869 daily observations. Returns and Standard Deviations are expressed in percentages. The Jarque–Bera statistic tests the normality of large samples using both skewness and kurtosis measures. LB(k) and $LB^2(k)$ are the Ljung–Box q-statistics for returns and squared returns, respectively, distributed as χ^2 with k degrees of freedom. For the autoregressive-conditional heteroskedasticity (ARCH) LM test, the null hypothesis is that ARCH effects are not present in the first 12 lags. Cross-correlation coefficients are measured by nonparametric Spearman's correlation coefficients. The t-statistics and p-values are provided in parentheses ( ) and [ ], respectively.
***Denotes the statistical significance at the 1 per cent level.

The measures for skewness show that with the exception of the distribution of returns for the Sri Lankan market, the return series are negatively skewed. The excess Kurtosis measures indicate that the distributions of all the return series are highly leptokurtic. Likewise, the Jarque–Bera statistics reject normality for each of the return series at the 1 per cent level of significance.

The Ljung–Box q-statistics – LB(k) and LB^2(k) – for lag lengths of 6 and 12 days are used to test for serial correlation in the return and squared return series. The null hypothesis of uncorrelated returns is rejected at the 1 per cent level of significance for the markets of Japan, India, Pakistan and Sri Lanka at both lag lengths used. The null hypothesis of homoskedastic returns (uncorrelated squared returns) is also rejected at the 1 per cent level for all markets at both lag levels. Linear dependencies may be due either to non-synchronous trading of the stocks that make up each index[12] or to some form of market inefficiency. Non-linear dependencies may be due to autoregressive conditional heteroskedasticity, as documented by several recent studies for both the US and foreign stock markets.[13] The ARCH Lagrange Multiplier (LM) tests (Engle, 1982) indicate that each market's returns strongly depend on their past values and exhibit strong ARCH effects, implying that the ARCH model is appropriate for data analysis in this study.[14] The ARCH effects may explain (at least partially) the observed thicker than normal distributional tails. Since the Jarque–Bera normality tests show that all the return series are not normally distributed, we examine the relationship among returns by using non-parametric correlations. All return series are positively correlated, but the cross-correlations among returns are relatively low.

Univariate EGARCH Model Estimation

We first estimate a univariate EGARCH (1,1) model for each of the five indices by restricting all cross-market coefficients measuring return and volatility spillovers to be zero. An EGARCH (1,1) model was determined to offer the best fit for the data series. The resulting coefficients from these models are presented in Table 3. Panel A provides estimates for Eq. (1). The first order autoregressive coefficient, α_1, is statistically significant for the Japanese, Indian, Pakistan and Sri Lankan markets, indicating that either non-synchronous trading or market inefficiency induces autocorrelation in the return series. The second order autoregressive coefficient, α_2, is also statistically significant for the Pakistan and Sri Lankan markets. However,

Table 3. EGARCH Model Estimation Results.

Parameters	US	JAP	IND	PAK	SRI
Panel A: Conditional mean equation coefficients					
α_0	0.0003*	−0.0003	0.0002	0.0002	0.0002
	(0.0001)	(0.0002)	(0.0003)	(0.0002)	(0.0001)
α_1	0.0239	0.0956***	0.1700***	0.1015***	0.4273***
	(0.0175)	(0.0165)	(0.0197)	(0.0085)	(0.0208)
α_2				0.0425**	0.0417**
				(0.0187)	(0.0208)
Panel B: Conditional variance equation coefficients					
a_0	−0.1609***	−0.1924***	−0.2026***	−0.3666***	−0.9019***
	(0.0293)	(0.0423)	(0.0566)	(0.0617)	(0.1045)
a_1	0.1174***	0.1649***	0.1811***	−0.0116	0.4836***
	(0.0133)	(0.0162)	(0.0218)	(0.0101)	(0.0234)
b_1	0.9823***	0.9776***	0.9750***	0.9537***	0.9046***
	(0.0032)	(0.0047)	(0.0067)	(0.0074)	(0.0106)
θ	−0.1047***	−0.0622***	−0.0270***	−0.0116	−0.0030
	0.0118	(0.0098)	(0.0094)	(0.0101)	(0.0157)
Log likelihood	9368.6	8822.2	8176.5	8038.5	9833.9
Wald statistic	175668.4	55691.9	42299.4	26000.5	12592.7
Panel C: Diagnostics on standardized and squared standardized residuals					
Jarque–Bera statistic	332.0	331.2	1268.4	2627.0	20766.5
LB(6)	11.3219	3.4443	13.9290	22.4325	29.0984
	[0.0790]	[0.7510]	[0.0300]	[0.0010]	[0.0000]
LB(12)	20.0903	12.2238	26.7866	35.1847	40.4759
	[0.0650]	[0.4280]	[0.0080]	[0.0000]	[0.0000]
$LB^2(6)$	1.3605	7.0264	8.7173	3.5142	1.8959
	[0.9680]	[0.3180]	[0.1900]	[0.7420]	[0.9290]
$LB^2(12)$	2.1665	11.7111	13.2885	6.0631	5.3730
	[1.0000]	[0.4690]	[0.3480]	[0.9130]	[0.9440]

Note: α_1 and α_2 are the coefficients on the first order and second order autoregressive process specified for the mean equations. a_1 is the measure of the autoregressive conditional heteroskedasticity (ARCH) effect. b_1 is the measure of volatility persistence. θ is the measure of asymmetric effect. The null hypothesis for Wald test is $a_1 = b_1 = 0$. Jarque–Bera statistic tests the normality of the standardized residual series. LB(k) and $LB^2(k)$ are the Ljung–Box q-statistics for the standardized residuals and squared standardized residuals distributed as χ^2 with k degrees of freedom. The standard errors and p-values are provided in parentheses ( ) and [ ] respectively.
***Denotes statistical significance at the 1 per cent level.
**Denotes at the 5 per cent level.
*Denotes at the 10 per cent level.

for the US market, α_1 is insignificant; this finding is consistent with previous studies such as Theodossiou and Lee (1993) and Koutmos and Booth (1995), indicating that the US market is more efficient than other markets. Conditional hetreoskedasticity is perhaps the single most important property describing the short-term dynamics of all markets.

The conditional variance is a function of past innovations and past conditional variances. Panel B provides estimates for Eq. (3). The relevant coefficients, a_1 (measuring the ARCH effect) and b_1 (measuring the degree of volatility persistence) are all statistically significant for all the markets. Furthermore, the values of b_1 coefficients are all close to one indicating a high degree of persistence in volatility. This volatility persistence is highest for the US, followed by the Japanese, Indian, Pakistan and Sri Lankan markets. The leverage effect, as measured by θ, or the asymmetric impact of past innovations on current volatility, is negative and statistically significant for the US, Japanese and Indian markets indicating that the volatility spillovers may also be asymmetric. The relative importance of the asymmetry, or leverage effect, can be measured by the ratio $|-1 + \theta|/1 + \theta$. Thus, the degree of asymmetry, based on the estimated θ coefficients, equals -1.23 for the US market, -1.13 for Japanese market and -1.06 for Indian market. These ratios indicate that the degree of asymmetry is highest for the US market (negative innovations increase volatility 1.23 times more than positive innovations), followed by the Japanese market (1.13 times) and the Indian market (1.06 times). The hypothesis that the return series are homoskedastic (i.e. $a_1 = b_1 = \theta$) is rejected at any significance level on the basis of the Wald test.[15]

Panel C reports the diagnostics on standardized and squared standardized residuals. The estimated Ljung–Box statistics show that the EGARCH model fully captures all linear and non-linear dependencies present in the US and Japanese return series, but only successfully accounts for the non-linear dependencies of the Indian, Pakistan and Sri Lankan return series. Our autoregressive formulations of the conditional mean and conditional variance equations appear to absorb all the non-linear serial correlations present in the original return series.[16] On the basis of Jarque–Bera statistics, the hypothesis of univariate normality is rejected for all the markets.

Price and Volatility Spillovers

We next estimate the univariate EGARCH (1,1) model given by Eqs. (7), (8) and (9) for each market to test for return and volatility spillovers. The results are shown in Table 4. Panels A, B and C report the return spillover coefficients, volatility spillover coefficients and the diagnostics on standardized and squared standardized residuals, respectively. The full model considers both return and volatility spillovers from the world source of shocks (US) and the regional source of shocks (Japan) to the three small emerging markets. In terms of first moment interdependencies (return spillovers), there are positive significant return spillovers from the US to India, Pakistan and Sri Lanka, respectively; all three US return spillover coefficients (0.0989, 0.0382 and 0.0269) are statistically significant at conventional levels. There is a positive significant return spillover from Japan to Pakistan,

Table 4.   Univariate ERGACH (1,1) Model of Return and Volatility
Spillovers Results.

Parameters	IND	PAK	SRI
Panel A: Return spillover coefficients			
α_0	0.0001	−0.0001	−0.0005
	(0.0002)	(0.0002)	(0.0001)
α_1	0.1684***	0.1053***	0.3864***
	(0.0195)	(0.0203)	(0.0205)
α_2		0.0439***	0.0682***
		(0.0152)	(0.0204)
β_1(from US)	0.0989***	0.0382**	0.0269***
	(0.0232)	(0.0180)	(0.0096)
β_2(from Japan)	−0.0346*	0.0600***	−0.0376***
	(0.0187)	(0.0185)	(0.0098)
Panel B: Volatility spillover coefficients			
a_0	−0.2149***	−0.2572***	−1.3001***
	(0.0615)	(0.0671)	(0.2050)
a_1	0.1872***	0.2584***	0.4569***
	(0.0218)	(0.0198)	(0.0226)
b_1	0.9729***	0.9472***	0.8459***
	(0.0076)	(0.0080)	(0.0194)
θ	−0.0282***	−0.0146	−0.0349**
	(0.0096)	(0.0105)	(0.0170)
c_1(from US)	0.0056*	0.0056	0.0209***
	(0.0029)	(0.0038)	(0.0064)
c_2(from JAP)	−0.0007	0.0097**	0.0096
	(0.0034)	(0.0045)	(0.0057)
Log Likelihood	8183.1	8048	9880
Wald statistic	36643.6	23930.8	11929.5
Likelihood Ratio (LR)	0.0016	0.0025	0.0094

Table 4. (Continued)

Parameters	IND	PAK	SRI
Panel C: Diagnostics on standardized and squared standardized residuals			
Jarque–Bera statistic	1410.0	2271.1	18821.1
LB(6)	14.3324	22.1950	26.3460
	[0.0260]	[0.0001]	[0.0000]
LB(12)	27.7540	34.8850	44.6270
	[0.0060]	[0.0000]	[0.0000]
$LB^2(6)$	8.1119	2.9370	1.6120
	[0.2300]	[0.8170]	[0.9520]
$LB^2(12)$	12.6056	5.5750	4.8370
	[0.3980]	[0.9360]	[0.9630]

Note: α_1 and α_2 are the coefficients on the first- and second-order autoregressive processes specified for the mean equations. a_1 is the measure of the autoregressive conditional heteroskedasticity (ARCH) effect. b_1 is the measure of volatility persistence. θ is the measure of asymmetric effect. The null hypothesis for Wald test is $a_1 = b_1 = \theta = c_1 = c_2$. $LR = 2*[ln(loglikelihood of unrestricted model) - ln(loglikelihood of restricted model)]$. The unrestricted model refers to the spillover model and restricted model refers to the univariate EGARCH (1,1) model. Jarque–Bera statistic tests the normality of the standardized residual series. LB(k) and $LB^2(k)$ are the Ljung–Box q-statistics for the standardized residuals and squared standardized residuals distributed as χ^2 with k degrees of freedom. The standard errors and p-values are provided in parentheses ( ) and [ ], respectively.
***Denotes statistical significance at the 1 per cent level.
**Denotes at the 5 per cent level.
*Denotes at the 10 per cent level.

but there are negative significant return spillovers from Japan to India and Sri Lanka. Again, all three Japanese return spillover coefficients (−0.0346, 0.0600 and −0.0376) are statistically significant. Moreover, the magnitude of the spillover coefficients varies from a low of 0.0269 from the US to Sri Lanka to a high of 0.0989, from the US to India.

Turning to second moment interdependencies (volatility spillovers), a statistically significant spillover effect exists from the US to India at the 10 per cent level of significance, from US to Sri Lanka at the 1 per cent level, and from Japan to Pakistan at the 5 per cent level. The magnitude of the volatility spillover coefficients also varies. Specifically, the coefficient from the US to Sri Lanka (0.0209) is greater than its counterparts from Japan to Pakistan (0.0097), and from the US to India (0.0056); these findings indicate that the US, proxying for the world factor as a source of shocks, has more impact on the Asian small markets. In addition, the coefficient measuring asymmetry, θ, is significant for the Indian and Sir Lankan markets, which means that any negative news (innovations) from the US market increase volatility more than positive news of similar size from the same market. Thus, both the Indian and Sri Lankan markets present evidence consistent with an asymmetric response of volatility to innovations from the US market. Numerically, bad news from the US market for Indian and Sri Lankan markets have 1.06 times, and 1.07 times the impact of good news as indicated by the relative asymmetry ratio. The spillovers are symmetric for the Pakistan market since the coefficient measuring asymmetry is insignificant.

Comparing the coefficients from the univariate EGARCH model (restricted model) with those of the spillover model (unrestricted model) (i.e. Tables 3 and 4, respectively), we can see that both sets of results are consistent. The coefficients α_1, α_2 (for the one-lag and two-lag conditional means) and b_1 (for the one-lag conditional variances) all are highly significant; b_1 is close to unity as well. These findings clearly indicate that both the returns and volatility of all three small markets respond to their own past information. Thus, current information for a market remains important for all future forecasts of the conditional mean and conditional variance of that market.

Conditional volatilities of the returns in the Pakistan and Sri Lankan markets respond symmetrically to their own past innovations; the θ coefficients reported in Table 3 for these two markets are insignificant. Also, evidence of asymmetric volatility transmission from either of the developed markets to the Pakistan market is not present; the θ coefficient reported in Table 4 for this market is insignificant. However, after taking into account volatility spillover, the Sri Lankan market becomes sensitive to news originating from the US market more strongly when the news is 'bad' than when the news is 'good'. The Indian market also responds asymmetrically to its own past innovations and also to world shocks; both the θ coefficients reported in Tables 3 and 4 are negative and significant. We use the likelihood ratio (LR) statistic to test the hypothesis that return and volatility spillovers from the two developed markets to three small markets are jointly zero (i.e. the univariate EGARCH model versus the spillover model). The null hypothesis cannot be rejected at any significance level, implying the importance of return and volatility spillovers. The Ljung–Box statistics for the standardized and squared standardized residuals reported in this unrestricted model indicate the presence of limited spillover effects as the values reported in the table are very close to those calculated for the restricted model. The Jarque–Bera normality test statistics indicate that standardized residuals for all three indices exhibit strong deviations from normality. In short, the existence of first and second moment interdependencies points to the presence of a global marketplace; however, the degree of interdependencies is limited.

Sub-period Price and Volatility Spillovers

The Asian financial crisis started in mid-1997 and lasted until the end of 1999. The most directly affected nations were from Southeast Asia, namely, Malaysia, Thailand, the Philippines and Indonesia. However, other countries soon became affected. Due to "financial contagion", markets fell across the globe and the implications of the Asian financial turmoil became far-reaching. For example, in the US the Dow Jones Industrial Average fell by 554 points on 27 October, 1997. The crisis badly affected Japan who was the biggest trading partner of the main Asian countries affected and the main supplier of foreign capital to Asian markets.

The results for the unrestricted model (i.e. univariate EGARCH (1,1) with spillover effect) for the three sub-periods are reported in Table 5. Coefficient a_1 (measuring ARCH effect) and b_1 (measuring volatility persistence) are significant for almost all markets in the three periods. The α_1 coefficient (measuring the return persistence) is significant on average, except for India during in-crisis period and for Pakistan during in- and post-crisis periods. The findings are consistent with the results reported in Table 4 for the entire period; that is, for these small emerging markets, past information can be used to forecast both stock market returns and variance. Finally, the Ljung–Box statistics for the standardized and squared standardized residuals indicate that the univariate EGARCH model with spillover effects are correctly specified.

For the pre-crisis period, there is evidence of return spillovers from Japan to all three small markets. There is also evidence of volatility spillovers from Japan to the Pakistan and Sri Lankan markets. However, these spillovers are symmetric since the θ coefficients (measuring the asymmetry) for both markets are insignificant. For the in-crisis period, the Indian market shows evidence of return spillovers from both the US and Japanese markets; the Pakistan market also shows signs of return spillovers from the Japanese market. There is no evidence of return spillovers for Sri Lankan market and also no evidence of volatility spillovers for any market. However, the θ coefficient is significant for the Indian and Pakistan markets, implying that both markets respond asymmetrically to their own past innovations. For the post-crisis period, there is evidence of both return spillovers and volatility spillovers from the US market to the Indian, Pakistan and Sri Lankan markets. In addition, there is some evidence of return spillovers from the Japanese to the Pakistan market and volatility spillovers from the Japanese to the Indian market. However, the volatility spillovers are only asymmetric in the Indian market as the coefficient θ is only significant for India. Thus,

Table 5. Subperiod Return and Volatility Spillovers Results.

Parameters	Pre-Crisis (1,172 Observations)			In-Crisis (654 Observations)			Post-Crisis (1,043 Observations)		
	IND	PAK	SRI	IND	PAK	SRI	IND	PAK	SRI
Panel A: Return spillover coefficients									
z_0	-0.0002	-0.0004	-0.0001	0.0005	-0.0003	0.0002	0.0002	0.0009**	0.0001
	(0.0005)	(0.0003)	(0.0001)	(0.0006)	(0.0007)	(0.0003)	(0.0004)	(0.0004)	(0.0002)
z_1	0.2817***	0.2227***	0.5988***	0.0572	0.0632	0.3804***	0.1096***	0.0011	0.3973***
	(0.0282)	(0.0332)	(0.0277)	(0.0389)	(0.0446)	(0.0393)	(0.0344)	(0.0349)	(0.0343)
z_2	0.0394								0.0066
	(0.0334)								(0.0351)
β_1 (from US)	-0.0005	0.0451	0.0292	0.1941***	0.1095	0.0352	0.1280***	0.0517*	0.0371***
	(0.0384)	(0.0475)	(0.0201)	(0.0531)	(0.0698)	(0.0258)	(0.0294)	(0.0274)	(0.0140)
β_2 (from Japan)	0.0770**	0.0577*	-0.0219*	-0.1064**	0.1175*	-0.0103	-0.0346	0.0368*	-0.0235
	(0.0387)	(0.0342)	(0.0127)	(0.0494)	(0.0648)	(0.0163)	(0.0284)	(0.0190)	(0.0147)
Panel B: Volatility spillover coefficients									
a_0	-0.1633***	-0.9776***	-1.0115***	-0.9785	-0.2762	-1.2784	-0.6184	-1.1255	-0.8053
	(0.0917)	(0.3355)	(0.2657)	(0.4558)	(0.1616)	(0.4107)	(0.1822)	(0.2765)	(0.2061)
a_1	0.1705***	0.3137***	0.5600***	0.0913	0.2003***	0.4254***	0.3496***	0.3410***	0.5784***
	(0.0282)	(0.0428)	(0.0482)	(0.0592)	(0.0354)	(0.0683)	(0.0567)	(0.0446)	(0.0412)
b_1	0.9762***	0.8645***	0.8784***	0.8858***	0.9352***	0.8544***	0.9266***	0.8882***	0.9127***
	(0.0093)	(0.0358)	(0.0191)	(0.0560)	(0.0205)	(0.0412)	(0.0224)	(0.0243)	(0.0146)
θ	0.0063	0.0299	0.0463	-0.0893***	-0.0569***	-0.0092	-0.0913***	-0.0329	-0.0467
	(0.0143)	(0.0243)	(0.0304)	(0.0293)	(0.0241)	(0.0359)	(0.0248)	(0.0248)	(0.0320)
c_1 (from US)	0.0068	-0.0106	-0.0030	-0.0036	0.0173	0.0152	-0.0222**	-0.0235**	-0.0232*
	(0.0056)	(0.0095)	(0.0113)	(0.0108)	(0.0109)	(0.0164)	(0.0095)	(0.0105)	(0.0122)
c_2 (from Japan)	-0.0039	0.0301***	0.0208**	0.0012	0.0163	-0.0194	0.0222**	0.0032	0.0073
	(0.0050)	(0.0090)	(0.0098)	(0.0160)	(0.0127)	(0.0168)	(0.0103)	(0.0100)	(0.0109)
Log Likelihood	3557.1	3585.0	4362.9	1754.8	1601.9	2278.7	2941.1	2918.5	3356.7
Wald statistic	18907.7	1291.3	3415.6	392.3	3494.8	1052.9	4538.4	2777.6	5517.5
Panel C: Diagnostics on standardized and squared standardized residuals									
Jarque–Bera statistic	725.0	180.9	632.4	126.7	550.9	78.8	53.4	461.4	16460.7

LB(6)	6.2091	14.2920	9.3241	9.1736	7.8576	12.1215	8.3227	7.5840	6.0126
	[0.4000]	[0.0270]	[0.1560]	[0.1640]	[0.2490]	[0.0590]	[0.2150]	[0.2700]	[0.4220]
LB(12)	13.8916	18.6630	18.2663	17.1463	16.4519	19.5879	15.1638	22.0721	15.3297
	[0.3080]	[0.0970]	[0.1080]	[0.1440]	[0.1710]	[0.0750]	[0.2330]	[0.0370]	[0.2240]
LB²(6)	8.2867	5.1431	1.9895	2.6644	1.9672	2.7444	2.7100	7.2896	0.8446
	[0.2180]	[0.5260]	[0.9210]	[0.8500]	[0.9230]	[0.8400]	[0.8440]	[0.2950]	[0.9910]
LB²(12)	10.7286	6.4961	4.5923	4.6227	3.9156	38.3501	9.5785	9.6050	2.2708
	[0.5520]	[0.8890]	[0.9700]	[0.9690]	[0.9850]	[0.0000]	[0.5910]	[0.6510]	[0.9990]

Note: α_1 and α_2 are the coefficients on the first order and second order autoregressive process specified for the mean equations. a_1 is the measure of the autoregressive conditional heteroskedasticity (ARCH) effect. b_1 is the measure of volatility persistence. θ is the measure of asymmetric effect. The null hypothesis for Wald test is $a_1 = b_1 = \theta = c_1 = c_2$. Jarque–Bera statistic tests the normality of the standardized residual series. LB(k) and LB²(k) are the Ljung–Box q-statistics for the standardized residuals and squared standardized residuals distributed as χ^2 with k degrees of freedom. The standard errors and p-values are provided in parentheses ( ) and [ ], respectively.

***Denotes statistical significance at the 1 per cent level.

**Denotes at the 5 per cent level.

*Denotes at the 10 per cent level.

the Indian market appears to respond asymmetrically to its own past innovations and to innovations from the two developed markets as well.

A comparison of the results from the three sub-periods reveals that during
the crisis the small markets are comparatively isolated. In more recent years,
however, these markets have grown more interdependent in the sense that
information affecting asset prices has become more global in nature. We
also find that during the pre-crisis period, these small markets are more
responsive to price changes in the Japanese market, which suggests that a
regional factor dominates the source of spillovers. However, during the
post-crisis period, the small markets have become more sensitive to news
originating in the US market, which indicates that the world factor is the
source of spillovers. Even though we find significant volatility spillovers in
these markets, the volatility transmission is not all asymmetric in the sense
that the bad news (a market decline) in one market has a greater impact on
the volatility of the other market to trade.

Discussion

Since governments have implemented financial liberalization policies, the
capital markets in South Asian countries have become more dependent
upon news from their developed market counterparts, which are often the
sources of capital outflows. This fact is confirmed by the findings of significant return spillovers from both the world's largest (US) and the region's
largest (Japanese) stock markets to all three South Asian stock markets.

The return and volatility spillovers observed from the US market to the
Indian market are hardly surprising as the US is India's biggest foreign trade
partner as well as its largest cumulative investor – both in Foreign Direct
Investment (FDI) and Foreign Portfolio Investment (FPI). According to the
International Financial Statistics Yearbook, for example, the FDI inflows
from the US constituted about 16 per cent of the total actual inflow into the
economy in 2001. Out of the 538 Foreign Institutional Investors (FIIs)
registered with the BSE, 220 were from the US. An investment of nearly
USD7 billion out of a total of USD13 billion by FIIs in the Indian capital
markets was from the US. This accounts for about 47 per cent of the net
investments made by the FIIs since 1993. However, FPI inflows are very
volatile. For example, in 1998, FDI inflows from the US were negative. As
Granger, Huang, and Yang (1999) highlighted, foreign investments to
emerging markets are extremely volatile and depend on changing economic
conditions. Since independence, Pakistan has had to depend on foreign

assistance in its development efforts. Japan is its largest donor and the biggest investor. According to the International Financial Statistics Year-book, the share of financial flows from Japan to Pakistan amounted to 91.9 per cent, 39 per cent and 59 per cent of total donations in 1998, 1999 and 2000, respectively. The total cumulative amount of net disbursement from Japan's Official Development Assistance (ODA) to Pakistan reached USD4 billion through 1999. As a result, it is not too surprising to find that the volatility of the Japanese capital market influences the volatility of Pakistan equity values. Due to the small size of Sri Lankan economy, export-oriented industries are extremely important. Sri Lanka and the US enjoy cordial trade relations. Since the proportion of exports to the US as a percentage of total exports has reached an average of 40 per cent during 1993–2001, according to International Trade Statistics Yearbook, we would therefore expect the volatility of the US economy to be transmitted to the Sri Lankan market.

It is interesting to see that the South Asian stock markets do not show any volatility spillovers from the US and/or Japan during the in-crisis period. The South Asian countries that were examined in this study have been relatively insulated from the 1997 financial crisis. One reason might be that the financial sectors of these counties might not have been liberalized to the extent that is evident in East Asian countries. Also, these countries, and in particular their companies, are less exposed to foreign debt.

5. CONCLUSION

This study investigates the magnitude and changing nature of the return and volatility spillovers from the US and Japan to the three small South Asian stock markets: namely India, Pakistan and Sri Lanka. We use a univariate Exponential Generalized Autoregressive Conditionally Heteroskedastic (EGARCH) spillover model to account for asymmetries in the volatility transmission mechanism, i.e. the possibility that bad news in a given market has a greater impact on the volatility of the returns of an other market than good news. We also attempt to distinguish world forces (the US) from regional factors (Japan). The tests cover the period 01/01/1993–31/12/2003. To examine whether or not there are structural shifts in the international market dynamics, the tests are also conducted for three sub-periods – pre-crisis, in-crisis and post-crisis.

A number of findings emerge from the analysis. First, for the entire period analysed, both world and regional factors are important in explaining returns and volatility in the three South Asian countries examined, although the world market influence tends to be greater. We find evidence of significant return spillovers from the US and Japan to all three small markets. We also document evidence of volatility spillovers from the US to Sri Lanka and from Japan to Pakistan at the 5 per cent significance level and from the US to India at the 10 per cent significance level. Second, the volatility transmission mechanism is asymmetric but only from the US stock market, i.e. negative innovations in US equity prices increase volatility in the Indian and Sri Lankan stock markets considerably more than positive innovations. Third, no volatility spillovers existed during the period of Asian crisis. More spillovers, and spillovers of greater intensity, were uncovered during the post-crisis period. In most cases, spillovers during the post-crisis period were not asymmetric. Finally, the relative importance of the world and regional market factors was influenced by the Southeast Asian financial crisis. The sub-period analysis revealed that before the crisis, regional factors were more important than their world factor counterparts; in other words, the Japanese stock market was the source of price and volatility spillover for the South Asia region. However, after the crisis, the world factors dominated the regional factors; that is, the US stock market has had a larger impact on small South Asian stock markets.

NOTES

1. Some researchers have extended this investigation to foreign exchange and to spot and future markets and uncovered evidence for the existence of spillovers among major currency markets (Baillie & Bollerslev, 1990; Engle, Ito, & Lin, 1991; Chin, Chan, & Karolyi, 1991; Cheung & Fung, 1997).

2. This phenomenon was originally motivated by the work of Black (1976), Christie (1982), French, Schwert, and Stambaugh (1987) and Nelson (1991). Its significance was evaluated by Pagan and Schwert (1990), Braun, Nelson, and Sunnier (1992), Glosten, Jagannathan, and Runkle (1993) and Engle and Ng (1993) by employing different variations of volatility models. Nelson (1991), Cheung and Ng (1992), Koutmos (1992) and Poon and Taylor (1992), among others, provide empirical evidence for the existence of a leverage effect.

3. See, Ng (2000), Chan-Lau and Ivaschenko (2002) and Worthington and Higgs (2004) for some evidence on this topic.

4. Many early studies failed to distinguish between world and regional factors as they were predominantly occupied with testing the influence of the world market (often US) on other markets. For example, see Hamao et al. (1990), Campbell and

Hamao (1992), Bekaert and Hodrick (1992), Bekaert and Harvey (1995), Harvey (1995), Karolyi (1995) and Karolyi and Stulz (1996).

5. Bollerslev, Chou, and Kroner (1992) suggest that the asymmetric response of volatility to innovations may be the result of a few extreme observations such as those associated with the October 1987 crash.

6. A competing model that also captures the asymmetric leverage effect is the Quadratic GARCH model proposed by Engle (1990). However, Engle and Ng (1993) find that the EGARCH performs better. Moreover, a significant body of previous evidence, summarized by Hamilton (1994), supports the use of the EG-ARCH model. On the basis of this evidence, the EGARCH model is employed in this study.

7. Likelihood ratios are calculated as follows: LR = 2*[ln (*log likelihood of unrestricted model*)-ln(*log likelihood of restricted model*)] The unrestricted model refers to either the EGARCH(1,2) or EGARCH(2,1) model and the restricted model refers to the EGARCH(1,1) model. Since we have a very small LR statistic for all markets, the lag truncation lengths $p = 2$ or $q = 2$ are not statistically significant. Based on these tests, we fit EGARCH (1,1) models for all markets.

8. Conventional standard errors tend to underestimate the true standard errors, especially for the parameters in the conditional variance equation (Susmel & Engle, 1994).

9. Even though the CSE had a "blue chips" index representing the top companies in the market, its composition changed in 1998. Therefore, it was decided to use the All Share Price Index.

10. See Campbell and Hamao (1989) for evidence on the dividend-price ratio for the Tokyo market.

11. Since Eastern trading time leads Western trading time by 1 day, we consider US returns with a 1-day lag in order to overcome problems associated with non-synchronous trading across five markets analysed. All three South Asian markets have overlapping trading hours with the Japanese market but not with the US market. Recent spillover investigations deal with this problem using open-to-close returns (Hamao et al., 1990; Bae & Karolyi, 1994; and Koutmos & Booth, 1995). However, this option was not available to us due to the difficulty of obtaining opening and closing prices for the South-Asian capital markets.

12. See Scholes and Williams (1977) and Lo and MacKinley (1988).

13. See, for example, Nelson (1991), Akgiray (1989) and Booth et al. (1992).

14. The LM test approach requires the estimation of the auxiliary regression model of $e_t^2 = constant + \sum_{i=1}^p d_i e_{t-i}^2 + error$, where e_ts are the OLS residuals, $i = 1, 2, \ldots p$; and $t = p + 1, p + 2, \ldots, m$. From the results of this auxiliary regression, a test statistic is calculated as $(N - p)*R^2$, which is expected to be distributed as Chi-squared (p) under the null hypothesis of no ARCH effects.

15. A non-linear Wald test is used to test the joint significance of the EGARCH model, as standard t-statistics do not work since we have a non-linear ML. The very large Wald statistic indicates the presence of an EGARCH volatility model.

16. Higher-order lags could not eliminate the linear serial correlation present in the Indian, Pakistan and Sri Lankan return series.

REFERENCES

Akgiray, V. (1989). Conditional heteroskedasticity in time series of stock returns: Evidence and forecasts. *Journal of Business, 62,* 55–80.

Bae, K. H., & Karolyi, G. A. (1994). Good news, bad News and international spillovers of stock return volatility between Japan and the US. *Pacific-Basin Finance Journal, 2,* 405–438.

Baele, L. (2002). *Volatility spillover effects in European equity markets: Evidence from a regime switching model.* Working Paper, Ghent University.

Baillie, R. T., & Bollerslev, T. (1990). Intra-day and inter-market volatility in foreign exchange rates. *Review of Economics Studies, 58,* 565–585.

Becker, K. G., Finnerty, J. E., & Gupta, M. (1990). The international relation between the US and Japanese stock markets. *Journal of Finance, 45,* 1297–1306.

Bekaert, G., & Harvey, C. R. (1995). Time-varying world market integration. *Journal of Finance, 50,* 403–444.

Bekaert, G., & Hodrick, R. J. (1992). Characterizing predictable components in excess returns on equity and foreign exchange markets. *Journal of Finance, 47,* 467–509.

Black, F. (1976). Studies of stock market volatility changes. *Proceedings of the American Econometrics, 31,* 307–327.

Bollerslev, T., Chou, R., & Kroner, K. (1992). ARCH modeling in finance: A review of the theory and empirical evidence. *Journal of Econometrics, 52,* 5–60.

Bollerslev, T., & Wooldridge, J. (1992). Qusai-maximum likelihood estimation and inference in dynamic models with time-varying covariances. *Econometric Reviews, 11,* 143–172.

Booth, G. G., Hatem, J., Vitranen, I., & Yli-Olli, P. (1992). Stochastic modeling of security returns: Evidence from the Helsinki stock exchange. *European Journal of Operational Research, 56,* 98–106.

Booth, G. G., Martikainen, T., & Tse, Y. (1997). Price and volatility spillovers in Scandinavian stock markets. *Journal of Banking and Finance, 21,* 811–823.

Braun, P., Nelson, D., & Sunier, A. (1992). *Good news, bad news, volatility and betas.* Working paper, University of Chicago.

Campbell, J. Y., & Hamao, Y. (1989). *Predictable stock returns in the United States and Japan: A study of long-term capital market integration.* Working Paper, National Bureau of Economic Research.

Campbell, J. Y., & Hamao, Y. (1992). Predictable stock returns in the United States and Japan: A study of long-term capital market integration. *Journal of Finance, 47,* 43–69.

Chan-Lau, J. A., & Ivaschenko, I. (2002). *Asian flu or Wall Street virus? Price and volatility spillovers of the tech and non-tech sectors in the United States and Asia.* IMF Working Paper.

Cheung, Y. W., & Fung, H. G. (1997). Information flows between Eurodollar spot and futures markets. *Multinational Finance Journal, 1,* 255–271.

Chueng, Y. W., & Ng, L. K. (1992). Stock price dynamics and firm size: An empirical investigation. *Journal of Finance, 47,* 1985–1997.

Chin, K., Chan, K. C., & Karolyi, A. (1991). Intra day volatility in the stock index and stock index futures markets. *Review of Financial Studies, 4,* 657–684.

Christie, A. A. (1982). The stochastic behavior of common stock variances: Value, leverages and interest rate effects. *Journal of Financial Economics, 10,* 407–432.

Engle, R. F. (1982). Autoregressive conditional heteroscedasticity with estimates of the variance of United Kingdom inflation. *Econometrica, 50,* 987–1008.

Engle, R. F. (1990). Discussion: Stock volatility and the crash of 87. *Review of Financial Studies*, *3*, 103–106.

Engle, R. F., Ito, T., & Lin, W. (1991). Meteor shower or heat waves? Heteroscedastic intra-daily volatility in the foreign exchange market. *Econometrica, 58*, 525–542.

Engle, R. F., & Ng, V. (1993). Measuring and testing the impact of news on volatility. *Journal of Finance, 48*, 1749–1777.

Eun, C., & Shim, S. (1989). International transmission of stock market movements. *Journal of Financial and Quantitative Analysis, 24*, 241–256.

Fratzscher, M. (2002). Financial market integration in Europe: On the effects of EMU on stock markets. *International Journal of Finance and Economics, 7*, 165–193.

French, K. R., Schwert, G. W., & Stambaugh, R. F. (1987). Expected stock returns and volatility. *Journal of Financial Economics, 19*, 3–29.

Glosten, L., Jagannathan, R., & Runkle, D. (1993). Seasonal patterns in the volatility of stock index excess returns. *Journal of Finance, 48*, 1779–1801.

Granger, C. W. J., Huang, B. N., & Yang, C. W. (1999). A bivariate causality between stock prices and exchange rates: Evidence from recent Asian flu. University of California at San Diego (UCSD) Economics Discussion Paper.

Hamao, Y., Masulis, R., & Ng, V. (1990). Correlations in price changes and volatility across international stock markets. *Review of Financial Studies, 3*, 281–307.

Hamilton, J. D. (1994). *Time series analysis*. NJ: Princeton University Press, Princeton.

Harvey, C. R. (1995). Predictable risk and returns in emerging markets. *Review of Financial Studies, 8*, 773–816.

Hilliard, J. (1979). The relationship between equity indices on world exchanges. *Journal of Finance, 34*, 103–114.

Hsieh, D. (1989). Modeling heteroskedasticity in daily foreign exchange rates. *Journal of Business and Economics Statistics, 7*, 5–33.

Joen, B. N., & Von Furstenberg, G. M. (1990). Growing international co-movement in stock price indexes. *Quarterly Review of Economics and Business, 30*, 15–30.

Kanas, A. (1998). Volatility spillovers across equity markets: European evidence. *Applied Financial Economics, 8*, 245–256.

Karolyi, G. A. (1995). A multivariate GARCH model of international transmissions of stock returns and volatility: The case of the United States and Canada. *Journal of Business and Economics Statistics, 13*, 11–25.

Karolyi, G. A., & Stulz, R. M. (1996). Why do markets move together? An investigation of US-Japan stock return comovements using ADRs. *Journal of Finance, 51*, 951–986.

Koch, P. D., & Koch, T. W. (1991). Evaluation in dynamic linkages across daily national stock indexes. *Journal of International Money and Finance, 10*, 231–251.

Koutmos, G. (1992). Asymmetric volatility and risk return tradeoff in foreign stock markets. *Journal of Multinational Financial Management, 2*, 27–43.

Koutmos, G., & Booth, G. G. (1995). Asymmetric volatility transmission in international stock markets. *Journal of International Money and Finance, 14*, 747–762.

Lo, A. W., & MacKinley, A. C. (1988). Stock market prices do not follow random walks. *Review of Financial Studies, 1*, 41–66.

Nelson, D. B. (1991). Conditional heteroskedasticity in asset returns: A new approach. *Econometrica, 59*, 347–370.

Ng, A. (2000). Volatility spillover effects from Japan and the US to the Pacific-basin. *Journal of International Money and Finance, 19*, 207–233.

Pagan, A., & Schwert, W. (1990). Alternative models for conditional stock volatility. *Journal of Econometrics, 52*, 245–266.

Poon, S. H., & Taylor, S. J. (1992). Stock returns and volatility: An empirical study of the UK stock market. *Journal of Banking and Finance,* 37–59.

Scheicher, M. (2001). The comovements of stock markets in Hungary, Poland, and the Czech Republic. *International Journal of Finance and Economics, 6*, 27–39.

Scholes, M., & Williams, J. T. (1977). Estimating betas from nonsynchronous data. *Journal of Financial Economics, 5*, 309–327.

Susmel, R., & Engle, R. F. (1994). Hourly volatility spillovers between international equity markets. *Journal of International Money and Finance, 13*, 3–25.

Theodossiou, P., & Lee, U. (1993). Mean and volatility spillovers across major national stock markets: Further empirical evidence. *Journal of Financial Research, 16*, 337–350.

Worthington, A., & Higgs, H. (2004). Transmission of equity returns and volatility in Asian developed and emerging markets: A multivariate GARCH analysis. *International Journal of Finance and Economics, 9*, 71–80.

A NOTE ON THE EQUILIBRIUM RELATIONSHIPS BETWEEN ISSUERS IN THE ASIA PACIFIC REGION

Jonathan A. Batten, Thomas A. Fetherston and Pongsak Hoontrakul

ABSTRACT

We investigate the relationships between the sovereign bonds issued in international markets by major Asia-Pacific issuers (China, Korea, Malaysia, Philippines and Thailand) and various benchmark US Treasury bonds (2, 5, 10 and 30 year maturities). The results suggest that the equilibrium relationship holds only between pairs of bonds of equivalent credit status. The dynamics of these processes highlight aggregation issues for portfolio managers constructing portfolios of sovereign Asian bonds of different credit ratings.

1. INTRODUCTION

Following the Asian Financial Crisis in the late 1990s there has been a considerable deterioration in the levels of foreign bank lending, while debt

Asia Pacific Financial Markets in Comparative Perspective: Issues and Implications for the 21st Century

Contemporary Studies in Economics and Financial Analysis, Volume 86, 167–176

ISSN: 1569-3759/doi:10.1016/S1569-3759(05)86008-5

issues in international markets have increased (Batten & Kim, 2001). Pricing in these offshore markets is usually based on a spread, which reflects the premium for default risk, above a riskless "benchmark" curve; in practice, generally the term structure of US government securities (De Almeida, Duarte, & Fernandes, 1998).

The objective of this note is to apply simple empirical techniques to investigate the relationships between sovereign bonds issued within the Asia-Pacific region and the underlying US Treasury benchmark[1] bonds with a maturity of 2, 5, 10 and 30 years. Such an analysis is essential to pricing and managing the risks of sovereign debt in international markets, while also providing an insight into the equilibrium relationship between different maturity classes of sovereign bonds and US Government benchmark bonds. Historically, studies investigating long-term equilibrium relationships have been restricted to securities of developed countries (for example, see Hiraki, Shiraishi, & Takezawa, 1996).

These issues are investigated using empirical models based on Batten, Hogan, and Pynnonen (2000) for the equilibrium relationships. The paper is set out as follows. In the next section, a brief discussion is provided on data and method employed in this study. The results are then presented and the final section allows for some concluding remarks (see Table 1).

2. DATA AND METHOD

Daily bond data was obtained from the Reuters Fixed Income Database for the period from 30 December 1999 to 28 November 2002 (749 daily observations). All bonds were fixed rate, semi-annual coupons priced on a 30/360-day basis. The yield to maturity (YTM) was calculated as the International Securities Markets Association (ISMA) yield to maturity, with indicative daily bids provided by market practitioners at the close of trading. To overcome potential distortions in yield due to illiquidity and the time path effects due to the bond approaching maturity, only liquid bonds and those with a modified duration of greater than 1 year were included in the final group of bonds. Only nine bonds issued by the governments of China (3 bonds), Korea (1 bond), Malaysia (1 bond), Philippines (3 bonds) and Thailand (1 bond) passed these simple tests and also had a complete set of price data. Table 1 reports this information as well as information on the issue date of each bond and its maturity. The price and yield to maturity of the bond at the end of the sample period (28 November 2002) are also reported. The correlations between the bond pairs, reported in Table 2, are

Table 1. Information on the Sovereign Bonds of Asian Issuers as at the 28 November 2002.

Issuer	Code	Coupon	Issued	Maturity	Rating	Price	YTM	Modified Duration
People's Republic of China	CHG08	7.3	12/9/1998	12/15/2008	BBB	118.41	3.928	5.017
People's Republic of China	CHU06	7.75	7/1/1996	7/5/2006	BBB	115.52	3.327	3.266
People's Republic of China	CHU04	6.5	2/2/1994	2/17/2004	BBB$^+$	105.43	2.472	1.319
Federation of Malaysia	MYG09	8.75	5/27/1999	6/1/2009	BBB$^-$	123	4.692	5.116
Republic of Korea	KOG08	8.875	4/7/1998	4/15/2008	A$^-$	124.14	3.978	4.385
Republic of Philippines	PHU24	9.5	10/14/1999	10/21/2024	BB$^+$	108.8	8.602	9.286
Republic of Philippines	PHG19	9.875	1/6/1999	1/15/2019	BB$^+$	99.25	9.965	7.834
Republic of Philippines	PHG08	8.875	4/2/1998	4/15/2008	BB$^+$	105.3	7.681	4.197
Kingdom of Thailand	THU07	7.75	4/10/1997	4/15/2007	BBB$^-$	115.46	3.994	3.772

Note: YTM is the ISMA yield to maturity of the bond. The designation "G" or "U" in the bond code refers to whether the bond was a global bond (G), or a Yankee bond (U).

Source: Reuters Fixed Income Database

Table 2. Correlations between Changes in Yields on Asian International Bonds and US Treasury Benchmark Bonds.

	CHU04	CHU06	CHG08	KOG08	MYG09	PHG08	PHG19	PHU24	THU07	US2	US5	US10
CHU06	0.295											
CHG08	0.081	0.119										
KOG08	0.073	0.204	0.222									
MYG09	0.103	0.144	0.091	0.292								
PHG08	0.042	0.111	0.049	0.172	0.237							
PHG19	−0.021	0.022	0.024	0.061	0.017	0.123						
PHU24	0.064	0.118	0.038	0.033	0.044	0.181	0.127					
THU07	0.084	0.200	0.157	0.131	0.054	−0.023	−0.032	0.010				
US2	0.083	0.117	0.078	0.128	0.095	0.016	−0.023	−0.007	0.036			
US5	0.187	0.285	0.196	0.154	0.082	0.090	0.012	0.055	0.203	0.238		
US10	0.148	0.270	0.100	0.109	0.091	0.057	−0.020	0.009	0.104	0.460	0.388	
US30	0.105	0.231	0.113	0.131	0.103	0.057	−0.037	0.042	0.075	0.341	0.279	0.473

generally low and are below 0.5. The highest correlation was between the US30 and US10 with a value 0.473. The correlations between the nearest maturity Asian international bonds are higher than between bonds of differing maturity.

Batten et al. (2000) denote the continuously compounded yield to maturity of a k period pure discount bond as $R^*(k,t), (k = 1, 2, \ldots)$. Using their notation, a general relationship between maturities of pure discount bonds is

$$R^*(k,t) = \frac{1}{k} \sum_{j=1}^{k} E_t[R^*(1, \ t + j - 1)] + A(k,t) \tag{1}$$

where $A(k,t)$ is a risk premium, with traditional theories of the term structure focusing on the properties of the premium. The pure expectation hypothesis asserts that $A(k,t)$ is zero and the expectation hypothesis that the premiums are constants. In our case of Asian sovereign bonds, there is a risk premium over an otherwise similar "risk-free" government bond, generally considered the equivalent US Treasury bond by the financial markets. Let $D(k,t)$ denote the risk premium for the Asian sovereign bond over the US government bond, and then from (1) we get the following model for the yield of the Asian sovereign bond

$$R(k,t) = R^*(k,t) + D(k,t) \tag{2}$$

Thus, using (2) we can write

$$R(k,t) - R(1,t) = R^*(k,t) - R^*(1,t) + D(k,t) - D(1,t)$$

$$= \frac{1}{k} \sum_{j=1}^{k} E_t[R^*(1, t+j-1)] - E_t[R^*(1,t)] + A(K,t)$$

$$+ D(k,t) - D(1,t)$$

$$= \frac{1}{k} \sum_{j-1}^{k-1} \sum_{i=1}^{j} E_t[\Delta R^*(1, t+i)] + A(k,t) + D(k,t) - D(1,t) \tag{3}$$

where $\Delta R^*(1, t+i) = R^*(1, t+i) - R^*(1, t+i-1)$

Given that $R^*(1, t+i)$ is $I(1)$ (integrated of order one), the differences $\Delta R^*(1, t+i)$ are therefore stationary implying that the (double) summation term in the last line of (3) is stationary. Therefore, the important result predicted from the theory is that the yield spread $R(k,t) - R(1,t)$ is stationary since the maturity premiums $A(k,t)$ and default risk premiums $D(k,t) - D(1,t)$ are stationary. The next section reports the results from the correlation and cointegration analysis.

3. RESULTS

Given that the risk premiums, $D(k, t)$ defined in Section 2, can be assumed stationary, theory predicts that the series should be cointegrated with a cointegration vector $(1, -1)$. To establish these relationships, Johansen unrestricted cointegration analysis was conducted using the daily bond data over the sample period. These tests have been applied by other authors on a daily yield time-series to determine the presence of a cointegrating relationship (In, Batten & Kim, 2003). Table 3 reports the corresponding likelihood ratio for various combinations of bond pairs between the various bonds. The Augmented Dickey-Fuller tests for stationarity of the spreads and the yields were also calculated but in the interest of brevity are not reported. The full sample test statistics show no evidence against the null hypothesis that there was a unit root in yield levels, but the data clearly rejects the null hypothesis that there was a unit root in the difference. A reasonable conclusion from these results is that each yield to maturity is integrated at order one (i.e. they are an $I(1)$ process) with all tests supporting the unit root hypothesis at the 1% level of significance for all the data series. However, all combinations of spread (levels) are non-stationarity, which suggests the spreads also follow $I(1)$ processes, or equivalently, that the stochastic trends which play the dominating role in the behaviour of the yields are independent of one another. The five lags proved to be sufficient to ensure that the residuals were not serially correlated.

There were 78 (13 by 12/2) possible combinations comprising six different pairs of US benchmark bonds, 36 pairs of bonds between US bonds and Asian bonds, and 36 different pairs of Asian bonds. Of the 78 possible bond pairs, only 34 (43.5%) were cointegrated at the 5% level. Of these 34 cointegrating pairs, 3 were between different pairs of US benchmark bonds (3/6 or 50%), a result which is inconsistent with the Expectations Hypothesis; 13 were between Asian bonds and US bonds (13/36 or 36.1% of all possible combinations) and 18 were between pairs of Asian bonds (18/36 or 50.0% of all possible combinations). The highest number of pairwise combinations was between the US 2-year benchmark (US2), which was cointegrated with all 12 other bonds. The other US bonds were generally not consistently cointegrated with any particular class or group of bonds.

Of those pairs of Asian bonds, it is interesting to note that with one exception the Philippines bonds were only cointegrated with one another and with the US 2-year benchmark bond. In fact the three pairwise combinations of China bonds and the three pairwise combinations of Philippines bonds were both 100% cointgerated – a result consistent with Expectations Theory.

Table 3. Bivariate Cointegration between Pairs of Bonds Comprising Asian International Bonds and US Treasury Benchmark Bonds.

	CHU04	CHU06	CHG08	KOG08	MYG09	PHG08	PHG19	PHU24	THU07	US2	US5	US10
CHU06	25.50**											
CHG08	29.28**	36.75**										
KOG08	35.40**	24.86	28.81*									
MYG09	30.45**	38.11**	40.81**	27.81*								
PHG08	22.26	16.43	17.42	21.60	20.24							
PHG19	23.49	16.67	18.09	20.08	19.71	34.81**						
PHU24	25.65*	18.02	19.09	23.01	22.31	39.73**	26.97*					
THU07	32.93*	28.41*	53.08**	38.00**	41.82**	19.28	17.42	20.87				
US2	61.35**	60.44**	56.78**	57.64**	61.87**	48.39**	49.20**	50.32**	51.66**			
US5	25.76*	19.76	24.69	22.32	21.79	15.82	17.11	19.46	17.45	53.99**		
US10	33.17**	23.86	24.41	28.47*	29.13*	20.46	20.49	22.55	22.39	56.36**	15.89	
US30	24.02	17.88	17.78	22.04	23.16	17.07	15.92	19.22	17.42	53.99**	12.40	16.63

Note: Johansen Cointegration Test at four lags.
*Critical level 5% (25.32);
**Critical level 1% (30.45).

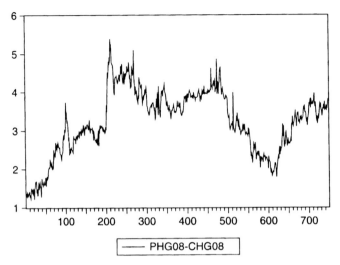

Fig. 1. Plot of the Spread between the Philippines and China Global 2008 Maturity
Bond.

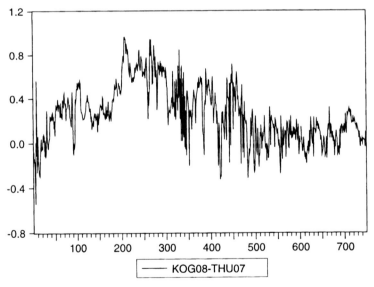

Fig. 2. Plot of the Spread between the Korea and Thailand Global 2008 Maturity
Bond.

If one excluded from the set of all pairs of Asian bonds, those pairs between with the same issuer (36–6), then the within group cointegrating pairs of Asian bonds was only 40%((18–6)/30). The reason for this result is that with one exception, the Philippines bonds were not cointegrated with the other Asian bonds. This is an important result for financial market participants since bundling groups of Asian issues into a portfolio of bonds may result in complex portfolio dynamics and difficulty in risk management.

To illustrate this complex behaviour, Figs. 1 and 2 plot the spread between two pairs of bonds: the PHG08-CHG08 and the KOG08THU07. Even though these bonds have equivalent maturity, the first pair is not cointegrated, while the second pair is cointegrated. The property of mean reversion expected from a cointegrating pair of bonds is evident in Fig. 2 (KOG08THU07), but not in Fig. 1 (PHG08-CHG08). In fact, in Fig. 1 the spread rose significantly from observation 1 to 460, then, declined to observation 620, and then, subsequently rose. Over the sample period the spread increased overall.

4. CONCLUSION

The objective of this note was to report the results of an examination of the equilibrium dynamics of Asian international bonds within a cointegration framework. The results from cointegration analysis suggest that the equilibrium relationship holds between pairs of bond of similar credit rating. The implication of this result is that there are definite limitations to the market approach for pricing and managing the risk of Asian bonds in international portfolios.

NOTES

1. Benchmark bonds of a specific maturity are interpolated from yields of selected on-the-run bonds using splining or other techniques (Kim, Moon, & Lee, 1998). Industry associations usually specify bonds, which are the most liquid, for this purpose.

ACKNOWLEDGEMENTS

The authors wish to thank Dr. Olarn Chaipravat of Fiscal Policy Research Institute of the Ministry of Finance, Thailand and Professor ShigeyukiAbe, Kyoto University for helpful comments on an earlier draft of this paper. We also acknowledge the support of the Sasin Graduate Institute of Business Administration and the Faculty of Commerce of Chulalongkorn University. The authors also wish to thank Reuters Asia Ltd. for providing the data used in this study, and participants at the Asia Pacific Finance Association (APFA) meeting in Bangkok, Thailand 22–25 July 2001 and the "International Bond and Debt Market Integration Conference" 31 May–1 June 2004, Institute for International Integration Studies, Trinity College, Dublin Ireland.

REFERENCES

Batten, J., Hogan, W., & Pynnönen, S. (2000). The dynamics of Australian dollar bonds with different credit qualities. *International Review of Financial Analysis, 9,* 389–404.

Batten, J., & Kim, Y.-H. (2001). Expanding long-term financing through bond market development: A post crisis policy task. In: Y.-H. Kim (Ed.), *Government Bond Markets in Asia*. Philippines: Asian Development Bank Manila.

De Almeida, C., Duarte, A., & Fernandes, C. (1998). Decomposing and simulating the movements of term structures of interest rates in emerging Eurobond markets. *Journal of Fixed Income, 8*(3), 21–31.

Hiraki, T., Shiraishi, N., & Takezawa, N. (1996). Cointegration, common factors, and the term structure of Yen offshore interest rates. *Journal of Fixed Income, 6*(3), 69–75.

In, F., Batten, J., & Kim, S. (2003). What drives the Japanese yen eurobond term structure. *Quarterly Review of Economics and Finance, 43*(3), 518–541.

Kim, B.-C., Moon, N.-S., & Lee, S.-B. (1998). Fitting the term structure of interest rates with a modified cubic smoothing spline. *The Journal of Financial Engineering, 5*(2), 147–159.

INVESTMENT PERFORMANCE

COUNTRY AND SECTOR EFFECTS IN ASIA PACIFIC MARKETS

Jianguo Chen, Yang Zhang and Ben R. Marshall

ABSTRACT

This paper focuses on the impact of country and sector effects in Asia Pacific equity market returns. Our study concludes that Asia Pacific market returns are mainly driven by country effects. Accordingly, country diversification is the most useful tool for managing portfolio risk. Recent evidence from developed markets indicates that country effect is no longer dominant and that sector exposure is of increasing significance in managing portfolio risk. We observed the same phenomenon; the difference is that it happened after the crisis period, not during the period as observed in the previous study.

1. INTRODUCTION

Investment in Asia Pacific markets is often encouraged because of relatively low correlation with developed equity markets. Recent research from developed markets has addressed the attention of the increasing importance of industrial factors in global equity markets returns. The rapidly growing economic integration in Asia Pacific has been the subject of considerable empirical investigation. That inspired us to observe whether it is also

Asia Pacific Financial Markets in Comparative Perspective: Issues and Implications for the 21st Century
Contemporary Studies in Economics and Financial Analysis, Volume 86, 179–197
Copyright © 2005 by Elsevier Ltd.
All rights of reproduction in any form reserved
ISSN: 1569-3759/doi:10.1016/S1569-3759(05)86009-7

reflected in the relative importance of country and industry factors in Asia Pacific stocks return.

Previous studies have indicated that greater integration among developed markets implies stronger co-movement between markets. That is an important concern for investors, given that international diversification works best when there is little co-movement between markets. The worldwide impact of the stock market crash in October 1987 highlighted how integrated markets have become.

The great challenge for international fund managers is that the market correlations seem to increase when the volatility of markets increase. This is troublesome for global fund managers or investors because the increased correlations occur at the same time when increased volatility is making diversification less effective.

Against this background, we address two contributions in this report. First, a cross-region analysis provides a comparison of the extent to which difference of country and sector effects occur between the Asia Pacific and developed markets. Our motivation stems from the fact that there are substantial differences across these regions in how economic and financial integration have progressed. Second, an observation period selected from July 1994 through January 2002 was selected. The advantage of starting in 1994 is that data include the 1997 Asian Financial Crisis as an important benchmark. Thus, we divide a time series analysis into three parts, namely, "pre-crisis, crisis, post-crisis", which enables us to assess how country and sector effects have changed over time.

Given the evidence of stronger segmentation among Asia Pacific markets, we conclude that country factor is the dominant influence in stock return, and thus country diversification is the most useful tool for managing Asia Pacific stock portfolio risk. Our study also confirms the increasing importance of the sectors effect and the declining but stable and continuing contribution of the country factor.

The report is organized as follows: Section 2, Literature Review; Section 3, Methodology; Section 4, Data Description and Test Results; and Section 5, Summary and Conclusion.

2. LITERATURE REVIEW

The relative importance of country versus industry on global stock returns has been addressed explicitly in a number of studies. Several key papers have found that the country of incorporation is of greater importance than industry for the main activity. Beckers, Grinold, Rudd, and Stefek (1992) used a factor model to explain the relative importance of country and industry, while controlling for relative company size, divided yield, price momentum and company-specific volatility. In a set of European companies, they found that several industries do impact stock returns, but that industry importance has declined over time and that country importance has increased over time.

Heston and Rouwenhorst (1994) and Heston (1995) showed that country-specific sources of return variation are dominant even in geographically concentrated and economically integrated regions such as Western Europe. They found that industrial structure explains very little of the cross-sectional difference in country return volatility, and that low correlation between country indices is mostly due to country-specific source of return variation.

Similarly, in a broader sample that includes emerging markets, Griffin and Karolyi (1998) claimed that global industry factors explain only around four per cent of the variation in national stocks. Accepting these conclusions, traditional top-down managers have adopted country selection as the critical tactical decision for portfolio management.

More recent researchers have found that industry effects are becoming more important. Lessard (1974) was the first who addressed how important differences in industrial composition are for explaining the variation in global stock returns. Baca, Garbe and Weiss (2000) and Brooks and Catao (2000) reported that the importance of global industry factors in explaining international return variation increased towards the late 1990s. Cavaglia, Brightman, and Aked (2000) showed that industry factors surpassed country effects in importance in the late 1990s, concluding that diversification across industries may now provide greater risk reduction than diversification across countries.

On a global basis, sectors have become more important in driving global share price performance, particularly in the 1990s. Recent research from Goldman Sachs suggests that global sector industry influence on share price have increased at the expense of local country influence especially in the last two years.

Much research has also explored the fact that correlation between international markets is often claimed to increase during a period of high stock market volatility. Therefore, the benefits of international diversification are reduced when they are most needed, that is, during periods of market turbulence. Solnik (1999, p. 121) claims, "an often-raised question is whether international correlation increases in periods of high turbulence".

The existing literature actually found mixed empirical evidence on the link between international correlation and stock market turbulence. Jeon and

Von Furstenberg (1990), Bertero and Mayer (1990), King and Wadhwani (1990) and Lee and Kim (1993) demonstrated a significant rise in the degree of co-movement in four major equity markets – British, French, German and US after the October 1987 crash.

Similarly, King, Sentana, and Wadhwani (1994) found that the increase in the correlation was only a transitory effect caused by the 1987 crash. In particular, Longin and Solnik (1995) tested the hypothesis of higher international correlation increase during periods of high stock market volatility. They confirmed that volatility is contagious and international correlation increases during periods of high stock market volatility. Erb, Harvey, and Viskanta (1994) found that correlations are higher during recessions than in growth periods.

Odier and Solnik (1993) and Lin, Engle, and Ito (1994) noticed that the international markets are more contagious in bear market periods than others. De Santis and Gerard (1997) found that the US stock price involves not only systematic risk premium (correlation to the world index), but also the country-specific risk premium. Although the systematic risk premium is reduced when market has a strong declining, the country-specific risk premium is, on the other hand, increasing, which makes international diversification still attractive.

On the other hand, Odier and Solnik (1993) and Solnik, Boucrelle, and Fur (1996) showed that the correlations between countries remain low, although they do appear to increase when market volatility increases. Sumel and Engle (1994) focused on hourly data of returns between New York and London stock markets, but even for the period including the 1987 crash, they did not find strong evidence of international volatility spillovers. In a more general setting, Ang and Bekaert (1999) obtained evidence of a high volatility and high correlation regime and a low volatility and low correlation regime.

The Asian financial crisis itself has elicited quite a few papers. The role of currency has received much attention. However, few papers have viewed the crisis from the perspective of an international portfolio investor. Limited literature documents the contribution of Asia Pacific markets to international diversification strategies as compared to co-movement of the Asia Pacific markets before and after this crisis. This subject therefore is important in this study and we aim to make a contribution.

3. METHODOLOGY

Following Heston and Rouwenhorst (1994), extended by Griffin and Karolyi (1998), we define a stock return depends on four components: (1) a region effect α; (2) sector effect β; (3) country effect γ; and (4) a firm-specific disturbance ε_{it}, where R_{it} is a stock return in month t that belongs to industry j and country k.

$$R_{it} = \alpha_t + \beta_{jt} + \gamma_{kt} + \varepsilon_{it} \tag{1}$$

We run the following cross-sectional regression of individual stock returns on sector and country dummies for each month, and obtain a time series of estimated sector and country coefficients which are used to measure how much country and sector effects account for the variation of Asia Pacific markets' aggregate return.

$$R_{it} = \alpha + \sum_{j=1}^{j} \beta_j I_{ij} + \sum_{k=1}^{k} \gamma_k C_{ik} + \varepsilon_i \tag{2}$$

where $_{i,AUS}$ is a dummy variable that equals one if the stock belongs to sector j and zero otherwise and C_{ik} a similar dummy variable that identifies stock that belongs to country k and zero otherwise. The J is the number of sectors and K the number of markets. Thus, in this study, the J and K in total are 10 sectors and 15 countries.

Eq. (2) cannot be used directly; there is an identification problem if dummy variables are defined for every country and industry. Thus, the following two restrictions are added to Eq. (2).

$$\sum_{j=1}^{10} \beta_j W_j = 0 \tag{3}$$

$$\sum_{k=1}^{15} \gamma_k V_k = 0 \tag{4}$$

where W_j and V_k are the value weights of sector j and country k in the region market portfolio. Subject to the restrictions on Eqs. (3) and (4), using Eq. (2), we obtained a time series of the estimates of the intercept (α_t), and country and sector coefficients (β_t and γ_t).

The estimate of the intercept, α gives the return of the value-weighted region market portfolio. The estimated coefficients of country variables can be interpreted as the 'pure' country effect relative to the value-weighted regional market portfolio and the coefficients of the industry variables can be interpreted as the estimated 'pure' sector effect relative to the value-weighted regional market portfolio.

The country behaviour can also be analysed by its industry combination. For example, a value-weighted Australian market index can be expressed as:

$$R_{\text{AUS}} = \varepsilon + \sum_{i=1}^{10} \chi_{i,\text{AUS}}\beta_i + \gamma_{\text{AUS}} \qquad (5)$$

$$[= (\text{Regionaleffect}) + (\text{Cumulativesectoreffect}) + (\text{Purecountryeffect})]$$

where $c_{i,\text{AUS}}$ is the proportion of the total market capitalization of sector i included in Australian market portfolio.

Eq. (5) states that Australian stock return differs from the regional market's return for two reasons: Australian unique sector composition (i.e. greater component of resource, basic industry and non-cyclical goods) and Australian country-specific return.

Similarly, a value-weighted information technology (IT) index can be expressed as:

$$R_{\text{IT}} = \alpha + \sum_{j=1}^{15} \theta_{j,\text{IT}}\gamma_j + \beta_{\text{IT}} \qquad (6)$$

$$[= (\text{Regionaleffect}) + (\text{Cumulativecountryeffect}) + (\text{Puresectoreffect})]$$

where $\theta_{j,\text{IT}}$ is the proportion of the country j market capitalization included in IT sector portfolio.

Thus, Eq. (6) states that the IT stock return differs from the region market's return for two reasons: because of its unique country composition (i.e. the selected set of eight countries indicates that IT is dominated by Taiwan while the sector has been developed only recently in New Zealand) and sector-specific return.

The model uses indicator variables only, which explains the cross-sectional difference between countries and sectors. It automatically recognizes that country-specific risk and industry factors are important factors in the market return. The country-specific risk is well supported by empirical evidences such as De Santis and Gerard (1997) and industry difference is also well documented in the previous literature such as Cavaglia et al. (2000).

We follow Rouwenhorst (1999) and Cavaglia et al. (2000) in using mean absolute deviations (MADs) to highlight the relative importance of country effects versus sectors effects in variation of Asia Pacific stocks return. We examined the amount of variation of country and sector effects over a period of nine years (109 months).

Cavaglia et al. (2000) have emphasized the ratio of industry and country MADs as a measure of their relative performance. A ratio greater than one means that sector effects dominate country effects in the test period. The opposite is true if the ratio is smaller than one. The implication of the MADs for portfolio managers is that if the ratio is greater than one, the return from a sectors-diversified portfolio on average will be more than the return from a countries-diversified portfolio.

4. DATA DESCRIPTION AND TEST RESULTS

Our data, taken from Global Equity Data Stream, covers 15 selected Asia Pacific countries and 10 broad sectors and spans the period from January 1994 to December 2002. The main advantage of using Global Equity Indices in examining the role of sector and country effects is that they are comprehensive and cover a large number of stocks. The FTA (Financial Times Actuaries) code covers 45 different Industries into 10 sectors as shown in Table 1. The value-weighted industry indexes cover from 60% to 80% of the market capitalization.

The 15 selected Asia Pacific markets are China, Hong Kong, Malaysia, Singapore, Thailand, Taiwan, Korea, Indonesia, India, Pakistan, Philippines, Sri Lanka, Canada, Australia and New Zealand. They are well representing the Asia Pacific region stock-market conditions. The US and Japan markets are excluded so that the estimating results will not be dominated by any one or two countries' condition. In addition, Morgan Stanley International Capital currently defines Hong Kong, Singapore, Canada, Australia and New Zealand as developed markets; and the others as Asian emerging markets.

The observation period selected is from January 1994 through December 2002. The regional annualized return rate movement in the period is depicted in Fig. 1. The advantage of starting in 1994 is that data include the 1997 Asian Financial Crisis, an important benchmark against which to assess how country and industry effects have changed over time.

On average, for each month, we examined 49 (of Indonesia) to 205 (of Canada) firms per country. Table 1 indicates that the number of firms and industries vary by country. Visually, the figure plots that for the 10 selected markets, finance is the dominant Sector, followed by cyclical service, IT industry and non-cyclical goods. For industrial sector indices, Canada dominated three sectors, resource, cyclical service and non-cyclical goods. Finance is dominated by Australia and IT is dominated the by Taiwan.

Table 1.   Breakdown Firms by Country and Sector, January 2002.

	RES	BI	GI	CYCG	NCYCG	CYCS	NCYCS	UTL	FINAN	IT	Total
China	5	30	10	9	10	11	2	11	8	4	105
Hong Kong	2	3	2	10	7	29	4	6	29	8	112
Malaysia	4	2	9	4	18	14	4	8	19	3	90
Singapore	2	4	27	2	11	22	2	1	22	9	108
Thailand	3	9	2	6	2	8	3	2	18	2	61
Taiwan	0	4	7	4	1	3	3	0	16	32	73
Korea	3	16	14	13	9	12	5	2	7	19	100
Indonesia	5	7	2	2	7	6	4	0	0	16	49
India	7	17	11	6	19	5	3	3	11	18	100
Pakistan	3	14	2	6	6	3	1	5	0	10	50
Philippines	1	1	2	1	7	7	4	3	1	23	50
Sri Lanka	1	2	6	3	13	9	1	0	0	15	50
Canada	64	25	13	10	24	34	0	11	11	13	205
Australia	18	16	10	2	19	6	3	5	51	2	139
New Zealand	9	6	1	2	8	16	2	5	9	0	62
Total	127	156	118	80	161	185	41	62	202	174	1354

Note: Sectors: RES, Resource; BI, Building materials; GI, Aerospace & defence; CYCG, Cyclical goods automobiles, household and textiles, etc.); NCYCG, Non-cyclical goods (food, beverage, etc.); CYCS, Cyclical service; NCYCS, Non-cyclical service; UTL, Utility; FINAN, Financials; IT, Information technology.

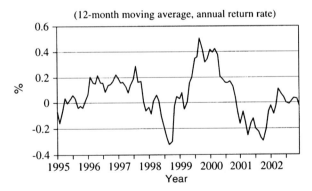

Fig. 1.   Asia Pacific Regional Return Rate. 15 Regional Countries Included are: China, Hong Kong, Malaysia, Singapore, Thailand, Taiwan, Korea, Indonesia, India, Pakistan, Philippines, Sri Lanka, Canada, Australia and New Zealand. The US and Japan Markets are Excluded so that the Estimating Results will not be Dominated by Any One or Two Countries' Condition.

Singapore on average dominated the general industry and China dominated basic industry sector. These different country dominances confirm that industrial compositions of Asia Pacific market indices are diverse.

We first computed correlation coefficients using US dollar-denominated monthly returns from the Data stream Global Equity Indices. With a selected set of 15 Asia Pacific stock markets and 10 sectors, our correlation analysis is divided into three periods: the first is 1994 through 1996 named "pre-crisis;" the second, 1997 through 1999 named "crisis;" and the third, 2000 through 2002 named "post-crisis". We then look into the markets and sectors correlation.

The average cross-markets correlation is 0.343 (from Table 2) and average sectors correlation is 0.608 (from Table 3), a clear indication that in the sample period, sectors correlation is almost double the markets correlation on average. The market correlation for the pre-crisis, crisis and post-crisis are 0.302, 0.385 and 0.301, respectively (Table 4); and the sector correlation averages for the three periods are 0.676, 0.684 and 0.482, respectively (Table 4). The sharp difference between the market and sector correlation happened in the first two periods; in the third period, the difference is reduced mainly because of the decline of the sector correlation.

The figures show that both market and sector correlations were a little higher during the crisis period, but declined and remained low after the crisis. This is consistent (although not strong here) with the contagion effect as raised by Solnik and Jacques (2000). This phenomenon was also reported by Erb et al. (1994) who also discovered evidence that markets correlations are high during recession but low on recovery.

We have also examined the market correlation with the regional index (in Tables 2–4). Similar results are obtained as those discussed with the cross-index correlations.

Market correlations can also be explained by dissimilarity of industrial composition between two equity markets. On average, the markets with dominant sectors (such as Hong Kong, Singapore, Taiwan, Canada and Australia) have higher correlation with the regional index.

To better explain the relative importance of country and sector effects, we used Eqs. (5) and (6) to compute the amount of variation explained by a time series of estimated country and sector coefficients.

Table 5 gives the variance of regional, country and sector effects for the value-weighted country and industry indices. Each country index return is decomposed into a regional effect plus a country "pure effect" and a sum of constituent sector effects. Each industry index return is decomposed into a regional effect plus a "pure sector effect" and a sum of the constituents of

Table 2. Country Correlation Coefficients from January 1994 through December 2002.

	Asia Pacific	China	Hong Kong	Malaysia	Singapore	Thailand	Taiwan	Korea	Indonesia	India	Pak	Phil	Sri L	Can	Aus
China	0.450	1.000													
Hong Kong	0.881	0.528	1.000												
Malaysia	0.664	0.415	0.562	1.000											
Singapore	0.798	0.360	0.742	0.603	1.000										
Thailand	0.622	0.270	0.468	0.540	0.577	1.000									
Taiwan	0.659	0.355	0.449	0.419	0.459	0.413	1.000								
Korea	0.594	0.161	0.400	0.297	0.418	0.594	0.418	1.000							
Indonesia	0.496	0.020	0.292	0.450	0.409	0.515	0.205	0.410	1.000						
India	0.416	0.054	0.221	0.218	0.238	0.083	0.315	0.256	0.183	1.000					
Pakistan	0.180	0.039	0.110	0.188	0.233	0.200	0.122	0.064	0.109	0.351	1.000				
Philippines	0.694	0.309	0.599	0.579	0.685	0.653	0.353	0.416	0.551	0.152	0.080	1.000			
Sri Lanka	0.244	0.161	0.161	0.159	0.163	0.077	0.092	0.237	0.107	0.291	0.311	0.048	1.000		
Canada	0.798	0.239	0.646	0.427	0.524	0.402	0.404	0.370	0.486	0.310	0.051	0.517	0.230	1.000	
Australia	0.760	0.215	0.624	0.377	0.584	0.477	0.390	0.494	0.410	0.291	0.093	0.486	0.213	0.644	1.000
New Zealand	0.610	0.155	0.482	0.347	0.492	0.388	0.323	0.434	0.387	0.213	0.015	0.440	0.269	0.534	0.688
Average	0.591							0.343							

Table 3. Industry Correlation Coefficients from January 1994 through December 2002.

Asia Pacific	RES	BI	GI	CYCG	NCYCG	CYCS	NCYCS	UTI	IT	FIN
RES	1.000									
BI	0.530	1.000								
GI	0.842	0.649	1.000							
CYCG	0.922	0.409	0.785	1.000						
NCYCG	0.776	0.445	0.834	0.764	1.000					
CYCS	0.769	0.516	0.731	0.629	0.601	1.000				
NCYCS	0.923	0.474	0.766	0.839	0.713	0.747	1.000			
UTI	0.794	0.324	0.524	0.659	0.493	0.571	0.737	1.000		
IT	0.643	0.595	0.633	0.550	0.483	0.678	0.600	0.510	1.000	
FIN	0.763	0.122	0.522	0.776	0.564	0.428	0.675	0.606	0.169	1.000
Average	0.910	0.506	0.781	0.803	0.699	0.764	0.831	0.632	0.667	0.567	1.000
Average	0.787					0.608				

Table 4. Country and Sector Correlation Coefficient's Sub-Periods Averages.

Years	Country Correlation		Sector Correlation	
	To Region	Each Other	To Region	Each other
1994–1996	0.571	0.302	0.833	0.676
1997–1999	0.624	0.385	0.834	0.684
2000–2002	0.555	0.301	0.692	0.482
1994–2002	0.591	0.343	0.787	0.608

country effects (Eq. (2)). The index excess return is defined as the difference between the country or sector return and regional index return.

The pure effect, cumulative effect and residual return are listed in Table 5 in different columns and the variances of the excess return are listed in the last column of the table. The ratios give the proportion of variance of a particular component relative to the variance of the index excess return.

Table 5 lists the results of the average variance over a period of 108 months (from January 1994 through December 2002). From the table we can see that the average country excess return variance (of 58.58) is much higher than the average sector variance (of 17.25). This information demonstrates that country factors are the dominant factors in Asia Pacific stock returns and pure country index is much less diversified than pure sector index.

Table 5.   Index Components Variance July 1994 through January 2002.

Index Country	Pure Country Effect		Cumulative Sector Effect		Residual Return		Excess Return
	Variance	Relative ratio	Variance	Relative ratio	Variance	Relative ratio	Total variance
China	93.17	0.85	1.72	0.02	12.68	0.12	109.31
Hong Kong	31.20	1.28	0.33	0.01	11.60	0.48	24.35
Malaysia	46.53	0.92	0.77	0.02	1.27	0.02	50.70
Singapore	29.12	1.52	0.40	0.02	10.16	0.53	19.17
Thailand	73.33	0.74	0.27	0.00	10.88	0.11	98.64
Taiwan	25.05	0.52	1.97	0.04	9.66	0.20	47.72
Korea	96.93	1.02	0.39	0.00	4.68	0.05	95.36
Indonesia	42.47	0.49	1.16	0.01	16.82	0.19	87.55
India	57.75	1.02	0.55	0.01	3.93	0.07	56.72
Pakistan	87.51	0.66	1.86	0.01	14.78	0.11	133.53
Philippines	41.75	1.06	0.49	0.01	6.12	0.16	39.36
Sri Lanka	37.19	0.50	1.02	0.01	9.88	0.13	74.70
Canada	9.63	0.88	0.37	0.03	1.95	0.18	10.89
Australia	9.96	0.86	0.57	0.05	3.12	0.27	11.54
New Zealand	16.14	0.84	0.89	0.05	2.89	0.15	19.18
Country Average	46.52	0.79	0.85	0.01	8.03	0.14	58.58

Index Sector	Pure Sector		Cumulative Country		Residual Return		Excess Return
	Variance	Relative Ratio	Variance	Relative Ratio	Variance	Relative Ratio	Total Variance
RES	8.46	0.37	4.65	0.20	13.76	0.60	23.03
BI	4.83	0.62	2.21	0.28	3.50	0.45	7.85
GI	5.15	0.42	2.40	0.19	6.65	0.54	12.34
CYCG	8.07	0.66	3.87	0.32	6.56	0.54	12.19
NCYCG	5.87	0.57	2.71	0.26	2.33	0.22	10.35
CYCS	3.15	0.74	0.80	0.19	5.02	1.17	4.28
NCYCS	9.34	0.50	2.96	0.16	4.95	0.26	18.81
UTI	11.02	0.66	3.35	0.20	6.70	0.40	16.81
IT	21.00	0.34	5.55	0.09	29.92	0.49	61.13
FIN	2.94	0.51	0.88	0.15	3.62	0.63	5.74
Sector Average	7.98	0.46	2.94	0.17	8.30	0.48	17.25

Note: Variances are in percent-squared per month, in multiple of 10,000. The table gives the variance of value-weighted country and sector index monthly returns from the Data Stream Global Indices from January 1994 to December 2002. Markets listed expect China have complete data. Each country index is decomposed into a pure country effect and the cumulative sum of sector effects using the dummy variable regression methods. Each industry index return is similarly decomposed into a pure industry effect and cumulative country effects. Ratios relative to the region market compute the ratio of the variance of that component relative to the variance of the index return in excess of region market return. Returns are defined in per cent per month.

The pure country variance actually is well captured by the pure country coefficients estimated with Eq. (2). On average, 79% of the variance is explained by the pure country effect. Only 1% of the pure country variance is explained by the cumulative sector effect and 14% by the residual return. The result is consistent with the previous literature (including Lessard, 1974; Grinold, Rudd, & Stefek, 1989; Beckers et al. (1992); Heston & Rouwenhorst, 1994; De Santis & Gerard, 1997) that country factors are dominant in capturing the variation of international stock returns.

Since the pure sector variance is quite well diversified, the pure sector coefficients estimated with Eq. (2) explains only 46% of the sector variance, and the cumulative country effect explains another 17%, leaving 48% of the sector variance unexplained in the residual value (ε in Eq. (2)).

Comparing the pure country variance between developed markets (Hong Kong, Singapore, Canada, Australia and New Zealand) and emerging markets (the others), we found that the former (less than 25) has generally much less excess return variance than the latter (greater than 39) (Table 5). This observation is consistent with the results of Heston and Rouwenhorst (1994), Heston (1995) and Griffin and Karolyi (1998). They conclude that country-specific sources of return variation are dominant and more pronounced for the emerging markets.

When comparing the pure country effect percentages between developed markets and emerging markets in the test, we found that there is no clear difference.

Another interesting observation from Table 2 is of the IT industry. Its total excess return variance is 61.13, much greater than the second highest of resource industry of 23.03. It is a clear indication that the IT industry index is not well diversified, consistent with the Taiwan dominance figure in Table 1.

Since our sample period covers the Asian financial crisis in 1997, dividing the period into pre-crisis (1994–1996), crisis (1997–1999) and post-crisis (2000–2002) makes sense. The periodical results are provided in Table 6. We can see from the table that the country excess return variance in the crisis period (at the value of 94.80) is actually more than double the variance in pre-crisis period (at the value of 31.84) and post-crisis period (at the value of 49.27). Referring to the result in Table 4, we know that there is no sharp increase of between-country correlation in the crisis period. Our results support the argument that country diversification is effective to deal with the financial crisis.

On the contrast, the sector variance is not the highest in the crisis period, and the sector diversification may not be effective to deal with the financial crisis.

Table 6. Index Components Variance Sub-Periods Averages.

Index Country	Pure Country Effect		Cumulative Sector Effect		Residua Returnl		Excess Return
	Variance	Relative Ratio	Variance	Relative Ratio	Variance	Relative Ratio	Total Variance
1994–996	24.05	0.76	0.28	0.01	4.80	0.15	31.84
1996–999	75.57	0.80	1.03	0.01	12.32	0.13	94.80
2000–002	39.96	0.81	1.16	0.02	7.08	0.14	49.27
1994–002	46.52	0.79	0.85	0.01	8.03	0.14	58.58

Index Sector	Pure Sector		Cumulative Country		Residual		Excess Return
	Average Variance	Relative Ratio	Average Variance	Relative Ratio	Average Variance	Relative Ratio	Total Variance
1994–1996	3.24	0.53	2.14	0.35	3.59	0.59	6.10
1996–1999	10.49	0.53	4.75	0.24	11.13	0.56	19.82
2000–2002	8.88	0.38	2.05	0.09	9.88	0.42	23.32
1994–2002	7.98	0.46	2.94	0.17	8.30	0.48	17.25

Note: Variances are in per cent-squared per month, in multiple of 10,000.

The conclusion from Table 5 about the pure country effect and pure sector effect is generally stable over different time periods including the special crisis period (in Table 6).

More intuitively, we use the mean absolute deviations or MADs (Rouwenhorst, 1999; Cavaglia et al., 2000) and the ratios of pure country and industry that measure the absolute and relative importance of country and sector effects. The results are shown in Fig. 2 and Table 7.

Similar to previous studies, the figure indicates that in the early period, the average country MADs are generally higher than the sector MADs (and the MAD ratio is less than 0.60), which suggests that the country effects account for most variation in Asia Pacific stock returns. In the recent post-crisis period, the country MAD has declined from 0.55 to 0.41 level and the sector MAD is moving in the opposite direction, increasing on average (Table 7). More detailed movements of the two MADs could be observed in

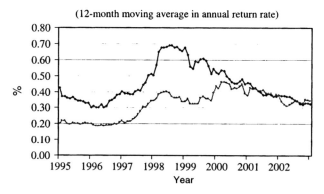

Fig. 2. Cap-Weighted Pure Factor MADs, January 1994–December 2002.

Table 7. Average Cap-Weighted Factor MADs and Ratios Sub-Periods Averages.

Years	Sector MAD	Country MAD	Sector–Country Ratio
1994–1996	0.199	0.344	0.580
1997–1999	0.327	0.553	0.592
2000–2002	0.389	0.411	0.945
1994–2002	0.319	0.447	0.713

Note: In annual return rate.

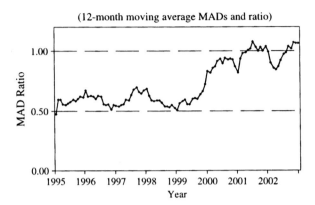

Fig. 3.   Cap-Weighted Pure Factor MAD Ratios, January 1995–December 2002.

Fig. 2. Both MADs are increasing from the beginning of 1997 to the middle of 1998 and both are decreasing after the middle of 2000.

The MAD ratios could be examined with the last column of Table 7 and Fig. 3. In both periods of pre-crisis and crisis, the MAD ratios are much lower than one, indicating that the country factors are the dominant influence in stock returns and country diversification is still effective even during the crisis period. This is no longer true in the post-crisis period; the MAD ratio on average is about 0.95, which is close to one. We can see from Fig. 3 that in the early period of 2000, the MAD was moving from about 0.60 to 0.95 and has remained in the level since then.

In summary, we have observed that our Asia Pacific sample firms' total variance increased sharply in the crisis period (Table 6) and declined to a much lower level after that. There is no obvious difference between country correlation in crisis period and non-crisis period (Table 4). The sector correlation decreased from the level of 0.68 (in the crisis) to the level of 0.48 (after crisis). Actually, the sector total variance (Table 6) and MAD (Table 7) have increased after the crisis period (Table 6) opposite to the relative movements of country component, all of these support the argument that sector diversification becomes more important in the recent (and after crisis) period, rather than in the crisis period.

Country diversification is relatively more effective before and in the crisis period, and in the post-crisis period, the sector effect is at the comparable level and sector diversification is about equally important for the Asia Pacific portfolio management.

Most recent study has found evidence from developed market, which suggests that country effects have declined and sector effects are more important to manage portfolio risk during a global downtown period. An important indication of how our conclusion differs from those of other studies in developed market is that this did not happen in the crisis period, instead it happened in the recovery period after the general downturn in the regional market.

5. SUMMARY AND CONCLUSION

We have examined the impact of country and sector effects in equity market returns for a selection of 15 Asia Pacific countries. Studying country and sector factors has an important implication for international diversification strategies.

Following Heston and Rouwenhorst (1994), extended by Griffin and Karolyi (1998), we assume that a regional return can be influenced by either country or industry factors. This model enables us to compare country effect without sector bias and vice versa.

The whole test period analysis shows that it is the country effects that dominate sector effects in explaining variation in Asia Pacific equity markets returns. Before and during the Asia Financial crisis period, country factors are the foremost effect. This observation also suggests that 'regionalism' is a strong influence upon the markets located within the Asia Pacific countries and is priced accordingly.

The new evidence from this study shows that the regional markets during the volatile financial crisis period, the country's correlation level and pure country effect remain the same as before. Different performance of pure sector effects happened in the recovery period; lower market volatility lowered the index correlation and lowered pure factor variance and country MAD. But the sector MAD is not lowered, rather it is increased to some extent, which makes the sector diversification equally important to the country diversification.

Recent evidence within developed markets by Baca, Garbe, and Weiss (2000) suggests that country effect is no longer dominant, and sector exposure became more important in managing portfolio risk during the global recession of August 1998. This study observes similar phenomenon; the difference is the time period in which this happens. We observed the phenomenon after the 1997 Asian financial crisis.

With that new observation, we hope this is helpful for investors or risk managers to understand how markets are integrated in order to develop effective diversification strategies accordingly.

For future study, it will be interesting to know the movement of risk price and risk factors before, during and after the Asian financial crisis (e.g. using the conditional risk model of De Santis and Gerard (1997)). Also in this study, we ignored the currency effect. A useful extension of this research by adding currency effect, since De Santis and Gerard (1998) shows that currency risk premium is important in international financial markets.

REFERENCES

Ang, A., & Bekaert, G. (1999). *International asset allocation with time-varying correlation.* NBER Working Paper 7056.

Baca, S. P., Garbe, B., & Weiss, R. A. (2000). The rise of sector effects in major equity market. *Financial Analysts Journal, 56*(5), 35–40.

Beckers, S., Grinold, R., Rudd, A., & Stefek, D. (1992). The relative importance of common factors across the European equity markets. *Journal of Banking and Finance, 16*(February), 75–95.

Bertero, E., & Mayer, C. (1990). Structure and performance: Global interdependence of stock markets around the crash of October 1987. *European Economic Review, 34*, 653–680.

Brooks, R., & Catao, L. (2000). *The new economy and global stock returns, IMF.* Working Paper WP/00/216.

Cavaglia, S., Brightman, C., & Aked, M. (2000). The Increasing Importance of Industry Factors. *Financial Analysts Journal, 56*(5), 4–54.

De Santis, G., & Gerard, B. (1997). International asset pricing and portfolio diversification with time-varying risk. *Journal of Finance, 52*, 1881–1912.

De Santis, G., & Gerard, B. (1998). How big is the premium for currency risk. *Journal of Financial Economics, 49*, 375–412.

Erb, C., Harvey, C. R., & Viskanta, T. E. (1994). Foresting international equity correlations. *Financial Analysts Journal, 50*, 32–45.

Griffin, J. M., & Karolyi, G. A. (1998). Another look at the role of industrial structure of markets for international diversification. *Journal of Financial Economics, 50*, 351–373.

Grinold, R., Rudd, A., & Stefek, D. (1989). Global factors: Fact or fiction? *Journal of Portfolio Management, 16*, 79–88.

Heston, S. L. (1995). Industry and country effects in international stock returns. *Journal of Portfolio Management, 21*, 53–58.

Heston, S. L., & Rouwenhorst, K. G. (1994). Does industry structure explain the benefits of international diversification. *Journal of Financial Economics, 36*, 3–27.

Jeon, B. N., & Von Furstenberg, G. M. (1990). Growing international co-movement in stock price indexes. *Quarterly Review of Economics and Business.* New York: Jhon Wiley & Inc.

King, M., Sentana, E., & Wadhwani, S. (1994). Volatility and links between national stock markets. *Econometrica, 62*, 902–933.

King, M., & Wadhwani, S. (1990). Transmission of volatility between stock markets. *Review of Financial Studies, 3*, 901–933.

Lee, B. S., & Kim, K. J. (1993). Does the October 1987 crash strengthen the comovments among national stock markets? *Review of Financial Economics, 3*, 89–102.

Lessard, D. R. (1974). World, national and industry factors in equity returns. *Journal of Finance, 29*, 379–391.

Lin, W.-L., Engle, R., & Ito, T. (1994). Do bulls and bears move across borders? International transmission and stock returns and volatility. *Review of Financial Studies, 7*, 507–538.

Longin, F., & Solnik, B. (1995). Is the correlation in international equity returns constant: 1960–1990? *Journal of International Money and Finance, 14*, 3–26.

Odier, P., & Solnik, B. H. (1993). Lessons for international asset allocation. *Financial Analysts Journal, 49*, 63–77.

Rouwenhorst, K. G. (1999). European equity markets and the EMU. *Financial Analysts Journal, 55*, 57–64.

Solnik, B. (1999). *International investments* (4th Ed.). Reading, MA: Addison Wesley.

Solnik, B., Boucrelle, C., & Fur, Y. L. (1996). International market correlation and volatility. *Financial Analysts Journal, 52*, 17–34.

Solnik, B., & Jacques, R. (2000). Dispersion as cross-sectional correlation: Are stock markets becoming increasingly correlated? *Financial Analysts Journal, 56*, 54–61.

Sumel, R., & Engle, R. F. (1994). Hour volatility spillovers between international equity markets. *Journal of International Money and Finance, 13*, 3–25.

US, EUROPEAN AND ASIAN INVESTORS IN THE JAPANESE STOCK MARKET

Akiko Kamesaka

ABSTRACT

This paper investigates aggregate buying and selling by foreign investors, subdivided into US, European and Asian investors, in the Japanese stock market over the period 1981–2004. The results indicate that in the late 1990s US investors began to take more active positions than other foreign investors, and traded with good timing from the middle of the 1990s. US investors were also generally better than other investors when completing net purchases. While European and Asian investors also traded with good timing, other foreign investors generally did not net purchase or sell with good timing.

1. INTRODUCTION

The financial world is increasingly becoming complicated and integrated. From 1997, most Asian economies suddenly fell into a serious crisis, and the world has experienced several other financial crises in the most recent decade. We now know that the main cause of the Asian crisis was due to

Asia Pacific Financial Markets in Comparative Perspective: Issues and Implications for the 21st Century
Contemporary Studies in Economics and Financial Analysis, Volume 86, 199–219
ISSN: 1569-3759/doi:10.1016/S1569-3759(05)86010-3

unhedged borrowing in foreign currencies. However, we still do not know very much about how foreign investors were speculating in currency, stock or other financial markets of the region. While Japan's financial market was already in crisis from the early 1990s, following the beginning of the Asian crisis several large Japanese financial institutions, including Yamaichi Securities Companies, Sanyo Securities Co. and the Hokkaido Takushoku Bank, began to experience financial difficulties.[1]

It goes without saying that foreign investors play an important role in the Japanese stock market. Monthly surveys conducted by Quick Co., a Japanese research company, indicated that from June 1996 to October 1999 more than half of all professional investors in Japan continued to answer that foreign investors were the investor group that drew the most attention[2] (Wakasugi, Ohta, & Asano, 2001). The Fact Book of the Tokyo Stock Exchange reports that foreign investor purchases and sales in 2003 in the three largest Japanese markets (Tokyo, Osaka and Nagoya) amounted to 137 trillion yen, comprising more than 30 percent of the total purchases and sales of 435 trillion yen. The Fact Book also indicates that 89.3 percent of all trades in Japanese listed stocks were executed at the Tokyo Stock Exchange, 4.6 percent at the Osaka Stock Exchange and 0.2 percent at the Nagoya Stock Exchange.[3] At balance date 2003, foreign investors owned 17.7 percent of all listed stocks, based on the yen value of stock prices at the end of March 2003.[4] This grew from only 6.4 percent in 1981 and 10 percent in 1995, with further increases in the flow and balance of foreign holdings following the end of the Asian crisis.

The Tokyo Stock Exchange collects information on the yen value of client purchases and sales from securities firms each month. All client orders are categorized into trading by securities companies, banks, insurance companies, investment trusts, nonfinancial corporations, individuals, foreigners, etc. Foreigner's trading is further categorized into US, European, South-East Asian (hereafter, abbreviated as Asian) and other foreign investors. Kamesaka, Nofsinger, and Kawakita (2003) found that foreign investors and securities companies trade with good market timing, while domestic individual investors and nonfinancial companies performed relatively poorly.[5] However, the trades of foreign investors across different regions have never been analyzed statistically.[6] In this paper, I focus on the behavior of four types of foreign investors in Japan: US, European, Asian and other foreigners. The sample period is from January 1981 to June 2004. It covers the bubble period of the latter half of 1980s, followed by the crash in the early 1990s, and the internet bubble period around 1999. I analyze foreign investor behavior before, during and after the crash by dividing the data into three subperiods: from January 1981 to December 1989 (before the crash or bubble period), from January 1990 to December 1998 (during the crash) and from January 1999 to June 2004 (after the crash).

Fig. 1 shows the value of the TOPIX index in local currency, and the Yen/Dollar (JPY/USD) exchange rate from 1972 to 2003. As shown, general stock prices rose sharply from the middle of 1980s and reached a historical maximum of 2884.8 in December 1989, falling sharply thereafter. JPY has gradually increased its value relative to USD. In this paper I employ the TOPIX to investigate and evaluate foreigners' investment flows, rather than the Nikkei Index, the other major Japanese stock price index. This is because the TOPIX is based on all listed stocks in the First Section of the Tokyo Stock Exchange. As at year-end 2003, there were 1,533 listed companies on the Tokyo Stock Exchange's First Section, all of which are included in the TOPIX index, whereas the Nikkei index includes only 225 major stocks.

2. EVIDENCE

Fig. 2 graphs the annual net investment flow of US, European, Asian and other foreign investors in Japan. As shown, US investors began to take more

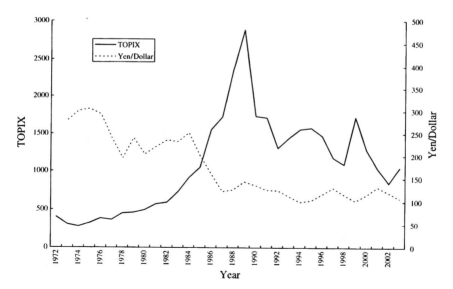

Fig. 1. Stock Index and Yen/Dollar Exchange Rate. *Note:* Closing Price of the TOPIX and Yen/Dollar Exchange Rate shown from Fiscal Years 1972 to 2003.

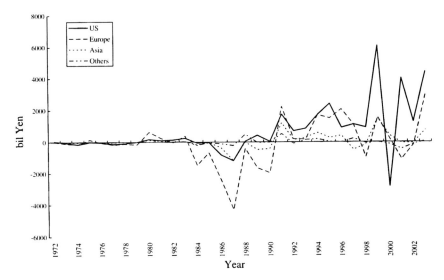

Fig. 2. Net Investment Flow of US, European, Asian and other Foreign Investors.
Note: Net Investment Flow of US, European, Asian and other Foreign Regions are
shown in Billion Yen from 1972 to 2003.

active positions from the late 1990s; they more actively changed their position in annual terms, and sold massively in 2000. They continued to be net
purchasers from 1988. On the other hand, European investors played the
largest role until the middle of the 1990s. European pension funds aimed to
make gains in the long term, and tried to realize profits before the crash was
expected. From the annual net investment flow, we can see that the trade
flows of all investor groups tend to move in the same direction: that is, when
European investors are net purchasers, US, Asian and foreigners of other
regions also tend to be net purchasers.

Table 1 lists the mean, standard deviation, minimum, maximum, median,
first-quarter and third-quarter of monthly buying and selling of fund flows
for each foreign investor group. The statistics are calculated by dividing
the dataset into three subperiods: 1981–1989, when the Japanese market
experienced continuous stock appreciation; 1990–1998, when the market
experienced a sharp decline and the Asian crisis; and 1999–2004, when the
market experienced the internet bubble and afterwards. The Net Purchases
(NP) and Net Purchases Ratio (NPR) of foreign investor group *i* during

Table 1. Summary Statistics of the Fund Flows of Different Foreign Investment Types.

		Mean	S.D.	Minimum	Maximum	Median	1st Qrt	3rd Qrt
Panel A: 1981–1989								
Purchases in billion yen	US	166.2	132.9	17.9	735.3	115.7	70.6	264.8
	Europe	561.6	342.0	90.7	1620.9	471.4	301.3	825.1
	Asia	241.1	188.9	30.7	710.5	138.6	95.5	407.7
	Others	112.6	105.3	4.4	510.9	69.6	30.6	189.6
Sales in billion yen	US	177.3	150.4	15.2	659.6	109.8	52.6	296.1
	Europe	659.7	428.3	113.3	1817.6	512.1	320.4	1011.4
	Asia	261.5	214.7	37.3	905.5	146.8	91.8	451.7
	Others	113.2	101.3	4.1	458.6	88.9	23.1	177.9
Net purchases in billion yen	US	−11.0	79.8	−371.1	293.7	−2.2	−32.9	29.6
	Europe	−98.1	196.9	−1063.1	489.7	−55.9	−180.4	24.3
	Asia	−20.3	67.1	−531.7	106.4	−9.8	−35.8	12.5
	Others	−0.6	29.7	−96.8	81.6	0.3	−14.7	9.7
Net purchases ratio	US	0.001	0.194	−0.391	0.613	−0.011	−0.134	0.123
	Europe	−0.065	0.135	−0.479	0.215	−0.060	−0.138	0.031
	Asia	−0.028	0.116	−0.416	0.242	−0.021	−0.090	0.047
	Others	0.000	0.139	−0.401	0.415	0.004	−0.074	0.094
	Return	0.016	0.043	−0.108	0.149	0.019	−0.008	0.042
	Yen/dollar	−0.003	0.036	−0.093	0.074	0.004	−0.029	0.020
Panel B: 1990–1998								
Purchases in billion yen	US	597.7	324.2	159.1	1493.5	488.5	310.2	854.6
	Europe	729.6	259.5	235.5	1489.1	677.8	544.0	918.2
	Asia	336.6	103.1	142.1	563.9	338.6	250.0	404.7
	Others	111.5	66.1	45.2	374.2	88.7	74.8	125.5

Table 1. (Continued)

		Mean	S.D.	Minimum	Maximum	Median	1st Qrt	3rd Qrt
Sales in billion yen	US	500.4	289.7	118.3	1276.2	417.7	247.3	698.6
	Europe	673.2	242.5	259.7	1504.3	651.5	476.1	862.9
	Asia	319.6	98.3	138.4	551.9	325.5	235.5	399.7
	Others	106.8	65.7	40.1	361.7	86.9	68.5	115.1
Net purchases in billion yen	US	97.3	190.9	−374.8	658.4	58.6	−13.4	184.7
	Europe	56.4	205.1	−666.5	618.3	53.7	−57.0	161.3
	Asia	17.0	79.4	−196.4	313.1	8.7	−23.5	62.7
	Others	4.6	34.8	−183.0	145.0	3.4	−7.1	19.6
Net purchases ratio	US	0.096	0.155	−0.243	0.496	0.078	−0.009	0.188
	Europe	0.040	0.128	−0.285	0.370	0.045	−0.043	0.121
	Asia	0.025	0.111	−0.216	0.402	0.017	−0.043	0.088
	Others	0.024	0.112	−0.505	0.380	0.024	−0.041	0.104
	Return	−0.009	0.066	−0.228	0.167	−0.010	−0.048	0.030
	Yen/dollar	−0.002	0.036	−0.156	0.100	−0.001	−0.021	0.019
Panel C: 1999–2004								
Purchases in billion yen	US	934.6	1019.6	108.4	3029.3	254.9	192.4	1954.8
	Europe	889.4	924.0	131.1	3344.1	339.3	187.5	1790.3
	Asia	442.6	467.5	72.9	1465.1	140.6	101.6	923.3
	Others	82.1	102.9	8.9	361.3	29.6	22.0	84.4
Sales in billion yen	US	868.2	998.3	107.2	3263.0	214.4	168.9	1773.9
	Europe	855.8	898.0	132.6	3363.7	306.5	193.0	1674.1
	Asia	411.7	433.1	71.3	1428.4	132.2	106.3	840.1
	Others	85.1	107.5	11.6	380.5	30.5	20.9	91.3
Net purchases in billion yen	US	66.4	306.3	−977.6	1170.8	27.3	1.9	67.2
	Europe	33.6	95.4	−194.5	393.5	19.7	−11.6	58.4

	Asia Others	30.9 −3.0	89.7 9.1	−140.1 −31.6	306.7 19.3	6.1 −1.4	−4.4 −6.1	26.9 1.3
Net purchases ratio	US	0.058	0.086	−0.201	0.301	0.057	0.005	0.104
	Europe	0.016	0.052	−0.134	0.118	0.026	−0.021	0.049
	Asia	0.021	0.060	−0.136	0.191	0.015	−0.017	0.064
	Others	−0.014	0.064	−0.148	0.187	−0.020	−0.058	0.023
	Return	0.001	0.050	−0.091	0.123	0.004	−0.039	0.041
	Yen/dollar	−0.001	0.029	−0.058	0.073	0.000	−0.020	0.013

month t are defined as follows:

$$NP_{it} = (PurchasingValue_{it} - SellingValue_{it}) \tag{1}$$

$$NPR_{it} = \frac{(PurchasingValue_{it} - SellingValue_{it})}{(PurchasingValue_{it} + SellingValue_{it})} \tag{2}$$

As indicated, both NP and NPR will be positive (negative) when the foreign investor group i buys more (less) equities than it sells, and will equal zero when purchases equal sales. NPR will equal one when all trades of foreign investor group i are buying, and will equal minus one when all trades of foreign investor group i are selling.

Panel A of Table 1 shows that in the 1980s more than half of all trades by foreign investors were conducted by European investors. The panel also shows that Asian investors took a larger role than US investors for the same period. The maximum and minimum values are at their most extreme for European investors. Panel B of the table shows that European investors continued to take the largest share of foreigners' purchases and sales in the 1990s. However, US investors then began to overtake European investors, and took on the highest values for purchases, net purchases and the net purchases ratio. Purchases and Sales in Panels A–C show that the aggregate trades of US, European and Asian investors, respectively, increased from the bubble period to during the crash, irrespective of the fall in stock prices, and from during the crash period to after the crash period. Panel C indicates that US investors began to play the largest role of all four groups after this period.

Table 2 presents the correlation coefficients between the flows of funds of each investor group across the three different subperiods. The results show that US, European and Asian investors tended to increase or decrease purchases, sales and net purchases at the same time, before, during and after the crash. However, while their purchases and net purchases increased when stock prices were increasing, sales do not appear to have any relation with the stock return. Therefore, there was an asymmetry between their purchases and sales and the stock return, and the asymmetry continued throughout the period under investigation. The investment flows, whether they are in gross or in net terms, also do not appear to display any relation with the JPY/USD exchange rate.

Table 3 examines the causality relationships between the net purchases of each foreign investor group and the index return using VAR analysis. While the Akaike information criterion and Schwarz' Bayes information criterion suggest that relatively longer lags should be included for the VAR, since most of the coefficients become insignificant after just a few months, the

Table 2. Correlation Matrix.

	US	Europe	Asia	Others	Return	Yen/Dollar
Panel A: 1981–1989						
Purchases						
US	1.000					
Europe	0.868	1.000				
Asia	0.885	0.938	1.000			
Others	0.874	0.894	0.889	1.000		
Return	0.151	0.305	0.229	0.129	1.000	
Yen/dollar	−0.001	−0.116	−0.059	−0.026	−0.114	1.000
Sales						
US	1.000					
Europe	0.933	1.000				
Asia	0.930	0.960	1.000			
Others	0.879	0.882	0.896	1.000		
Return	−0.004	0.089	0.070	0.028	1.000	
Yen/dollar	−0.021	−0.085	−0.065	0.000	−0.114	1.000
Net purchases						
US	1.000					
Europe	0.740	1.000				
Asia	0.689	0.793	1.000			
Others	0.493	0.603	0.548	1.000		
Return	0.260	0.337	0.420	0.361	1.000	
Yen/dollar	0.038	−0.015	0.041	−0.093	−0.114	1.000
Net purchases ratio						
US	1.000					
Europe	0.692	1.000				
Asia	0.606	0.778	1.000			
Others	0.536	0.725	0.639	1.000		
Return	0.333	0.478	0.469	0.334	1.000	
Yen/dollar	−0.058	−0.135	−0.079	−0.149	−0.114	1.000

Table 2. (*Continued*)

	US	Europe	Asia	Others	Return	Yen/Dollar
Panel B: 1990–1998						
Purchases						
US	1.000					
Europe	0.778	1.000				
Asia	0.577	0.772	1.000			
Others	−0.228	0.178	0.318	1.000		
Return	0.246	0.227	0.299	0.007	1.000	
Yen/Dollar	0.049	0.059	−0.015	−0.079	−0.032	1.000
Sales						
US	1.000					
Europe	0.715	1.000				
Asia	0.656	0.830	1.000			
Others	−0.157	0.391	0.365	1.000		
Return	−0.055	−0.080	0.020	−0.067	1.000	
Yen/dollar	0.028	0.084	0.059	−0.049	−0.032	1.000
Net purchases						
US	1.000					
Europe	0.651	1.000				
Asia	0.638	0.651	1.000			
Others	0.038	0.175	0.372	1.000		
Return	0.502	0.382	0.363	0.141	1.000	
Yen/dollar	0.041	−0.024	−0.092	−0.058	−0.032	1.000
Net purchases ratio						
US	1.000					
Europe	0.676	1.000				
Asia	0.716	0.652	1.000			
Others	0.248	0.242	0.393	1.000		
Return	0.507	0.327	0.303	0.123	1.000	
Yen/Dollar	0.006	0.031	−0.070	−0.062	−0.032	1.000

Panel C: 1999–2004

Purchases

	US	Europe	Asia	Others	Return	Yen/dollar
US	1.000					
Europe	0.962	1.000				
Asia	0.970	0.981	1.000			
Others	0.777	0.873	0.856	1.000		
Return	0.141	0.066	0.056	-0.128	1.000	
Yen/dollar	-0.066	-0.023	-0.020	0.058	-0.167	1.000

Sales

	US	Europe	Asia	Others	Return	Yen/dollar
US	1.000					
Europe	0.978	1.000				
Asia	0.980	0.982	1.000			
Others	0.885	0.878	0.889	1.000		
Return	-0.009	0.024	-0.016	-0.143	1.000	
Yen/Dollar	0.014	-0.017	0.000	0.061	-0.167	1.000

Net purchases

	US	Europe	Asia	Others	Return	Yen/dollar
US	1.000					
Europe	0.342	1.000				
Asia	0.582	0.423	1.000			
Others	0.229	0.152	0.429	1.000		
Return	0.495	0.416	0.367	0.246	1.000	
Yen/dollar	-0.265	-0.060	-0.107	-0.065	-0.167	1.000

Net purchases ratio

	US	Europe	Asia	Others	Return	Yen/dollar
US	1.000					
Europe	0.437	1.000				
Asia	0.555	0.580	1.000			
Others	0.104	0.285	0.236	1.000		
Return	0.601	0.518	0.531	0.272	1.000	
Yen/dollar	-0.263	-0.257	-0.247	-0.065	-0.167	1.000

Table 3. VAR Statistics.

		US	Europe	Asia	Others	Return	Yen/Dollar
Panel A: 1981–1989							
US	-1	0.1948	0.0703	-0.1568	-0.0855*	0.0000	-
	-2	0.0391	-0.4008	0.0316	0.0143	0.0000	-
	-3	0.1739	0.6139**	0.1336	0.0958*	0.0001	-
Europe	-1	0.0510	0.3963*	0.0438	-0.0008	-0.0001	-
	-2	0.0685	0.4099*	0.2188*	0.0513	0.0002**	-
	-3	0.1326	0.3108	-0.0293	-0.0158	-0.0001	-
Asia	-1	0.1276	-0.0270	0.4293**	0.1953**	0.0003**	-
	-2	-0.2255	-0.6493	-0.3397	-0.1866**	0.0000	-
	-3	-0.3719	-0.7346	-0.0424	-0.1159	-0.0002	-
Others	-1	0.0542	1.4421*	-0.2558	0.2640*	-0.0002	-
	-2	0.0671	-1.4728*	-0.3626	0.1507	-0.0003	-
	-3	-0.1580	-1.0845	0.2054	0.2083	0.0002	-
Return	-1	-58.9584	-698.2140*	-41.3113	-67.4989	0.0430	-
	-2	-337.6810*	-986.2250**	-426.3160**	-93.4062	-0.1650	-
	-3	-161.0100	-710.4730*	-25.2501	29.9193	0.1114	-
Yen/dollar	-1	-38.8169	169.0910	-268.1200	29.9193	-0.1977	-
	-2	7.7106	281.8410	79.2528	92.6521	0.0366	-
	-3	254.8640	-619.2360	-53.6281	-45.0747	0.0034	-
Constant		18.9231*	24.1536	10.5398	4.6488	0.0180***	-
Adjusted R^2		0.2724	0.5056	0.2758	0.3253	0.1005	-
F-test		1.5901*	3.2048***	2.1123**	2.2052**	1.9051**	-
Panel B: 1990–1998							
US	-1	0.4093**	0.1035	-0.0738	-0.0523	0.0000	-
	-2	-0.1466	-0.1554	0.0764	0.0123	0.0000	-
	-3	0.0855	0.1228	0.0044	-0.0236	0.0000	-

Europe	−1	0.1395	0.3810**	0.0274	−0.0054	0.0001
	−2	−0.0251	0.2823**	0.0196	0.0139	0.0000
	−3	−0.0620	−0.1548	−0.0173	−0.0036	0.0000
Asia	−1	−0.3688	0.4312	0.4890***	0.1339*	0.0001
	−2	0.1824	−0.3830	−0.0793	0.0159	−0.0001
	−3	0.3349	0.3324	−0.0216	−0.0298	0.0000
Others	−1	−0.4832	−0.3581	−0.1187	0.1765	0.0001
	−2	−0.2310	−0.4056	0.1838	−0.0790	−0.0006***
	−3	0.7884	0.8173	0.6496***	0.1339	0.0002
Return	−1	534.1840	−65.8281	246.1380*	41.5995	−0.0245
	−2	−109.9610	−391.0480	−162.2320	16.9619	0.0132
	−3	−613.7340*	−156.9900	−200.3610	32.2777	−0.0145
Yen/dollar	−1	−265.1380	−26.6600	9.0284	137.8600	−0.1485
	−2	1117.2400**	−123.8210	285.8280	−103.8840	0.0443
	−3	−343.3540	666.4720	−278.2990	90.0313	0.1803
Constant		58.3922**	14.5007	4.5430	8.0793	−0.0071
Adjusted R^2		0.1524	0.2931	0.2432	0.0139	−0.0063
F-test		0.9067	1.2989	1.1484	0.7114	1.1063
Panel C: 1999–2004						
US	−1	0.7552***	−0.1370*	0.1837***	0.0086	0.0000
	−2	−0.0445	0.1044	−0.0880	−0.0029	0.0000
	−3	0.2701*	0.0243	0.1251***	0.0205***	0.0001
Europe	−1	0.3383	−0.1423	0.6601***	0.0058	0.0000
	−2	−0.2246	−0.1498	−0.0265	0.0196	0.0000
	−3	0.6122*	0.1794	0.2595***	0.0056	0.0001
Asia	−1	0.1039	0.5158**	0.0780	−0.0311	0.0001
	−2	−1.7211***	0.0234	−0.3167**	0.0030	−0.0003*
	−3	0.3064	−0.1709	−0.0703	−0.0569***	0.0000
Others	−1	3.1306	−1.2176	0.7103	0.1736	−0.0007
	−2	−2.5551	2.2851	−4.1160***	−0.1178	0.0009
	−3	−2.1929	1.7682	−0.0597	0.1396	0.0001

AKIKO KAMESAKA

Table 3. (*Continued*)

		US	Europe	Asia	Others	Return	Yen/Dollar
Return	−1	−516.3220	411.5340	−188.2880	−1.0143	0.0787	–
	−2	514.1870	135.6050	97.4990	35.6136	0.2245	–
	−3	−248.3010	−92.8360	−24.4458	−5.3016	0.0170	–
Yen/dollar	−1	688.2920	187.8320	516.3150*	22.1579	0.1093	–
	−2	−402.3480	59.0827	−48.2303	17.4442	0.2284	–
	−3	−27.7280	−450.0270	69.0654	−14.9377	−0.0820	–
Constant		−0.8366	23.9482*	−11.1991	−2.3190*	−0.0010	–
Adjusted R^2		0.5849	0.2352	0.6511	0.3860	0.0052	–
F-test		2.0910**	1.5017	6.2118***	2.6660***	0.9094	–

* $p < 0.1$.
** $p < 0.05$.
*** $p < 0.01$.

results of three-month lag are shown. Panel A of the table indicates that before the crash period, European, Asian and other foreign investors, respectively, tended to be the net purchasers after their own net purchases: that is, after the month they net purchase, we expect net purchasing in the following month. The same panel also shows that US, European and Asian investors tended to be net purchasers a few months after a price fall. Stock returns are shown to have increased following European and Asian investors' net purchases during 1980s.

Panel B shows the results of the long crash period in the 1990s. During this subperiod, US investors were net purchasers after their own net purchases of the previous month. European and Asian investors were also net purchasers after their own net purchases. US, European and Asian investors tended to be net purchasers after a few months' stock price decline, after observing the symptoms of price recovery. Panel C shows that US investors continued to be net purchasers after their own net purchases of the previous month from the late 1990s, during and after the internet bubbles. However, the relation between the net purchases and that of the previous month disappeared in this period for each of the other foreign investor groups, respectively. Asian investors tend to buy after the US and European investors' net purchases during this period. Considering the increase in the size of the US investor trade after the middle of the 1990s (Table 1), US investors then began to exert the largest influence on the Japanese stock market.[7]

In order to evaluate which foreign investor groups traded with good timing, I estimate the aggregate one-month following return after foreigners' net purchases or net sales based on each foreign investor group's net investment flow (Grinblatt & Titman (1993) and Kamesaka et al.(2003)):[8]

$$\text{Aggregate Following One Month Returns}_{it}$$
$$= \sum^{s=t}(\text{PurchasingValue}_{is} - \text{SellingValue}_{is})IR_{s+1} \qquad (3)$$

whereas, I denote an indicator function that takes either one or zero under the conditions defined later in this section.

Fig. 3 presents the performance measure of each of the four groups of foreign investors after their net purchase, by imposing a condition to Eq. (3) that I takes a value of one when (Purchasing Value$_{is}$ − Selling Value$_{is}$) > 0, and zero, otherwise. Earlier studies do not distinguish between positive returns after net purchase (net purchase before stock price increase) from negative returns after net sales (net sales before stock price falls). However, here they are separated by the inclusion of the indicator function. In this

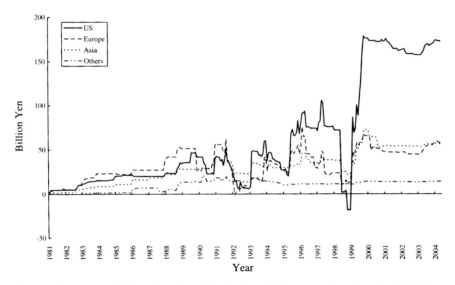

Fig. 3. Aggregate Following One-Month Stock Returns after Foreign Net Purchase. *Note:* Aggregate Following One-Month Stock Returns after Net Purchase of US, European, Asian and other Foreign Investors are shown using Monthly Dataset for the Period 1981–2004.

figure, foreign investor i's trade is evaluated by the following month's return only when positive net purchases by investor i are observed. Eq. (3) adds this monthly evaluation measure up to time t, such that Fig. 3 ensures the stability of each foreigner's trade performance throughout the period. The figure clearly shows that US investors were performing best in the Japanese stock market. Their superior performance was achieved mainly in 1999, during the period of the internet bubble. While US investors suffered large losses after the Asian crisis, they made much larger gains during the internet bubble. The performance of European and Asian investors show similar patterns to US investors. That is, after losses following the Asian crisis, recovery was achieved. The differences in performance among US, European and Asian investors are most apparent in 1999, with the apparent superiority of US investors mainly brought about by active purchasing.

Fig. 4 captures each foreign investor group's performance after their net sales, by imposing a condition to Eq. (3), that I takes a value of one when (Purchasing Value$_{is}$ − Selling Value$_{is}$) < 0, and zero, otherwise. In Fig. 4, foreign investor i's trade is evaluated by the following month's return only when positive net sales by investor i are observed. When we observe net sales

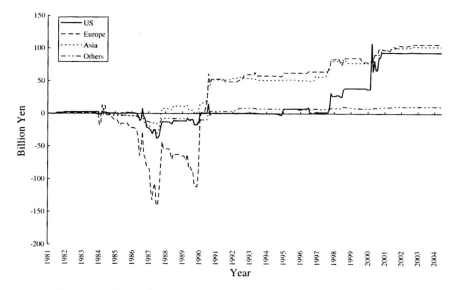

Fig. 4. Aggregate Following One-Month Stock Returns after Foreign Net Selling. *Note:* Aggregate Following One-Month Stock Returns after Net Selling of US, European, Asian and other Foreign Investors are shown using Monthly Dataset for the Period 1981–2004.

by foreign investor i, (Purchasing Value$_{is}$ − Selling Value$_{is}$) will be negative, and if we observe negative stock return after they sell, it means that they have net sold before a stock price fall, which can be used to suggest that they have successfully sold before the stock price fall. If this is indeed the case, we may expect to observe positive performance values as defined in Eq. (3) for Fig. 4. The results indicate that the performance of US, European and Asian investors are at the same level when the data period from January 1981 to June 2004 is aggregated. One difference is that European and Asian investors sold with good timing, especially in the early 1990s, whereas US investors sold with good timing only after 1997, and after the Asian crisis had begun. Fig. 4 shows that European investors were selling with bad timing from the middle of the 1980s to the late 1980s, however, these sales were mainly from stocks invested before the beginning of the data period; that is, they started to invest in the 1970s, and sold after capital gains in the stock price bubble of the mid-1980s. The dataset employed in this manuscript is only available after 1980 and there appears to be no possible means of evaluating European investors' net sales in the 1980s. It is, however, likely that they sold at a higher price than they had previously purchased, and gained from their long-term investments in Japan.

Summing up Figs. 3 and 4, US, European and Asian investors were buying and selling with good timing. US investors performed relatively better, especially after the internet bubbles in the late 1990s, and they were also particularly better when net purchasing.[9] European and Asian investors also performed well; however, other foreign investors did not make profit or losses from investing in Japan. Previous studies have also shown that foreign investors are the market winners in Japan, while in this study it has been shown that European and Asian investors were performing relatively better until the early 1990s, while US investors began to perform better after the middle of the 1990s.

3. CONCLUSIONS

This paper investigates over 20 years' aggregate trade performance of US, European and Asian investors in the Japanese stock market. While the Tokyo Stock Exchange collects the yen value of aggregate purchases and sales each month, the trades of foreign investors of different regions have never been analyzed statistically in any previous work. The sample period employed is from January 1981 to June 2004, and covers the bubble period of the second half of the 1980s, followed by the crash in the early 1990s. The study examines the behavior of foreign investors in different regions, before, during and after the crash by dividing the data into three subperiods: from January 1981 to December 1989 (before the crash or bubble period), from January 1990 to December 1998 (during the crash) and from January 1999 to June 2004 (after the crash).

The results before, during and after the crash indicate that all foreign investors increased their purchases, sales and net purchases (purchases less sales) at the same time. They increased their purchases and net purchases while stock prices were increasing, however, no relation was found between sales and stock returns. Therefore, an asymmetry exists between purchases, sales and stock price returns, and this asymmetry continues to exist regardless of the changes in the Japanese stock market. Foreign investors of each region tended to increase their net purchases after each investor's own net purchases of the previous month and after a few months' stock price fall before and during the crash period. However, these tended to disappear after the crash period. The stock prices tended to increase after European and Asian investors' net purchases during the 1980s, however, the relation disappears in the 1990s and thereafter.

By evaluating the one-month following return, I also observe positive stock returns following each foreign investor's net purchases, and negative stock returns after net sales. US investors performed extremely well by net purchasing during the internet bubble around 1999. The overall performance of net sales did not differ among US, European and Asian investors. However, I should also note that the European investors sold after the stock price appreciation from the middle of the 1980s, and it is likely that they gained from investing in Japan by selling stocks they bought in the 1970s.

NOTES

1. Ito (2000) details the failures of Japanese financial institutions before and after the Asian crisis

2. The Quick Co. sends questionnaires to over 300 professional stock investors each month, with the response rate exceeding 50 percent since the commencement of the surveys.

3. There was also 5.9 percent of off-the-board trade in the year 2003.

4. The Tokyo Stock Exchange reports investor groups' stock holding based on closing prices in March, since the accounting year ends in March for most Japanese firms.

5. Kamesaka (Murase) (1999, 2003) also find foreigners trading with good market timing in the Japanese market. Hamao and Mei (2001) also analyze the Japanese market. Choe, Kho, and Stulz (1999, 2000) find domestic investors have better information than foreigners. Kim (2000) finds that foreigners out-perform domestic individuals in large stocks, however, under-perform in small stocks. Kamesaka and Wang (2001) find that foreign purchases from domestic investors out-perform domestic investors' purchases from foreign investors in Indonesia before the Asian crisis. Kamesaka and Wang (2005) analyze Thailand's stock market and find that foreigners consistently traded with good timing before, during and after the Asian crisis, regardless of the large changes in market conditions.

6. Shirota (2002) documents related statistics and a calendar of events regarding foreign investors in Japan.

7. In spite of these results, Japanese investors tend to gain an understanding of the total purchases and sales of the four groups of foreign investors by understanding the positions of European investors (Kusano, 2001). They therefore tend to underestimate the effect of trading by US investors.

8. Kamesaka (Murase) (1999, 2003) also use this measure to evaluate investment performance of main investor groups in Japan using weekly and monthly data, respectively.

9. US investors' superiority in overall market timing remains, even when their trade performance is evaluated using a three-month following returns or US dollar-based stock returns.

ACKNOWLEDGMENTS

The author would like to thank Yoshitaka Kurosawa, Mikiyo Niizeki, Jun Shirota, Yoshiro Tsutsui, Katsunari Yamaguchi and other participants at the Japanese Economic Association, the Japan Society of Monetary Economics and the Nippon Finance Association meetings for helpful comments on earlier versions of this paper. Financial support from the Japan Society for the Promotion of Science, Grants-in-Aid for Young Scientists (B15730164) and a competitive grant from the Ryukoku University Research Institute for Social Sciences are also gratefully acknowledged.

REFERENCES

Choe, H., Kho, B., & Stulz, R. (1999). Do foreign investors destabilize stock markets? The Korean experience in 1997. *Journal of Financial Economics, 54*(2), 227–264.

Choe, H., Kho, B., & Stulz, R. (2000). *Do domestic investors have more valuable information about individual stocks than foreign investors?* Ohio State University Working Paper.

Grinblatt, M., & Titman, S. (1993). Performance measurement without benchmarks: An examination of mutual fund returns. *Journal of Business, 66*(1), 47–68.

Hamao, Y., & Mei, J. (2001). Living with the 'enemy': An analysis of foreign investment in the Japanese equity market. *Journal of International Money and Finance, 20*(5), 715–735.

Ito, T. (2000). The stagnant Japanese economy in the 1990s: The need for financial supervision to restore sustained growth. In: T. Hoshi & H. Patrick (Eds), *Crisis and change in the Japanese financial system* (pp. 85–107). Dordrencht: Kluwer.

Kamesaka, A. (Murase, A.) (1999). Stock investment performance of main investor groups in Japanese market. In: H. Baba (Ed.), *Myth and reality of Japanese firms.* Tokyo, Japan: Daito Bunka University Institute of Business Research Book Series No. 16. Reprinted in *Review of Monetary and Financial Studies,* (17), 66–78 (2001) (in Japanese).

Kamesaka, A. (2003). Investor groups in Japan. In: T. Hayashi & K. Matsuura Y. Yonezawa (Eds), *Financial problems in Japan.* Tokyo, Japan: Nippon Hyouron Sha (in Japanese).

Kamesaka, A., Nofsinger, J., & Kawakita, H. (2003). Investment patterns and performance of investor groups in Japan. Pacific Basin Finance Journal, 1–22.

Kamesaka, A., & Wang, J. (2001). *Foreign and domestic investors in Indonesia.* Ryukoku University and University of New South Wales Working Paper, presented at the Ministry of Finance, Indonesia.

Kamesaka, A., & Wang, J. (2005). *The Asian crisis and investor behavior in Thailand's equity market.* Presented at the American Economic Association meetings 2005 in Philadelphia.

Kim, W. (2000). Do foreign investors perform better than locals? *Information asymmetry versus investor sophistication.* KDI School of Public Policy and Management Working Paper.

Kusano, T. (2001). QSS stock research and behavior of foreign investors. In: T. Wakasugi, H. Ohta, & Y. Asano (Eds), *Formation of investors' expectation and market price movement. (Tousika no Yosoukeisei to Souba doukou.)* Tokyo, Japan: Nikkei BP Planning Inc. (in Japanese).

Shirota, J. (2002). *Foreign investors in the Japanese stock market.* Tokyo, Japan: Toyo Keizai Inc. (in Japanese).

Wakasugi, T., Ohta, H., & Asano, Y. (Eds) (2001). *A supplement to formation of investors' expectation and market price movement. (Tousika no Yosoukeisei to Souba doukou.)* Tokyo, Japan: Nikkei BP Planning Inc. (in Japanese).

THE OPTIONS HOLDING CONCENTRATION PROBLEM: EVIDENCE FROM AUSTRALIAN LISTED CORPORATIONS

Tyrone M. Carlin and Guy Ford

ABSTRACT

The literature on executive options has burgeoned over the past decade. While early literature tended to expound the benefits associated with the adoption of options plans, more recent literature has taken on a more cautionary tone. Recent empirical research has suggested a range of conditions under which the adoption of options plans might result in unanticipated outcomes. This paper adds to the literature by discussing options holding concentration, which we define as the proportion of options outstanding under a firm's executive options plan held by a firm's board and the top five non-board executives. We examine previous empirical literature on executive options plans and some of the incentive problems associated with the implementation of such plans, which have been reported in the literature. On the basis of these discussions, we discuss why it might plausibly be expected that options holding concentration could represent a variable with the power to explain the degree to which incentive problems are encountered by organisations, which employ

Asia Pacific Financial Markets in Comparative Perspective: Issues and Implications for the 21st Century
Contemporary Studies in Economics and Financial Analysis, Volume 86, 221–234
ISSN: 1569-3759/doi:10.1016/S1569-3759(05)86011-5

executive options schemes. We report observed options holding concentration for a sample of Australian listed corporations between 1997 and 2002, but demonstrate that while significantly inversely associated with firm size, holdings concentration does not appear to be associated with factors which point towards organisational risk taking and cash payment policy choices. We discuss possible reasons for our findings and suggest potential future research extensions flowing from our work.

INTRODUCTION

Debates about the use of options as a component of employee compensation have burgeoned in the past few years. Much of the heat in this debate has surrounded the contentious issue of how best to account for and report on the financial consequences of using options as an element of remuneration (Core & Guay, 2001; Hall & Murphy, 2002). It is this element in particular of the wider debate which has attracted a considerable degree of attention from the business press, thus bringing the argument into the public domain.

However, concern about the use of options plans has by no means been limited to issues of financial reporting and disclosure. A considerable body of literature has now developed in which the key thematic element relates to the incentive compatibility consequences of the adoption of options plans as a component of employee remuneration. The accumulation of knowledge embodied in this stream of literature is now giving rise to concern that, contrary to the agency theory derived expectations of the value of options as tools for mitigating principal agency problems and thus generating improved shareholder value creation outcomes (Jensen & Meckling, 1976; Jensen & Murphy, 1990), a range of perverse, value-destroying incentives may be introduced as a result of the implementation of options-based compensation plans. Examples of problems identified in the literature thus far include evidence of opportunistically timed disclosures to capital markets (Aboody & Kasnik, 2000), questionably motivated share buyback programmes (Yermack, 2001; Aboody & Kasnik, 2001), material changes to dividend policy (Lambert, Lanen, & Larcker, 1989) and changes to the risk profile of projects undertaken by firms (Chen, 2002).

In this paper, we examine one little researched aspect of the options debate, the question of options holding concentration, and present empirical evidence on whether holding concentration appears to be associated with the types of problems evident from the literature discussed above.

The remainder of this paper proceeds as follows. In the next section, we expand our discussion of the potential for the use of options plans to introduce incentives for option recipients to act in ways which are not necessarily commensurate with the objective of shareholder value creation. We then define options holding concentration and present our arguments as to why we view the phenomenon as potentially problematic. In light of these arguments, we present data on the degree to which options holding concentration appears to be associated with a range of financial factors, including size, leverage and dividend policy. Finally, we provide analysis of our empirical results and present our conclusions.

OPTIONS AND INCENTIVE PROBLEMS

As discussed above, the use of options has been argued to represent an effective means of overcoming many agency difficulties by directly tying managerial wealth outcomes to share price, and thus to the wealth outcomes of a firm's body of shareholders at large.[1] That at least is the theory. However, we have also referred to the growing body of evidence that share options schemes associated with a range of dubious behaviour on the part of executives.

This represents a clear threat to good firm governance, since the vehicle adopted by many boards of directors to modify incentive sets with a view to greater alignment between the interests of managers and shareholders may in fact in many settings represent a Trojan horse for the stimulation of the opposite effect. In part, this can be attributed to poor contract design.

The case of Sprint Telecommunications provides a useful insight into one reason why this may be so. It is common for options plans to contain "change of control" clauses, by which executives who have been the recipients of options grants have their interests conserved in the event that board membership or stock ownership changes sufficiently to yield control to another party, with potential implications for terms and conditions of employment, or indeed, loss of employment. Such a clause existed within the Sprint executive options plan, in which change of control was defined to incorporate a range of situations, including that in which shareholders voted to approve a mooted merger or disposal of the business.

However, the fact that a meeting of shareholders votes to approve a merger or business disposal does not mean that such events will actually transpire, for example as a result of regulatory (e.g. antitrust) intervention. In Sprint's case, in the aftermath of an outside acquisition proposal, shareholders met and approved the disposal of the business, which in turn triggered Sprint's executive option plan change of control clause. This caused immediate vesting of options held by executives, many of whom are reported to have exercised their rights (while the share price was boosted by the mooted acquisition deal) and immediately left the company (Monks, 2003). Ultimately, the acquisition did not proceed, due to a range of antitrust considerations. This type of situation seems difficult to reconcile with the objective of shareholder wealth creation. Corporate value appropriation seems a label which rings truer.

In other cases, the desired incentive alignment outcome is subverted by the expedient of executives entering into third party contractual arrangements which have the effect of relieving the executives of all or part of the risk which would otherwise burden them as a result of their receipt of executive options. Over recent years, financial institutions have engineered a range of mechanisms effectively allowing managers to realise value from and or reconfigure the risk profile of their options holdings, including fences and zero cost collars (Ali & Stapledon, 2000; Bettis, Bizjak, & Lemmon, 1999; Ellis, 1998). That this possibility is not explicitly excluded from many executive options plans also represents a material contractual design flaw.

A third species of contractual design flaw apparent in many executive options plans is the lack of control for the indiscriminate reward of managers irrespective of actual performance in situations where equity valuations are rising in general. Allowing the value of executive options to vary solely based on the underlying share price has been described as giving rise to a situation where the options are "wildly capricious in their distribution of rewards, inefficient as motivators and inordinately expensive for shareholders." (Cairncross, 1999). Despite this, the incorporation of devices which strip out the impact of whole of market price movements leaving managers exposed to that component of price change explained by outperformance relative to peers has been reported to represent the exception rather than the rule (Meulbroek, 2001).

The existence of these types of contractual design flaws (and others not catalogued here), while damaging, does not explain the full extent of scepticism voiced as to the likelihood that executive options schemes will fail to appropriately align the interests of managers with those of the shareholders as a general body. Conceivably, opportunistically timed voluntary information disclosures (Aboody & Kasnik, 2000) released strategically prior to grant dates (where bad news releases may depress share price and thus exercise price), and vesting dates (where good news releases may increase share prices and thus option holder wealth) may take place irrespective of other contractual design weaknesses.

Similarly, there is no reason to believe that the decision to adopt higher risk profile projects (as described by Chen, 2002), or the decision to restrict dividend payments (as described by Lambert, Lanen, & Larcker, 1989) is excluded merely because of the absence of the types of contractual design flaws discussed above. The same could be argued in relation to the propensity to engage in price supporting or inflating share buybacks to the possible exclusion of dividend payments or net present value (NPV) positive project investments (as discussed in Aboody & Kasnik, 2001). Rather, there is reason to believe that these are problems which are general in their character, and can therefore be anticipated to present themselves, to some extent, wherever executive options schemes are in place. We contend, however, that there may be reasons to expect that the likelihood of the types of behaviours described above manifesting themselves and their materiality may be accentuated as a result of the variable of particular interest within this study, options holding concentration. The next section of this paper defines this phenomenon and provides our intuition as to why it is a variable of potential explanatory interest in the context of research into incentive compatibility problems associated with executive options schemes.

HOLDING CONCENTRATION DATA AND PROBLEM CONTENTION

The term "holding concentration" refers to a measurement of the degree to which the ownership of options issued pursuant to an organisation's executive options scheme is concentrated in the hands of a select group of senior actors, defined in this study to include the board (including executive and non-executive members), the chief executive officer and highest remunerated five non-director executives employed by the firm. Thus holdings concentration represents the percentage of outstanding options issued by an organisation held by the group of senior actors defined above. On the basis of disclosures contained within the annual financial statements of a sample of Australian listed public corporations, it is possible to gather data on options issuance and holdings to this level of detail.

Our sample consisted of the 100 largest corporations (as measured by market capitalisation) whose equity securities were listed for quotation on the Australian Stock Exchange (ASX) as at 1997. We gathered data relating to the options plans and in place within these corporations, as well as other operational and financial variables of interest, for a six-year period ending in

2002.[2] Of the 100 companies in our sample, only 17 had no option plan of any sort in place during the period spanning 1997 through 2002. Therefore, 83% of the companies in our sample did have an options plan in place at some stage during the six years studies.

Based on financial statement disclosures made by the companies in our sample, we were able to measure the degree of options holding concentration (as defined above) for each organisation with an options plan in place during each of the years under consideration. This data is set out in Table 1.

Our data suggest a significant degree of holdings concentration in large publicly listed Australian corporations. In the only other published research of which we are aware which touches on this issue, Blasi, Kruse, and Bernstein (2003, p. 190) suggest senior executive holding concentration in top 100 U.S.-based firms at around 33%. It would therefore seem that at least in aggregate, the Australian experience is similar to that of the United States.

Though options holding concentration has not received a high volume of attention in the literature on executive options, earlier work does offer some conjectures on the questions of the situations in which options holding concentration is likely to be most defined as well as the problems which might arise as a consequence. Blasi et al. (2003) suggest that options holding concentration is most likely to be pronounced in larger, more established enterprises. They also suggest that smaller, more dynamic enterprises are less likely to experience high options concentration. Further, they argue that less concentrated options ownership is likely to be associated with lower rates of corporate malfeasance, implying that higher options holding concentration may be associated with greater manifestation of undesirable wealth transfer behaviour.

Although they provide many interesting and useful insights, Blasi et al. (2003) do not provide structured arguments in favour of these conjectural statements. However, in relation to the question of the relationship between options holding concentration and corporate wealth appropriations by option holders, a possible theoretical explanation goes as follows. Altering capital-structure mix, systematic alteration of firm risk profile, the management of information flows between the firm and capital markets, the timing of options issue and vesting and the management of dividend and buyback policy are all initiated by a very narrow but powerful constituency within a firm.

In firms with high options holdings concentration this same constituency would stand to gain disproportionately from wealth transfers generated as a result of choices made with respect to these types of policies which are aimed at maximising option holder (rather than shareholder) value. In other

Table 1. Concentration of Option Holdings among Senior Management (Average Holdings by Company) 1997–2002.

Year	Board Chair(%)	CEO (%)	Executive Director (%)	Non Executive Director (%)	Board Senior Executive (%)	Non Board Senior Executive (%)	Total Senior Executives(%)[a]
1997	14	31	15	12	40	7	40
1998	14	26	15	10	34	12	42
1999	10	20	11	8	26	11	38
2000	14	19	15	11	27	10	40
2001	11	20	12	9	28	12	38
2002	9	17	14	10	24	17	40

[a]This is the sum of all board option holdings (irrespective of position on board, executive or non-executive status) as well as the holdings of the top 5 non-board executives employed by the firm.

words, the narrow decision-making constituency holding a disproportionate exposure to outstand options has both the means and the motive necessary to give effect to the actions which endanger shareholder wealth creation and therefore represent poor governance outcomes.

DATA ANALYSIS

since previous authors have conjectured a relationship between firm size and the degree to which options holdings are concentrated in a select group of senior actors within an organisation, we collected data on two measures of firm size, total assets and total revenue, with a view to examine correlations between these variables and observed options holding concentration.

Further, because earlier empirical literature has demonstrated that the existence of options plans can introduce perverse incentives for shareholder wealth destruction (and managerial wealth appropriation), we were interested to determine whether there appeared to be any meaningful association between factors which might proxy for the types of phenomena discussed earlier in this paper (reductions in dividend payouts, increases in share buybacks, increases in leverage) and options holding concentration.

In order to facilitate analysis of this question, we also gathered data on firm leverage, interest cover ratios and dividend payout ratios. Our basis for gathering data on these ratios was as follows. As discussed above, previous empirical literature has produced evidence that there exist relationships between dividend and other cash payment policy, capital structure and risk profile, and the use of executive options by organisations. It has been demonstrated that in those organisations where executive options are employed, there is a greater propensity to employ share buybacks, to reduce dividend payouts and to increase risk profile. We use leverage, interest cover and dividend payout ratios as data points, which point towards the existence of these phenomena.

If options holding concentration accentuates these types of problems, as conjectured above, then one would expect to identify positive correlations between options holding concentration and leverage, and negative correlations between options holding concentration and interest cover, and options holding concentration and dividend payout. We have used the Pearson correlation coefficient as the basis for measuring the degree of linear association between options concentration and the variables selected for the study. The positive correlation with leverage would be anticipated on the basis that the small group of senior managers in receipt of options are able to take exerted steps to increase risk, which should be visible via increases in leverage. In turn, this would reduce interest cover (hence our expected negative correlation). Further, since managers in receipt of options would arguably prefer to deploy cash towards share buybacks rather than dividend payments, it could be plausible to argue that higher concentration would be negatively correlated with dividend payout ratios.

Our total available dataset consisted of 352 observations gathered from our sample of Australian listed corporations between (and including) 1997 and 2002. We analysed a total of six variables, options holding concentration (as defined earlier in this paper), total assets and total revenues (as proxies for firm size), leverage and interest cover (as proxies for degree of risk) and dividend payout ratio (as an indicator of firm cash payment preferences). Descriptive statistics for the total data set are set out in Table 2. (Assets and revenues were measured in millions of Australian dollars, all other variables were measured as ratios or percentages as appropriate).

Our results are presented in Table 3. We find that correlation coefficients between options holdings concentration and the selected variables run contrary to the expectations discussed above on the basis of work by Blasi et al. (2003). While the coefficients for firm size (both assets and revenue) did appear to be statistically significantly associated with options holding concentration (at the $p = 0.01$ level, 2-tailed), the direction of the correlation (for both total assets and total revenue) was inverse to that discussed by Blasi et al. (2003). That is, they asserted that options holding concentration would be observed most acutely in larger organisations, whereas, at least in our sample, there was an inverse correlation between size and concentration. This suggests that in larger Australian listed companies with options plans, options are spread more widely throughout the organisation than in relatively smaller organisations.

Table 2. Data Descriptive Statistics.

	N	Minimum	Maximum	Mean	Std. Deviation
Concentration	352	0.00	1.00	0.3705	0.30439
Total assets	352	13.00	377387.00	20273.8574	56495.91665
Total revenue	352	1.00	33145.00	4037.7665	7009.69988
Leverage	352	−3.55	23.34	3.9763	4.62127
Interest cover	352	−67.20	206.00	7.0779	18.94246
Dividend payout	352	−21.72	8.84	0.5033	1.54109
Valid N (listwise)	352				

Table 3. Data Correlations.

		Concentration	Total Assets	Total Revenue	Leverage	Interest Cover	Dividend Payout
Concentration	Pearson correlation	1	-0.233**	-0.292**	-0.120*	0.008	-0.009
	sig. (2-tailed)	—	0.000	0.000	0.025	0.884	0.866
	N	352	352	352	352	352	352
Total assets	Pearson correlation	-0.233**	1	0.636**	0.694**	-0.097	-0.014
	sig. (2-tailed)	0.000	—	0.000	0.000	0.069	0.787
	N	352	352	352	352	352	352
Total revenue	Pearson correlation	-0.292**	0.636**	1	0.329**	-0.061	0.004
	sig. (2-tailed)	0.000	0.000	—	0.000	0.254	0.943
	N	352	352	352	352	352	352
Leverage	Pearson correlation	-0.120*	0.694**	0.329**	1	-0.138**	-0.003
	sig. (2-tailed)	0.025	0.000	0.000	—	0.010	0.953
	N	352	352	352	352	352	352
Interest cover	Pearson correlation	0.008	-0.097	-0.061	-0.138**	1	-0.006
	sig. (2-tailed)	0.884	0.069	0.254	0.010	—	0.915
	N	352	352	352	352	352	352
Dividend payout	Pearson correlation	-0.009	-0.014	0.004	-0.003	-0.006	1
	sig. (2-tailed)	0.866	0.787	0.943	0.953	0.915	—
	N	352	352	352	352	352	352

*Correlation is significant at the 0.05 level (2-tailed);
**Correlation is significant at the 0.01 level (2-tailed).

There was weak evidence of a statistically significant association between leverage and options concentration (at the $p = 0.05$ level), but again, the direction of this association appears to run inverse to the expectations we derived from Blasi et al.'s (2003) work on concentration. However, this apparent statistically significant association may be no more than a data artefact. When we re-examined the correlation coefficients between our studied variables after excluding financial institutions from our sample (reducing the number of total observations to 296), leverage was no longer significant, but both total assets and total revenue remained so. The lack of significant correlation between leverage and options concentration in non-financial firms is not entirely unexpected, given that changes in leverage are unlikely to substantially increase the size of potential payoffs to equity holders (or holders of options). While it is true that higher leverage may increase returns to equity holders (through conventional mechanisms such as the tax deductibility of interest expenses), the potential for higher cash flows is significantly enhanced if senior management engage in the acquisition of riskier assets, such as may be achieved through corporate acquisitions or investment in non-core activities. This fits with the reasoning presented by Chen (2002) that firms with large executive option plans are likely to carry more volatile assets. If we were to identify a link between leverage and options concentration, it would perhaps be more likely to reflect asset substitution on the part of senior executives: the investment of debt proceeds into assets carrying a greater speculative component than that envisaged by the holders of the debt at origination.

In neither dataset was there any statistically significant association between concentration and interest cover, or concentration and the dividend payout ratio.

CONCLUSIONS

The data we have presented in this paper suggest options holding concentration is a significant feature of the options plans of publicly listed Australian corporations. The effect is less pronounced in the largest companies in our sample. This suggests that even though an elite group of senior executives within the largest listed corporations may be receiving significant quantities of options, the distribution of these instruments throughout these organisations is sufficiently diffuse that the ultimate degree of observed options holding concentration is lower than the mean observed value for the sample as a whole. This result runs contrary to discussions of options holding concentration based on the U.S. data, and may suggest structural variations between the form of plans adopted by large U.S. corporations and their Australian counterparts.

Apart from size-based measures, we did not detect statistically significant associations between measures of leverage or dividend payout rate and options holding concentration. Though the arguments as to why managers in receipt of options might prefer to see cash deployed to uses other than dividend payments have been long established in the literature, there was no apparent suggestion in our data that a high concentration of options holding in the hands of those who set dividend policy (the board and very senior executives) was associated with the dividend payout behaviour of the firms in our sample.

This may be explained by the existence of institutional factors in Australia not present in the United States during the period of our study, most particularly Australia's dividend imputation system (a means of avoiding double taxation of corporate profits), which in Australia renders dividends a more tax-effective form of return for many investors than capital gains (Kohler, 2001). Even if Australian managers in receipt of options desired to reduce dividend payments in favour of alternative means of distributing cash, strong investor demand for dividends, coupled with the high visibility of dividend policy might effectively mitigate any incentives to change dividend policy which would otherwise be stimulated by options holding and accentuated by high options holding concentration.

Similarly, there appeared to be no significant association between leverage (which we used as a proxy for risk appetite) and options holding concentration. We do not interpret this result as bringing into question the results reported by other authors such as Chen (2002), who suggested that the adoption of options plans did result in measurable increases in risk burdens adopted by business enterprises. Rather, it may be that the presence of any material executive options plan is sufficient to stimulate this outcome such that high options concentration is not additively explanatory. Alternatively, it may be that the risk proxies we adopted in this study were incapable of measuring the types of risk responses to options plans made by Australian managers. This would be so if firms maintained similar capital structures in the presence of options plans as without, but changed operational risk profiles in a manner not readily transparent via variables reported in periodic financial statements.

Finally, though apart from size measures there appeared to be little evidence of significant statistical association between our measures of options holding concentration and selected financial variables, this does not exclude significant relationships between options holding concentration and other operational, structural and institutional factors. For example, due to the relatively restricted sample size, we have not examined industry grouping as a possible associated variable.

Nor in this paper have we examined structural characteristics such as board structure (for example, proportion of executive versus non-executive directors, whether or not the CEO also fills the role of board chairman and so on), which might plausibly be associated with options holding concentration. Therefore, we posit that options holding concentration remains a variable of considerable interest for future investigation.

NOTES

1. It has been estimated in some earlier literature that the degree to which a CEO's wealth is sensitive to changes in the market capitalisation of the firm by which they are employed, in the absence of strong equity holdings, or equity-based exposures such as those created by options, is very low. For example, in a seminal article by Jensen & Murphy, the authors estimated that the sensitivity of a median CEO's salary and bonus payments to a $1,000 change in firm market capitalisation was 6.7 cents. See Jensen and Murphy (1990).

2. In two cases, we were unable to collect data for the entire six-year period. In the first case, a firm within the sample became insolvent and was delisted, and in the second , a firm within the sample was acquired and subsequently delisted. We collected data on these organisations for the period during which they remained listed going concerns.

ACKNOWLEDGEMENTS

The authors gratefully acknowledge funding jointly provided by the Australian Stock Exchange (ASX) and Macquarie University, without which the research leading to the production of this paper would not have been possible.

REFERENCES

Aboody, D., & Kasnik, R. (2000). CEO stock option awards and the timing of corporate voluntary disclosures. *Journal of Accounting and Economics, 29,* 73–100.

Aboody, D., & Kasnik, R. (2001). *Executive stock option compensation and corporate cash payout policy.* Working Paper, Graduate School of Business, Stanford University.

Ali, P., & Stapledon, G. (2000). Having your options and eating them too: Fences, zero cost collars and executive share options. *Company and Securities Law Journal, 18,* 277–282.

Bettis, J., Bizjak, J., & Lemmon, M. (1999). *Insider trading in derivatives securities: An empirical examination of the use of zero cost collars and equity swaps by corporate insiders.* Working Paper, Arizona State University.

Blasi, J., Kruse, D., & Bernstein, A. (2003). *In the company of owners: The truth about stock options and why every employee should have them.* New York: Basic Books.

Cairncross, F. (1999). Survey: Pay: Who wants to be a billionaire? The Economist, May 8, 14–17.

Chen, Y. (2002). *Executive stock options and managerial risk taking,* Working Paper, University of Houston.

Core, J., & Guay, W. (2001). Stock option plans for non-executive employees. *Journal of Financial Economics, 61*(2), 253–287.

Ellis, R. (1998). Equity derivatives, executive compensation and agency costs. *Houston Law Review, 35,* 399–451.

Hall, B., & Murphy, K. (2002). Stock options for undiversified executives. *Journal of Accounting and Economics, 33,* 3–42.

Jensen, M., & Meckling, W. (1976). Theory of the firm: Managerial behaviour, agency costs and ownership structure. *Journal of Financial Economics, 3,* 305–360.

Jensen, M., & Murphy, K. (1990). CEO incentives: It's not how much you pay but how. *Harvard Business Review, 68*(May-June), 138–153.

Kohler, A. (2001). Taxation's double trouble. *Australian Financial Review, 31*(July), 38.

Lambert, R., Lanen, W., & Larcker, D. (1989). Executive stock option plans and corporate dividend policy. *Journal of Financial and Quantitative Analysis, 2*(4), 409–425.

Meulbroek, L. (2001). *Restoring the link between pay and performance: Evaluating the costs of relative performance based (indexed) options.* Harvard Business School Working Paper 01-021.

Monks, R. (2003). Equity culture at risk: The threat to Anglo-American prosperity. *Corporate Governance An International Review, 11*(3), 164–170.

Yermack, D. (2001). *Executive stock options: Puzzles, problems and mysteries.* Working Paper, Stern School of Business.

LOSS AVERSION ASSET PRICING MODEL PERFORMANCE: EMPIRICAL EVIDENCE FROM FIVE PACIFIC-BASIN COUNTRIES

David Ng and Mehdi Sadeghi

ABSTRACT

This paper studies the empirical application of an asset pricing model derived from the irrational individual behavior of loss aversion. Previous research using loss aversion asset pricing finds conclusive evidence that estimations match market equity premium and volatility using simulation data. We find that within its empirical application, the estimated errors are comparable to errors estimated from the capital asset pricing model. This study of the correlations between rational and irrational asset pricing model from the empirical results finds validity for both estimated values. Finally, we see the importance of cultures, economic development and financial development on asset pricing through an empirical examination of five pacific-basin countries in the estimation of asset pricing models.

Traditional asset pricing theory fails to estimate the excessive volatility and equity premiums that are persistent in equity markets. *Loss aversion* theory

Asia Pacific Financial Markets in Comparative Perspective: Issues and Implications for the 21st Century
Contemporary Studies in Economics and Financial Analysis, Volume 86, 235–271
ISSN: 1569-3759/doi:10.1016/S1569-3759(05)86012-7

is a segment of behavioral finance. It is a representation of the additional disutility felt by an investor when faced with a loss of monetary value. This paper continues the work and the simulation results of Barberis and Huang (2001) through an application of their loss aversion asset pricing model to empirical data from a number of countries. The analysis of empirical data allows the pairing of estimated and market values, leading to a comparative analysis between the asset pricing model, the market values as well as the capital asset pricing model (CAPM). The use of a number of countries within the sample allows the analysis of the impact from varying cultures, and economic and financial market developments on the estimation of asset prices.

The fundamental theory of asset pricing is derived from the *efficient market hypothesis* (EMH), which assumes that the buyer will always buy on purely economic grounds. This price incorporates all relevant information that influences the expected discount rate and earnings of an individual company. Empirically, however, the EMH fails to estimate the observed high equity premiums and volatility leading to adjustments to the hypothesis, such as the strong and weak forms of the EMH, the January effect or the stickiness of prices, to cope with market anomalies. These models either force an irrational behavior on a rational asset pricing model, or use statistical methods to generate models without theoretical reasoning. In the 1990s, the focus shifted to the theoretical implications of changes in individual psychology. *Behavioral finance*, as it is called, attempts to examine individual psychological behavior and how this human psychological patterns would have theoretical impact on asset pricing models. This paper studies the specific individual behavior of loss aversion initially examined by Kahneman and Tversky (1979) in their prospect theory.

Prospect theory focuses on the individual's behavior when faced with various prospects. Kahneman and Tversky (1979) find through experimental evidence that a risk-adverse individual would prefer a risk-adverse behavior when facing pure gain prospects, but would prefer a risk-seeking behavior when facing pure loss prospects, called 'a reflection of risk' behavior. Barberis, Huang, and Santos (2001) incorporate the ideal of the additional disutility from a loss in equity value in a lifetime utility maximization asset pricing model. This additional disutility is experimentally concluded to follow a general process of editing and evaluation of the prospect, a process replicated by Barberis et al. (2001). The additional application of mental accounting and narrow framing theory considered by Kahneman and Tversky (1984) resulted in a relative match of estimated equity premium using simulation evidence in Barberis and Huang (2001).

This study focuses on the application of individual framing loss aversion asset pricing with prior gains and losses on empirical data from five countries, Australia, the United States, Hong Kong, Japan and Singapore. While Barberis and Huang (2001) estimate returns that are capable of matching average returns and volatility, they use a simulation of 500 stocks for 10,000 time periods to calculate their average means and variances. The use of empirical data allows the pairing of estimated returns and market values, providing a more rigorous test of the asset pricing model and a greater analysis of its predictive powers. The use of empirical estimations also allows the analysis of its comparative abilities against the CAPM to test the differences from a rational and irrational asset pricing model. Finally, the use of five pacific-basin countries allows the impact of each individual country's culture, its economic development as well as its financial market's development to impact on the estimated results. A mixture of these rational and irrational behaviors in each country will lead to an interesting comparison of the CAPM and the loss aversion model. The remainder of the paper is organized as follows: Section 1 derives the hypothesis of the paper from its motivation. Section 2 discusses the literature from which Barberis and Huang (2001) derive their asset pricing model and the associated parameters that govern individual behavior. Section 3 presents the derivation of the asset pricing model, data specifications and the estimation methodology. The extensive study of both literature and derivation of the model is essential as previous research does not delve deeply into its past. Section 4 discusses the empirical results as well as the sensitivity tests that enable a clear view of the impact that investor behavior has on the asset pricing model. Section 5 discusses the estimations, results and limitations. Section 6 concludes the findings of this paper. Plots may be found as attachments.

1. MOTIVATION AND HYPOTHESES

The ideal of the loss aversion asset pricing model would, without a doubt, have significance for contemporary asset pricing theory if validated. The loss aversion asset pricing model is based on strong theoretical background. The model itself is an adaptation of the lifetime utility maximization of an individual from Merton (1971), where its bequest function is adapted to account for annual adjustments of portfolios by individuals. The evaluation and editing processes have been examined by Kahneman and Tversky (1979) and Barberis et al. (2001) add its adjustments to the maximization equation using parameters from experimental results. Although, how comparable is the estimation from this sound theoretical asset pricing model to real market values? The evidence from Barberis et al. (2001) has been positive. However, this result is from the comparison of summary statistics of the *simulated* portfolio aggregate observation of the loss aversion model compared to the portfolio values from the NYSE from 1926 to 1995, a comparison of 50,000 observations to 70 market observations. One of the goals of this *empirical* application is the specific pairing of estimated and market values such that the test of the loss aversion asset pricing model is more rigorous. It also allows the results to have a more predictive meaning, with estimated returns matched against its actual market return value.

To test the abilities of the loss aversion asset pricing model, we have to test the biasness of its estimated errors. If on an average, the estimated returns are equal to the market return value, then the average estimated errors should neither be significantly positive or negative. Thus, the first hypothesis is thus drawn from this motivation;

H_0. The asset pricing model does not, on average, over or under estimate returns vs.

H_1. The asset pricing model does, on average, over or under estimate returns.

Previous research, due to the use of simulations, does not have the option for comparative analysis using market values as well as different asset pricing models. The use of empirical data allows the estimation of returns from multiple asset pricing models while holding all market values constant. Thus, there is a consistent pairing of estimated returns for comparative purposes. On the calculation of errors, the abilities of individual asset pricing models can be compared to the market values as well as to each other. As a comparison of the irrational loss aversion model, the model used for comparison would be the rational CAPM. This leads to the second hypothesis;

H_0. The estimated errors for the *asset pricing model indicates the model is no better or worst than the CAPM vs.

H_1. The estimated errors for the *asset pricing model indicates the model is better or worst than CAPM.

One of the interesting possibilities from the application of irrational asset pricing would be its role in varying countries. If a country had a specific record for high levels of equity market participation, would irrational investor behavior be more evident? Does the role of a less developed, more speculative market have a greater role in the price of an asset compared to its rational value? Through the application of both the rational CAPM and the irrational loss aversion asset pricing model, a comparison of the results maybe lead to casual relationships about the importance of irrational behaviors. The use of sensitivity analysis on the parameters that govern the loss aversion model would also display the estimative abilities to match market values. This leads to the third and final hypothesis:

H_0. A comparison of estimated errors between countries would reveal consistency vs.

H_1. A comparison of estimated errors between countries would not reveal consistency.

2. LITERATURE REVIEW

This research paper deals with the empirical application of the loss aversion asset pricing model and thus relies on previous theoretical developments from Barberis and Huang (2001). Their individual stock analysis is derived from the previous work of Barberis et al. (2001) dealing with portfolio loss aversion. Their research is based on the work of Benartzi and Thaler (1995) dealing with portfolio re-evaluations as well as with the application of prospect theory studied by Kahneman and Tversky (1979). The following section begins with a brief overview of the development of loss aversion and the importance of the initial endowment of individuals when considering prospects: the prior gains and losses variable as used by Barberis et al. (2001). Next, the development and testing of its application to asset pricing using portfolios will be discussed. The literature reviewed considers each aspect of the loss aversion asset pricing model, while the paper by Barberis et al. (2001) ties the individual theories together and develops the asset pricing model.

The ideal of loss aversion was first considered by Kahneman and Tversky (1979) because of the flaws in the application of expected utility theory to prospects. Using the results of experiments dealing with choices between prospects with different probabilities and gains, they found that the axioms of expected utility theory are violated through the ideals of loss aversion. The critical part of their research in relation to the loss aversion asset pricing model lies in the differing evaluations of prospects depending on the coded gains or losses. Given a simple single prospect, an individual would be risk-seeking if they were provided with two gain prospects, but would have a reflection of risk behavior to risk-aversion when dealing with two loss

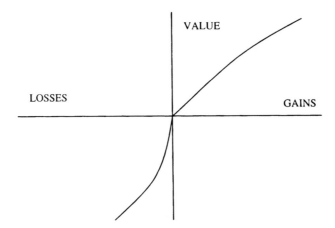

Fig. 1.   A Hypothetical Value Function.

prospects. Through a series of experiments with varying gains/losses and probabilities in prospects, they found that the evaluation of prospects leads to an expected utility that is concave for a gain, convex and steeper for a loss, and would be highly dependent on the initial reference point of the prospect (see Fig. 1).

As an extension to their simple prospects, Kahneman and Tversky (1984) extended into multi-attributed prospects and prospect framing. *Framing* is the changing of the wording of simple prospects, where the editing of choices would differ when considering, say, a monetary prospect and a prospect dealing with the number of deaths in a hospital. Multi-attributed prospects deals with the aggregation of all positive and negative aspects of various prospects resulting in a *mental accounting*, that takes account of not only simple probabilities but also of human irrationality in the editing and evaluation process. Framing and mental accounting provides the experimental proof that is required to apply prospect theory to games that are more complex than two choice games as outlined in the original paper by Kahneman and Tversky (1979). This understanding paves the way to its use in complex multi-attributed assets such as individual stocks or portfolios as used by Barberis and Huang (2001).

The endowment effect is an extension of the prospect theory's belief that the initial reference point plays a vital role in the risk-behavior of the individual. Kahneman, Knetsch, and Thaler (1990) used experiments finding the median asking price to sell an asset is 1.8–6 times higher than the median asking price to buy an asset.[1] Thus, disutility of the seller of the asset is greater than the utility of the buyer of the asset. Using this experiments, Kahneman and Tversky (1991) found the significance of this research. This research leads specifically to the study of prospect dealing with complex prospects by Thaler and Johnson (1990) whom isolated the actual effect of loss aversion, where an individual would experience an increase in their risk-adverse once they have developed a history of losses greater than gains. The result is a reflection effect where an individual becomes more risk-seeking once they have a history of gains greater than losses. This study provides the basic evaluation process used by Barberis et al. (2001) in their estimation of the loss aversion asset pricing model. The distinction between a gain and loss is dependant first on its initial reference position, where, if an individual is experiencing a prior gain, they become more risk-seeking, while if the individual is experiencing a prior loss, they become more risk-adverse. In estimation, Barberis et al. (2001) adjust through the use of an additional disutility loss variable when dealing with a prior loss as well as taking into account the impact of 'house-money' where prior gains increase the barrier if an asset is classified as a loss.

In 1992, Tversky and Kahneman extended their experiments of prospect theory to consider prospects of continuous rather than discrete probabilities.[2] In the analysis of the median gain value chosen from experiments involving mixed gains and losses prospects with equal probability, a non-linear regression was used to find that additional disutility involved with a loss prospect is 2.25. The utility evaluation weight given to a positive prospect was 0.61, whereas the weight given to a negative prospect was 0.69. These specific estimated coefficients are used by Barberis et al. (2001) as the parameters in the loss aversion asset pricing model. These parameters are an experimental estimate of individual behavior.

In an attempt to prove that portfolio re-evaluations may have a significant impact on the equity premium puzzle, Benartzi and Thaler (1995) applied the advanced prospect theory framework to simulations of asset classes and risk-free assets. They found that the editing and evaluation process of the prospect theory produces an intersection of utility when the portfolio is re-evaluated on an annual basis when compared to the risk-free rate of return. Barberis et al. (2001) use this simulation result to argue that, while the bequest of an individual is a portfolio of assets that is held for a lifetime period, an individual would re-evaluate this portfolio to try and gain the maximum return rather than have a constant portfolio as stated by Merton (1971). From this simulation result, Barberis and Huang (2001) base their individual stock adjustments to an annual basis with the use of 'tax reasons' as an additional theoretical proof.

Barberis et al. (2001) combine these experimental and simulation results to produce the loss aversion asset pricing model. Their model starts with the basis of a lifetime utility maximization function as suggested by Merton (1971). They modify the bequest function with the simulation results of Benartzi and Thaler (1995). The prospect theory is proven to have applications to various assets including individual stock analysis through the experiments by Kahneman and Tverksy (1984) among others discussed above. Finally, many of the individual parameters are taken from the estimated values from Tversky and Kahneman (1992). Using this model, they estimate a duel model comparing a model of consumption only against a model that also includes market return changes. They find that the consumption model fails to match historical returns, while a simulation of the consumption and portfolio returns does have comparative ability to the aggregate statistics of the market. To test an asset pricing model using only portfolio data for estimation and results would not provide too much insight into the model's capacity. Thus, as a further extension, Barberis and Huang (2001) incorporate individual assets to the loss aversion asset pricing model to test the comparative abilities of the portfolio simulation against a model that allows for individual stocks. They have found that this application of mental accounting and narrow framing allows the simulated estimated returns to more closely match the average returns and volatility over the simulated period compared to the portfolio. Barberis and Huang (2001) provide a result that provides conclusive simulation evidence for the possibilities of the loss aversion asset pricing model to match the historical aggregate statistics. It is the aim of this study to conduct an empirical application of the same theoretical model in order to provide more robust proof that the loss aversion asset pricing model has greater significance in estimation and prediction of asset values.

3. DATA AND METHODOLOGY

For this research to have validity and comparative ability, the empirical application must replicate the theoretical loss aversion asset pricing model of Barberis and Huang. The derivation of the loss aversion asset pricing model from its utility maximization will be briefly discussed before we apply it to an empirical database. This discussion is considered in Section 3.1, which explains the loss aversion asset pricing model as well as the calculations of input data. Section 3.2 discusses the nature of the data acquired and the validity of each sample. Section 3.3 examines the methodology used for the estimation of the asset pricing models. With the empirical application, there appeared to be a theoretical problem in replicating the exact iterative process used by Barberis and Huang (2001) in estimation of returns. We believe that the estimative procedure used is valid as it is based from the same theoretical model and the same theoretical steps. This is examined further in Section 3.3.

3.1. The derivation of the model

As with most asset pricing models, the loss aversion asset pricing model is derived from the theoretical lifetime utility maximization of an individual as developed by Merton (1971). To allow estimations of loss aversion to be made, Barberis et al. (2001) have adapted the utility maximization to include the editing and evaluation processes for individual stocks, rather than using the portfolio bequest function of Merton. The following theoretical model derivation is simply an explanation of the loss aversion asset pricing model first developed by Barberis et al. (2001) and further adapted by Barberis and Huang (2001). We believe that recent papers are not as expressive with the exact derivation of the model and thus have included a more extensive explanation within this section. The adapted lifetime consumption maximization used by Barberis and Huang (2001) can be stated as;

$$E \sum_{t=0}^{\infty} \left[\rho^t C_t^{1-\gamma} / (1 - \gamma) + b_0 C_t^{-\gamma} \rho^{t+1} \sum_{i=1}^{n} v(X_{i,t+1}, S_{i,t}, z_{i,t}) \right]$$

This is subject to the standard budget constraint:

$$W_{t+1} = (W_t + Y_t - C_t) R_{f,t} + \sum_{i=1}^{n} S_{i,t} (R_{i,t+1} - R_{f,t})$$

The adaptation to loss aversion comes from the b_0, which accounts for the utility derived from the portfolio. With the aggregate consumption variable, it creates a scaling factor to ensure a stationary evaluation of individual stock as wealth increases over time. The $v(\cdot)$ is a representation of the editing and evaluation of individual stocks, a process of prospect theory. This is summed to form the aggregate and discounted to present values. Previous cumulative prospect theory implies that loss aversion is modeled as $V(x) = x^a$ if $x \geq 0$ or $-\lambda(-x)^\beta$ if $x < 0$. Given that prior positions would create a change in an investor's risk-behavior as implied by Thaler and Johnson, Barberis et al. (2001) modify the evaluation function to include the impacts of prior gains or losses. Barberis and Huang (2001) use the same theory with a prior neutral position of 1 or when $z_{i,t} = 1$ and implies the $\upsilon(\cdot)$ function as $\upsilon(X_{i,t+1}, S_{i,t}, 1) = X_{i,t+1}$ if $X_{i,t+1} \geq 0$ or $\lambda X_{i,t+1}$ if $X_{i,t+1} < 0$ whereas given a prior gain position, where the $z_{i,t} \leq 1$, the $\upsilon(\cdot)$ function is derived as;

$$\upsilon(X_{i,t+1}, S_{i,t}, z_{i,t}) = \begin{cases} X_{i,t+1} & \text{if } R_{i,t+1} \geq z_{i,t}R_{f,t} \\ X_{i,t+1} + (\lambda - 1)S_{i,t}(R_{i,t+1}z_{i,t}R_{f,t}) & \text{if } R_{i,t+1} < z_{i,t} R_{f,t} \end{cases}$$

Given a situation of a prior loss or when $z_{i,t} > 1$, the $\upsilon(\cdot)$ function is assumed as:

$$\upsilon(X_{i,t+1}, S_{i,t}, z_{i,t}) = \begin{cases} X_{i,t+1} & \text{if } R_{i,t+1} \geq z_{i,t}R_{f,t} \\ \lambda(z_{i,t}) X_{i,t+1} & \text{if } R_{i,t+1} < R_{f,t} \end{cases}$$

where $\lambda(z_t) = \lambda + \kappa(z_{i,t} - 1)$. The $(\lambda - 1)$ is a representation of additional disutility from experiencing a loss. The $\lambda(z_t)$ function and the κ variable is a representation of experiencing a loss while under a prior loss. Both Barberis et al. (2001) and Barberis and Huang (2001) did not incorporate the additional 'break even' effect found in the experimental results of Thaler and Johnson. When one considers that the valuation of the market is proportional to the stock value, the $\upsilon(X_{i,t+1}, S_{i,t}, 1)$ can be rewritten as $S_{i,t}\upsilon(R_{i,t+1}, z_{i,t})$, since the gain from an individual stock is assumed to be $X_{i,t+1} = S_{i,t} R_{i,t} - S_{i,t} R_{f,t}$, where $R_{i,t+1}$ is the return for the individual stock at time $t + 1$ and $R_{f,t}$ is the risk-free rate of return at time t. Given a $z_{i,t} \leq 1$, the $\upsilon(\cdot)$ function can be derived as;

$$S_{i,t}\upsilon(R_{i,t+1}, z_{i,t}) = \begin{cases} R_{i,t+1} - R_{f,t} & \text{if } R_{i,t+1} \geq z_{i,t} R_{f,t} \\ S_{i,t}(z_{i,t}R_{f,t} - R_{f,t}) + \lambda S_{i,t}(R_{i,t+1} - z_{i,t}R_{f,t}) & \text{if } R_{i,t+1} < z_{i,t} R_{f,t} \end{cases}$$

and where $z_{i,t} > 1$, the $\upsilon(\cdot)$ function is derived as;

$$S_{i,t}\upsilon(R_{i,t+1}, z_{i,t}) = \begin{cases} R_{i,t+1} - R_{f,t} & \text{if } R_{i,t+1} \geq R_{f,t} \\ \lambda(z_{i,t})(R_{i,t+1} - R_{f,t}) & \text{if } R_{i,t+1} < R_{f,t} \end{cases}$$

where

$$\lambda(z_t) = \lambda + \kappa(z_{i,t} - 1)$$

The dynamics of the prior gains or losses variable is assumed to follow the process of $z_{i,t} = 1 + \eta[z_{i,t-1}(\text{R-bar}/R_{i,t}) - 1]$ where η is the factor that accounts for how long a prior gain or loss in the past effects the variable at the current point and R-bar is a constant that ensures the median value of the prior gains and losses variable remains at 1. The prior gains and losses variable is represented by z_t.

Barberis and Huang (2001) also describe a few more additional variables and their processes. The following replicates these variables and their descriptions. The consumption is assumed to follow a lognormal distribution of $\text{Ln}(C_{t+1}/C_t) = g_c + \sigma_c \, \eta_{t+1}$ and where the process for dividends is assumed to follow a lognormal distribution of $\text{Ln}(D_{i,t+1}/D_{i,t}) = g_i + \sigma_i \, \varepsilon_{i,t+1}$. Barberis and Huang (2001) calculate returns as;

$$R_{i,t+1} = \frac{P_{i,t+1} + D_{i,t+1}}{P_{i,t}} = \frac{1 + P_{i,t+1}/D_{i,t+1}}{P_{i,t}/D_{i,t}} \cdot \frac{D_{i,t+1}}{D_{i,t}}$$
$$= \frac{1 + f_i(z_{i,t+1})}{f_i(z_{i,t})} \cdot \frac{D_{i,t+1}}{D_{i,t}} = \frac{1 + f_i(z_{i,t+1})}{f_i(z_{i,t})} \, e^{g_i + \sigma_i \, \varepsilon_{i,t+1}}$$

where

$$f_i(z_{i,t}) = P_{i,t}/D_{i,t}$$

The function between $f_i(z_{i,t})$ and $P_{i,t}/D_{i,t}$ is described as the expectations for future returns influencing the price dividend (P/D) ratio. An individual experiencing a prior loss would have lower expectations for future cash flows increasing the discount rate used and lowering the P/D. An individual experiencing a prior gain would have a higher expectation for future cash flows, decreasing the discount rate used and increasing the P/D.

From the lifetime utility maximization, Barberis and Huang (2001) derives the individual stock estimation optimization for the individual as;

$$1 = b_0 \rho E[v(\{(1 + f_i(z_{i,t+1}))/f_i(z_{i,t})\} \, e^{g_i + \sigma_i \, \varepsilon_{i,t+1}}, z_{i,t})]$$
$$+ \rho e^{g_c - \gamma g_c + 1/2\gamma^2 \sigma_c^2 (1 - w^2)} E[\{(1 + f_i(z_{i,t+1}))/f_i(z_{i,t})\} e^{(\sigma_i - \gamma w \sigma_c)\varepsilon_{i,t+1}}]$$

The optimization of the investor's lifetime utility is derived from an application of the *Bellman's equation* to investor lifetime utility maximization, a step taken by Penati and Pennacchi (2001). We will use the definition of the Bellman's equation taken from Suen (2003–2004), Woodward (2003) and Provencher (1998) defined as:

$$V(x_t) = \max_{z_t} E\left[u(z_t, x_t, \varepsilon_t) + \beta V(x_{t+1})\right]$$

The application of the Bellman's equation uses the maximization variable as consumption and stock price value subject to the state variables of wealth and the prior gains and losses variable. β is given as the discount factor and the errors is taken as the dividend growth error as in BH. Taking the first-order conditions of Consumption: $0 = C_t^{-\gamma} - \rho R_{f,t} E[V_w(W_{t+1}, z_{t+1})]$ where $V_w = \delta V/\delta W_t$ and Stock prices; $0 = b_0 C_t^{-\gamma} E[v(R_{i,t+1}, z_{i,t})] + E[V_w(W_{t+1}, z_{t+1}) R_{i,t+1} - V_w(W_{t+1}, z_{t+1}) R_{f,t}]$ Penati and Pennacchi (2001) show that it is straightforward to find the standard envelope condition as: $C_t^{-\gamma} = V_w(W_t, z_{i,t})$. Applying this envelope condition to the first order condition for consumption, $0 = C_t^{-\gamma} - \rho R_{f,t} E[V_w(W_{t+1}, z_{t+1})]$, we find $1 = \rho R_{f,t} E[C_{t+1}/C_t]^{-\gamma}$ or $R_{f,t} E[C_{t+1}^{-\gamma}] = C_t^{-\gamma}/\rho$. From the equality equation and the standard envelope condition and applying to the first order condition for share prices, the optimization is achieved, as stated by Penati and Pennacchi (2001):

$$1 = b_0 \rho E\left[v\left(R_{i,t+1}, z_{i,t}\right)\right] + \rho E\left[\left(C_{t+1}/C_t\right)^{-\gamma} R_{i,t+1}\right]$$

Once the asset pricing model is stated to deal with aggregated individual behavior as a whole, then the individual and aggregate consumption becomes the same. Thus the replacement of the individual consumption allows the utility optimization to hold on average. From consumption maximization, the risk-free rate of interest can be derived as;

$$1 = \rho R_{f,t} E[C_{t+1}/C_t]^{-\gamma}$$

or

$$R_{f,t} = e^{\gamma g_c - 1/2\gamma^2 \sigma_c^2}/\rho$$

Using the assumption of a lognormal distribution of dividends and consumption as well as the equation for the calculation of returns for a period, the aggregate investor utility optimization can be rewritten as:

$$1 = b_0 \rho E[v(\{(1 + f_i(z_{i,t+1}))/f_i(z_{i,t})\} e^{g_i + \sigma_i \, \varepsilon_{i,t+1}}, z_{i,t})]$$
$$+ \rho e^{g_i - \gamma g_c + 1/2\gamma^2 \sigma_c^2(1 - w^2)} E[\{(1 + f_i(z_{i,t+1}))/f_i(z_{i,t})\} e^{(\sigma_i - \gamma w \sigma_c)\varepsilon_{i,t+1}}]$$

3.2. Data Specifications

All data was retrieved from the 'DataStream' database of information unless stated otherwise. Data was collected from Australia, the United States, Japan, Singapore and Hong Kong. The data included the market value of each individual share, the dividend yield of each individual share, the private consumption of each country as well as a typical rate of risk-free debt return form each country.

The market value used is the market capitalization removing the need for individual numbers of shares as well as problems associated with buy-backs, splits and other schemes. Consumption is selected as 'Private Consumption, current price not adjusted' figures from the IMF International Financial Statistics to provide consistency. Consumption is then used to generate the lognormal consumption process required for the asset pricing model. The price to dividend ratio is calculated as the market capitalization value for the stock divided by the dividend payment for the same period.

The dividend paid per an annual period is calculated as the dividend yield multiplied by the market capitalization value. This dividend yield does not include any special or once-off dividend payments. The dividend paid is used to generate the lognormal dividend process although this leaves out the removal of any stock that does not pay dividends for three consecutive periods.

The 10 year government bond is selected as the risk-free rate of return from Australia, Japan and the United States, while the Prime rate was selected for Hong Kong and Singapore due to the lack of a substitute. With the use of empirical data, the estimation uses annual observed risk-free rates of return with the discount variable ρ becoming time-dependent. Barberis and Huang's calculation of the $z_{i,t}$ requires a continuous stream of returns, but is matched with a return equation that requires continuous dividend payments. Empirically, dividend payments cease and start at random, thus requiring returns to be calculated as simply as the market capitalization value plus the dividend paid divided by the past market capitalization value.

On initial purchase of a stock, the z value is set to a value of 1 where the investor has experienced neither gain nor loss. Shares that existed prior to the range of the sample are assumed to be purchased at the start of the sample. The dynamic, autoregressive prior gains and loss equation is applied to periods after the initial purchase of the stock. The authors require the z variable to be calculated from dividend returns only when it seems fruitless to ignore capital gains as returns to the individual stock.

The R-bar constant is designed to ensure an equally distributed z variable above and below prior neutrality. This distribution is achieved through the use of the R-bar as a benchmark in the calculation of z such that a return that exceeds this benchmark is evaluated as a gain. By using the median return of the country, half of the returns used to calculate z would theoretically be considered as a gain.

Psychological preference parameters are assumed to be the same as those used by Barberis and Huang (2001). The curvature of the consumption curve is assumed to be unity for simplicity. The loss aversion parameter, λ, is assumed to be 2.25 from experimental evidence by Tversky and Kahneman (1992). The additional aversion of a loss when the individual is experiencing prior losses, κ, is assumed to be 3 from simulation evidence by BS. The persistence of prior gains and losses, η, is set at 0.9 to remove autocorrelation in the price to dividend ratio used in the simulation of BHS. The relative importance of market gains and losses for individual utility, b_0, is set at 0.45. Combined with the discount rate and aggregate consumption, it equates to an equal weighting between consumption and market forces for an individual utility.

3.3. Methodology

3.3.1. Loss Aversion Model
In previous research, the simulation of the loss aversion asset pricing model focused on the estimation of returns from a simulated dividend error, drawn with the parameters from market values. Estimation resulted from the use of an iteration to find a convergence between the function that solves returns and $z_{i,t}$ simultaneously (denoted $h(\cdot)$), and the functional relationship between the P/D and the $z_{i,t}$ variable. Using the estimation of these two functions, Barberis et al. (2001) and Barberis and Huang (2001) could proceed with the estimation of returns from simulations of randomly drawn dividend errors.

Within the empirical application, the exact replication of the estimation model by Barberis and Huang (2001) was difficult. While previous research mentions their iteration process, replication of the same methods were difficult and ultimately, not meet with any useful success. Without this exact replication, we rely on an adaptation of their asset pricing model to estimate returns and to provide estimated errors. We believe our methods are valid as the basis of the estimative procedure is derived from the same estimation models as that used by Barberis and Huang (2001). There were a few proxies used within the estimation, but these are discussed and tested within the results to consider their relevance and abilities.

The $f(\cdot)$ function should be estimated by using regressions of empirical data. The $h(\cdot)$ variable remains unadjusted, as it is simply the function relating the calculations of returns of the dynamic z equation. Thus, the $h(\cdot)$ is derived

$$z_{i,t+1} = 1 + \eta[z_{i,t}(R_t/R_{i,t+1}) - 1]$$

and

$$R_{i,t+1} = [(1 + f(z_{i,t+1}))/f(z_{i,t})]e^{g_i + \sigma_i \varepsilon_{i,t+1}}$$

$$z_{i,t+1} = 1 + \eta[z_{i,t}(R_t f(z_{i,t})e^{-g_i - \sigma_i \varepsilon_{i,t+1}})/(1 + f(z_{i,t+1})) - 1] = h(z_{i,t}, \varepsilon_{i,t+1})$$

Empirically, the estimation of $h(\cdot)$ would be difficult as it requires the $f(z_{i,t+1})$, which in turn would require the $z_{i,t+1}$, which then requires the $h(\cdot)$, resulting in a vicious cycle. The solution lies in the ability to estimate $f(z_{i,t+1})$ without the $h(\cdot)$ function, but still ensuring the optimization of investor lifetime utility and allow the calculation of z from the $h(\cdot)$ function. The lifetime utility optimization will reveal the possibility of deriving the $f(z_{i,t+1})$ from $f(z_{i,t})$. The utility curvature and the relative importance of market gains and losses are assumed constant throughout the model. The consumption average and standard deviation is dependent on the country, but constant for all stocks. The average and standard deviation of dividend growth, as well as the correlation between the errors and consumption errors are constant to individual stocks. Thus, the variables that change with each country, stock and time period is the $f(z_{i,t+1})$, $f(z_{i,t})$ and the $\varepsilon_{i,t+1}$. Since the $\varepsilon_{i,t+1}$ is taken from market values at $t+1$ its value is known to the individual allowing a derivation of $f(z_{i,t+1})$ from $f(z_{i,t})$.

The derivation of the functional form between $f(z_{i,t+1})$ and $f(z_{i,t})$ (denoted $j(\cdot)$ for simplicity) must also take into consideration the evaluation process from a prior gains and losses perspective. Within the utility optimization equation, the $v([(1+f_i(z_{i,t+1}))/f_i(z_{i,t})]e^{g_i+\sigma_i\varepsilon_{i,t+1}}, z_{i,t})$ can also be rewritten as $v(R_{i,t+1}, z_{i,t+1})$. Thus, given a stock that has gained in value (when $R_{i,t+1} \geq z_{i,t}R_f$ for a prior gain and $R_{i,t+1} \geq R_f$ for a prior loss), the $j(\cdot)$ function would be;

$$f_i(z_{i,t+1}) = \left\{(1+b_0\rho R_f)/\left(pe^{g_i-\gamma g_c+(1/2)\gamma^2\sigma_c^2(1-w_{ci}^2)} \times E_t\left[e^{(\sigma_i-\gamma\,w_{ci}\,s_c)\varepsilon_{i,t+1}}\right.\right.\right.$$
$$\left.\left.\left.+b_0\rho E_t\{e^{g_i+\sigma_i\,\varepsilon_{i,t+1}}\}\right]\right)\right\} \times f_i(z_{i,t}) - 1$$

When a stock that has loss in value while experiencing a prior gain (defined as $R_{i,t+1} \leq z_{i,t}R_f$), the $j(\cdot)$ function would be:

$$f_i(z_{i,t+1}) = \left\{[1 - b_0\,\rho\,(z_{i,t}R_{f,t} - R_{f,t}) + b_0\rho\lambda z_{i,t}R_{f,t}]/\left(pe^{g_i-\gamma g_c+(1/2)\gamma^2\sigma_c^2(1-\omega_{ci}^2)}\right.\right.$$
$$\left.\left.\times E_t\left[e^{(\sigma_i-\gamma\,\omega_{ci}\,\sigma_c)\varepsilon_{i,t+1}}\right] + b_0\rho\lambda E_t\left[e^{g_i+\sigma_i\varepsilon_{i,t+1}}\right]\right)\right\} \times f_i(z_{i,t}) - 1$$

When a stock that has loss in value while experiencing a prior loss (defined as $R_{i,t+1} \leq R_f$), the $j(\cdot)$ function would be:

$$f_i(z_{i,t+1}) = \left\{[1 + b_0\rho(\lambda + \kappa(z_{i,t} - 1))R_{f,t}]/\left(pe^{g_i-\gamma\,g_c+(1/2)\gamma^2\sigma_c^2(1-\omega_{ci}^2)}\right.\right.$$
$$\left.\times E_t\left[e^{(\sigma_i-g\omega_{ci}\sigma_c)\varepsilon_{i,t+1}}\right] + b_0\rho(\lambda + \kappa(z_{i,t} - 1))E_t\left[e^{g_i+\sigma_i\varepsilon_{i,t+1}}\right]\right)\right\}$$
$$\times f_i(z_{i,t}) - 1$$

Thus follows the estimation procedure. The $f(\cdot)$ function is used on $z_{i,t}$ to find $f(z_{i,t})$. Using the $j(\cdot)$ function, the $f(z_{i,t})$ is used to find $f(z_{i,t+1})$. $f(z_{i,t+1})$ is used to find $z_{i,t+1}$ using the $h(\cdot)$ function. The $z_{i,t+1}$ is used to calculate returns and estimate errors. Initially, the theoretical model is used as the first comparison, with the regression of the relationship between P/D and $z_{i,t}$. However, the rather dismal predicability of the regression[3] compared to the market value of $f(z_{i,t})$, which is available to the individual at the time, leads to the dropping of the theoretical model as the base. Instead the Market Implied Loss Aversion Model (MILAM), a model using the market-implied values of the price to dividend ratios, is used as the comparison. Thus, with the $f(z_{i,t})$ taken from the P/D at time t, and the estimation of return is simply the application of the $j(\cdot)$ function, the $h(\cdot)$ function can be used to find ... and ... the $z_{i,t+1}$, the $P/D_{i,t+1}^{\text{predict}}$. Errors are calculated as:

$$\varepsilon_{i,t+1} = \left(P/D_{i,t+1}^{\text{predict}} \times \text{Dividend}_{i,t+1} - MV_{i,t+1} \right)/MV_{i,t+1} \times 100$$

where $\varepsilon_{i,t+1}$ is the estimated percentage error for stock i at time $t+1$, $P/D_{i,t+1}^{\text{predict}}$ is the price to dividend ratio estimated for stock i at time $t+1$, $\text{Dividend}_{i,t+1}$ is the dividend payment for stock i at time $t+1$ and $MV_{i,t+1}$ is the market capitalization value for stock i at time $t+1$. Absolute values are taken with the necessity to consider the statistics of both forms of errors.

One further difficulty arose from this empirical application of the MILAM. It would be difficult for an individual to know the actual return for $t+1$ to evaluate the possible gains and losses in the $j(\cdot)$ function at time t. Rather, a proxy is used, where the investor would expect a return greater than the risk-free rate if errors in dividend growth are positive and judge returns would be less than the risk-free rate if errors in dividend growth are negative. The assumption lies in corporate finance behavior, where a change from normal dividend payment behavior would signify expectations for future earnings. A cut in dividends may signify future difficulties and a need to stash retained profits while an increase in dividends may signify excess cash and higher earnings in the future. A test of the reliability of the proxy would determine if this assumption holds.

3.3.2. Capital Asset Pricing Model

The possibilities of the loss aversion asset pricing model are well established from the results of simulations. One significant benefit of empirical research is the ability of a comparative analysis against other asset pricing models, in this case, the rational simplistic CAPM. The estimation of errors would allow a comparison of the relative biasness of each of the estimated errors as well as the ability to determine which model is more proficient in the estimation of absolute percentage errors. The CAPM is estimated simply as $R_{i,t} = R_{f,t} + \beta_i(R_{m,t} - R_f)$, where $\beta_i = \sigma_{i,m}/\sigma_m^2$. The market return, $R_{m,t}$, is calculated at each period as the market value plus the dividend payment, divided by the previous market value. The market portfolio is simply the aggregation of all individual stocks' market capitalization value. Market dividend payments are the aggregation of individual total dividend payments. Individual stock, β_i, are calculated from the covariance between returns of the individual stock and the market value, $\sigma_{i,m}$, for those that exist at the time divided by the variance of the market portfolio returns, σ_m^2. The risk-free rate of return $R_{f,t}$ is not static, but changes with each year.

To estimate the errors for comparative analysis, the estimated CAPM return for a period is the beta of the individual stock multiplied by the market premium $(R_{m,t} - R_{f,t})$, with the risk-free rate added to the individual stock premium.

$$\varepsilon_{i,t+1} = (R_{i,t+1}^{\text{predict}} - R_{i,t+1})(MV_{i,t}/MV_{i,t+1}) \times 100$$

Errors are calculated as a percentage, with the difference between the CAPM expected return and the real market return multiplied by the previous market capitalization value, divided by the current real market value multiplied by 100. These are then taken also as an absolute number, with both error forms having statistics taken. The CAPM is used initially as a benchmark for the theoretical model, using the biasness of estimated errors and the general ability to match historical returns of the absolute percentage errors. Future asset pricing models derived from the loss aversion individual behavior may be tested in its ability to outperform its previous model, but would always be tested against the CAPM.

4. RESULTS

4.1. Capital Asset Pricing Model

Table 1 reports the summary statistics and hypothesis tests for the estimated errors for the CAPM. Panel A reports the summary statistics for the percentage errors of the CAPM. A significance test providing statistical results is reported in Panel C. The results are rejections of the null hypothesis for the countries of the United States of America, Japan and Singapore, while the null hypothesis is only retained at the 1% critical level for the countries of Australia and Hong Kong. By considering the implications of the median

Table 1. Summary Statistics and Hypothesis Tests for each Country for
the CAPM Estimation Errors.

	Number	Mean	S. D.	Median	Skewness	Kurtosis
Panel A – Percentage errors						
Australia	3,366	4.351	114.475	−5.966	35.512	1655.276
United States	14,912	3.779	50.337	−2.148	5.449	170.375
Hong Kong	6,061	10.643	377.624	9.778	−39.453	2175.693
Japan	8,767	5.721	32.958	2.031	1.940	15.789
Singapore	2,792	8.657	88.496	3.638	−6.343	118.552
Panel B – Absolute percentage errors						
Australia	3,366	33.707	109.485	21.028	39.815	1935.707
United States	14,912	26.6	42.901	17.590	12.480	295.359
Hong Kong	6,061	75.153	370.222	31.519	41.555	2316.405
Japan	8,967	23.283	24.016	17.329	4.265	45.988
Singapore	2,792	41.768	78.495	23.382	10.310	165.704552

Panel C – Hypothesis tests (H0: Mean = 0; H1: Mean≠0)

	Df	Test Statistic	p-Value	Result
Australia	3,365	2.204808961	0.028	Retain
United States	14,911	9.167331755	0.000	Reject
Hong Kong	6,060	2.19402103	0.028	Retain
Japan	6,766	16.25218778	0.000	Reject
Singapore	2,791	5.168014157	0.000	Reject

Note: Panel A reports the summary statistics of the percentage errors calculated from the estimation of CAPM returns. Panel B reports the summary statistics of the absolute percentage errors calculated from the estimation of the CAPM returns. Panel C reports the t-statistics for the hypothesis. The t-statistics if distributed from a t distribution with Number-1 degrees of freedom. The critical test used is a 1% level. This test uses the mean, number and standard deviation of the percentage errors statistics for each country.

values, which range from −5.966 in Australia to 9.778 in Hong Kong, it can be considered that the CAPM estimated percentage errors are comparatively unbiased compared to the theoretical loss aversion asset pricing model.

Comparing the standard deviations of the percentage errors, it is interesting to see a country specific behavior. For those countries whom the significance test was rejected, the standard deviation had decreased dramatically compared to the theoretical model, while for the countries that have a retained result, the standard deviation had actually increased. Fig. 2 plots the histogram of estimated percentage errors from the estimation of CAPM. The high level of kurtosis reveals the distribution of estimated

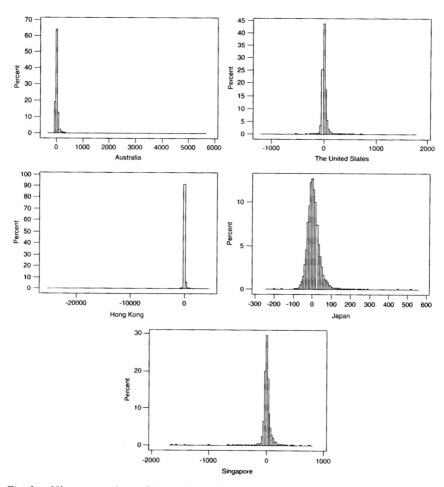

Fig. 2. Histogram plots of the estimated percentage errors from the application of the capital asset pricing model. The high level of kurtosis can be readily seen in every country's estimated error except for Japan. The negative skew for Hong Kong and Singapore is evident in the high negative errors of low probabilities whilst in Australia, the high positive skew is evident in the high positive errors of low probabilities.

returns from the CAPM has high errors with low probabilities. However, the mixture of both positive and negative skews and the general distribution of errors would imply that in general, the CAPM is a relatively unbiased estimator of observed returns.

Panel B reports the summary statistics for the absolute percentage errors of the CAPM. Here, we find that the means are all below 50% with the exception of Hong Kong, and median values are definitely below 50%, with the lowest being Japan, with a median percentage error of 4.265%.

4.2. Market Implied Loss Aversion Model

The necessity of finding a relationship between the Price to Dividend ratio and the prior gains and losses variable is removed when using market implied values. Estimation follows the use of the market implied $f(z_{i,t})$ and the error in dividend growth in $t + 1$. These are applied to the $j(\cdot)$ function to estimate the $f(z_{i,t+1})$. The $j(\cdot)$ function is defined as:

$$f_i(z_{i,t+1}) = [(1 + b_0\rho R_f)/(pe^{g_i - \gamma \, g_c + (1/2)\gamma^2 \, \sigma_c^2(1-\omega_{ci}^2)} \times E_t[e^{(\sigma_i - \gamma \, \omega_{ci}\sigma_c)\varepsilon_{i,t+1}}$$
$$+ b_0\rho E_t e^{g_i + \sigma_i \, \varepsilon_{i,t+1}}])] \times f_i(z_{i,t}) - 1$$

for gains regardless of prior position,

$$f_i(z_{i,t+1}) = \left([1 - b_0\rho(z_{i,t}R_{f,t} - R_{f,t}) + b_0\rho\lambda z_{i,t}R_{f,t}]/\left(pe^{g_i - \gamma \, g_c + (1/2)\gamma^2\sigma_c^2(1-\omega_{ci}^2)}\right.\right.$$
$$\left.\left. E_t[e^{(\sigma_i - \gamma\omega_{ci}\sigma_c)\varepsilon_{i,t+1}}] + b_0\rho\lambda \, E\lambda_t[e^{g_i + \sigma_i\varepsilon_{i,t+1}}]\right)\right) \times f_i(z_{i,t}) - 1$$

for losses where the investor is experiencing a prior gain,

$$f_i(z_{i,t+1}) = \{[1 + b_0\rho(\lambda + \kappa(z_{i,t} - 1))R_{f,t}]/(pe^{g_i - \gamma \, g_c + (1/2)\gamma^2\sigma_c^2(1-w_{ci}^2)}$$
$$\times E_t[e^{(\sigma_i - \gamma \, w_{ci}\sigma_c)\varepsilon_{i,t+1}}] + b_0\rho(\lambda + \kappa(z_{i,t} - 1))E_t[e^{g_i + \sigma_i\varepsilon_{i,t+1}}])\} \times f_i(z_{i,t}) - 1$$

for losses where the investor is experiencing a prior loss.

The $h(\cdot)$ function uses the estimated $f(z_{i,t+1})$ and observed $f(z_{i,t})$ to estimate returns over the period. Estimation stops here with the estimation of the next period using a new market implied P/D ratio. Table 2 looks at the summary statistics for the estimated percentage errors and absolute percentage error as well as the hypothesis tests for biasness and comparative studies.

Panel A reports the summary statistics for the percentage errors calculated from the MILAM. The degree of bias seems dependant on the country, where Hong Kong and Singapore exhibit strong positive bias, Japan exhibits only slight positive bias and Australia and the United States exhibit slight negative bias. Again, the t-hypothesis test of significance is used in part to consider the bias of the estimator, but the summary statistics are also considered. To test the estimated percentage errors of the MILAM mode,

Table 2. Summary Statistic and Hypothesis Tests for each Country for
the MILAM Estimation Errors.

	Number	Mean	S. D.	Median	Skewness	Kurtosis
Panel A – Percentage errors						
Australia	2,672	−5.908	44.413	−11.933	4.523	47.513
United States	13,410	−2.769	36.861	−8.969	3.949	48.855
Hong Kong	4,030	23.819	203.808	−7.661	26.268	1075.585
Japan	7,999	3.887	37.331	−1.700	1.628	7.301
Singapore	2,254	14.981	80.380	0.147	3.259	23.674
Panel B – Absolute percentage errors						
Australia	2,672	28.610	34.476	21.724	7.294	100.918
United States	13,410	24.995	27.232	19.531	7.563	133.660
Hong Kong	4,030	59.526	196.370	29.370	28.835	1227.335
Japan	7,999	27.205	25.855	21.301	3.380	22.891
Singapore	2,254	45.498	67.930	27.890	5.200	37.622

Panel C – Hypothesis tests (H_0: Mean = 0; H_1: Mean$\neq$0)

	Df	Test Statistic	p-Value	Result
Australia	2,671	−6.874914808	0.000	Reject
United States	13,409	−8.69869369	0.000	Reject
Hong Kong	4,029	7.418240873	0.000	Reject
Japan	7,998	9.311842395	0.000	Reject
Singapore	2,253	8.846539032	0.000	Reject

Panel D – Two sample hypothesis tests (H0: Mean$_{MILAM}$ = Mean$_{CAPM}$; H1:
Mean$_{MILAM}\neq$Mean$_{CAPM}$)

Australia	4,176	−2.55	0.011	Retain
United States	25,560	−3.80	0.000	Reject
Hong Kong	9,669	−2.75	0.006	Reject
Japan	16,319	10.15	0.000	Reject
Singapore	5,019	1.81	0.071	Retain

Note: Panel A reports the actual percentage errors calculated from the model's estimation
deviation from the market values for the 20 years ending 2003. Panel B reports the absolute
percentage error calculated from the model's estimation deviation from the market values.
Panel C reports the *t*-test hypothesis for the mean of the percentage errors for each country
using a 1% critical level. Panel D reports the two samples *t*-test hypothesis between the estimation errors of the MILAM and the CAPM.

the *t*-hypothesis test seeks to conclude if average errors are equal to zero, or
not equal to zero. Panel C reports the results of the *t*-hypothesis test. The
estimated *t*-statistic is found to be significant implying the estimated percentage errors of the MILAM is biased for all countries. While the

hypothesis tests support the argument that the MILAM is biased, a few normative statements can be made. As a comparison to the theoretical loss aversion asset pricing model, the biasness of the estimated errors is dramatically reduced. A significant factor in the rejection of all hypothesis tests of significance maybe due to a lower estimated standard deviation of percentage errors. As a benchmark, the MILAM has a smaller standard deviation compared to the CAPM for all countries except for Japan.

As a comparison, errors estimated in the Asian countries remains positive as with previous asset pricing models, while errors estimated in Australia and the United States had a negative bias where previouly it was positive. Although inconclusive, the impact of individual behavior and the increase in the ability of loss aversion in the MILAM may explain the countries mass market psychology having varying impact on the MILAM, while the CAPM is unaffected. Fig. 3 plots the histogram of the estimated percentage errors of the estimated MILAM. The combination of the estimated skew and kurtosis reveals the distribution of errors that is concentrated on a negative value close to zero, but also has high estimated errors but with low probabilities. However, the estimated kurtosis is lower for all countries when the MILAM is compared against the CAPM.

Panel B reports the summary statistics for the absolute percentage errors calculated from the MILAM model. On an average, estimation of errors was below 50% except for Hong Kong, which had average absolute errors of 59.526%. When dealing with the median errors, all countries had errors below 30%, with the United States having the lowest median absolute percentage error of 19.531% and Hong Kong having the highest of 29.370%. An analysis of errors is useless without a valid comparison. Two sample t-tests are used to compare the means of absolute percentage estimated errors of each country.

Panel C reports the test statistics and results comparing the MILAM and the CAPM means for each country. The hypothesis test seeks to determine if the estimated errors for the MILAM are equal to the CAPM, or if they are different. The results for a comparative analysis of the MILAM to the CAPM find an interesting mixture of results. The test statistics are found to be negative and positive, as well as insignificant in some of the countries. At the 1% critical level, both Australia and Singapore have an insignificant difference between the estimated average absolute percentage estimated errors of the two asset pricing models. For Japan and the United States, there is a significant difference between the average absolute percentage estimated errors, whereas the United States statistics are negative, the statistic for Japan is positive. For Hong Kong, there is a weak negative significant

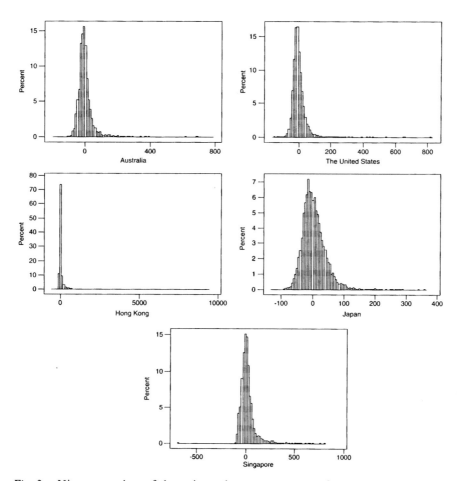

Fig. 3. Histogram plots of the estimated percentage errors from the application of the MILAM. For all countries except for Hong Kong, the lower kurtosis is evident in the greater density of probable errors around zero. The lower skew of the distribution for all countries except for Hong Kong is observed as a more equal distribution of errors around zero.

difference between average absolute percentage errors. The difference between the MILAM and the CAPM cannot provide significant empirical evidence to conclude that either asset pricing models is superior to the other. Two-fifths of the countries have insignificant differences in errors estimated between the CAPM and MILAM. In addition, the significance of the two countries, where MILAM fares better than CAPM is matched by the highly significant country of Japan, where the CAPM is estimated better than the MILAM. The rationality of individual behavior seems most evident in Japan, where the test statistic has the highest significant difference. The negative significant statistics for Hong Kong and the United States would imply the opposite, where the absolute percentage error estimated for the MILAM is superior to that of CAPM. The results for Hong Kong are perhaps the most surprising as in all previous asset pricing models, this country has been the most difficult to estimate a return close to that observed.

4.3. Analysis of Assumptions: Dividend Growth Error Proxy and CAPM estimated returns proxy

In the empirical application of the MILAM, one of the key assumptions made was the use of the dividend error as proxy for the returns over the period. The necessity for the investor to proxy future returns is evident in the application of the model, since the estimation of the price to dividend ratio allows the estimation of the return itself. The question arises 'how reliable is this proxy?' With the estimation of the CAPM, there is an additional proxy available, the estimated rate of return from the CAPM. Would this produce a better proxy for the MILAM? Table 3 reports on the findings of the reliability of the dividend errors as a proxy for market return as well as the CAPM estimated returns, in terms of the number of correctly specified periods and the proportion of correctly specified periods to total. A period is defined as correctly specified if the evaluation procedure followed for real returns and the errors in dividend growth are the same. The evaluation function is theoretically defined as; For $z_t \leq 1$

$$v(R_{i,t+1}, z_{i,t+1}) = R_{i,t+1} - R_f \text{ for } R_{i,t+1} \geq z_{i,t}R_{f,t} \text{ or } \varepsilon_{i,t+1} \geq 0$$

$$v(R_{i,t+1}, z_{i,t+1}) = (z_{i,t}R_{f,t} - R_{f,t}) + \lambda(R_{i,t+1} - z_{i,t}R_{f,t})$$
$$\text{for } R_{i,t+1} < z_{i,t}R_{f,t} \text{ or } \varepsilon_{i,t+1} < 0$$

For $z_t > 1$

$$v(R_{i,t+1}, z_{i,t+1}) = R_{i,t+1} - R_f \text{ for } R_{i,t+1} \geq R_{f,t} \text{ or } \varepsilon_{i,t+1} \geq 0$$

$$v(R_{i,t+1}, z_{i,t+1}) = \lambda(z_{i,t})(R_{i,t+1} - R_{f,t}) \text{ for } R_{i,t+1} < R_{f,t} \text{ or } \varepsilon_{i,t+1} < 0$$

where the definition of gains and losses is first set in the observed returns and then the errors in dividend growth. The proportion of correctness would imply the reliability of the dividend error as a proxy for real market returns.

Table 3. Ratio of Positive Relationships Between Dividend Errors and Market Observed Returns, and CAPM Estimated Returns and Market Observed Returns.

	Correctly Specified	Incorrectly Specified	Proportion
Australia	1,374	1,255	0.522632
United States	6,858	6,023	0.532412
Hong Kong	2,260	1,767	0.561212
Japan	4,049	3,949	0.506252
Singapore	1,173	1,080	0.520639
Australia	2,018	611	0.76759224
United States	10,048	3,361	0.74934745
Hong Kong	3,271	8,15	0.800538424
Japan	6,193	1,806	0.774221778
Singapore	1,736	518	0.770186335

For all countries, when using the dividend as the return proxy, the proportion is slightly above 50% of the periods estimated, with the lowest being 0.506252 in Japan and the highest being 0.561212 in Hong Kong. A proxy that is 50% accurate is sufficient for the empirical application of the loss aversion asset pricing model. However, it can hardly be considered as a good proxy for observed returns.

For all countries, when using the estimated CAPM return as the proxy, the proportion of correctly specified periods to total periods ranged between 75% and 80%. With this increase in the reliability of the proxy, would this have a significant impact on the loss aversion asset pricing model?

4.4. Market Implied Loss Aversion Model using CAPM Returns (MICLAM)

The estimation of the MICLAM follows the same procedure used in the estimation of the returns in the MILAM except the proxy changes from the error in dividend growth to CAPM estimated returns. The $j(\cdot)$ and $h(\cdot)$ functions remain the same in the estimation of returns, but only the evaluation of stock returns would change from $R_{i,t+1}$ to $R_{i,t+1,CAPM}$ to incorporate the new proxy. Table 4 reports the summary statistics, the hypothesis tests as well as the comparative analysis to previous models.

Panel A reports the estimated percentage errors from the MICLAM. While for the countries of Australia, the United States and Japan the estimated errors seem to be slightly biased, for Hong Kong and Singapore,

Table 4. Summary Statistics and Hypothesis Tests for each Country for
the MICLAM Estimation Errors.

	Number	Mean	S. D.	Median	Skewness	Kurtosis
Panel A – Percentage errors						
Australia	2,672	−2.741	47.346	−9.266	5.231	61.838
United States	13,410	−0.854	38.081	−6.989	4.485	62.067
Hong Kong	4,030	26.044	202.514	−4.042	26.591	1099.887
Japan	7,999	6.064	38.485	0.629	1.809	9.252
Singapore	2,254	16.540	79.169	2.317	3.093	22.306
Panel B – Absolute percentage errors						
Australia	2,672	28.610	37.819	20.373	8.274	124.488
United States	13,410	24.870	28.850	18.892	8.337	159.541
Hong Kong	4,030	59.263	195.390	28.808	29.112	1249.737
Japan	7,999	27.723	27.372	21.245	3.719	27.636
Singapore	2,254	45.372	66.946	27.315	5.032	35.435

Panel C – Hypothesis tests (H_0: Mean $= 0$; H_1: Mean$\neq 0$)

	Df	Test Statistic	p-Value	Result
Australia	2,671	−2.992007555	0.003	Reject
United States	13,409	−2.596855126	0.009	Reject
Hong Kong	4,029	8.163027669	0.000	Reject
Japan	7,998	14.09153818	0.000	Reject
Singapore	2,253	9.918758169	0.000	Reject

Panel D – Two sample hypothesis tests (H_0: Mean$_{MICLAM}$ = Mean$_{MILAM}$; H_1: Mean$_{MICLAM}\neq$Mean$_{MILAM}$)

Australia	5,296	0.000	1.000	Retain
United States	26,729	−0.37	0.714	Retain
Hong Kong	8,057	−0.06	0.952	Retain
Japan	1,594	1.23	0.219	Retain
Singapore	4,505	−0.06	0.950	Retain

Note: Panel A reports the actual percentage errors calculated from the model's estimation deviation from the market values for the 20 years ending 2003. Panel B reports the absolute percentage error calculated from the model's estimation deviation from the market values. Panel C reports the t-test hypothesis for the mean of the percentage errors for each country. The t-test uses a t-distribution with the number of observations – 1 degrees of freedom. The statistic is calculated from the mean, standard deviation and number of observations in each country and uses a critical level of 1%. Panel D reports the two samples t-test hypothesis between the estimation errors of the MICLAM and the MILAM.

there appears to be a stronger positive bias. Hypothesis tests of significance are used to test the significance of the average estimated percentage errors for the MICLAM. The results are reported in Panel C, where the rejections of the tests are similar to the results from the MILAM model. In a comparison between the MILAM and the MICLAM, the significance of the estimated errors are lower for all countries except for Japan with the countries of Australia and the United States approaching insignificance using a critical value of 1%. These decreases in significance are directly due to the increase in the standard deviation for all countries except for Japan. The distribution of the estimated errors can be seen in Fig. 4. The comparison of the estimated errors to those of the MILAM is similar in terms of the kurtosis as well as the skew of the distribution. The estimated errors are still observed with the behavior of high errors but with low probabilities.

Panel B reports the summary statistics for the MICLAM. The average absolute percentage error ranges from 24.87% in the United States to 59.263% in Hong Kong. The median values fair slightly better, with the range from 18.892% in United States to 28.808% in Hong Kong. For all countries except for Singapore, the increase in the accuracy of the proxy actually increases the skew and the kurtosis of the estimated absolute error. The importance of the MICLAM lies in its comparison to the MILAM, of which Panel D reports the two sample test statistics, which examine whether there are significant differences between the estimated absolute percentage errors. The results of the hypothesis test finds that with an increase in the accuracy of the proxy there are insignificant differences between the two asset pricing models for all countries at the 1% critical level. For Australia, the statistic is especially interesting, as the absolute error is identical for the MICLAM and the MILAM, while their estimated percentage errors differ. Disregarding the significance of the statistics, it would seem that three countries in which the MICLAM fairs better are Hong Kong, Singapore and the United States, while the country where the MILAM fairs better is Japan. The comparison of the standard deviations of each country in Panel B finds decreases for all countries except for Australia and the United States. This gives mixed results, as smaller deviations means a greater reliability in estimation, but this only occurs in three-fifths of the sample countries.

4.5. CAPM and Loss Aversion Asset Pricing

From the results of the comparison between the theoretical loss aversion set pricing models and CAPM, a possible conclusion would simply be the difficulty of both the CAPM and the loss aversion asset pricing models in

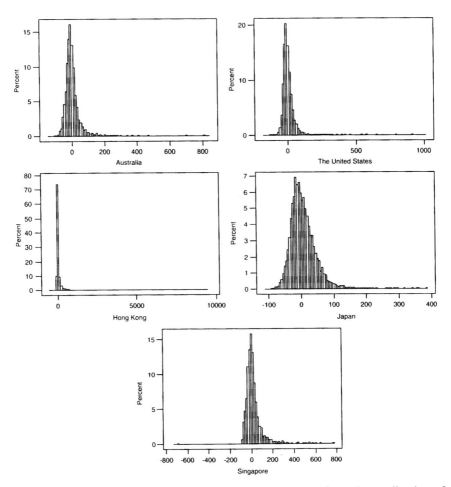

Fig. 4. Histogram plots of the estimated percentage errors from the application of the MICLAM. For all countries except for Hong Kong, the kurtosis is seen to be more dense around zero than the CAPM, but less dense than the MILAM.

estimating returns in all countries. The possibility of a combination of both the rational and irrational aspects of individual behavior in the two asset pricing models have been considered in previous results. To further expand on this possibility, a study is made into the relationships between the estimated returns of the CAPM, the MICLAM and the real individual stock returns.

Table 5. Correlations Between CAPM, MICLAM and Observed Returns.

Correlation Between	CAPM and Returns	MICLAM and Returns	CAPM and MICLAM
Panel A – Average			
Australia	0.352464	0.00493	0.199971
United States	0.370063	0.284744	0.185631
Hong Kong	0.140835	0.506154	0.288497
Japan	0.544633	0.117226	0.163659
Singapore	0.69075	0.262756	0.34757
Panel B – Standard deviation			
Australia	0.296078	0.477025	0.485454
United States	0.220171	0.260699	0.319796
Hong Kong	0.479463	0.274876	0.428046
Japan	0.207533	0.304258	0.286794
Singapore	0.253761	0.394077	0.373244

Panel C – Paired t-test (H_0: $\sigma_{CAPM.R} = \sigma_{MICLAM.R}$ H_1: $\sigma_{CAPM.R} \neq \sigma_{MICLAM.R}$)

	Df	Test Statistic	p-Value	Result
Australia	264	10.72	0.000	Reject
United States	850	6.80	0.000	Reject
Hong Kong	443	−14.84	0.000	Reject
Japan	486	29.37	0.000	Reject
Singapore	202	14.53	0.000	Reject

Note: Panel A reports the country's average correlation as calculated on an individual stock weighted average basis. Panel B reports the standard deviation of correlations in each country. Panel C reports the paired t-tests used in determining the significance of the difference in correlation between the CAPM and the MICLAM against returns.

Table 5 displays the correlations between the estimated returns for the MICLAM, the estimated returns for the CAPM and the observed returns for each country. In a comparison between the correlation of the CAPM returns with observed returns in each country, there is an observed negative non-linear relationship, where the greater the correlation, the lower the average absolute percentage error. In contrast, the correlation between the MICLAM estimated returns and real returns does not appear to have any steady relationship at all. The United States has the lowest absolute average error, but has a correlation similar to that of Singapore, which has approximately twice the absolute error. A study of the standard deviations of individual stock correlations within each country and a paired t-test to see if there is significant difference is reported in Panels B and C. Of the five countries, only Japan, Hong Kong and the United States had a significant difference in the estimated absolute errors between the CAPM and the MICLAM. The appropriateness of the CAPM estimation for Japan is re-inforced by the significantly larger correlation for the CAPM compared to the MICLAM. The ability of loss aversion to model market reactions is justified by the larger correlation of the MICLAM compared to the CAPM in Hong Kong.

The correlation between the estimated returns for the CAPM and MICLAM is reported in Panel A. The results reveal that the estimation of one asset pricing model does not match the estimation of its rival. In Australia, the United States and Japan, the correlation ranges from 0.16 to 0.20, while Hong Kong has a correlation of 0.29 and Singapore has a cor-relation of 0.34. Thus, if the CAPM estimates a change, the MICLAM would only estimate a change that is approximately 20% of that of the CAPM. The higher correlation in Singapore might explain the insignificant difference in estimated errors between the CAPM and MICLAM. There does appear to be a greater consistency in the correlations between CAPM and MICLAM than between the asset pricing models and the market return values. The generally lower correlation between the estimated values from the two asset pricing models would imply that the abilities of the CAPM in estimating returns is similar, but different from the abilities of the MICLAM in estimating returns.

4.6. Sensitivity Analysis of Key Investor Assumptions

One of the broad assumptions made from the empirical analysis of the loss aversion asset pricing models is the assumption about the parameters that govern loss aversion in investors. The empirical analysis assumes that the same parameters used in the simulation application of the theoretical model in the Barberis and Huang are used in empirical application. Table 6 reports the finding of changes to each parameter to observe the empirical reaction to investor parameters in each country. The choices of the changes to each parameter are replicated from the sensitivity analysis completed by BHS.

Panel A reports the impact of changes to the relative importance of mar-ket returns compared to changes in consumption. The sensitivity analysis holds all other factors constant while changing the b_0 parameter. Changes in the parameter ranges from a value of 0 or where the investor is believed to care only about consumption to a value of 100 or where the investor cares

Table 6. Sensitivity of Estimated Errors for MICLAM to Investor
Utility Parameters.

Panel A	$b_0 = 0$	$b_0 = 0.45$	$b_0 = 0.7$	$b_0 = 2$	$b_0 = 100$
Australia	28.6475	28.61018	28.6026	28.58783	28.57977
United States	24.91844	24.86995	24.86429	24.85817	24.85944
Hong Kong	61.44569	59.26302	58.81829	58.00881	57.35678
Japan	27.99543	27.72256	27.67234	27.58979	27.54052
Singapore	46.42306	45.37191	45.15637	44.75847	44.43383
Panel B	$\kappa = 0$	$\kappa = 1$	$\kappa = 3$	$\kappa = 5$	$\kappa = 10$
Australia	28.60698	28.60837	28.61018	28.6114	28.61139
United States	24.87045	24.8702	24.86995	24.86979	24.8695
Hong Kong	59.24215	59.25073	59.26302	59.27129	59.28445
Japan	27.72094	27.72159	27.72256	27.72332	27.72464
Singapore	45.36756	45.36911	45.37191	45.37422	45.37859

Panel C		$\lambda = 1.5$		$\lambda = 2.25$		$\lambda = 3$
Australia		28.62762		28.61018		28.5981
United States		24.89296		24.86995		24.85732
Hong Kong		60.54855		59.26302		58.36512
Japan		27.87008		27.72256		27.62392
Singapore		45.95363		45.37191		44.96423

Panel D		$\eta = 1$		$\eta = 0.9$		$\eta = 0.8$
Australia		28.64552		28.61018		28.63046
United States		24.89597		24.86995		24.85335
Hong Kong		59.14371		59.26302		58.81941
Japan		27.85506		27.72256		27.67818
Singapore		45.37267		45.37191		45.62346

Note: Estimated absolute percentage errors from the MICLAM models are collected from a series of sensitivity analysis on the parameters that judge the investor's loss aversion. The model is estimated with a single change to parameters and compared to the benchmark of the parameters used in the MICLAM. Panel A reports the impact of changes to b_0, the parameter that controls for how much the investor cares about financial wealth fluctuations. Panel B reports the impact of changes to κ, the parameter that controls the increase in loss aversion after a prior loss. Panel C reports the impact of changes to λ, the parameter that controls for the investor's loss aversion. Panel D reports the impact of changes to η, the parameter that governs how long-lasting the effects of prior gains and losses are. The average absolute percentage errors are provided in each panel. For each change in the parameters, all other parameters are held constant.

only about the return from the risky asset. There appears to be a clear relationship shown within all countries with an increase in the b_0 decreasing average absolute estimated error. In all countries except for Australia, the increase in the importance of market movements would also decrease the estimated standard deviation.

Panel B reports the statistics for changes in the parameter that controls for loss aversion after a prior loss, the κ. This ranges from a value of 0–10, where the greater the κ, the faster the change in risk-aversion and when κ is equal to 0, then losses has the same impact on utility, regardless of prior gains or losses. The results are consistent across countries with the absolute average percentage error appearing to be insensitive to κ parameter, as the changes are approximately 0.01% for all countries except for the United States, which recorded a change of less than 0.01%. Thus, empirical evidence shows that investors fail to account fully for the disutility of a loss following a prior loss. Note that these results are the opposite to those found by BHS, who find that increasing the additional loss aversion due to a loss following a prior loss would increase excess returns to historical values.

Panel C reports the statistics for changes in the parameter that controls for loss aversion, λ. This ranges from a value of 1.5–3, with the theoretical value set at 2.25. A lower λ would reflect a loss having a lesser impact on an investor's disutility compared to a higher λ value. For the estimated absolute average percentage errors, the results seem to mirror those found during the sensitivity analysis of the relative importance of market returns to changes to consumption. While there is a definite negative relationship between increases in loss aversion and the estimated error, there is a greater fall in errors estimated in the Asian regional countries of Hong Kong with a change of 3.61%, in Japan with a change of 0.88% and in Singapore with a change of 2.15% compared with the change in absolute errors in Australia of 0.10% and in the United States of 0.14%. For all countries, the estimated standard deviation decreases as the impact of a loss on disutility increases.

Panel D reports the statistics for changes in the parameter that controls for the persistence of a prior gain or a loss, η, ranging from a value of 1–0.8. This would measure the level of autocorrelation, with a value of 1 indicating a prior gain or loss that is only affected by the past period's gain or loss, whereas a value of 0.8 would indicate a decreasing impact of previous prior gains or losses.

The results are more interesting, indicating that the persistence of prior gains or losses is country specific rather than investor specific. One just has to look at the downward parabola of the estimated absolute error for Australia and compare this with the upward parabola for Hong Kong, the differences between averages and standard deviations can be clearly seen. Since η is derived from removing autocorrelation in the price to dividend ratio, the summary statistics in Table 1 shows that each country's price to dividend ratio is thoroughly different compared to others and thus, so would the impact of η movements.

5. DISCUSSIONS OF RESULTS

5.1. Contributions and Implications of Empirical Application

In its application to empirical data, the paper sought to argue the significance of the loss aversion asset pricing model through its unbiased estimation of returns and through its comparison to a benchmark asset pricing model. However, on estimation of the initial theoretical loss aversion asset pricing model, it was found to have two major deviations from its simulation application. The estimated functional relationship is empirically weak with estimated coefficients of determination well below 10% in most countries. Also, the proxy for the observed return used in the evaluation of individual stock returns is found to be inaccurate. The MILAM is developed to ratify the first fault by assuming a market-implied price to dividend ratio, which effectively increases the functional relationship between the price to dividend ratio and the prior gains and losses variable to a perfect coefficient of determination.

In its comparative analysis with the CAPM, the conclusion that can be drawn is that both the CAPM and the MILAM are incapable of successfully estimating returns that match those observed. While the results of the estimation using regressions are not included, we find that the increase in the coefficient of determination for the estimation of $f(\cdot)$ has a positive effect on the estimative ability of the loss aversion asset pricing model. For the purpose of comparative analysis, the estimated errors are comparable to the CAPM in terms of estimated absolute errors. Taking the significance of the difference in absolute estimated error, MILAM is found to be superior in the United States and Hong Kong, while found inferior in Japan. As a further extension, the proxy used for the MILAM and theoretical model is replaced by the estimated returns from the CAPM, to form the MICLAM model. However, the estimated errors are found to be insignificantly different from those of the MILAM for all countries.

Throughout the paper, the parameters that govern the specific loss aversion behavior exhibited in individuals are assumed to be the same as those used by Barberis and Huang (2001) and can be extended to application to countries other than the United States. The significance of this assumption is tested in the third hypothesis of the paper; does individual behavior remain consistent across countries? The analysis of changes to parameters and their impact on various countries lead us to conclude that there is perhaps a regional cultural impact on individual behavior in some aspects. Apart from the parameter that rules the autocorrelation of the prior gains and losses variable, all other parameters behave in a consistent manner. For the relative importance of market returns compared to changes of consumption and the loss aversion factor, there is a negative relationship. The additional disutility of a loss following a prior loss has a consistent relatively insignificant effect on estimated absolute errors. However, while the relationship is consistent, the impact from the change in the parameter appears to have a regional impact. Increases to the b_0 and λ has a greater impact on those countries associated with the Asian region compared with Australia and the United States. While the relationships in the Asian countries are evident in all tests of the parameters, the conclusions are drawn from insignificant results and thus, are not truly conclusive in their findings. The use of a regional influence on individual behavior maybe actually a proxy for specific information that would relate to Hong Kong, Japan and Singapore but would not relate to Australia and the United States. Further studies into various other countries in differing regions may provide a more conclusive result.

This study thus argues that empirical evidence supports the conclusion of previous simulation results that the loss aversion asset pricing model plays an important role in the evaluation of individual stock returns. Its application to empirical data extends the abilities of the loss aversion individual behavior from prior research by its comparability to the CAPM in all five of the countries sampled. To conclude to a specific superiority of either of the models would be difficult as neither of the models can accurately estimate observed returns. The significance of loss aversion can be seen in the overall negative relationship in the b_0 and the λ parameters to the absolute estimated errors. However, the significance of the CAPM estimates in a comparison between Japan and the United States clearly provides a role for the risk measurement of rational investor behavior.

5.2. Limitations of Assumptions

Previous research on the loss aversion asset pricing model has resulted in estimations due to the use of an iteration method to solve the functions of

$f(\cdot)$ and $h(\cdot)$ simultaneously. This paper uses the same theoretical background as that used by Barberis et al. (2001) as well as the extension by Barberis and Huang (2001). However, in its empirical application, the methodology does not follow, step by step, the same methods used in previous research. In its empirical application, the iteration process could not be replicated to any useful conclusion. With the introduction of market implied values as well as proxies, we use a derivative of the theoretical model that we believe has the same heart as that used by Barberis and Huang (2001). Thus while we can conclude that the loss aversion asset pricing model is comparable to the CAPM, we cannot make a distinctive comparison between the results derived from this paper and previous research. If the exact simulation can be replicated using empirical data, then a more consistent proof of the loss aversion model would result.

The lack of the exact procedure used within the loss aversion estimation by Barberis et al. (2001) leads to the use of first the dividend errors as the proxy for expected returns for time $t + 1$, and then the later proxy of the CAPM estimated returns. However, from the statistics suggested, neither of these are perfect proxies for the expected returns as, even with the CAPM estimated returns, there is at least a 20% estimated proxy error rate. How this would relate to the actual estimation of the loss aversion is unknown, but it may have significant impact on estimated errors.

6. CONCLUSION

Within this paper, we use an empirical application of an alternative asset pricing model developed by Barberis et al. (2001) and further expanded by Barberis and Huang (2001). Through the estimation of this model using empirical evidence, we hope to provide the first comparison between estimated returns from this recent innovative model against both the real market values as well as with the rational based CAPM. Using an estimation of the empirical loss aversion asset pricing model on the stock markets of Australia, the United States, Hong Kong, Japan and Singapore, we find surprising results.

While the loss aversion model is found to be significantly biased when compared period to period, stock to stock, against the market value, we find that the results are very comparable to the basic CAPM. On noticing the differences in significance of errors for various countries between the CAPM and the loss aversion model, we have tested for the possibilities of country dependant factors as well as for correlations between estimated errors of the

CAPM and the loss aversion model. The results, while not conclusive, are revealing. In a comparison of the MILAM and the CAPM for the countries in question, it is found, the MILAM estimates significantly better for the United States as well as Hong Kong, while the CAPM is significantly better than the MILAM in Japan. This has the implication that irrationality of the loss aversion has specific benefits in certain countries over others. The analysis of sensitivity test of the relative importance of stock market values and the additional disutility of losses, there is a much higher sensitivity to its movements when comparing Asian countries compared to those of western influenced countries. With this information, asset pricing within the Asian countries should take greater consideration of individual behaviors and irrationalities within their theoretical models and estimations.

Lastly, there appears to be a significant difference in the correlations between the estimated errors of the MILAM with the market values and the CAPM with market values. With the estimated correlations slightly positive, we can surmise that the estimation of returns from the CAPM and the MILAM use significantly different methods. When one considers that both models estimate comparably the market return value, and both have a low correlation and different correlations with the market, then the inclusion of the loss aversion theory to rational models should provide a benefit to the estimation of future returns. With the incorporation of a theoretical behavioral finance model to that of rational theory, then perhaps, the estimation of asset prices can include in some small part both the significance of rational thoughts as well as irrational human psychological behavior.

NOTES

1. Despite excessive data mining to find the most correct functional form and the use of three separate methods in finding the appropriate model, the highest squared correlation achieved was 0.217, for only one country. While this maybe acceptable in most regressions using samples ranging from 2,140 observations to 12,737 observations, the easily accessible $f(z_{i,t})$ would be akin to using a functional relationship with a coefficient of 1.

2. Their experiment was two-staged. Initially, simple prospects had to be transformed into complex continuous probability prospects. From these continuous prospects, experiments were used to find the boundary value between accepting and rejecting a range of prospects with different values, probability and expected values.

3. Despite excessive data mining to find the most correct functional form and the use of three separate methods in finding the appropriate model, the highest squared correlation achieved was 0.217, for only one country. While this maybe acceptable in most regressions using samples ranging from 2,140 observations to 12,737

observations, the easily accessible $f(z_{i,t})$ would be akin to using a functional relationship with a coefficient of 1.

REFERENCE

Barberis, N., & Huang, M. (2001). Mental accounting, loss aversion and individual stock returns. *The Journal of Finance, LVI*(4), 1247–1295.

Barberis, N., Huang, M., & Santos, T. (2001). Prospect theory and asset prices. *Quarterly Journal of Economics, 116*, 1–53.

Benartzi, S., & Thaler, R. (1995). Myopic loss aversion and the equity premium puzzle. *The Quarterly Journal of Economics, 110*, 73–92.

Kahneman, D., Knetsch, L., & Thaler, R. (1990). Experimental tests of the endowment effect and the Coase Theorem. *Journal of Political Economy, XCVIII*, 1325–1348.

Kahneman, D., & Tversky, A. (1979). Prospect theory: An analysis of decision under risk. *Econometrica, 47*, 263–291.

Kahneman, D., & Tversky, A. (1984). Choices, values, and frames. *American Psychologist, XXXIX*, 341–350.

Merton, R. C. (1971). Optimum consumption and portfolio rules in a continuous-time model. *Journal of Economics Theory, 3*, 373–413.

Penati, A. & Pennacchi, G. (2001). Prospect Note XXVIII: Prospect Theory and Asset Prices. University of Illinois, Finance 400.

Provencher, B. (1998). Some Simple Analytics of Bellman's Equation, Dynamic Resource Economics, University of Wisconsin, Madison, www.aae.wisc.edu/provencher/ aae760hp/lec18_98.pdf

Suen, W. (2003–2004). Permanent Income Hypothesis. Lecture notes no. 27, School of Economics and Finance, University of Hong Kong, www.econ.hku.hk/~hrneswc/micro/ permanent.html

Thaler, R., & Johnson, E. (1990). Gambling with the house money and trying to break even: The effects of prior outcomes on risky choice. *Managerial Science, 36*, 643–660.

Tversky, A., & Kahneman, D. (1991). Loss aversion in riskless choice: A reference-dependent model. *Quarterly Journal of Economics, CVII*, 1039–1061.

Tversky, A., & Kahneman, D. (1992). Advances in prospect theory: Cumulative representation of uncertainty. *Journal of Risk and Uncertainty, 5*, 297–323.

Woodward, R. (2003). Dynamic Programming with Continuous State and Continuous Control Variables – Theory and Practice, *Production Economics and Dynamic Optimisation, Agec 637*, College of Agriculture and Life Sciences, Texas A&M University, http:// agecon.tamu.edu/faculty/woodward/637/notes/12.pdf

A SPECIAL AND UNDERVALUED STOCK MARKET IN TAIWAN

Yao-Chun Tsao and Wen-Kuei Chen

ABSTRACT

The 'managed stock' market in Taiwan is neglected by the authorities and general investors. In this paper, we explore the link between financial trait and stock price changes in this special market.

Overall, we analyze and discuss managerial implications for institutional investors, general investors and the authorities as well.

1. INTRODUCTION

The stock market in Taiwan has fairly developed since 1960s. It helps many businesses to expand and strengthen themselves and provides the public with a proper channel for investment. Besides, it leads to the upgradation of industries and enhancement of competitiveness. Owing to the rapidly enlarging scale of the stock market and the magnificent foreign funds inflow, Taiwan has emerged as one of the most important stock market in Asia.

Like the other Asian countries, Taiwan's economy was affected by financial risk in Asia and global depression around 1998. Taiwan's stock market seriously plunged. And there are many business distress cases that occurred in that particular time. Most reasons include abnormal trade,

Asia Pacific Financial Markets in Comparative Perspective: Issues and Implications for the 21st Century

Contemporary Studies in Economics and Financial Analysis, Volume 86, 273–289
ISSN: 1569-3759/doi:10.1016/S1569-3759(05)86013-9

insider trading and assets deceit, etc. Take for example, the Jui-Lien Corporation, Han-Yang Group (Kuo-yang, Kuang-Yu), Hsin-Chu-Chun Group (Ya-Se technology, Tai-fang, Pu-ta), Kuang-San Group (Shun-Ta-Yu, Chung-Chi), Jung-Chou Group (Ta-Kang, Yu-Li), Sakura Group (Taiwan Sakura, Sakura construction), Lien-Cheng, Ta-Ying, Hsin-Yen, Ta-Yung-Hsing, Chin-Wei, Chung-Ching-Chi, Ming-Chia-Li, Feng-An, Hsin-Tai-Shen Copper, Kuo-Tsan Car, Chung-Chiang, Chang-Yi, Hung-Fu, Huang-Pu, Jen-Hsiang, Chien-Mei, Tung-Lung, Yu-Mei, etc.

Regulations are designed to delist, listed companies from stock market mostly focus on those investors are unwilling to invest, such as extreme stockholder concentration, rare trading volume and turnover, too much lower stock price and/or market value. But the practical delisted events generally are due to individual financial affairs. That is, most listed firms were announced to stop trading temporarily or delisted by the authority because of their financial distress. The next question is what is the future of these? Many of them were transfered to the managed stock market for trading again. Our concern is how about their performance by staying there!

In the period of our study, 'managed stock' market included the following 13 firms: Tong Lung (code 8705), Victor (code 8707), Tah Chung (code 8708), YiShin (code 8710), CAC (Chinese Automobile Company, code 8712), TIDC (Taiwan Industrial Development Corporation, code 8718), Hung Fu (code 8719), Ensure (code 8720), Sun Home (code 8721), TaTeh (code 8722), Taiyu (code 8723), Lee Tah (code 8724) and Sun Splendor (code 8725). In the viewpoint of investment strategy, we should not ignore the significance of 'managed stock' market. Virtually, 'managed stock' market still holds its own value and intrinsic importance. For this reason it is taken for granted that the authorities should care about 'managed stock' market, and pay more attention to its stock price and financial performance. In other words, even if a firm with financial distress is listed in 'managed stock', the authority is obliged to supervise as serious as it could. For general investors, they should pay attention to 'managed stock' market, because it might be another ground that can make fortune.

2. RESEARCH PURPOSE

Accordingly, the business financial distress was generally ascribed to either artificial mistakes or incorrect policy decision. In fact, a firm's financial distress is just like a chronic disease. It does not happen suddenly, but gradually in separate stages. The signals of its first stage are the shortage of operating funds and delay in payment; the second stage is the stage of unbalanced financial affairs. Its phenomena are fund turnover difficulty and debts default; the latter leading to bankruptcy. The firm loses the ability to pay off all debts.

Some listed firms stop trading in TSE (Taiwan Stock Exchange) or OTC (Over-the-Counter) owing to their financial distress. Then, the firms that are regarded worthy to operate by the authorities will apply to list as 'managed stock' on OTC. They are allowed to improve themselves within a period. Once they are listed in 'managed stock' market, they will be delisted if their performance does not get better before the deadline.

The study focuses on whether the firms show signs of worse financial status before financial distress; whether their financial status improves after being transfered as 'managed stock' and how these stocks are priced? In addition, whether the 'managed stocks' get valuation as relatively as TSE or OTC markets?

Therefore, our research investigates the relative changes of 'managed stock' between stock price and financial performance before and after being listed in the stock market in an effort to catch on to the connection between financial distress and stock price pattern.

3. LITERATURE REVIEW

The literatures discussed on 'managed stock' in Taiwan are fairly limited. Most of them examine advantage/disadvantage and feasibility of the 'managed stock' market. We introduce some informative research offerings of 'managed stock' for comprehension.

Also, we have provided the definitions and regulations of managed stock in the appendix for your reference (see the appendix).

As we know, 'managed stocks' are listed on the special market after being delisted in TSE or OTC. We find that most of them matching these requirements encounter either hardship in financial condition or shortage of capital. Therefore, we must examine more literatures on the reasons for of financial distress, and discover the connection and possible relation it has with stock price.

3.1. Financial Causality

Financial crisis incessantly occurred in Taiwan in the late twentieth century. Not only did it cause prices plummet, but also influenced the performance of the whole stock market of Taiwan. Moreover, the un-performing loan and default of the companies caused the financial institution to worsen and frail. There was also a contagion spill over into other well-conditioned companies, and economic development was impeded. The problem is so serious, that it was beyond imagination.

Actually, analyzing a firm's financial distress sheds some light on the causes. Financial analysis is central to business valuation and business-lending decision (Foster, 1978; Palepu, Bernard, & Healey, 1997). Generally, financial distress results from either artificial mistakes or incorrect policy decisions. Some important tracking indexes and financial ratios that are precisely related with the financial distress diagnosis are listed in Table 1.

We can precisely scout the uncertainty of whether financial distress occurs by following each financial index. This helps us take further preventive measures and tactics. This paper deals with some precedent studies, based on which we have observed the trends of eight financial ratios – 'Debt ratio', 'Current ratio', 'Quick ratio', 'Accounts receivable turnover ratio', 'Average days for sale of goods', 'Return on total assets', 'Earning per share' and 'Cash flow ratio' – to discern the signal of financial distress in advance.

Theoretically, there are many causes for a firm to be listed in 'managed stock' market. From our data analysis, the causes for these 13 'managed stock' companies are: one is because false and concealed items of accounts; one is because the operation items of the business change substantially. Another three come from the negative net assets, and the remaining eight are from the records of refusal transactions by the financial company or of check deposit shortage for payment (Table 2). All signs comply with literatures claimed above. As a result, the performance of financial ratio can be the measurement and linkage with price performance (see Table 2).

4. METHOD

The samples of this paper are 13 specific firms listed on 'managed stock' market at the end of June 2003. They are Tong Lung, Victor, Tah Chung, YiShin, CAC, TIDC, Hung Fu, Ensure, Sun Home, TaTeh, Taiyu, Lee Tah and Sun Splendor. The main reasons why the authority was forced to delist the listed firms were the effects of the latter's financial distress. Thus, we summarize eight key financial ratios of 'managed stock' firms in recent years for empirical study, and also analyze the performance and trend analysis of these financial ratios.

Table 1. Literature Review Summary for Financial Distress.

Researcher	Advocate
Zmijewski (1984)	Develop weighted profit bankruptcy prediction model including three critical independent variables: ROA, Debt Ratio and Current Ratio
Lai (1989)	Four financial indexes: Net return on investment, debt ratio, quick ratio and operating income of this quarter – operating income of previous quarter/ operating income of previous quarter
Yin (1994)	Five low – current ratio, total assets turnover ratio, return on total assets, return on total capital, operating income ratio One high – Inventory turnover ratio
Tsai (1995)	Six financial indexes – Total liability/total assets, quick assets/current liability, operating grass profit/operating income, earning after income tax, stock accounts value, and stock cash divided
Chu (1996)	Seven financial indexes: – Return on stockholder's equity, current assets ratio, debt ratio, accounts receivable turnover ratio,selling growing ratio, revenue ratio and return on total assets
Cooper, Leung, Mathews, and Carlson (1998)	Advocate 18 ratio types for different users. The most important ratio is liquidity and the second one is profitability
Li (2000)	Stage of beginning – Inventory begins to be un-salable and accounts receivable appears to be in arrears and unreceivable. Stage of worsening – profitability declines sharply. Stage of striving – be lack of operating fund
Chang, Chiu, and Hsu (2000)	(1) Higher debt ratio and too more financial leverage. (2) All profit ratio is much lower than companies. (3) Accounts receivable turnover ratio goes average worse, and so does Inventory ratio
Hsiao (2001)	Seven critical financial indexes – Debt ratio, current ratio, quick ratio, inventory turnover ratio, fixed assets turnover ratio, net income/revenue ratio, earning per stock
Swamy (2002)	Adopt four groups of financial ratios to diagnosis corporate sickness: Liquidity ratios, profitability ratios, turnover ratios, and operating efficiency ratios
Pan (2002)	Four financial indexes – Operating income/sales income ratio, inventory/ sales income ratio, total assets growing ratio, and fixed assets/total assets ratio
Yu (2002)	The common phenomena – such as lack of ability for paying debt, too higher debt ratio, too low profit, and so forth
Milauskas (2003)	The most five critical financial ratios are: Liabilities to net worth, current ratio, ROA, ROS and ROE

Table 2. Reasons and Regulations for DeListed Firms.

Name	Main Reasons	Relative Regulations
Tong Lung	The consolidated financial report shows negative net assets	In accordance with operating rules of the Taiwan Stock Exchange Corporation – Paragraph 9 of Article 50-1
Victor	The false and concealed items of accounts still exist at the time of the final confirmation of judgment	In accordance with operating rules of the Taiwan Stock Exchange Corporation – Subparagraph 14-2 of Paragraph 5 of Article 50-1
Tah Chung	The scope of the business of the company changed substantially	In accordance with operating rules of the Taiwan Stock Exchange Corporation – Paragraph 8 of Article 50-1
YiShin	Records of refusal of transaction by a financial institution or insufficient funds on check deposit	In accordance with operating rules of the Taiwan Stock Exchange Corporation – Paragraph 8 of Article 50-1
CAC	Records of refusal of transaction by a financial institution or insufficient funds on check deposit	In accordance with operating rules of the Taiwan Stock Exchange Corporation – Paragraph 8 of Article 50-1
TIDC	Records of refusal of transaction by a financial institution or insufficient funds on check deposit	In accordance with operating rules of the Taiwan Stock Exchange Corporation – Paragraph 8 of Article 50-1
Hung Fu	Records of refusal of transaction by a financial institution or insufficient funds on check deposit	In accordance with operating rules of the Taiwan Stock Exchange Corporation – Paragraph 8 of Article 50-1
Ensure	Records of refusal of transaction by a financial institution or insufficient funds on check deposit	In accordance with operating rules of the Taiwan Stock Exchange Corporation – Paragraph 8 of Article 50-1
Sun Home	The consolidated financial report shows negative net assets	In accordance with operating rules of the Taiwan Stock Exchange Corporation – Paragraph 9 of Article 50-1
TaTeh	Records of refusal of transaction by a financial institution or insufficient funds on check deposit	In accordance with operating rules of the Taiwan Stock Exchange Corporation – Paragraph 8 of Article 50-1
Taiyu	Records of refusal of transaction by a financial institution or insufficient funds on check deposit	In accordance with operating rules of the Taiwan Stock Exchange Corporation – Paragraph 8 of Article 50-1
Lee Tah	Records of refusal of transaction by a financial institution or insufficient funds on check deposit	In accordance with operating rules of the Taiwan Stock Exchange Corporation – Paragraph 8 of Article 50-1
Sun Splendor	The consolidated financial report shows negative net assets	In accordance with operating rules of the Taiwan Stock Exchange Corporation – Paragraph 9 of Article 50-1

Moreover, we draw a comparison between the trend charts of the most valuable figure of four dominant financial ratios. They are debt ratio, current ratio, account receivable turnover ratio and return on total assets. From the figures of annual stock prices (the end of month) it is possible to observe whether the trend of the charts present positive or negative correlation with their stock performance.

For statistical and economic information, we scrutinize managed stocks in different time level to examine whether they get better or worse with *t* test and signed ranks test. As a standard example, we take Tong Lung, which is in a better condition than the other 'managed stock' firms. We enumerate Price/Earning ratio (P/E ratio) of Tong Lung, average P/E ratio on OTC, and average ratio of other sector stocks on OTC to examine if the relative values of a 'managed stock' is undervalued by investors or not.

5. DISCUSSION

5.1. Critical Financial Ratio

In this section we explain the reasons based on which the important financial ratios are adopted in this paper.

1. Debt ratio shows how large the debt is in total assets with a view to know the situation of financial structure. The higher the debt ratio a company owns, the more credit risk a company has. This index is for the purpose of measuring a company's long-term capacity to pay debts. Therefore, it is appropriate to examine whether the status of a company's capital is strongly sufficient or not.

2. Cash flow ratio measures the multiple in cash flow from operations divided by current debt. And net cash flow indicates that a company will produce how much net cash flow of operating activities in the future. This paper omits this ratio because its meaning is just similar to that of current ratio.

   Current ratio measures a company's short-term capacity to pay debts and the risk of poor turnover in short time. Practically, it is more suitable to take the industry average for standard level.

   To the greater extent, current ratio is very essential in the use of determining a company's capital. Much higher current ratio means that the capital need not be manipulated better enough. In contrast, very low current ratio means poor capital turnover capacity, tending to result in a company's failure to emergency operations.

Quick ratio, having close resemblance to current ratio, estimates a company's capacity to pay a short-term debt. Therefore, this paper merely takes current ratio to gauge a company's capacity to pay the short-term debt.

3. Higher accounts receivable turnover ratio shows if cash of accounts receivable is received promptly. In contrary, lower ratio means that the cash is received slowly. Investors can compare a company's turnover ratio at different time levels. If the turnover ratio decreases continually or sharply, it could be a potential trouble for the company.

As regards to the other index – average days for cash receipts. It is reasonable that we just take accounts receivable turnover ratio for assessing turnover ability, because their functions are the same. With the same reason, this study excludes inventory for cash receipt as well.

4. Return on total assets presents the efficiency of return by exerting assets. Higher return ratio implies higher efficiency of return. Lower return ratio means lower efficiency or excessive investment assets.

For this reason, it is logical that this paper adopts return on total assets to estimate a company's capacity of earning.

Earning per share also shows a company's capacity of earning. We herein exclude it because of its same application as return on total assets.

5.2. Comparison between Stock Price and Financial Performance

In this section, we compare trends of financial ratio with stock price to explore the connected implication. We combine them and brief them in Tables 3 and 4[1].

In Tables 5 and 6, we can identify the stock returns and relative testing hypothesis of the 13 'managed stocks'. Table 6 shows the average stock returns of the half year before delisting is less than the mean value of the half year after being listed as managed stocks. The variance of the half year before delisting is more than the variance of the half year after being listed. Also, t statistics of the half year before delisting and after being listed in 'managed stock' market implies insignificant, differences in return. On the other hand, t-test of the one year before delisting and after being listed in 'managed stock' market implies that the average of the one-year before delisted is much less than one year after listed. Implying the stock performance one year after being listed in 'managed stock' market rises significantly. To further explore the robustness of our study, we analyze the data by

Table 3. Linkage between Price Performance and Financial Performance (before Listed).

Name	Performance before Listed	Financial Ratio				Combined Index	Price vs. Index
		Debt ratio	Current ratio	Accounts receivable turnover ratio	Return on total assets		
Tong Lung	→	+Worsen	−Worsen	+Better	−Worsen	→(Worsen)	Positive direction
Victor	→	+Worsen	−Worsen	−Worsen	−Worsen	→(Worsen)	Positive direction
Tah Chung	→	+Worsen	−Worsen	−Worsen	−Worsen	→(Worsen)	Positive direction
YiShin	→	+Worsen	−Worsen	−Worsen	−Worsen	→(Worsen)	Positive direction
CAC	→	+Worsen	−Worsen	+Better	−Worsen	→(Worsen)	Positive direction
TIDC	→	+Worsen	−Worsen	+Better	−Worsen	→(Worsen)	Positive direction
Hung Fu	→	+Worsen	−Worsen	−Worsen	+Better	→(Worsen)	Positive direction
Ensure	→	+Worsen	−Worsen	−Worsen	+Better	→(Worsen)	Positive direction
Sun Home	→	+Worsen	−Worsen	−Worsen	+Better	→(Worsen)	Positive direction
TaTeh	→	−Better	−Worsen	+Better	−Worsen	*(Not changed)	Irrelevance
Taiyu	→	+Worsen	−Worsen	−Worsen	−Worsen	→(Worsen)	Positive direction
Lee Tah	→	+Worsen	−Worsen	−Worsen	+Better	→(Worsen)	Positive direction
Sun Splendor	→	+Worsen	−Worsen	−Worsen	−Worsen	→(Worsen)	Positive direction

Table 4. Linkage between Price Performance and Financial Performance (after Listed).

Name	Performance after Listed	Financial Ratio				Combined Index	Price vs. Index
		Debt ratio	Current ratio	Accounts receivable turnover ratio	Return on total assets		
Tong Lung	→	−Better	+Better	−Worsen	+Better	↓ (Better)	Positive direction
Victor	→	+Worsen	−Worsen	−Worsen	+Better	→ (Worsen)	Positive direction
Tah Chung	→	+Worsen	−Worsen	+Better	+Better	* (Not changed)	Irrelevance
YiShin	→	+Worsen	−Worsen	−Worsen	+Better	→ (Worsen)	Positive direction
CAC	→	+Worsen	−Worsen	+Better	−Worsen	→ (Worsen)	Positive direction
TIDC	→	+Worsen	−Worsen	+Better	+Better	* (Not changed)	Irrelevance
Hung Fu	→	+Worsen	−Worsen	−Worsen	−Worsen	→ (Worsen)	Positive direction
Ensure	→	+Worsen	+Better	+Better	−Worsen	* (Not changed)	Irrelevance
Sun Home	→	+Worsen	−Worsen	+Better	−Worsen	→ (Worsen)	Positive direction
TaTeh	→	−Better	−Worsen	−Worsen	+Better	→ (Worsen)	Positive direction
Taiyu	→	+Worsen	−Worsen	−Worsen	+Better	→ (Worsen)	Positive direction
Lee Tah	→	+Worsen	−Worsen	−Worsen	+Better	→ (Worsen)	Positive direction
Sun Splendor	→	+Worsen	−Worsen	+Better	+Better	* (Not changed)	Irrelevance

Table 5.   Returns of Individual Stock (before and after Listed).

Name	−1 year (%)	−0.5 year (%)	0.5 year (%)	1 year (%)
Tong Lung	−87.74	−6.81	−40.09	338.67
Victor	−230.24	−13.43	−84.77	−92.47
Tah Chung	−93.16	−94.62	61.29	1.00
YiShin	−63.95	−79.25	−93.64	−98.72
CAC	−97.30	−73.00	−45.28	−65.09
TIDC	−91.92	−84.18	−53.36	−47.15
Hung Fu	−11.11	135.29	1.00	200.00
Ensure	−59.62	−65.39	−61.00	−10.55
Sun Home	−37.02	−10.16	80.06	−41.47
TaTeh	−53.24	−73.78	−27.74	−69.94
Taiyu	202.16	6.25	21.42	80.06
Lee Tah	−47.72	−57.40	78.26	63.04
Sun Splendor	−56.65	−86.40	28.57	1.00

Table 6.   Difference Test for Stock Returns.

Items	−0.5 year	0.5 year	−1 year	1 year
Mean	−0.39	−0.10	−0.56	0.20
Variance	0.39	0.36	0.87	1.60
t-value		−1.23		−2.03
P ($T < = t$), single tail		0.12		0.03
Critical value		1.78		1.78
No. of samples			13	

Wilcoxon signed ranks test (Table 7). And the same answers fully support our induction about the significant differences one year before and one year after these stocks were listed in the managed stock market (Table 8).

Synthesizing these statistical analyses, in light of investment returns, the stock performances of 'managed stock' before delisting from Securities and Exchange Commission (SEC) or Over The Counter (OTC) are extremely poor. However, the firms evidently go improve after being listed in 'managed stock' market for a certain time.

5.3. The Traits of 'Managed Stock' Returns

It is interesting that 9 out of the 13 firms – Tong Lung, Tah Chung, CAC, Hung Fu, Ensure, Sun Home, TaTeh, Lee Tah and Sun Splendor –

Table 7. Wilcoxon Signed Ranks Test.

	N	Mean Rank	Sum of Ranks
Before 5 year – After 5 year		7.11	64.00
Negative ranks	9[a]	6.75	27.00
Positive ranks	4[b]		
Ties	0[c]		
Total	13		
Before 1 year – After 1 year		8.22	74.00
Negative ranks	9[d]	4.25	17.00
Positive ranks	4[e]		
Ties	0[f]		
Total	13		

[a]Before 5 year < after 5 year.
[b]Before 5 year > after 5 year.
[c]Before 5 year = after 5 year.
[d]Before 1 year < after 1 year.
[e]Before 1 year > after 1 year.
[f]Before 1 year = after 1 year.

Table 8. Significance.

	Before 5 year – After 5 year	Before 1 year – After 1 year
Z	−1.293[a]	−1.992[b]
Asymp. Sig. (2-tailed)	0.196	0.046

[a]Based on positive ranks.
[b]Wilcoxon signed ranks test.

performed well in the half year after being listed in 'managed stock' market. Four out of thirteen –Victor, YiShin, TIDC and Taiyu – were eventually losers.

In addition Tong Lung, Hung Fu and Ensure were the only firms whose stock returns evidently rose in one year after being listed in 'managed stock' market (see Tables 5 and 6). The other 10 firms, including – Tah Chung, CAC, Sun Home, Sun Home, TaTeh, Lee Tah and Sun Splendor reversed downward after half year. As a result, if investors had held these stocks even while the firms were being listed in 'managed stock' market, they could have still made profits in the short-term. But in the viewpoint of long-term, you are not so sure whether lasting excessive profits exist there.

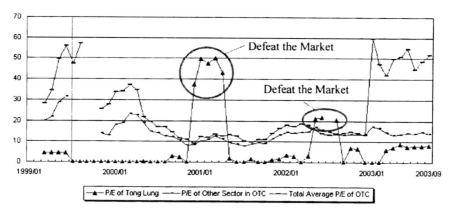

Fig. 1. Comparison of P/E.

5.4. Relative Market Performance vs. Tong Lung Case

Fig. 1 shows that the P/E of Tong Lung is far lower than the P/E of other sector stocks in OTC and total average P/E of OTC after it was listed in 'managed stock' market, except during December 2000–April 2001 and May–August 2002. In other words, we find that the stock price of Tong Lung is undervalued for most periods even though it is the most outstanding company in the managed stock market.

6. CONCLUSIONS

According to the results, we conclude by providing some concrete suggestions from three different dimensions.

1. *For general investors.* General investors may pay more attention to 'managed stock' market. In effect, it might be a source of making fortune. And for the investors already plunged into 'managed stock' market, they should be aware of the risk as well as attribute of 'managed stock', and take note of the fundamental changes for reference to adjust their portfolios.
2. *For the securities authority.* Considering the fundamental performance and stock price status of 'managed stock', they are not evaluated precisely by comparison with TSE and OTC Market. The explainable excuse is that investors have a subjective conception to regard 'managed stock'

market as an inferior market. As for the authority, it is noticeable that the stock price of individual stock in 'managed stock' market is much lower than the intrinsic value. Maybe that is deserved to discuss if the promotion of managed stock market is necessary.

3. *For institutional investors.* From our viewpoint, 'managed stock' is not safe for investment because of its mortal illiquidity. The individual stock with better financial status will enjoy the excellent stock performance when 'managed stock' gradually goes from bad to good. Hence, it may be a good choice for institutional investors to wait until the firms are listed again in TSE.

NOTES

1. Owing to the limitation of the length of article, this paper does not enumerate detailed financial ratio figures and analyses of each managed stock company, but these are available on request.

ACKNOWLEDGMENT

We would like to express our thanks to anonymous reviewers for kind suggestions and to Heng-Yi Zheng in NKFUST for her thoughtful assistance with this study.

REFERENCES

Chang, C. M., Chiu, C. H., & Hsu, W. C. (2000). Discussion of listed firms financial distress. *Accounting Research Monthly*(178), 48–59.
Chu, H. W. (1996). *Research of financial warning system of national listed Firms.* Ph.D. dissertation, Graduate Institute of Accounting, National Chengchi University.
Cooper, B. J., Leung, P., Mathews, C., & Carlson, P. (1998). *Accounting and finance for managers* (New Zealand Edition). Brisbane: Jacaranda-Wiley.
Foster, G. (1978). *Financial statement analysis.* New Jersey: Prentice-Hall.
Hsiao, H. Y. (2001). *Research in earning management of depressed company – Take listed firms for an example.* Ph.D. dissertation, Department of Accounting, National Cheng Kung University.
Lai, S. C. (1989). *Comparison research of normal and failure company.* Ph.D. dissertation, Graduate Institute of Business Administration, National Cheng Kung University.
Li, S. C. (2000). *Stages and symptoms of financial distress for listed firms.* Ph.D. dissertation, Graduate Institute of Business Administration, National Central University.

Milauskas, S. (2003). Taking the mystery out of financial ratios. *Journal of Forestry, 101*(1), 4.

Palepu, K. G., Bernard, V. L., & Healey, P. M. (1997). *Introduction to business analysis and valuation*. Cincinnati: South-Western College Publishing.

Pan, H. N. (2002). *A model for Taiwan listed electronic firms financial distress warning.* Ph.D. dissertation, Department of Financial, Chauyang University of Technology.

Swamy, M. R. K. (2002). How to diagnose corporate sickness using the Wall-Dunning Index of Credit Strength? *Journal of Financial Management and Analysis, 15*(2), 76–84.

Tsai, C. T. (1995). *A neural network research for predicting difficulty situation in listed firms.* Ph.D. dissertation, Graduate Institute of Accounting, National Cheng Kung University.

Yin, K. T. (1994). *Prediction of Taiwan listed firms demoting-analysis by logit model and financial ratios.* Ph.D. dissertation, Graduate Institute of Business Administration, National Cheng Kung University.

Yu, C. C. (2002). *Comparison research of heredity neural network in financial distress warning model.* Ph.D. dissertation, Department of Financial, Soochow University.

Zmijewski, M. E. (1984). Methodological issues related to the estimation of financial distress prediction models. *Journal of Accounting Research, 24*(Suppl.), 59–82.

APPENDIX

Definitions and regulations of 'managed stock'

a) Forty days prior to the delisting of securities as approved by the Competent Authority, this Corporation shall publicly announce such facts, and inform the OTC trading exchanges and such company that the securities may by applied for as managed stocks.

b) A public issuer meeting one of the following conditions and without any of the conditions under Operation Rules Article 13 and Article 13-1 of OSE for Trading Securities on OTC Markets (the "Operation Rules") are, with the written recommendation of more than two underwriters, qualified to apply for trading in managed stock market.

   (1) Where trading of the stocks on OTC market is terminated pursuant to Article 12-2 of the Operation Rules; or

   (2) Where the issuer is a listed company whose listing on the Taiwan Stock Exchange is terminated.

c) GreTai Securities Market Rules Governing Securities Trading on OTC Markets — Article 13:

   (1) Where any condition specified in Article 282 of the Company Law exists, and a court has prohibited the transfer of its shares pursuant to Subparagraph 5 of Paragraph 1 of Article 287 of the Company Law.

   (2) Where the securities transfer institution established at the location of the GreTai is withdrawn, or a dummy transfer institution is

established such that no transfers are processed, and upon the order of the GreTai to correct the situation within a certain time period, no correction is made.

(3) Where any document or information that has been submitted is suspected to be untrue, and upon the request of the GreTai to explain the matter, no reasonable explanation is provided within the prescribed time period.

(4) Where the most recent financial report publicly announced and reported under Article 36 of the Securities and Exchange Law shows a negative net worth at the same figure of the paid-in capital; provided, when a company records as a deduction from shareholders equity the cost of shares bought back by it pursuant to Article 28-2 of the Securities and Exchange Law or of shares held in said company by subsidiaries thereof, the par value of treasury stock held in said company by the company and subsidiaries thereof may be deducted from the paid-in capital in the calculation of the above-stated ratio.

(5) Where the financial report publicly announced and registered pursuant to Article 36 of the Securities and Exchange Law was not produced pursuant to relevant laws and regulations and generally accepted accounting principles, and such violations were serious and corrections or rewrites were not made within the specified time period; or the CPA audit report for the publicly announced and registered semi-annual or annual financial statement contained a disclaimer of opinion or an adverse opinion.

(6) Where there exists any circumstance set forth in Article 9 of the GreTai Procedures for Verification and Disclosure of Material Information of OTC Companies, Article 7 of the GreTai Procedures for Press Conferences Concerning Material Information of OTC Companies, Article 11 of the GreTai Procedures for the Ordinary and Extraordinary Management of Financial Business of OTC Companies, Article 8 of the GreTai Procedures for Verification and Disclosure of Material Information of Foreign Securities, or Article 6 of the GreTai Regulations Governing Information Reporting by OTC Securities Companies, were such violation was serious, and there is the need to suspend trading in its securities.

(7) Where an OTC company has violated an undertaking it gave when applying for OTC listing.

(8) Where there is any other condition for which the trading of securities on the OTC market shall be suspended in accordance with GreTai regulations or opinions of the GreTai.

d) GreTai Securities Market Rules Governing Securities Trading on Over-the-Counter Markets — Subparagraph 1 of Article 13:

(1) Where the stocks have been listed on Taiwan Stock Exchange Corporation.

(2) Where the stocks have been changed to ordinary stocks traded on the OTC Market pursuant to Article 12-5 of these Rules.

(3) Where the application and the attached documents contain false statement or omission in connection with significant issues or facts.

(4) Where the most recent financial report publicly announced or reported under Article 36 of the Securities and Exchange law shows that the net worth is twice the paid-in capital.

(5) Where the issuer has any of the conditions under Article 9, Article 10, Article 11, Paragraph 2 of Article 17, Subparagraph 1 through Subparagraph 7 of Paragraph 1 of Article 315, and Article 397 of the Company Law or other conditions, and its corporate registration is revoked or the company is dissolved by the relevant competent authority.

(6) Where the issuer has any of the conditions under Article 251 or Article 271 of the Company Law or other conditions, and the approval is revoked by the relevant competent authority.

(7) Where an application for re-organization is dismissed pursuant to Article 285-1, paragraph 3, subparagraph 2 of the Company Law and such dismissal becomes final.

(8) Where the issuer is adjudicated bankrupt by the court and such adjudication becomes final.

(9) Where the stocks have been traded as OTC managed stocks for a period of longer than 2 years.

(10) Where any circumstance set forth in Paragraph 1 of Article 13 of these Rules continues to exist six months after the Competent Authority has approved suspension of OTC trading of the stocks pursuant to application by the GreTai.

(11) Where the issuer has materially violated the contract for trading securities on the OTC Market or these Rules, or where other significant event occurs, and the GreTai decides that it is improper for the issuer to trade as managed stocks on the OTC Market.

(12) Where there is any other matter for which it is necessary to terminate the trading of managed stocks on the OTC Market.

INSTITUTIONS, MARKETS AND POLICY

THE DERIVATION, DEVELOPMENT, AND EFFECTS OF FINANCIAL REFORM IN 10 COUNTRIES OF EASTERN ASIA: COMPARISONS BETWEEN PRE- AND POST-ASIA FINANCIAL CRISIS

Shu-Ling Lin

ABSTRACT

The current work studies the cause, process, and effects of financial reform in 10 countries in Eastern Asia for the period of 1993–2002, especially focusing upon comparisons between pre- and post-Asia financial crisis. This study utilizes Mann–Whitney U test and Intervention Analysis to explore the different effects of the changes of GDP, stock index, exchange rate, CPI index, and the changes of the unemployment rate before and after the Asia financial crisis. It shows the consistent relationship between stock index, exchange rate, CPI index, and the changes of unemployment rate.

Asia Pacific Financial Markets in Comparative Perspective: Issues and Implications for the 21st Century
Contemporary Studies in Economics and Financial Analysis, Volume 86, 293–337
Copyright © 2005 by Elsevier Ltd.
All rights of reproduction in any form reserved
ISSN: 1569-3759/doi:10.1016/S1569-3759(05)86014-0

1. INTRODUCTION

Since July 1997, Thailand was the beginning of a string of financial crises. Over the past seven years, the countries that were most impacted include Indonesia, Malaysia and others in South Eastern Asia. It was originally thought that with the assistance provided by the International Monetary Fund (IMF), the chaotic state of the financial market would subside. However, it continued on to Korea and further attacked Japan causing all of Asia to be overshadowed with the financial crisis. Other than China and Hong Kong maintaining a steady exchange rate, the currencies of other Asian countries have substantially devaluated when compared with the US dollar.

Due to the importance of the reconstruction of the financial markets, each country has adopted its policies for financial reform, but the content of the policies are not unified. Some of these changes are self-mastering reforms while others are brought about due to the pressure inflicted by IMF. Some of these reforms are taking on measures that are more open, while others are tightening restrictions. The short-term effectiveness of the implementation of each country's policies, too, is not unified. Due to the effect macroeconomics (the drop in the fluctuation rate of GDP and devaluation of exchange rates) has upon microeconomics, we can discover in previous documentation that most explore the macro-perspective, and few delve into the stability which may be produced due to the macro changes.

As such, this study focuses upon and explores the causes, processes and reforms which surround the 10 countries of Eastern Asia. It further compares the differences and effectiveness. Additionally, through the fluctuation rate of GDP, stock indexes, exchange rates, currency inflation, unemployment rates and other macro-variables found in the 10 countries of Eastern Asia during the period from 1993 to 2002, we utilize Mann–Whitney U test and Intervention Analysis to compare the differences for pre- and post-financial crisis in Asia. This is also used in further analyzing the concrete effectiveness of the financial reforms of 10 countries of Eastern Asia. The purpose of this research includes:

1. Exploring the causes, process and effects of the economic crisis in the 10 countries in Eastern Asia, processes of financial reforms and the effect of the reforms.
2. Utilizing Mann–Whitney U test and Intervention Analysis to compare pre- and post-Asia financial crisis and the impact the financial reforms of the 10 countries of Eastern Asia had upon the fluctuation rate of GDP,

stock index, exchange rate, currency inflation, and fluctuation rate of the unemployment rate. It also compares the differences.

2. LITERATURE REVIEW

2.1. Causes, Process and Effects of Financial Reform of the 10 Countries in Eastern Asia

The causes of the financial crisis, the processes of financial reform and the effects of financial reform are separately listed below by country for the 10 countries of Eastern Asia (Japan, China, Taiwan, Indonesia, Hong Kong, Malaysia, Thailand, The Philippines, Singapore, and Korea). (Table 1–10)

2.2. Effectiveness of Financial Reform

In the past, scholars from Taiwan and overseas have explored the documentation regarding the effects financial reforms have had upon each country and the elements surrounding them. Theoretically, it can be divided into four categories: bank mergers, bad assets and asset securitization; stock markets and foreign exchange markets; funds moving offshore; governmental elements, etc. A brief summary of each documented research is listed below along with the conclusion.

Lin's thesis studies the exchange rate information of the nine Asian countries (Thailand, Malaysia, The Philippines, Korea, Hong Kong, Indonesia, Taiwan, China and Japan) from 1995 to 2003. It also analyzes the foreign exchange systems, and how foreign exchange trends are affected by the government, the economy, and changes in policy. It further utilizes three risk value models (history simulation theory, variation – total variation theory and bootstrap theory), and analyzes the nine countries/regions during pre- and post-financial crisis, and the fluctuation in the risk value of the foreign exchange rate. The research found that exchange rate risk value for Indonesia's rupiah was high (negative value), and that currencies in Korea, Thailand, Malaysia, China and Hong Kong were the most stable.

Chen's (2000) thesis analyzes the statistical information using Asian Development Bank (ADB), and focuses upon 6 countries including Thailand, Malaysia, Indonesia and The Philippines (the 4 tigers) and Korea and Taiwan (2 of the 4 dragons) to explore pre- and post-1997 financial crisis, each country's economic structure, financial government, and the effectiveness of

Table 1. The Content and Effect of the Financial Reform on Thailand (July 1997).

Background to the Reform Development	The Content of the Reform Development		The Effects of the Reform	
	Macroeconomic	Microeconomic	Macroeconomic	Microeconomic
1. Due to the inappropriate currency and exchange policies, ineffective financial structure reform, uncertain policies and high current account deficit has led to a decrease in its once high credit rating. 2. Shows that overly high foreign debt is difficult to defend against. Opportunistic investments increase credit risk though a great deal of documentation shows that the deficit is 6% higher than national production. 3. Restrictions on foreign exchange have been lifted.	1. Foreign exchange and investments: (1) Revised the foreign exchange policies: requires that exporters deposit foreign currency sales into the bank within 7 days of the Forex settlement. (2) Investment bank-type financial markets will greatly increase. (3) Encourage foreign investment 2. Stocks and securities: (1) Open and deregulated financial market. (2) Developing the bond market, established stock market securities fund, Thailand	1. Lifted multi-sector operational restrictions: (1) Expanding the operational and service scope of financial institutions, and moving closer to the full service bank. (2) In September 2000, Thailand's Central Bank approved its commercial banks to deal in securities, loans and short sell services. 2. Capital sales management (1) Revised commercial banking law and financial corporate law and gave BOT controls and replaced the management in financial institutions. (2) Financial Institutions Development Fund (FIDF) to take responsibility for reconstructing and assisting financial institutions, and assist the central bank in handling financial crisis problems.	1. Fluctuation rate of GDP: From US$ 32.56256 billion (1997, Q3), it increased to US$ 33.04719 billion (2002.Q4) 2. Stock price: Stock index was 544.54 (1997, Q3) and fell to 356.48 (2002, Q4). 3. Exchange rate Thai currency exchange rate with US$: 36.3 (1997, Q3) devaluated to 43.1 (2002, Q4). 4. Fluctuation of the unemployment rate: From 3.5% (1997) it dropped to 1.80% (2002, Q4).	1. Number of institutions and mergers: 42 Thai finance companies were forced to close (August 1997). Within a 3-month period, the number increased to 58 companies. In order to combine the market, the government encouraged securities companies and financial companies to merge with banks. 2. Number of individuals in the finance industry: The number of individuals in the financial

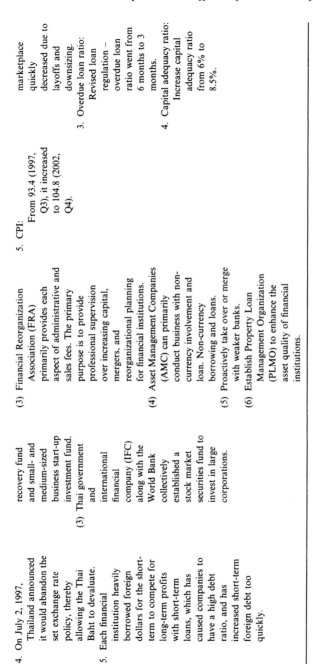

4. On July 2, 1997, Thailand announced it would abandon the set exchange rate policy, thereby allowing the Thai Baht to devaluate.

5. Each financial institution heavily borrowed foreign dollars for the short-term to compete for long-term profits with short-term loans, which has caused companies to have a high debt ratio, and has increased short-term foreign debt too quickly.

recovery fund and small- and medium-sized business start-up investment fund.

(3) Thai government and international financial company (IFC) along with the World Bank collectively established a stock market securities fund to invest in large corporations.

(3) Financial Reorganization Association (FRA) primarily provides each aspect of administrative and sales fees. The primary purpose is to provide professional supervision over increasing capital, mergers, and reorganizational planning for financial institutions.

(4) Asset Management Companies (AMC) can primarily conduct business with non-currency involvement and loan. Non-currency borrowing and loans.

(5) Proactively take over or merge with weaker banks.

(6) Establish Property Loan Management Organization (PLMO) to enhance the asset quality of financial institutions.

5. CPI:
From 93.4 (1997, Q3), it increased to 104.8 (2002, Q4).

marketplace quickly decreased due to layoffs and downsizing.

3. Overdue loan ratio: Revised loan regulation – overdue loan ratio went from 6 months to 3 months.

4. Capital adequacy ratio: Increase capital adequacy ratio from 6% to 8.5%.

Note: Source of Statistical Information: (1) DATASTREAM; (2) South Eastern Asia Business Investment Research Quarterly Review.

Table 2.   The Content and Effect of the Financial Reform on Indonesia (October 1997).

Background to the Reform Development	The Content of the Reform Development		The Effects of the Reform	
	Macroeconomic	Microeconomic	Macroeconomic	Microeconomic
1. Dissolved the maximum interest limit of 1983. 2. Relaxed the limit of foreign debt for commercial banks. 3. Deregulated the banking sector allowing foreign banks to enter the marketplace and compete. All restrictions relating to the opening of branches of foreign banks were lifted. 4. Rescinded regulation that would not allow foreign investment to be directly wired. 5. Government supervision was too laxidasical; it was tempted into neglecting overseeing the operations. 6. The pressure due to the serious problematic fluctuation of the rupiah has caused runs on banks by depositors. The reduction in liquidity will increase the interest rate. 7. The anti-Chinese riots of 1998 then led to financial crisis and then on to political crisis.	1. Foreign exchange and investments: (1) Announced that foreign investments are now allowed. (2) Loosened restrictions on banks that perform foreign wire transfers. 2. Lifted multi-sector operational restrictions: Lifted restrictions on the operational and service scope of banking institutions.	1. Asset management services: (1) They achieved the right of operation for banks and strictly oversee the loan and credit aspects with regard to commercial banking. (2) Established Indonesia Bank Reorganization Association (IBRA) to take responsibility for overseeing the reorganization process for banks and to assist in managing assets. (3) IBRA established Asset Management Unit (AMU) to take charge of purchasing banks' overdue loans.	1. Fluctuation rate of GDP: From US$ 36.39828 billion (1997, Q3), it increased to US$ 45.09382 billion by (2002, Q4). 2. Stock price: After 1997, the stock index began to fall. It fell from −2722 (1997, Q4) to −38012.4 (2002, Q4). 3. Exchange rate Indonesian currency exchange rate with US$: 4650 (1997, Q4) devaluated to 8950 (2002, Q4). 4. Fluctuation of the unemployment rate: From 4.3% (1997) it increased to 8.1% (2002, Q4).	1. Number of institutions and mergers: The government forced the closure of 16 banks (Dec. 1997). These banks discontinued operations and their licenses were cancelled. Four state-run banks announced mergers (1998). 2. Capital adequacy ratio: Capital adequacy ratio increased from 4% (1998) to 8% (1999), and then to 10% (2000). 3. Number of individuals in the finance industry: Those in the financial marketplace have suffered layoffs and downsizing.

4. NPL: —[a]

5. CPI: From 95.2 (1997, Q3), it rose to 104.6 (2002, Q4).

(4) Encouraged bank mergers.
(5) New Financial Regulatory Association (FRA) has taken the verification service and made it independent of the Central Bank.
(6) The guarantee of LC provided to depositors by the banks.
(7) In 1998, IBRA planned to establish the deposit insurance organization within two years.

8. In order to maintain a low currency inflation rate, they implemented large amounts of subsidizing so the government could control the price of goods.
9. The Indonesian government utilized monetary squeeze policy to limit overseas borrowing and to strengthen the effect of bank management measures.
10. Each financial institution heavily borrowed short-term foreign capital and competed under the notion of short-term borrowing, long-term profits, which has caused companies to have a high debt ratio, and has increased short-term foreign debt too quickly.

Note: Source of Statistical Information: (1) DATASTREAM; (2) South Eastern Asia Business Investment Research Quarterly Review.
[a] Unable to find this information for the chart.

Table 3. The Content and Effect of the Financial Reform on Malaysia (1997).

Background to the Reform Development	The Content of the Reform Development		The Effects of the Reform	
	Macroeconomic	Microeconomic	Macroeconomic	Microeconomic
1. Over the past 10 years, Malaysia has taken a more conservative approach to its foreign debt management. Regardless of whether it is private or public enterprise, they all have strict government management policies regarding loans. 2. From 1987 to 1997, there was an average annual growth in the fluctuation of GDP of 8.8%. Additionally, currency inflation remained at 3.4%. 3. Ringgit is determined by the management of fluctuation and market function. 4. The index of Kuala Lumpur dropped 35.1% and 44.8% in the latter 6 months of 1997 and the first 6 months of 1998 respectively. 5. The total debt as of September 1998 was RM$ 667 billion.	1. Foreign exchange and investments: Other than foreign investments in banks remaining at 30%, foreign investment in telecommunications companies was increased from 49% to 61%. Securities industry was increased to 49%, while a small amount of those can reach 70%. Wholesale and retail increased to 51%, this is the same as insurance companies. 2. Stocks and Securities: (1) Stocks distributed by Malay companies can be purchased at high prices, whereas foreign companies can only be purchased at the market price.	1. Capital sales management (1) Prohibits banks from loaning money to affiliates. (2) Prohibits banks from loaning money to the same individual or entity that exceeds 25% the total capital amount. 2. Number of mergers: In June 1998, over half of the financial institutions had merged, and three new companies were established. They include Danaharta, Danamodal and Corporate Debt Restructuring Committee (CDRC). 3. Overdue loan ratio: Danaharta will purchase overdue loans from financial	1. Fluctuation in GDP: Actual fluctuation in GDP grew to 6.1%. From 22158.2 in 1997 (Q4) to 25169.7 in 2002 (Q4). 2. Stock index: KLCI stock index 731.24 rebounded 27.8%. 594.44 from 1997 (Q4) went to 646.32 in 2002 (Q4). 3. Exchange rate: In March 1998, the Ringgit was equivalent to US$ 3.67, which rebounded 22.2%. Afterwards, it stabilized at 1:3.8. 4. Fluctuation of the unemployment rate: There is no method by which it could rebound to come within 3% of the	1. Number of institutions and mergers: In 1998, the Malaysia Central Committee ordered that the 39 financial institutions merge to become 5 or 6. 2. Number of individuals in the finance industry: —[a] 3. Capital adequacy ratio: —[a] 4. NPL: It had already dropped to 12.4% in the middle of 1999.

(2) The Malaysian government spent RM$ 60 billion to support the stock market.

3. Reserve deposit ratio

(1) On June 26, 1998, Malaysia Central Bank announced that the legal reserve deposit ratio decreased by 2%, from 10% to 8%. By doing so, it allowed for RM$ 8 billion to enter the marketplace to decrease interest rates.

(2) Malay citizens began wiring their overseas deposits back to Malaysia, and they received immunity for income taxes.

institutions to ensure that NPL is managed.

4. Other

(1) The highest allowed loan rate is 8.5% for the small- and medium-sized business funds in the service, manufacturing and farming industries.

(2) The highest allowed loan rate is 5% for the small- and medium-sized business working capital funds.

(3) Export and foreign trade regulations have loosened.

standard. After the reforms, it remained at 3.1% and 3.2%.

5. CPI or inflation rate: 102.73 in 1997 (Q4) went to 101.8 in 2002 (Q4).

Note: Source of Statistical Information: (1) DATASTREAM; (2) South Eastern Asia Business Investment Research Quarterly Review.
aUnable to find this information for the chart.

Table 4. The Content and Effect of the Financial Reform on Japan (April 1998).

Background to the Reform Development	The Content of the Reform Development		The Effects of the Reform	
	Macroeconomic	Microeconomic	Macroeconomic	Microeconomic
1. In May 1989, Japanese banks began implementing tight monetary policy to stop the bubble economy from expanding. The rediscount rate increased dramatically when it reached 6% in August 1990 because of the plummeting of Japan's stock market and real estate values, which in turn caused companies to declare bankruptcy and had a domino effect on the entire economy. 2. Problems with poor claims caused the assets of Japan's banking industry to worsen. 3. Japan's financial marketplace has also shown a trend of divesting; foreign investors have slowly withdrawn.	1. Foreign exchange and investments: (1) Liberalization of foreign exchange services: foreign exchange banks, foreign exchange booth and specified foreign exchange dealers. They are able to freely operate foreign exchange services. (2) Liberalization of foreign capital trade: Rescinded the requirement that required approval or reporting of multinational investment, foreign liquidation and asset trade, and also simplified the paperwork following said activities.	1. Capital sales management: (1) Handling bankrupt financial institutions according to Financial Reconstruction Law. (2) Using capital adequacy ratio to determine the healthiness of a financial institution via Financial Function Early Strengthening Law and assist banks that do not have sufficient capital. (3) Financial asset securitization and increase the circulation of secured securities via Special Purpose Companies (SPC) policies.	1. Rate of fluctuation in GDP: It rose from US$ 436.172 billion (1997, Q1)to US$ 443.657 billion (2002, Q4). 2. Stock index: The fluctuation in the stock prices has been great. It soared from 394 points (1997, Q1) to 71,523 points(1999, Q1) showing that the Japanese government's numerous policies have been accepted by investors. However, it later plummeted to 2091 points (2002, Q4). 3. Exchange rate: Japanese yen was once at JY$ 117.9398 (1997, Q3), and	1. Mergers and number of financial institutions: Since 1999, 12 of Japan's cosmopolitan banks merged into 4 large financial enterprises. 2. Number of individuals in the finance industry: Those in the finance industry experienced layoffs and downsizing. 3. Capital adequacy ratio: At the end of 1999, the capital adequacy ratio for large banks offering international services increased to 11.79%. The capital adequacy ratio for local banks not offering international services also reached 9.69%.

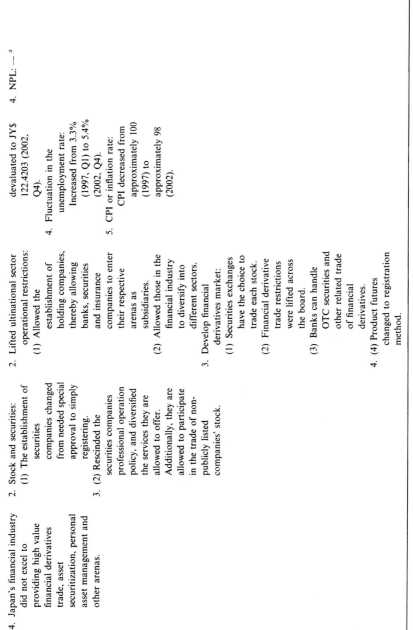

4. Japan's financial industry did not excel to providing high value financial derivatives trade, asset securitization, personal asset management and other arenas.

2. Stock and securities:
   (1) The establishment of securities companies changed from needed special approval to simply registering.
3. (2) Rescinded the securities companies professional operation policy, and diversified the services they are allowed to offer. Additionally, they are allowed to participate in the trade of non-publicly listed companies' stock.

2. Lifted ultinational sector operational restrictions:
   (1) Allowed the establishment of holding companies, thereby allowing banks, securities and insurance companies to enter their respective arenas as subsidiaries.
   (2) Allowed those in the financial industry to diversify into different sectors.
3. Develop financial derivatives market:
   (1) Securities exchanges have the choice to trade each stock.
   (2) Financial derivative trade restrictions were lifted across the board.
   (3) Banks can handle OTC securities and other related trade of financial derivatives.
4. (4) Product futures changed to registration method.

devalued to JY$ 122.4203 (2002, Q4).
4. Fluctuation in the unemployment rate: Increased from 3.3% (1997, Q1) to 5.4% (2002, Q4).
5. CPI or inflation rate: CPI decreased from approximately 100 (1997) to approximately 98 (2002).

4. NPL: —ª

Note: Source of Statistical Information: (1) DATASTREAM; (2) Ching-wen Cheng (2001). Japan's financial reform and prospects. Taiwan Economic Research Quarterly Review, 24(7), 18–23.
ªUnable to find this information for the chart.

Table 5. The Content and Effect of the Financial Reform on China (1998).

Background to the Reform Development	The Content of the Reform Development		The Effects of the Reform	
	Macroeconomic	Microeconomic	Macroeconomic	Microeconomic
1. Corporate economic effectiveness dropped resulting in serious loss.	1. Foreign exchange and investment:	1. Asset services management:	1. Fluctuation rate of GDP: It increased from US$ 25.55 billion(1997) to US$36.938 billion.	1. Mergers and the number of financial institutions: The number of financial institutions slightly dropped from 226,145 (1997) to 222,090 (1998).
2. Due to massive amounts of bad assets in the financial institutions, the asset to debt ratio is too high. 20% of the total assets of state-owned commercial banks are bad assets. The banking system has reached a point of high risk.	(1) Set exchange rates were utilized during the financial crisis. (2) The liberalization and implementation of foreign currency savings and loan rates began in 2000. Additionally, it foresaw that over the following 3–5 years, RMB savings and loan rates would be liberalized.	(1) Rescinded all restrictions regarding size of loans for state-owned commercial banks. (2) Beginning in the latter part of 1998, trust and investment companies slowly began merging and being taken over. The goal of authorities was to decrease the number of trust and investment companies to approximately 40 during 2001.	2. Stock index: The Shanghai B stocks were opened to foreign investors. The index before the crisis had a high of nearly 90. It then plummeted to approximately 25 (1999, Q1), however, it later rebounded to 120.65 points(2002, Q4).	2. G. Number of individuals in the finance industry: The number of employees working at financial institutions fell from almost 10,000 to approximately 5,000.
3. The origin of the investment capital is irrational. Hid the worries of inflation.	(3) In December 2000, the People's Bank decided to slowly increase the exchange rate fluctuation area to 10–15%.	(3) Established Asset Management Company (AMC) to specialize in the handling of the long-term bad assets of the 4 state-run commercial	3. Exchange rate: It has remained very stable averaging US$1 being equal to between RMB$ 8.25 and RMB$ 8.3.	3. Capital adequacy ratio: —a 4. NPL: Four financial asset management companies took on the bad assets of four large commercial banks. Of those,
	2. Stock and securities: (1) Established People's Bank Supervisory Bank and the Trust Industry. China Securities		4. Fluctuation in unemployment rate: It rose from 3.1% (1997) to 4% (2002).	approximately 71% had already performed asset liquidation. After

Regulatories Commission oversees the futures and securities industries. China Insurance Regulatory Commission oversees the financial industry and the supervisory sytems in place within the insurance industry.

(2) Strengthened forces stopping the underground trade of RMB and securities of value.

(3) Beginning December 2000, B stocks with foreign investors were allowed to be traded in the marketplace.

3. Reserve deposit ratio In March 1998, the People's Bank dropped the reserve deposit ratio rate from 13% to 8%.

banks. Debt-to-Equity Swap policy was also implemented.

(4) Established 5 levels of loan distinction policy. Loans are separated into normal, attention needed, secondary, suspicious and loss.

2. Central bank institutional reform:
Reform of the management system at the People's Bank took place in order to prevent the involvement of unrelated levels of government. Abandoned the original 32 provincial branches and changed them into 9 interprovincial branches.

5. CPI or inflation rate: CPI dropped from 105.2 (1997, Q1) to 99.04 (2002, Q4). There is a slight deflation phenomenon.

ridding themselves of bad assets, four state-owned commercial banks were able to control the overdue loan ratio to 20%.

Note: Source of Statistical Information: (1) DATASTREAM; (2) Keng-Hsiao Lin (2000). *China's banking system structure and reform.* Master's thesis, Taiwan University International Business Research.
[a] Unable to find this information for the chart.

Table 6. The Content and Effect of the Financial Reform on Taiwan (Latter Portion of 1998).

Background to the Reform Development	The Content of the Reform Development		The Effects of the Reform	
	Macroeconomic	Microeconomic	Macroeconomic	Microeconomic
1. The financial crisis began in Q3 of 1997.	1. Foreign exchange and investment:	1. Asset services management:	1. Fluctuation rate of GDP: It increased from US$ 6595.1 billion (1998, Q4) to US$ 7205.6 billion (2002, Q4).	1. Mergers and number of financial institutions: (1) The number of financial institutions dropped from 482 (1998) to 418 (August 2002). Hence the effectiveness of mergers.
2. After 1998 land mine shares effect caused a local financial crisis.	(1) Established foreign exchange bank policies. Banks which wish to offer foreign exchange services must receive approval from authorities.	Public fund management companies, investment trusts and investment consultants are unable to be fully empowered to perform these services for their clients.	2. B. Stock index: It dropped from 635.79 (1998) to 441.05 (2002).	(2) 14 financial holding companies merged with 53 banks, securities, insurance and financial peripheral institutions.
3. In 2000, governmental parties taking their place, while America's high-tech stocks suffered setbacks.	(2) Individuals and companies have Forex settlement amounts of US$ 5 million and US$ 50 million. However, those exceeding NT$ 500,000 must fill out a declaration form.	2. Lifted multinational operational restrictions: Established financial holding companies thereby allowing banks an avenue by which to enter these arenas by using a subsidiary.	3. Exchange rate: It devaluated from 32.216 (1998) to 34.753 (2002).	2. Number of Individuals in the finance industry: It decreased from 119,529 (1998) to 115,575 (June 2002).
4. Out-of-date financial system.	(3) Currently, foreigners (those who have not registered and been approved by the government) must fill out a declaration form for Forex settlement amounts exceeding NT$ 100,000.	3. Develop financial derivatives market: (1) Currently there are 3 kinds of futures products: Taiwan stock index futures, electronics and finance/insurance stock index futures.	4. Fluctuation rate of unemployment: It increased from 2.7% (1998) to 5.2% (2002).	3. Capital adequacy ratio: —[a]
5. There was a lack of financial information and little supervisory oversight.		(2) Banks now have the choice at which exchange rate they use for New	5. CPI or inflation rate: The inflation rate decreased from 1.7% (1998) to −0.2% (2002).	4. NPL: It increased from 4.93% (December 1998) to 6.39% (June 2003). There was an uprising trend after the financial reform.
6. As they were unable to establish a system of controls, bad loans and bad accounts were continually occurring causing the banks' overdue loan ratio to remain very high.				

2. Stock and securities:
   (1) The limit on investments in the stock market was increased to 50%, and the limit was lifted on January 1, 2001.
   (2) QFII wire transfer amounts were increased to US$ 120 million in November 1999.
   (3) Securities brokers and futures brokers needed approval before being established.
   (4) The handling fee for securities trading began using a tiered system.
   (5) Prohibits collective market outside trading.
   (6) Ratio of investments in the stock market by insurance companies cannot exceed 35%.

Taiwan Dollars and another 23 different new financial services

Note: Source of Statistical Information: (1) DATASTREAM; (2) Ministry of Finance, Financial Division.
[a]Unable to find this information for the chart.

Table 7. The Content and Effect of the Financial Crisis on Singapore (1998).

Background to the Reform Development	The Content of the Reform Development		The Effects of the Reform	
	Macroeconomic	Microeconomic	Macroeconomic	Microeconomic
Similar to Hong Kong, it is called a regional financial center. It was affected by neighboring countries due to the financial crisis, which caused Singapore banks to reap more profits than losses.	1. Foreign exchange and investment: (1) Lifted restrictions on uses of Singapore Dollar in foreign markets. Restrictions on borrowing by foreigners also increased to 1 billion. (2) Maintained the principle of Singapore Dollar being international. 2. Securities and stock (1) Decreased the IPO standards for companies, and simplified the IPO process for foreign companies in Singapore, thereby increasing the number of publicly listed companies. (2) Liberalized the fees for handling the sale and purchase of stock.	1. Asset services management: (1) State-run companies can take their surplus capital and have it managed by private fund. (2) Loaning foreign capital fund management companies entered the standard for the Singapore market. The standard for legal/corporate officer of foreign capital trust needn't pay stock tax as it was decreased to 5 billion dollars. (3) The Singapore government issued Singapore $ 25 billion to hasten and succeed at becoming Asia's fund management center. (4) Simplified the process for a legal/juridical/corporate officer to establish an investment trust and business communiqué forms.	1. The fluctuation rate of GDP: It increased from US$ 84.3 billion (1998) to US$ 85.8 billion (2002). 2. Stock index: From 1452.79 (1999) to 1768.56 (2001). 3. Exchange rate: It devaluated from 1.612 (1998) to 1.7341 (2001). 4. Fluctuation in the unemployment rate: It increased from 3.2% (1998) to 4.4% (2002). 5. CPI or inflation rate: The inflation rate dropped from −0.3% (1998) to −0.4% (2002).	1. Mergers and number of financial institutions: —[a] 2. Number of individuals in the finance industry: —[a] 3. Capital adequacy ratio—[a] 4. NPL: —[a]

(3) The limit of stock investment ratio by insurance companies was increased to 45%.

(4) Revised corporate law allowing for publicly listed companies to purchase their own stock.

(5) The Singapore Stock Exchange Discussion Panel suggested improvements in exchange for personnel, broader commissions, terms and new products and services. This was done to make Singapore's marketplace more global and more competitive.

2. Develop financial derivatives markets:

(1) Singapore Stock Exchange and SIMEX merged to create SGX-DT, and they established a private stock company allowing them to closely join on commercial policies, and later engage in major investing.

(2) Primary financial products include Euro-Yen interest rate futures, MSCI TaiEx futures, options, and Nikkei stock average futures. In the future, they plan to add Malaysia, Hong Kong and other Asian countries' stock index futures, exchange rate futures and other financial derivatives.

Note: Source of Statistical Information: (1) DATASTREAM; (2) Singapore Statistics Bureau. http://www.singstat.gov.sg/index.html.

[a]Unable to find this information for the chart.

Table 8. The Content and Effect of Financial Reform on Korea (December 1997).

Background to the Reform Development	The Content of the Reform Development		The Effects of the Reform	
	Macroeconomic	Microeconomic	Macroeconomic	Microeconomic
1. Overly relied upon large companies and focus industries. 2. The government controlled bank loans with policies, which made for companies overly investing and price slashing. There were also losses in exports. 3. High debt ratio and short-term foreign debt increased too quickly. 4. Each financial institution began short-term borrowing large amounts of foreign capital to compete for long-term profits with short-term loans.	1. Foreign exchange and investment: (1) Rescinded the limitations on the foreign currency fluctuation rate on US and Japanese currencies making WON a freely fluctuating currency. (2) Allow foreigners to open savings and trust accounts in Korean financial institutions for 1 year or more. They are also able to distribute foreign securities. (3) Permit companies or financial institutions to borrow money from overseas for one year or less and property investment.	1. Asset management sales: (1) Bad asset management fund was established, and KAMCO was authorized to assist in handling bad financial assets for each financial institution. (2) In accord with the financial supervisory organization establishment act, the FSC was officially established. All of the previous supervisory duties handled by the ministry of finance and the central bank were turned over to the FSC. The FSC take full responsibility for promoting and implementing internal financial restructuring. (3) The FSC separated banks into three categories (unapproved, controlled/approved,	1. Fluctuation rate of GDP: It increased from US$ 62,856.76 million (1997, Q4) to US$ 113,148.3 million (2002. Q4). 2. Stock index: It increased from 297.9 points (1998, Q2) to 1028.1 points (1999, Q4), and then slowly dropped to 627.6 points (2002. Q4). 3. Exchange rate: The exchange rates went from WON$ 1390.8:US$ 1 (1998. Q3) to WON$ 1186.1:US$ 1 (2002. Q4).	1. Mergers and number of financial institutions: After the reorganiziation of Korean financial institutions, the number of banks decreased from 6,117 in 1997 to 5,183 in 1998. 2. Number of individuals in the finance industry: Until 1998 and within 3 years, the number of employees decreased by more than 38,000, which is equal to about 33.6%. 3. Capital adequacy ratio: —[a]

(4) Privatization of the operation of foreign exchange business.

2. Stock and securities:
   (1) Limit at which foreigners can invest in the stock market was increased from 26% to 55%, and then the limitation was rescinded on May 25, 1998.

3. (2) The limitation of foreign ownership in state-run public businesses was increased from 25% to 30%.

and approved) and designed a reform plan for each of them.

2. Lifted Multinational operational restrictions:
   (1) Capital structure reform agreement was signed with 64 companies. Decreased the number of subsidiaries and affiliates making them more professional companies.
   (2) Develop financial derivatives markets:
   (3) All who go through foreign exchange banks will not be limited with regard to derivatives markets trading.

4. NPL:
   From its peak of 13.6%, it dropped to 5.6% at the end of 2001.

4. Fluctuation rate in unemployment rate: It slowly grew from 2.6% (1999, Q4) 8.5% (1999, Q1), and then dropped to 3% (2002, Q4).

5. CPI or inflation rate: CPI increased from 79.7 (1997, Q4) to 98.6 (2002, Q4).

Note: Source of Statistical Information: (1) DATASTREAM; (2) Finance Department at Korea First Bank, Explore South Korean Banking Financial Reforms and Management Post-Asia Financial Crisis, Korea First Bank Economic Newsletter, No. 445, April 2002: p. 36: (3) The Bank of Korea website, http://www.bok.or.kr/svc/frame_eng.html.
[a]Unable to find this information for the chart.

Table 9. The Content and Effect of Financial Reform on Hong Kong.

Background to the Reform Development	The Content of the Reform Development		The Effects of the Reform	
	Macroeconomic	Microeconomic	Macroeconomic	Microeconomic
1. Hong Kong's economic structure relies heavily upon the financial and service industries' high profits and quick returns.	1. Foreign exchange and investment: In order to stabilize the Linked Exchange Rate System of the Hong Kong dollar, Hong Kong's financial management bureau recalled Hong Kong dollars creating a currency reduction and an increased interest rate. Hong Kong government paid out US$ 8.8 billion to protect the Hong Kong dollar in August 1998.	1. Financial derivatives market: (1) Hong Kong futures exchange began accepting exchange fund bills and notes as security for buying and selling stock options and futures since December 13, 1999. (2) Establish the Tracker Fund and slowly released the government-held stock.	1. The Fluctuation rate of GDP: It slowly rebounded from US$ 39979.34 million (1998, Q1) to US$ 42385.4 million (2002, Q4).	1. Mergers and number of financial institutions The approved number of institution headquarters decreased from approximately 366 (1997) to approximately 232 (2002).
2. From October 17, 1983, Hong Kong began using the Linked Exchange Rate System, which brought the exchange rate to HKD$ 7.8:US$ 1.	2. Stock and securities: From August 14, 1998, the Hong Kong government has strongly been protecting the stock market. It utilized US$ 15 billion from the foreign exchange fund to purchase over HKD$ 110 billion in blue chip stocks.		2. Stock index: Hong Kong Hang Seng Index rebounded from 7883.45 points (1998, Q2) to 9321.29 points (2002, Q4).	2. Number of individuals in the finance industry: The number of individuals working in the finance industry increased from 410,000 (1998) to 475,000 (2002).
3. The growth rate of Hong Kong's fluctuation rate of GDP cannot compare with Hong Kong's currency growth rate and Hong Kong's real estate price index growth rate.			3. Exchange rate: From HKD$ 7.7363:US$ 1 (1997, Q4) to HKD$ 7.7987:US$ 1 (2002, Q4).	3. Capital adequacy ratio: The capital adequacy ratio of local Hong Kong banks increased from 18.5% (1998) to 18.7% (1999),
4. During the first two years of the financial crisis, Hong Kong Hang Seng Stock Index experienced 139% growth.			4. The fluctuation rate of the unemployment rate: Increased from 1.1% (1997, Q4) to 3% (2002, Q4).	

3. Finance policy:
   Several tax reforms
   have been proposed
   including a decrease
   in personal income
   tax, corporate/
   business tax, and it
   also increased each
   tax accommodation
   hoping to decrease
   the financial
   burdens of most
   individuals and
   businesses in Hong
   Kong, thereby
   stimulating the
   economy.
   Additionally,
   developing
   numerous public
   foundation
   construction plans
   to accommodate for
   the growth needed
   to create more jobs
   in the workforce.

5. CPI or inflation rate:
   In view of CPI, it
   shows that there
   may be currency
   reduction as it
   went from 106.2
   (1998, Q2) to
   93.9 (2002, Q4).

   and then
   dropped to
   16.6% in 2001.

4. NPL:
   It increased from
   1.07% (1997) to
   5.72% (1999),
   and then slowly
   decreased to
   3.42% (2002).

Note: Source of statistical information: (1).DATASTREAM; (2). Hong Kong Monetary Authority, http://www.info.gov.hk/hkma/.

Table 10. The Content and Effect of Financial Reform on The Philippines (1998).

Background to the Reform Development	The Content of the Reform Development		The Effects of the Reform	
	Macroeconomic	Microeconomic	Macroeconomic	Microeconomic
1. El Nino caused great havoc and loss to the agricultural industry, and adding the political unrest to that has made for financial instability. 2. Due to the Mexican financial crisis and the financial instability in The Philippines in 1995, foreign investors left The Philippines, which caused the peso to devaluate. As such, The Philippine government started to interfere with the foreign exchange market, but the peso was still very difficult to prevent devaluation. The government needed to abandon the strategy of targeting the US dollar. The government implemented currency reduction policy and increased short-term interest rates, thereby bringing growth to the financial marketplace	1. Foreign exchange and investment: Purchasing foreign currency limitations went from 20% to 5%, whereas selling foreign currency went from 10% to 20% lowering the OTC buy/sell limit on foreign currency of US$ 10,000. 2. Stocks and securities: (1) Even at the most critical time, the government does not interfere with the stock market opening it for more people to invest. Established a committee to accelerate the increased capital and increased size of publicly listed companies. They allowed the brokers which had not yet lost their stock market membership	1. Asset services management: The Philippines deposit insurance company began supervising 1 commercial bank, 7 financial companies and 44 local banks. The Philippines Central Bank utilized stricter supervisory standards for financial institutions. It prepared to redefine bad debt in order to have a healthier economy. 2. Developing financial derivatives market: January 7, 1998 opened no capital, long-term foreign exchange to control and restrain the opportunistic demand for currency market US dollars. In March, they announced limitations on NDF to prevent opportunists from playing the exchange market. In April 1998, they announced that over the next 18 months, the banking system would not renew contracts with NDF.	1. Fluctuation rate of GDP: It dropped from US$ 8289.43 million (1997, Q2) to US$ 4919.634 million (1998, Q3), and then increased to US$ 5483.713 million (2002, Q4). 2. Stock index: The Philippines Stock Index decreased from 1072.2 points (1997, Q3) to 662.3 points (1997, Q4), and then dropped to 412.6 points (1998, Q3) where it stopped and then rebounded in Q1 of 2000 to 1089.2 points. After this, it dropped to 219.9 points (2002, Q4) due to government instability. 3. Exchange rate: The peso devaluated from 26.376: US$ 1	1. Mergers and the number of financial institutions: It increased from 17,297 (1997) to 19,297 (1999), and then decreased to 17,944 (2002). 2. Number of individuals in the finance industry: It increased slowly from 696,000 (1997) to 731,000 (2000, Q1), and then decreased at the end of 2000 to 678,000. 3. Capital adequacy ratio: —[a] 4. Overdue loan ratio: It increased from a 7,360.2 pesos NPL (1997) to 160,001 thousand pesos (1998). At the end of 2002, 24,510.2 pesos showing that bad debts continued to increase after the financial reform.

economy. However, due to the increase in capital costs, companies lost profits and some announced bankruptcy causing a huge increase in bad debt. Domestic credit is growing, and commercial banks' deposits have grown immensely. Along with all of this, the stock market dropped by 45%.

status to discontinue operations. (2) Liberalization of investments increasing the foreign investment holding amount to increase from 49% to 60%. 3. Fluid management Adjusted the crucial interest rate and discontinued the next evening borrowing policy to strengthen its liquidity. Increased required liquid reserve to prevent currency inflation after the depression. Decreased the legal reserve rate, and increased surplus reserve rate to help decrease loan costs and make funds more accessible.

3. Strengthen banking systems: Increasing the lowest requirement for bank capital to ensure the healthiness of the bank and to decrease moral crises. Increase the transparency of the banking system, and announce that the NPL, percentage of loans and other information will be included in borrowing interest rates and quarterly reports. Stricter standards were put into place for the establishment of a new bank.

(1997, Q2) to 34.35: US$ 1 (1997, Q3), and then devaluated even further to 53.385: US$ 1 (2002, Q4). 4. Fluctuation rate of the unemployment rate: The average in 1997 was 8.7%, and slowly increased to 11.4% in 2002. 5. CPI or inflation rate If we take 1994 as a base of calculating, the currency inflation rate in 1997 was 5.9%, and it was 3.1% in 2002. There is an indication of currency reduction.

Note: Source of Statistical Information: (1) DATASTREAM; (2) BANGKO SENTRAL NG PILIPINAS, http://www.bsp.gov.ph/.
aUnable to find this information for the chart.

the policies which came about due to the crisis. The research found that (1) due to domestic savings not commonly being sufficient to support investors' needs, they relied upon foreign assistance for a long time, which created a long-term deficit. Of those, Thailand was the worst of the 4 tigers, Malaysia was second and The Philippines was not very serious. Of the 4 dragons, South Korea had current account deficit, while Taiwan had a very strong economic structure. These have historically all had current account surplus. (2) Capital market had a disorderly opening creating short-term hot money attacking stock and foreign exchange markets expediting the collapse of the financial marketplace. Other than Taiwan, the other five Eastern Asian countries were unable to have a stable domestic financial marketplace after the opening of the capital market. They also stabilized domestic pricing and balanced the budgets for the ministry of finance creating a weak economic structure that is lacking because of the opening of the capital market which brought about a surge of international capital.

Li's (2001) thesis researches the stock markets and foreign exchange markets of 10 Asian countries/regions (Japan, China, Hong Kong, Taiwan, Korea, Singapore, Thailand, Malaysia, Indonesia and The Philippines) by using MA(1)-GARCH(1,1) model from March 17, 1994 to October 31, 2000 for the fluctuation of the stock market and foreign exchange market of each country. The result of the research was that (1) it observed the time that there was comparatively more fluctuation in the exchange rate, and the stock market prices were also fluctuating; (2) there has been no observed systematic relationship between the fluctuation found in the exchange rate and the stock market; (3) hypothetically, the instability in the fluctuation in the exchange rate is due to market investor's anticipated devaluation, which thereby affected the stock market by driving the stock prices down and increased fluctuation. This was seen prior to the financial crisis. We did not discover anticipated devaluation with regard to a majority of the stock market returns. They had a negative transfer effect. After the financial crisis, anticipated devaluation had a negative transfer effect on all stock market regards with the exception of China. The exchange market fluctuation is, in fact, one of the reasons the fluctuation in the stock market occurred; (4) after the financial crisis, the stock market and exchange market rates of return in America, Japan, Hong Kong and Singapore had an increasing trend when compared with the stock market rates of return and the fluctuating transfer effect in each Asian country. This shows that the international capital market is moving toward a trend that compiles daily. Investors investing in the stock market not only need to take the economic foundation of the country where the investment will be made into consideration, but also must not neglect the financial trends globally and regionally. By doing so, investors can lower the investment risk.

Liu's (2000) thesis wishes to analyze eight Asian countries from an international investor's perspective, and to explore the relationship among Asian stock markets, the global stock market and exchange rates. It further delves into the macroeconomic variables of the world and each country to forecast exceeding returns in the stock market. It also takes the Asian financial crisis into consideration with regard to the model. The models utilized for the study were OLS and GARCH (1,1). It discovered that using local information to forecast exceeding returns in the stock market in Asian new countries was better than using global information. This result was the same as that proven by Harvey (1995), however, the difference was that this research found that global information and global indexes have a greater level of influence upon the stock markets in Asian countries. This proves the globalization that has taken place in the Asian stock market over the past 10 years. Additionally, it can substantially forecast that the exceeding returns in each county's stock market are not all the same, and that collectively speaking, each country's interest rate is an important factor that is prevalent in the forecasting of the economic variables of the respective countries. GARCH(1,1) model fits well with the forecasted exceeding returns in the stock markets of some countries like Indonesia, Korea, Singapore, and Thailand, but regarding their forecasting abilities and forecasting results, the OLS and GARCH(1,1) models were used and showed no substantial difference in each country's stock market forecasting base. It discovered that not until after the Asian financial crisis occurred did they find the notable relationship with the exchange rates. After the financial crisis, forecasting models began experiencing major structural changes, which means that they had elements that could affect the stock market returns. These structural changes created a sample foreign investment strategy, which was not highly effective due to this.

Chih-Ping Li's (2000) thesis explores the role played by similar funds in the midst of the Asian financial crisis. The research utilized capital flow data and changes in the stock markets and exchange markets in Malaysia, Thailand, Indonesia, Singapore, The Philippines, Korea and Hong Kong to show: (1) Stock prices and foreign capital began moving overseas mostly prior to the time of the financial crisis. (2) Foreign capital flows only account for a small amount of local stock market volume or market value. It is extremely unlikely that this was the main cause of the Asian financial crisis. (3) Foreign capital flow decreased after the crisis. Foreign investors became very cautious before investing in Asia. (4) Foreign capital flow and local stock markets' rates of return are not really related. It is difficult to conclude whether local or foreign investors had better information before and after the financial crisis. Additionally, we also explored the net value of 23 closed national funds and the market price for pre- and post-financial crisis and any correlation they may have. First, with regard to the causality of funds' net value and market price, we found that half of the US funds' market prices did not have a significant relationship with the net value of Asian funds. However, the net value of all of Asia's funds has a significant causality relationship with US market prices. In analyzing the value at risk (VAR) model, the substantial proof and results show that the attack on the net value rate of return had its greatest effect the first quarter on market price rate of return for pre- and post-Asian financial crisis (positive). Regarding the variable for market price return rules, the net value rate of return for the first quarter was described as reaching as high as 33.8%. Thereafter, increases were limited.

According to the *Indian Express Newspaper* dated September 9, 1998, a large majority of Malaysia's economy relies upon the export of electronic products. As such, when the global information and technology markets began to suffer, Malaysia reacted immediately. At this time, Ringgit increased in value while the currencies in Japan and other countries devaluated. Moreover, short-term capital was flowing overseas and there was capital preparation for loss. Prior to 1998, Malaysia's domestic investments never seemed to grow and made a change for the better. Due to the financial crisis, Malaysia took over management and increased its controls. Malaysia controlled the exchange rate to remain at US$1 being equal to approximately $4 Ringgits. At the same time, they controlled the exchange rate market, they also restricted opportunists' plans for the Ringgit. The Ringgit devaluated 40% due to the Asian financial crisis.

3. RESEARCH DESIGN AND STATISTICAL METHODS

3.1. Establishing Hypothesis

1 *The fluctuation rate of GDP for the 10 Eastern Asian countries was higher for post-Asian financial crisis than pre-Asian financial crisis.* During the economic crisis, the 10 Eastern Asian countries were all affected. During the financial crisis, the fluctuation rate of GDP in Taiwan decreased. This paper proves that after each country's government had actively

implemented reforms, the average fluctuation rate of GDP (μ_2) for the 10 Eastern Asian countries was greater after the financial reform policy implementation than the average fluctuation rate of GDP (μ_1)before the Asian financial crisis. Moreover, the hypothesis is $H_0 : \mu_1 = \mu_2; H_1 :$ $\mu_1 < \mu_2$

2 *The stock index for the 10 Eastern Asian countries was higher for post-Asian financial crisis than pre-Asian financial crisis.* The Asian financial crisis adversely affected the stock indexes of the 10 Eastern Asian countries causing them to rapidly plummet. Through the financial reforms that each country adopted, we saw an increase. Although the increase experienced by each country was different, for example, the Korean stock index rebounded to its pre-financial crisis standard. Though the Thai stock index slightly increased, it still lingered around the lower points. This paper proves that after the implementation of financial reform policies for the 10 Eastern Asian countries for post-Asian financial crisis, the average stock index (μ_2) for each country was higher than pre-financial reform average stock index (μ_1). The hypothesis is $H_0 : \mu_1 = \mu_2; H_1 :$ $\mu_1 < \mu_2$.

3 *The standard of the exchange rate for the 10 Eastern Asian countries was lower for post-Asian financial crisis than pre-Asian financial crisis.* As the documentation shows, the foreign exchange rate standard devaluated quite seriously for each of the 10 Eastern Asian countries during the Asian financial crisis, with the exception of Singapore and Taiwan. As such, this paper tests and proves the comparison after the implementation of each country's financial reform policies. It takes the average exchange rate (μ_2) for the 10 Eastern Asian countries after the Asian financial crisis and compares it with the average exchange rate (μ_1) prior to the Asian financial crisis and finds that it is lower. It is then experimented and revaluated. The hypothesis is: $H_0 : \mu_1 = \mu_2; H_1 : \mu_1 > \mu_2$.

4 *The standard of the inflation rate (CPI) for the 10 Eastern Asian countries was lower for post-Asian financial crisis than pre-Asian financial crisis.* Due to the instability of the exchange rate, the 10 countries of Eastern Asia faced pressures of inflation during the Asian financial crisis. This paper tests and proves that after the implementation of each country's financial reform policies, the average inflation rate (μ_2) for the 10 Eastern Asian countries after the Asian financial crisis was lower than the average inflation rate (μ_1) before the Asian financial crisis. The hypothesis is: $H_0 :$ $\mu_1 = \mu_2; H_1 : \mu_1 > \mu_2$.

5 *The fluctuation rate of the unemployment rate for the 10 Eastern Asian countries was lower for post-Asian financial crisis than pre-Asian financial*

crisis. During the financial crisis, each country's businesses faced difficult trials. Layoffs and downsizing were among the methods by which companies were able to stay afloat or redeem themselves. This, in turn, created a high rate of fluctuation of the unemployment rate. If each country's post-financial crisis financial reforms were successful, it would create more jobs thereby clearly decreasing the fluctuation rate of the unemployment rate. This paper tests and proves that after the implementation of each country's financial reform policies, the average fluctuation rate of the unemployment rate (μ_2) of the 10 countries of Eastern Asia was lower than the average fluctuation of the unemployment rate (μ_1) during pre-Asian financial crisis. The hypothesis is: $H_0 : \mu_1 = \mu_2; H_1 : \mu_1 > \mu_2$.

3.2. Statistical Methods

Mann–Whitney U test and Intervention Analysis were separately utilized to prove whether a significant difference was found in pre- and post-Asian financial crisis for the fluctuation rate of GDP, stock index, exchange rate, inflation rate, and fluctuation rate of the unemployment rate for the 10 Eastern Asian countries after financial reforms. The structure of the Intervention Analysis model utilizes ASTSA statistical software structure transformation function. Intervention effect utilizes Statistica statistical software to calculate. Additionally, Mann–Whitney U test utilizes SPSS statistical software to calculate. These statistics calculate U as

$$U = \left[n_1 n_2 + \frac{n_1(n_1 + 1)}{2} \right] - W$$

4. EMPIRICAL RESULTS AND ANALYSIS

The descriptive statistical values from 10 Eastern Asian macroeconomic variables show that Malaysia experienced the highest fluctuation rate of GDP, and Indonesia had the second highest. Indonesia and Japan had the highest differences in the stock index. Additionally, the exchange rate in Indonesia experienced extreme amounts of change. The Philippines had the highest amount of change in the inflation rate, with Thailand and Korea following. Hong Kong had the highest fluctuation rate of the unemployment rate with Korea and The Philippines following. (Table 11)

Table 11. Descriptive Statistical Values of the Macroeconomic Variables for the 10 Countries of Eastern Asia.

Variables	Observation	Minimum	Maximum	Mean	Standard Deviation
△ GDP					
Thailand	40	−0.28	0.21	6.577E−02	8.766E−02
Indonesia	40	−0.4	0.64	1.817E−02	0.169
Malaysia	40	−0.199	0.131	0.050	0.659
Japan	40	−0.0.9	0.17	4.109E−03	5.742E−02
China	10	−0.23	0.12	4.680E−02	0.100
Taiwan	40	−0.1	0.07	7.293E−03	3.789E−02
Singapore	10	−0.02	0.11	5.094E−03	4.889E−02
Korea	39	−4.6	0.19	0.009	0.094
Hong Kong	39	−1.2	0.10	0.013	0.058
The Philippines	39	−2.4	0.27	0.004	0.115
Stock index					
Thailand	40	253.82	1682.85	714.011	445.607
Indonesia	40	−46743	11577	−8793.07	15745.332
Malaysia	40	373.52	1275.32	834.212	231.060
Japan	40	80.00	71523.00	3231.0750	11204.293
China	40	25.41	212.85	76.680	42.439
Taiwan	40	5486.10	7944.50	6826.733	618.766
Singapore	23	576.60	2266.54	989.814	492.929
Korea	40	297.90	1050.50	729.367	192.986
Hong Kong	40	6388.86	17406.54	11263.718	2785.671
The Philippines	40	219.90	1179.30	758.703	256.448
Exchange Rate −US$					
Thailand	40	24.65	48.15	34.067	8.4257
Indonesia	40	2071	14900	5857.112	3722.755
Malaysia	40	2.46	4.06	3.216	0.637
Japan	40	84.49	139.99	113.626	11.768
China	40	5.72	8.71	8.069	0.783
Taiwan	40	25.58	35.03	30.083	3.283
Singapore	40	1.40	1.85	1.614	0.146
Korea	39	−0.27	1.23	0.207	0.258
Hong Kong	39	−0.16	0.34	0.040	0.135
The Philippines	39	−0.33	0.58	0.021	0.2254
CPI (%)					
Thailand	40	73	105	92.54	10.738
Indonesia	40	90.9	104.6	96.407	4.356
Malaysia	40	101.20	105.73	102.959	1.197
Japan	40	97.10	101.60	99.335	1.128
China	40	97.80	126.90	106.507	8.937
Taiwan	40	85.21	101.22	95.977	4.581
Singapore	40	91.50	102.40	98.645	3.085
Korea	40	72.60	107.90	91.770	10.710
Hong Kong	40	76.40	106.80	95.692	8.300

Table 11. (*Continued*)

Variables	Observation	Minimum	Maximum	Mean	Standard Deviation
The Philippines	40	89.76	168.10	130.613	25.142
△ Unemployment Rate					
Thailand	10	−0.3	2.89	0.186	0.957
Indonesia	10	−0.32	0.64	0.132	0.285
Malaysia	21	−1.579	2.903	0.753	0.9.95
Japan	40	2.30	5.40	3.920	0.966
China	10	2.60	4.00	3.130	0.400
Taiwan	40	−0.19	0.28	4.138E−02	0.115
Singapore	10	−0.3	0.78	8.296E−02	0.299
Korea	40	1.80	8.50	3.642	1.772
Hong Kong	40	1.60	7.60	3.987	1.865
The Philippines	40	7.40	13.90	9.895	1.743

Source: Datastream and *Taiwan Economic Journal* database.

4.1. Comparison of the Difference in the Macroeconomic Variables for the 10 Eastern Asian Countries for Pre- and Post-Asian Financial Crisis: Mann–Whitney U Test

(1) *Comparison of the difference of the fluctuation rate of GDP for the 10 Eastern Asian countries for pre- and post-Asian financial crisis.* With a 95% confidence level, Hong Kong's average fluctuation rate of GDP distribution was different for pre- and post-Asian financial crisis. Its p-value was 0.018, and had already reached the level of significance of 5%. The fluctuation rate of GDP distribution of the remaining nine countries was the same for pre- and post-Asian financial crisis. This shows that the average fluctuation rate of GDP of the remaining nine countries did not display a significant difference meaning that during pre- and post-Asian financial crisis, Hong Kong's fluctuation rate of GDP is significantly different, while the average fluctuation rate of GDP in the other nine countries shows no significant difference. (Table 12)

(2) *Comparison of the difference in the stock index for the 10 Eastern Asian countries for pre- and post-Asian financial crisis.* With a 99% confidence level, the average stock index distribution in Thailand, Indonesia, Malaysia, Singapore, Korea, and The Philippines was different for pre- and post-Asian financial crisis. Its p-values were 0.000, 0.000, 0.000,

Table 12.   Comparison of the Fluctuation Rate of GDP for the 10 Eastern Asian Countries for Pre- and Post-Asian Financial Crisis – Mann–Whitney *U* Test.

Country	Mann–Whitney *U* Statistical Measurement	Wilcoxon *W* Statistical Measurement	*Z* Test	Near Significance (Two-Tailed)	2*(Single-Tailed significance)
Thailand	198.000	172.000	−0.054	0.957	0.968
Indonesia	408.000	382.000	−0.757	0.449	0.461
Malaysia	166.000	376.000	−0.674	0.500	0.513
Japan	187.00	397.00	−0.352	0.725	0.738
China	10.000	25.000	−0.522	0.602	0.690
Taiwan	177.000	387.000	−0.622	0.534	0.547
Singapore	6.000	21.000	−1.358	0.175	0.222
Korea	147.000	337.000	−1.208	0.227	0.235
Hong Kong	106.000	316.000	−2.360	0.018	0.018**
The Philippines	188.000	398.000	−0.056	0.955	0.967

Significance levels at
*10%;
**5%.

0.002, 0.005 and 0.000, all of which reached a 1% level of significance. Additionally, with a 90% confidence level, the average stock index distribution in Japan and Hong Kong was different for pre- and post-Asian financial crisis. Its p-value was 0.043, and it reached a 5% level of significance. The average stock index distribution in others like Taiwan and China was the same for pre- and post-Asian financial crisis showing that the average stock indexes in Taiwan and China have not yet showed significant difference, meaning that the average stock index for Japan, Hong Kong, Thailand, Indonesia, Malaysia, Singapore, Korea and The Philippines showed a significant difference for pre- and post-Asian financial crisis, while the average stock indexes of Taiwan and China did not show significant difference.˙ (Table 13)

(3) *Comparison of the difference in the exchange rate for the 10 Eastern Asian countries for pre- and post-Asian financial crisis.* With a 99% confidence level, the average stock index distribution of the 10 Asian countries was different for pre- and post-Asian financial crisis. Its p-value was 0.000, and they all reached a 1% level of significance meaning that there truly is

Table 13. Comparison of the Stock Index for the 10 Eastern Asian Countries for Pre- and Post-Asian Financial Crisis – Mann–Whitney U Test.

Country	Mann–Whitney U Statistical Measurement	Wilcoxon W Statistical Measurement	Z Test	Near Significance (Two-Tailed)	2*(Single-Tailed Significance)
Thailand	7.000	217.000	−5.221	0.000***	0.000***
Indonesia	19.000	229.000	−4.896	0.000***	0.000***
Malaysia	39.000	249.000	−4.355	0.000***	0.000***
Japan	131.000	341.000	−1.866	0.062*	0.063*
China	195.000	405.000	−0.135	0.892	0.904
Taiwan	33.000	186.000	−0.744	0.457	0.493
Singapore	1.000	211.000	−2.647	0.008***	0.002***
Korea	98.000	308.000	−2.759	0.006***	0.005***
Hong Kong	125.000	335.000	−2.029	0.042**	0.043*
The Philippines	63.000	273.000	−3.706	0.000***	0.000***

Notes: Significance levels at
*10%;
**5%; and
***1%.

a significant difference in the exchange rates of the 10 Eastern Asian countries for pre- and post-Asian financial crisis. (Table 14)

(4) *Comparison of the difference in the consumption price index (CPI) for the 10 Eastern Asian countries for pre- and post-Asian financial crisis. With a 99% confidence level, the CPI distribution of the 10 Asian countries was different for pre- and post-Asian financial crisis.* Its p-value was 0.000, and they all reached a 1% level of significance, meaning that there truly is a significant difference in the CPI of the 10 Eastern Asian countries for pre- and post-Asian financial crisis. (Table 15)

(5) *Comparison of the difference in the fluctuation rate of the unemployment rate for the 10 Eastern Asian countries for pre- and post-Asian financial crisis. With a 95% confidence level, the fluctuation rate in the unemployment rate distribution of the 10 Asian countries was the same for pre- and post-Asian financial crisis.* Its p-value did not reach a 1% level of significance meaning that there was not a significant difference in the fluctuation rate in the unemployment rate of the 10 Eastern Asian countries for pre- and post-Asian financial crisis. (Table 16)

Table 14. Comparison of the Exchange Rate for the 10 Eastern Asian Countries for Pre- and Post-Asian Financial Crisis – Mann–Whitney U Test.

Country	Mann–Whitney U Statistical Measurement	Wilcoxon W Statistical Measurement	Z Test	Near Significance (Two-Tailed)	2*(Single-Tailed Significance)
Thailand	20.000	230.000	−4.869	0.000***	0.000***
Indonesia	0.000	210.000	−5.410	0.000***	0.000***
Malaysia	0.000	210.000	−5.630	0.000***	0.000***
Japan	80.000	290.000	−3.246	0.001***	0.001***
China	82.000	292.000	−3.193	0.001***	0.001***
Taiwan	3.000	213.000	−5.329	0.000***	0.000***
Singapore	5.000	215.000	−5.275	0.000***	0.000***
Korea	20.000	230.000	−4.869	0.000***	0.000***
Hong Kong	9.500	219.500	−5.156	0.000***	0.000***
The Philippines	4.000	214.000	−5.302	0.000***	0.000***

Significance levels at
*10%;
***1%.

Table 15. Comparison of the CPI for the 10 Eastern Asian Countries for Pre- and Post-Asian Financial Crisis – Mann–Whitney U Test.

Country	Mann–Whitney U Statistical Measurement	Wilcoxon W Statistical Measurement	Z Test	Near Significance (two-tailed)	2*(Single-Tailed Significance)
Thailand	0.000	210.000	−5.411	0.000***	0.000***
Indonesia	0.000	210.000	−5.413	0.000***	0.000***
Malaysia	100.500	310.500	−2.694	0.007***	0.006***
Japan	99.500	309.500	−2.723	0.006***	0.006***
China	1.000	211.000	−5.385	0.000***	0.000***
Taiwan	1.000	211.000	−5.383	0.000***	0.000***
Singapore	21.000	231.000	−4.844	0.000***	0.000***
Korea	0.000	210.000	−5.411	0.000***	0.000***
Hong Kong	85.500	295.500	−3.098	0.002***	0.001***
The Philippines	0.000	210.000	−5.410	0.000***	0.000***

Significance levels at
*10%;
***1%.

Table 16. Comparison of the Fluctuation Rate of the Unemployment Rate for the 10 Eastern Asian Countries for Pre - and Post-Asian Financial Crisis – Mann–Whitney *U* Test.

Country	Mann–Whitney *U* Statisitical Measurement	Wilcoxon *W* Statistical Measurement	*Z* Test	Near Significance (Two-Tailed)	2*(Single-Tailed Significance)
Thailand	13.000	28.000	−1.926	0.054	0.059
Indonesia	28.000	119.000	−0.444	0.657	0.703
Malaysia	21.500	31.500	−1.132	0.257	0.275
Japan	198.500	408.500	−0.041	0.968	0.968
China	11.500	26.500	−0.216	0.829	0.841
Taiwan	129.00	402.00	−0.216	0.829	0.841
Singapore	5.00	20.00	−1.567	0.117	0.151
Korea	190.000	400.000	0.000	1.000	1.000
Hong Kong	142.500	332.500	−1.335	0.182	0.184
The Philippines	169.000	359.000	−0.590	0.555	0.569

Significance level at
*1%.

4.2. Comparison of the Difference in the Macroeconomic Variables for the 10 Eastern Asian Countries for Pre- and Post-Asian Financial Crisis: Intervention Analysis

(1) *Comparison of the difference in the fluctuation rate of GDP for the 10 Eastern Asian countries for pre- and post-Asian financial crisis.* Analysis and results using intervention analysis show that Taiwan's fluctuation of GDP was higher for post-Asian financial crisis than for pre-Asian financial crisis. Its p-value was 0.0972, and it reached a 10% level of significance. Additionally, the fluctuation rates of GDP for Indonesia, Hong Kong and Thailand were also higher post-Asian financial crisis than for pre-Asian financial crisis. However, they did not reach a level of significance. Conversely, the fluctuation rate of GDP for The Philippines was lower for post-Asian financial crisis than for pre-Asian financial crisis. Its p-value was 0.0013, and it reached 1% level of significance. Additionally, the fluctuation rate of GDP for Japan, Korea and Malaysia was lower for post-Asian financial crisis than for pre-Asian financial crisis. However, they did not reach a level of significance. (Table 17)

(2) *Comparison of the difference in the stock index for the 10 Eastern Asian countries for pre- and post-Asian financial crisis.* Analysis and results using intervention analysis show that the stock index of The Philippines

and Korea was higher for post-Asian financial crisis than for pre-Asian financial crisis. Its p-values were 0.0102 and 0.0348, and it reached a 5% level of significance. Additionally, the stock index for Japan and China were also higher for post-Asian financial crisis than for pre-Asian financial crisis. However, they did not reach a level of significance.Conversely, the stock index for Malaysia was lower for post-Asian financial crisis than for pre-Asian financial crisis. Its p-value was 0.0368, and it reached a 5% level of significance. Additionally, the stock index for Indonesia, Hong Kong and Thailand was lower for post-Asian financial crisis than for pre-Asian financial crisis. However, they did not reach a level of significance. (Table 18)

(3) *Comparison of the difference in the exchange rate for the 10 Eastern Asian countries for pre- and post-Asian financial crisis.* Analysis and results using intervention analysis show that the exchange rates of Malaysia, Thailand, The Philippines, Singapore and Korea devaluated for post-Asian financial crisis. Its p-values were 0.0000, 0.0000, 0.00004, 0.00097 and 0.0000, and it reached a 1% level of significance. Additionally, the exchange rate for Indonesia also devaluated for post-Asian financial crisis. However, they did not reach a level of significance.Conversely, the exchange rates for Japan, China, Taiwan and Hong Kong revaluated for post-Asian financial crisis. However, they did not reach a level of significance. (Table 19)

(4) *Comparison of the difference in the CPI for the 10 Eastern Asian countries for pre- and post-Asian financial crisis.* Analysis and results using intervention analysis show that the CPI of Thailand and Singapore was higher for post-Asian financial crisis than for pre-Asian financial crisis. Its p-values were 0.0634 and 0.0845, and it reached a 10% level of significance. Additionally, the CPI for The Philippines was also lower for post-Asian financial crisis than for pre-Asian financial crisis. The other remaining countries all showed an increase; however, they did not reach a level of significance. (Table 20)

(5) *Comparison of the difference in the fluctuation rate of the unemployment rate for the 10 Eastern Asian countries for pre- and post-Asian financial crisis.* Analysis and results using intervention analysis show that the fluctuation rates of the unemployment rate of Japan, Taiwan and The Philippines were higher for post-Asian financial crisis than for pre-Asian financial crisis, but did not reach a level of significance. Conversely, the fluctuation rates of the unemployment rate of Hong Kong and Korea were lower for post-Asian financial crisis than for pre-Asian financial crisis; however, they did not reach a level of significance. (Table 21)

Table 17. Comparison of the Fluctuation Rate of GDP for the 10 Eastern Asian Countries for Pre- and Post-Asian Financial Crisis – Intervention Analysis.

	Transformation	Model	MS Residual	Parameter						
				Constant	AR(1)	AR(2)	MA(1)	MA(2)	Intervention	Forecast
Japan	ln(x), D(1) (interrupted) ARIMA	(1,1,1)	0.00319							
Coefficient				15.3722	0.4075		1.13	0.7961	-0.00283	4411331
p					0.0000		0.0000	0.0000	0.9612	
Taiwan	ln(x), D(2) (interrupted) ARIMA	(1,2,1)	0.00346							
Coefficient				11.0677	-0.102		1.7231		0.070983	77478.42
p					0.0000		0.0000		0.0972*	
Indonesia	ln(x), D(1) (interrupted) ARIMA	(1,1,1)	0.00262							
Coefficient				0.0385	1.0331		1.4964		0.043881	4186.328
p					0.0000		0.0000		0.4093	
Hong Kong	ln(x), D(1) (interrupted) ARIMA	(2,2,2)	0.00173							
Coefficient				10.4581	0.2014	-0.8489	2.0921	-2.1564	0.010793	38137.8
p					0.0000	0.0000	0.0000	0.0000	0.6780	
Malaysia	ln(x), D(1) (interrupted) ARIMA	(2,1,2)	0.00380							
Coefficient				9.9525	0.3126	-0.944	0.2504	-2.1968	-0.07168	24948.15
p					0.0000	0.0000	0.0370	0.0000	0.2846	
Thailand	ln(x), D(2) (interrupted) ARIMA	(2,2,1)	0.00125							
Coefficient				6.8919	-0.1369	-0.2544	1.6702		0.012876	1443.301
p					0.0170	0.0000	0.0000		0.6192	
The Philippines	ln(x), D(2) (interrupted) ARIMA	(2,1,1)	0.00861							
Coefficient				0.0109	-1.262	-0.3176	-1.5777		-0.312228	5132.677
p					0.0000	0.0000	0.0000		0.0013***	

Korea	ln(x), D(1) (interrupted ARIMA) (0,0,1)				
Coefficient	0.01298	11.6395	−1.1286	−0.29074	111674
p			0.0000	0.2030	

Notes:
(1) As the GDP data for China and Singapore are insufficient, the time sequence model could not be built.
(2) The method established by time sequence intervention model interjects elements that have infinite effect as a hypothesis.
(3) Korea GDP time sequence intervention model is divided into hypothetical intervention of elements that have infinite effect and progressively decreasing effect.

Significance levels at
*10%;
***1%.

Table 18. Comparison of the Stock Index for the 10 Eastern Asian Countries for Pre- and Post-Asian Financial Crisis – Intervention Analysis.

	Transformation	Model	MS Residual	Parameter							Forecast
				Constant	AR(1)	AR(2)	MA(1)	MA(2)	Intervention	δ	
Japan	ln(x), D(1) (interrupted ARIMA)	(2,1,2)	1.7891								
Coefficient				0.0539	−0.7349	−1.0194	−0.6894	−2.2998	0.584340		
p					0.0000	0.0000	0.0000	0.0000			
China	ln(x), D(1) (interrupted ARIMA)	(2,1,2)	0.10773								116.1077
Coefficient				4.1650	−0.7354	−0.8101	−1.7486	−1.9862	0.214324		
p					0.0000	0.0000	0.0000	0.0000	0.4401		
Indonesia	None (interrupted ARIMA)	(2,0,2)	4626E6								143702.8
Coefficient				3392.111	0.3005	−0.7919	−0.0061	−2.1921	−1373.000		
p					0.0000	0.0000	0.385	0.0000			
Hong Kong	ln(x), 2*D(2) (interrupted ARIMA)	(2,2,1)	0.06210								7806.179
Coefficient				9.1923	−1.3522	−0.6987	−1.5502		−0.00331		
p					0.0000	0.0000	0.0000		0.9841		
Malaysia	ln(x), D(1) (interrupted ARIMA)	(1,1,1)	0.03619								651.9111
Coefficient				0.0303	1.0006		1.5333		−0.424263		
p					0.0000		0.0000		0.0368**		
Thailand	ln(x), D(2) (interrupted ARIMA)	(2,2,2)	0.10604								300.354
Coefficient				−0.0446	−1.2095	−0.5189	−1.2285	0.5496	−0.06085		
p					0.0000	0.0000	0.0000	0.0000	0.8136		
The Philippines	ln(x), D(1) (interrupted ARIMA)	(2,1,1)	0.04463								192.0845
Coefficient				6.8023	0.2193	0.1052	0.6087		0.40614	−0.1606	
p					0.1350	0.6030	0.0000		0.0102**	0.6194	

Korea	ln(x), D(1) (interrupted ARIMA)	(1,1,0)	0.04361		δ
Coefficient				6.7239	−0.03722	0.232777	−0.55688	626.153
p					0.8850	0.0348**	0.0011***

Notes:

(1) As the data for Taiwan and Singapore are insufficient, the time sequence model could not be built.

(2) The method established by time sequence intervention model interjects elements which have infinite effect.

(3) The time sequence intervention model for Korea, The Philippines and Hong Kong is divided into hypothetical intervention of elements which have infinite effect and progressively decreasing effect.

(4) δ – progressively decreasing parameter.

Significance levels at
* 10%;
** 5%;
*** 1%.

Table 19. Comparison of the Exchange Rate for the 10 Eastern Asian Countries for Pre- and Post-Asian Financial Crisis – Intervention Analysis.

| | Transformation | Model | MS Residual | Parameter | | | | | | |
				Constant	AR(1)	AR(2)	MA(1)	MA(2)	Intervention	Forecast
Japan	ln(x), D(1) (interrupted ARIMA)	(2,1,2)	0.00315							
Coefficient				4.6582	-0.0525	-0.4999	-0.3315	-1.9127	-0.01665	123.1326
p					0.3280	0.0000	0.0000	0.0000	0.7796	
China	ln(x), D(1) (interrupted ARIMA)	(0,1,1)	0.00450							
Coefficient				2.0442			0.008636		-0.01121	8.361307
p							0.9730		0.8720	
Taiwan	ln(x), D(1) (interrupted ARIMA)	(1,1,1)	0.00070							
Coefficient				3.288062	0.8903		1.5866		-0.006673	35.24328
p					0.0000		0.0000		0.8179	
Indonesia	ln(x), D(1) (interrupted ARIMA)	(1,1,0)	0.03166							
Coefficient				7.714475	0.7926				0.189990	9159.872
p					0.0000				0.3028	
Hong Kong	ln(x), 2*D(1) (interrupted ARIMA)	(2,2,0)	0.00000							
Coefficient				2.045695	-0.6655	-0.3952			-0.001097	7.798774
p					0.0000	0.0100			0.2424	
Malaysia	ln(x), (interrupted ARIMA)	(0,0,2)	0.00296							
Coefficient				0.93531			-1.1993	-0.6905	0.372197	3.747969
p							0.0000	0.0020	0.0000***	
Thailand	ln(x), D(1) (interrupted ARIMA)	(0,1,1)	0.00337							
Coefficient				3.229554			0.007099		0.432058	43.42568
p							0.9770		0.0000***	
The Philippines	ln(x), D(1) (interrupted ARIMA)	(2,1,1)	0.00280							
Coefficient				3.275787	-0.6078	0.0465	-1.4497		0.274665	54.03982
p					0.0000	0.0090	0.0000		0.00004***	
Singapore	ln(x), (2) (interrupted ARIMA)	(2,2,2)	0.00119							
Coefficient				0.390465	-0.885	-0.8977	-0.6068	-2.0684	0.089250	1.729051
p					0.0000	0.0000	0.0000	0.0000	0.00097***	
Korea	ln(x), D(1) (interrupted ARIMA)	(0,1,2)	0.01000							
Coefficient				11.63945			-0.8786	0.1656	0.475764	1221.685
p							0.0050	0.5800	0.0000***	

Significance level at
***1%.

Table 20. Comparison of the Consumer Price Index (CPI) for the 10 Eastern Asian Countries for Pre- and Post-Asian Financial Crisis – Intervention Analysis.

	Transformation	Model	MS Residual	Parameter					Intervention	Forecast
				Constant	AR(1)	AR(2)	MA(1)	MA(2)		
Japan	ln(x), D(1) (interrupted ARIMA)	(2,1,2)	0.00002							
Coefficient				4.590766	-0.8087	-0.0516	0.869	-2.4826	0.004083	98.09498
p					0.0000	0.0000	0.0000	0.0000	0.4453	
China	ln(x), D(1) (interrupted ARIMA)	(1,1,2)	0.00018							
Coefficient				-0.00451	0.623		0.6274	-1.3684	0.008094	99.74793
p					0.0030		0.0030	0.0000	0.4531	
Taiwan	ln(x), D(1) (interrupted ARIMA)	(1,1,1)	0.00008							
Coefficient				4.5206	-0.398		-1.5789		0.006823	100.4732
p					0.0000		0.0000		0.4865	
Indonesia	ln(x), D(1) (interrupted ARIMA)	(1,1,1)	0.00002							
Coefficient				0.002285	-0.6198		-1.5785		0.000407	104.9782
p					0.0000		0.0000		0.9308	
Hong Kong	ln(x), (2) (interrupted ARIMA)	(0,2,1)	0.00012							
Coefficient				4.4938			0.7776		0.006241	93.33694
p							0.0000		0.4253	
Malaysia	ln(x), D(1) (interrupted ARIMA)	(2,1,2)	0.00002							
Coefficient				-0.00112	0.3174	-0.5239	0.586	-2.1473	0.005466	101.4287
p					0.0000	0.0000	0.0000	0.0000	0.2163	
Thailand	ln(x), D(1) (interrupted ARIMA)	(1,1,2)	0.00004							
Coefficient				4.402342	0.9275		0.9685	0.7929	0.011240	105.606
p					0.0000		0.0000	0.0760	0.0634*	
The Philippines	ln(x), D(1) (interrupted ARIMA)	(2,1,1)	0.00006							
Coefficient				0.018737	0.1609	0.9236	-1.4847		-0.004225	170.1362
p					0.0000	0.0000	0.0000		0.5257	
Singapore	ln(x), D(1) (interrupted ARIMA)	(2,1,1)	0.00001							
Coefficient				4.5633	1.4847	-0.456	1.4405		0.006584	101.8729
p					0.0000	0.0000	0.0000		0.0845*	
Korea	ln(x). D(1) (interrupted ARIMA)	(2,1,2)	0.00010							
Coefficient				0.012442	0.6341	0.4728	1.1601	0.5599	0.008209	109.1265
p					0.0000	0.0000	0.0000	0.0000	0.4738	

Significance level at
*10%.

Table 21. Comparison of the Fluctuation Rate of the Unemployment Rate for the 10 Eastern Asian Countries for Pre- and Post-Asian Financial Crisis – Intervention Analysis.

	Transformation	Model MS Residual	Parameter						
			Constant	AR(1)	AR(2)	MA(1)	MA(2)	Intervention	Forecast
Japan	ln(x), D(1) (interrupted ARIMA) (1,1,1)	0.00119							
Coefficient			0.0212	1.0066		1.505		0.008890	5.501633
p				0.0000		0.0000		0.8022	
Taiwan	ln(x), D(1) (interrupted ARIMA) (2,1,2)	0.06949							
Coefficient			0.0776	−0.5481	0.4046	−1.3164	0.6331	0.016850	5.134394
p				0.0000	0.0000	0.0000	0.0000	0.9485	
Hong Kong	ln(x), D(1) (interrupted ARIMA) (2,1,2)	0.01353							
Coefficient			0.0027	−0.3432	−0.9449	−0.911	−2.5053	−0.034338	7.163612
p				0.0000	0.0000	0.0000	0.0000	0.7450	
The Philippines	ln(x), D(1) (interrupted ARIMA) (1,1,1)	0.03187							
Coefficient			2.2088	−0.1682		1.6429		0.048031	11.04287
p				0.0000		0.0000		0.7180	
Korea	ln(x), D(1) (interrupted ARIMA) (2,1,2)	0.03185							
Coefficient			−0.0049	0.2571	−0.8295	0.7116	−2.1974	−0.084475	3.585424
p				0.0000	0.0000	0.0000	0.0000	0.6538	

Note: There was insufficient data for Thailand, Indonesia, Malaysia, China and Singapore. Therefore, it was not possible to contruct a time sequence model.

5. CONCLUDING REMARKS

After the surprise attack of the 1997 Asian financial crisis, each country realized that its present financial measures were insufficient; so they slowly began financial reforms. There are many aspects of the content of the Thai reforms. It was primarily the establishment of many financial-specific re-structuring institutions. With regard to financial laws, Thailand actively revised commercial banking law, loan law and exchange rate management policies. Regarding securities and stock markets, Thai government dis-tributed government securities to replace the loss created by financial in-stitutions' development funds, and made the short-term debt long-term. Indonesian financial reform content primarily focuses upon strengthening financial supervisory systems and restructuring financial institutions. It also rescinded all restrictions limiting banks in areas of operation. Ma-laysia's financial reform primarily encouraged financial mergers. In June 1998, the Ministry of Finance invested and established an asset manage-ment company to purchase overdue loans from financial institutions and also dismiss the Central Bank of its management duties of overdue loans at financial institutions. Additionally, Corporate Debt Restructuring Committee was established in July 1998 to assist companies in solving their debt problems. In August 1998, the Central Bank invested and es-tablished an investment company to assist financial institutions in in-creasing their capital adequacy ratio. Japan's financial reform was primarily the passing of the Financial Reconstruction Law and Financial Function Early Strengthening Law to handle bankruptcies and unhealthy financial institutions. Regarding China, the most serious problem was the bad loan ratio for state-run banks. In 1998, a financial asset management company was established to handle state-run bank problems. Taiwan's financial reforms focused mostly upon building an effective organization, improving financial institution operational systems, and increasing its op-erational efficacy. There were several other reforms, which related to the strong development of the stock market, and it also began addressing issues with over banking and high overdue loan ratios. Singapore's pri-mary financial reforms were enhancing the size of the stock market, con-tinually developing SIMEX, and proactively marketing futures products to stimulate Singapore's economy, thereby making Singapore's products more competitive. Korea rescinded its foreign exchange restrictions, loos-ened limitations upon foreign investments, strengthened asset management services, caused its financial company operations to become more special-ized, and developed financial derivatives products. Hong Kong invested vast amounts of foreign exchange reserve to strongly guard the stock market and the exchange market, to decrease taxes, and to develop financial derivatives products. The Philippines restricted the buying and selling of the peso to enhance asset management services and to strengthen bank organizational systems.

From the results of the Mann–Whitney U test, we find that there was a significant difference in the fluctuation rate of GDP in Hong Kong for pre- and post-Asian financial crisis. The fluctuation rate of GDP for the other nine countries did not show a significant difference. Regarding the stock index, other than Taiwan and China not indicating a significant difference in the average stock index for pre- or post-Asian financial crisis, the stock index of the others (Japan, Hong Kong, Thailand, Indonesia, Malaysia, Singapore, Korea and The Philippines) all showed a significant difference. Additionally, all 10 Eastern Asian countries showed a significant difference in the exchange rate standards and consumer price indexes for pre- and post-Asian financial crisis. Conversely, the fluctuation rate in the unemployment rate for all 10 Eastern Asian countries did not show significant difference.

From the analysis and results of Intervention Analysis, we found that the fluctuation rate of GDP for Taiwan was higher for post-Asian financial crisis. Conversely, the fluctuation rate of GDP for The Philippines was lower for post-Asian financial crisis. With regard to the stock index, the stock indexes of The Philippines and Korea were higher for post-Asian financial crisis. Conversely, the stock index for Malaysia was lower for post-Asian financial crisis. The exchange rates in Malaysia, Thailand, The Philippines, Singapore, and Korea all devaluated with regard to the Asian financial crisis. Moreover, the CPI in Thailand and Singapore were higher for post-Asian financial crisis. None of the 10 Eastern Asian countries reached level of significance for the fluctuation rates for the unemployment rate, showing that the unemployment rate in not affected by Asian financial crises.

Generally speaking, other than the fluctuation rate of GDP, the analysis and results of Mann–Whitney U test and Intervention Analysis proved to be unanimous. Even so, a relationship does not exist between the financial reform variables (legal effectiveness, overdue loan ratio (NPL) in the banking industry, capital adequacy ratio, financial innovation, number of individuals employed in the finance industry, and mergers and numbers of financial departments) and macroeconomic variables (fluctuation rate of GDP, stock index, exchange rate, CPI, and fluctuation rate of the unemployment rate) for the 10 Eastern Asian countries.

ACKNOWLEDGMENTS

The author would like to thank Chih-Yuan You, Chiu-Ju Hou, Chiao-Ling Lai, Ya-Ping Hong, Jui-Ju Chen and Ting-Ya Yang who are students in the college department at Fu-Jen Catholic University for their assistance in gathering and organizing information.

REFERENCES

Chen, J. -C. (2000). *The Impacts on Eastern Asian countries by international capital flows: The case of Eastern Asian financial crisis.* Taiwan, ROC: Master thesis, Institute of Mainland China Studies, National Sun Yat-Sen University.

Cheng, C. W. (2001). The future and reform of financial reform in Japan. *Taiwan Economic Research Journal, 24*(7), 18–23.

Harvey, C. R. (1995). Predictable risk and returns in emerging markets. *Review of Financial Studies, 8,* 773–816.

Li, C. P. (2000). *The role of foreign institutional investors in the Asia financial crisis.* Taiwan, ROC: Master thesis, Graduate Institute of Finance, Taiwan University.

Li, W. Y. (2001). *Volatility research of stock and exchange rate markets in Asia countries.* Master thesis, Graduate Institute of Economic, Sow-Chou University.

Lin, K.-H. (2000). *The build and reform of banking system in Mainland China.* Taiwan, ROC: Master Thesis of graduate Institute of International Business from National Chi-Nan University.

Liu, H. J. (2000). *Forecasting of Asian emerging stock market returns and the effects of Asian crisis.* Master thesis, Graduate Institute of Financial Management, Central University.

DEVELOPING A FINANCIAL DERIVATIVES MARKET IN CHINA

Jing Chi and Martin Young

ABSTRACT

While China is currently moving toward the full development of its own financial derivatives markets, to date, China's experience with these has been a negative one. This paper examines the importance to China of developing a fully integrated financial derivatives market from both the economic and financial market perspectives. It examines the best way forward for derivative trading, both market based and over-the-counter, and the types of products best suited to both, given the current state of the Chinese financial markets. Consideration is given to market structure, regulation, trading and settlement systems and international cooperation.

1. INTRODUCTION

During the last two decades, the development and expansion of financial derivatives have been one of the most remarkable events in finance. According to the IOMA (the Institute of Management and Administration) derivatives market survey, when equity markets were falling in 2002, the derivatives volumes actually increased by 39%. Financial derivatives, such

Asia Pacific Financial Markets in Comparative Perspective: Issues and Implications for the 21st Century
Contemporary Studies in Economics and Financial Analysis, Volume 86, 339–359
ISSN: 1569-3759/doi:10.1016/S1569-3759(05)86015-2

as futures, options and swap contracts have become popular risk management tools that not only have risk sharing properties, but also offer productive investment opportunities. Moreover, they facilitate the completeness of the financial markets and the gathering of information that is not available from trading in the underlying assets. As the largest emerging economy, China, however, abandoned its financial derivatives market after some unregulated and illegal derivatives trading in the mid-1990s. This paper focuses on the way forward for the redevelopment of an official financial derivatives market in China, and the major issues surrounding this redevelopment. Consideration is also given to China's over-the-counter (OTC) derivatives market.

The reasons why China needs to develop a financial derivatives market are quite straightforward and are fundamentally the same as those that led to the development of financial derivative markets in places such as the United States and Europe. Whenever exchange rate risk, interest rate risk and equity price risk exist, there is a need for derivative products that can help to hedge these risks. Therefore, as well as discussing the need for developing a financial derivatives market in China, interesting questions to address are, why the financial derivatives market did not work in China in the mid-1990s; what the key issues are for the financial derivatives market to work successfully in China today; how to develop this market; and what relationships can be developed with other international derivatives markets?

Section 2 of this paper discusses the background and history of the Chinese financial derivatives markets and the benefits of having derivatives as a necessary component of China's capital markets. In Section 3, we investigate, and give suggestions on, how to develop a formal financial derivatives market in China with regard to the regulatory environment, potential products and market structure. Development of the OTC derivatives market is examined in Section 4, with the focus being on its regulation and the products traded. Possible relationships and cooperations between the Chinese derivatives markets and other international derivatives markets are discussed in Section 5 with conclusions given in Section 6.

2. BACKGROUND AND BENEFITS OF FINANCIAL DERIVATIVES TRADING IN CHINA

Financial derivatives trading in China officially began in the early 1990s with the Hainan Stock Exchange starting to trade a stock index futures product based on the Shenzhen composite stock index on March 10, 1993. Then in October 1993, futures market trading in Government bond futures started up as part of the Shanghai and Shenzhen Stock Exchanges' operations. There were 37 government bond futures contract-series written on seven different government bonds during 1993–1995. The stock index contracts had a very short life on account of a large number of trading violations. The bond contract did somewhat better for a while, especially after October 1994,[1] but again this trading was not well regulated.

There were two particular features of government bond futures trading in China that would have serious implications for the trading of derivatives on these assets. During the late 1980s and early 1990s, the inflation rates in China were very high, often reaching double digits. In order to compensate investors for holding government bonds, the Chinese government gave bondholders a subsidized interest rate at maturity, in addition to the stated coupon rate on the bonds. The other feature was that, instead of paying out the coupon rate on a semi-annual basis, as is the case with most government issued bonds, the government sold bonds at face value and paid the principal and all interest accrued at maturity. These features made the pricing of both the physical bonds and their related futures products very difficult with serious implications for the delivery of long or short positions (Chen & Zhou, 2004). In particular the government had the ability to change maturity values at maturity. This led to severe speculation in the market, especially prior to the maturity of a government bond. In addition, the exchanges' trading and settlement systems were not sophisticated enough to monitor or control unregulated trading. This culminated in the extreme case of the trading and speculation on the "327" futures contract in February 1995.

The "327" futures contract was based on a three-year government bond issued in 1992, with the total issued amount of 24 billion yuan. Its maturity was June 1995 and its coupon rate was 9.5% plus any possible subsidized rate from the government at maturity to compensate for excessive inflation. During the first half of February 1995, the price of this particular contract ranged from 147.80 to 148.30 yuan. Some institutional investors thought that the inflation rate had reached its peak in January 1995, so they started to sell a large amount of "327" futures contracts believing the contract to be overpriced. However, other institutional investors were still buying the "327" futures contract based on their expectations of the forthcoming subsidized rate and the fact that the price of the "327" futures contract was trading higher in other markets, mostly unofficial, than in Shanghai. On February 23, 1995, Liaoning Guofa company obtained advanced information on the subsidized rate to be paid on the bond from the government This rate was high and outside market expectations so the company started to buy huge amounts of "327" futures contracts, pushing price up by 2 yuan within 1 min and another 3.77 yuan after 10 min. This price change would have led to huge losses for some companies that were on the selling side of the contract, even bankruptcy had the companies not been government controlled. In order to protect their own interests, one of the selling companies, Wanguo Securities Company sold "327" futures contracts worth 140 billion yuan in the last 8 min before the market closed, decreasing the price from 152 yuan to 147.5 yuan.[2] The impact of this price change, if maintained, would mean that the company would profit by 4.2 billion yuan. Due to this price manipulation, the huge number of contracts entered into over these last 8 min was subsequently cancelled.[3] On May 17, of the same year, the government ordered an end to official financial futures trading in China.

After this event, the only financial product of a derivative nature that officially trades in China is the bond repurchase product. There are, or have been, other derivative market operations in China from time to time. Derivatives on commodities are traded on three exchanges currently, the Zhengzhou Commodity Exchange, the Dalian Commodity Exchange, and the Shanghai Futures Exchange. The Zhengzhou Commodity Exchange is the smallest of these, trading cotton, mung bean and wheat futures. The Shanghai Futures Exchange trades aluminum, copper, fuel oil and rubber futures and for the 2003 year had a turnover of approximately 40 million contracts. The Dalian Commodity Exchange is the largest of the three exchanges with a volume of approximately 60 million contracts in 2003 (IOMA Derivatives Market Survey, 2003). The contracts traded on this exchange are corn and soybean futures contracts. These markets have not caused problems for the Chinese government, however, so have been left to operate largely unhindered. The magnitude of the problems with financial derivatives trading, however, was such that China has now been almost a decade without an official financial derivatives market.

While China's experience to date with financial derivatives has not been a good one due to the immaturity of the market and very poor regulation, it should be remembered that financial derivatives markets are a very new development globally. In the United States, the first commodity derivatives trading began in Chicago at the Chicago Board of Trade in 1849. However the first financial derivates trading did not begin until 1972 when the Chicago Mercantile Exchange began trading futures contracts on seven foreign currencies. These were the world's first official financial futures contracts. In Europe, the oldest financial derivative market was the London

International Financial Futures Exchange, or LIFFE, which began trading financial futures in 1982. The real growth in financial derivative trading has occurred since the early 1990s so it can be argued that China will not be far behind other counties if it is able to develop a sound financial derivative market in the near future.

Although financial derivatives trading have been suspended for some time in China, the government is now trying to reopen and develop this market due to its potential benefits for the Chinese economy. These benefits relate primarily to the three main economic functions of derivatives as documented by Gibson and Zimmermann (1996a). They are risk sharing and market completion, implementation of asset allocation decisions, and information gathering. All are important, especially for a major financial market such as that of China. First, risk sharing is seen as the major economic function of derivatives, and derivatives can offer an efficient allocation of economic risks if well structured. For example, a portfolio manager can hedge overall stock market exposure by buying index put options or selling index futures contracts. In relation to market completion, the arguments here are of a more theoretical nature, but it has been shown by Ross (1976) and Hakansson (1982) that options do complete markets and that in doing so provide an appropriate mechanism for the efficient allocation of risk.

Second, derivatives can provide a useful and cost-effective method for the implementation of asset allocation decisions. Static strategies represented by buy-and-hold investments and are easily implemented and can be enhanced by the cheap diversification and leverage opportunities that derivatives provide. A static strategy can, therefore, become a dynamic one through the use of the options and futures products of the derivatives market.

Finally, it should be noted that risk and information are related. In fact it would be reasonable to argue that information surrounding the risk considerations in financial markets is paramount in the investment decision-making process. Derivative markets will therefore provide a significant amount of information to the financial system in general. Grossman (1988a, b) first illustrated the information role of options. First, options trading provide their own price relative supply and demand information that can impact on the underlying market. Options prices can also be used to calculate implied volatility, giving valuable information to traders in the cash markets. Moreover, due to the superiority of options as speculative vehicles, the marginal benefit of becoming informed is obvious, which results in a greater information search by market participants. The increase in public information lowers information asymmetry and the spread, improves liquidity and reduces the variance of the pricing error, therefore, making the underlying markets more efficient. Kumar, Sarin, and Shastri (1998) find empirical evidence for this argument. Though the information role of futures contracts is less obvious, Grossman (1977) provides theoretical evidence to show that derivative trading has a positive impact on the price discovery process in the cash markets.

China's economic growth over the last 20 years now make it essential to complete the market with the introduction of a credible financial derivatives market. Since 1980s, China's GDP has grown by nearly 8% per year, and China's two stock markets have grown rapidly since their foundation in 1990. The Shanghai Stock Exchange is now the second largest stock exchange in Asia, next to the Tokyo Stock Exchange. It is clear that a financial derivatives market is essential for the continued expansion of China's economy and its financial market system. This will also help provide Chinese financial institutions and corporations with appropriate hedging and risk management tools. The Chinese government has made some progress toward the development of an OTC derivatives market. In March 2004, the China Banking Regulatory Commission (CBRC) introduced the first set of rules and enabled financial institutions to engage in OTC derivative transactions in China. This initiative will be discussed in detail later. To date, however, there are no plans finalized for the development of a financial derivatives exchange, though discussion on how this should be done is now underway in China.

3. DEVELOPING A FORMAL FINANCIAL DERIVATIVES EXCHANGE

At this point, the question is no longer whether or not China needs to develop a financial derivatives exchange, but what challenges need to be overcome to achieve this and how these challenges can be met. In this section, we focus on the development of a formal derivatives exchange, and discuss its regulation, potential products and market structure.

3.1. Regulating a Formal Financial Derivatives Exchange in China

The first and main challenge for developing a derivatives market in China is with its regulatory environment. As mentioned early, the lack of regulatory control bought about the demise of financial derivative trading in China in the mid-1990s. The newness of the market and lack of knowledge of investors can cause high speculation, price manipulation and gambling in this market. The objectives of derivatives regulation are to ensure the integrity of markets, to deter manipulation and to protect market participants from losses resulting from fraud or the insolvency of counterparties. To set up sound and successful derivatives markets, certain regulatory requirements need to be met. Craig Donohue (2004) the CEO of Chicago Mercantile Exchange (CME), mentioned three fundamental requirements for developing a formal futures and options market in his remarks to the Shanghai Derivatives Forum on May 28, 2004. First, an Exchange must ensure that all market participants have equal and immediate access to accurate and fully transparent market information. Second, an exchange must ensure standardized practices and rules for market participants and it must have the ability to detect, deter and punish individuals or entities that engage in market manipulation or unsound business practices. Third, an exchange must guarantee the financial performance of all transactions in its markets, as well as the safety and soundness of the related banking, settlement and custodial functions necessary to support market transactions.

Before exploring in detail the regulatory system that China should develop for its derivatives market, it is important to understand the risks involved in this market. According to Gibson and Zimmermann (1996a, b), there are three categories of risks associated with derivatives markets (i.e. explicit risks, implicit risks and estimation risks). First, explicit risks consist of the various market risks coming from taking positions in derivatives instruments and thus from the resulting risk exposure to the underlying assets. Second, implicit risks contain all the risks associated with the use of derivatives in the particular market environment in which one is operating. These include risks such as credit risk, liquidity risk, settlement risk, operational risk and legal risk. Third, estimation risks stem from the fact that information is never complete and its interpretation is seldom perfect. All market participants and regulatory bodies face estimation risk to some degree. Three contributors to these estimation risks, as detailed by Gibson and Zimmermann (1996a, b) are, lack of information disclosure and market transparency; lack of knowledge or educational training among different market participants; and inappropriate risk incentives offered to market participants.

In terms of measuring and controlling the risks discussed above, market risks are generally measured by the volatility of the underlying assets' relative price changes. The complex mathematical models have allowed for the efficient use of hedging policies, computerized trading programs and day-to-day monitoring of the deviation from the optimal market risk exposures within a corporation. The market risk of derivatives should not be our focus, since such risk is only meaningful on an overall portfolio basis, after considering both derivatives and cash market positions and offsetting between them. Sound regulation is important to manage the second and third categories of risks in the derivatives markets. In the Chinese financial markets, the risks such as the credit risk, accounting and disclosure risks and systematic risk, in particular, need to be addressed.

Credit risk is the loss of a contract if the counterpart is unable to fulfill its obligation. In the early 1990s a series of reports were released on derivatives and financial stability, led by work carried out by the Bank of International Settlements, Basle.[4] Within these reports credit risk is the risk most examined. The difficulties involved in measuring credit risk come from the absence of a robust technology to measure default risk. In China, there is no formal credit rating company in the market. The state-owned banks rather than agencies such as Standard and Poors usually carry out the credit rating of corporations. However, outdated technology and the connected system (since all banks and major financial institutions belong to the government) make credit ratings questionable in China. Credit risk can also stem from the poor trading and settlement systems in an exchange. For instance, in the mid-1990s, there were two clearinghouses operating under the two stock exchanges, responsible for the settlement of derivative transactions in China. Although, there were margin requirements set for derivatives trading, the level of monitoring was not sufficient, and the margin check took place after the trading day ended. In order to manage credit risk properly, the following measures are necessary. First, is the need for a dynamic and advanced credit rating and risk measurement and management system. Second, is the need for direct credit risk reduction mechanisms, such as intra-day and daily marking-to-market procedures and appropriate capital adequacy requirements. Most standardized exchanges now have computerized continuous trading systems that can work together with marking-to-market, margin calls or clearing operations. Kroszner (1999) uses a comparative institutional analysis to explore how innovations in organizational and contractual design and governance for financial institutions and markets have evolved privately to address regulatory challenges, particularly with respect to risk management. His focus in relation to futures exchanges is in the development of clearinghouses. In his opinion, the historical development of futures clearinghouses and how they address risk issues has been largely overlooked in the both academic literature and practice. He finds that a clearing-house providing high credit quality helps to enhance the liquidity of standardized futures contracts traded on exchanges. Daily variation settlements by clearinghouses can also limit the counterpart risks. Third, is the need to implement indirect credit risk reduction mechanisms, such as netting and settlement agreements between the official market participants and their non-official counterparts.

Internationally software that manages the risk positions of the market participants has become ever more important. CME developed its proprietary SPAN Margining System a decade ago, which literally created the industry standards in this area. CME has licensed the SPAN system to more than 47 exchanges and clearinghouses around the world, and one of its most recent licensees is the Shanghai Futures Exchange. It would seem logical for any financial derivatives exchange in China to adopt the same or a similar system.

Accounting and disclosure risks are another important issue in China. Information transparency and standardized disclosure are crucial for risk management given the complicated characteristics of derivatives trading. Although, the Chinese government has made considerable effort to promote international accounting standards in its financial markets, information transparency has been a severe problem since the foundation of the securities markets. Insider trading is rife, and information is not accessible to all market participants at the same time. Considerable work needs to be done in this area to improve the situation as information standardization and frequent and full disclosure at all levels is necessary for an efficient and credible financial derivatives market. Also, since the majority of investors in the Chinese financial markets are individual investors, educating these investors on derivatives trading and the accurate interpretation of information is very important.

Finally, consideration should be given to systematic risk, which can be defined as the risk caused by the failure of one financial institution or section of the market to the whole market. Any severe market, credit or liquidity variation that causes losses in a transaction or financial institution could generate a systematic crisis. In China, systematic risk is a major concern of the government, since almost all the financial institutions in China are state-owned. Any loss will be the loss of the government at the end. For example, the clearinghouses in China use a central counterparty system, which means that the clearinghouse is the counterparty for each transaction for all investors. In this case, if one side of the transaction fails, the transaction between the clearinghouse and the other party can still be fulfilled, leaving the problem existing between the defaulting party and the clearinghouse. Since both of them may well belong to the government, at the end of the day, it is the government who bears the loss. This was a major reason for the government closing the financial derivatives markets in the mid-1990s. Another risk that is also related to systematic risk, and is somewhat unique to the Chinese financial market is that of moral risk. As mentioned earlier, the exchanges, the clearinghouses and almost all financial institutions are state-owned,[5] and bankruptcy law in China cannot be implemented on most state-owned corporations as in theory. Therefore, some managers working in the financial institutions are willing to take extra risk, since if they win, they get the benefit through the company, while if they lose, the government is going to pay. Moral risk is very hard to control and takes a long time to manage, since it comes from the economic system and the quality of the people. Regarding regulation to manage the systematic and moral risk, the key point is to have efficient risk measurement and monitoring tools. More importantly, education and confidence building are necessary to ensure the traders and corresponding managers have correct moral standards and sufficient knowledge on derivatives trading.

3.2. Potential Products for a Formal Derivatives Market in China

While the order of derivatives product development in the United States and Europe was currency products first, followed by interest rate products and then equity-based products, the reverse may well be the case for China moving forward. Equity price risk can be reasonably well defined at this time in China, but with exchange rate and interest rate controls in place in China, determining and hedging exchange rate risk and interest rate risk are likely to be more problematic. It therefore follows that when designing market-based derivative products for China, we need to consider not only the characteristics of the major derivative products traded in the main securities markets of the world but also the special features of the Chinese markets.

Currently, the most popular traded financial derivative products are currency futures, interest rate futures, stock index futures and options on these products to hedge foreign exchange risk, interest rate risk and systematic risk in the stock market. However, in China, the exchange rate between RMB Yuan and US dollar was fixed at around 8.28 Yuan/$ by the government until recently, and the government also fixes the interest rate to stabilize the economy. The Yuan is now operating under a tightly managed float. In this case, the common currency futures and interest rate futures may not necessarily be appropriate products to develop at this moment within a formal financial derivatives exchange given the political risk surrounding both. Hedging currency risk against currencies such as the US dollar, Japanese

Yen, Euro or Pounds Sterling, has already found significant demand within China's growing OTC market, but regulators have not allowed yuan-de-nominated derivative products to trade in this market to date.

In the international market place Chinese yuan derivative products have grown significantly in popularity in recent times as the Chinese economy becomes more global and international investors and corporations gain greater exposure to the Chinese economy. Also 10 offshore banks received licenses in late 2004 to trade currency derivatives in an OTC market in China for the benefit of Chinese companies. As will be discussed later, OTC markets tend to pose less risk-related problems than official derivative exchanges, and with a managed, and probably undervalued yuan, the trading of currency derivative products in an official exchange environment should not proceed prior to the adoption of a free-floating yuan.

In relation to interest rate risk, this risk is again mainly political given the way interest rates are currently set in China. It is very difficult for any market to operate efficiently or effectively if the major risk faced is a political one, so it is reasonable to believe that currency and interest rate derivative products are unlikely to be developed successfully in an official derivatives exchange until there is a move to more market-driven pricing in both these areas.

On the other hand, the stock markets in China have enjoyed tremendous growth in the past 10 years, and the Shanghai Stock Exchange is now the second largest stock exchange in Asia. However, stocks, bonds and a small number of bond repos are the only products traded on the Shanghai Stock Exchange. Investors do not have other investment alternatives to hedge their risk, while in China the risk in the stock market is high. In addition, although the majority of investors in China are individual investors, since 1998, the government strongly encouraged the development of institutional investors, such as close-end funds, open-end funds, pension funds, securities companies and insurance companies. This growing number of institutional investors needs sophisticated investment instruments to hedge positions and to further develop their product range. Therefore, individual stock and stock index futures and options become the most obvious products for development given the current Chinese market conditions.

Stock index futures are futures contracts based on a specific stock index in the marketplace. The two counterparties agree to buy or sell the stock index at a future time and at an agreed price. The settlement of the transaction is usually in cash. In China, there are two major stock exchanges – the Shanghai and Shenzhen Stock Exchanges. They are both non-profit organizations under the supervision of the China Securities Regulatory Commission (CSRC).

When founded in the early 1990s, they had equal positions and the same goals. In 2000, the CSRC wanted to differentiate them by targeting the Shanghai Stock Exchanges as the main board in China for blue chips, while targeting the Shenzhen Stock Exchanges as a high-tech board like NASDAQ. However, the Internet bubble collapsed worldwide in 2000. To avoid market risk, the Chinese NASDAQ has not been established up to now. To keep the development of the Shenzhen Stock Exchange moving forward, a Small and Medium Enterprises Board was set up in June 2004. From this time on, the Shenzhen Stock Exchange will keep all the listed companies that went public before 2000 in Shenzhen and absorb all small and medium companies to be listed subsequently.

In terms of current market indices, there are three kinds of market indices on each stock exchange. These are all-share indices for both markets, the Shanghai 30 index and Shenzhen 40 index (30 or 40 representative companies in each market), and the industry indices. Ideally, all-share indices are a good underlying asset for index futures since they represent the whole market. However, since they consist of over 1,000 stocks in both markets, it is very hard to construct a matching product, while the Shanghai 30 index and Shenzhen 40 index have too few stocks to give a good representation of the whole market. The example of FTSE-100 index on the London Stock Exchange or the QQQ product representing the top 100 stocks on NASDAQ could be good models for an index futures product in China. Constructing a stock index or exchange traded fund based on 100 stocks traded either on the Shanghai or the Shenzhen Stock Exchange, with consideration given to company size, liquidity of trading and industry representation, can be a good starting point for the a Chinese stock market index futures product. To further hedge risk in the stock markets and be able to produce more combinations of trading strategies, stock options (call and put) on these 100 individual stocks included in the index also need to be developed. In an interesting development in late 2004, CME entered into talks with the Shanghai Stock Exchange to develop stock index futures and other financial derivative products though no details are available at the time of writing this paper as to what, if any, decisions have been made.

There are two issues that should be addressed in conjunction with the development of stock and stock index futures and options trading. These are short selling and securities lending on all the stocks involved in the derivatives trading. At this point in time, short selling is not permitted on the Chinese stock exchanges and no market has yet developed for securities lending. If short selling can effectively occur in the derivatives market, it should also be an option in the cash market. Also securities lending is an important part of the market dynamics of short selling. The potential for a very large and active stock and stock index derivatives market in China is great, however, given the size of the Chinese equity markets as shown in Table 1. While stock turnover in China cannot match the $US 1 trillion per month that is currently seen on the New York Stock Exchange, it is still very large by international standards. The Chinese bond market volume (see Table 2) is also of a size that should be able to support active derivative trading at some future date, as was the case in the past.

3.3. Market Structure of a Formal Derivatives Market in China

When comparing the growth of derivatives trading and exchange development worldwide, we find that there are significant regional differences.

Table 1. Statistical Summary on the Equity Market in China, 1999–2003.

	1999	2000	2001	2002	2003
A or B share listed companies	949	1088	1160	1224	1287
Total market capitalization (billion yuan)	2,647.12	4,809.09	4,352.22	3,832.91	4,245.77
Negotiable market capitalization (billion yuan)	821.40	1,608.75	1,446.32	1,248.46	1,317.85
Stock turnover (billion yuan)	3,331.86	6,282.67	4,030.62	2,999.25	3,411.83
Total investors (thousand)	44,819.7	58,011.3	66,504.1	68,840.8	70,254.1

Source: China Securities Regulatory Commission, Statistical Information.

Table 2. Statistical Summary on the Bond Market in China, 1999–2003.

Year	1999	2000	2001	2002	2003
Turnover of T-bonds Spots (billion yuan)	530.09	415.75	481.56	870.87	575.61
Turnover of T-bonds Repurchase (billion yuan)	1,289.05	1,473.37	1,548.76	2,441.97	5,299.99

Source: China Securities Regulatory Commission, Statistical Information.

In the United States, financial derivatives tend to be traded in different markets from existing cash exchanges. For example, both the Chicago Board of Trade and CME remain independent of the large equity exchanges, such as the New York Stock Exchange and NASDAQ. In Europe, however, major derivatives markets are now part of mainstream exchanges. In many countries, like France, Germany, Netherlands and Spain, the derivatives market was taken over by the cash exchange. Since, the Shanghai Stock Exchange is now the main board in China, and equity-based derivative products are likely to be the major part of any financial derivatives market at this time, it could be argued that this trading should be launched either on, or under the umbrella of the Shanghai Stock Exchange. The current talks between the Shanghai Stock Exchange and CME indicate that the Shanghai Stock Exchange holds a similar view.

In terms of trading systems, electronic systems now dominate in financial derivative markets globally. The major markets of the US still have the open outcry trading system, but in every case there is an electronic systems sitting behind, at least for order routing and trade execution. The development of a state-of-the-art electronic derivatives trading system for financial derivatives within China is quite achievable. China's two stock exchanges started in the early 1990s and began with electronic trading systems from the start. These systems have been further developed over time and are regarded as being of a very high standard. It could well be prudent, however, to adopt one of the internationally accepted trading systems such as CME's GLOBEX®, Euronext-LIFFE's LIFFE-Connect^{TM} or the electronic trading system run by Eurex. While any of these options may be a more expensive long-term, it would have two major benefits. First, it would give a very clear signal to the international derivative marketplace that China was serious about derivative trading and second, it would made the development of international relationships easier out into the future. Given the relative strengths of the systems mentioned above, LIFFE-Connect^{TM} may well be the best choice, however, if the Shanghai Stock Exchange does take on the financial derivatives trading, its relationship with CME may well mean GLOBEX® is the preferred choice of trading systems despite its recent drop in popularity.

In relation to trading systems, another issue to decide is whether to adopt a market maker system of trading or whether to have an order driven system. In the US markets, the market makers dominate. In the two major exchanges of Europe, the situation is a little different. Eurex operates with a mix of market maker and broker order flow. At Euronext, however, up until recently only the Amsterdam operation has had a market maker system of trading in place. Euronext is made up of Euronext-LIFFE, Euronext-Amsterdam,

Euronext-Paris, Euronext-Lisbon, and Euronext-Brussels and in 2004 Euronext completed the integration of all its markets. All are now on the LIFFE-Connect^{TM} trading platform so the system now caters for both order driven and market maker order flow. Euronext-LIFFE itself has started introducing market makers for some of its products. While the presence of market makers may well be good for a Chinese financial derivatives market later on, we would strongly argue that, at least in the short term, an order driven system should be adopted given the level of moral risk that exists in China. A well-regulated and trusted broker network needs to be established first to build up both local and international trust in the financial derivatives market. Once this is done, there may well be scope for the introduction of market makers.

4. AN OVER-THE-COUNTER DERIVATIVES MARKET

Financial derivatives are not only traded in structured and regulated markets. A very large percentage of all financial derivative contracts traded globally are OTC trades since the individually tailored products can meet market participants' specific needs better. OTC derivatives are a recent financial phenomenon that started in the early 1980s after the debt crisis in developing countries. However, there is a very great demand for customized as opposed to standardized products. For example, in the United States through the 1990s, for every dollar value of exchange traded derivative contacts there were approximately 8$ value of OTC contracts. According to the International Swap Dealers Association (ISDA), the notional value of OTC derivatives market grew from around 24 trillion dollars in 1992 to over 100 trillion dollars in 2000.

Although, OTC derivatives markets are seen as being less regulated than formal derivatives exchanges, at the Financial Markets Conference of the Federal Reserve Bank of Atlanta on February 21, 1997, Alan Greenspan (1997), pointed out that "in the case of the institutional off-exchange derivatives markets, it seems abundantly clear that private market regulation is quite effectively and efficiently achieving what have been identified as the public policy objectives of government regulation". He finds no evidence that the prices of OTC contracts have been manipulated, since with settlement in cash rather than through delivery it is hard to control or manipulate the prices of OTC derivatives products. In addition, as prices of OTC contracts are not used directly as the basis for pricing other transactions, any price distortions would not affect other market participants and certainly not the whole economy. Greenspan also documents that institutional participants in the OTC derivative markets have demonstrated their ability to protect themselves from losses through fraud and counterparty insolvencies due to the threat of legal damages and fear of loss of the dealer's good reputation. Therefore, Greenspan concludes that there appears to be no need for government regulation of off-exchange derivative transactions between institutional counterparties.

Although this may be the case in most developed economies, due to the moral risk existing in the Chinese financial markets, one still needs to watch closely the risk involved in the OTC derivatives markets in China, especially for those contracts brokering for clients. Kroszner (1999) studies the regulations in the financial markets and explains that while clearinghouses have been successful in managing risk for exchange traded contracts, a new type of organization form, called the derivatives product company (DPC), has developed to provide some of the benefits of the clearinghouse system, while keeping the flexibility and decentralization of the OTC market. For example, the International Swap Dealers Association, a private trade association, provides a "master agreement" that offers standard definitions of terms and guidelines for the formulation of OTC contracts, but the contracts are individually tailored. In addition, Kroszner (1999) believes that credit rating agencies play an important certification role as third-party monitors in the OTC markets. He argues that, "credit rating agencies are the effective regulators in setting standards for capital, collateral and conduct, much like clearinghouses and government regulators, but do not have a direct financial stake in the transactions". Table 3 shows the characteristics of alternative structures for trading derivatives as given by Kroszner (1999).

As for the products, the popular OTC derivatives products are currency and interest rate swaps, and more recently credit derivatives. Although currency derivatives are now the main growth area for Chinese-based OTC transactions, equity-based derivatives can be traded in an OTC environment and are likely to have more appeal in China, at least in the short term. A very successful example that can be followed is the customized equity markets derivatives product, Contracts for Difference (CFD), offered by many major UK brokers. CFDs are derivatives contracts between stockbrokers and investors, which are based either on listed UK stocks or on market indexes. These contracts operate very much like a futures product with similar payoff characteristics. Besides trading commissions, brokers get financing charges from customers going long and pay interest to customers going short.

On March 1, 2004, the regulatory authorities in China began a new initiative to help develop OTC derivatives trading with the setting up of a

Table 3. Characteristics of Alternative Structures for Trading Derivatives.

Prior to Organized Exchanges (forward)	Exchange with Clearinghouse	OTC Markets with Derivative Product Companies (DPCs)
Decentralized	Centralized	Decentralized
Unorganized	Organized	Organized
No standardization	Standardized contracts	Customized contracts in framework of broad standards (ISDA)
High transaction costs	Low transaction costs	Low transaction costs
Very high monitoring costs	Monitoring costs: • High if no central guarantor • Low if clearinghouse guarantor	Monitoring costs: Low due to rating agencies and risk models

Source: Kroszner (1999), pp. 609.

structured system for its operation. The intention was to enable the major financial institutions and enterprises to hedge their foreign currency positions as well as for brokers to develop customized derivatives products, and this is now being achieved to a large extent. At the time the spokesperson for the initiative stated that "this new initiative is to avoid opening up financial derivatives business in a simple way, but to specify qualifications, standardize trading behaviors, manage trading risk and ensure financial safety" (China Daily, 4/2/04). The details of this new initiative are as follows. Approved financial institutions within China can apply to the China Banking Regulatory Committee to take part in the OTC derivatives trading. In order to gain approval, however, there are a number of conditions that need to be met. The business must be specifically to hedge the institution's own risk or to be a product offered to the institution's customers. The institutions must show that they have a good risk management system in place and be able to show that good and effective communication exists among the front, middle and back offices. The manager directly responsible for the derivative trading operation must have a minimum of five years experience in derivatives trading and risk management, with two other team members having a minimum of two years similar experience. Two additional team members must have the clear responsibility for risk management and modeling and risk analysis respectively. The institution must also show that it has sufficient current assets to support the proposed business. While this move to develop

OTC trading is clearly a positive one, it needs to be viewed as just one part of the Chinese financial derivative market development.

5. INTERNATIONAL COOPERATION AND THE DERIVATIVES MARKET IN CHINA

As China's economy continues to develop and becomes more integrated with the global economy, people are also interested in the question of how internationalized a financial derivatives market in China can be. To become an internationalized financial derivatives market, first of all, the Chinese derivatives market needs to meet international industry standards. Over the last 10 years, in particular, trading and settlement systems have become extremely efficient and sophisticated. The Shanghai Stock Exchange itself has state-of-the-art trading and settlement technology, but it is interesting to note that the best trading systems, such as those of CME and Euronext-LIFFE have found wider popularity and a Chinese financial derivatives market might well be advised to adopt technology from outside as mentioned earlier. Adopting internationally accepted trading, settlement and risk management systems can be seen as an effective way in which China can move toward global industry standards.

As the integration between China and the global economy has developed, hedging risk in China will become more of an issue for foreign operators as well as those in China itself. This issue can also be considered from the viewpoint of other major financial derivatives exchanges, particularly those of the United States and Europe. Yuan-based derivative products are already well established in a number of international derivative exchanges. Not only can there be further substantial growth in this area, but a Chinese financial derivatives market could well take back some of this business if structured correctly. International cooperation is a real option for China with many cross-country partnerships having developed in recent times as globalization expands. The Shanghai Stock Exchange and CME cooperation could well be the beginning of international derivative market cooperation for China.

6. CONCLUSIONS

This research is aimed to assist policy makers, in particular, to move forward with the credible development of an official financial derivatives market in China. A summary of our recommendations is as follows. Developing a credible financial derivatives market is an essential part of the whole process of financial market development in China. This development should take place within a reasonably short-time frame. The European model of having the derivative market attached to the physical market should be adopted, particularly given the fact that stock-based derivative products are the ones most likely to be developed first. Although there are two stock exchanges in China, given that the Shanghai Stock Exchange is the main board after the restructuring in 2000, it is our view that the Shanghai financial derivatives market should be developed first as part of the Shanghai Stock Exchange operation. The trading system used by the exchanges should be an internationally recognized one to help ensure an international acceptance of these new exchanges. In particular, we recommend that consideration be given to adopting the LIFFE-Connect^{TM} trading system used by the Euronext exchanges. Settlement and risk management systems should also be internationally recognized ones.

In relation to products traded, individual stock and stock index futures and options should be traded in the first instance. Exchange traded currency and interest rate futures and options should wait for exchange rate and interest rate deregulation in China. We consider that both the Shanghai and Shenzhen Stock Exchanges should develop indices based on the 100 top stocks on which to base the stock index contracts. As part of the development of these markets, controlled short selling and stock lending systems should be developed.

The regulatory system has been a major concern and challenge for the development of the financial derivatives market in China. There are three main kinds of risk involved in a financial derivatives market, i.e. explicit risks, implicit risks and estimation risks. Among these, in the Chinese financial market, credit risk, accounting and disclosure risk, systematic risk and moral risk are our major focuses. Risks are analyzed in the Chinese context and suggestions are provided to improve the regulatory system to manage these major risks.

The OTC market should continue to develop within the structure laid down recently within China. Although the regulatory system in the OTC market in most western countries is not a major concern for the government, due to the moral risk involved in the Chinese derivatives market, certain measures may be needed, such as the possible implementation of DPC. Equity-based derivatives, such as CFD could be traded in this market in the near future along with currency derivatives. We believe that, with due care, exchange-based financial derivatives trading can successfully return to

China in the near future, along with further expansion of the OTC market, based on the structures suggested above.

NOTES

1. The monthly trading volume in the government bond futures market exceeded that in the spot market by about 500% after October 1994 (Chen & Zhou, 2004).
2. After the price increase, the margin that Wanguo Securities Company had available was totally wiped out. However, due to unregulated trading and the settlement system of the Shanghai Stock Exchange, Wanguo Securities Company was able to keep on trading (selling) the futures contract without making any further margin payments.
3. At that time, the margin requirement was 2.5%, which means that the maximum trading of the futures contracts was 40 times of the total issuing amount of the government bonds. However, due to the lack of monitoring and margin checking after trading, securities companies and broker firms did not trade based on how many bonds they had or on how much margin they could pay. Trading became pure speculation, with securities companies and broker firms trying to push prices into the range that favored them.
4. The reports published by the Bank of International Settlements, Basle were "Recent developments in international interbank relations" (1992) and "Risk management guidelines for derivatives" (1994).
5. Both the Shanghai and Shenzhen Stock Exchanges are non-profit organizations operating under the supervision of the China Securities Regulatory Commission.

REFERENCES

Chen, C., & Zhou, Z. G. (2004). *The rise and fall of the government bond futures market in China*. Working Paper. California State University, Northridge.
Donohue, C. S. (2004). Developing China's derivatives market infrastructure: Challenges and opportunities. Remarks to the Shanghai Derivatives Forum on 28 May 2004.
Gibson, R., & Zimmermann, H. (1996a). Analyzing and monitoring derivatives' risk: An economic perspective. *Derivatives Use, Trading and Regulation, 2*(1), 47–66.
Gibson, R., & Zimmermann, H. (1996b). Analyzing and monitoring derivatives' risks – Part 2. *Derivatives Use, Trading and Regulation, 2*(2), 119–128.
Greenspan, A. (1997). Government regulation and derivative contracts. Remarks at the Financial Markets Conference of the Federal Reserve Bank of Atlanta, Coral Gables, Florida on 21 February 1997.
Grossman, S. (1977). The existence of futures markets, noisy rational expectations, and informational externalities. *Review of Economic Studies, 64*, 431–449.
Grossman, S. (1988a). An analysis of the implications for stock and futures price volatility of program trading and dynamic hedging strategies. *Journal of Business, 61*, 275–298.
Grossman, S. (1988b). Insurance seen and unseen: The impact on markets. *Journal of Portfolio Management Summer*, 5–8.

Hakansson, N. H. (1982). Changes in the financial market: Welfare and price effects and the basis theorems of value conservation. *Journal of Finance, 37,* 977–1004.

IOMA Derivatives Market Survey. (2003). World Federation of Exchanges, 2004 Institute for Financial Markets, Futures and Options Fact Book.

Kroszner, R. S. (1999). Can the financial markets privately regulate risk?: The development of derivatives clearinghouses and recent over-the-counter innovations. *Journal of Money, Credit and Banking, 31,* 596–618.

Kumar, R., Sarin, A., & Shastri, K. (1998). The impact of options trading on the market quality of the underlying security: An empirical analysis. *Journal of Finance, 53,* 717–732.

Ross, S. A. (1976). Options and efficiency. *Quarterly Journal of Economics, 90,* 75–89.

ENCOURAGING GROWTH IN ASIA WITH MULTI-PILLAR FINANCIAL SYSTEMS

Mukund Narayanamurti and Jonathan A. Batten

ABSTRACT

Post-crisis policy measures in Asia have focussed on banking sector and market reform. The paper argues that in order to propel growth, banking and market reform in Asia must be undertaken with the view that they are not mutually exclusive competitive tradeoffs. Rather banks and markets must be viewed as complementary supportive pillars in a financial system. Additionally, legal and functional reform must be undertaken simultaneously. The paper proposes that a likely consequence of doing so will enable creating a four-pillared multi-dimensional growth paradigm in the region to help restore and promote growth.

1. INTRODUCTION

Post-crisis policy prognosis in Asia has focussed on the historical dualism between banks and markets. Notable are the attempts made by authors such as Greenspan (1999, 2000), Davis (2001) and Demirguc-Kunt and Levine

Asia Pacific Financial Markets in Comparative Perspective: Issues and Implications for the 21st Century
Contemporary Studies in Economics and Financial Analysis, Volume 86, 361–415
Copyright © 2005 by Elsevier Ltd.
All rights of reproduction in any form reserved
ISSN: 1569-3759/doi:10.1016/S1569-3759(05)86016-4

(1999) to spur the development of multiple avenues of intermediation in bank centric economies. In particular these tasks have addressed the need to develop equity and bond markets, enhance transparency and disclosure, develop optimal regulatory structures and adequately pace financial reform.

Initial diagnosis of the malady gripping Asia was divided between two schools of thought: the fundamental and the panic-stricken (Kahler, 2000). Fundamentalists attribute structural and macroeconomic deficiencies to have coincided simultaneously in activating the crisis (Christoffersen & Errunza, 2000; Corsetti, Pesenti, & Roubini, 1999). The panic-stricken view on the other hand, claim that the crisis was fuelled by self-fulfilling prophecies prompting investor trepidation, causing in turn financial panic (Noble & Ravenhill, 2000; Kahler, 2000). The fact that Asian economies enjoyed unprecedented levels of growth pre-crisis, and because countries with similar economic frameworks went unscathed meant that the arguments proposed by the panic-stricken view seemed more plausible.

Concurrence with the panic-stricken view triggered policy efforts to develop multiple avenues of intermediation (Shirai, 2001; Sharma, 2001). While these efforts have been impressive their focus has been anachronistic, by failing to appreciate that in an environment with increasingly borderless economies, financial and real sector linkages need to be established. Policy efforts have principally failed to appreciate that financial and real sector reform, due to their nexus need to be conducted simultaneously.

This paper aims to bridge this gap by exploring the linkages between financial system design and the real sector in Asia. A multi-pillar paragon is constructed revolving around the previously considered mutually exclusive concepts of banking, financial markets, the law and functional reform. By doing so the major queries gripping crisis management and resolution in the region are addressed.

For instance, why have South East Asian economies promoted the dominance of banks in their financial systems? Has this dominance arisen due to the banking sector's ability to promote growth? If so, then why has growth slumped post-crisis? Additionally, why has the development of capital markets, particularly bond markets been impeded in South East Asia? Does the underlying legal system hinder the development of multiple avenues of intermediation? Besides, has South East Asia's institutional focus prevented functional reform in the region?

Restoration of growth in East Asia is vital as prior to the crisis. Dalla (1995) notes that while the region accounted for only 6% of world output, it contributed to more than one-fourth of the GDP attributable to emerging economies. Moreover, Dalla (1995) highlights that East Asia's GDP was about one-fifth the size of U.S. GDP, and greater than countries such as the United Kingdom. In addition the global economy grew at less than half the rate enjoyed by East Asia, which averaged growth through the mid-1980s and early 1990s equivalent to 7.8% (Dalla, 1995). A period in which developed economies are facing high rates of retirement, and low rates of growth in the labour force, developing regions such as East Asia with its high savings rate and low wage labour sectors, are to serve as propellers to growth in global productivity (Summers, 1999). A reflection of the region's significance is depicted by it serving as a growth model to other developing countries.

The overall objective is to establish how financial sector development can potentially impact on growth. By doing so the negative growth rates faced by the region upon commencement of the crisis in 1997 can be reversed. Included in the country set are Thailand, Indonesia, Malaysia and Korea.[1] The reason for choosing these four countries is due to key similarities depicted in their financial systems, in particular their experiences with financial and capital account liberalization. While these similarities have existed, the four nations have had varying degrees of success in areas such as capital market development.

Four secondary aims are used to help establish the primary objective of restoring growth. The first aim is to identify why South East Asian banks which helped to promote growth in the past (Birdsall et al., 1993), succumbed when national governments adopted open capital accounts. The second aim is to investigate how markets can reduce the possibilities of crisis by reducing dependence on banks (Yam, 1997; Herring & Chatusripitak, 2000). In particular an attempt is made to assess how financial deepening promotes growth and aids market discipline (Batten & Kim, 2000). The third aim is to explore if the legal system in South East Asia is conducive to financial development. In particular, shareholder and creditor rights protection, ownership structures and the potentialities for equity and debt market development is investigated. The fourth aim is to evaluate the level of functional reform adopted in South East Asia. A functional perspective is far more important than an institutional perspective (Merton & Bodie, 1995), as functions persist longer than institutions. A "non-leapfrog approach" is used to demonstrate that South East Asian economies are likely to take time to evolve. The major implication is that by not leapfrogging financial development, the need for the real economy to be stabilized before being deregulated is recommended (McKinnon, 1973).

The paper adopts a flow of fund analysis, utilizing secondary data drawn from the Bank for International Settlements (BIS). With approximately

US$ 370 billion flowing through to all emerging economies during the peak of the crisis, and with South East Asia at one stage claiming as high as 38% of these funds, the nature and direction that these funds assume is crucial to our understanding of boom–bust cycles (Batten & Kim, 2000). The paper is structured as follows: Section 2 reviews the literature in the area of financial intermediation, financial and real sector linkages and financial architecture. Section 3 highlights the propositions to be investigated. Section 4 makes specific policy recommendations centred on the impediments identified in Section 3, while Section 5 allows room for some concluding remarks.

2. LITERATURE REVIEW

2.1. The Changing Trend in Financial Contracting

In envisaging to build virtually borderless economies reflective of a single collaborated global system, there is a requirement that current efforts be concentrated on improving the economic growth of nations by whole-heartedly focussing on the structure, conduct and performance of these nations financial systems. At the heart of this above statement lies the financial activity which is considered a synonym for financial intermediation (Bryant, 1987). Bryant (1987) defines financial intermediation as a process of reconciliation between the needs of savers and investors.

Walter (1993) highlights the various conduits through which financial assets flow within and between national economies. Clearly the classical model of intermediation is based around the services generated through banks and their ability to create standardised contracts yielding to the users of the funds an optimal combination of transaction costs, flexibility and liquidity. Against this backdrop, as economies grow enabling markets to establish functional and geographical linkages an attempt is made to capture the finer gains of dynamic efficiency evidenced through product and process innovations (Walter, 1993). This is clearly reflective of Walter's (1993) competing modes of contracting based around markets attempting to unfold. These alternative modes are relevant in relation to the South East Asian crisis economies as they strive to avoid the possibility of financial obsolescence by endeavouring to achieve strategic, competitive and dynamic efficiency gains through the speedy but incremental development of efficient capital markets.

Other approaches by authors such as Stiglitz and Weiss (1981) and Davis (2001) clearly point out that as a response to asymmetric information problems, a structure for intermediation theory arises on the grounds that there tends to be adverse selection before lending and moral hazard after lending has taken place. Diamond (1984) highlights that intermediaries overcome asymmetries of information through their function of delegated monitoring, as a result of enjoying a cost advantage in relation to the collection of information. By doing so the intermediary serves an important function by preventing duplication of effort and the well-publicised free-rider problem (Diamond, 1984). Santos (2000) concludes that it is the provision of liquidity services that helps to justify the liability side of the bank's balance sheet, and the provision of monitoring services that helps to explain the asset side. Diamond and Rajan (1998) confirm that it is advantageous for intermediaries to provide liquidity services as compared to other institutions, due to its significance to both investors and borrowers.

Allen and Santomero (1998) in their paper argue that theories of financial intermediation should focus more on risk management and participation costs, as they are activities which are central to the current chores of intermediaries. Essentially by shifting the focus in intermediation theory towards risk management and participation costs, accommodation is being made for financial innovation as it grips the world economy (Sholtens & Wensveen, 1999). Allen and Santomero (1999) reinforce the role of risk management by referring to standard financial theory, which portrays the crucial function of financial markets to be facilitation of risk sharing, while banks undertake intertemporal smoothing of risk in bank-centred economies.

Therefore, in the bank-centric financial systems of Thailand, Korea, Indonesia and Malaysia with little competition from alternative sources of finance a role for intertemporal smoothing can be instituted and justified. Thus, as a medium of fostering crisis management in the due course of time, if competition from markets increases, then the form of risk management will change, involving for instance the extensive use of derivatives. By espousing the significance of risk management and participation costs we are incorporating both static and dynamic aspects of intermediation theory and therefore able to better reflect the significance of financial innovation (Allen & Santomero, 1999).

South East Asia also enjoyed an unprecedented inflow of capital from overseas banks. As a consequence of the asymmetries of information the international banks often delegated the role of lead monitor to local banks. This was especially true in the case of Korea, but was widely prevalent in the other South East Asian economies as well. BIS banks[2] often lent to the local banks rather than directly to the local firms, due to the information asymmetries that existed as a result of the financial environment displaying significantly poor transparency and disclosure. It is due to this extensive prevalence of information asymmetries that Davis (2001) feels assured that even if multiple avenues of intermediation develop, banks will continue to play the lead role in these economies to help solve these imperfections.

However, as Merton (1993) rightly points out, it is financial market innovations that often create risk management business for banks. This is reflective of the symbiotic relationship that is shared between intermediaries and markets. It basically signifies how as markets change and evolve the type of risk management undertaken will change. This change is essentially what is more reflective of market-based systems. However, according to Allen and Gale (2000) the current trend towards market-based systems, maybe nothing more than a result of the majority of research being centred on the United States and the United Kingdom.

2.2. Financial and Real Sector Linkages

King and Levine (1992) throw light on the pivotal interaction between the financial and real sector by highlighting that in countries where intermediaries have played a dominant role in the organisation of industry, those countries have systematically outperformed other countries over time.

There are different mediums through which financial activity may propagate the real sector. Thakor (1996) by portraying a paradigm of financial and real sector linkages shows that financial system design matters substantially because of its real consequences. These real consequences force us to view the financial structure implications of design from the perspective of a wider audience rather than along only the architectural desires of the financial community.

Therefore in the case of Asia, while multiple avenues of intermediation may help reduce the probability of financial crises and thereby reduce real sector shocks, these economies may in hindsight need to proceed further along their economic development curves for multiple avenues to actively flourish. However as Davis (2001) rightly shows, the existence of multiple avenues will help an economy in the event of a particular avenue being engulfed in financial turmoil. This is directly significant to Asia as there was an overreliance on bank-based finance due to underdeveloped alternative sources of finance.

2.3. Architecture and Designing an Optimal Financial Structure Mix

The constitution of the financial sector is of paramount significance since it aids and directs overall financial development, which has been shown to positively influence long run growth. Any prospective study of financial structure configuration must include a reflection of how the United States and Germany are at polar extremes, portraying as a result the differing social and economic frameworks that are required in market-based systems (U.S. & U.K.) as compared to bank-based systems (Germany and Japan) (Allen & Gale, 2000).

As financial systems are critical to ensuring allocative efficiency in an economy, there must exist certain pillars, which support and enable accomplishment of this objective. Goldsmith (1969) describes financial structure as a combination of intermediaries and markets. This definition is furthered here by laying down pillars in terms of the roles to be played by banks, markets, regulation and financial services. Therefore, the work of Walter (1993) and Levine (2000) is in essence combined to show that ultimately a financial system irrespective of whether it is bank based or market based should serve as a catalyst to growth in the real sector, by providing sound financial services in a regulated environment. Accordingly, the following are the four pillars depicting Levine's (2000) views on the optimal structure underpinning a modern financial system's architecture.

2.3.1. Bank-based View {pillar #1}

Gerschenkron (1962), Diamond (1984), Bryant (1987), Dewatripoint and Tirole (1992), Allen and Gale (2000) and Levine (2000) among others, have noted that in order for markets to achieve their potential in allocative efficiency it is critical that they are helped by intermediaries in overcoming frictions that affect financial systems.

Bank-based systems enjoy a number of advantages: First, banks serve as delegated monitors (Diamond, 1984). Second, Shleifer and Summers (1988) suggest that banks are extremely well positioned to make credible long-term commitments. Third, Allen and Gale (2000), Rajan and Zingales (1999) and Gerschenkron (1962) highlight that banks are particularly adept at leading growth during the early stages of economic development, as there might be a lack of an appropriate financial and legal framework. Fourth, banks provide more efficient risk-sharing opportunities through the intertemporal smoothing of risk as compared to markets, which provide cross-sectional risk sharing (Allen & Gale, 2000). Lastly, banks enable the functioning of efficient payment and settlement systems (Dewatripoint & Tirole, 1992);

enable the easing of liquidity risk (Diamond & Dybvig, 1983); apart from providing their traditional advantageous functions of lowering transaction costs (Benston & Smith, 1976) and reducing informational asymmetries (Akerlof, 1970; Leland & Pyle, 1977).

Bank-Based systems are beset with a number of disadvantages as well. These disadvantages may be summarised as follows: First, there exists the inability of banks to provide multiple evaluations in situations when there are large differences in opinions regarding firms' production processes (Allen, 1992). Second, Levine (2000) highlights that banks may as a result of their superior informational levels extract rents and expected future profits from a firm. Lastly, Levine (2000) throws light on the German industry where there have been significant instances of collusion between bankers and firm managers.

2.3.2. Market-based Systems {pillar #2}

Fujita (2000) states that financial systems in different countries have emerged in different historical contexts, requiring as a result that every nation's financial system be awarded its own unique spatial recognition. Why then are market-based systems gaining such universal popularity when building financial systems is clearly a country-specific task?

There are two major reasons that help explain this global trend. First and foremost, as Allen and Gale (2000) so rightly point out, government intervention has come to be recognised as a fallen approach. Government intervention failures have come to be viewed as costly as market failures have been at different stages of economic history (Allen & Gale, 2000). Furthermore, in an era of systemic financial crises portrayed heavily in the form of banking panics, the United States and United Kingdom have managed to condense and magnify a sparkling picture of market-based systems (Allen & Gale, 2000). Market-based systems have been shown to be prone to cyclical shocks, but this fact has been less emphasised lately, due to growing interest in developing nations to develop alternative means of finance in bank-centric economies. The rationale behind this is to reduce the effect of banking sector shocks through viable efficient markets.

The major proponents of this view include Allen (1992), Allen and Gale (2000), Levine (2000), Levine and Beck (2000) and Fujita (2000) among others. The major advantages of the market-based view maybe summarised as follows: First, markets enable efficient financing by reducing the costs of using a middleman in an era of declining costs associated with direct financing (Mayer & Vives, 1993). Second, Allen and Gale (2000) and Holmstrom and Tirole (1993) pinpoint that markets through the acquisition and dissemination of information enable efficient decision making. As such by trading in liquid and large markets informational advantages can be gained about firms which help in the efficient allocation of resources (Allen & Gale, 2000).

Third, Diamond (1967) shows that markets enable efficient risk sharing. Markets by engaging in cross-sectional risk sharing enable investors to design portfolios that suit their individual needs. Fourth, markets serve as efficient external corporate governance mechanisms by exerting corporate control (Jensen & Meckling, 1976). Allen and Gale (2000) show how this has an impact of aligning managers interest with those of the shareholders as poorly managed firms can be acquired by firms that are capable of pursuing superior management policies.

Lastly, as Allen (1992) shows markets are necessary for the aggregation of diverse opinions in industries that are of monopolistic or oligopolistic nature witnessing very rapid technological change. As such where there is divergence in opinions of investors on what constitutes an optimal production process for the firm, the market aggregates such opinions as compared to banks playing the role of a delegated monitor (Allen, 1992).

Similar to bank-based systems market-oriented economies are plagued with certain disadvantages. Firstly, Allen and Gale (2000) show that markets expose investors to market risk; the possibility that changes in market information and investor sentiments will cause volatility in asset values. Allen and Gale (2000) suggest that it is here that intermediaries through intertemporal risk smoothing protect investors from having to liquidate assets at fire sale values. Secondly, Stiglitz (1985) shows that by markets revealing information to all investors, provide individual investors with lesser initiative to research and collect firm-specific information. This phenomenon is typically reflective of market-oriented economies where there is concern of under-investment in information.

Third, Boot and Thakor (2000) reveal how banks by fostering long-term relationships can enable firms to concentrate on more productive long-term investment decisions. This attribute of relationship banking is clearly missing in markets, as contracts are not tailor-made and renegotiated on as they are generally standardised and transaction oriented. Lastly, while large and liquid markets reflect allocative efficiency, establishing this size for effectiveness translates into higher participation costs for investors making markets costly to use (Allen & Gale, 2000).

Markets like intermediaries espouse positive real sector effects. Holmstrom and Tirole (1993) find that stock prices contain information that not only helps in aiding managerial compensation, but also helps to facilitate superior real decisions. Additionally, stock markets according to Thakor (1996) enable a more efficient real sector by reducing the effects of effort-avoidance and overinvestment moral hazard, both of which would exist in the event of dependence on the banking sector.

In conclusion, while viewing intermediaries and markets as being worlds' apart, in reality the picture portrayed is one for intermediaries *and* markets rather than intermediaries versus markets. As Allen and Gale (2000) and Davis (2001) so rightly show, intermediaries are more often than not required for the efficient exploitation of increasingly complex markets. Besides the nature of incompleteness of markets compels intermediaries to solve the various frictions bestowed in them to enable the operation of smooth well-functioning financial systems.

2.3.3. Law and Finance View {pillar #3}

Due to the fiduciary nature of the financial services industry and the high social costs associated with institutional failures, regulation is a central aspect of every financial system (Walter, 1993). Within this framework financial regulation portrays an attempt to enable the satisfactory dissemination of information, the evaluation of financial institutions, instruments and markets and the supervision of the core financial services extended by a nation's financial system.

Allen (2001) highlights that a framework for financial regulation must particularly in developing countries come to resemble the U.S. system of regulation due to its proven worth. In Asia this would involve a shift away from regulatory structures designed to satisfy the pre-requisites of government and political bodies towards institutional investors. This changing paradigm is essentially a response to the dynamics of global capital mobility. Therefore, it is most likely that a paragon of regulation epitomising investor protection (shareholder and creditor) is likely to become one of the most important policy centre-stones in Asia's financial architecture.

This view is principally advocated by Levine (2000), who shows that it is basically the quality of financial services as determined by the legal system which promotes growth. These views are reflective of Laporta, Lopez-de-Silanes, and Shleifer (2000a) and Laporta, Lopez-de-Silanes, Shleifer, and Vishny's (1997, 1998, 1999, 2000b)[3] emphasis on viewing finance as a set of contracts whereby enforcement mechanisms and the legal framework are pivotal to promoting economic growth. Laporta et al. (2000b) believe that it is the legal rules shaped by the respective legal families that denotes the shape and influence of financial markets and not vice versa. Clearly from this perspective it is the legal rules that define the possible frontiers of intermediaries and markets.

The quality of investor protection varies drastically across different legal origins (Laporta et al., 1998). As the ensuing analysis depicts, despite their geographical nearness Asian economies reflect legal origins that vary significantly causing the implications of the resultant legal rules affecting capital market development to differ significantly. Why do different legal origins afford different qualities of protection thereby affecting financial system configuration and stability?

Laporta et al. (2000b) suggest that this occurs because the foundations upon which legal rules are based vary significantly between common law and civil law countries. In this regard, Laporta et al. (2000b) conclude that while common law may be affected by certain vague fiduciary duty principles, they afford greater protection to investors than the clearly demarcated civil law rules that, they believe can be overcome by insiders that are imaginative.

This in conclusion has clear policy implications, as legal frameworks will continue to grow and evolve in response to social and financial system changes and challenges. Therefore, the broad implication for developing nations would be to develop a regulatory framework that ensures the efficient provision of financial services by intermediaries and markets, while enabling overall financial and economic development. This in turn will help to accommodate for increasingly borderless economies and the dynamics of capital mobility. By doing so these nations can develop what they view at a particular point in time to be an optimal regulatory framework in order to spark the development of a particular avenue of finance (e.g., capital market development). Therefore, the configuration of their legal rules can change shape based on their respective policy agenda.

2.3.4. Financial Services View {pillar #4}

It is perceived that a financial system espouses certain primary functions centred on its ability to ensure efficient allocation of scarce resources in an often turbulent financial environment. As such this function is taken to be stable across borders and depicts that chief economic functions are represented in similar vein across different geographical territories (Merton & Bodie, 1995). This suggests that irrespective of who performs these functions, these functions remain stable and constant over time.

As such the core financial services that have been pronounced to administer growth include aiding of liquidity, risk management, exertion of corporate control and savings mobilization (Levine, 2000). It is the provision of these services that promotes growth rather than the source of provision.

Levine (2000) and Levine and Beck (2000) show through their extensive empirical research that classifying systems as bank-based or market-based is not particularly effective but that the legal system and the financial services provided affect financial development and economic growth. It is quite inconsequential as to whether economic growth is fostered through a bank-based system or a market-based system. As Allen and Santomero (1998) and particularly Merton and Bodie (1995) so clearly highlight a functional perspective is far more important than an institutional perspective.

Merton and Bodie (1995) state that the multiplicity of institutional forms that have been seen to exist over time are followers of economic functions, whereby the economic functions serve as conceptual anchors for analysing the financial system. A functional perspective assumes that the economic functions to be performed are given such that while the source of accomplishment of these functions maybe inconsequential, there is a need to help establish the best institutional structure within the current framework to enable establishment of these functions. In viewing the financial system as an innovation spiral, Merton and Bodie (1995) place emphasis on the ultimate financial services as provided by the financial system, as they believe that it is this end product which remains constant over time rather than altering functions to suit institutional structures.

3. KEY PROPOSITIONS AND ANALYSIS

In developing propositions that are relevant to South East Asia, it is important that these propositions are transportable across borders to other emerging and converging economies. There are four propositions that are scripted in the form of reform proposals aimed at helping to re-establish pre-crisis growth rates in post-crisis Asia. By being centred on a particular pillar of financial market development, the propositions provide a conceptual understanding to the theories and issues addressed.

3.1. Proposition One: Banking Reform is Crucial in Post-Crisis Asia so as to Enable the Re-establishment of Pre-crisis Growth Rates

The three major forms of capital flowing into Asia may be categorised as foreign direct investment, portfolio equity investment and international bank lending. Bank capital (in the form of inter-bank lending, lending to the public sector and to the private sector) from BIS reporting banks was the single most volatile source of capital. Of major policy concern has been the inability of domestic banks to redirect this international capital in a productive growth enhancing way. For example the 68th Annual BIS Report (1998) shows that until the breakout of the crisis in 1997 Malaysia, Thailand, Indonesia and Korea had not endured a single year where real GDP growth was less than 5% since Malaysia in 1986.

The significance of banks in supporting growth is clearly reflected by Shirai's (2001) analysis which finds that the size of outstanding bank loans to GDP for the period 1990–1999 averaged 90% for Thailand, 80% for Malaysia, 50% for Indonesia and 40% for Korea. Besides the size of bank loans in terms of external finance ranged from about 30% in Malaysia, 45% in Korea, 70% in Thailand and approximately 65% in Indonesia for the period ranging from 1990 to 1999 (Shirai, 2001). This is consistent with Yam (1997) who finds that the majority of the financing needs of the region are and will be met by banks.

This suggests that it is important that banks continue to foster growth in an era of large amounts of international lending being directed to developing regions. Asian banks have failed in this regard on a number of accounts as is summarised in the ensuing discussion. Therefore for pre-crisis growth rates to return, banking reform is crucial to enable the banking system to withstand swings in investor sentiments and other deficiencies underpinning these crisis-hit economies.

3.1.1. Maturity Mismatches, Foreign Currency Lending and Asset Bubbles

Easy global liquidity coupled with a policy of financial liberalisation in the crisis-struck countries through the early and mid-1990s attracted large amounts of international bank lending. International bank lending to the four countries peaked at US$ 231.8 billion in December 1996, but the commencement of the crisis in 1997 saw this amount fall to US$ 161.8 billion by September 2001 (refer to Table 1). Clearly the major provider of funds to all four countries was Japan. Grenville (2000) notes that the major reason for Japan's extensive funding to the region was in order to transfer funds for production to low-cost and lower-wage countries. Besides the interest rate differential made Japanese loans attractive to banks in Asia as they could borrow at lower rates and re-lend at higher domestic interest rates. However, commencement of the crisis saw a reduction in loans being extended by Japan to all four countries with Indonesia and Malaysia facing the largest

Table 1. Consolidated International Claims of BIS Teporting Banks on Individual Countries.

	Total	Austria	Belgium	Canada	Denmark	Finland	France	Germany	Ireland	Italy	Japan	Netherlands	Portugal	Spain	Sweden	Switzerland	United Kingdom	United States
Thailand																		
Dec-95	63842	514	1161	813	48	188	3739	4977	2	358	38998	1329	—	49	307	1511	2822	7026
Dec-96	72114	668	1298	1118	97	253	4642	6914	30	461	39475	1838	—	103	592	1591	4660	8374
Dec-97	61912	645	764	768	25	127	5026	6463	74	338	35081	2071	—	142	475	1330	2361	6222
Dec-98	49834	452	530	549	53	711	3874	5105	—	514	24008	5817	—	148	388	699	1775	5211
Dec-99	41292	296	416	—	—	668	3652	4980	—	231	15541	5678	7	37	229	927	4390	4240
Dec-00	34842	206	294	306	—	449	2110	4411	—	157	12772	4964	3	1	247	653	4164	4105
Sep-01	33112	120	139	222	—	387	2082	4248	—	134	11787	4464	15	1	263	552	4515	4183
Indonesia																		
Dec-95	43851	1087	1441	346	112	52	3417	3893	2	64	22467	2780	—	70	60	1001	2727	4332
Dec-96	54316	1357	2982	589	115	108	4828	5508	5	104	23453	2915	—	143	147	1516	3834	6712
Dec-97	55864	1478	1667	913	68	99	4950	6367	53	184	22834	3305	—	242	288	2025	4492	6899
Dec-98	44557	1524	798	471	56	212	4085	5811	3	140	16973	3856	—	168	71	1609	3814	4966
Dec-99	43734	1451	440	642	—	208	3655	8407	—	160	13102	4375	—	131	33	1374	4485	5271
Dec-00	38813	1457	439	853	—	196	2896	7277	—	139	10936	3776	—	91	63	1697	4411	4582
Sep-01	35178	194	291	663	—	173	2726	8496	—	115	9643	3522	—	78	53	1547	3956	3721
Malaysia																		
Dec-95	19640	37	74	357	7	27	2207	2249	2	97	7323	462	—	2	38	280	1158	5320
Dec-96	27112	68	249	531	12	25	2643	3857	2	167	9172	1251	—	1	92	458	1417	7167
Dec-97	31414	190	375	552	3	35	2885	7839	24	222	9276	1340	—	25	53	782	2014	5799
Dec-98	25681	162	209	685	3	8	2335	5052	27	83	7364	1243	—	103	17	601	2040	5749
Dec-99	34919	156	195	—	—	20	2478	2890	—	73	6829	1304	19	135	19	657	12815	7348
Dec-00	34991	174	230	—	—	7	2348	2951	—	119	6388	1431	12	51	14	566	13617	7076
Sep-01	33773	142	195	—	—	2	1824	3147	—	123	6334	1296	—	16	50	721	12762	7149
Korea																		
Dec-95	62809	530	1954	961	88	90	7487	7318	10	1010	22809	1371	—	299	381	1082	4312	13107
Dec-96	78308	1269	3731	1474	204	170	9370	9977	54	1208	25722	2261	—	469	428	1582	6203	14186
Dec-97	77147	741	1433	1968	25	61	11861	9849	49	806	21290	2078	—	526	174	3127	7803	15356
Dec-98	63081	564	725	1587	10	22	7905	8568	11	598	18294	2907	—	145	197	1759	6193	13596
Dec-99	63158	578	629	1984	—	13	9192	7677	—	366	13548	3092	81	267	157	3283	6491	15800
Dec-00	60011	669	737	1751	—	53	8155	7489	—	701	11000	3236	140	178	76	2242	6789	16795
Sep-01	59915	454	516	1667	—	34	7318	7117	—	701	11450	3083	59	148	66	3575	6865	16862

Note: (in millions of U.S dollars) By nationality of reporting banks
Source: Bank for International Settlements, BIS statistics for consolidated international claims of BIS Reporting banks on individual ountries
for the year ended 1995,1996,1997,1998,1999,2000 and for September 2001.

reduction. A certain portion of this reduction was compensated for by increased funding by European banks but the total volume of loans in absolute terms diminished nonetheless.

A major area of concern pertaining to international bank lending to the region was related to the maturity structure of the loans extended (refer to Table 2). A staggering amount of the loans were of a short-term nature ranging from 68% for Thailand, 64.4% for Indonesia, 58.1% for Malaysia and 77% for Korea in the year 1996.

A major consequence of this burgeoning volume of short-term loans was that it was directed towards long-term non-tradeable sectors such as property, therefore causing a maturity mismatch (Gochoco-Bautista, Oh, & Rhee, 2000). The constant injection of capital into these financial systems

Table 2. Consolidated International Claims of BIS Reporting Banks.

	Thailand	Indonesia	Malaysia	Korea
Up to and including 1 year				
Dec-95	43606	27578	7895	54275
Dec-96	45702	34248	11178	67506
Dec-97	38512	35104	14419	58795
Dec-98	24003	23702	9310	29698
Dec-99	14206	19035	7749	35076
Dec-00	10305	20096	6994	32799
Sep-01	9451	18169	6882	31981
Over 1 year and up to 2 years				
Dec-95	3536	3157	1147	2553
Dec-96	4829	3589	721	4107
Dec-97	4165	3691	916	5242
Dec-98	3395	3096	1029	8270
Dec-99	2626	3039	1290	6736
Dec-00	2311	2561	1590	4794
Sep-01	1590	2126	1531	2864
Over 2 years				
Dec-95	13599	12331	5727	12027
Dec-96	16344	15331	7326	15884
Dec-97	13824	17311	9417	16675
Dec-98	11900	16496	8174	16974
Dec-99	9995	17028	7269	11021
Dec-00	9253	15763	9569	10913
Sep-01	8297	14583	9467	10584

Note: (in millions of U.S. dollars) By Maturity
Source: Bank for International Settlements, BIS Consolidated banking Statistics (by maturity) for the year ended 1995, 1996, 1997, 1998, 1999, 2000 and September 2001.

propelled property prices to record highs, enabling banks to feel secure in undertaking property as viable collateral. Significant underpricing of risk as evidenced through narrow interest margins being accepted by banks caused banks and investors to be vulnerable to sudden declines in asset prices (e.g., property). When reversals in bank capital amounted to a US$ 100 billion between 1996 and 1998 asset prices began to slump, as prices were unsustainable without further injections of capital into the system (Williamson, 2000). The resultant consequence was banks being saddled by large volumes of non-performing loans (NPLs) as a result of property being used as collateral (Williamson, 2000; Yam, 1997).

In addition to the maturity mismatches, currency mismatches existed as well. The BIS Report (1998) notes that almost 40% of funds lent were yen denominated and the rest were denominated in dollars. Indonesia was the most extreme with almost one-third of domestic banks balance sheets denominated in foreign currency. The single most important factor causing such a mismatch was the pegged exchange rate in all four countries causing 'mis-perceptions of the risks undertaken.

The majority of the international bank lending (Table 3) was directed towards the banking sector in Korea while in the other three countries it was directed towards the non-bank private sector.[4] Batten and Kim (2000) highlight this irregularity in the case of Korea as a consequence of the degree of concentration of the banking sector in this country, and due to the rather complex financial arrangements between the Korean chaebols.

Asia therefore serves as an outstanding example of how rapid credit expansion can cause asset bubbles, the deflation of which tends to retard growth setting in recessionary cycles. As Grenville (2000) shows, the level of credit expansion was beyond what could have been meaningfully absorbed by these nations. In an environment beset with high levels of risk and uncertainty it is critical that prudential regulation assumes greater importance. However, despite rising uncertainties in the financial environment, only Hong Kong, Philippines and Singapore consistently met higher than required capital ratios (BIS Report, 1998). Besides, bank assets were very poorly diversified in all four countries as a consequence of bank loans being directed towards certain strategic sectors supported by a developmental role for banks rather than a commercial one.

A major factor that created excessive liquidity is stated to have been the existence of explicit and implicit government guarantees. Therefore, a number of variables corresponded in creating a systemic capital account crisis. It is clear from the work of McKinnon (1973, 1991) that, it was important for all four countries to have directed their efforts towards

Table 3. Consolidated International Claims of BIS Reporting Banks on Individual Countries.

Years	Total	Sectors Banks	Public Sector	Non-Bank Private Sector
Thailand				
Dec-95	62699	25763	2277	34659
Dec-96	70002	25904	2276	41822
Dec-97	66096	25080	1810	39206
Dec-98	47390	15271	1938	30181
Dec-99	32144	7312	2008	22824
Dec-00	26334	5747	2023	18564
Sep-01	23649	5334	2089	16226
Indonesia				
Dec-95	44496	8948	6707	28841
Dec-96	55489	11788	6942	36759
Dec-97	58999	12445	6840	39714
Dec-98	45584	5935	6650	32999
Dec-99	41151	4757	8454	27940
Dec-00	39922	4936	7658	27328
Sep-01	36346	4606	7488	24252
Malaysia				
Dec-95	16652	4419	2086	10147
Dec-96	22228	6504	1992	13732
Dec-97	27571	9904	1740	15927
Dec-98	21129	6013	1850	13266
Dec-99	18168	3921	2615	11632
Dec-00	20710	3786	3491	13433
Sep-01	20165	3161	4125	12879
Korea				
Dec-95	77493	49949	6169	21375
Dec-96	99883	65896	5677	28310
Dec-97	96365	58310	3978	34077
Dec-98	67590	39637	5448	22505
Dec-99	64162	38575	5198	20389
Dec-00	58047	33681	5209	19157
Sep-01	53389	30602	5015	17772

Note: (in millions of U.S. dollars) By sector
Source: Bank for International Settlements, BIS Statistics for Consolidated claims of BIS Reporting banks on individual Countries for the year ended 1995, 1996, 1997, 1998, 1999, 2000 and September 2001.

ensuring that the macroeconomy and the real economy was stabilised, prior to liberalising their capital accounts. The outcome of not having done so created an environment where the administration of monetary policy became exigent, as it was uncertain as to whether interest rates must be raised to defend the currency, or, whether it should be lowered to enable debtors to help settle debts and thereby reduce credit risk.

Therefore for Asian banks in future to positively impact on economic growth, should account for the spiral manifestations that are likely to be represented when international capital flows to a region beset with significant distortions. Essentially, Asian banks must appreciate that capital account liberalisation is not without its hazards. In particular a cost–benefit analysis where costs are measured in terms of the perils of excess liquidity should be conducted.

3.1.2. NPLs and Asset Management Units (AMU)

The significance of banking in Asia becomes more pronounced due to the absence of alternative sources of finance. The resultant effect is that the effect of imprudent decisions in the sector comes to bare a key outcome on the entire financial sector. As reflected from the analysis thus far conducted, factors such as the developmental orientation of banks, unhedged foreign currency borrowing and asset bubbles place a severe strain on the entire financial sector.

As Allen (2001) shows of all the critical variables that affected these crisis economies, the creation of asset bubbles (caused through excessive lending by banks to low-credit borrowers which in turn was directed to long-term non-tradeable sectors such as property) resulted in a large proportion of loans provided being unserviced. As noted earlier, this comes to bare a huge upshot because of the large fall in capital injections to the region causing asset prices to fall and collateral values to plummet due to unsustainability in prices.

The International Monetary Fund (IMF) (1998) defines a NPL as any loan that is essentially deemed to have a distinct possibility of a loss. The four East Asian economies were saddled with extraordinary volumes of NPLs, with the quantum of NPLs to GDP being 70% in Thailand, 53% in Indonesia, 42% in Malaysia and 35% in Korea, respectively (Cooke & Foley, 1999).

Cooke and Foley (1999) highlight a number of problems with NPLs. First, they highlight that earning assets in the financial sector diminish quite substantially. Secondly, a huge amount of management resources are directed towards NPL problems all of which could have otherwise been used towards other more productive ends (Cooke & Foley, 1999). Thirdly, banks may either end up being extremely averse towards risking their capital or might conversely choose to take on even riskier loans in order to increase capital (Cooke & Foley, 1999). In the event of banks being risk averse when making loans, the net effect is a credit crunch situation that will drastically retard the real sector.

Gochoco-Bautista et al. (2000) suggest two ways of resolving NPLs: firstly, through AMU and secondly, through a systematic process of bank restructuring. Besides, Gochoco-Bautista et al. (2000) state that a combination of flow and stock solutions are crucial in stabilising banks when saddled with NPLs. Dziobek (1998) shows that market-based solutions ranging from financial, structural and operational measures are pivotal in enabling a government reform troubled insolvent institutions.

Included in Dziobek's (1998) structural measures is the creation of AMU. Cooke and Foley (1999) state an AMU as an institution that is established to acquire, manage and resolve the non-performing assets of troubled institutions. AMU have been known to be moulded in two main forms – bank-based and government-based. The four East Asian economies have largely focussed their AMU on centralised government-based models, but have at times acknowledged the benefits of bank-based models incorporating them into case-specific hybrid models.

The benefits of government-based centralised units are popular in Asia because government-based units can develop optimal strategies to recover the best values of assets taken over from troubled institutions. Also by centralising asset management and disposition functions (both of which are not possible when using bank-based units because of the existence of multiple sub-units) transparency in the operations of the AMU is achieved (Cooke & Foley, 1999). Also the many disadvantages of bank-based units force economies particularly when crisis hit to strongly consider the use of government-based units, as decentralised approaches tend to be less optimal when promoted as a recipe of crisis management.

Deterioration in asset quality in Asia was a result of financial liberalisation that spawned excessive risk taking by banks so as to remain competitive in the face of increased competition (this was a result of poorly framed banking laws overseeing the issue of banking licenses). The financial impact of NPL's on the real economy is mainly manifested in the form of a credit crunch as stated earlier. Governments therefore in reforming their banking sectors, should bring about a speedy resolution of troubled institutions by simultaneously considering the legal, economic and social factors confronting their crisis resolution strategies.

3.1.3. Deposit Insurance and Financial Development

In bank-dominated environments regulation fosters stability, which is vital for economic well-being and development (Santomero, 1997). The justification for regulation stems from the premise that banks are conduits for liquidity, monitoring and information aggregation services which leaves them vulnerable to market failures stemming from asymmetries of information between buyers and sellers (Santos, 2000). The major rationale underpinning regulation is the systemic risk argument (Santos, 2000), which is centred around the possibility of bank runs arising from the provision of liquidity services by banks (Diamond & Dybvig, 1983). This argument is based on the possibility of bank runs arising due to maturity mismatches caused by financing long-term illiquid loans (assets) with liquid deposits (liabilities). The principal concern in such a setting is the effect of investor panic resulting in a run, which precipitates a disruption of productive investments due to a recall of bank loans.

Clearly, Asian banks faced investor panic in the midst of the crisis leaving banks heavily subjected to runs. Banks in Indonesia, Malaysia, Thailand and Korea burdened with burgeoning NPLs created depositor panic as real estate and equity prices plummeted. This compelled a reassessment by depositors of the strength of the banking system given that regulatory settings were highly questionable. Engulfed by such an environment, governments in these countries responded with financial safety nets, which manifested a string of institutional mechanisms expected to prevent contagious spillovers within the financial sector.

As these measures were drawn up as a policy of crisis management rather than voluntary reform they were far from comprehensive. The most important response was characterised in terms of implicit and explicit government guarantees to stem the flow of fleeing and panicking investors. These guarantees termed deposit insurance aim to prevent bank runs and preserve the stability of the financial system by insuring depositors of the principal and interest on their deposits with banks despite the banks being insolvent (Choi, 1999). A deposit insurance scheme promotes stability by reinforcing the rights and responsibilities of depositors, financial institutions and the government through interplay between these parties which is ever so crucial given the significance of the financial sector to the overall economy (Choi, 1999).

Besides deposit insurance schemes by fostering broad consumer protection programmes provide ample protection to smaller less sophisticated depositors who have informational and monitoring disadvantages as compared to larger borrowers (Santomero, 1997). The major drawbacks associated with deposit insurance are generally based around promoting excessive risk taking by banks creating moral hazard, and lower monitoring by depositors as they start to view a bank deposit as virtually a government deposit (Santomero, 1997).

Deposit insurance can either be explicit or implicit. An explicit insurance scheme is one which is governed by law compelling the government to provide protection and states explicitly the terms of the provision such as the coverage limit, administration of the scheme, and sources and uses of funding, etc. (Choi, 1999). An implicit scheme on the other hand is one where the government is not obliged to provide protection and where funds for assistance are not clearly earmarked (Choi, 1999). Clearly, as the Asian countries developed safety nets as a prescription of crisis response, only Korea portrayed a comprehensive explicit insurance scheme.

Choi (1999) highlights that, the Korean Deposit Insurance Corporation (KDIC) is responsible for insuring the deposits of the participants in the financial sector in Korea, while Malaysia Bank, Negara provides an implicit guarantee, but in the past has been shown to cover only commercial banks without any compensation for the depositors of other failed institutions. The Indonesian Bank Restructuring Agency administers the provision of an implicit guarantee and works closely with the established AMU so as to help deal with the large volume of NPLs destabilising the insolvent banks (Choi, 1999). Thailand through the Financial Institutions Development Fund has in the past administered the provision of an implicit blanket guarantee. However, there have been recent efforts to set up a comprehensive explicit insurance scheme to be managed by a new institution the Deposit Insurance Authority, so as to enable the provision of a comprehensive scheme to foster confidence in the banking sector.

Implicit schemes fail to clearly distinguish between protection being provided to failed institutions and depositors therefore often providing assistance to insolvent institutions (Choi, 1999). Secondly, implicit schemes place unprecedented pressure upon taxpayer funds as compared to an explicit scheme which gathers insurance premiums to cover the costs (Choi, 1999). Therefore, Korea offers the only significant deposit protection programme, which is capable of being compared to universal best practices.

An area of concern, however, exists with regard to insurance premiums, which are currently charged at a flat rate rather than a differential rate (risk-based). In a setting where informational frictions persist, it is important that moral hazard stemming from excessive risk taking is curtailed with either a risk-based insurance premium or risk-related capital standards (Sharpe, 1978). However, when bank risks are observable only with error, these two mechanisms must go hand in hand in such an informationally asymmetric setting. A major rationale for a flat rate premium may be due to the complexities involved in fair pricing (risk-based) deposit insurance premiums. Another area of concern is centred on the KDIC not being allowed to partake as a receiver during resolution. This is critical while ensuring effective implementation of the "least cost principle" in enabling the resolution of insolvent institutions.

In retrospect the underlying question is whether Korea should serve as a reasonable paradigm of duplication to its regional partners? And are explicit deposit insurance schemes actually transportable? The effectiveness of a depositor insurance scheme is dependent on the country's institutional design and setting (Demirguc-Kunt & Kane, 2001). Kane (2000) highlights transparency, deterrency and accountability to be critical dimensions of an institutional environment, the accomplishment of which is important before adopting an explicit deposit insurance scheme. For Malaysia, Indonesia and Thailand to follow Korea's paragon, they must first focus their architectural efforts towards institutional building and towards a strong environment of contract enforcement. This in turn will enable an explicit scheme to favourably impact on financial activity (Cull, Senbet, & Sorge, 2000).

The extensive relationship between financial development and economic growth has already been established. Therefore as a policy prescription for Malaysia, Indonesia and Thailand for reform through deposit insurance to propel growth, crisis management should be focussed on improving institutional settings, legal systems and market discipline. Failure to institute such a reform agenda could result in a premature implementation of explicit schemes, which have shown to be positively correlated to banking crises when not supported by such measures (Demirguc-Kunt & Kane, 2001).

3.1.4. Orientation of Banks: "Managed" Versus "Commercial"

Banks in order to reflect prudence in decision-making need to be viewed as stand-alone institutions that are governed by commercial considerations alone. However, the rationale behind government interventions blurs the concept of a commercial enterprise and compels banks to lean towards a developmental orientation rather than a commercial one. Clearly in East Asia government intervention in the banking sector took the form of lending being directed to certain strategic sectors marked out by the government itself based on its economic policy.

The ability of any government, however, to foster a policy of managed development in an era of globally integrated markets is bound to spark certain inefficiencies. As Gochoco-Bautista et al. (2000) highlight, governments in East Asia through their developmental policy promoted governance problems, unprofitability in the sectors they effectively subsidised and generated major resource allocation and monitoring inefficiencies. An environment of managed development is at odds with the perceived objectives of financial liberalisation and deregulation, which promotes a backdrop of free markets. Therefore, in East Asia economic policy (financial liberalisation and deregulation) was at odds with the developmental policy of the state.

The incentive for a policy of managed development in East Asia can be traced to certain interlocking relationships that exist between banks, governments and corporations in these countries. Berle and Gardiner (1932) based their seminal work on the grounds of ownership of a firm being widely held and there being a clear distinction between ownership and management. These findings however come under criticism in East Asia where concentrated firm ownership structures exist. The reason for this is due to the extensive prevalence of family-owned and state-owned businesses often leaving no clear demarcation between the owners and managers of the firm.

The significance of firm ownership to a system of managed development promoted by governments stems from the close relationships that corporations often share with governments in East Asia (Backman, 1999). This is ever so consistent with the case of Indonesia where the Suharto family controlled almost 17% of the total stock market capitalisation and owned 417 listed and unlisted firms (Classens, Djankov, & Lang, 1999). Classens et al. (1999) find as an implication of this magnitude of firm concentration that it diminishes as a country's institutional and economic development improves, i.e. as countries become wealthier, concentration reduces.

From the perspective of a developmental orientation to banking in East Asia, concentrated firm ownership has resulted in these controlling family businesses setting up banks as part of their conglomerates so as to fuel and fund their investment decisions and destinations. As Backman (1999) shows almost all the private Indonesian banks that existed during the crisis were part of a major conglomerate. In Thailand as well almost every private bank had one controlling shareholder. The chief reason underpinning this set-up was the desire of these family-owned businesses to use public deposits to fuel their investments. This spells inefficiency because banking as an activity depends on being exposed to the fates of multiple clients rather than the fate of a single client. The major rationale to using a bank in the conglomerate structure to fund investments was to ensure that the very essence of banking profits, which is determined through spreads was kept within the firm.

Malaysian banks are considered to be peculiar in their own way because of being able to portray significant independence and non-financial interests. However, as Sharma (2001) shows, this odd feature of independence becomes compromised when there is dealing between parties of similar ethnic groups.

Korea throws an insight into these interlocking relationships as well but from a different standpoint. In Korea banking laws have been framed in such a way that no shareholder can hold more than a small amount of a bank's total equity (Backman, 1999). Nevertheless, there exists as a response to this positive feature a negative. The government in Korea controls all the decision-making at the existent private banks, forcing the Korean chaebols as a result to accept the government's policy of using the funding provided to them to fund socially beneficial projects (Backman, 1999). Backman (1999) notes that the resultant effect is extremely cheap bank credit that is often over supplied.

These interlocking relationships portray that a policy of developmental banking maybe inevitable as due to the vested interests existing between these parties. The power to control the actions of the government, corporations and banks often lies with the same people.

If banks propel growth then the macroeconomic environment must display fundamentals that enhance a commercial orientation rather than a developmental one. East Asian economies espoused weak fundamentals by attempting to balance open capital accounts, fixed exchange rate regimes and an independent monetary policy all of which are mutually incompatible (Summers, 1999). As Gochoco-Bautista et al. (2000) show, capital outflows, high interest rates and unsound economic policies create undesirable outcomes.

Economic policy in Asia must keep pace with the desired level of financial liberalisation and deregulation, if not as has been the case, capital account liberalisation maybe premature. Therefore, policy options to overcome the developmental orientation of Asian banks may include increasing the level of competition and foreign participation in the financial sector. It may also include as suggested by Goldstein and Turner (1996) enhancing the transparency of the government's involvement in the banking sector. This is suggested in the light that state-owned banks have often been shielded from the public despite having been saddled with a large number of NPLs. Goldstein and Turner (1996) further suggest that in keeping with the economic significance of banks, promoting a culture where each solvent bank directs a certain percentage of its lending to strategic sectors maybe desirable. Lastly, it is suggested that privatisation of state-owned banks is crucial to improving the efficiency of banking.

The implementation of these and other requisites to enable a commercial orientation to banking may only be achieved when the stage of the developmental process engulfing the economy is taken into consideration, i.e. financial liberalisation and deregulation. This will enable factors such as competition and foreign participation to favourably rather than unfavourably impact on the banking sector.

3.2. Proposition Two: Market Reform is Crucial in Post-Crisis Asia so as to Enable the Re-establishment of Pre-Crisis Growth Rates

The availability of a suite of financing alternatives will enable East Asian corporations to facilitate development more efficiently. Greenspan (1999, 2000) clearly shows that the existence of multiple avenues of intermediation can help to protect an economy when either its banking or securities markets are engulfed in crisis. Asian economies are beginning to adopt an "Anglo Saxon" structure to their financial systems to help increase the level of protection against banking crises. Therefore as suggested by Davis (2001), Knight (1998) and Stone (2000) securities market development has gathered significant pace in Asia.

Banks have clearly contributed to the East Asian miracle, and therefore it maybe argued that there is no need for any radical overhaul of regional financial systems (Birdsall et al., 1993). However, excessive reliance on the banking sector has spawned inefficiencies manifested through maturity and currency mismatches, asset bubbles and NPLs, excessive government intervention and moral hazard through implicit guarantees. The resultant effect has been banking panics due to a significant loss of investor confidence. Moreover, as banking systems in Asia were highly leveraged and subject to regulatory imperfections, the possibilities of systemic crises through banking sector failures was largely magnified (Hakansson, 1999).

Markets on the other hand by acquiring and disseminating information, facilitating in risk-sharing and by aggregating diverse opinions to fund industrial ventures help to serve as attractive alternative sources of finance as compared to banks (Allen & Gale, 2000). However, analysis by authors such as Allen and Gale (2000) (in studying bank-based and market-based systems) has tended to refer to markets largely in terms of stock markets with very little reference to debt markets. Therefore, the attempt made in the ensuing discussion is to analyse the probable development of bond markets (government and corporate) given the potentialities for growth in the region with its high domestic savings rate (Batten & Kim, 2000).

Equity markets are clearly well developed in the region, which is consistent with the intent of East Asian firms to smooth out their highly extended debt-equity ratios (caused due to extensive bank borrowing) through equity financing (Sharma, 2001). The rationale behind well-developed equity markets but undeveloped bond markets lies in the difference between debt and equity contracts, because equity contracts provide its holders with a prorate share of profits, a proportionate vote in corporate governance matters and unlimited upside potential all of which are not provided by debt contracts, the development of equity markets tends to lead bond markets due to its perceived attractiveness (Herring & Chatusripitak, 2000).

The consequences of operating a financial system with a banking sector and equity market but with no bond market can be quite dire. As Herring and Chatusripitak (2000) show, it will prevent the establishment of effective market-determined interest rates, over extend the banking sector, discourage entrepreneurial ventures (due to a lack of alternative sources of industrial financing) and prevent savings mobilisation. Moreover, as Batten and Kim (2000) show, a lack of efficient bond markets will prevent the refinancing needs of the region being met, besides thwarting high growth outcomes from being reached due to savings not being optimally directed. Therefore, the underlying objective that a well-functioning bond market is likely to serve in South East Asia is the promotion of market discipline and stability in financing. This is likely to augment the entire financial system because market discipline will be administered by promoting a strong system of financial reporting, a robust community of financial analysts and a comprehensive system of bankruptcy proceedings, all of which will stimulate confidence in the economy besides providing financial deepening which is ever so important in propelling economic growth.

3.2.1. Trends in International and Domestic Bond Markets

The decline in international bank lending to the four crisis economies (Refer Table 1) from a peak of US$ 231.8 billion in 1996 to US$ 161.8 billion in September 2001 has compelled a reassessment of the Asian crisis as largely as a liquidity crisis. Due to this reduction in lending significant interest in international bond, money and equity markets was generated. However, the total amount of international bonds issued attributable to the region amounted to US$ 82.1 billion in 2001, which was still small and incomparable to the amount of intermediated debt financing for the period (US$ 161.8 billion).

The total amount of international bonds issued by the four Asian economies ranged from US$ 43.5 billion in 1995 to peak at US$ 94.2 billion in 1997. The Republic of Korea was the largest issuer of bonds during this period with international bonds increasing from US$ 25.1 billion in 1995 to US$ 49.7 billion in 1997. Brown, Batten, and Fetherston (2002) note that the majority of the international issues of the region have focussed on the U.S.

Yankee Bond market by quasi-government or sovereign borrowers. This large degree of interest espoused by U.S. investors in emerging market debt is at odds with the apparent disinterest that U.S. financial intermediaries have shown in directing credit to the region. Brown et al. (2002) explain this anomaly in terms of the ability of the U.S. financial system to offer high levels of investor protection to its investors when investing in emerging market debt due to the transparency and strength of its legal system.

Trends depicted in international money market issues suggest that their attractiveness is diminishing. The amount of issues by the four economies in the international money markets peaked in 1996 at US$ 6.3 billion before declining to settle at US$ 1.1 billion in 2001. Once again the majority of the issues were by Korean borrowers (amounting to US$ 5.6 billion in 1996). This large reduction in international money market issues suggests that borrowers tend to have a preference for securities with greater maturities.

International equity issues ranged from US$ 4 billion in 1995 to US$ 9.9 billion in 2001 for the four countries. The significant rise in 2001 is a consequence of a large equity issue by Korean borrowers during the year to the amount of US$ 6.9 billion.

On the whole despite international bond, money market and equity issues provided an additional source of liquidity to South East Asian borrowers. The substantial decrease in international bank lending between 1996 and 2001 to the tune of US$ 70 billion was clearly not offset. The resultant effect has been a shift in focus towards domestic bond markets to help address the regions liquidity concerns.

3.2.2. Trends in Domestic Bond Markets
A number of striking observations stem from an analysis of domestic debt securities markets in the four South East Asian countries (refer Table 4). Firstly, some of the markets are extremely small in size rendering no data being reported or collected for countries such as Indonesia. Secondly, of the four countries Korea clearly has the largest bond market with domestic debt securities outstanding equal to US$ 292.7 billion in 2001. The negative aspect that maybe related to the Korean market though is that only 27% are public sector issues. Malaysia has a reported US$ 81.8 billion outstanding in domestic debt securities as in 2001 and is 31% larger as compared to its size in 1995. However, only 38% was attributable to public sector issues. Thailand has enjoyed a substantial rise in the order of 143% from 1995 to 2001 resulting in domestic debt securities outstanding equating to US$ 38.7

Table 4.   Domestic Debt Securities by Sector.

Country	Year End	Public Sector	Financial Institution	Corporate Sector	Private Sector Total	Total
		A	B	C	$D = B + C$	$E = A + D$
Thailand	1995	11.2	1.2	3.5	4.7	15.9
	1996	11.6	2.3	5.1	7.4	19
	1997	6.5	1.3	2.8	4.1	10.6
	1998	19.4	1.6	3.4	5	24.4
	1999	25.9	1	4.8	5.8	31.7
	2000	25.9	0.4	4.9	5.3	31.2
	2001	30.1	2.9	5.7	8.6	38.7
Malaysia	1995	32.4	14.4	15.6	30	62.4
	1996	30.2	19.4	23.5	42.9	73.1
	1997	19.4	16.8	20.8	37.6	57
	1998	22.7	14.8	24.4	39.2	61.9
	1999	24.7	7.2	34.1	41.3	66
	2000	28.3	5.8	42.3	48.1	76.4
	2001	30.6	6.9	44.3	51.2	81.8
Korea	1995	41.3	106.9	79.1	186	227.3
	1996	43.9	104.7	90.4	195.1	239
	1997	25.4	51.7	53.2	104.9	130.3
	1998	51.2	86.9	101.9	188.8	240
	1999	72.7	87.6	105.1	192.7	265.4
	2000	73.3	89.7	106.3	196	269.3
	2001	77.3	97.9	117.5	215.4	292.7
Indonesia	1995	—	—	—	—	—
	1996	—	—	—	—	—
	1997	—	—	—	—	—
	1998	—	—	—	—	—
	1999	—	—	—	—	—
	2000	—	—	—	—	—
	2001	—	—	—	—	—

Note: (in billions of U.S. dollars)
Source: Bank for International Settlements, BIS Domestic Debt Securities (By Sector) for the year ended 1995,1996,1997,1998,1999,2000,2001.

billion. An encouraging factor is that 77% of issues are attributable to the public sector.

Clearly the level of domestic debt securities issued coupled with international issues (bonds, money market and equity issues) has not helped to meet the refinancing needs of the region given the large reversals and declines observed in international bank lending to the region. This begs us to ask the question as to why domestic bond markets are not more developed?

3.2.3. Impediments to Bond Market Development in Asia
There are a number of obstacles that have prevented the development of substantial domestic bond markets in South East Asia. These impediments are as follows:

3.2.3.1. Lack of Liquid and Substantial Government Bond Markets Inhibiting the Development of a Benchmark Yield Curve. The development of corporate bond markets is a function of effective long-term government bond markets. Government bond markets are crucial as they help in pricing corporate debt securities by establishing a benchmark yield curve.[5] Governments essentially issue bonds to fund the gap between tax receipts and current expenditures (Herring & Chatusripitak, 2000). Credit risk is not an important consideration with government debt securities, and therefore can serve as an optimal benchmark for the pricing of issues of corporate borrowers where credit risk is of concern.[6]

South East Asian economies have found a lesser reason to nurture the development of bond markets due to a tradition of fiscal surpluses. Shirai (2001) highlights the significance of fiscal soundness in preventing the development of robust bond markets in South East Asia, by specifically referring to the case of Thailand where the Budget Law prohibits the issuance of government debt in the absence of a deficit. For corporate debt securities to be effectively priced it is imperative that the government bond market is liquid and has a large number of issues of varying maturities. From analysing Table 4 it is clear that apart from Thailand where public sector issues accounted for 77%, the proportion of total debt issued by the public sector is low in Korea and Malaysia where public sector issues accounted for 27% and 38% of the total debt, respectively. This therefore highlights insufficient liquidity in government bond markets and is of particular policy concern given the role of the government bond market in serving as a benchmark.

It is crucial that governments not only issue securities regularly but also do so at varying maturities, e.g. three month, six month, 1 year, 3 years, 5 years, 10 years, etc. Shirai (2001) notes that, the maturity structure of government debt securities is of a real concern in post-crisis Korea; while the Thai government has only recently made efforts to increase the maturity on its issued debt (Herring & Chatusripitak, 2000). The maturity on Malaysian bonds does seem to portray extension to longer maturities, but it is of concern that the number of Malaysian government bonds with maturities longer than 15 years has diminished from 52% pre-crisis to 38% post-crisis (Shirai, 2001). Moreover, it must be remembered that in the past where maturity structures have been deemed to be appropriate the real concern has been that issues have been too irregular thereby preventing institutional investors from actively timing the maturity profile on their portfolios.

As Herring and Chatusripitak (2000) highlight, in an environment of fiscal surpluses the development of a bond market is likely to conflict with the government's desire to reduce borrowing. The four South East Asian economies would do well to take a leaf out of the success enjoyed by Hong Kong. Hong Kong enabled the development of a benchmark yield curve with the use of Exchange Fund Bills and Notes to fund its international expenditures rather than concentrating on the net debt position of its government as the sole criteria for issuing debt (Herring & Chatusripitak, 2000). Also, there is something to learn from the success enjoyed by Singapore, where the Government Investment Corporation through its role in debt and investment management has enabled the development of a benchmark infrastructure despite a tradition of fiscal surpluses (Batten & Kim, 2000).

Therefore, the development of a benchmark yield curve is crucial for the creation of an effective corporate bond market. Until the supply and demand of government securities is increased it is unlikely that investors would have enjoyed sufficient favourable experiences to encourage them to invest in corporate debt securities.

3.2.3.2. Lack of Deep Efficient Derivative Markets to Facilitate Risk Transformation. It is often argued that in countries with poor economic environments not conducive to domestic bond market development the ability to tap international markets is crucial. As previously stated, the U.S. Yankee bond market has been particularly attractive to the four crisis economies. The U.S. investors have shown great interest in the debt issued by these emerging economies because their international issues have been of significantly large sizes, with attractive spreads (therefore compensating U.S. investors for holding emerging market debt) and have been marketed impressively through roadshows etc. (Batten & Kim, 2000).

However, international bond issues are generally made against a backdrop of risk transformation capability generated through active derivative markets. This is of substantial relevance as international bond issues tend to be denominated in non-local currencies. Therefore as Batten and Kim (2000) suggest, emerging market issuers in order to prevent probable translation losses will undertake a foreign currency swap from foreign to local currency and an interest rate swap from fixed to floating rate coupons. This is nevertheless a function of active derivative markets existing in the region.

BIS (2002) survey data suggests the contrary with regard to the Asian economies whose foreign exchange and derivatives trading volume (foreign exchange derivatives and interest rate derivatives) is compared to Hong Kong and Singapore, both of which are considered advanced economies and regional paragons. For all the four crisis economies trading volume in foreign exchange derivatives as a percentage of GDP is small. There is little or no trading in interest rate derivatives. The small size of the derivative markets reflects extreme difficulties in transforming risk. Moreover, the BIS Triennial Survey (2002)[7] suggests that the foreign exchange markets in all four countries is largely segmented which drastically inhibits fair pricing of products. Segmentation maybe interpreted as concentration with the total number of participants in the foreign exchange markets for all four countries standing at 35 for Thailand, 15 for Indonesia, 9 for Malaysia and 71 for Korea (BIS Triennial Survey, 2002). However, the striking feature is that 75% of the trading volume is attributable to only 11 participants for Thailand, 9 for Malaysia, and 14 for Korea[8] (BIS Triennial Survey, 2002).

While it has been argued that the attractiveness of holding bonds in a portfolio is dependent on being able to hedge interest rate and foreign exchange exposures, it must be remembered that developing derivative markets is dependent on bond markets. The relationship therefore is bidirectional. Therefore, both bond and derivative markets need to be reformed and developed in an orderly simultaneous manner to help address the liquidity and risk management issues of the region.

3.2.3.3. Narrow Issuer and Investor Base in Government and Corporate Bond Markets. There are a number of factors that prevent the supply of government and corporate bonds in South East Asia. As has already been discussed there is reluctance on the part of governments to issue bonds during periods of fiscal surpluses. With corporations however, there are two main factors that have traditionally hindered supply.

Firstly, South East Asian corporations have depicted extremely poor financial health with a large majority of firms depicting extremely high debt to equity ratios. In an environment where bankruptcy laws are poorly framed and implemented, unless these highly leveraged firms receive high credit ratings it is unlikely that they will feel sufficiently confident that their issues will be invested in by the market. Rhee (2000) throws light on the case of Indonesia where the PEFINDO rating agency reported that less than a third of bond issues prior to the crisis received a credit rating above investment grade.

Secondly, as Shinasi and Smith (1998) show, repressive regulations can drastically hamper the development of bond markets. As Rhee (2000) highlights, company law in Asian economies more often than not states the amount of corporate debt that can be raised by a firm and the minimum size of corporate issues. It is imperative that the government does not interfere with the forces of demand and supply by attempting to lead the market with such repressive regulations. Thirdly, the majority of the issues in corporate bond markets in Asia (particularly in Thailand and Indonesia) are by banks rather than non-financial firms. Korea and Malaysia are the only real exceptions to this pattern where manufacturing firms and large public entities have tended to dominate issues respectively (Shirai, 2001).

The narrow investor base in the four crisis economies is attributable to three main factors. Firstly, governments have more often than not attempted to create captive demand for bonds by forcing institutional investors to hold government bonds at administered rates rather than market-driven rates, therefore making bonds unattractive (Shirai, 2001). Secondly, households in Asia have shown a preference for traditional bank deposits over other forms of investing. Shirai (2001) highlights this trend as a consequence of the risk-averse nature of Asian borrowers who prefer liquid and short-term assets such as deposits. Thirdly, it is imperative that while banks may be the largest investors in government and corporate bonds, it is the development of non-bank financial intermediaries such as mutual funds, pension funds and insurance companies that can help create significant investments in domestic bond markets. This would involve engaging in an effort that changes the configuration of regional financial systems where non-bank intermediaries come to dominate in much the same way as the U.S. economy.

The main objective that multiple avenues of intermediation helps to establish is greater stability in corporate financing, in general over time and most importantly during periods of crisis (Davis, 2001). It is however uncertain as to whether plain economic and financial variables when introduced in a particular mix can prompt the development of markets such as bond markets in environments where banks play a lead role. For instance the U.S. economy through the separation of investment banking and commercial banking activities coupled with its legal structure, financial and economic policies and the wave of financial panics and cyclical shocks endured by it through history, may have worked together to develop more arm's length financing mechanisms. This is often compared to Europe where the promotion of universal banking with alternative legal structures (civil law) may have prompted the development of more relationship-based financing.

Therefore, in the development of multiple avenues of intermediation it must be remembered that while financial mixes can be created so as to enable development in a particular area (e.g., bond markets), there often tends to exist certain fundamental national factors often stronger and more compulsive than financial and economic factors, that may well demand an alternative course of action.

3.3. Proposition Three: Legal Reform is Crucial in Post-Crisis Asia so as to Enable the Re-establishment of Pre-Crisis Growth Rates

Central to resurrecting South East Asia's financial architecture is to enable the development of their legal and judicial frameworks thereby fostering the evolution of their financial systems (i.e. banks and markets). While dependence on the banking sector may persist, a legal structure enabling the protection of both creditors and shareholders must exist. In a number of countries there exists poor investor protection, which is espoused by excessive expropriation of investors (shareholders and creditors) by controlling shareholders and management.

Laporta et al. (1997, 1998, 1999, 2000a, 2000b) show that there exist significant differences in corporate financing patterns across countries due to differences in legal protection being offered to investors. Therefore, the focus applied here is on a corporate governance approach[9] to the legal system to help explain the legal and institutional settings in South East Asia.

The attempt made here is to firstly portray the high levels of expropriation evident in South East Asia during the crisis. Secondly, we wish to link this outcome to the levels of investor protection evident. Thirdly, an attempt is made to find a causal linkage between the level of investor protection and the level of ownership concentration in the region and to evaluate any possible effects this may have on the legal systems' evolution. Lastly, the breadth and depth of the equity and debt markets as a consequence of these effects is evaluated. The core objective is to note if the legal approach is influencing financing patterns and the development of the financial system. If this can be established then reform in this area is crucial as financial development (through deepening) has positive real sector consequences (King & Levine, 1993).

3.3.1. Expropriation of Minority Shareholders
Expropriation refers to the possibility that controlling shareholders and management, through the diversion of corporate opportunities and theft etc. may prevent investors that finance firms from enjoying the materialisation of their investments (Laporta et al., 2000b). Expropriation of investors

(particularly minority shareholders) is representative of Jensen and Meck-ling's (1976) theory on the consumption of perquisites by managers which lies at the heart of the agency conflict between management and sharehold-ers. Investors are unlikely to finance firms if their cash flow and control rights are not well protected by the underlying legal system and enforcement mechanisms.

South East Asian economies portrayed significant levels of expropriation during the Asian crisis, where management was able to transfer cash and company assets to help save affiliated failing companies, to pay off the personal debts of management and in some cases to finance the interests of certain political parties (Johnson, Boone, Breach, & Friedman, 2000). Such trends do not promote the development of active stock and bond markets where investors draw security from their defined cash flow and control rights. Even banks suffer, as bankruptcy laws despite being well defined are poorly enforced (Johnson et al., 2000). Therefore, an evaluation of why creditors and shareholders in South East Asia are poorly protected by their legal and enforcement systems is warranted, in order to help explain the extensive prevalence of expropriation in the region. Such an analysis will also help to highlight possible avenues where legal protection may be im-proved, and in doing so help reduce the expropriation mechanism.

3.3.2. Investor Protection in South East Asia

Investors as the providers of finance to firms enjoy a number of rights: for instance the rights of shareholders to vote for directors, to call extraordinary shareholders meetings and to participate in shareholders meetings etc. Sim-ilarly, creditors enjoy rights during the process of bankruptcy, the re-possession of collateral etc. The law protects these rights, while market regulators and the courts administer their enforcement (Laporta et al., 2000b). Accordingly, it is imperative that these rights and their enforcement mechanisms are administered efficiently so as to help promote security and confidence in investors when financing a firm.

Laporta et al. (1998) show that different countries protect their investors to different degrees due to differences in their respective legal families and the quality of their enforcement mechanisms. Laporta et al. (1998) clearly highlight the varying levels of protection imparted to shareholders and creditors in the four South East Asian countries. In reviewing shareholder rights, Laporta et al. (1998) highlight that common law countries afford the best protection and French civil law countries such as Indonesia the worst. Furthermore, Laporta et al. (1998) note that, Korea (German civil law) offers poor protection and is comparable to that of Indonesia, while

Thailand despite being of common law origin offers poor protection as it does not specifically provide its minority shareholders with significant powers to withstand oppression and pre-emptive rights to new issues, both of which are offered by Malaysia.

An analysis of creditor rights awarded suggests as expected, acceptable levels of protection to creditors consistent with these countries being of bank-based origin. As Laporta et al. (1998) show, Malaysia offers the best protection, while Indonesia, Thailand and Korea offer acceptable standards of protection as well.

In terms of enforcement, Malaysia offers the most efficient levels of enforcement well above common average law, clearly reflective of the size and need of its stock market (Laporta et al., 1998). The surprising feature underscored is that of Korea, which despite being of German civil law origin renders poor enforcement mechanisms, which according to Laporta et al. (1998) deviates from the general trend because, while the legal rights afforded by countries do not vary based on the level of economic development, enforcement mechanisms tend to be higher in richer countries particularly of Scandinavian and German civil law origin.

Reasons for the substantial differences between countries, in the levels of protection afforded to investors are due to differing levels of government intervention (Laporta et al., 1999). As Gochoco-Bautista et al. (2000) highlight, governments in East Asia through their developmental policy promoted governance problems, unprofitability in the sectors and they effectively subsidised and generated major resource allocation and monitoring inefficiencies. Laporta et al. (1999) find this to be consistent with the trend observed in Asia where civil law countries particularly Indonesia and Korea depicted significant government intervention in attempting to regulate economic activity. This is not to say that Malaysia and Thailand were free from government intervention. In fact Malaysia and Thailand also espoused significant developmental roles attributable to banks as administered by the state. The consequence of heavy government intervention is that it prevents the effective establishment of a legal and enforcement system, which protects the rights of investors as this may significantly vary from the objectives of the government, especially where corruption and nepotism towards certain sectors are of the highest order.

The evidence is therefore conclusive that excessive expropriation of investors exists due to poor investor protection being afforded by the law in the four South East Asian countries. When this effect is compounded with poor enforcement systems, investors are left with fewer incentives to provide firms with external finance.

3.3.3. Excessive Prevalence of Concentrated Ownership and Family-Owned Businesses

A major consequence stemming from excessive expropriation caused due to poor investor protection is concentration of firm ownership (Laporta et al., 2000b). It should be noted however that, ownership concentration can be beneficial as large shareholders can actively monitor managers (Shleifer & Vishny, 1986). The general conclusion is that ownership concentration is warranted in an environment of poor investor protection as it substitutes for legal protection enabling large shareholders to receive a return on their investment.

Therefore in Asia, where investor protection has been found to be poor, corporate ownership structures can be expected to be highly concentrated. In terms of composition, South East Asian economies are found to be heavily dominated by family owned businesses.

Classens et al. (1999) show that Indonesia represents firms that are the most highly concentrated with 57.7% of stock market capitalisation attributable to the top 10 families, while the top 10 families in Korea, Thailand and Malaysia account for 26.8%, 46.2% and 24.8% of market capitalisation, respectively. From these figures it is clear that not only are firms in East Asian countries highly concentrated but that family control adds to the level of concentration (Classens et al., 1999).

As East Asian firms are mainly family owned and signify excessive concentration, it may be argued that the Berle and Means (1932) notion of a dispersed corporation is a myth particularly in South East Asia. In this regard, Classens et al. (1999) show that only 6.6% of firms in Indonesia, 51.1% of firms in Korea, 8.2% of firms in Thailand and 16.2% of firms in Malaysia are widely held.

The main conduits through which control is enhanced in East Asian corporations is through the use of pyramid structures, cross shareholdings and by instituting family members in management, all of which enables expropriation of minority shareholders (Classens et al., 1999). Therefore, as Shleifer and Vishny (1997) suggest, the real agency conflict is one between controlling shareholders and minority shareholders rather than the traditional one between outside investors and management.

The central governance issue that concentrated firm ownership creates, in an environment of close linkages between corporations and the government, is that legal and regulatory development maybe significantly impeded (Classens et al., 1999). Therefore, in conclusion we find that ownership concentration is justified due to poor investor protection. However, the relationship develops into bi-directional sense whereby the tight links between businesses and the government render evolution of the legal system stagnant.

3.3.4. Corporate Financing Patterns in South East Asia

It has already been established that when investor protection is good the avenues for expropriation are fewer due to which investors are more willing to provide finance to firms. Therefore as Laporta et al. (1997) predict, countries with higher levels of investor protection have more developed capital markets. Clearly if creditor rights are well protected then the development of debt markets will be augmented, irrespective of whether it is biased towards bank lending or through bond markets. Similarly, the promotion of active shareholder rights that are well enforced will promote the development of equity markets.

The extensive prevalence of expropriation of minority shareholders in South East Asia has already been portrayed to exist as a consequence of poor shareholder and creditor rights and inferior enforcement mechanisms. In this regard, one of the effects of poor investor protection was found to be excessive concentration of firm ownership, which due to convoluted relationships in Asia was found to impede legal development.

A further effect of the poor levels of investor protection is the underdeveloped nature of the regions financial markets. This is due to the reluctance of investors to finance firms due to the possibility of expropriation.

Laporta et al. (1997) test this aspect of investor protection and note that Malaysia enjoys a ratio of outsider held stock market to GNP of 148% (which is much higher than the common law average of 60% and is representative of its large stock market), while Thailand has a ratio of 56%, Indonesia 15% and South Korea 44%, respectively. Additionally, Laporta et al. (1997) find that for all four countries the number of listed domestic firms per one million people is below their legal family's average. With regard to IPO's per million people, Laporta et al. (1997) find that Malaysia was the only one of the four countries to be above its legal family's average. In general, Laporta et al. (1997) find that barring Malaysia, which has an active stock market, Thailand, Indonesia and Korea portray poor results with regard to their equity markets.

With regard to aggregate debt as a share of GNP, Laporta et al. (1997) show that Malaysia and Thailand have scores of 84% and 93% respectively, which is well above the common law average of 68%, while Indonesia and Korea reflect 42% and 74% respectively, which is slightly lower than their legal families averages. However, the results in this category seem to be broadly consistent with the view that creditor rights for all four countries was above average, clearly representative of their bank-based systems. However, the impeding factor was found to be poor enforcement mechanisms that seemed to reduce the benefit gained through strong creditor rights.

From the analysis undertaken in this section it is evident that the legal system by influencing the quality of investor protection provided affects the corporate financing patterns of firms, by determining the development of equity and debt markets. Investor protection is found to influence the development of the financial system through its effect on financial markets. Beck, Levine, and Loayza (2000) help to establish linkages between financial development and the real sector through savings enhancement, capital accumulation and resource allocation. Batten and Kim (2000) show through capital market development financial deepening helps to benefit the real sector.

Therefore, it is crucial that while equity and debt markets may be proposed for development the underlying features of the encompassing legal system must be taken into consideration. For example in Asia, the quality of creditor rights has been depicted as good, however as the quality of enforcement is poor, bond market development could be potentially impeded as market participants depend upon arms length financing as compared to a relationship framework, which is enjoyed by banks (Sharma, 2001). Therefore, the governance approach to the legal system is an appropriate method for determining the potentialities in an economy for external sources of finance.

3.4. Proposition Four: Functional Reform is Crucial in Post-Crisis Asia so as to Enable the Re-establishment of Pre-Crisis Growth Rates

Financial systems display certain core functions centred on their ability to transfer and pool economic resources, manage risk, price information and solve contracting problems caused due to incentive barriers (Merton & Bodie, 1995). As such these functions are taken to be stable across borders and depict that chief functions are represented in similar vein across different geographical territories (Merton & Bodie, 1995). A consequence of this setting is that policy focus should be laid on a functional perspective rather than an institutional perspective.

The core financial services that have been pronounced to administer growth include aiding of liquidity, risk management, exertion of corporate control and savings mobilization (Levine, 2000). It is quite inconsequential as to whether bank-based or market-based systems are more adept at promoting growth through the provision of financial services. Debates promoting the merits of bank-based and market-based systems and their ability to stimulate growth seem rather weak when viewed from the perspective that the United States and Germany, which exist at polar extremes have enjoyed largely similar growth rates. The institutional focus adopted in Asia centred on a desire to build purely bank-based or market-based systems should be abandoned. Such a constricted policy focus fails to accommodate for the dynamics of institutional change. By focussing entirely on either banking reform or market reform, rather than treating them cumulatively financial system evolution is impeded.

A functional perspective therefore promotes the co-evolution of intermediaries and markets, rather than viewing them as mutually exclusive competitive tradeoffs. Markets and intermediaries in fact share a symbiotic relationship. As Merton (1993) states, it is financial market innovations that create risk management business for banks. Additionally, banks and markets can propel growth in one another by enabling financial development (Demirguc-Kunt & Maksimovic, 1998). The focus in policy efforts has been too fixated on the static tradeoffs between banks and markets rather than on the complementary dynamic relationship between the two.

This is critical as overall financial development has been shown to be robustly linked to growth (Levine, 2000). Levine (2000) finds that better-developed financial systems influence growth by impacting on total factor productivity (TFP) growth, which in turn feeds into real GDP growth. This is critical to Asia's resurgence, as the IMF (2001) reports that growth in the ensuing decade in the region is to be stimulated through TFP growth rather than capital accumulation. In addition the legal environment is of paramount significance, as the enforcement of good legal codes will enable growth-enhancing financial services to be generated. As Rajan and Zingales (1998) show, an improvement in the legal system propagates the co-evolution of banks and markets.

The analysis in this section aims to achieve a twin objective. First and foremost the level of development of the financial sector in South East Asia is investigated. Secondly, as Asian economies espouse significant incentive barriers to efficient contracting, evolution of regional financial systems is likely to take time. Therefore, a non-leapfrog approach whereby financial liberalisation is appropriately paced is recommended.

3.4.1. Financial Sector Development in Asia

It has been deduced that in order to promote growth overall financial sector development is important. Financial sector development is commonly measured by portraying the size of the domestic banking sector and stock markets. Demirguc-Kunt and Levine (1999) analyse the size of the four

South East Asian economies by distinguishing them based on their level of GDP per capita and show that the size of the banking sector in all four countries is large.

Demirguc-Kunt and Levine (1999) also find that Malaysia has an extremely large stock market while the size of the stock market in the other three countries seems moderate. This is consistent with Laporta et al. (1998) who show that the level of shareholder protection, evidenced through legal rights and contract enforcement is poor in Korea, Indonesia and Thailand. In this regard, Demirguc-Kunt and Levine (1999) find that common law countries such as Malaysia tend to be more market based as compared to countries from other legal origins.

Moreover in an environment of significant information asymmetries such as Asia, a "lemons" problem tends to engulf the equity market. This occurs because outside investors cannot observationally differentiate between good and bad firms, resulting in the stock of both firms being valued at their intermediate price. At such an equilibrium price, Froot (1995) suggests that only bad firms are likely to issue stock while good firms are unlikely to do so. Therefore, the market is likely to view an equity issue as a negative signal about the quality of the firm. This might well have been a de-motivating factor preventing South East Asian firms from issuing significant equity.

In addition the IMF (1999, 2001) reports that in the case of Thailand and Malaysia, local firms faced extremely low levels of profitability post-crisis as compared to pre-crisis, when earnings were comparatively stable. Froot (1995) finds that when firms face stable earnings or low profitability (both of which were the case with Asia, pre- and post-crisis) as compared to high profitability, they tend to rely largely on debt finance. This seems to be consistent with the corporate financing patterns evidenced in the region. Furthermore, Demirguc-Kunt and Levine (1999) find a positive correlation between the overall size of the financial sector and GDP per capita in all four countries, and conclude broadly that richer countries have larger financial sectors. Therefore, as Demirguc-Kunt and Levine (1999) show, as Indonesia depicts low GDP per capita it seems only logical that the overall level of financial development in the country is low. Therefore, a range of factors seem to have caused the extremely poor levels of financial development portrayed in Asia. This as stated earlier is likely to have real consequences due to the financial sector's ability to stimulate growth.

3.4.2. Non-Leapfrogging Liberalisation
The central conduit through which South East Asian economies have attempted to influence financial development is by spurring financial and

capital account liberalisation (Demirguc-Kunt & Detragiache, 1998). The underlying rationale promoting a process of deregulation in the region was the perceived benefits of competition that financial liberalisation brings to the financial sector (Kawai & Takayasu, 1999).

3.4.2.1. Capital Account Liberalisation. Kawai and Takayasu (1999) highlight that in the case of Thailand three factors propelled capital account liberalisation. First and foremost, Kawai and Takayasu (1999) highlight that foreign capital helps to spur the development of efficient production and management systems. Secondly, Kawai and Takayasu (1999) state that capital account liberalisation is warranted due to competitive pressures from domestic and international sources to enable foreign institutions to partake in industry. Thirdly, Kawai and Takayasu (1999) highlight that liberalisation was sparked due to bilateral and multilateral pressures caused by dominant trading partners such as the United States, and by supra-nationals such as the World Trade Organisation.

The central reason as to why the above-mentioned benefits failed to materialise in terms of promoting growth is because they were not sufficiently supported through empirical research. To the contrary as Stiglitz (2000) purports there is strong evidence pointing to the destabilising effects of capital account liberalisation. These negative effects seem to have been widely prevalent in the case of Asia.

First, between 1996 and 1998 South East Asia faced capital flight to the tune of a US$ 100 million, causing asset bubbles as commodity prices were unsustainable without further capital injections (Williamson, 2000). Second, a capital account crisis in Thailand caused due to swings in capital flows resulted in contagion. The consequence was manifested in terms of investor panic being precipitated in other "peer" countries with similar financial and macroeconomic variables. Third, liberalisation is generally undertaken based on the perceived benefits that long-term flows such as foreign direct investment (FDI) are likely to bring (Stiglitz, 2000). The perils of short-term bank flows, which affected South East Asia are seldom discussed. Fourth, South East Asian economies pursued open capital accounts with fixed exchange rate regimes. The resultant effect was that the macroeconomy was neglected due to monetary policy being restricted to maintaining the exchange rate peg.

3.4.2.2. Financial Liberalisation. South East Asian economies essentially failed to appreciate the positive relationship between financial liberalisation and financial fragility. The reason for the failure was because the traditional literature in this area has been too fixated on the order of economic liberalisation as forwarded by McKinnon (1991) and Edwards (1987). While the sequencing of financial liberalisation is crucial and validated, it by no means assures stability post-liberalisation. This is because as Demirguc-Kunt and Detragiache (1998) show, financial fragility surfaces several years after liberalisation has been undertaken.

What is the economic rationale for financial liberalisation to cause financial fragility? The centrepiece during the process of deregulation is the lifting of controls on interest rates. When interest rates are market determined, banks as they are no longer subject to ceilings are able to finance high-risk high return projects. Demirguc-Kunt and Detragiache (1998) show that while this may be desirable, the private benefits tend to outweigh the social benefits thereby rendering the economy vulnerable to adverse shocks. Moreover, in an environment of developmental banking and implicit and explicit government guarantees (both of which were present in South East Asia), banks funding risky projects is more likely to affect economy-wide stability (Demirguc-Kunt & Detragiache, 1998).

In addition in South East Asia, liberalisation spurred increased competition in the banking industry. Demirguc-Kunt and Detragiache (1998) find that the resultant effect in such a setting is banking licenses espousing a lower value causing riskier lending practices.

The most crucial pillar supporting efficient liberalisation is the existence of strong institutional structures enabling judicial efficiency, low corruption and enforcement of the rule of the law (Demirguc-Kunt & Detragiache, 1998). Laporta et al. (1998) find that enforcement mechanisms in South East Asia are poor in general. The major reason being that enforcement mechanisms tend to be better in richer countries as compared to the poorer South East Asian economies (Laporta et al., 1998).

Therefore in conclusion, financial liberalisation in order to facilitate financial development and growth should be undertaken in a gradual and non-leapfrog manner. By non-leapfrog it is suggested that firstly, the order of economic liberalisation should be appreciated. Secondly, the causal linkage between financial fragility and liberalisation should be adequately weighed. Lastly, institutional structures should be improved before attempting to deregulate the economy.

4. RECOMMENDATIONS

In response to the impediments that have been highlighted to hinder the active implementation of banking, market, legal and functional reform, the following recommendations are made.

4.1. Minimise the Developmental Orientation of Banks

South East banks have shown to lack a commercial orientation. Policy-based lending by Asian banks under the influence of the government has resulted in the core functions of screening and monitoring provided by the banking system to be drastically affected. Directed lending essentially distorts fiscal management, as the government budget does not accommodate for resultant inefficiencies (Gochoco-Bautista et al., 2000).

Goldstein and Turner (1996) are right in recommending that it maybe desirable for banks to direct a small percentage of their lending to strategic sectors. However, such practices should be minimised as government intervention in the credit allocation process prevents free market forces from functioning. Moreover, concentration in the banking sector should be diminished as competition enables efficiency gains to be achieved. In spurring competition it must be appreciated that the system overseeing the issue of banking licenses is sound. While it is desirable to fund high-risk high return projects, the resultant private and social benefits that stem must be in sync (Demirguc-Kunt & Detragiache, 1998).

4.2. Develop Optimal Regulatory Structures to Oversee the Banking Sector

As South East Asia has embraced a policy of financial liberalisation, its banking systems need to be well regulated. Risk-based regulation is essential to stimulating an Asian banking resurgence. While the provision of deposit insurance is an integral part of ensuring investor protection, moral hazard needs to be accommodated. Korea with the only comprehensive explicit deposit insurance scheme currently charges a flat rate insurance premium. In an environment of significant moral hazard it is pivotal that risk-based insurance premiums are used. Furthermore, ceiling and coinsurance limits on the deposit insurance scheme must be promoted as they help to limit moral hazard.

South East Asian banks must comprehensively implement the Core Principles of Effective Banking Supervision as forwarded by the Basle Accord. In doing so the prescribed capital requirements inclusive of off-balance sheet items must be subscribed to enable construction of optimal value-at-risk models (Gochoco-Bautista et al., 2000). In addition asset-liability management, loan classification and accounting for NPLs must be given priority. Accounting for NPLs appropriately helps to ensure that supervisory systems can serve as early warning indicators.

Development of optimal regulatory structures must serve a dual objective. First and foremost globally accepted prudential regulations and supervisory standards promoted by supranationals such as the Asian Development Bank, the IMF and the BIS should be implemented. Secondly, regulatory gaps must be blocked to ensure that bank managers are compelled to run banks with a commercially oriented objective, thereby compelling allegiance to serving as efficient monitors to depositors.

4.3. Maturity Mismatches and Unhedged Foreign Currency Borrowing Must be Minimised

Asian banks in welcoming international capital in the future must ensure first and foremost that the maturity structure of their debt is lengthened, and secondly in the event of the loan being denominated in a foreign currency, that it is hedged. Friedman (1999) rightly points out that the Asian crisis was triggered largely by domestic banks in the region re-lending loans acquired from overseas banks to domestic borrowers without hedging the resultant currency exposure. Friedman (1999) highlights that the implicit guarantees afforded by Asian governments served as a major cause triggering such recklessness.

Options such as Chilean style taxes (Eichengreen, 1999) that impose an unremunerated reserve requirement are desirable in extending the maturity of the debt. Additionally to prevent maturity mismatches short-term loans should not be made to borrowers attempting to finance long-term non-tradeable assets such as property. Also, borrowers' financial position should be thoroughly scanned so as to ensure the highest financial standing. This in turn will enable loans to be made out on the pre-requisite of the borrower's ability to repay rather than on the value of the collateral, which is always a sub-optimal option.

4.4. Increase the Participation of Mutual Funds and Pension Funds in Domestic Bond Markets

South East Asian economies in order to stimulate demand for corporate and government bonds need to promote the participation of non-bank intermediaries in the financial sector. Korea depicts the largest corporate bond market in the region estimated at 27.3% of GDP (Batten & Kim, 2000), while the size of it non-bank intermediaries is estimated at 59% of GDP (Demirguc-Kunt & Levine, 1999). The large size of its bond market is often attributed to the role played by investment trust corporations (ITC) and investment trust management companies (ITMC) who serve as dominant investors in corporate bonds in Korea (Shirai, 2001). ITCs and ITMCs grew rapidly in Korea due to the preference of the public to invest in them as compared to banks, due to the lack of confidence in the banking sector (Shirai, 2001).

In Malaysia, Shirai (2001) notes that the employee provident fund (EPF) has dominated investing in domestic bond markets. Shirai (2001) notes that a consequence of a lack of institutional investors, suggests that in Malaysia there exist significant concerns that pricing mechanisms and maturity structures are government administered rather than being market oriented. Thailand and Indonesia reflect small asset management sectors as well. Shirai (2001) notes specifically in the case of Indonesia that, insurance companies prefer bank deposits as compared to other investments.

In order to spur familiarisation in corporate bonds the role of institutional investors besides commercial banks needs to be enhanced. While economies of scale and scope suggest that it is improper to make comparisons with capital markets in the U.S., it is important to appreciate that a major factor propelling the development of the U.S. corporate bond market has been the substantial influence of non-bank intermediaries in investing in corporate bond issues (Shinasi & Smith, 1998). The development of pension funds and mutual funds in Asia will spur corporate governance in the region besides helping to ignite demand in nascent bond markets. Focus should therefore be laid on deregulating the asset management industry in South East Asia, by abandoning repressive captive regulations on institutional investors in the construction of their portfolios. The resultant effect will be greater participation in domestic capital markets by non-banks.

4.5. Improve the Size and Efficiency of Regional Derivative Markets

In an environment in which domestic debt markets are less developed as compared to norms in advanced economies, international markets need to be tapped. The Triennial Survey by the BIS (2002) suggests that the overall size of domestic derivative markets in South East Asia is small, depicting poor risk transformation capabilities. Barring Korea there is virtually no reported trading volume in interest rate derivatives, while trading volume in foreign exchange derivatives in all four nations is moderate.

Rhee (2000) notes that South East Asian countries have essentially relied on equity index futures to hedge equity investments. For market makers such as institutional investors to be attracted to investing in domestic bond markets, the availability of a suite of hedging opportunities is important. Therefore, short-term and long-term interest rate hedging instruments that facilitate the development of primary and secondary systems in bond markets should be promoted (Rhee, 2000). In addition South East Asia should develop effective futures markets with a range of underlying features (relating to settlement) to spur the development of long-term bond markets.

4.6. Develop Conducive Regulatory Structures for Securities Markets

A vital channel through which South East Asia can enable the development of domestic bond markets is by propelling the reform of regulatory structures. In particular governments must establish strict regulatory standards, which reflect strong legal codes and enforcement mechanisms. Also central bank independence must be established from the functions of the office of debt management.

Non-residents holding of domestic securities must be encouraged. In order to access global capital South East Asia must espouse a low net regulatory burden. Therefore, as Shinasi and Smith (1998) recommend where possible withholding taxes, turnover taxes and stamp duties should be abandoned. It must be remembered that institutional investors are likely to be attracted to investing in domestic bond markets only if market processes are market determined. The common trend in Asia for governments to issue bonds at below market rates, and in creating captive demand must be abandoned. In totality, regulatory structures must, as Batten and Kim (2000) suggest, promote the simultaneous accomplishment of currency stability and financial reform.

4.7. Investor Protection through Functional Convergence should be Improved

South East Asian corporations have been shown to provide their investors poor protection, triggering as a consequence significant instances of expropriation. Poor anti-director and moderate creditor rights coupled with weak enforcement mechanisms has rendered evolution of domestic financial systems stagnant. While reform measures to improve investor protection and to reduce concentrated ownership maybe recommended, implementation of such measures is impeded due to the vested interests that stem from the close linkages between conglomerates and governments.

Laporta et al. (2000b) define functional convergence as a process that is heavily market oriented but nonetheless manages to increase the quality and level of investor protection. Laporta et al. (2000b) and Mitton (2002) strongly recommend the use of American Depository Receipts (ADR) as a method of overcoming the limitations of a weak legal regime by opting into a more attractive one. ADR's compel non-US firms to meet the disclosure requirements prescribed by U.S. listing requirements. By doing so minority shareholders of non-US firms are aided as higher accounting and regulatory standards need to be met.

The use of a major audit firm is another method recommended in improving shareholder protection. As Mitton (2002) highlights large audit firms demand greater disclosure quality of their clients. Backman (1999) points out that the 'Big Five' audit firms have all established operations in South East Asia either directly or through affiliations with local firms. The 'Big Five' firms are more likely to do a good job of ensuring high disclosure quality as their reputation costs are higher (Michaely & Shaw, 1995), and because of the high political costs of audit failures (Watts & Zimmerman, 1986). Moreover, large audit firms are more likely to detect earnings management in their clients (Gore, Pope, & Singh, 2001), and by doing so protect ultimate shareholder funds.

Establishing an efficient market for corporate control helps to further discipline firms in legal environments not conducive to protecting investors. As Laporta et al. (2000b) state, when firms from friendlier legal regimes acquire a firm in a less favourable legal setting, the minority shareholders are offered avenues for better protection that help to reduce possibilities for expropriation.

The use of market-based functional reform measures are important in Asia, as prescribing purely legally oriented reforms requires indepth regulatory and judicial reform that may not always be feasible. The use of ADRs, major audit firms and takeover devices are vital to ensuring promotion of confidence in investors to participate in arm's length financing in South East Asia.

4.8. Cross Border Mobility of Capital Needs to be Limited

Capital controls refer to a system of defending an economy's prevailing market position (Cohen, 2000). Proponents for capital mobility draw on an influential analogy between capital mobility and free markets for ordinary goods and services. However, as the Asian crisis depicts, in a setting of information frictions such linkages are severely constricted (Cohen, 2000). Thus the use of capital controls by China and its ability to have ridden out the crisis comparatively unscathed portrays that in a region beset with asymmetries of information capital mobility may in fact worsen economic welfare.

Malaysia further proved through the success of its capital controls adopted post-crisis that free flowing capital in conjunction with a fixed exchange rate regime renders less potent monetary policy. Therefore, until domestic financial systems are capable of directing capital to growth-enhancing outcomes, it seems logical to prescribe limiting inflows to emerging economies, as excess liquidity may be more harmful than useful.

4.9. Need to Regulate the Different Types of Capital Inflows

Reisen and Soto (2001) find that in emerging economies such as South East Asia, FDI and portfolio equity inflows significantly impact on growth. Short-term bank flows are shown to be associated with crises especially in the event of their reversal (Rodrik & Velasco, 1999). Excessive dependence on short-term bank flows in Asia created maturity mismatches and asset bubbles due to significant investment in non-tradeables such as property.

FDI on the other hand should be encouraged as it depicts lower levels of reversibility during crises periods and is less affected by distortions in economic settings. Moreover, Borenstzein, Gregario, and Lee (1998) find that FDI by complementing domestic investment enables positive technology spillovers. However, while portfolio equity flows facilitate governance, Cohen (2000) recommends that in the case of South East Asia, portfolio equity flows seeking capital gains rather than dividends should be strictly regulated as they have been shown to be more speculative.

4.10. Financial Liberalization Must be Adequately Paced

Summers (1999) highlights that, emerging economies have historically endured the inflow of capital without the resultant precipitation of crises as frequently and markedly. This in turn reflects that developing and transition economies under ideal conditions are capable of dealing with the large inflows of capital directed to their financial systems.

South East Asian economies need to direct their policy efforts towards seeking capital commensurate with the strength and capacity of their domestic financial systems (Summers, 1999). In doing so the key is to pace financial liberalisation so that the quality and level of prudential regulation and risk management is adequately appraised (Summers, 1999).

5. CONCLUSION

Asia imposes a special policy challenge, due to the extensive degree of deviation evident from the features of its financial systems and the predictions of standard theoretical models. Asian banks for instance failed to serve as efficient monitors and solvers of information asymmetries. The excessive lending by the banking sector to fund the acquisition of non-tradeables such as property, suggests a failure to effectively screen borrowers. The resultant effect was a maturity mismatch, triggering in turn a large volume of NPLs.

Banks faced lesser incentives to alter their behaviour due to the existence of implicit guarantees (barring Korea), which enabled insolvent institutions to be bailed out. Failure to implement risk-based explicit insurance schemes meant that the real sector was severely drained of valuable taxpayer funds.

Intermediation theory states that banks negate risk by diversifying their loan portfolios. A developmental orientation to banking in Asia, however, meant that bank fortunes were often tied to a single client. Excessive foreign currency borrowing, NPLs, implicit deposit insurance schemes and a developmental orientation created a chain effect, wherein Asia suffered from a severe liquidity crunch, thus affecting the real sector and retarding investment activity.

Market reform in Asia has been found to be impeded due to the absence of institutional investors, poor demand and supply of quality government and corporate bond issues, lack of a benchmark infrastructure and poorly developed derivative markets. Markets promote efficiency in the banking sector, through the provision of market-determined interest rates, which portrays the true cost of funds. Besides, the potentialities for growth in domestic bond markets are large given the region's high savings rate. For high growth outcomes to be reached in Asia, the development of multiple avenues of intermediation is important so as to help reduce the effect of future crisis in a particular avenue.

Legal and functional reform must be undertaken simultaneously to facilitate banking and market reform. Therefore, while banks and markets maybe viewed as supportive pillars to an effective growth paradigm, the legal system and ultimate financial services provided are complementary pillars. In Asia the legal system, through the quality of investor protection provided is seen to affect the corporate financing patterns of firms, by influencing the development of the region's equity and debt markets.

Moreover, attempts made to stimulate the banking sector and the capital markets of the region through capital and financial liberalisation must

involve a non-leapfrog approach. The results of the analysis undertaken suggest that, capital flight, asset bubbles, contagion and currency
collapses in Asia were natural outcomes of failing to appreciate the linkage
between liberalisation and fragility. By portraying the causes of the
crisis and impediments to reform, the paper has essentially highlighted
that for high growth outcomes to be reached, post-crisis reform must involve the adoption of a multi-dimensional approach. In particular through
the linkages established between the four pillars the paper shows that
reform packages that espouse a restricted policy focus are unlikely to
succeed.

NOTES

1. It is to be noted that the term Asia, South East Asia and East Asia are used as
substitutes for one another and refer to Thailand, Indonesia, Malaysia and Korea,
except where obvious reference to the contrary is made.

2. BIS banks refers to international banks reporting to the Bank for International
Settlements.

3. Henceforth LLSV.

4. The total amount of international bank lending to the banking sector in Korea
was 66% in 1996 and 57.3% in September 2001. On the other hand, lending to the
non-bank private sector in Thailand, Malaysia and Indonesia averaged 62.5% in
1996 and 66.4% in September 2001.

5. Shinasi and Smith (1998) define a benchmark security (in this case government
bonds) as one that is used for the purpose of pricing other securities. It is also
expected that as the benchmark securities have been chosen to serve as a benchmark,
there is sufficient liquidity (espoused through heavy trading) and that they have been
issued at varying maturities.

6. Batten and Kim (2000) state that a benchmark yield curve is constructed through a process of interpolation that enables a continuous curve to be
constructed (from a range of government securities of different maturities)
which ultimately serves as a benchmark for the pricing of corporate securities.
The authors go on to highlight that the crucial factor involved in establishing
the yield of a corporate security is to add a time-varying spread to the risk free
government rate.

7. The BIS Triennial Survey (2002) refers to a triennial central bank survey of
foreign exchange and derivatives market activity in 2001 undertaken by the BIS's
Monetary and Economic Department.

8. Data on the number of participants accounting for 75% of trading volume in
Indonesia is not available.

9. Laporta et al. (2000b) refer to corporate governance as an approach whereby
investors protect themselves against expropriation by controlling shareholders and
management.

REFERENCES

Akerlof, G. A. (1970). The market for lemons: Qualitative uncertainty and the market mechanism. *Quarterly Journal of Economics, 84*, 488–500.

Allen, F. (1992). Stock markets and resource allocation. In: C. Mayer & X. Vives (Eds), *Capital markets and financial intermediation*. Great Britain: Cambridge University Press.

Allen, F. (2001). Financial structure and financial crises. *International Review of Finance, 2*(1–2), 1–19.

Allen, F., & Gale, D. (2000). *Comparing financial systems*. Cambridge MA: MIT Press.

Allen, F., & Santomero, A. (1999). *What do financial intermediaries do?* Wharton Financial Institutions Centre, Working Paper, University of Pennsylvania.

Allen, F., & Santomero, A. M. (1998). The theory of financial intermediation. *Journal of Banking and Finance, 21*, 1461–1485.

Backman, M. (1999). *Asian eclipse: Exposing the dark side of business in Asia*. New York: Wiley.

Bank for international settlements (1998). *Financial intermediation and the Asian crisis*. In the 68th Annual BIS Report.

Bank for international settlements (2002). *Triennial bank survey of foreign exchange and derivatives market activity in 2001*. Monetary and Economic Department.

Batten, J., & Kim, Y. (2000). *Expanding long-term financing through bond market development: A post crisis policy task*. Asian Development Review, Working Paper.

Beck, T., Levine, R., & Loayza, N. (2000). Finance and sources of growth. *Journal of Financial Economics, 58*, 113–139.

Benston, G., & Smith, C. (1976). A transaction cost approach to the theory of financial intermediation. *Journal of Finance, 31*(2), 215–231.

Berle, A., & Gardiner, M. (1932). *The modern corporation and private property*. New York: MacMillan.

Birdsall, N., Campos, E., Corden, W. M., Kim, C., Pack, H., Sabot, R., Stiglitz, J., & Uy, M. (1993). *The East Asian miracle: Economic growth and public policy*. New York: Oxford University Press.

Boot, A. W. A., & Thakor, A. V. (2000). Can relationship banking survive competition? *Journal of Finance, 55*(2), 679–713.

Borenstzein, E., Gregario, J., & Lee, J. (1998). How does foreign direct investment affect economic growth. *Journal of International Economics, 45*(1), 115–135.

Brown, K., Batten, J., & Fetherston, T. A. (2002). International bank lending and the Asian crisis. In: N. Mercuro & P.R. Smith (Series Eds), *The international review of comparative public policy*. In: N.R. Sabri (Ed.), *International financial systems and stock volatility: Issues and remedies*.

Bryant, R. C. (1987). *International financial intermediation*. Washington, DC.: Brookings Institution.

Choi, J. (1999). *Structuring a deposit insurance system from the Asian perspective*. In: *Rising to the challenge in Asia: A study of financial markets* (Vol. 2). Special Issues. Asian Development Bank.

Christoffersen, P., & Errunza, V. (2000). Towards a global financial architecture: Capital mobility and risk management issues. *Emerging Markets Review, 1*, 3–20.

Classens, S., Djankov, S., & Lang, L. H. P. (1999). *Who controls East Asian corporations*. World Bank, Working Paper.

Cohen, B. J. (2000). Taming the phoenix? Monetary governance after the crisis. In: G. W. Noble & J. Ravenhill (Eds), *The Asian crisis and the architecture of global finance*. Cambridge: Cambridge University Press.

Cooke, D., & Foley, J. (1999). The role of the asset management entity: An Asian perspective. In: *Rising to the challenge in Asia: A study of financial markets* (Vol. 2) Special Issues. Asian Development Bank.

Corsetti, G., Pesenti, P., & Roubini, N. (1999). What caused the Asian currency and financial crisis. *Japan and the World Economy, 11*, 305–373.

Cull, R., Senbet, L. W., & Sorge, M. (2000). *Deposit insurance and financial development*. World Bank, Mimeo.

Dalla, I. (1995). *The emerging Asian bond market*. Washington, DC.: World Bank.

Davis, P. E. (2001). *Multiple avenues of intermediation, corporate finance and financial stability*. IMF, Working Paper no. WP/01/115.

Demirguc-Kunt, A., & Detragiache, E. (1998). *Financial liberalization and financial fragility*. World Bank, Development Research Group.

Demirguc-Kunt, A., & Kane, E. J. (2001). *Deposit insurance around the globe: Where does it work?* World Bank, Mimeo.

Demirguc-Kunt, A., & Levine, R. (1999). *Bank-based and market-based financial systems: Cross-country comparisons*. World Bank, Development Research Group.

Demirguc-Kunt, A., & Maksimovic, V. (1998). Law, finance, and firm growth. *Journal of Finance, 53*(6), 2107–2137.

Dewatripoint, M., & Tirole, J. (1992). Efficient governance structure: Implications for banking regulation. In: C. Mayer & X. Vives (Eds), *Capital Markets and Financial Intermediation*. Great Britain: Cambridge University Press.

Diamond, D. (1984). Financial intermediation and delegated monitoring. *Review of Economic Studies, 51*, 393–414.

Diamond, D., & Dybvig, P. (1983). Bank runs, deposit insurance and liquidity. *Journal of Political Economy, 91*, 401–419.

Diamond, D., & Rajan, R. (1998). *Liquidity, risk, liquidity creation and financial fragility: A theory of banking*. University of Chicago, Mimeo.

Diamond, P. (1967). The role of a stock market in a general equilibrium model with technological uncertainty. *American Economic Review, 57*, 759–766.

Dziobek, C. (1998). *Market-based policy instruments for systemic bank restructuring*. IMF, Working Paper no. WP/98/113.

Edwards, S. (1987). Sequencing economic liberalization in developing countries. *Finance and Development, 24*(1), 26–29.

Eichengreen, B. (1999). Toward a new international financial architecture: A practical post-Asia agenda. Institute for International Economics.

Friedman, B. M. (1999). Comments on Delong, J. B., financial crisis in the 1980s and 1990s: Must history repeat. *Brookings Papers on Economic Activity, 2*, 280–289.

Froot, K. A. (1995). Incentive problems in financial contracting: Impacts on corporate financing, investment, and risk management policies. In: R. C. Merton & Z. Bodie (Eds), *A conceptual framework for analysing the financial environment, the global financial system – A functional perspective*. Harvard: Harvard University Press.

Fujita, K. (2000). Asian crisis, financial systems and urban development. *Urban Studies, 37*(12), 2197–2217.

Gerschenkron, A. (1962). *Economic backwardness in historical perspective. A book of essays.* Cambridge, MA: Harvard University Press.

Gore, P., Pope, P. F., & Singh, A. K. (2001). *Non-audit services, auditor independence and earnings management.* Working paper, Lancaster University.

Greenspan, A. (1999). Do efficient capital markets mitigate financial crises? Speech to the financial markets conference of the Federal Reserve Bank of Atlanta, 19th October.

Greenspan, A. (2000). Global challenges. Speech to the financial crisis conference. Council on Foreign Relations, New York, 12th July.

Grenville, S. (2000). Capital flows and crises. In: G. W. Noble & J. Ravenhill (Eds), *The Asian crisis and the architecture of global finance.* Cambridge: Cambridge University Press.

Gochoco-Bautista, M. S., Oh, S., & Rhee, S. G. (2000). *In the eye of the Asian financial maelstrom: Banking sector reforms in the Asia-Pacific region.* In: *Rising to the Challenge in Asia: A Study of Financial Markets* (Vol. 1) – An Overview. Asian Development Bank.

Goldsmith, R. W. (1969). *Financial structure and development.* New Haven, CT: Yale University Press.

Goldstein, M., & Turner, T. (1996). *Banking crises in emerging economies: Origins and policy options.* BIS, Working Paper no. 46.

Hakansson, N. H. (1999). *The role of a corporate bond market in an economy – and in avoiding crises.* University of California, Berkeley, Working Paper.

Herring, R. J., & Chatusripitak, N. (2000). *The case of the missing market: The bond market and why it matters for financial development.* Asian Development Bank Institute, Working Paper Series no. 11.

Holmstrom, B., & Tirole, J. (1993). Market liquidity and performance monitoring. *Journal of Political Economy, 101*(4), 678–709.

International Monetary Fund. (1998). Toward a framework for financial stability. World Economic and Financial Surveys, IMF.

International Monetary Fund. (1999). Malaysia selected issues. IMF, Country Report, no. 99/86.

International Monetary Fund. (2001). Thailand selected issues. IMF, Country Report no. 01/147.

Jensen, M., & Meckling, W. R. (1976). Theory of the firm: Managerial behaviour, agency costs, and ownership structure. *Journal of Financial Economics, 3*, 305–360.

Johnson, S., Boone, P., Breach, A., & Friedman, E. (2000). Corporate governance in the Asian crisis. *Journal of Financial Economics, 58*, 141–186.

Kahler, M. (2000). The new international financial architecture and its limits. In: G. W. Noble & J. Ravenhill (Eds), *The Asian crisis and the architecture of global finance.* Cambridge: Cambridge University Press.

Kane, E. J. (2000). *Designing financial safety nets to fit country circumstances.* World Bank, Mimeo.

Kawai, M., & Takayasu, K. (1999). The economic crisis and banking sector restructuring in Thailand. In: *Rising to the challenge in Asia: A study of financial markets* (Vol. 11) – Thailand. Asian Development Bank.

King, R. G., & Levine, R. (1992). Financial intermediation and economic development. In: C. Mayer & X. Vives (Eds), *Capital markets and financial intermediation.* Great Britain: Cambridge University Press.

King, R. G., & Levine, R. (1993). Finance and growth: Schumpeter might be right. *Quarterly Journal of Economics, 108*(3), 717–738.

Knight, M. (1998). *Developing countries and the globalisation of financial markets.* IMF, Working Paper no. WP/98/105.

Laporta, R., Lopez-de-Silanes, F., & Shleifer, A. (2000a). *Government ownership of banks.* Harvard University, Harvard, Mimeo.

Laporta, R., Lopez- de- Silanes, F., Shleifer, A., & Vishny, R. W. (1997). Legal determinants of external finance. *Journal of Finance, 52*(3), 1131–1150.

Laporta, R., Lopez- de- Silanes, F., Shleifer, A., & Vishny, R. W. (1998). Law and finance. *Journal of Political Economy, 106*(6), 1113–1155.

Laporta, R., Lopez-de-Silanes, F., Shleifer, A., & Vishny, R. W. (1999). The quality of government. *Journal of Law Economics and Organisations, 15*(1), 222–279.

Laporta, R., Lopez-de-Silanes, F., Shleifer, A., & Vishny, R. W. (2000b). Investor protection and corporate governance. *Journal of Financial Economics, 58*, 3–27.

Leland, H. E., & Pyle, D. H. (1977). Informational asymmetries, financial structure, and financial intermediation. *Journal of Finance, 32*, 371–387.

Levine, R. (2000). *Bank-based or market-based financial systems: Which is better?* Carlson School of Management, University of Minnesota.

Levine, R., & Beck, T. (2000). *Industry growth and capital allocation: Does having a bank-based system or a market based system matter.* University of Minnesota.

Mayer, C., & Vives, X. (1993). *Capital markets and financial intermediation.* Great Britain: Cambridge University Press.

McKinnon, R. I. (1973). *Money and capital in economic development.* Washington: Brookings Institution.

McKinnon, R. I. (1991). *The order of economic liberalization.* Baltimore: Johns Hopkins University Press.

Merton, R. C. (1993). Operation and regulation in financial intermediation: A functional perspective. In: P. Englund (Ed.), *Operation and regulation of financial markets.* Stockholm: The Economic Council.

Merton, R. C., & Bodie, Z. (1995). *A conceptual framework for analysing the financial environment. The global financial system – A functional perspective.* Harvard University Press.

Michaely, R., & Shaw, W. (1995). Does the choice of auditor convey quality in an initial public offering. *Financial Management, 24*(4), 15–30.

Mitton, T. (2002). A cross-firm analysis of the impact of corporate governance on the East Asian financial crisis. *Journal of Financial Economics, 64*, 215–241.

Noble, G. W., & Ravenhill, J. (2000). Causes and consequences of the Asian financial crisis. In: G. W. Noble & J. Ravenhill (Eds), *The Asian financial crisis and the architecture of global finance.* Cambridge: Cambridge University Press.

Rajan, R. G., & Zingales, L. (1998). Financial dependence and growth. *American Economic Review, 88*, 559–586.

Rajan, R. G., & Zingales, L. (1999). Which capitalism? Lessons from the East Asian crisis. *Journal of Applied Corporate Finance, 11*(3), 40–48.

Reisen, H., & Soto, M. (2001). Which types of capital inflows foster developing country growth. *Journal of International Finance, 4*(1), 1–14.

Rhee, S. G. (2000). Rising to Asia's challenge: Enhanced role of capital markets. In: *Rising to the challenge in Asia: A study of financial markets* (Vol. 1) – *An overview*, Asian Development Bank.

Rodrik, D., & Velasco, A. (1999). *Short-term capital flows.* NBER, Working Paper no. 7364.

Santomero, A. (1997). *Deposit insurance: Do we need it and why?* Wharton Financial Institutions Centre, Working Paper, University of Pennsylvania.

Santos, J. A. C. (2000). *Bank capital regulation in contemporary banking theory: A review of the literature.* BIS, Working Paper no. 90.

Sharma, K. (2001). The underlying constraints on corporate bond market development in South East Asia. *World Development, 29*(8), 1405–1419.

Sharpe, W. F. (1978). Bank capital adequacy, deposit insurance and security values. *Journal of Financial and Quantitative Analysis, 13,* 701–718.

Shinasi, G. J., & Smith, T. R. (1998). *Fixed income markets in the United States, Europe and Japan: Some lessons for emerging markets.* IMF, Working Paper no. WP/98/173.

Shirai, S. (2001). Overview of financial market structures in Asia – Cases of the Republic of Korea, Malaysia, Thailand and Indonesia. Asian Development Bank Institute Research Paper, 25.

Shleifer, A., & Summers, L. (1988). Breach of trust in hostile takeovers. In: A. Auerbach (Ed.), *Mergers and acquisitions, NBER.* Chicago: University of Chicago Press.

Shleifer, A., & Vishny, R. (1986). Large shareholders and corporate control. *Journal of Political Economy, 94,* 461–488.

Shleifer, A., & Vishny, R. (1997). A survey of corporate governance. *Journal of Finance, 52,* 737–783.

Sholtens, B., & Wensveen, D. V. (1999). A critique on the theory of financial intermediation. *Journal of Banking and Finance, 24,* 1243–1251.

Stiglitz, J. E. (1985). Credit markets and the control of capital. *Journal of Money, Credit and Banking, 17*(2), 133–152.

Stiglitz, J. E. (2000). Capital market liberalization, economic growth, and instability. *World Development, 28*(6), 1075–1086.

Stiglitz, J., & Weiss, A. (1981). Credit rationing in markets with imperfect information. *American Economic Review, 71,* 393–410.

Stone, M. A. (2000). *The corporate sector dynamics of systemic financial crises.* IMF, Working Paper no. WP/00/114.

Summers, L. H. (1999). Building an international financial architecture for the 21st century. *Cato Journal, 18*(3), 321–329.

Thakor, A. (1996). The design of financial systems: An overview. *Journal of Banking and Finance, 20,* 917–948.

Walter, I. (1993). *High performance financial systems; blueprint for development. ISEAS current economic affairs.* Singapore: Institute of South-East Asian studies.

Watts, R. L., & Zimmerman, J. L. (1986). *Positive accounting theory.* NJ: Prentice-Hall.

Williamson, J. (2000). *Development of the financial system in post-crisis Asia.* Asian Development Bank, Working Paper.

Yam, J. (1997). Mr. Yam looks at Asian banking in a regional and global context. Address at the ADB-IIF Forum on Developing Asian Financial Markets, Fukuoka, Japan.

A PERSPECTIVE ON JAPAN'S CORPORATE BOND MARKET

Peter G. Szilagyi

1. INTRODUCTION

In the past decade, academic research has been awash with proposals on how Japan should reform, redesign and administer its bank-based financial system (Schinasi & Smith, 1998; Kuratani & Endo, 2000; Hattori, Koyama, & Yonetani, 2001; Rhee, 2001; Baba & Hisada, 2002; Batten & Szilagyi, 2003). Until the late 1980s, this unique regime, involving banks having cross-ownership with industry, was a driving force behind Japan's post-war economic miracle. However, the burst of the asset bubble, and the subsequent prolonged ailing of both the banking sector and the economy as a whole suggests that during the bubble period, the monitoring effectiveness of banks was compromised by a lack of independence from industry and the absence of external discipline. This banking crisis ultimately impaired the corporate sector's fund-raising ability, while trapping excess liquidity in the financial system through a lack of attractive investment choice afforded to risk-averse Japanese investors.

Japanese policymakers have made concerted efforts to resolve these problems and focused on capital market deregulation and liberalization. But, a key element of the reform agenda, the development of the corporate

Asia Pacific Financial Markets in Comparative Perspective: Issues and Implications for the 21st Century
Contemporary Studies in Economics and Financial Analysis, Volume 86, 417–434
Copyright © 2005 by Elsevier Ltd.
All rights of reproduction in any form reserved
ISSN: 1569-3759/doi:10.1016/S1569-3759(05)86017-6

bond market has received perhaps unduly modest attention. Since the 1980s, extensive changes in the financial environment have helped the Japanese market to become second only to its US counterpart. Today, the market's key role in the financing of Japanese firms is highlighted by the fact that it represents 17.1% of GDP, comparable to 22% in the US, as of June 2004. On the other hand, the spectacular growth of Japan's corporate bond market conceals the fact that it continues to lag the US and UK markets in most key aspects of development, effectiveness and diversity. At the same time, and as a result, it continues to struggle to attract borrowers with yen needs from the Euroyen market.

The literature has proposed various problems that impede further development of the corporate bond market, and market-based mechanisms in general. Baba and Hisada (2002) emphasize that Japan's bank-based financial system ultimately remains strongly path dependent. The on-going dominance of banks indicates that the raison d'étre of banks remains, and makes the regime unlikely to shift rapidly towards the market-based system of the US. At the same time, Japanese firms have continued to focus on reducing debt rather than step up investment since 1997. They have also remained heavily reliant on cheap finance provided by public financial institutions at below-market prices. The system is reinforced by the extreme risk-aversion of Japanese households, which continue to keep the bulk of their savings in currency and deposits. Households favour the holding of riskless postal savings in particular, which are then channelled into public financial institutions, distorting capital market competition in the process. Meanwhile, the Japanese government continues to run excessive deficits and issue vast amounts of government bonds (JGB), largely designed to mop up excess liquidity that the banking sector and investment and pension funds cannot or will not place with corporate borrowers or channel overseas.

This paper advocates that the development of the corporate bond market is instrumental in ensuring the medium-term recovery of Japan's financial system. An improved market, providing a platform where excess liquidity is channelled to domestic and international borrowers, would help resolve the extreme waste of financial resources that is currently seen. The remainder of the paper is as follows. Section 2 discusses recent developments in Japan's financial system, and highlights the regime's main problems. Section 3 provides a brief overview of existing theory on financial systems. An analysis of Japan's corporate bond market is provided in Section 4. Section 5 allows for some concluding remarks and defines future direction for academic and regulatory attention.

2. RECENT DEVELOPMENTS IN JAPAN'S FINANCIAL SYSTEM

The close bank–firm relationships that comprise the backbone of Japan's financial system are uniformly credited as one of the driving forces behind Japan's post-war economic miracle. Banking relationships have been extensively investigated in the theoretical literature and are shown to have substantial benefits in developing countries in particular. Banks help resolve information asymmetries that arise from the imperfection of markets, and may ease the resulting liquidity constraints in the corporate sector (Leland & Pyle, 1977). In addition, banks enable the intertemporal and cross-sectional smoothing of risk, foster the efficient exploitation of markets, as well as provide the traditional advantageous functions of delegated monitoring (Diamond, 1984; Boyd & Prescott, 1986), and lower transaction costs (Benston & Smith, 1976). The key role of close bank ties in resolving financial distress of the firm is also emphasized (Hoshi, Kashyap, & Scharfstein, 1991). The unique financial system in Japan, involving banks having cross-ownership with industry and thereby establishing large self-funding conglomerates or *keiretsu*, evolved as a mechanism to perform these tasks expeditiously.

It is the same Japanese system, however, that has shown how the monitoring effectiveness of banks may be compromised by a lack of independence from industry and the absence of external discipline. Bank-based financial regimes such as Japan's work well only when bank management is sound, and there are no large and persistent shocks to the system. During the time of Japan's bubble economy, banks' lending practices became increasingly slack, especially with respect to loans collateralized by real estate. When the asset bubble collapsed in the late 1980s, the crisis triggered a serious non-performing loan and debt overhang problem, which compromised the banking sector's ability to intermediate, and is largely blamed for Japan's prolonged economic stagnation. For the bad loan burden confronting the banking sector, there is no immediate answer other than improvements in internal control mechanisms and the eventual dismantling of the cross-ownership structures with industry – a solution complicated by the impact that such restructuring would have on an already fragile stock market and economy. On the other hand, the banking crisis impaired the corporate sector's fund-raising ability, while trapping excess liquidity in the financial system through a lack of investment choice afforded to Japanese investors.

In response to the crisis of the banking sector, Japanese regulators have made concerted efforts to liberalize and develop the country's capital markets. Nonetheless, the financial system is still fundamentally dominated by banks, and the corporate bond market remains in its relative infancy in terms of issuer base and infrastructure. At the same time, the banking crisis has significantly eroded borrowing conditions for the corporate sector, and small- and medium-sized firms in particular. Corporate flow of funds data released by the Bank of Japan is contained in Table 1. The table shows that, willingly or not, Japanese corporations have substantially curtailed their borrowing from banks. The data indicate that corporate borrowing from private institutions declined from a peak of ¥ 469.1 trillion in March 1993, the end of Japan's fiscal year 1992, to ¥ 296 trillion in March 2004. At the same time, the corporate sector has consistently posted net savings, owing to a deceleration of business fixed investment as well as the repayment of excessive debt. On the other hand, borrowing in the form of marketable debt has increased somewhat, providing evidence for gradual disintermediation in the Japanese system. This shows that the banks' position is weakening

Table 1.   Financial Assets and Liabilities of Japanese Non-Financial Corporations (Trillions of Yen).

	Assets			Liabilities		
	1989FY	1996FY	2003FY	1989FY	1996FY	2003FY
Currency and deposits	195.0	179.3	201.8			
Loans	25.2	30.8	28.4	533.3	603.5	437.1
Loans by private financial institutions				427.2	434.6	296.0
Loans by public financial institutions				66.6	89.0	86.3
Loans by the non-financial sector	19.8	24.6	24.0	30.4	61.6	37.5
Securities other than shares	39.3	21.4	36.3	110.5	147.0	113.4
Local government securities	0.2	0.3	0.7	2.8	3.9	2.8
Public corporation securities	1.5	0.3	2.0	36.9	61.6	34.8
Industrial securities	2.0	3.4	1.7	22.2	53.4	52.9
External securities issued by residents	0	0	0	35.4	19.5	9.7
Commercial paper	5.5	3.7	6.1	13.3	8.6	12.1
Shares and other equities	255.0	143.0	131.5	586.2	404.0	440.2
Trade credits and foreign trade credits	261.2	268.3	213.7	210.2	208.6	167.8
Outward direct investment	8.3	17.4	15.3			
Outward investment in securities	20.2	22.7	40.5			
Total assets	878.8	759.1	734.8			
Total liabilities				1,522.7	1,456.1	1,246.4
Financial surplus or deficit				−643.8	−697.0	−511.5

Source: Flow of Funds Accounts (various issues). Bank of Japan, Research and Statistics Department, http://www.boj.or.jp/en/index.htm.

against those large, creditworthy borrowers that either want to distance themselves from their main banks or simply seek cheaper funding in the capital markets. Banks also find it difficult to compete with public financial institutions that provide cheap funding in the lower segment of the market, at rates that are determined outside of the market mechanism in line with policy objectives.

The same trend is apparent from the banks' flow of funds data, contained in Table 2. The table shows that bank lending has fallen significantly from its peak of ¥ 748.4 trillion in March 1998 to ¥ 633.4 trillion in March 2004. Since bank assets have actually grown over the same period, this points to major structural changes on banks' balance sheets, and provides support for Oyama and Shiratori's (2001) claim that the Japanese banking sector is essentially oversized. Indeed, banks have faced a substantial excess liquidity problem, as government policy, typically protective of troubled banks, has reinforced rather than weakened their ability to attract household savings. Banks, impaired in their risk-taking capacity, have channelled excess liquidity into a variety of low-risk investments, and in particular into government securities. This has led to the adverse situation where banks support the government's slack fiscal policy,[1] and often indirectly finance their own bailouts, while at the same time hurt their own profitability and future recovery.

3. THEORY OF THE FINANCIAL SYSTEM

The concerted efforts of Japanese regulators to deregulate and liberalize the country's capital market borrow their rationale from the rapidly expanding theoretical literature on comparative financial systems. Levine (2000) identifies four competing views of financial structure, and emphasize that all four boost their own merits. The *bank-based view* (Boot & Thakor, 1997; Rajan & Zingales, 1999) affirms the role of banks within the financial system. The *market-based view* (Hellwig, 1991; Rajan, 1992) regards markets being more appropriate in achieving capital allocation efficiency. The *law and finance view* (Benston & Smith, 1976; La Porta, Lopez-de-Silanes, Shleifer, & Vishny, 2000) primarily emphasizes the role of the legal system in generating financial development. Finally, the *financial services view* (Levine, 1997; Allen & Santomero, 1998; Boyd & Smith, 1998) considers the provision of financial services as the most important issue within the financial system.

It is the financial services view that stresses that banks and markets might act as complements in providing financial services for improving

Table 2. Financial Assets and Liabilities of Japanese Banks (Trillions of Yen).

(Trillion Yen)	Assets			Liabilities		
	1989FY	1996FY	2003FY	1989FY	1996FY	2003FY
Currency and deposits	149.5	144.7	159.8	706.0	802.7	893.2
Loans	669.3	730.9	633.4	184.8	167.7	164.2
Housing loans	46.3	75.0	116.5			
Consumer credit	17.6	18.1	10.8			
Loans to companies and governments	568.1	602.0	465.0	21.0	48.5	24.0
Securities other than shares	126.3	135.9	259.3	59.9	76.2	41.4
Financing bills	0.1	0.2	41.6			
Central government securities and FILP bonds	49.3	55.1	122.9			
Local government securities	9.7	15.4	15.6			
Public corporation securities	15.4	12.4	15.8			
Bank debentures	14.4	17.7	12.5	55.8	75.4	30.4
Industrial securities	5.8	12.8	22.9	2.3	0.1	9.9
External securities issued by residents	2.3	2.4	4.7	1.8	0.7	0.3
Commercial paper	4.2	1.5	5.6	0.0	0.0	0.9
Shares and other equities	72.5	53.5	55.3	112.1	61.0	75.8
Of which: shares	71.5	51.8	29.0	108.3	56.7	35.8
Outward direct investment	6.4	6.4	13.6			
Outward investment in securities	17.9	21.8	35.9			
Total assets	1097.2	1124.3	1204.3			
Total liabilities				1127.7	1136.8	1225.5
Financial surplus or deficit (transactions)				−30.5	−12.5	−21.2

Source: Flow of Funds Accounts (various issues). Bank of Japan, Research and Statistics Department, http://www.boj.or.jp/en/index.htm.

information and transaction costs (Boyd & Smith, 1998; Huybens & Smith, 1999). Bolton and Freixas (2000) propose a model of segmented markets, wherein equilibrium riskier corporations prefer bank loans, the safer ones tap the bond market, and the ones in-between prefer to issue both equity and bonds. This segmentation of financing is broadly consistent with the stylized facts evident in developed financial markets. But, Davis and Mayer (1991) find that banks and bond markets are not perfect substitutes under more general conditions either. Even for large companies, the financing of high-risk projects – entailing a large degree of informational asymmetry – requires the involvement of banks, which therefore retain a central function. This is consistent with Ongena and Smith's (2000) investigation of multiple-bank relationships, which finds that firms also maintain more relationships in countries with unconcentrated but stable banking systems and active public bond markets.

These and other academic studies lead to the conclusion that banks and capital markets may coexist efficiently. And, notwithstanding the success of bank-based systems such as those of Germany and Japan, there may be benefits from developing capital markets in a bank-based system. The literature proposes a wide array of these. Takagi (2002) emphasizes the lower average cost of external finance by exposing the banks to competition; the building of a more efficient capital structure that helps manage agency costs; better control of management due to external market discipline; improved efficiency of resource allocation by provision of price signals for investment decisions; and greater encouragement for the financing of innovation. Dinc (2000) specifically shows that, crucially for Japan, credit market competition forces banks to also give loans to lower quality borrowers they would have refused otherwise. Weinstein and Yafeh (1998) emphasize the lower dependence on banking relationships, while Sharma (2001) proposes a possible reduction of maturity mismatches, occurring as a result of firms borrowing short term in order to finance long-term projects.

From the investors' point of view, Batten and Szilagyi (2003) conclude that in Japan's case, the current liquidity trap burdening the financial sector provides a further incentive to develop the capital market. At the same time, fostering the capital market may also increase the financial system's ability to withstand prolonged volatility shocks. Schinasi and Smith (1998) argue that securities markets may be capable of pricing financial risks as well as banks, while distributing financial risks more widely, if not also more efficiently. A smaller concentration of risks and potential losses in local banking and payment systems, vulnerable to the ill-effects of moral hazard, may be desirable due to the heavy support of public safety nets.

The literature on the transition from a bank-based financial system to a market economy identifies the importance of financial system reform, not only to aid the transition, but also to ensure a strong basis for future economic growth (Beck, Levine, & Loayza, 2000). Successful financial sector reform, including the development of market-based forms of financing, will importantly require and encourage the effective development of other policy reforms. However, to be successful, property rights and bankruptcy laws must also be enforced, tax systems revised and state-owned enterprise privatized. These views are important for Japan, which has adopted a wide selection of reforms since the "Big Bang" initiative of 1996, but must now tackle a broad reform agenda of which financial market reform generally, and corporate bond market development more specifically, is but a part.

In order to better understand the appropriate process of reform necessary to improve market-based financing mechanisms, it is first necessary to understand the reasons behind the lack of their development in developed financial markets. Smith's (1995) survey of markets for corporate debt securities in the major industrial countries and international markets provides a basis for understanding these issues, by investigating some of the reasons for the underdevelopment of domestic bond markets and the consequences of corporations shifting debt financing needs from banks to securities markets. Other authors, including Batten and Kim (2001), Sharma (2001) and Cheung and Chan (2002) provide a reform agenda for Asia-Pacific economies in the post-crisis period. These authors all agree that in order to develop bond markets, there is a need to build stronger legal and regulatory frameworks, to improve investor protection, to encourage adequate disclosure of information and to foster best practices by listed companies and financial intermediaries.

It is also insightful to reflect upon the experience of those countries that have recently developed or expanded their domestic securities markets. For example, Thorat (2002) provides a perspective on the experience of India in developing government securities markets from the 1990s. It is important to note that this process was undertaken with regard to the appropriate sequence of infrastructure development, including the enlargement of products and participants to ensure appropriate liquidity, an appropriate regulatory framework for valuation, accounting and disclosure, and risk management and settlement capability.

4. THE SPECIAL CASE OF JAPAN'S CORPORATE BOND MARKET

It is undisputable that the reason why Japan's corporate bond market is lagging behind in terms of development owes to a very unique set of factors that define Japan's financial system and present economic and financial environment. In a recent paper, Batten and Szilagyi (2003) provide an overview of the major issues and impediments, and progress appears to have been measured since then.

Before the 1980s, the capital market in Japan was highly regulated, immature and segmented along banking relationships. Then, the financial system underwent a process of dramatic deregulation and liberalization, a breaking point of which was the revision of the Foreign Exchange Control Law in the late 1980s. The revision allowed Japanese firms to issue unsecured foreign bonds, and triggered a huge flight of borrowers from the domestic to the Euroyen and other Eurobond markets in search for lower cost of funds, less regulation and greater flexibility. This prompted the rapid decline of the local bond-underwriting cartel of Japanese banks, the *kisaikai*, which ultimately had to revise its terms of issuance in the domestic market as well, bringing tremendous growth in domestic bond issuance. At the same time, previously stringent equity market regulations were also relaxed, resulting in a substantial shift towards equity rather than debt finance. This first wave of financial market deregulation in Japan is discussed in detail by several authors, including Kester (1991) and Weinstein and Yafeh (1998).

The second wave of liberalization was forced by the burst of the bubble economy and the subsequent prolonged ailing of the banking sector and the economy in general. The Japanese authorities have strived to mitigate these problems by relaxing and abolishing financial regulations that impeded the strengthening of capital markets and the activation of capital market transactions. The "Big Bang" initiative of 1996 (i) abolished the eligibility standards for bond issuance; (ii) abolished the securities transaction tax, the bourse tax and made withholding tax exemptions; (iii) improved conditions for both exchange and over-the-counter (OTC) trading; (iv) deregulated trustee, underwriting and brokerage commissions; (v) introduced OTC sales of investment trusts; (vi) liberalized securities derivatives; (vii) fully liberalized cross-border capital and foreign exchange transactions; (viii) reformed the pension system; and, crucially, (ix) approved entry by banks, securities companies and insurance companies in each other's business.

The authorities' liberalization efforts have been accompanied by advances in information technology (IT) and globalization. The three factors work together to increase the effectiveness of Japanese capital markets, shifting the competitive balance with banks at the expense of the latter. Baba and Hisada (2002) describe how IT innovation and financial engineering facilitate the quantification of the risk-return profiles of financial products, foster securitization techniques and encourage arbitrage trading. At the same time, globalization should increase the substitutability of domestic and foreign financial assets, possibly boosting market activity with the involvement of foreign investors. IT development and globalization also erode banks' comparative advantage in information production, and force them to pursue more objective profitability measures, and diversify their business more into investment banking.

But, as has been mentioned, the main problems of the market come down to issues related to supply and demand. Fig. 1 below shows that the yen-denominated corporate bond market has failed to produce a major takeoff since it bottomed out at US$ 629.2 billion at the end of 2001. In June 2004, there were US$ 789.2 billion of corporate bonds outstanding in the market. While many have expressed concerns over the potential crowding-out effect of on-going expansion of the JGB market, these appear unwarranted given the persistent household surpluses, which must be continually channelled into financial assets. On the other hand, there is moderate competition among borrowers to offer potentially liquid securities, largely due to sluggish demand for funds, and because the deterioration in the credit quality of many Japanese firms appears to have eroded public confidence in the security issuing process. The market also remains homogeneous relative to its US counterpart, as very highly rated issues dominate, while the high-yield junk bond market is virtually absent due to limited demand by investors as well as limited access by potential borrowers. It is notable that the market

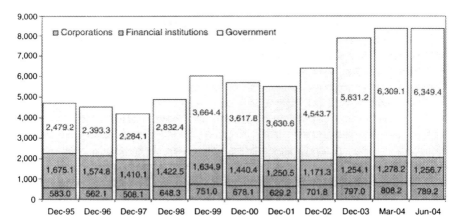

Fig. 1. Outstanding Yen-Denominated Bonds in Japan. (Billions of US Dollars). *Source*: Asian Development Bank, AsianBondsOnline, http://www.asianbondsonline .com.

remains highly concentrated, with the top three issuers accounting for 37.8% of the market in December 2004. Much issuance is limited to specific sectors such as electricity, land transport and transport equipment, wholesale, retail and telecommunications. In more recent years, supply in the market has become more diverse in term of credit ratings, issuer base and maturities, but this diversification process is measured and unlikely to accelerate in the near future.

A persistent problem of the market is that it still struggles to gain ground against the very competitive international Euroyen market. Table 3 shows that the vast majority of non-Japanese residents with yen needs continue to tap the Euroyen market – this despite a recent gradual recovery in the local Samurai market for non-resident issuers. This is a non-trivial issue from the viewpoint of Japanese policymakers, since non-resident issuance could greatly contribute to the easing of the liquidity trap burdening the country's financial system as well as encourage more active issuance by resident borrowers. It is interesting to observe, however, that even resident borrowers are increasingly turning to the Euroyen market – international yen-denominated issuance by

Table 3. Issuance in the Samurai and Euroyen Markets (Billion Yen).

	Samurai Issuance by Non-Japanese Residents	Euroyen Issuance by Non-Japanese Residents	Euroyen Issuance by Japanese Residents
1987	630.7	2,993.9	520.0
1988	809.9	2,213.0	0.0
1989	1,222.8	3,557.9	12.0
1990	1,236.0	4,980.9	747.0
1991	704.5	3,290.4	3,288.3
1992	1,175.1	3,328.0	3,006.0
1993	1,693.4	5,102.1	2,282.5
1994	1,230.7	10,194.2	691.7
1995	1,616.5	10,884.5	411.3
1996	3,933.7	12,909.9	955.6
1997	2,176.2	17,872.6	926.9
1998	412.3	12,328.6	566.2
1999	1,036.8	13,918.2	1,429.6
2000	2,919.0	16,771.9	1,260.4
2001	2,019.0	17,256.7	1,531.5
2002	2,118.7	12,322.3	2,040.5
2003	2,391.8	11,085.7	2,718.6
2004	2,774.3	8,881.7	3,129.2

Source: Japanese Ministry of Finance, http://www.mof.go.jp/english/e1c009.htm.

Japanese borrowers has more than doubled in the past few years, from ¥ 1.3 trillion in 2000 to ¥ 3.1 trillion in 2004.

Credit spread data obtained from the Asian Development Bank (ADB) indicates that, in the investment-grade segment at least, demand is increasing for corporate bonds. Spreads, measured as the difference in yields between corporate bonds and JGBs of matched maturities, have substantially narrowed since the financial instability during 1997–1998. Nishioka and Baba (2004) point out that strong monetary easing by the Bank of Japan under the zero interest rate policy and the subsequent quantitative monetary easing policy has facilitated this trend. The figures contained in Table 4 show that spreads continued to narrow in 2004 at almost all maturities in all ratings classes.

From Fig. 2 it appears that the narrowing of credit spreads is largely due to more aggressive purchases by banks and other private financial institutions battling excess liquidity. Nishioka and Baba (2004) explain that at the same time, the narrowing of yields spreads on lower-rated bonds in particular has alarmed more risk-conscious investors such insurance and

Table 4.   Credit Spread of LCY Corporate Bonds versus LCY Government Bonds.

Ratings/Tenor	Nov. 30, 2004	Oct. 31, 2004	Dec. 31, 2004
	AAA-rated		
1-year	16	14	13
3-year	40	43	46
5-year	81	82	
	AA-rated		
1-year	11	12	12
3-year	41	43	44
5-year	80	82	82
10-year	161	164	152
	A-rated		
1-year	18	19	26
3-year	53	55	66
5-year	94	96	111
10-year	176	180	
	BBB-rated		
1-year	29	30	48
3-year	67	70	96
5-year	112	146	149

Source: Asian Development Bank, AsianBondsOnline, http://www.asianbondsonline.com.

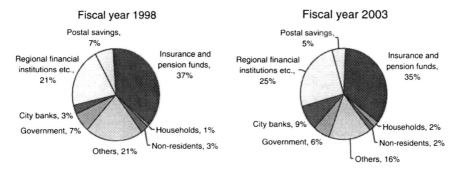

Fig. 2. Holders of Corporate Bonds in Japan. *Source:* Flow of Funds Accounts and Banking Accounts of Domestically Licensed Banks (Various Issues). Bank of Japan, Research and Statistics Department, http://www.boj.or.jp/en/index.htm. In: Nishioka, S. & N. Baba (2004). Changing Investor Structure of Japanese Corporate Bond Market under Zero Interest Rate Environment. Bank of Japan Review 2004-E-4.

pension funds and non-residents, cautious of a large potential capital loss in the event of a reversal of credit spreads.

It must be noted that a boost in demand at many market segments remains hindered by the underdevelopment of Japan's institutional investor base, and the risk aversion of existing institutional investors. Many institutional investors use single-A credit ratings and above as an internal criteria for investment, rather than the BBB recommendation of Standard and Poor's. Given that credit downgrades have hugely outnumbered upgrades in Japan in recent years, this is a major problem for lower rated corporations that consider tapping the domestic bond market. Securities investment trusts, which could help build up the lower segments of the market, have also been slow to develop. Some impetus for growth of these trusts was initially provided by the introduction of OTC sales by banks and other institutions and the liberalization of derivatives dealings, but the fact that the concept of these trusts is not deeply rooted in Japan's financial and legal system cannot be overlooked.

A more prosaic reason why the less risk-conscious institutional investor base has failed to develop is the extreme risk aversion of Japanese households. Fig. 3 shows that in June 2004, a staggering 55% of household investments lay in currency and deposits, up from 44.1% in March 1989, which compares with just 13.2% in the US. This trend is largely driven by the postal savings system, whose virtually risk-free deposits offer a highly advantageous risk-return profile, mitigating any incentive for households to

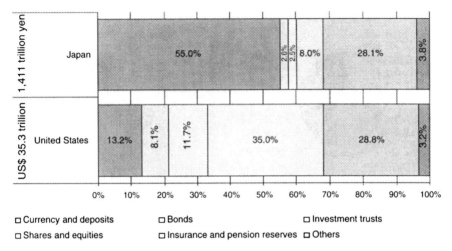

Fig. 3. Financial Assets Held by Japanese Households (as at End of September 2004). *Notes:* Households, by Definition of the Bank of Japan, Include Business-Like Elements such as Own-Account Workers. *Source:* Flow of Funds Accounts, Bank of Japan, Research and Statistics Department, http://www.boj.or.jp/en/index.htm; and Flow of Funds Accounts of the United States, Federal Reserve Bank, http://www.federalreserve.gov/releases/z1/current/data.htm. In: Flow of Funds (3rd Quarter of 2004) – Japan and U.S. Overview. Bank of Japan, Research and Statistics Department.

take on risk on their own initiative. At the same time, household investment in securities and securities investment trusts have been on the decline. The share of equities fell spectacularly, from 23.3% to 8% between March 1989 and June 2004, coinciding with the huge decline in the Japanese stock market from the late 1980s. Over the same period, household investment in other securities also fell from a high of 9.9% to 4.9%.

The concern over Japanese investors having limited appetite for evaluating and trading in credit risk is somewhat exacerbated by the fact that most foreign investors are increasingly uncomfortable holding large positions in Japanese debt. Between December 2000 and June 2004, foreign holdings of JGBs dropped from 5.9% to 3.3% of the total outstanding amount. Currency risk aside, foreign investors are alarmed in particular by a potential increase in yields, associated with the on-going growth of the JGB market and a sentiment of increasing oversupply. Accordingly, the rating agency Standard and Poor's downgraded both Japan's local and foreign currency by three notches, from AAA to AA, between February 2001 and April 2002.

Despite sluggish growth in the market, it is positive news that developments in market infrastructure have enhanced liquidity in recent years. ADB data[2] reveal that the turnover ratio of Japanese corporate bonds grew from 0.33 in 1999 to 0.82 in 2003. Overall, trading volume more than doubled between 1999 and 2003, from US$451.6 billion to US$ 1,020.1 billion. On the other hand, the ADB figures also show that turnover is significantly higher even in the Korean and Malaysian markets, at 1.44 and 1.10, respectively. Importantly, this suggests that in Japan the price information available to market participants for resource allocation decisions may be unreliable even relative to other markets in the region.

5. CONCLUDING REMARKS AND FUTURE DIRECTION

The collapse of Japan's bubble economy in the late 1980s triggered a serious non-performing loan and debt overhang problem, which compromised the banking sector's ability to intermediate, and is largely blamed for Japan's prolonged economic stagnation. The banking crisis has impaired the corporate sector's fund-raising ability, while trapping excess liquidity in the system through a lack of investment choice afforded to Japanese investors. For the bad loan burden confronting Japanese banks, there is no immediate answer other than improvements in internal control mechanisms and the eventual dismantling of the cross-ownership structures with industry. This however is a lengthy process, while the system's reduced ability to intermediate is an acute problem that threatens Japan's medium-term ability to recover. This paper has argued that the development of Japan's corporate bond market should provide a key contribution to the recovery of Japan's financial system and its entire economy, but has found that the market continues to lag its US and UK counterparts in development, efficiency and diversity.

For the market mechanisms to work more efficiently, further improvements in Japan's market infrastructure are indispensable in the broadest sense of the word. The key areas where development is necessary have been identified by several studies, including Schinasi and Smith (1998), Kuratani and Endo (2000), Hattori et al. (2001), Rhee (2001), Baba and Hisada (2002) and Batten and Szilagyi (2003). Since these papers were published, some progress has been made. In August 2002, Japan's Financial Services Agency adopted a comprehensive program for promoting securities markets reform, focusing on three broad areas: (i) providing easy access to securities markets by everyone; (ii) establishing a fair and transparent market investors can confidently invest in; and (iii) establishing an efficient and competitive market. Key advances include the introduction of the Law Concerning Book-Entry Transfer of Corporate Bonds in January 2003, which is to completely replace the outdated bond registration law. The new book-entry transfer system, to be launched in 2006, consolidates settlement processes, thus enabling the future adoption of straight-through-processing (STP) and paving the way for greater market liquidity. At the same time, steps have been taken to improve corporate governance and implement internationally consistent accounting and auditing standards, enhance auditor oversight and independence, strengthen the rules applicable to securities analysts, as well as promote the development of securities exchanges.

It is evident that there remains room for development in practically all areas, however. Necessary infrastructural improvements include sufficient market transaction volume and the reduction of distortions in price information; high quality, across-the-board disclosure, ideally on a real-time basis; further improvement of clearing and settlement systems; strengthening of market surveillance functions and frameworks; and removal of regulation that limits access to the issuing, underwriting and trading process. At the same time, further improvements in the corporate governance system are required, including better accounting and business standards and practices, and a more active market for corporate control. Legal tasks include improvements in antitrust and insolvency laws, further limitation of banks' market power, easing of restrictions on institutional investors, as well as the long-awaited further partial withdrawal of deposit insurance and introduction of dual income taxation, both now under way. More generally, it is imperative that a diverse and multilevel market participant base be developed, which comprises a variety of, individual and institutional investors, investment banks, credit rating firms and investment analysts. The internationalization of market participants is all but a key element of this strategy, which requires the enhanced competitiveness of the Japanese market in the global setting.

NOTES

1. With an outstanding US$ 6.3 trillion in government bonds, Japan's public debt was 154.5% of GDP in 2003, by far the highest among the G7 countries. However, The Economist (2004) notes that much of this debt is a result of intra-governmental lending, and the government owes only 46% of GDP to external parties. On the other hand, the budget deficit reached 7.42% in 2003 and is expected to remain at around 5–10% of GDP in the near to medium term.

2. http://www.asianbondsonline.com.

REFERENCES:

Allen, F., & Santomero, A. M. (1998). The theory of financial intermediation. *Journal of Banking and Finance, 21*, 1461–1485.

Baba, N., & Hisada, T. (2002). *Japan's financial system: Its perspective and the authorities' roles in redesigning and administering the system.* IMES Discussion Paper 2002-E-1, Bank of Japan, Institute for Monetary and Economic Studies (IMES).

Batten, J., & Kim, Y.-H. (2001). Expanding long-term financing through bond market development: A post crisis policy task. In: Y. -H. Kim (Ed.), *Government bond markets in Asia.* Manila: Asian Development Bank.

Batten, J. A., & Szilagyi, P. G. (2003). Why Japan needs to develop its corporate bond market. *International Journal of the Economics of Business, 10*(1), 85–110.

Beck, T., Levine, R., & Loayza, N. (2000). Finance and the sources of growth. *Journal of Financial Economics, 58*(1–2), 261–300.

Benston, G., & Smith, C. W. (1976). A transaction cost approach to the theory of financial intermediation. *Journal of Finance, 31*(2), 215–231.

Bolton, P., & Freixas, X. (2000). Equity, bonds, and bank debt: Capital structure and financial market equilibrium under asymmetric information. *Journal of Political Economy, 108*(2), 324–351.

Boot, A. W. A., & Thakor, A. (1997). Financial system architecture. *Review of Financial Studies, 10*(3), 693–733.

Boyd, J. D., & Smith, B. D. (1998). Capital market imperfections in a monetary growth model. *Economic Theory, 11*, 241–273.

Boyd, J. H., & Prescott, E. C. (1986). Financial intermediary coalitions. *Journal of Economic Theory, 38*, 211–232.

Cheung, S., & Chan, B. Y. (2002). Bond markets in the Pacific rim: Development, market structure and relevant issues in fixed income markets. *Asia Pacific Development Journal, 9*(1), 1–21.

Davis, P., & Mayer, C. P. (1991). Corporate finance in the euromarkets and the economics of intermediation. CEPR discussion paper no. 570. *Centre for Economic Policy Research,* 1–32.

Diamond, D. W. (1984). Financial intermediaries and delegated monitoring. *Review of Economic Studies, 51*(3), 393–414.

Dinc, I. S. (2000). Bank reputation, bank commitment, and the effects of competition in credit markets. *Review of Financial Studies, 13*(3), 781–812.

Economist, The. (2004). Grey hair, red ink, but blue skies? *The Economist,* 24 June.

Hattori, M., Koyama, K., & Yonetani, T. (2001). *Analysis of credit spread in Japan's corporate bond market.* BIS Papers No. 5., Bank for International Settlements.

Hellwig, M. (1991). Banking, financial intermediation and corporate finance. In: A. Giovanni & C. Mayers (Eds), *European financial intermediation* (pp. 35–63). Cambridge: Cambridge University Press.

Hoshi, T., Kashyap, A., & Scharfstein, D. (1991). Corporate structure, liquidity, and investment: Evidence from Japanese industrial groups. *Quarterly Journal of Economics, 106*(1), 33–60.

Huybens, E., & Smith, B. (1999). Inflation, financial markets, and long-run real activity. *Journal of Monetary Economics, 43*, 283–315.

Kester, W. K. (1991). *Japanese takeovers: The global contest for corporate control.* Cambridge, MA: Harvard Business School Press.

Kuratani, M., & Endo, Y. (2000). *Establishing new financial markets in Japan.* NRI Papers No. 6, Nomura Research Institute.

La Porta, R., Lopez-de-Silanes, F., Shleifer, A., & Vishny, R. W. (2000). Investor protection and corporate governance. *Journal of Financial Economics, 58*(1–2), 3–29.

Leland, H. E., & Pyle, D. H. (1977). Informational asymmertires, financial structures, and financial intermediation. *Journal of Finance, 32*(2), 371–387.

Levine, R. (1997). Financial development and economic growth: Views and agenda. *Journal of Economic Literature, 35*(2), 688–726.

Levine, R. (2000). *Bank-based or market-based financial systems: Which is better?* Minneapolis, MI: Carlson School of Management, University of Minnesota.

Nishioka, S., & Baba, N. (2004). *Changing investor structure of Japanese corporate bond market under zero interest rate environment.* Bank of Japan Review 2004-E-4.

Ongena, S., & Smith, D. C. (2000). What determines the number of bank relationships: Cross-country evidence. *Journal of Financial Intermediation, 9*(1), 26–56.

Oyama, T., & Shiratori, T. (2001). *Insights into the low profitability of Japanese banks: Some lessons from the analysis of trends in banks' margins.* Bank of Japan, Discussion Paper 01-E-1, Bank Examination and Surveillance Department.

Rajan, R. (1992). Insiders and outsiders: The choice between informed and arm's-length debt. *Journal of Finance, 47,* 1367–1400.

Rajan, R. G., & Zingales, L. (1999). *Financial systems, industrial structure, and Growth.* Mimeo.

Rhee, S. G. (2001). *Further reforms of the JGB market for the promotion of regional bond markets.* Bond market development in Asia (pp. 217–236). Paris: Organization for Economic Co-Operation and Development (OECD).

Schinasi, G. J., & Smith, T. R. (1998). *Fixed income markets in the United States, Europe and Japan: Some lessons for emerging markets.* IMF Working Paper No. 98 (12): 1–70. International Monetary Fund, Washington, D.C.

Sharma, K. (2001). The underlying constraints on corporate bond market development in Southeast Asia. *World Development, 29*(8), 1405–1419.

Smith, T. D. (1995). Markets for corporate debt securities. IMF Working Paper No. 95/67: 1–77. International Monetary Fund, Washington, D.C.

Takagi, S. (2002). Fostering capital markets in a bank-based financial system: A review of conceptual issues. *Asian Development Review, 19*(1), 67–97.

Thorat, U. (2002). Developing bond markets to diversify long-term development finance: Country study of India. *Asia-Pacific Development Journal, 9*(1), 45–63.

Weinstein, D. E., & Yafeh, Y. (1998). On the costs of a bank-centered financial system: Evidence from the changing main bank relations in Japan. *Journal of Finance, 53*(2), 635–672.

CORPORATE GOVERNANCE AND SOCIAL RESPONSIBILITY: COMBATING MONEY LAUNDERING IN THE ASIA PACIFIC REGION

Bonnie Buchanan

ABSTRACT

Corruption can take many forms. One of the most alarming aspects of corruption has been the impact of money laundering on financial markets. The amount of money laundered in the Asian region is estimated at approximately $200 billion, or one-fifth the global total. Some of the Asia-Pacific countries still lack any consistent anti-money laundering legislation. The Asia-Pacific region is also home to five of the six remaining non-cooperative countries and territories on The Financial Action Task Force's 2004 list. In this paper, I present a clinical examination of the impact of money laundering and Off-shore financial centres on Asia Pacific financial markets. I describe the money laundering cycle, tools and techniques utilized in the Asia-Pacific region as well as anti-money laundering measures and regulation.

Asia Pacific Financial Markets in Comparative Perspective: Issues and Implications for the 21st Century

Contemporary Studies in Economics and Financial Analysis, Volume 86, 435–452
ISSN: 1569-3759/doi:10.1016/S1569-3759(05)86018-8

Corporate social responsibility is the commitment of business to contribute to sustainable economic development by working with employees, their families, their local community and society at large to improve their lives in ways that are good for business and for development.

IFC Definition

1. INTRODUCTION

In the Asia-Pacific region corporate social responsibility has been one of the more enduring themes of the past year. This is largely because the region was rocked by a number of corporate governance scandals – the largest since the financial crisis of 1997–1998. These scandals include Seibu railway, which was ordered to delist after it was revealed that the company had falsified shareholder data for more than 40 years. China Aviation Oil revealed it had lost more than US$550 million in derivatives trading. These events threw the spotlight on deficiencies surrounding internal corporate governance controls in the companies. The past couple of years have also witnessed growth in new or amended rules around the Asia-Pacific region, in areas such as accounting, auditing standards and in corporate governance regulations.

During the last few years in addition to improved corporate governance regulation, combating corruption has become a top priority for many countries in the Asia-Pacific region. The challenge of controlling corruption remains daunting for both the public and private sector. Multinational companies and international finance companies have also had to adapt to increased international regulation in order to prevent tax avoidance, tax evasion and money laundering in the region.

The high cost of corruption has primarily been the motivating factor for many policy makers in recent years. Mauro (1995) argues that corruption lowers investment and thereby lowers growth, suggesting there is evidence that bureaucratic efficiency may be at least as important a determinant of investment and growth as political stability. Corruption worsens inequality and poverty (Gupta, Davoodi, & Alonso-Terme, 2002), reduces investment rates (Mauro, 1996), and lowers economic growth (Tanzi & Davoodi, 1997).

Now that markets operate on a 24-h basis, globalization has benefited participants not only in the legal economy, but also in the illegal economy as well. Corruption can take many forms. Dearden (2003) distinguishes between petty and grand corruption. Petty corruption, more prevalent in developing countries, is usually associated with low levels of public sector pay, where minor bribes become an important and often unrecognized source of income.

Grand corruption, on the other hand, usually entails large amounts of money being stolen by corrupt senior officials and political leaders in developing countries as well as large bribes being paid by international businesses.

One of the most alarming aspects of corruption has been the impact of money laundering on financial markets. According to IMF estimates, somewhere between $500 billion and $1.5 trillion, or up to 5 percent of gross world product, is laundered through global financial institutions each year.[1] According to one former U.S government official, "Globalization has rapidly democratized money laundering".[2]

Money laundering is a global phenomenon and an international challenge. As globalization has evolved, money launderers have been able to conduct their trade with greater ease, sophistication and profitability. Increased competition between borders has also compressed the associated transaction costs of money laundering. As new financial instruments and trading opportunities have been created and liquidity of financial markets has improved, it has also allowed money-laundering systems to be set up and shut down with greater ease.

Money laundering tends to allocate dirty money around the world on the basis of avoiding national controls, because tainted money tends to flow to countries with less stringent controls. Globalization has improved the ability of money launderers to communicate, allowing them to spread transactions across a greater number of jurisdictions, thereby increasing the number of legal obstacles that may be put up to hinder investigations. Underground, or alternative remittance systems, have also attracted the attention of law enforcement and regulatory agencies.

Global money laundering imposes significant costs on the world economy by damaging the effective operations of national economies. As financial markets slowly become corrupted, the public's confidence in the international financial system is eroded. As financial markets become increasingly risky and less stable, the rate of growth of the world economy is eventually reduced. The continued presence of money laundering confuses the difference between the change in rates and prices and exacerbates volatility in financial markets. For example, in August 2003, the financial market reacted negatively to reports regarding alleged money laundering activities against First Gentleman Jose Miguel Arroryo. The negative news caused the Philippine peso to plunge.[3] Finally, failure to take notice of money laundering problems will result in incorrect policy setting.

In the Asia-Pacific region, the growth of money laundering has hastened due to a number of factors. Firstly, many economies in the region are still based on cash transactions and this presents a problem when dealing with

Western based regulation, which considers large cash transfers as being "suspicious transactions". Secondly, in countries like India and Pakistan there are the Hawala and Hundi banking systems. These underground banking and remittance systems effectively leave no paper trail, and so it becomes increasingly difficult to distinguish money laundering from legitimate transactions. The region also contains the major narcotic production areas such as the Golden Crescent of Afghanistan, Iran and Pakistan and the Golden Triangle of Thailand, Myanmar and Laos. Finally, in China, activities involving the production of counterfeit cigarettes, computer software and music CDs etc. generates an enormous quantity of funds that must be laundered.

Tax havens, or Off Shore Financial Centres (OFCs), are also closely linked with the problem of money laundering. Money launderers consider OFCs an ideal avenue because it offers the advantages of secrecy and a low tax regime. Dearden (2003) estimates that approximately $6 trillion to $7 trillion is held in 100 OFCs around the world. This amount is believed to be held equally between companies and individuals. Corruption associated with OFCs will clearly reduce the ability of a government to sustain its corporate taxation base and this will shift the burden to personal and indirect taxation.

Some of the Asia-Pacific countries still lack any consistent anti-money laundering legislation. FATF maintains what can be considered a "black list" of countries that fail to maintain adequate anti-money laundering controls. The Asia-Pacific region is home to five of the six remaining NCCTs on FATFs 2004 list.

In this paper, I present a clinical examination of the impact of money laundering and OFCs on Asia Pacific financial markets. In the next section, I describe the money laundering cycle and the more common tools and techniques utilized in the Asia-Pacific region. In Section 3, I detail the extent of the problem in the region. Anti-money laundering measures and regulation in the Asia-Pacific region are addressed in Section 4 and Section 5 concludes.

2. THE MONEY LAUNDERING PROCESS: AN OVERVIEW

Money laundering is diverse and widespread. The removal of barriers to the free movement of capital along with technological driven change has brought global markets, financial flows and information even closer together. Simply stated, money laundering is intended to process criminal profits through the financial system in order to obscure their illegal origins and make them appear legitimate. A wide variety of criminal activity such as illegal arms sales, smuggling, drug trafficking, human trafficking, prostitution rings, activities of organized crime, embezzlement, insider trading, bribery and fraud, political corruption can produce large profits and create the incentive to make them appear legitimate.

Money laundering often involves a complex series of transactions and numerous financial institutions from many jurisdictions. Domestic money laundering refers to money generated by crime and laundered in the banking system of the same country. Transnational money laundering refers to criminal activity and laundering separated by one or more national borders. Buchanan (2004) provides an overview of the global impact of money laundering.

It is not just enough to hide the proceeds of illegal activities. Equally important in the laundering process is to render the proceeds reusable for other purposes. To accomplish this, non-bank financial institutions such as bureau de change, check cashing services, insurers, brokers and traders are increasingly utilized by money launderers.

The money laundering process is more broadly classified into three basic steps: placement, layering and integration. Firstly, the purpose of placement is to avoid detection by the authorities and remove the cash as far as possible from the proceeds' illegal origins. The placement stage is accomplished by changing the bulk cash derived from criminal activities into a more portable and less suspicious form by depositing those proceeds into the mainstream financial system. The laundering mechanism is at its most vulnerable during placement because most illegal activity generates cash profits, which is bulky and difficult to conceal in large amounts. As a result, the money launderer has to find a solution to move large masses of cash into a more manageable form for introduction into the financial system. Such solutions could include using front corporations to deposit cash or check cashing businesses to convert cash to negotiable instruments such as traveller's checks, cashiers checks and money orders.

Layering, the second stage of the money laundering process takes place after the funds have entered the financial system. This particular stage involves creating a web of financial transactions that in terms of their frequency, complexity and volume often resemble legitimate financial activity. A paper trail becomes increasingly difficult to reconstruct due to the web of parallel and serial transactions. In transnational money laundering OFCs can perform an important function in the layering stage because it usually involves more than two or three jurisdictions. In an attempt to hide its true origins, the funds are often wire transferred into a financial or banking system through offshore accounts.

The final stage of the money laundering process is known as integration. Integration involves reintegrating the washed or cleansed funds with formal sector economic activity. There are a variety of financial instruments used to accomplish this task such as letters of credit, bonds, bank notes, bills of lading and guarantees.

Lilliey (2003) maintains that the money laundering cycle is encouraged and achieved by countries that fall into the following categories. The first category is a country that has a highly developed banking system where there are compliant professional advisors and so money laundering can be subsequently hidden. On the other hand, the "washing" cycle could also be quickly achieved in a country with an underdeveloped banking and legal system where there is little risk of detecting money laundering. Listed below are common techniques and tools associated with money laundering.

2.1. Common Techniques and Tools of Money Laundering in the Asia-Pacific Region

Most of the money laundering typologies commonly used in the Asia-Pacific region are identical to typologies frequently used around the world. These include wire transfers, opening accounts at financial institutions in false names, false invoicing, smurfing, shell companies and alternative remittance systems. These will be discussed in turn.

2.1.1. Smurfing
Smurfing, or structuring, usually involves the use of multiple cash deposits, each being smaller than the minimum cash reporting requirement. The U.S. 1970 Bank Secrecy Act requires that certain banks or other financial institutions retain records and report certain financial transactions over US$10,000. This minimum reporting requirement of US$10,000 is also used in other jurisdictions around the world. In Asia, smurfing is typically accomplished through the bank accounts of accomplices known as "Tua Peh Kong", or "ants" (Tan, 2002).

2.1.2. Front Companies
Front companies can be used to layer and integrate the illegal proceeds of fraudulent commercial trade. These companies are considered to be effective in the money laundering cycle for two reasons. Any business that is cash rich

can serve as a front company and this may include check cashing businesses, travel agencies, liquor stores and restaurants. Import/export companies can also serve as front companies and typically use three operations to launder money, namely, double invoicing, undervaluation and overvaluation of goods and financing exports. First of all, in order to operate, front companies do not necessarily require the complicity of a financial institution. Secondly, detection is more difficult if front companies are also conducting legitimate business, particularly ones that are exempt from Currency Transaction Reports.

2.1.3. Misinvoicing
One other common money laundering transaction is the misinvoicing of international trade transfers. False import letters of credit and customs declarations can conceal cross border transfers of illegal proceeds. Fraudulent valuation of goods by international traders can also reach large inflated amounts.

2.1.4. Offshore Financial Centres
OFCs are a popular mechanism to route laundered funds. FATF defines an OFC as a corporation or institution "that does not conduct any commercial or manufacturing business or any other form of commercial operation in the country where their registered office is located."

In recent years, OFCs have been viewed as contributing to the increased instability of the international financial system, increasing the administrative costs and compliance burdens on both tax authorities and tax payers. Errico and Musalem (1999) claim that offshore banks exploit the risk-return trade-off by being more profitable than onshore banks, and in many instances are also more leveraged.

OFCs are typically characterized by absolute secrecy and confidentiality, minimal or no taxes on business or investment income, no withholding taxes, light and flexible supervisory regimes. Other red flags to watch out for include corporate structures that can be bought quickly and cost effectively, no exchange controls, predominant use of a major currency such as the US dollar, the absence of normal accepted company supervision, the ability to disguise the ownership of corporate vehicles through the use of nominee directors and bearer shares and the absence of normally accepted company reporting requirements for companies. The OFCs secrecy laws and the sheer volume of wire transfer transactions can hamper subsequent investigations of laundered funds by regulatory.

Since the 1997–1998 Asian financial crisis, global attention has increased regarding OFCs. Countries and territories in the Asia-Pacific region which have OFCs include: Australia, Cook Islands, Guam, Hong Kong, Japan, Macau, Malaysia (Labuan), Marianas, Marshall Islands, Micronesia, Nauru, Niue, Philippines, Singapore, Thailand, Vanuatu and Western Samoa. The features of a select group of Asian OFCs may be found in Table 1.

2.1.5. Wire Transfers

A common transaction used to layer illicit funds is electronic funds transfers, or wire transfers. The Society for Worldwide Interbank Financial Telecommunications (SWIFT) operates internationally in addition to the Clearing House Interbank Payments System (CHIPS) (which provides a central role for New York Clearing House banks), and Fedwire (acting for the Federal Reserve System member banks). If two banks are members of the same wire transfer system, then they are considered to be the only two banks in the wire transfer chain. Or, on the other hand, correspondent banks can be used to route the transfers through one or more intermediary banks.

2.1.6. E-Commerce

With the emergence of the Internet e-commerce, and in particular the e-banking industry, has been recognized as a potential avenue for money launderers. Paper trails can be obscured if transactions are conducted in cipher, making it increasingly difficult to investigate and prosecute a possible money laundering offence. Simply stated, electronic records are easier to manipulate than paper records.

The FATF feels that a financial institution will encounter more difficulties in detecting money laundering activities if customers are allowed to open a new electronic account without a link to an existing traditional account (Tan, 2002). It also becomes difficult for financial institutions to detect suspicious transactions among the thousands of transactions conducted daily at a financial establishment.

2.1.7. Alternative Remittance Systems

During the last decade the FATF, UN, OECD and Interpol have expressed concerns about the possible use of alternative remittance systems for money laundering. Shehu (2003) estimates that there are approximately 3000 alternative remittance systems in the Asia-Pacific region alone, categorized broadly into either the Indian hawala/hundi system or Chinese fei chi'en system. In 2001/2002, the U.S. Treasury identified the hawala as the chief means of money laundering in Pakistan. Alternative remittance systems

Table 1. Characteristics of Two Offshore Financial Centres.

OFC	Activities and Restrictions	Prudential Regulations	Tax Privileges	Role of Regulators
Malaysia (Lubuan)	Offshore banks may only operate in the International Off-shore Financial Centre (IOFC) on the island of Labuan	Stringent bank secrecy rules No exchange controls are in place	Minimal taxation	Monitored by the Labuan Offshore Financial Services Authority
Singapore	Offshore banking is operated through Asian Currency Units (ACUs). These are operational units whose function is to conduct business in the Asia Dollar Market. Onshore commercial centres and merchant banks may also operate ACUs. The Monetary Authority of Singapore (MAS) in this case would license the ACUs as distinct accounting entities	ACUs are exempt from a number of key prudential regulations, including reserve requirements (usually 6 percent), minimum liquid asset ratio (not less than 18 percent), investment limitations and some of the limitations on credit facilities	No withholding or income tax on non-resident ACUs depositors	MAS supervises ACUs. Regular inspections are carried out
	ACUs are prohibited from conducting business denominated in Singapore dollars and may accept deposits and make loans in foreign currencies. ACUs also cannot accept time deposits of less than 250,000 Singapore dollars		ACUs are taxed at a concessionary rate of 10 percent compared with the corporate tax rate of 26 percent	No formal deposit insurance scheme. The MAS does not have an obligation to act as a lender of last resort. The 1996 Banking Act was amended to allow foreign regulators to inspect the Singaporean of banks under their oversight

Source: Errico and Musalem (1999).

have been used for illegal activities including currency control evasion, tax evasion, purchase of illegal arms and laundering money. It is possible though that illegal money never enters the mainstream financial system, but instead goes through an underground banking system, such as the Hawala and Hundi system in India, or Chop or fei chi'en (flying money) parallel banking systems in China.

These informal money remittance systems are based on honor and ethnic ties and represent a highly efficient channel to launder money. The way they operate is as follows: a person can deposit cash with a Hawala or Chop money exchanger and in exchange receive a chit, ticket or some sort of marker. Despite a rather ordinary appearance (though they can be impossible to replicate), the markers are actually coded bearer notes. Whereas the Chinese system uses "chits" or "chops", the Hawala system is based on codes and messages transmitted via telephone, facsimile and e-mail. When presented to a moneychanger in another country, the bearer will receive the same amount of cash, less a commission (usually 5–15 percent of the amount). The underground banking system can be extremely complex or it could even be as simple as someone in a grocery store using e-mail or a cell phone to send money to another country. A chief feature is that no money will actually cross the border and little if any paperwork will be compiled to document what has taken place. The challenge for regulatory authorities is to find the "golden thread" that indicates the presence of a parallel banking system in the first place. Schramm and Taube (2003) describe the evolution of the Hawala system.

3. THE EXTENT OF MONEY LAUNDERING IN THE ASIA-PACIFIC REGION

Without a doubt, money laundering involves enormous sums relative to overall economic activity. Given that most law enforcement estimates use actual data on reported crimes and that reported crimes are a fraction of all crimes, the real magnitude of money laundering is significantly understated in most of the literature. Tanzi (1996) presents an estimate of US$300 billion to US$500 billion of "dirty money" entering the international capital market each year. Schneider and Enste (2000) estimate the size of the underground economy in OECD countries ranges from 5–28 percent of GDP and 8–63 percent of GDP in transition economies. In 1999, the United Nations Human Development report estimated that global criminal activity generates $1.5 trillion each year while other estimates have claimed that money laundering could be as high as $3 trillion per annum. However, the most publicized global money laundering size estimate has been provided by FATF. The FATF estimates that money laundering comprises approximately 2 percent of global GDP.

There have been alternative estimates as to the size and extent of the money-laundering problem. Quirk (1996) provides a wide range of estimates of the size of underground economies, as a percentage of Gross Domestic Product (GDP) – for example in the Asia-Pacific Rim area: Australia 4–12 percent, Japan 4–15 percent and the United States 4–33 percent.

Walter (1990) claims that the underground economy accounts for anywhere between 7 percent and 10 percent of a developed country's GDP. In less developed countries the size of the underground economy may be significantly higher. Kumar (1996) provides an estimate for India, where the informal economy has been estimated to account for between 18 and 21 percent of India's Gross National Product (GNP). Lilliey (2003) presents an estimate that place the amount of money laundered in the Asian region at approximately $200 billion, or one-fifth the global total.

Despite the variation in the above estimates, what becomes apparent is that macroeconomic policymakers cannot ignore the effects of money laundering. Simply stated, money laundering can shift money demands from one country to another and this will result in misleading monetary data. The misleading monetary data will in turn have adverse consequences on interest rates, exchange rates and asset prices in economies. Gradually, the governance of the banking system is undermined, the financial market becomes corrupted and public confidence in the international financial system is eroded. This in turn increases the risk and instability of the financial system. Overall, these effects eventually reduce the growth rate of the world economy. Quirk (1996), in a study of 18 industrial countries, finds that significant reductions in annual GDP growth rates were associated with increases in the laundered criminal proceeds between 1983 and 1990.

Even though it is considered a violation of the foreign exchange law, the hawala remains pervasive in India. Shehu (2003) estimates that the hawala constitutes the equivalent of 40 percent of Indian GDP, or as much as $680 billion passes through the financial system. In 1998 it was reported that criminal organizations had used alternative remittance systems to send approximately US$265.5 million from Japan to various countries in Asia and the Middle East.

There is also the additional difficulty of measuring the impact of offshore financial centres. The Asian financial crisis was characterized by a series of large capital inflows influenced by pegged exchange rates, financial liberalization leading to increased liquidity, foreign exchange and credit exposure. Onshore banks and corporations were encouraged to tap international capital markets through offshore financial institutions due to regulatory and tax advantages.

In 1993, the establishment of the Bangkok International Banking Facilities (BIBFs) led to a significant increase in short-term offshore borrowing, which encouraged unhedged domestic lending to finance equity and real estate purchases. The BIBFs intermediated about two-thirds of total short-term inflows in 1995. Total lending in foreign exchange by BIBFs between 1993 and 1996 increased by 38 percent annually, reaching a total of US$32 billion by the end of 1996.

By the end of December 1997, the international offshore centre off Labuan had 52 offshore banks (including 17 domestic) with short-term liabilities amounting to US$10.2 billion. In Malaysia, a review of offshore operations revealed significant losses which one bank had not previously recognized. In the aftermath of the crisis, Malaysia committed to protect depositors of Malaysian banks as well as offshore banks.

In the next section, I discuss various international anti-money laundering efforts that have evolved in recent years to address the problem of money laundering in the Asia-Pacific region.

4. GLOBAL ANTI-MONEY LAUNDERING MEASURES

International efforts to fight money laundering also intensified with the establishment of FATF in 1989. The G7 group of nations founded the FATF with the primary purpose of examining measures to combat money laundering. Originally, the FATF had a mandate of five years but this has repeatedly been renewed in response to concern about money laundering. The FATF is currently an inter-governmental body comprising 29 countries and two international organizations (the European Commission and Gulf Cooperation Council). Asia Pacific members can be found in Table 2.

At the heart of FATF's mission is a set of 40 recommendations, which are intended to set out criteria to identify money laundering, prosecute and enforce convictions. Recommendations 1–3 sets out the general framework, and the role of the country's legal system in the prosecution of money laundering is detailed in recommendations 4–7. Recommendations 4–7 also provide measures regarding asset confiscation that should be provided for in a country's law. Recommendations 8–29 provide the role of a country's

Table 2. Asia Pacific Group – Anti-Money Laundering Features.

Country	Established an Anti-money Laundering System?	FATF Member?	Formed a Financial Intelligence Unit?	Capability to Report Suspicious Transactions?
Australia	Yes	Yes	Yes	Yes
Bangladesh	Strengthening		Yes	Yes
Brunei Darussalem	Yes		No	Yes
Cambodia	N/A		N/A	N/A
Chinese Taipei	Yes		Yes	Yes
Cook Islands	Strengthening		Yes	Yes
Fiji	Yes		Yes	Yes
Hong Kong, China	Strengthening	Yes	No	Yes
India	Strengthening		Yes	Yes
Indonesia	Strengthening		Yes	Yes
Japan	Yes	Yes	Yes	Yes
Korea, Republic of	Yes		Yes	Yes
Macau, China	Yes		Yes	Yes
Malaysia	Strengthening		Yes	Yes
Marshall Islands	N/A		N/A	N/A
Mongolia	Strengthening		No	Developing
Nepal	Strengthening		Yes	Yes
New Zealand	Yes	Yes	No	Yes
Niue	Strengthening			Yes
Pakistan	Yes		Developing	Yes
Palau	Yes		Developing	Yes
Philippines	Strengthening		Yes	Yes
Samoa	Yes		Yes	Yes
Singapore	Yes	Yes	Yes	Yes
Sri Lanka	Strengthening		No	Yes
Thailand	Yes		Yes	Yes
USA	Yes	Yes	Yes	Yes
Vanuatu	Yes		Yes	Yes

Source: Asia/Pacific (APG) Group on money laundering.

financial system in preventing money laundering. This particular group of recommendations also entail customer identification and record keeping requirements and due diligence provisions. Recommendations 30–40 describe measures to improve cooperation between regulatory agencies and law enforcement agencies.

Review of compliance with the FATF 40 Recommendations is based upon mutual evaluation by FATF peers. The FATF publishes the results from the mutual evaluation and annual self-assessment exercises, and in some cases identifies where infractions have occurred. However, the extent of the non-compliance is not described. Using 25 criteria based on the forty recommendations, the FATF also evaluates non-members, without their consent, and this is termed the NCCTs exercise. This exercise results in a NCCTs list, equivalent to a "name and shame" list. Table 3 details the

Table 3. Non-Cooperative Countries and Territories (NCCTs) List 2000–2003.

2000	2001	2002	2003	2004
Bahamas	Cook Islands	Cook Islands	Cook Islands	Cook Islands
Cayman Islands	Dominica	Dominica	Egypt	Indonesia
Cook Islands	Egypt	Egypt	Guatemala	Mynamar
Dominica	Guatemala	Grenada	Indonesia	Nauru
Israel	Grenada	Guatemala	Myanmar	Nigeria
Lebanon	Hungary	Indonesia	Nauru	Philippines
Liechtenstein	Indonesia	Marshall Islands	Nigeria	
Marshall Islands	Israel	Myanmar	Philippines	
Nauru	Lebanon	Nauru	Ukraine	
Niue	Marshall Islands	Nigeria		
Panama	Myanmar	Niue		
Philippines	Nauru	Philippines		
Russia	Nigeria	Russia		
St Kitts and Nevis	Niue	St Vincent and the Grenadines		
St Vincent and the Grenadines	Philippines	Ukraine		
	Russia			
	St Kitts and Nevis			
	St Vincent and the Grenadines			
	Ukraine			

Source: Financial Action Task Force.

NCCT lists between 2000 and 2004. As mentioned before, five of the six non-cooperative countries and territories in the 2004 list are from the Asia-Pacific region (Table 3).

The idea behind the NCCT list is that the named countries may have pressure exerted on them by the international community to work with the FATF in order to bring about legal, regulatory and law enforcement changes in compliance with international money laundering control standards. Financial transactions with a NCCT listed country are subject to heightened scrutiny by financial institutions in FATF member countries.

The efforts of the FATF have also extended to the creation of a number of regional anti-money laundering organizations such as the Asia/Pacific Group on Money Laundering (APG), the Caribbean Financial Action Task Force (CFATF) and the Select Committee of the Council of Europe. In the aftermath of the Asian financial crisis the OECD formed the Financial Stability Forum (FSF), which examines the degree of supervision and co-operation with other OFCs. FATF regional bodies are becoming increasingly important, especially with the establishment of the Eurasian Group on Money Laundering and Financing of Terrorism. As of the end of 2004, China was expected to enter the FATFs.[4]

On a more country specific basis, in 2003, the FATF faced the possibility that it might have to sanction the Philippines after it failed to address deficiencies in its procedures to combat dirty money. The country was given a one month deadline to strengthen its anti-money law.[5] Under the Second Non-Bank Governance Program, the Asian Development Bank approved a US$150 million loan to help the Philippines establish an effective anti-money laundering scheme and strengthen the country's financial sector.[6] Essentially the loan is intended to help the Philippines address corruption in financial markets, improve transparency, strengthen investor protection and promote the mobilization of domestic savings.

In February 2003, the Asia Development Bank announced it would provide a US$1 million technical assistance grant to help develop nonbanking and capital markets and counter money laundering in support of Vietnam's financial reforms.[7]

The Asia Pacific Economic Council (APEC) group includes 21 Pacific Rim nations: Australia, Brunei, Canada, Chile, China, Hong Kong, Indonesia, Japan, Malaysia, Mexico, New Zealand, Papua new Guinea, Peru, the Philippines, Russia, Singapore, south Korea, Taiwan, Thailand, the U.S. and Vietnam. The APEC group met post-September 11, 2001 to address the strengthening of laws against money laundering and terrorist financing.[8]

In May 2001, the Cook Islands joined the Asia Pacific Group on Money Laundering.[9] By November 2001, the Cook Islands, Federated States of Micronesia, Fiji, Nauru, Palau, Samoa and Vanuatu had established anti-money laundering laws. At the time, legislation was still considered inadequate in Nauru. The Pacific Islands Prudential Regulation and supervision Initiative (PIPRSI) have also been established in an attempt to reduce the likelihood that these nations will fall victim to financial crimes.

In Singapore the Evidence Act has been broadened allowing courts to accept electronic evidence in prosecutions. The 1997 Corruption, Drug Trafficking and Serious Offences Act contain serious penalties for persons involved in money laundering. A cybercrime task force was formed in 2000 to address the problems associated with e-commerce and financial crimes.

5. CONCLUSION

Money laundering remains a global phenomenon. International efforts continue to be made to address the problem of money laundering, particularly in the Asia-Pacific region. The proposed new Basel Capital Accord identifies credit, market, interest rate and operational risk as four types of risk that banks closely need to monitor.[10] Operational risk refers to " ... the risk of direct or indirect loss resulting from inadequate or failed internal processes, people and systems or from external events." In a money-laundering context, operation risk is the most important. Banks still remain a very vulnerable part of the money laundering process. Thus, to cover this risk, regulators need to make sure that banks have adequate measures in place to minimize the abuse of their services by money launderers. Added to that is the additional difficulty of monitoring possible money laundering via e-commerce transactions. Ways to combat money laundering through e-commerce could include the reinforcement of current customer identification requirements, stronger "know your customer" rules, prohibiting unlicensed financial institutions from offering their services and improving technological capabilities to detect suspicious online transactions.

In this paper, I have presented a clinical examination of the money laundering process and global efforts to address anti-money laundering regulation in the Asia-Pacific region. To resolve the problems associated with money laundering will require co-operative links among regulatory, law enforcement agencies and the public and private sector both within and across borders. A coordinated response will be required for detection and investigation of this transnational activity.

NOTES

1. Russian Organized crime: Crime without punishment", *The Economist*, 28 August 1999.
2. Jonathan M. Winer, How to clean up dirty money, *The Financial Times*, 23–24 March 2002.
3. Philippine Peso hit by money laundering allegations, *Asia Pulse*, 20 August 2003.
4. Statement issued by G20 ministers in Berlin, *Reuters News*, 22 November 2004.
5. Manila stocks seen down on dirty money Law worries, *Reuters News*, 17 February 2003.
6. ADB to help Philippines set up anti-money laundering regime, *Asia Pulse*, 4 September 2003.
7. ADB to provide further US$ 1 MLN for Vietnam financial markets, *Asia Pulse*, 24 February 2003.
8. Asia-Pacific finance chiefs seek to block terror financing, David Williams. Agency France-Press, 5 September 2002.
9. Cook Islands outlines measures against money lsaundering, *BBC Monitoring Asia-Pacific*, 22 October, 2001.
10. Refer to www.bis.org.

REFERENCES

Buchanan, B. (2004). Money laundering – a global obstacle. *Research in International Business and Finance, 18*, 115–127.
Dearden, S. (2003). The challenge to corruption and the international business environment. In: J. Kidd & F. J. Richter (Eds), *Corruption and governance in Asia*. (pp. 27–42) New York.
Errico, L., & Musalem, A. (1999) *Offshore banking: An analysis of micro- and macro-prudential issues*. IMF Working Paper. Wp/99/5 56p.
Gupta, S., Davoodi, H., & Alonso-Terme, R. (2002). Does corruption affect income inequality and poverty? *Economics of Governance, 3*(1, Heidelberg March), 23–45.
Kumar, B. V. (1996). Unaccountable funds and underground banking – An Indian perspective. In: Rider Barry & Ashe Michael (Eds), *Money Laundering Control*. Ireland: Rand Hall, Sweet and Maxwell.
Lilliey, P. (2003) In: J. Kidd & F.J. Richter (Eds), Asian money laundering explosion, fighting corruption in Asia – Causes, effects and remedies. Singapore: World Scientific Co. Ltd.
Mauro, P. (1995). Corruption and growth. *Quarterly Journal of Economics, 10*(3), 661–712.
Mauro, P. (1996) *The effects of corruption on growth, investment and government expenditure*. International Monetary Fund Working Paper. 96/98.
Quirk, P. J. (1996) *Macroeconomic implications of money laundering*. IMF Working Paper, 96/66, pp. 1–33.
Schneider, F., & Enste, D. (2000). Shadow economies: Size, causes and consequences. *The Journal of Economic Literature, 38*(1), 77–114.
Schramm, M., & Taube, M. (2003). Evolution and the institutional foundation of the Hawala system. *International Review of Financial Analysis, 12*, 405–420.

Shehu, A. Y. (2003). The Asian alternative remittance systems and money laundering. *Journal of Money Laundering Control, 7*(2), 175–185.

Tan, S. T. (2002). Money laundering and e-commerce. *Journal of Financial Crime, 9*(3), 277–285.

Tanzi, V. (1996). *Money laundering and the International Financial System.* IMF Working Paper, 96/55. pp. 1–14.

Tanzi, V., & Davoodi, H. (1997) Corruption, public investment and growth. IMF Working Paper. 95/139 Washington: International Monetary Fund.

Walter, I. (1990). *The secret money market* (376 pp.). New York: Harper & Row.

www.bis.org Basel Committee on Banking Supervision, Operational Risk.

A TEST OF THE RESPONSE TO A MONETARY POLICY REGIME CHANGE IN NEW ZEALAND [☆]

David Tripe, John McDermott and Ben Petro

ABSTRACT

In March 1999, the Reserve Bank of New Zealand changed its method of implementing monetary policy from targeting settlement cash to specifying an (official) Overnight Cash Rate (OCR). This paper explores some of the impacts of this, by comparing market movements before and after the change.

We find that, since the introduction of the OCR, key lending interest rates have been found to be more responsive to changes in official monetary policy, with a significant shortening of the half-life of interest rate changes. This suggests that monetary policy is now more efficient, while the speed of response supports the case for regarding the New Zealand banking market as competitive.

[☆] An earlier version of this paper was presented at the 7th New Zealand Finance Colloquium in Palmerston North in February 2003.

Asia Pacific Financial Markets in Comparative Perspective: Issues and Implications for the 21ˢᵗ Century
Contemporary Studies in Economics and Financial Analysis, Volume 86, 453–467
Copyright © 2005 by Elsevier Ltd.
ISSN: 1569-3759/doi:10.1016/S1569-3759(05)86019-X

1. INTRODUCTION

One of the Reserve Bank of New Zealand's objectives as enshrined in its governing legislation is that it should be promoting a financial system that is not only sound, but also efficient. Among the areas in which efficiency is to be pursued is in respect of the implementation of monetary policy. This study looks at the impact of a change in the procedures for implementation of monetary policy on the efficiency with which that policy achieves its goals.

Monetary policy assumed a particular significance in New Zealand as it was the primary instrument used to try and combat the severe inflation which had characterised the New Zealand economy for much of the 1970s and 1980s. A formal inflation targeting regime (the world's first) was adopted following the enactment of the Reserve Bank of New Zealand Act (1989), and as public confidence that inflation levels would be lower grew during the 1990s, the previously high interest rates gradually reduced.[1]

As inflation and interest rates have reduced, there have been changes to the Reserve Bank's approach to monetary policy, both in terms of the inflation target and the instruments used. A key change was on 17 March 1999, when the Reserve Bank of New Zealand (RBNZ) switched to use of an Official Cash Rate (OCR) as its basic monetary policy instrument. This sets the basic rates at which banks can borrow and lend overnight from the RBNZ, with actual rates 25 basis points above and below the OCR.[2] This change in monetary policy instrument has provided an opportunity to review the operation of monetary policy in New Zealand, and more particularly to understand something about the pass-through from the policy rate to both short and longer-term interest rates in the New Zealand economy.

The OCR is set eight times a year (although the RBNZ has power to intervene intra-meeting) and can remain unchanged for long periods of time (it was held steady at 6.50% for 10 months during 2000). As with official interest rates in other countries, a change in the OCR is well publicised, and even though it is only an overnight rate, it potentially influences interest rates all along the yield curve, although effects are stronger for shorter maturities, where the arbitrage effects of an official rate change are strongest. The OCR's effects are weaker at longer maturities, which are more influenced by interest rate and inflation expectations. Movements of longer term rates might be expected to be more important for monetary policy, as they would be more likely to influence firms' and households' spending decisions.

Brookes and Hampton (2000) reviewed the new OCR regime one-year into its existence. They concluded that the new system was working well and that it appeared to be effective, simple, transparent and efficient. Their main focus was on the effects on short-term interest and exchange rate volatility, transaction volumes and market behaviour. International comparisons showed that, since the OCR's inception, the average daily change in overnight interest rates had reduced significantly, and that New Zealand rates were less volatile than those of Australia, Canada, the USA and the UK.

The reduction in cash rate volatility since the OCR has been implemented is highlighted in Fig. 1. Under the previous regime, the cash rate was market determined and fluctuated frequently. Banks sought to influence the cash rate to benefit trading positions by shifting other parts of the yield curve as well as influencing the cash rate at which they could borrow or lend overnight, with this reflected in high volatility in New Zealand interest rate markets.

The reduced volatility of the cash rate in New Zealand has coincided with reduced volatility in longer term money market rates including the 90-day bank bill rate and the one to three-year swap rates. Brookes and Hampton (2000) also suggested that the reduced volatility of short-term interest rates since the OCR's introduction might have enabled banks to reduce margins on floating rate mortgages, but they provided no evidence to support this.

This paper investigates this relationship between the cash rate, money market interest rates and interest rates charged by financial institutions in New Zealand. The interest rates examined are the standard floating and one, two and three year fixed residential mortgage rates, over the period from

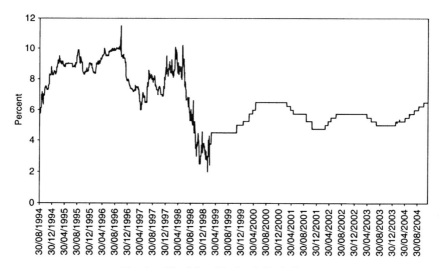

Fig. 1. The New Zealand Cash Rate.

July 1994 to August 2001. These are the lending rates most widely publicised and discussed in the New Zealand market, which reflects the significance of residential mortgage lending in New Zealand banks' assets. Moreover, the rates advertised are the rates charged, rather than being a base or prime rate subject to an additional margin.

Because we are looking at pass-throughs, we would expect to generate some insights into the operation of monetary policy in New Zealand, and in particular, on the effects that arise from a change in the instruments used for implementation of monetary policy.

In the next section of the paper, we review some institutional characteristics of the New Zealand market against the background of prior research, which will help us develop some expectations with regard to results. In Section 3 we look at the method employed and data used for this research, while Section 4 discusses the results and concludes.

2. FEATURES OF THE NEW ZEALAND MARKET

There are a number of institutional and historical characteristics of the New Zealand banking market that affect the way in which prior research relates to that reported in this paper. Cottarelli and Kourelis (1994) have argued that the effectiveness of monetary policy hinges on a set of structural parameters, not directly controlled by central banks, and it is thus reasonable to expect that differences in financial system structure between countries may in turn lead to differences in the way in which monetary policy has its effect.

One of the key features of the New Zealand market is the emphasis on property lending, and residential mortgage lending in particular. This is at least in part a consequence of the high inflation of the 1970s and 1980s, when property assets were seen as a good vehicle for preserving wealth. Moreover, property provided good opportunities to increase wealth if funds could be borrowed to allow investors to utilise gearing. Following the liberalisation of borrowing in the 1980s, banks looked to respond to customer demand and increase their lending in this sector, a process that was further encouraged by the adoption of the 1988 Basel Capital Accord for banks in the early 1990s.

The emphasis on residential mortgage lending has continued, and according to Reserve Bank of New Zealand data, lending for housing comprised 50.2% of M3 claims as at 30 June 2004.[3] Because of the importance of housing lending, the interest rates applying to it are widely advertised, and are seen as important in competition between the banks. Even though most New Zealand banks operate some sort of base rate system for some of their lending, comparable to what is referred to as the prime rate in the United States, it is the housing lending rates that attract public attention.

Residential mortgage lending rates are adjusted according to a process somewhat similar to that which applies to that applying to prime rate changes in the United States (Mester & Saunders, 1995). The changes occur primarily in response to changes in the underlying cost of funds: for floating rates, the relevant rates are the overnight and 90-day bank bill rates, while for fixed rate lending, the relevant market rates are the corresponding swap rates. The emphasis on the swap rates reflects the predominantly short maturity of New Zealand bank funding, which means that banks must enter into interest rate swaps where they pay fixed, receive floating (usually 90-day bank bill), if they wish to avoid significant exposure to interest rate risk. For these longer term fixed rates, the relevant swap rates are thus the marginal cost of funds. Money market rates are important as all the major New Zealand banks have some dependence on wholesale funding (making them more responsive to changes in market rates). A further consequence of this is that major banks tend to have more or less identical floating rates, with any differences in fixed rates also tending to be very small.

In some contexts, loan default rate has been perceived as being a factor influencing loan interest rates (Ho & Saunders, 1981).[4] Since the early 1990s, however, New Zealand banks have had very low levels of losses in their loan portfolios, reflecting generally favourable economic conditions, and there is no indication that loan loss experience has had any impact on residential mortgage interest rates. In any case, if any one bank had been affected, competitive pressures would make it very difficult to charge a standard lending rate that was significantly different from that charged by its competitors.

Ho and Saunders also postulated that there should be a positive relationship between interest rate volatility and banks' interest margins. In this case, if interest rate volatility in New Zealand has reduced with the introduction of the OCR, the consequent reduction in uncertainty as to banks' cost of funds should have led to a reduction in the margin between the lending rates and the underlying money market rates.

Another factor identified as important in terms of banks' lending rates is competitive conditions (Berger & Hannan, 1989). In the New Zealand context it is considered reasonable to look at a single national market for residential mortgage lending (except in rare circumstances, the rates charged are uniform across the whole country). Between 1996 and 2003 the

Herfindahl–Hirschman Index (a standard measure of industrial concentration) for banks' residential mortgage lending ranged between 1673 and 1940. In terms of the US Department of Justice criteria, this would normally be regarded as indicative of relatively high concentration (Rhoades, 1993; Amel, 1996). On the other hand, exploratory research using the Rosse-Panzar statistic failed to find any evidence for anything more disadvantageous to consumers than that the New Zealand market was characterised by monopolistic competition (Smith & Tripe, 2001). The New Zealand banking market is seen as contestable, with no quantitative barriers to entry or exit. We also note that the banks appear to compete vigorously in the market for residential mortgage lending, so that there is no obvious reflection of inadequate competition.

We note that banks are active in both floating and fixed rate lending, with fixed rate lending originally promoted during the 1990s as away for banks to reduce the interest rate risk applying to non-interest sensitive liabilities. Fixed rate lending has now become a major part of banks' portfolios, reflecting both borrower concern at the potentially adverse trends in the level of floating rates, and the relative prevalence of negatively sloping yield curves for residential mortgage loans, which has meant that headline fixed rates have often been lower than headline floating rates. Thus, at 30 June 2004, only 31.0% by value of loans were at floating rates. The term of fixed rates is inclined to be relatively short: at 30 June 2004, 44.6% by value of fixed rate loans were due to reprice within 12 months.[5] The majority of fixed rate lending is fixed for one, two or three years.

Another feature of the New Zealand system is the way the Reserve Bank communicates its views on both current and expected future monetary policy positions: with the OCR in place, this has included a desired interest rate level. The bank strives for openness, which does not appear consistent with traditional precepts in relation to monetary policy, which are inclined to stress the importance of uncertainty in driving banks' responses. Cottarelli and Kourelis (1994), however, have argued that announcements by the central bank of a change in a benchmark interest rate can reduce uncertainty about other banks' responses, causing the relative administered rate (in this case the floating mortgage rate) to adjust relatively more promptly. As a result of the introduction of the OCR, which specifies an interest rate level, we therefore expect a prompt and direct pass-through to floating mortgage rates (subject only to significantly different changes in the 90-day rate). This change would also be likely to have been assisted by the reduction in volatility of the overnight rate, which should have reduced switching costs for banks of changing their residential mortgage lending rates.

It does not necessarily follow, however, that longer term rates should respond in the same way. One issue is the way that longer-term rates respond to changes in short term rates. The other issue, which we explore in this research, is in the way longer-term fixed rates respond to changes in the swap rates that underpin banks' cost of funds. A relatively prompt and direct pass-through would be presumed to indicate a relatively competitive market, providing for the efficient operation of monetary policy.

3. EMPIRICAL RESULTS

Our data set consists of daily observations of money market and retail lending interest rates. The data span the period from 30 August 1994 to 7 December 2004 offering a total of 2,585 observations. A full listing of data source and methods is given in the appendix. Our sample provides a rich body of data for studying the link between wholesale and retail interest rates since the monetary policy implementation regime was altered considerably during this timeframe. This offers a unique nature experiment for us to examine the behaviour of banks under different regimes.

Our aim is to test whether there has been a shift in the (long-run) relationship between lending rates and money market interest rates after the introduction of the OCR regime. The OCR regime has clearly reduced the volatility of money market rates. The standard deviations of the daily money market rates for our pre post-OCR samples are shown in Table 1. While the new regime will have altered the time-series properties of money market rates in some respects our central concern is with the longer-run properties, specifically whether the degree of pass-through from wholesale to retail market has changed.

First, we need to establish the time-series properties of the interest rate data to see if the possibility of a (long-run) or cointegrated relationship exists. We do that by employing unit root statistics to test the null hypothesis that interest rates follow a unit root process. Unit roots in individual

Table 1. Standard deviations of daily interest rate changes, before and after the introduction of the OCR regime.

	Cash	90 Days	1-year swap	2-year swap	3-year swap
Pre-OCR	1.814	1.525	1.255	1.003	0.899
Post-OCR	0.637	0.637	0.657	0.615	0.601

rates would imply nonstationarity in the rates but if the spreads between the rates are stationary then there must be (long-run) or cointegrating relationships between the rates. Second, we test for cointegration using a residual-based test. A useful by-product of this test is that average pass-through is estimated. Finally, we will use a Wald test to determine whether there is any change in the long-run relationships.

3.1. Unit Root Tests

We applied two sets of unit root tests to the data, both the augmented Dickey–Fuller (ADF) tests and the seminonparametric Phillips–Perron (PP) modifications of those tests. To control for the presence of serial correlation, lags of the first difference are included in the ADF regression while nonparametric adjustments are made to the PP regression. The number of lags in the ADF regression was determined using the general-to-specific lag selection procedure of Ng and Perron (1995) and Hall (1994), with the maximum lag set to 10. Results from the PP unit root test were computed using the Bartlet kernel and with lag lengths determined by the data-dependent method of Andrews (1991). Both testing procedures indicate that all the interest rates examined in this paper are integrated of order one and so the possibility of cointegration between lending rates and money market rates exists (Table 2).

3.2. Cointegration Tests

We commence with the standard model for cointegration, which in the context of this paper is

$$L_t = \alpha + \beta M_t + \varepsilon_t \tag{1}$$

where L_t is the lending rate at time t, M_t the money market rate at time t and ε_t a stationary error term that may be serially correlated and heterogeneously distributed. The error term may even be correlated to differences of the regressor introducing an endogeneity problem when estimating the cointegrating relationship. Using an asymptotically efficient estimator that makes an explicit correction for endogeneity can circumvent this problem. In particular, the cointegrating regression can be estimated using Phillips and Hansen's (1990) fully modified estimator, Park's (1992) canonical cointegrating regression, or Stock and Watson's (1993) dynamic OLS

Table 2. Unit Root Test for Interest Rates.

Interest Rate	ADF Test	PP Test
Money market rates		
90 day bank bill	$-1.37(2)$	$-1.30(0.62)$
1-year swap	$-1.36(1)$	$-1.34(3.60)$
2-year swap	$-1.53(0)$	$-1.54(1.88)$
3-year swap	$-1.73(0)$	$-1.73(0.08)$
Lending rates		
Floating	$-1.32(0)$	$-1.32(0.19)$
1-year fixed	$-1.46(0)$	$-1.47(1.27)$
2-year fixed	$-1.29(0)$	$-1.30(1.39)$
3-year fixed	$-1.62(0)$	$-1.63(1.11)$

Note: The results allow for serial correlation by including lagged first difference in the case of the ADF test or using a lag window in the case of the PP test. The number of lags in the ADF test was determined using the modified Hannan–Quinn method with the maximum lag set to 27. The number of lags required to control for serial correlation is shown in parentheses. Results from the PP unit root test were computed using the Bartlett kernel and with bandwidth determined by the data-dependent method of Andrews (1991). The 5% critical values is -2.86 (Hamilton, 1994, p. 763). The required bandwidth is shown in parentheses.

estimator, which are all asymptotically efficient in the presence of serial correlation and endogeneity.[6]

We use Stock and Watson's dynamic OLS estimator, which was independently proposed by Saikkonen (1991), and found to be asymptotically efficient under very general conditions. To implement the dynamic OLS estimator, one simply regresses the lending rate onto contemporaneous levels of the money market rate, leads and lags of their first difference, and a constant.

The results of the Phillips–Ouliaris (1990) $Z(t)$ residual-based tests for cointegration, computed using the residuals from the Stock and Watson dynamic OLS cointegrating regression of Eq. (1), reject the null hypothesis of no cointegration between lending rates and money market rates at the 5% significance level for all time horizons and all subperiods (Table 3). There is a long-run link between money market and lending rates over the whole sample period despite the diverse monetary policy implementation regimes being in place.

We also report the estimated coefficients of the cointegrating regression for both pre- and post-OCR periods together with the full sample period. The estimated slope coefficients in the fixed interest markets are all close to unity indicating a high degree of pass-through from wholesale to retail rates.

Table 3.   Cointegration Tests between Lending and Money Market
Rates.

Time Horizon	Pre-OCR			Post-OCR			Full Sample		
	α	β	$Z(t)$	α	β	$Z(t)$	α	β	$Z(t)$
Floating	3.18	0.83	−5.64	1.88	1.00	−6.97	2.36	0.92	−8.47
1 year	0.96	1.03	−5.00	1.20	0.98	−5.75	0.85	1.04	−7.48
2 year	1.22	1.02	−4.14	1.41	0.95	−6.29	0.66	1.07	−6.19
3 year	1.38	1.00	−4.09	1.36	0.97	−9.00	0.74	1.07	−6.45

Note: Parameter estimates have been obtained from Stock and Watson (1993) dynamic OLS
estimation of the cointegrating regression equation (1). The lags and leads were determined
using the general-to-specific approach, starting from a maximum of 10 leads and lags and
sequential reducing them until the longest lag or lead is significant. The coefficient estimates on
the lead and lagged first differences are omitted for reasons of space. $Z(t)$ is the Phillips–
Ouliaris (1990) residual-based cointegration test – the 5% critical value for this test is − 3.37; an
asterisk (∗) indicates that the null hypothesis of a cointegration can be rejected at the 5% level
of significance. The Phillips–Ouliaris (1990) cointegration test was computed using the residuals
from the Stock and Watson (1993) dynamic OLS cointegrating regression of Eq. (1), the
Bartlett kernel, and lag lengths were determined by the data-dependent method of Andrews
(1991).

However, for floating interest rates there seems to a marked difference in this
slope coefficient. In the pre-OCR regime the coefficient is much less than
unity, while in the post-OCR regime it is exactly one. This suggests the degree
of pass-through in floating interest rates rose sharply following the introduction of the OCR regime. We will formally test this proposition below.

3.3. Regime Change Test

The final task is to test whether the slope coefficients from the pre-OCR
sample are less than the slope coefficients from the post-OCR sample. To do
this we use a Wald test that has been suitably corrected for the error term
being serially correlated and heterogeneously distributed and correlated
with first differences of the regressor (see Stock and Watson (1993) for
details). This test has the usual Chi-square asymptotic distribution.

The Wald statistics are 369.8, 54.3, 241.9 and 212.5 for the equations and
the floating, one-, two- and three-year horizons, respectively. All these results are significantly in excess of the 5% critical value of 3.84. This provides
very strong evidence of a significant change in how mortgage market pricing
has operated following the introduction of the OCR regime. The biggest

change has occurred in how retail floating mortgages price off the wholesale market.

4. DISCUSSION AND CONCLUSION

The previous section has shown that the pass-through from money market rates to loan rates has been stronger for floating interest rate loans since the OCR has been in place, and that volatility in both money market and loan rates has been reduced. These findings are broadly consistent with the general precepts outlined in Section 2. The quick responses would seem to be generally consistent with a competitive banking market, and with a speedy reaction by the banks in their interest rates to changes in monetary policy settings by the Reserve Bank of New Zealand. The effectiveness of the Reserve Bank's action may, however, be limited to some extent by the increasing proportion of banks' loan portfolios that is at fixed interest rates. An investigation of pass-through along the yield curve, from short-term rates to the swap rates that underpin banks fixed rate lending is beyond the scope of this paper.

Bank policy plays an important role in the level of pass-through. This includes loss-leading campaigns to build market share, the structure of balance sheets and regulatory capital requirements. Market share is sometimes chosen by banks as a policy over profitability and margins are reduced as a result. Regardless of fluctuations in money market rates, banks forego profit in attempt to gain new customers. These campaigns tend, however, to be temporary and the lending rates often return to 'market' levels once specific targets have been reached. This sort of situation has been evident in late 2004, with the banks waging a vigorous campaign to try and report the lowest rate for two-year fixed rate lending. In these sorts of campaigns the banks have actively encouraged borrowers to switch, with fees for new loans commonly being negative (in that the banks will often offer to contribute to borrowers' legal fees relative to switching mortgage providers).

The final issue is volatility reduction and its effect on the degree of pass-through and the margin. The New Zealand wholesale interest rate market is a lot more transparent since the OCR has been in place, with changes in the OCR publicised as soon as they occur, and with these changes filtering through to residential mortgage rates, particularly the floating rate. The changes normally take effect immediately for new borrowers but with a time lag of approximately a month for existing borrowers. Changes are less rapid further along the yield curve.

Under the previous cash rate regime, a cash rate movement did not always lead to a change in lending rates. The likelihood of the cash rate being at a different level over the next few days was high given the volatile nature of the market. If a bank were to change lending rates, especially the floating rate, whenever the cash rate changed, they would be doing so frequently, with a consequent increase in costs. These costs include customer notification, system alteration costs and re-training/educating staff. Banks would therefore charge a higher margin to smooth revenue and compensate themselves for their volatile cost of funds. This is also evident in the volatility of the spread, which has also reduced since the OCR has been in place.

The degree of pass-through is now greater for floating rate loans (see Wald test in the previous section). Banks are able to budget their cost of funds in the knowledge that the lending rates and money market rates will have a stronger relationship to the OCR, which has become a benchmark for lending rates.

The impact of monetary policy on the real economy depends on the pass-through of policy levers like the OCR being rapid and complete. Certain factors such as competition will prevent pass through being one for one but the implementation of the OCR has given the Reserve Bank more control over the economy, as money markets now have a closer relationship with the corresponding lending rates.

This paper has examined the effects of the OCR implementation on residential lending rates in New Zealand. We find that since 17 March 1999 there has been a significant decline in the volatility of both underlying money market rates and margins. There has also been a significant structural change in the relationship between the money market and relevant lending rates, with margins relative to floating rates having widened, whereas those relative to the one- to three- year fixed rates have narrowed.

NOTES

1. Both overnight and 90-day rates had consistently been in excess of 10% up until 25 June and 16 May 1991, respectively.

2. Details of the OCR and the background to it are provided in Archer, Brookes, and Reddell (1999).

3. Total lending to the household sector comprised 50.2% of claims, or 57.5% of claims on New Zealand resident, non-M3 counterparties. Data have been derived from Reserve Bank of New Zealand data tables C4 and C7. The figures for lending for housing as part of M3 are very close to the total figures for assets secured by residential mortgage, as reported by each of the banks in their quarterly disclosure

statements. This is despite the M3 data identifying lending by purpose rather than by security, and the lack of complete correspondence between the group of institutions whose balance sheets are reported as part of M3 and the set of all registered banks.

4. Note that the Ho and Saunders (1981) dealership approach would also be consistent with there being a stable margin between loan rates and the underlying cost of funds.

5. Data on the term structure and related interest rates applying to New Zealand banks' residential mortgage loan portfolios reported in the statistical table HSSR-Part E, available on the Reserve Bank's web-site at http://www.rbnz.govt.nz.

6. Ordinary least-squares (OLS) estimation could be used to yield a super-consistent estimate of the cointegrating vector, where the endogeneity problem vanishes asymptotically. However, OLS estimation has rather poor small sample properties, is not asymptotically efficient, and yields non-standard distributions of the estimators. Consequently, standard test of linear restriction cannot be used in the OLS framework, a severe disadvantage given we wish to use a Wald test to examine if the degree of pass-through has varied over regimes.

7. Reserve Bank of New Zealand data are available on its web-site at http://www.rbnz.govt.nz.

REFERENCES

Amel, D. F. (1996, January). Trends in the structure of federally insured depository institutions. *Federal Reserve Bulletin, 82*(1), 1–15.

Andrews, D. W. K. (1991). Heteroskedasticity and autocorrelation consistent covariance matrix estimation. *Econometrica, 59*, 817–888.

Archer, D., Brookes, A., & Reddell, M. (1999). A cash rate system for implementing monetary policy. *Reserve Bank of New Zealand Bulletin, 62*(1), 51–61.

Berger, A. N., & Hannan, T. H. (1989). The price–concentration relationship in banking. *The Review of Economics and Statistics, 71*(2), 291–299.

Brookes, A., & Hampton, T. (2000). The official cash rate one year on. *Reserve Bank of New Zealand Bulletin, 63*(2), 53–61.

Cottarelli, C., & Kourelis, A. (1994). Financial structure, bank lending rates, and the transmission mechanism of monetary policy. *IMF Staff Papers, 41*(4), 587–623.

Hall, A. (1994). Testing for a unit root in time series with pretest data-based model selection. *Journal of Business and Economic Statistics, 12*, 461–470.

Hamilton, J. D. (1994). *Time Series Analysis*. Princeton, NJ: Princeton University Press.

Ho, T. S. Y., & Saunders, A. (1981). The determinants of bank interest margins: Theory and empirical evidence. *Journal of Financial and Quantitative Analysis, 16*, 581–600.

Mester, L. J., & Saunders, A. (1995). When does the prime rate change? *Journal of Banking and Finance, 19*, 743–764.

Ng, S., & Perron, P. (1995). Unit root tests in ARMA models with data-dependent methods for the selection of the truncation lag. *Journal of the American Statistical Association, 90*, 268–281.

Park, J. (1992). Canonical cointegrating regressions. *Econometrica, 60*, 119–143.

Phillips, P. C. B., & Hansen, B. E. (1990). Statistical inference in instrumental variable regression with I(1) processes. *Review of Economic Studies, 57*, 99–125.

Phillips, P. C. B., & Ouliaris, S. (1990). Asymptotic properties of residual-based tests for cointegration. *Econometrica, 58,* 165–193.

Rhoades, S. A. (1993, March). The Herfindahl–Hirschman index. *Federal Reserve Bulletin,* 188–189.

Saikkonen, P. (1991). Asymptotically efficient estimation of cointegration regressions. *Econometric Theory, 7,* 1–21.

Smith, R., & Tripe, D. (2001). *Competition and contestability in New Zealand's banking system.* Paper presented at the 14th Australasian Finance and Banking Conference, Sydney. Available at http://centre-banking-studies.massey.ac.nz.

Stock, J., & Watson, M. (1993). A simple estimator of cointegrating vectors in higher order systems. *Econometrica, 61,* 783–820.

APPENDIX: DATA

Lending rate data for this research were obtained from the National Bank of New Zealand (NBNZ), while Fixed Interest Securities (FIS) provided money market and cash rate data. The cash rate data utilised were the RBNZ's inter-bank rate for New Zealand settlement banks to square up cash positions at the end of each business day.[7] The bank bill rate used is the mid rate as at 10:30 am each business day, with this derived from rate-setting activity by participating banks, and which is also used as the benchmark for daily derivative settlements. The swap rates are the semi annual rates at the close of business (4:30 pm) each day. The lending rates used are the floating and one to three-year fixed rate mortgages for residential borrowers. The sample period was 30 August 1994 to 7 December 2004.

One weakness identified is that the lending rate data have been obtained from only one source. The loan market is far from homogenous and there are a number of factors which banks consider when they set lending rates, including cost of funds, contract terms of the loan including maturity, repayment clauses, collateral and fee structures. We have, however, assumed that a bank would receive negative publicity for not conforming with the rest of the market and would lose market share over time. Any differences in rates between the main mortgage providers are likely to be negligible, with a difference of 5–10 bp the norm. Obviously some banks will have cheaper access to funding or offer 'special' rates to entice new clientele but we also assume that over time that this has a minimal effect on the general movements in interest rates.

Another weakness relates to the source of data for swap rates. The rates used in this research are termed as semi annual i.e. the floating leg of the swap is paid/reset at semi annual intervals. The swap rates used to hedge the fixed rate loans are predominantly priced on a quarterly basis, i.e. the floating leg of the swap is reset/paid at quarterly intervals. Whilst this will affect the spread (the current difference between a 2 year semi-annual and a 2 year quarterly rate is 4 bp), the difference between semi-annual and quarterly rate will remain relatively constant over time.

There will also be a lag in the lending rate changes. In some instances rates charged to customers will not be altered for up to a month, to allow for systems changes and customer notification. Banks may participate in asymmetric price setting behaviour depending on whether the change in money market rates is a decrease or an increase. The actual cost of providing these funds will also not be entirely accurate. Banks use derivative instruments such as Forward Rate Agreements (FRAs), options and forward starting swaps to mitigate potential losses as a result of adverse interest rate movements. The spread is therefore a snapshot in time, valid for the observed day only.

The way the data have been recorded assumes that all loans made on that day are funded at the actual rate for the money market instrument on that day. This is not the case: derivative instruments may have been used, and loans will therefore often be placed in time series buckets and hedged as a group rather than individually.

THE PROSPECTS OF A REGIONAL MONETARY INSTITUTION FOR THE ASIA PACIFIC

Justin W. Iu

ABSTRACT

The Asian Monetary Fund, proposed during the 1997–1998 Asian Financial Crisis, was an attempt by East Asian nations to develop collective policy responses to financial crises and provide rapid distribution of emergency funding. It was envisaged that policy prescriptions would exhibit greater regional sensitivity and prevent contagion. The proposal was rejected because of the perceived perpetuation of moral hazard, duplication and conflict with the International Monetary Fund and belief that historical disunity would prevent successful collaboration. This paper advocates, in the context of international financial architecture reform, enhanced East Asian regionalism is crucial to prevent and manage future financial crises.

1. INTRODUCTION

Efforts to reform the international financial architecture have tended to focus on national markets and global organisations while largely ignoring

Asia Pacific Financial Markets in Comparative Perspective: Issues and Implications for the 21st Century
Contemporary Studies in Economics and Financial Analysis, Volume 86, 469–505
ISSN: 1569-3759/doi:10.1016/S1569-3759(05)86020-6

the place of regional-level institutions. However, a noticeable feature of the 1997–1998 Asian Financial Crisis (hereafter 'the Crisis') was that it exhibited a distinctly regional character. That is, countries within East Asia experienced the most immediate and extensive distress. This being the case, it becomes pertinent to discuss the development of a regionally based, rapid response mechanism capable of dealing with the occurrence of future financial crises.

At the height of the Crisis, the Japanese Government proposed the creation of a regionally based monetary institution known as the Asian Monetary Fund (AMF). The proposal to create the AMF came as a direct response to the diminishing faith of East Asian governments in the ability of international policy makers to prescribe solutions to the incidence of financial crises. The proposal was an attempt to pool the foreign currency reserves of members in order for the AMF to act as a regional lender of last resort providing liquidity in the event of a crisis (Sakakibara, 2000).

The AMF was intended to provide a quick distribution of funds, with low conditionality, to defend Asian countries against speculative attacks and balance of payment problems. Supporters of the AMF suggested that by being based within the region, more appropriate and culturally sensitive policy responses could be formulated to prevent prolonged and severe periods of economic turmoil. Importantly, the AMF was to redress criticisms in International Monetary Fund (IMF) prescriptions (below). Indeed, the AMF was mooted as an alternative to the existing international financial institutions, such as the IMF, as a means of protecting East Asian states against the vagaries of volatile capital flows.

1.1. The Story So Far

The original proposal called for a commitment of $US100 billon to create the AMF. Half of this amount was to be pledged by Japan with the remaining half contributed by other regional powers including China or Singapore (Narine, 2002). The initiative was, however, effectively rejected at an international level by insurmountable opposition, which emanated primarily from the United States. Having succumbed to the initial opposition, the AMF was reincarnated in 1998 as the New Miyazawa Plan. Funding would still be based on lower conditionality determined by regional surveillance. The total amount was reduced from $US100 billion to $US30 billion. The mechanics of distribution would be through a series of bilateral swaps between members. In either case, funding could have enabled countries to guarantee sovereign bond issues, which were necessary to support expenditures.

In a further development, the members of the Association of South East Asian Nations (ASEAN) and their dialogue partners China, Japan and Korea agreed to the Chiang Mai Initiative in 2000. The basis of the Chiang Mai initiative was similar to the Miyazawa Plan in that Bilateral Swap Arrangements were the centrepiece. It was to provide quick activation and disbursement in the advent of a financial crisis through coordinated decision-making (Park, 2000). The Chiang Mai Initiative was seen as a historic "first step towards the creation of a full-fledged monetary facility" (Chang & Rajan, 2001, p. 107).

The Chiang Mai Initiative brought the region together to meet the mutual objective of financial stability in a less formal way than AMF. Sakakibara (2000) suggested these elements should be formally institutionalised via an AMF. Bergsten and Park (2002) recommend that the creation of the AMF be attempted only after a fuller range of regional financial linkages are established under Chiang Mai Initiative. But with the initiative in place Chang and Rajan (2001) conclude that "creation of a regional monetary facility would be a natural evolution ... and a recognition of the region's commonality of interests" (p. 113).

Despite the progress made through Chiang Mai and ever since the AMF movement was first abandoned, there have been signs that the establishment of the AMF remains an unfulfilled policy aspiration within East Asia. In the course of 2003, several high-profile politicians and commentators renewed calls for East Asian states to work towards regional cooperation on monetary policy through an AMF. Former Japanese Vice-Minister for Finance Eisuke Sakakibara, for example, said "I strongly endorse the establishment of an AMF, the time has come for us to make some solid progress". Notably, the Prime Ministers of Thailand and Malaysia have also lent their support to the concept. At a meeting of regional leaders in 2004, Malaysian Prime Minister Badawi once again broached the subject. Thus, as the post-crisis reform of the international financial architecture continues to proceed, it is opportune to reconsider the case for (and against) establishing the AMF.

The notion underlying the creation of the AMF – that benefits can be gained from familiarity with the specific needs of countries – was sound. However, obtaining the consensus required for effective regional cooperation is fraught with difficulties. Political and cultural imperatives often have a greater role in determining the success of multilateral cooperation than economic linkages (that already exist within the region). East Asia is a dynamic region with many and varied cultural traits. Such diversity and competing national interests have caused significant conflicts and tensions throughout the region's history.

In this context, the primary purpose of this paper is to reconsider the challenges to achieving the integration of East Asian monetary policy as imagined under the AMF and advocate that collective action in East Asia is crucial to prevent and manage future financial crises. Moreover, the paper will determine the validity of the initial rejection of the idea, because the benefits of regionalism and a regional institution can contribute to the stability of international markets. This is a critical aspect that needs attention within the reform of international financial architecture.

The remainder of the paper shall focus on three substantive themes. First, an exploration of current economic linkages and institutional similarities between East Asian states will be conducted. The second part of this paper examines historical, political and cultural conflicts within the region that impact upon the potential to achieve collective action in the region. By adopting a political perspective it is hoped that the imbalance towards economic issues in the literature will be redressed. Finally, evidence of existing regional ties will be shown as supporting the creation of the regional monetary response mechanism and also the ability of Asian countries to combine with common purpose.

2. BUILDING THE CASE FOR THE AMF

2.1. The Need for Reform

International financial markets are, by their nature, characterised by volatility. Bhagwati (1998) attributes such volatility to the unrestricted movement of financial capital. While risk caused by capital mobility is largely unavoidable, to the extent governments are unwilling to institute restrictions on capital flows, better attempts at reducing the severity and frequency of crises caused by the situation are imperative (Fischer, 1999). The unpredictability of short-term capital flows above all needs to be controlled so that the potentially devastating effects of future crises can be managed (Stiglitz, 2002; King, 1999). The ability to manage crises relies heavily on the construction of the international financial architecture.[1]

The international financial architecture has been defined in various ways. The World Bank (2000) suggests the international financial architecture "refers broadly to the framework and set of measures that can help prevent crises and manage them better in the more integrated international financial environment" (p. 1). Thus, a principal function of the international financial architecture is responding to the occurrence of financial crises. From this it can be inferred that the international financial architecture comprises two main facets: rules and the institutions that set those rules. The institutions work to preserve an environment within which market participants can interact in an orderly fashion, to ensure the stability of capital markets and limit potential crises.

The task of controlling and preventing instability in modern financial markets continues to be borne by the international financial institutions created under the Bretton Woods Agreement of 1944. (Respective national regulators also play a role in the discipline of domestic markets, although the duty for responding to international crises falls predominantly on international institutions). However, following a series of financial crises at the end of the 20th century in Latin America, Russia and Asia, these institutions were increasingly forced to justify their relevance.[2] Much of the criticism came from a growing awareness that both the institutions themselves *and* the financial system over which they presided were inadequate for coping with contemporary market problems, including increased capital mobility (Haggard, 2001).

Among the primary complaints was that the central tenet of Bretton Woods – fixed exchange rates – was abandoned in 1971 and replaced with a system of floating exchange rates. Yet, the institutions that oversaw this development did not adapt. The concern is that as the issues facing the world are now very different from when Bretton Woods was signed, its institutions have become antiquated. This has meant the international financial architecture failed to equally distribute the benefits and risks of capital mobility. Indeed, there is a virtually palpable feeling that the outcomes of the system are unsatisfactory.

The IMF especially came under tremendous scrutiny. The responsibility for maintaining global financial stability is firmly entrenched in the IMF's original mandate. As the Crisis deepened and instability gripped more nations within the region, the task of finding a solution fell largely upon those at the IMF. It is an important element of the international financial architecture, acting as a quasi-international lender of last resort for those countries who face liquidity or balance of payments issues. As Fischer (1999) states "[t]he role of the lender of last resort is to offer an assurance of credit, given under certain limited conditions, which will stop a financial panic from spreading – or better still, stop it from even getting worse" (p. 86). Sadly, the approaches recommended by the IMF failed to inspire.[3]

The stability of the international financial system greatly depends on the existence of institutions capable of adequately dealing with the periodic crises, which can severely disrupt modern financial markets. As it stands, the existing international financial architecture is not equipped to deal with the crises that will confront it in the future (Eichengreen, 2000). There is a need, therefore, to seriously address fundamental issues in this period of relative calm, given the risk that the next crisis may be much worse (Sakakibara, 2000). The inevitable consequence has been the call for the reform of existing systems and structures of the international financial architecture – especially to the key institutions and the way in which they govern.

2.2. Causes Determine Responses

Noble and Ravenhill (2000) observe that there is great disagreement on the "lessons and policy prescriptions to be drawn from the unhappy events of 1997–98" (p. 8). Much seems to hinge on the identification of the causal factors of crisis. Kahler (2000) saw two interpretations of the causes and consequences of the Crisis developed in the literature: "'fundamentalists', who assigned financial crisis to ill-chosen national economic policies, and the 'panic-stricken', who were convinced that many crises were self-fulfilling" (p. 237). Each view generated its own set of prescriptions (Narine, 2002).

Fundamentalists argued that the structure of national financial markets left East Asian economies severely exposed to potential shocks. Under this view, numerous aspects of the international financial architecture need to be improved in order to enhance the stability of domestic financial markets. Moskow (2002) argued reform of financial institutions in emerging economies needed to account for structural flaws. Recommendations included strengthening the banking and financial sectors, heightened transparency, bailing-in the private sector, sequencing capital account liberalisation, capital account controls, exchange rate flexibility and the implementation of international standards (Stiglitz, 2002; Eichengreen, 1999; King, 1999; Rogoff, 1999; OECD, 1998).

Undoubtedly, the Crisis exposed flaws in the economies, with many lacking institutional fundamentals capable of handling external shocks. However, the prescriptions of the main international financial institutions were also deemed to have contributed to perpetuating the crisis (Stiglitz, 2002). With this in mind, proponents of the alternative body of literature argued that the Asian growth model was not inherently flawed. Quite the opposite in fact, as prior to the crisis Asian economies were lauded for their growth model to the extent that it was identified as one that should be followed in the West (Beeson, 2001). Indeed, in the pre-crisis period many Asian countries enjoyed strong growth – particularly the fabled 'Asian tigers'.

Proponents of the panic-stricken view argued that reform should concentrate on the supply side of international finance rather than on domestic economies (Park & Wang, 2001). The focus here was on the role of international capital mobility and negative impacts of capital account liberalisation (Stiglitz, 2002; Bhagwati, 1998). For example, Beeson (1999) suggested that international capital flows were just as much the cause of the Crisis than a history of authoritarianism or crony capitalism. Nevertheless, after the Crisis the Asian growth model was persecuted as riddled with flaws and Western models of markets were advocated. East Asian governments staunchly defended their decisions against the claim that the Asian method of achieving economic growth was intrinsically defective.

Bhagwati (1998) argued the "claims of enormous benefits from free capital mobility are not persuasive. Substantial gains have been asserted, not demonstrated" (p. 7). Former IMF Senior Deputy Managing Director Stanley Fischer too conceded "there is as yet little econometric evidence bearing on the benefits or costs of open capital markets" (Fischer, 1999, p. 95). Further damaging was the fact that countries such as India, which had capital controls, suffered less during the crisis (King, 1999). The rapid recovery in terms of economic growth (Park & Wang, 2001) also pointed to the flawed perception of structural inadequacies.

Although the causes remain heavily contested, one constant became evident. Both sides of the causal debate highlighted the role of the IMF in providing emergency funds to support the Crisis Economies (Little & Olivei, 1999). Of particular concern were the conditionalities attached to IMF loans. East Asian governments who were recipients of funding disputed – albeit with limited success – many of the proposed solutions that emanated from the international policy makers. It was argued the prescriptions were inappropriate for borrowing countries and the IMF failed to account for regional sensitivity instead applying a 'one-size-fits-all' approach to correcting crises.

As it happened many of the initial IMF prescriptions did fail disastrously (see below). Maintaining the status quo, where IMF directives must be strictly adhered to regardless of suitability, became clearly undesirable. Ultimately, calls were made for the creation of a regional institution to combat the underlying problems in the IMF. Much of the impetus stemmed from the inability of the IMF to provide policy prescriptions that account for regional idiosyncrasies. Arguably, a regional response mechanism could address the shortcomings that had detracted from the ability of the IMF to successfully intervene in the Crisis. Hence, the idea of an AMF was born.

There are signs that in the current period of relative financial calm the reform process is losing momentum. Park (2000) interprets the slow progress of reform as encouraging the formation of regional action in Asia. Instead of waiting for a new architecture to evolve, East Asia should adopt a more proactive stance and work to create their own system of defence (Park & Wang, 2001). Hence, considering the plausibility of a regional body that could facilitate a concerted effort to draw upon regional reserves and manage financial instability is a valuable endeavour. The remainder of this section expands on three areas where an AMF can address the failures mentioned above.

2.3. Contagion

One of the principal themes to come out of the Crisis was that of contagion. Contagion occurs as a crisis spreads from one country to another like a contagious disease. The Crisis eventually reached beyond Asia, but regional countries endured the hardest and most immediate fallout. When the Thai baht was initially devaluated the ramifications steadily flowed through the region first to Korea, then to Malaysia and then Indonesia. The economic argument in favour of creating the AMF was predicated on the concept of contagion. That is, absent an effective international response, regional efforts to combat the onset of a crisis are mutually beneficial to all countries within a region.

The degree of contagion of a crisis is largely a function of the binds between national economies (Manzano, 2001). Significant economic connections exist between countries in the region. Taking the ASEAN membership, for example, in terms of both imports and exports for 2001, approximately 40% of total trade is concentrated within the 10 countries.[4] This suggests maintaining stability is required to ensure these obligations are fulfilled. The implication is that if something were to affect the ability of one country to meet its obligations, the likely impact would be on its trading partners and not just the country that defaults.

The amount of Foreign Direct Investment received by ASEAN members is also indicative of the close economic bonds between countries in the region. In 2001, foreign investment sourced from within Asia totalled 35% of total global sources. This contribution is approximately on par with funding from Europe and substantially greater than that of the US. Again, while these figures are somewhat inconclusive, they imply that if funding from Asian neighbours were to cease, then the consequences would be significant. When the amount invested in the region is taken as a percentage of supplying country Gross domestic product (GDP) then the case for drawing on regional resources through an AMF improves.

The seeds for collective action derived from contagion are well founded. Economic linkages create a terrific incentive to act because each country depends on the stability of others. The utility of exploiting peer pressure in this situation cannot be understated (Kahler, 2000; Noble & Ravenhill, 2000). As countries in close proximity will rapidly feel the externalities of financial disturbances caused by their neighbours, a case is made for regional cooperation in surveillance and monitoring (Manzano, 2001; Kahler, 2000). This being the case, having a regional mechanism could be a more natural way of enforcing financial discipline (Manzano, 2001).

So, despite the international nature of finance the impact of crises are likely to be felt first in the region and so demand regional responses. Unfortunately, the existence of contagion failed to entice countries to contribute the substantial amounts necessary to fund regional efforts. Instead, they called upon the IMF to provide funding. Regrettably, the IMF was perceived as being slow to prevent the spread of contagion. The discussion below elaborates on reasons why East Asian states may have found it more prudent to act collectively.

2.4. Conditionality and Regional Responsiveness

Countries that request funding from the IMF are typically required to undertake certain conditions prior to loans being made. Conditions – or conditionalities as they are known – are imposed essentially as a means of ensuring the resources are used efficiently and for the purpose intended. During the Crisis many IMF conditions also sought to open Asian financial markets. The arguments advanced in defense of conditionality contend structural changes reduce the possibility of contagion, facilitate financial market integration and trade, all of which should subsequently produce benefits to the overall global economy. Reassurances of such benefits should have in theory ruled out the rejection of and protests against conditionality. However, during the Crisis the issue of conditionality came under intense criticism (Park & Wang, 2001).

Feldstein (1998) observes that while 'fundamentalists' campaigned for strict conditionalities to be attached to IMF aid packages, many of the structural adjustments and austerity requirements demanded caused a great deal of disquiet within borrowing countries. Chang and Rajan (2001) surmised that the opinion of the opposition was that conditionality was "overly intrusive and unwarranted in view of what they considered as being a 'liquidity' crisis" (p. 103). Furthermore, it was thought that by requiring conditionalities the IMF had exceeded its original mandate and the IMF should not be involved with structural issues (Lipscy, 2003; Eichengreen, 1999). This became known as the IMF *mission creep.*

Rogoff (1999) states "many Asian leaders feel that G-7 and IMF conditions on loans to their countries were far more stringent than those imposed on Mexico and Brazil, despite the fact that until the crisis, Asian countries had been seen as models of growth for the rest of the developing world" (p. 27). Indeed, it was questioned why all of a sudden a facet of Asian business practices like crony capitalism caused a crisis? (Narine, 2002; Beeson, 2001; Sakakibara, 2000). The conditions were also seen to evoke neo-colonist feelings combining a lack of empowerment and the ceding of national sovereignty. Eichengreen (2000) suggested the result was that the necessary support for IMF reforms was unable to be canvassed. The sense of domestic ownership is crucial to the successful implementation of international standards (Park & Wang, 2001).

It was argued that the IMF failed to acknowledge the basic principle that directives that do not suit the particular needs of borrowing countries, but are transplanted or ordered from outside the country, will not succeed. This is because such reforms will lack commitment, breed resentment and so, not achieve the desired goals. Eichengreen (1999) acknowledged differences in economic, legal and cultural settings that worked to prevent IMF recommendations. Instead, when changes are developed from within a country there may be more awareness of the country-specific sensitivities and thus, may work better. With ownership there is a greater chance that reform policies will be adopted (Manzano, 2001). Noble and Ravenhill (2000) believe that a greater sense of community is building because of the shared perception of the unnecessary harshness of conditionalities attached to IMF programmes. In this context, the establishment of an AMF was seen as an important mechanism through which necessary changes could be facilitated. This remains the case as Asian financial markets continue in their phase of reform.

The rebuttal to those who rejected conditionality was that countries displayed an unwillingness to bear the short-term discomfort for the long-term gain. Although Bhagwati (1998) asserted "countries have lost the political independence to run their economic policies as they deem fit. That their independence is lost not directly to foreign nations but to an IMF increasingly extending its agenda, at the behest of the US Congress" (p. 9). The reduction in national sovereignty caused by international finance became too much to bear for proud Asian nations and shaped a desire to reclaim control over outcomes (Park & Wang, 2001; Cohen, 2000; Kahler, 2000).

The IMF was also heavily criticised for the absence of regional sensitivity in prescribing solutions (Amyx, 2000; Little & Olivei, 1999). Even if the imposition of conditionalities was accepted, there remained a significant concern that, for the most part, the conditionalities were quite inappropriate for Asia. Too often, argued its critics, had the IMF applied a traditional 'one-size-fits-all' approach to correcting crises and done so without success. For example, it failed to understand the impact of fiscal restrictions in Asia (Narine, 2002). Undoubtedly, the failure to account for regional, political and cultural idiosyncrasies led to the strongest opposition to the IMF. The IMF advocated policies that were relatively questionable, given the circumstances of the Crisis Economies, in fact, in some cases things were actually made worse (Stiglitz, 2002).

What may work well in developed economies may not be appropriate for emerging economies (Moskow, 2001). The clearest example of this was the IMF's advocacy of open capital markets. It has been argued that the bank-centric nature of Asian economies impeded their ability to absorb external shocks during the Crisis (Batten & Kim, 2000). So, crisis countries were told to open their capital markets in order to diversify their sources of funding. The criticism of this IMF prescription was that it forced developing countries, which did not have adequate internal institutions, to adopt policies only recently implemented by developed nations (Stiglitz, 2002; Kahler, 2000; Noble & Ravenhill, 2000).

La Porta, Lopez-De-Silanes, Shleifer, and Vishny (1998) provided data on the strength of the legal system in selected Asian countries based on measures of judicial efficiency, rule of law and corruption. Their results were representative of the fact that some countries are more equipped than others to support legal structures required to protect foreign capital. For example, the crisis economies of Indonesia and Thailand rated well below other countries in the region in their respective abilities to enforce investment laws. Arguably, a regional institution like the AMF would be more cognizant of these flaws and ensure conditions accounted for the varying stages of development in sequencing reforms. Demands for liberalising financial markets provide a good illustration of how local knowledge may have given rise to the sequential introduction of reforms that account for country-specific environments.

Furthermore, Tadesse (2002) argues prescribing the shift to open financial markets for all countries at the same time is flawed because developing countries, like those in Asia, do not have adequate infrastructure to support open markets and will do better maintaining a bank-based system. Indeed, evidence on the effectiveness of market liberalisation remains inconclusive. Recent research tends to conclude that neither closed banking systems nor open markets are superior (Beck & Levine, 2002). Rather, the choice between the two should be made according to circumstances. The performance of the IMF judged in these terms leaves much to be desired.

2.5. Regulatory Capture and the Washington Consensus

In seeking to explain why the IMF was so regionally inept in its management of the Crisis, critics found some useful guidance offered by the concept Western Hegemony. The structure of the international economy, with tendencies to either openness or closure, is largely determined by ideological influences (Horowitz & Heo, 2001). With the triumph of capitalism and the end of the Cold War it appeared that the advocacy of free markets would dominate. Trade boarders were opened and, in time, attention turned to freeing capital flows. Unfortunately, as Bhagwati (1998) emphasized, the rules governing 'trade in widgets' did not equate to trade in capital. Why then did the IMF pursue market liberalisation?

Park and Wang (2001) state that a "few rich industrial countries control the decision-making process as well as the operations of the IMF" (p. 16). Thus, the IMF was susceptible to regulatory capture and political decision-making that advances the interests of those select nations and not necessarily potential borrowers. In relation to why members of the G-7 bailout troubled economies, Rogoff (1999) believes that "some genuine (albeit modest) altruism is involved, but self-interest is clearly the main reason" (p. 27).

Narine (2002) argues that in the handling of the Crisis the IMF was "revealed as a blunt instrument of American economic policy" (p. 9). Worse still Noble and Ravenhill (2000) considered "the shock of the crisis offered a rare opportunity to mobilise the political energy for reform. In practice, the US government took advantage of the crisis to push long-sought trade goals" (p. 22). The story of US national interest is told with regard to increasing market access to crisis countries (McFarlane, 2001; Eichengreen,

1999; Beeson, 1999). Not surprisingly there is a perception that sees the IMF as serving the US – that uses its disproportionate influence to advance its own objectives (Lipscy, 2003; Chang & Rajan, 2001; Rajan, 2000; Narine, 2002). Many similar remarks proliferated from the IMF's handling of crises in Mexico and Russia.[5]

Bhagwati (1998) claims "Wall Street's financial firms have obvious self-interest in a world of free capital mobility since it only enlarges the arena in which to make money" (p. 11). It has begotten what he labelled a "Wall Street-Treasury complex", which seeks to promote capital account convertibility and the use of the IMF to bailout investment banks who avoid the risks (p. 12). Sakakibara (2000) notes recognition of these interests meant "world opinion has certainly moved from market fundamentalism or the Washington consensus" (p. 4). The perception of regulatory capture by Western vested interests supported the calls for the reform of the main international financial institutions.

Narine (2002) summarises the sentiment of the last sections concisely: "[t]he IMF's mishandling of Asia, combined with the inadequate and predatory American response, has had serious repercussions in the region. To many Asians, the IMF demonstrated that it lacks the expertise to manage financial relations in the region" (p. 9). The recognition that the manner in which the IMF responded was flawed imparts an obvious need for cultural sensitivity bearing local expertise both at the top level and on the ground.

At the most extreme, the arguments against the IMF called for its abolition (Calomiris, 1998). As Eichengreen (1999) puts it: "[i]f the problem is that the Fund's decisions are distorted by the parochial concerns of national government, then greater independence from those governments is the logical solution" (p. 32). More moderate opinions called for greater voice to be given to developing nations on the executive boards of the IMF (Park & Wang 2001).[6] Others called for the establishment of a regional institution to carry out the functions once viewed as the sole domain of the IMF. Here again, campaigners for an AMF were adamant that the institution would yield superior policy results on the merits of regional sensitivity.

2.6. Comparative Advantage and Sustaining the Asian Growth Model

Successful diagnosis of financial crises largely depends on a familiarity with particular contextual environments. The IMF proved during the Crisis that its knowledge of the circumstances prevailing in East Asia was deficient (above). This being the case, it was asserted that a regionally based monetary institution would have a comparative advantage over the IMF with respect to the prescription of remedies to correct the onset of a financial crisis in East Asia. Resources such as local knowledge could be readily drawn upon as a means of improving conditionality. Narine (2002) suggests that this would have been useful to the IMF who had limited expertise with regard to East Asia. Indeed, the absence of an Asian division within the IMF prior to the crisis is often noted (Stiglitz, 2002).

Observing financial conditions of neighbours is somewhat easier than when conducted from afar (Noble & Ravenhill, 2000). Working collectively through the AMF would have provided East Asian neighbours the ability to offer regional insights and perhaps have been able to warn of the impending disaster. The bilateral nature of swap arrangements under the proposal is conducive to considering reforms from within the historical and socio-economic context of the parties (Amyx, 2000). Moreover, regional institutions can accomplish the design and monitoring of reform more effectively, given comparative advantage (Kahler, 2000).

In a practical sense, the amount of human resources required to construct, implement and enforce new international standards also pose a problem, given the relatively small size of the IMF (Eichengreen, 1999). This provides a window for the growing number of skilled personnel in Asia to contribute (Park & Wang, 2001). The participation of locally trained staff could redress the fact that even worse than failing to account for regional factors, the IMF considered *no* factors at all. The involvement of a regional body in the policy process ought to negate much of the criticism directed at the appropriateness of prescriptions (Rajan, 2000).

Eichengreen (1999) notes the "complaint that the IMF's structural interventions are arbitrary and capricious at least partly explains the backlash they have provoked" (p. 6). Chang and Rajan (2001) assert "a regional monetary facility might be better able than the IMF to reach a genuine consensus on policy reform to ensure greater ownership of a programme of reform" (p. 114). Importantly, this comparative advantage could combat hostility to externally imposed conditionality. These arguments are congruent with those which purport transitions and reforms handled internally are often smoother than those dictated from outside (see above).

An alternative perception of comparative advantage also exists in the literature. Instead of arguing that comparative advantage begets ownership of reform programmes – that would still implement IMF conditionality – proponents argue the AMF would provide policy makers with the ability to uphold the East Asian model of growth. For instance, Chang and Rajan (2001) contend the AMF was an attempt "to sustain the East Asian development model and remain supportive of the countries that adopted it" (p. 103). In this respect, the AMF would provide members with a means to resist the "Wall Street-Treasury complex" and offer an alternative to the conditions imposed by the IMF. As such, the AMF was to be an important tool to advance the normative agenda of countries in the region.

Belief in the sustainability of export-led growth informed much of these arguments (Hughes, 1999). In this guise, one of the central objectives of the AMF would be to contribute to policy dialogue and advocate the positions of member nations and resist the Anglo-American model (Rajan, 2000; Narine, 2002). Support came from those who believed that overall, pre-crisis policies such as relationship-based business, were sound – particularly as evidenced by the enormous growth in the region (Noble & Ravenhill, 2000). Indeed, the model employed by the Asian tiger economies appear more suited to the development goals.

The provision of emergency funding with conditionality suited more to East Asian circumstances would have enabled many countries to refuse to abide by some of the more questionable IMF prescriptions. For example, interest rates were raised to such a level that they had disastrous effects on real economies, notably forcing the foreclosure on many business loans (Narine, 2002). Also, bank closures forced 'bank runs' in Indonesia (Stiglitz, 2002; Park & Wang, 2001). In the most extreme case, the Indonesian government was unable to pay coupons on its bonds and subsequently defaulted requiring further assistance!

Narine (2002) suggests that the AMF "would, implicitly, protect these economies from being forced into structural adjustments that would run contrary to the political and social goals of the state government" (p. 13). So despite the IMF advocating the Anglo-American conception of the world founded purely on ideology, Beeson (1999) believes that models are less likely to converge post-crisis. Hughes (1999) and Higgott (1998) also reject the convergence theory.

If the AMF had formed, prescriptions based on the so-called 'Asian values' would have perhaps resulted in vastly different outcomes. The much-vaunted case of Malaysia proved that countries that did not follow IMF prescriptions could still manage the crisis (Sakakibara, 2000; Hughes, 1999). This signals that knowledge of a country's true state of affairs can conjure more accurate policy replies. Thus, a locally sponsored AMF intuitively offers a real ability to resolve information asymmetries and adverse selection of prescriptions. The AMF would sound the challenge to the hegemony of liberal capitalist democracies and create a cause for an alternative voice that reaffirms sovereign rights to control policy directions.

The term 'Asian Values' has been popularised in the battle against the IMF-led reform agenda.[7] Differences between Western democracy and cultural traits exhibited throughout Asia resonate profoundly when the resistance debate is considered. Culture is seen as an impediment to the adoption of practices from other countries. Uniting behind a common sense of shared values provides the countries supporting the AMF a substantial weapon in the fight for financial self-determination. Whether these values will be enough to surmount long-standing political tensions remains to be seen – as the concept of Asian values remains contested (Sen, 1997).

There is a perception among East Asian countries that their views are not represented in the governance of the international financial system (Noble & Ravenhill, 2000). The cause, argued Beeson (2001), is that by acting in isolation states would find it difficult to have an impact on processes and outcomes – individually, these countries do not possess an effective voice. Here, advocates of the AMF saw it as an opportunity for regional nations through collective action to achieve a say in policy directions and assist governments to regain control of decision-making lost to markets. In fact, some, like Sakakibara (2000), promote the use of proactive measures (like the AMF) by the countries at the 'periphery' of the system as a means of accomplishing change.

2.7. Limited IMF Resources and a Lack of Western Funding

The inability of the international community to act with sufficient speed at the time of the Crisis also raised significant questions regarding the ability of the present financial architecture to deal with the occurrence of crises. In particular, concerns revolved around the financial capacity of the IMF and whether it had sufficient funds to supply countries in need (Park & Wang, 2001). Much of the debate centred on the commitment levels of Western developed nations to contribute to preventing the onset of crisis and crisis management (Stiglitz, 2002; Hughes, 1999).

Reluctance can be attributed to the fact that countries that have shallow economic relationships with crisis countries can escape the effects of financial panic. As long as countries remain unaffected by a crisis, they will not have the urgent political incentive to assume the costs of donating funds to the international lender of last resort – in most countries altruism is dictated by political realism (Lipscy, 2003; Sakakibara, 2000). Rogoff (1999) concluded "[a]ll evidence suggests that the G-7 is simply not prepared to put up the kind of resources needed to preclude a broad-based attack on developing country debt" (p. 28).

In this light, it has been suggested that the US did not contribute because its interests in Asia were not high enough and thus, the US did not have an adequate incentive to assist in the bailout (Lipscy, 2003). This observation can also explain the US intervention in Mexico. Kahler (2000) identified that the need for "active crisis management to limit contagion" should have been a key lesson from US involvement in the Mexican bailout in the early 1990s. Instead, the result was a US refusal to offer such lending to Asia (p. 240).

With such mentalities at play, a regional institution comprising members with significant economic linkages should be created in East Asia to fill the void left by the reluctant members of the G-7. Indeed, with the absence of global altruism the hardest hit nations might be forced to look closer to home for support. Should the need arise, an institution like the AMF can assist in a purely financial capacity as a regional lender of last resort when the IMF's resources are stretched too far (Park, 2000; Rajan, 2000).

The conspicuous absence of leading developed nations in the funding of crisis aid packages signifies the need for a proactive East Asian approach to crisis management. Nevertheless, there were some who doubted the region retained adequate foreign reserves to make the undertaking viable. Kahler (2000) believed interventions sourced from beyond the G-7 and international financial institutions would be too costly for economies already beset by crisis and further threaten stability in the international financial system.

On the other hand, much more evidence was presented that collectively, East Asian countries were capable of contributing and did contribute a substantial amount of funding – especially Japan (Lipscy, 2003; Chang & Rajan, 2001; Rajan, 2000; Hughes, 1999). Their capability stemmed largely from balance of payment surpluses and foreign exchange reserves (Narine, 2002). What is more, Narine (2002) argues, the main contributors to the AMF held more than twice the amount of funds required meaning the "region possessed more than adequate resources to effectively deal with the problem" (p. 8).

Therefore, Narine (2002) construes that "having a regional body to co-ordinate such rescues is not a great departure from established practice and increases efficiency" (p. 11). In fact, this strong pragmatic basis for the idea was as Lipscy (2003) argued "based on the premise that the US would not act as vigorously in the event of a similar crisis in Asia" as that of Mexico (p. 94).

Table 1 shows that East Asian countries had large amounts of reserve holdings at the time of the Crisis and have built substantial reserves since

Table 1.   Foreign Reserve Positions 1997 and 2002 (in $US Millions).

Country	1997	2002
China	142,762	291,128
Indonesia	16,587	30,969
Japan	219,648	416,186
Korea	20,368	121,345
Malaysia	20,788	34,222
Philippines	7,266	13,144
Singapore	71,289	82,021
Thailand	26,179	38,046
Vietnam	1,986	4,121

Source: IMF International Financial Statistics July 2003.

that time. Presented in this light it appears East Asia has sufficient capacity to respond to a financial crisis in the first instance to such an extent that liquidity could be restored without IMF contribution. To do so may have spared East Asia the misery of recession and social dislocation (Park, 2000). The challenge becomes drawing on these reserves in a collective manner in the future through the AMF.

3. OPPOSITION TO THE AMF

Despite the purported benefits of the AMF there was a realisation, both in the academic literature and other commentaries, that the proposal would face considerable opposition. It has been noted that the US proved to be the party most against the creation of the AMF (Lipscy, 2003; Narine, 2002). The European Union and the IMF also rejected the idea (Lipscy, 2003; Park & Wang, 2001; Park, 2000). It became clear that the AMF constituted a serious threat to the established hierarchy within the international financial architecture, if not a radical departure from the extant model.

The vehement opposition of the US can be traced to the perception that the regional body would challenge its regional hegemony (Chang & Rajan, 2001). The US was focused on protecting its own self-interest and political influence in the region, as it feared the AMF would transfer power to Japan – the dominant contributor to the facility (McFarlane, 2001; Cohen, 2000). Indeed, as the AMF was to be funded from reserves within the region it was seen to represent a means to avoid dependency on IMF loans and, therefore, the pressures of the Washington consensus. Evidently, this was an unacceptable proposition and so several points of resistance emerged.

3.1. Duplication and the Central Role of the IMF

The issue of the AMF causing unnecessary duplication has been identified as a primary reason against its creation. To have both an international and regional body with similar or identical objectives adds little value to the existing IMF-centred system (Lipscy, 2003). This is particularly so when reform seems to have reaffirmed the position of the Bretton Woods financial institutions as the main instruments for maintaining stability (Kahler, 2000). Thus, one of the main concerns of the US was about the potential competition an AMF would give to the central role of the IMF (Lipscy, 2003; Park & Wang, 2001; Cohen, 2000). The problem with this scenario is that it not only weakens the authority of the IMF, but can also obscure the need to reform domestic institutions of borrowers (Noble & Ravenhill, 2000).

Such an argument appeared to offer intuitive appeal. However, whether it was the intention of the AMF to compete with the IMF is unclear. Throughout the initial debates, proponents of the AMF offered constant assurances that the two monetary institutions would act in unison and not competition – with the AMF complementing the lead role of the IMF (Kuroda & Kawai, 2003). Indeed, the relationship would be much like that between regional development banks and the World Bank (Chang & Rajan, 2001). Where the AMF would be truly complementary without duplication, then it would be supported. Hans Kohler (2002), Managing Director of the IMF, said this at a press conference in Prague, 20 September 2000. In reality, the assurances did not allay the opposition because the financial independence of the AMF makes possible policy independence.

From another perspective the existence of an alternative place to obtain funding was viewed as allowing potential borrowers to 'play off' the competing institutions against each other. Here, the concern was that relatively 'cheaper' finance would create moral hazard with the institution offering the least restricted lending conditions securing more of the business of troubled governments (discussed below). Supporters of the AMF dispute this interpretation as they believe trading off the IMF with the AMF will ultimately lead to superior policy results, given that advice and not only funding will enable institutions to retain their customer base (Eichengreen, 1999). Competition in this sense is required because if it did not occur and the two institutions existed without differentiation then there would be no need for a regional institution.

The rationale behind the belief that creating a regional institution is irrelevant was (and is) supported by the claims that the IMF is undergoing major reform in an effort to correct faults in its operations (Corden, 2001; Park & Wang, 2001). The IMF (2001) asserts that there are positive signs that it has learnt some lessons from its actions during the Crisis. For instance, there have been moves to make the IMF more transparent and conditionality has been amended to provide greater national 'ownership' of programmes.[8] Proponents argued that efforts should concentrate on these initiatives rather than on creating an entirely new organisation – even in the midst of reform of the wider architecture. Unfortunately, to argue that reform of the IMF reduces the need for new institutions ignores the fact that "[a]part from an increase in the transparency of the IMF's own operations, other changes in the organization have been minimal" (Kahler, 2000, p. 248).

3.2. Moral Hazard

A prescriptive function for any monetary institution is required because of the existence of moral hazard. Noble and Ravenhill (2000) mention the conditionality attached to IMF loans is aimed at reducing moral hazard. Opponents to the AMF have attacked the less stringent conditionality associated with AMF funding, suggesting it would lead to moral hazard (Park & Wang, 2001). If it is believed that countries will be automatically rescued by a fund then it may promote less than optimum decision-making. This may include less fiscal restraint. Based upon moral hazard it is argued, "the AMF would create unnecessary incentive for Asian countries to postpone adjustment" (Lipscy, 2003, p. 96).[9] It is not clear why regional institutions would be more susceptible to moral hazard than the IMF has been in the past (Park, 2000).

Among the many criticisms of the IMF include the contention that the IMF is a source of moral hazard (Park & Wang, 2001). However, Eichengreen (2000) dismisses this on the basis that the IMF plays a more important function in assisting countries maintain investor confidence. If this were the case then why would the same argument not hold when applied to a regional institution? Fischer (1999) states: "[m]oral hazard is something to be lived with and controlled, rather than fully eliminated" (p. 93).[10] Thus, moral hazard has been used as an excuse to block Asian regionalism by countries – particularly the US – who are unwilling to contribute their own funds to crisis management (Lipscy, 2003; Sakakibara, 2000; Park, 2000). Arguably, the AMF intended to impose less restrictive standards, although still high enough to prevent moral hazard.

3.3. Lack of History

Critics of the AMF pointed to the fact that Asia lacked a history of collective action. It was emphasized that the absence of a collective history was precisely the challenge that confronted those wanting to establish the regional organisation. This is because the ability for countries to cooperate relies heavily on past experiences. It was argued, any potential engagement would be impeded where the parties did not have a long record of cooperation or goodwill. This being the case, it was thought the AMF was bound to fail and that time would be better spent concentrating on domestic reforms and improving the IMF.

The plausibility of regional financial institutions was evidenced primarily by reference to the European Central Bank, which has among other things been able to integrate the economies of the European Union and implement a common currency. The marked difference between the collective histories of Europe and Asia was used to refute this and, moreover, highlighted the requirement for historical solidarity. Asia might not be ready for the AMF because it lacks a tradition of 'integrationist' thinking and existing agreements needed for cooperation – especially when compared to the European experience (Park, 2000; Eichengreen, 1997, 1999). This would nullify any ability to exploit comparative advantage and draw upon regional resources for collective action.

It was inferred earlier that the success of the AMF in crisis prevention depended, at least in part, on the ability of the institution to exert influence for change. This depends on the willingness of members to submit to regional peer pressure that demands the undertaking of necessary policy adjustments (Rajan, 2000). Without a collective history, critics were unsure whether potential members could be able to agree upon sanctions to borrowing members who do not conform with conditions set – especially if they are domestically unpopular? Eichengreen (1999) implied the potential difficulty in exerting peer pressure was a consequence of lack of history. Thus, not only is the provision of funding a critical issue but in addition the capability to enforce conditionalities is essential.

The sanctioning of other governments' non-compliance with IMF pre-scriptions via peer pressure has not been particularly effective among Asia (Kahler, 2000). This is compared to European countries that were able to conclude the Maastricht Treaty, which sets out very specific responsibilities. The point was further demonstrated by reference to the fact associational bodies between Asian countries are not supranational institutions but rather networks with foundations of consensus, limited direct cooperation and non-interference in domestic affairs of members (Beeson, 2001; Eichengreen, 1997). This is attributed to the fact sovereignty is still jealously guarded by East Asian states (Beeson, 2001). Eichengreen (1999) claimed: "proposals to create new international institutions to deal with the crisis problem are politically unrealistic" because there is "no appetite for powerful suprana-tional bodies with the power to usurp the traditional prerogatives of sov-ereign national states" (p. 2).

Finally, the contention that merely holding similar values across countries would automatically facilitate cooperation between Asian countries was argued to be problematic. There remains significant diversity in both the cultures and stages of development in Asia that would make immediate unification, similar to the European model, very difficult (Sakakibara, 2000). Whether countries in the region can harness the pain experienced during the Crisis to set aside historical animosities and expedite the process of jointly developing a regional defence mechanism, that would entail some sacrifice of sovereignty to protect members from threat of future crises, is unknown (Narine, 2002). There are signs that East Asian countries are prepared to do so (Park, 2000). Indeed, the practical necessity for a regional institution may offer a glimmer of hope and counter the 'lack of history' argument. The means by which Asia's differences can be overcome will be explored in the following section.

4. OVERCOMING POLITICAL IMPEDIMENTS TO COLLECTIVE ACTION IN EAST ASIA

Sizeable economic interconnectivity exists between countries in Asia, which is an important precursor to regional co-operation. Although influential, whether economic interests alone are enough to appease political grievances remains to be seen. Bayoumi, Eichengreen, and Mauro (1999) claim "the essential preconditions for a durable regional arrangement are political rather than economic" (p. 2). Indeed, while the economic arguments are pervasive they often play second fiddle to political ones (Lipscy, 2003; Kahler, 2000; Beeson, 1999). Bluntly, King (1999) suggests any attempt to create a new lender of last resort will be constrained for the basic reason "it's the politics, stupid" (p. 7).

One of the key points raised in opposition to the creation of the AMF was that Asia lacked the history of collective action needed to establish a viable monetary cooperative. There is much evidence indicating that lingering historical conflicts will potentially have a negative impact on meaningful and mutually beneficial monetary cooperation between key Asian states in the future. This would make any attempt to integrate politically unfeasible. While such challenges would make handing sovereignty over to a regional institution no more tenable than existing at the behest of a Washington-controlled IMF, it is important amidst current reform to contemplate whether enough political will exists in the region to overcome these deep animosities.

Determining how receptive any country may be to external pressures or how inclined they may be to working collectively with other countries is a subjective matter. Many questions, such as those dealing with leadership and enforcement, are difficult to answer. For instance, Noble and Ravenhill (2000) pose "[c]ould Japan effectively impose conditionality on Indonesia, for example, or Singapore on Malaysia?" (p. 31). Perhaps, because of this the majority of the literature focused on economic considerations (Lipscy, 2003). Unfortunately, few researchers have pondered the political impediments to regional monetary union. Rajan (2000) for instance, considered these arguments beyond scope of his paper. Addressing collective history requires a consideration of political issues. Discussion will now turn to some of the political dynamics in Asia that may help or hinder the creation of the AMF.

Several political hurdles confront East Asian states wanting to engage in collective action through the establishment of the AMF. Cohen (2000) queries whether there are sufficient political preconditions in the region for the establishment of a new regional monetary institution. The situation is very much a function of the lack of an extensive history of positive interaction between parties. Historical conflicts have particularly impinged upon attempts for collaboration and cooperation. The history of East Asia is littered with examples of animosity sourced from post-colonial tension, territorial disputes and remnants of the World War II.[11] While this perhaps differs little from the experience of other regions, Asia has proven less capable of overcoming past hostilities. Thus, what could be worse than a fragmented history of collaboration than a history of repeated conflict coupled with deep-seated suspicion and hatred?

Manzano (2001) sees political considerations preventing appropriate collective responses from eventuating particularly where political will is lacking. Therefore, attempts to canvass support for increasing regional
cooperation under the AMF must accommodate the dynamics of domestic political accountabilities. This task becomes difficult because of the susceptibility to resistance based on the self-interest of domestic social and
political elites. This is especially so when considering the degree of concentrated control seeking to maintain dominance in East Asia. It should be
recognised then that a challenge confronting the plan for the AMF is the
fact domestic authorities would still wield enormous regulatory powers
(Rogoff, 1999).

Corrupt links between the private sector and government generally create
a situation where political interests are likely to impinge upon the success of
domestic regulatory change. The so-called 'crony capitalism' is often attributed to Asian countries. As such, there is the potential for the use of a
regional body like an AMF as a means of maintaining control by existing
elites (Beeson, 2001; Narine, 2002). The degree of concentrated ownership in
Asia, as shown by Claessens, Djankov, and Lang (2000) reveals that resistance to change and potential to control the AMF become possible.

Besson (2001) suggests "the temptation for power-holders to construct
and defend economic rules of the game that favor their own interest is often
irresistible" (p. 492). This is especially the case when reforms confront existing systems as in Indonesia, Japan, Korea and Thailand (Noble &
Ravenhill, 2000). Levine (1997) notes, in discussing domestic changes, "political and legal impediments to financial development are apparently difficult to change" (p. 710). As we have seen earlier these problems are not
unique to Asia but permeate in the IMF. Nevertheless, the situation will
contribute to the problems associated with establishing an AMF.

4.1. The Question of Leadership: An Asian Hegemon

Cohen (2000) identified leadership as one of the most crucial issues to the
success of regional integration. Strong leadership encourages participation
and can facilitate reconciliation. In terms of financial leadership two con-
tenders immediately emerge in Japan and China. Japan long held the status
as Asia's largest financial centre and as such became the most obvious
candidate for leadership of regional financial institutions. Japan's membership of the G-7, in particular, means it has an important role promoting
regional cooperation (Park & Wang, 2001). With regard to the AMF

initiative, Japan attempted to draw on this fact to assert its leadership ambitions by being the original instigator of the concept. Indeed, as Japan would have contributed the majority of the funds, its credentials seemed assured.

Noble and Ravenhill (2000) point out that "[p]olitical energy is often, perhaps usually, generated by a political or economic crisis – often a crisis arising from the failures of the old system" (p. 12). As the Crisis deepened Japan sought to summon the political energy among its Asian neighbours and proposed the creation of an AMF. Although Japan has been criticised for the timing of the announcement (Chang & Rajan, 2001) – at a stage when things were at their height – it was an opportunity to counter IMF dominance in the region. Importantly, the idea was supported by most nations in East Asia as a means of maintaining financial stability (Lipscy, 2003; Chang & Rajan, 2001; Park & Wang, 2001). Yet, this did not easily translate into pragmatic implementation.

There are significant problems with hegemonic Japan (Nordhaug, 2002). Even before the onset of the Crisis the Japanese economy was facing serious decline (Horowitz & Heo, 2001). Also, the shine on the Yen had decidedly waned as its value fell relative to other currencies. The Dollar-denominated nature of many of the region's balance sheets compounded the problems with advocating greater use of the Yen. With a weak economy and currency Japan may find it difficult to argue for leadership. Japan's inability to implement international standards also detracts from its leadership aspirations. For instance, Japan failed to adequately regulate Basel capital adequacy (Eichengreen, 1999; Rogoff, 1999).

From a normative perspective Rajan (2000) notes that there are "historical reasons for the failure of Japan to accept or be accepted as a regional economic hegemon" (pp. 4–5). Most evidently, the wounds inflicted during WWII remain fresh. For instance, the Nanjing Massacre, the infamous Thai–Burma railroad and atrocities in Singapore are all sources of sensitivity. The political response throughout the region to Japanese Prime Minister's visits to war memorials in 2002 is testament to this. The implication of a negative relationship in the past means "it is still unlikely that Japan is prepared to exercise regional leadership, or that its leadership would be accepted by other Asian states" (Narine, 2002, p. 14).

One other factor that may limit the ability for Japan to assume leadership of the AMF is that it has often failed to be totally open regarding its national interests. Lipscy (2003) argued the AMF was purely based on advancing Japanese self-interest as "Japanese banks stood at the greatest risk in the event of a major conflagration" (p. 98). Thus, with more ties to the region than the US, Japan sought to protect its own interests rather than any sense of regional altruism. Japan must be up front with its national interests. Hughes (1999) provides another indictment pointing to Japan's quick reversal of support for the initial AMF when US forces lodged their opposition. This view is supported by Nordhaug (2002).

The enduring challenge is as Cohen (2000) questions whether Asians are "prepared to bury historical suspicions of Japanese motivations and interests? Japan might well aspire to a strategy of market leadership, but it is unclear whether others in the area would voluntarily follow" (p. 197). Park (2000) contends "China will find it very difficult to support any regional arrangements dominated by Japan" (p. 21). Lipscy (2003) notes that the US tried to exploit this position by lobbying China to oppose the AMF by emphasizing the threat of a "Japanese hegemony" (p. 96). It did so successfully.

China's qualification for regional leadership is fast expanding. Hughes (1999) recognises that China is contesting the leadership of the region. Eichengreen (2003) also notes that China is becoming increasingly active in regional affairs. With China's entry into the World Trade Organization and its status as the most populace nation in the world, it has staked its claim to regional supremacy. Control of the world's largest domestic market solidifies this opinion.

In the course of the Crisis, China became an active participant in recovery programmes. Desire to assert its leadership credentials in the region saw China contribute significantly to crisis management teams during the crisis. It offered support through the IMF and unilaterally, which represents not only compassion for its neighbours but also ability to lead. However, enduring reservations regarding human rights and security issues may also impede acceptance of China's position at the head of the AMF.

A choice between Japan and China seems difficult, as presented in this light both have their respective positive and negative qualities. Any decision is made even more complicated when we consider historical tensions as unlikely to mean other countries will "prefer the dictates of local powers over the IMF" or, moreover, may make regional leadership "even more unpalatable than taking the IMF's medicine" (Narine, 2002, p. 16). It is imperative then to determine whether a *greater collective goal* could exist on a regional level that would supplant the clash of individual positions. Ostensibly, the prevention of another outbreak of financial crisis matches this criterion.

The obstacle to be cleared then is whether countries within the region are prepared to overlook, for example, the problems with Japan and support the

AMF. The initial backing indicated that this is possible and that the severity of the economic imperatives will help overcome political problems. Moreover, the initial contributions to bailout package sources from within the region also imply that not only are the resources readily available but that there is a willingness to support regional efforts – whoever the leader.

4.2. Existing Regional Arrangements

The existence of numerous regional associations and groupings provides evidence that while a long history of collective action is absent, an emerging future of cooperation awaits Asia. This is in stark contrast to the suggestion that Asia lacks the tradition of integration required for such arrangements. The ability to overlook historical conflicts has resulted in the propagation of institutional linkages that are in no way spurious. These existing collaborations underpin the creation of new institutions. As the explicit purpose of some of these relationships is the promotion of economic regionalism, creating a monetary facility is a natural intensification of such efforts (Rajan, 2000). Several existing associations between potential members of the AMF will be examined and used to refute claims that collective history does not exist in East Asia.

The Association of South East Asian Nations (ASEAN) was formed in 1967 and is perhaps the premier regional body within the South East Asia. It currently represents the interests of 10 member countries.[12] The aims and purposes of ASEAN concentrate on promoting shared economic growth, social progress and cultural development with peace and stability fundamental goals. Among the more important ASEAN-initiated dialogues include the ASEAN + 3 Summits, the ASEAN Regional Forum, the ASEAN Free Trade Area and the ASEAN Vision 2020 for economic integration. The Bali Summit of 2003 saw the ASEAN nations agree to form an ASEAN Economic Community by 2020. This implies financial cooperation through ASEAN is a possibility.

The actions of ASEAN are guided by the *"Treaty of Amity and Cooperation"* (1976) that establishes the principles of mutual respect for sovereignty and non-interference. This non-interventionist strategy in the internal affairs of its members has largely contributed to the survival of ASEAN (Narine, 2002). More relevant to this discussion is the relatively little action taken by ASEAN in the wake of the Crisis. This failure to coordinate a regional response has damaged the prestige and purpose of the organisation (Narine, 2002).

In 1998, the ASEAN Finance Ministers agreed to initiate the *ASEAN Surveillance Mechanism* to complement IMF surveillance. The premise as always was consensus and informality using peer pressure (Manzano, 2001; Beeson, 1999). It has become apparent that the data required for this body to function have not been entirely forthcoming (Narine, 2002). The danger is that without the requisite information any attempt to offer purposeful policy prescriptions will be nullified. This will consequently hamper the ability to influence country behaviour (Manzano, 2001).

ASEAN was intended to promote the interests of South East Asia as a collective political voice, rather than for any specific economic goals (Narine, 2002). The important question in the context of this paper is whether ASEAN can facilitate the creation of an AMF? Significantly, ASEAN has been able to issue a 'Common ASEAN Position on Reforming the International Financial Architecture'. This shows positive signs that the region is willing and can work together to improve stability in financial markets.

The most pertinent commentary on the difficulties to be overcome when creating a regional organisation can be taken from the ASEAN website. It says: "each man brought into the deliberations a historical and political perspective that had no resemblance to that of any of the others" but despite this the agreement was made.[13] The defining feature was the fact that it had been forged at a time when great urgency was needed and collective action seen as the way for mutual benefit. Importantly, it was founded on the advocacy of regional interests against those that would seek outside influences. This offers the blueprint of hope for the AMF.

Established in 1989, the Asia-Pacific Economic Cooperation (APEC) operates as a forum brought together for the aim of enhancing economic growth and sense of community within the Asia-Pacific region. Now with 21 member economies, the main objective of APEC is the reduction of trade barriers between countries under the 1994 '*Bogor Goals*'.[14] Several members suffered severely during the crisis and are potential members of the AMF. Notably, the US is also a member of APEC. This may hinder future plans for an AMF given first the US opposition to the initiative and second the desire of East Asia to gain independence from US influence in domestic financial affairs.

One of the great strengths APEC purports to exploit is the non-binding, voluntary consensus nature of its decision-making process. Adopting this approach makes possible the accommodation of the disparate position of members, yet has little possibility of threatening existing regional interests (Beeson, 1999). The consequence is that even with economic management as its principal concern APEC, much like ASEAN, was absent in mobilising a response to the Crisis (Beeson, 1999). Nevertheless, the existence of APEC again shows the willingness of countries in the region to work together for the achievement of common prosperity.

In 1997 members of APEC agreed on the Asian Regional Co-operation to Promote Financial Stability. Known as the *Manila Framework* it was to act in complement at the regional level around a primary role of the IMF. It would be based on four pillars: regional surveillance, enhanced co-operation to strength regulatory frameworks, increased crisis response capacity and supplementing IMF resources (Lipscy, 2003; Chang & Rajan, 2001).

But without an institutional setting it is little more than a high level forum (Chang & Rajan, 2001). Indeed, Hughes (1999) goes so far as to suggest "although the meeting certainly marked progress in regional financial co-operation, at the same time it was also clearly a toothless substitute for the AMF as first envisaged"(p. 24). If taken at face value the Manila Framework is indicative of the willingness of the region to act collectively. It was a compromise to the AMF and importantly had US support.

4.2.1. Other Regional Initiatives
The beginning of 2003 saw the clearest indication that Asian countries were willing to cooperate in a financial capacity for the advancement of regional prosperity. With the launch of the *Asian Bond Fund* countries within the region agreed to establish a regional bond fund that would work to develop regional capital markets (BIS, 2003). Underpinning the venture would be the issuance of sovereign bonds in US dollars that will aid in the development of domestic bond markets in Asia.

Also relatively new is the *Executives' Meeting of East Asia and Pacific Central Banks and Monetary Authorities* (EMEAP). Comprising 11 of the regions' senior monetary officials the aims again are cooperation and dialogue.[15] It is hoped that groupings such as the EMEAP "might weave the sort of fabric of related ties that could one day support more ambitious strategies of monetary alliance. But despite such efforts there is still little tradition of true financial solidarity – to say nothing of political solidarity – across the region" (Cohen, 2000, p. 197).

The Asian Development Bank (ADB) was established in 1966 as a multilateral development finance institution. It is the clearest example that Asian nations can work in unison within a regional context and not disrupt the working of international organisations. The place of the AMF in the international financial architecture can be modelled on the functional relationship between the ADB and the World Bank. Indeed, Park and Wang

(2001) conclude any "Asian regional initiative should contribute to the stability of the international financial system, as the Asian Development Bank
has done for global development finance for over 30 years" (p. 56).

5. CONCLUSION

The case for the AMF was reconsidered in this paper in the context of the
reform of the international financial architecture. The AMF was presented
as an opportunity to draw upon regional resources – financial and knowledge – in order to manage potential instability in East Asia financial markets. Support for creating the AMF was premised on combating contagion
through the provision of emergency funding and comparative advantage in
policy prescription. The theoretical and practical underpinning of these
reasons appeared to be sound.

The AMF was stifled at its inception by the 'Washington Consensus',
which opposed the idea on the basis that competing with the IMF would
exacerbate moral hazard concerns. Rejection was also justified using Asia's
apparent lack of collective history as indicating the pursuit was futile. These
reasons seemed politically motivated more that anything else. Indeed, moral
hazard claims were refuted using evidence of the IMF's own susceptibility to
the problem. Furthermore, the existence of a number of regional associations countered the belief that East Asian states were unwilling to embark
upon collective dialogue.

Pauly (2001) remarks "there will be no way to move to effective global
governance without having first achieved more effective national or, in some
cases, regional governance" (p. 2). Overall, as it was discussed in this paper
there is a place for the AMF, as a regional institution, within the new
international financial architecture. If economic linkages remain intact then
political factors are the only obstacle. The urgency of reform may force
greater expediency in overcoming this issue. Park and Wang (2001) question
whether "the international community need another global crisis or two
before reaching the political consensus that seems almost impossible at this
juncture?" (p. 5).

5.1. Enduring Challenges and Directions for Future Research

If the AMF is to be seriously pursued in the near future several challenges
will require attention. First, Noble and Ravenhill (2000) ask a fundamental

question in "[w]hat is the appropriate geographical definition of the region?" (p. 31). The answer to that question has significant implications for the future AMF in terms of membership and control. Would the membership base be extended to include South Asian countries such as India or Pacific countries such as Australia or New Zealand. There are strong cases for including these nations given their abilities to weather the storm during the Asian Crisis.

Further, while many of the regional financial institutions involve the US, given the attempt to avoid US influence in the region it is unlikely that the US would be a member as it is in APEC. Given the power of the US, it appears relatively difficult to completely avoid it. Key players would also need to determine the place of Taiwan. Noble and Ravenhill (2000) suggest "Taiwanese participation is very unlikely to be acceptable to China" (p. 31) Rajan (2000) acknowledges that "[i]n the end, however, membership is going to be determined at least partly by geopolitical considerations and biases rather than pure economic rationale" (p. 15).

Finally, the role of the AMF in aiding the move towards a common currency for Asia also needs to be resolved. Should a common currency be adopted in East Asia, the AMF would have a significant role in managing monetary policy. Research developing the type of functionalities and responsibilities that the AMF would play is warranted in this context. Serious consideration of how the varying national financial architectures could sustain collective policy is also imperative.

NOTES

1. For example, controlling capital flows through adequate regulation and matching of maturities can prevent unexpected shocks. The focus of this paper is on constructing institutions to respond to shocks where these elements do not exist.

2. While domestic institutions also played a significant role in causing the Crisis and will have a role in preventing future crises, the focus of this paper is on the role of the IMF. Other than those issues discussed under the section dealing with 'Causes', further discussion is beyond the scope of this paper.

3. It is not the purpose of the paper to dissect every decision that the IMF made during the Asian Financial Crisis. See Stiglitz (2002) for a commentary on the main criticisms of IMF prescriptions made during the crisis.

4. Figures provided in the appendix.

5. Eichengreen (1999) suggests that the IMF is "excessively politicized" with its programmes in Mexico serving "the interests of creditor countries by providing financial assistance that allowed foreign portfolio investors to be repaid at the expense of the taxpayers in the crisis country" (pp. 31–32). See also Meltzer (1998).

Further, there are implications that for Russia "IMF policies were used to further US security objectives rather than in the pursuit of financial stability" (Eichengreen, 1999, p. 32).

6. See Park and Wang (2001) for a discussion of the some of the challenges that confront the reform of the quota-voting system.

7. See Zakaria (1994) for a further discussion of Asian values with views from Lee Kuan Yew.

8. Further, new facilities aimed at rapid action such as *contingent lines of credit* have been initiated. See IMF (2001) for more detailed discussion.

9. Certainly, if the AMF were seen as a way of maintaining the negative aspects of relationship-based financial transactions, so prevalent in Asia, then moral hazard concerns would arise. This appears less likely considering the reforms to national banking systems taking place. Perhaps, the encouragement of AMF is supported by chaebols in Korea and of keiretsu in Japan.

10. Controlled through regulation, private sector monitoring and imposing cost on those that make mistakes.

11. Several cases highlight this point: China and the South China Sea, the invasion of Cambodia by Vietnam, lingering memories of Japanese cruelty during WWII.

12. Indonesia, Malaysia, Philippines, Singapore and Thailand. Brunei Darussalam joined on 8 January 1984, Vietnam on 28 July 1995, Laos and Myanmar on 23 July 1997, and Cambodia on 30 April 1999.

13. http://www.aseansec.org/7069.htm.

14. Australia; Brunei Darussalam; Canada; Chile; People's Republic of China; Hong Kong, China; Indonesia; Japan; Republic of Korea; Malaysia; Mexico; New Zealand; Papua New Guinea; Peru; The Republic of the Philippines; The Russian Federation; Singapore; Chinese Taipei; Thailand; United States of America; Vietnam.

15. Australia, China, Hong Kong, Indonesia, Japan, South Korea, Malaysia, New Zealand, the Philippines, Singapore and Thailand.

REFERENCES

Amyx, J. (2000). Political impediments to far-reaching banking reforms in Japan: Implications for Asia. In: G. Noble & J. Ravenhill (Eds), *The Asian financial crisis and the architecture of global finance* (pp. 132–151). Cambridge: Cambridge University Press.

Bank for International Settlements (BIS). (2003). *Launch of the Asian Bond Fund.* http://www.bis.org/press/p030602b.htm.

Batten, J., & Kim, Y. H. (2000). Expanding long-term financing through bond market development: A postcrisis policy task. *Asian development bank conference on government bond markets and financial sector development in developing Asian economies*, 28–30 March.

Bayoumi, T., Eichengreen, B., & Mauro, P. (1999). On regional monetary arrangements for ASEAN. *Prepared for the ADB/CEPII/KIEP conference on exchange rate regimes in emerging market economies, Tokyo,* 17–18 December.

Beck, T., & Levine, R. (2002). Industry growth and capital allocation: Does having a market- or bank-based system matter? *Journal of Financial Economics, 64*, 147–180.

Beeson, M. (1999). Reshaping regional institutions: APEC and the IMF in East Asia. *Pacific Review, 12*(1), 1–24.

Beeson, M. (2001). Globalization, governance, and the political-economy of public policy reform in East Asia. *Governance: An International Journal of Policy and Administration, 14*(4), 481–502.

Bergsten, C. F., & Park, Y. C. (2002). *Toward creating a regional monetary arrangement in East Asia.* Asian Development Bank Institute Research Paper 50.

Bhagwati, J. (1998). The capital myth: The difference between trade in widgets and dollars. *Foreign Affairs, 77*(3), 7–12.

Calomiris, C. (1998). The IMF's imprudent role as lender of last resort. *The Cato Journal, 17*(3), 275–294.

Chang, L., & Rajan, R. (2001). The economics and politics of monetary regionalism in Asia. *ASEAN Economic Bulletin, 18*(1), 103–118.

Claessens, S., Djankov, S., & Lang, L. (2000). The separation of ownership and control in East Asian Corporations. *Journal of Financial Economics, 58*, 81–112.

Cohen, B. (2000). Taming the phoenix? Monetary governance after the crisis. In: G. Noble & J. Ravenhill (Eds), *The Asian financial crisis and the architecture of global finance* (pp. 192–212). Cambridge: Cambridge University Press.

Corden, W. M. (2001). The world financial crisis: Are the IMF prescriptions right? In: S. Horowitz & U. Heo (Eds), *The political economy of international financial crisis* (pp. 41–61). Singapore: Institute of Southeast Asian Studies.

Eichengreen, B. (1997). International monetary arrangements: Is there a monetary union in Asia's future? *Brookings Review, 15*(2), 33–35.

Eichengreen, B. (1999). Strengthening the international financial architecture: Where do we stand? Prepared for the East–West center workshop on international monetary and financial Reform, Honolulu, 1–2 October.

Eichengreen, B. (2000). The International Monetary Fund in the wake of the Asian crisis. In: G. Noble & J. Ravenhill (Eds), *The Asian financial crisis and the architecture of global finance* (pp. 170–191). Cambridge: Cambridge University Press.

Eichengreen, B. (2003). What to do with the Chang Mai Initiative? Asian economic papers, Winter.

Feldstein, M. (1998). Refocusing the IMF. *Foreign Affairs, 77*(2), 20–33.

Fischer, S. (1999). On the need for an international lender of last resort. *Journal of Economic Perspectives, 13*(4), 85–104.

Haggard, S. (2001). Politics, institutions and globalization: The aftermath of the Asian financial crisis. *American Asia Review, XIX*(2), 71–98.

Higgott, R. (1998). The politics of economic crisis in East Asia: Some longer term implications. *Centre for the Study of Globalisation and Regionalism Working Paper, 2*, 1–21.

Horowitz, S., & Heo, U. (2001). Explaining precrisis policies and postcrisis responses: Coalitions and institutions in East Asia, Latin America, and Eastern Europe. In: S. Horowitz & U. Heo (Eds), *The political economy of international financial crisis* (pp. 3–13). Singapore: Institute of Southeast Asian Studies.

Hughes, C. (1999). *Japanese policy and the East Asian currency crisis: Abject defeat of quiet victory?* Centre for the Study of Globalisation and Regionalisation Working Paper No 24, 1–53.

International Monetary Fund (IMF). (2001). Public Information Notice (PIN) No. 01/92, http://www.imf.org/external/np/sec/pn/2001/pn0192.htm.

International Monetary Fund. (2002). *Direction of trade statistics yearbook*, Washington.

International Monetary Fund. (2003). *International Financial Statistics*, Vol. LVI, 7 July.

Kahler, M. (2000). The new international financial architecture and its limits. In: G. Noble & J. Ravenhill (Eds), *The Asian financial crisis and the architecture of global finance* (pp. 235–260). Cambridge: Cambridge University Press.

Kohler, H. (2002). Reform of the international financial architecture: A work in progress, Speech given at the Central Bank Governors' Symposium, Bank of England Conference Center, July 5, http://www.imf.org/external/np/speeches/2002/070502.htm.

King, M. (1999). Reforming the international financial system: The middle way, money marketeers at the Federal Reserve Bank of New York, 9 September.

Kuroda, H., & Kawai, M. (2003). *Strengthening regional financial cooperation in East Asia.* Pacific Economic Papers, forthcoming.

La Porta, R., Lopez-De-Silanes, F., Shleifer, A., & Vishny, R. (1998). Law and finance. *Journal of Political Economy, 106*(6), 1113–1155.

Levine, R. (1997). Financial development and economic growth: Views and agenda. *Journal of Economic Literature, XXXV*(June), 688–726.

Lipscy, P. (2003). Japan's Asian Monetary Fund proposal. *Stanford Journal of East Asian Affairs, 3*(1), 93–104.

Little, J. S., & Olivei, G. (1999). Rethinking the international monetary system: An overview. New England Economic Review November/December, 3–24.

Manzano, G. (2001). Is there any value-added in the ASEAN surveillance process? *ASEAN Economic Bulletin, 18*(1), 94–102.

McFarlane, B. (2001). Politics of the World Bank-International Monetary Fund nexus in Asia. *Journal of Contemporary Asia, 31*(2), 214–240.

Meltzer, A. (1998). Asian problems and the IMF. *The Cato Journal, 17*(3), 267–274.

Moskow, M. (2002). Symposium keynote address: Financial infrastructure in emerging economies. *Journal of Financial Intermediation, 11*, 354–361.

Narine, S. (2002). ASEAN and the idea of an "Asian Monetary Fund": Institutional uncertainty in the Asia Pacific. Paper for UNU Seminar 'Non-Traditional Security in Asia: Governance, Globalization, and the Environment', 15 March.

Noble, G., & Ravenhill, J. (2000). Causes and consequences of the Asian financial crisis. In: G. Noble & J. Ravenhill (Eds), *The Asian financial crisis and the architecture of global finance* (pp. 1–35). Cambridge: Cambridge University Press.

Nordhaug, K. (2002). Regional economic integration, US hegemony and East Asian regionalism. Paper for the XIII nordic political science association meeting, Aalborg, 15–17 August.

OECD, (1998). Report of the working group on international financial crises. http://www.oecd.org/subject/fin_architecture/ebooks/ifcrep.pdf.

Park, Y. C. (2000). Beyond the Chiang Mai Initiative: Rationale and need for decision-making body and extended regional surveillance under the ASEAN + 3 framework. ASEAN + 3 deputies meeting, Bangkok, 22 October. http://sobac.kornet.net/~ycpark/pub/00bc.pdf.

Park, Y. C., & Wang, Y. (2001). What kind of international financial architecture for an integrated world economy. Asian Economic Panel, 26–27 April, Cambridge, MA, USA, pp. 1–70.

Pauly, L. (2001). Reforming global governance. CIS Working Paper 2001–2004.

Rajan, R. (2000). Examining the case for an Asian monetary fund. CIES Discussion Paper 0002.

Rogoff, K. (1999). International institutions for reducing global financial instability. *Journal of Economic Perspectives, 13*(4), 21–42.

Sakakibara, E. (2000). East Asian crisis – Two years later. *12th annual bank conference on development economics,* Washington, 18–20 April.

Sen, A. (1997). Human rights and Asian values. *The New Republic, 217*(2–3), 33–40.

Stiglitz, J. (2002). *Globalization and its discontents.* Australia: Allen Lane, The Penguin Press.

Tadesse, S. (2002). Financial architecture and economic performance: International evidence. *Journal of Financial Intermediation, 11,* 429–454.

World Bank. (2000). International financial architecture: An update of bank activities. For the September 25, 2000 Development Committee, http://lnweb18.worldbank.org/DCS/DevCom.nsf/0/48b5ffa456f42b7585256959005882be/$FILE/DC-2000-20(E)-IFA.pdf.

Zakaria, F. (1994). Culture is destiny – A conversation with Lee Kuan Yew. *Foreign Affairs, 73*(2), 109–126.

APPENDIX: 2001 DIRECTION OF TRADE STATISTICS IN US MILLIONS

Imports	China	Indonesia	Japan	Korea	Malaysia	Philippines	Singapore	Thailand	Vietnam	Asia	World
China	—	3,888	483	23,389	6,205	1,945	5,143	4,713	1,011	86,183	243,521
Indonesia	3,120	—	7,046	3,608	1,719	146	3,773	1,502	302	17,440	33,511
Japan	57,780	14,883	—	17,221	12,824	6,418	5,382	10,353	2,604	148,432	349,089
Korea	13,303	4,474	26,633	—	4,126	1,819	3,011	1,589	386	36,385	141,098
Malaysia	3,804	2,241	14,211	2,958	—	1,839	9,293	2,927	318	30,924	73,866
Philippines	953	760	6,098	1,950	928	—	1,793	897	280	10,776	31,358
Singapore	7,195	a	16,091	3,823	20,094	2,555	—	5,159	4,932	49,057	116,000
Thailand	3,711	1,364	13,881	2,121	3,078	1,129	2,854	—	327	20,307	62,058
Vietnam	1,985	373	1,954	1,905	521	69	2,316	877	—	10,932	16,602

Exports	China	Indonesia	Japan	Korea	Malaysia	Philippines	Singapore	Thailand	Vietnam	Asia	World
China	—	2,827	44,958	12,521	3,220	1,620	5,792	2,337	1,804	87,601	266,620
Indonesia	3,535	—	13,530	4,068	2,038	691	7,081	1,240	389	24,621	64,874
Japan	30,948	6,405	—	25,292	11,012	8,188	14,713	11,873	1,777	161,692	403,496
Korea	18,190	3,280	16,506	—	2,628	2,535	4,080	1,848	1,732	53,182	150,439
Malaysia	3,821	1,563	11,770	2,963	—	1,288	14,913	3,360	474	38,663	88,005
Philippines	793	133	5,054	1,044	1,112	—	2,308	1,358	62	10,646	32,664
Singapore	5,329	a	9,341	4,688	21,122	3,085	—	5,304	2,105	65,098	121,751
Thailand	2,863	1,366	9,964	1,229	2,722	1,156	5,287	—	797	23,048	65,113
Vietnam	919	248	2,368	351	289	255	772	297	—	4,017	13,572

Source: IMF (2002). [a]Singapore does not report direction of trade statistics with Indonesia.

NOTES ON CONTRIBUTORS

Zaleha Abdul Shukor is a senior lecturer in Accounting at the School of Accounting, Universiti Kebangsaan Malaysia. She obtained Masters of Commerce from Macquarie Uni, Australia and BSc (Acctg) from Syracuse Univ, NY. She is pursuing her PhD at Universiti Teknologi MARA, Malaysia. Her research interests include, financial reporting and capital market-based research.

Jonathan A. Batten is Visiting Professor of Finance at Seoul National University in Korea, Professor of Management (Finance) at Macquarie University, Sydney and co-editor of Research in International Business and Finance. Jonathan has published work in many journals, including *The Journal of Business Ethics*, *The Journal of International Business Studies*, *The International Review of Financial Analysis and Physica A* and has recently co-edited a volume, *European Fixed Income Markets: Money, Bond and Interest Rate Derivatives*, as part of the Wiley Finance series.

Bonnie Buchanan is a lecturer in the Department of Finance, University of Melbourne, Australia. She obtained her PhD from the Department of Finance, University of Georgia, USA in 2000. Her research interests include corporate governance, law and finance and fraud and money laundering. She has published papers in several international finance journals, including *Research in International Business and Finance*, *Advances in Financial Economics*, *Journal of Financial Case Research* and *Journal of Financial Education*.

Tyrone M. Carlin is a professor of Management at the Macquarie Graduate School of Management (MGSM), Sydney, Australia. His current research interests lie in interdisciplinary work in the areas of corporate governance and corporate financial reporting as well as public sector financial management. He has published articles in these areas in a range of international journals including *Management Accounting Research, Financial Accountability & Management, Public Management Review, Australian Accounting Review, Sydney Law Review, University of New South Wales Law Review* and *Australian Business Law Review.* He co-edits the *Journal of Law & Financial Management.*

Jianguo Chen is a senior lecturer in the Department of Finance, Banking and Property, Massey University, New Zealand. He obtained his PhD from the department of Economics and Finance, University of Mississippi, USA in 1999. His research interests include corporate governance, capital structure, dividend policy and foreign exchange exposure in equity returns. He has published papers in several international finance journals, including *Pacific Basin Finance Journal, Quarterly Review of Economics and Finance* and *Emerging Market Finance Journal.*

Wen-Kuei Chen is the professor of graduate school of management at I-Shou University. Holding his masters degree and PhD degree from Case Western Reserve University, he has many years of experience as a senior business counselor as well as excellent achievement in stock-market research and administration. More than his academic offerings, he got the best personal honor from Chinese society for Quality in 2003.

Jing Chi is a senior lecturer in the Department of Finance, Banking and Property, Massey University, New Zealand. Jing worked in Huatai Securities Company in China for two years, responsible for IPOs and M&A, before she went to England for further studies. During her PhD study, Jing also worked part-time as Analyst in the London Stock Exchange. Jing received her PhD from the University of Reading in England in 2003. Her academic publications and research interests are in the area of Chinese IPOs, Corporate Finance, Financial Derivatives and Financial markets.

Kevin James Daly has taught on a full-time basis at the University of Brighton, University of Adelaide, the University of Western Sydney and been visiting lecturer at the National University of Ireland Galway and Dublin City University Business School. The major emphasis in his research is in the areas of financial integration, international finance, risk management and applied financial economics. Kevin has published across a broad spectrum of international journals including; *Journal of Applied Financial Economics, Australian Economic Review, Journal of Applied Financial Economics, Journal of Economic Studies, Singapore Economic Review, International Review of Financial Analysis, Review of International Business and Finance.* Kevin has published a number of books including: *Financial*

Volatility and Real Economic Activity, Ashgate 1999 and *Finance in Asia* Edward Elgar 2006.

Craig A. Ellis is currently a Senior Lecturer in Finance at the University of Western Sydney in Australia, from where he gained his PhD in 1998. His research interests include nonlinear time-series analysis, technical analysis and forecasting. He has published papers in and refereed numerous articles for international finance and econophysics journals including *International Review of Financial Analysis, Economics Letters, Physica A* and *Atmospheric Environment*.

Thomas A. Fetherston is Professor of Finance at the University of Alabama Birmingham. He is editor of the journal *International Review of Financial Analysis* and co-editor of *Research in International Business and Finance*. His previous books include *Asia-Pacific Fixed Income Markets: An Analysis of the Region's Money, Bond and Interest Derivative Markets*, co-edited with Jonathan A. Batten and published by John Wiley & Sons, Singapore. *European Fixed Income Markets and Their Derivatives*, Jonathan Batten, Thomas A. Fetherston and P.G. Szilagyi, London: John Wiley, 2004.

Guy Ford is a senior lecturer in Management at the Macquarie Graduate School of Management (MGSM), Sydney, Australia. His research areas are in the areas of risk and performance measurement, corporate finance and corporate treasury management. He has published work in these areas in international and domestic journals and presented papers at a number of international conferences. He is the co-author of two books, *Readings in Financial Institutions Management* and *Financial Markets and Institutions in Australia*. He co-edits the *Journal of Law & Financial Management*.

Abeyratna Gunasekarage is a Senior Lecturer in Finance at the Waikato Management School, New Zealand. He graduated BSc (Honors) from the University of Sri Jayewardenepura, Sri Lanka and obtained both MAcc and PhD from the University of Dundee, Scotland. He has published on dividend policy and Market efficiency in European and Australasian journals.

Pongsak Hoontrakul is distinctively known in both academic and practitioner worlds. Academically he is a senior research fellow at Sasin of Chulalongkorn University, Thailand. Capital market, derivative products, banking and financial economics are among his recent studies. His current researches are in information economics, travel industry and new economy. Internationally, he is a member of International Advisory Council of Schulich School of Business, York University, Toronto and a past member of World Economic Forum, Geneva. Commercially, Dr. Pongsak serves as a Chairman of Audit Committee and independent director of United Overseas Bank (Thai) Plc. In the political areas, his past positions included the advisor to Deputy Prime Minister (for ICT) and the advisor to the Parliament Committee for Economic Affairs and Human Rights. Currently, he is an advisor to the Senate Committee for Fiscal, Banking and Financial Institution.

Muhd Kamil Ibrahim is a Professor of Accounting of Universiti Teknologi MARA (UiTM), Shah Alam, Malaysia. He obtained his MAcc degree from the University of Dundee, Scotland, and PhD from University of Wales, Bangor. He is founder and Director of UiTM-ACCA Financial Reporting Research Center (UiTM-ACCA FRRC). Dr. Muhd Kamil has authored or co-authored four books, and more than 200 articles. Previously, he was Head of the Education Development Center, Head of the Center for Continuing Education and Dean of Faculty of Sports Science and Recreation. Currently, Dr. Muhd Kamil is Special Assistant to the Vice Chancellor.

Justin W. Iu was an Associate Lecturer in Finance with the School of Accounting, Economics and Finance at Deakin University, Australia. His research interests include the reform of the international financial architecture, corporate governance and public policy.

Bang Nam Jeon, Professor of Economics and International Business, Bennett S. LeBow College of Business, Drexel University, Philadelphia, PA. He has a PhD in Economics from Indiana University. His research interests include international commercial policy, international financial linkages, and foreign direct investment and host-country policies in Asia Pacific countries. He has published articles in various economics and international business/finance journals including *Brookings Papers on Economic Activity, Journal of international Money and Finance, Journal of Economic Integration, Journal of Asian Business, Transnational Corporations* (United Nations), *Journal of the Japanese and International Economies, Quarterly Review of Economics and Business, Journal of Economics and Business, Journal of Policy Modeling*, and *Pacific Basin Finance Journal*.

Akiko Kamesaka is an associate professor in the School of Business Administration, Aoyama Gakuin University, Japan. Her research interests include international capital flows, institutional investors and behavioral finance. She received Ibbotson Associates Japan Research Award at APFA/PACAP/FMA Finance Conference in July 2002 for her paper entitled "Investment Patterns and Performance of Investor Groups in Japan". She presented her paper entitled "The Asian Crisis and Investor Behavior in Thailand's Equity Market" at the American Economic Association meetings 2005 in Philadelphia. She has published papers in several economics and finance journals, including *Pacific Basin Finance Journal* and *Journal of Economics and Business*.

Jagjit Kaur is an Associate Professor of Accounting at Universiti Teknologi MARA (UiTM), Shah Alam, Malaysia. She obtained her Master degree from Macquarie Uni, Australia, and PhD from Deakin University (under a Deakin University Scholarship for International Students).

Colm Kearney is Professor of International Business in the School of Business Studies, and Research Associate in the Institute for International Integration Studies at Trinity College Dublin. Prior positions include Professor of Finance and Economics at the University of Technology Sydney, and Professor of Economics at the University of Western Sydney. He has published widely in the area of international finance, focussing on exchange rate systems, volatility transmission, and the new international financial architecture. His homepage is at www.internationalbusiness.ie.

Shu-Ling Lin is an Associate Professor at the Department of International Trade and Finance, Fu-Jen Catholic University. Her main research and teaching areas are financial market and institution, corporate finance, etc. in Asia Pacific countries. She has published articles in various international business/finance journals including *Research in Finance, Research in International Business and Finance, International Journal of Services Technology and Management, Collaborative Research in Econometrics and Quantitative Finance* and *Collaborative Research in Quantitative Finance, Risk Management and Econometrics*.

Ben R. Marshall is a lecturer in the Department of Finance, Banking and Property, Massey University, New Zealand. His research interests include market efficiency with respect to technical trading strategies, arbitrage within sports betting markets, the effect of investor psychology on financial markets and the relationship between liquidity and stock returns.

John McDermott is the Chief Economist at ANZ National Bank. John previously worked at the Reserve Bank of New Zealand as a Manager in the Economics Department and as member of the Monetary Policy Committee. John has also worked at the International Monetary Fund in the Research, Asian, and Middle Eastern Departments. He holds a PhD from Yale University, and has published in several fields of economics, including international finance, monetary and fiscal policy.

Hamezah Md Nor is a lecturer in Accounting at Universiti Kebangsaan Malaysia (UKM). She obtained B.Accounting and Masters Accounting from UKM. Her research interests include financial reporting, environmental reporting and capital market-based research.

Cal Muckley is a lecturer in Finance in the Department of Economics and Finance at Durham Business School. He obtained his MSc degree from Dublin City University and is currently completing his PhD dissertation at the University of Dublin, Trinity College. During his doctoral studies Cal spent periods, as a visiting doctoral scholar, both at the New York University Stern School of Business and at Tilburg University in the Netherlands. His academic publications and research interests are in the areas of international finance and applied time series econometrics.

Mukund Narayanamurti graduated with Honors in Finance from Deakin University, Australia. He currently works as a Senior Consultant at KPMG Tax Australia. He also has a research affiliation with the School of Accounting, Economics and finance at Deakin University, Australia. His research interests include the development of multiple avenues of intermediation in Asia, and the effects of financial sector development on economic growth.

David Ng obtained a Bachelor of Finance with Honors and a Bachelor of Economics majoring in Applied Econometrics in 2003 at the Macquarie University in Sydney, Australia. He is currently managing a family business.

Ben Petro has a Masters degree in Business Studies (in Banking) from Massey University and is employed at the Wellington treasury of ANZ Investment Bank.

David Power is Professor of Business Finance at the University of Dundee. He graduated BComm from the National University of Ireland, obtained his MSc from the London School of Economics and was awarded his doctorate in Stock Market Overreaction from the University of Dundee. He has published widely in international journals on corporate financial communications in both developed and emerging markets.

Mehdi Sadeghi is a lecturer in finance, the Department of Accounting and Finance, Macquarie University, Sydney Australia. He has a PhD from the University of Kentucky, United States. His research interests include, testing the efficiency of capital market, empirical application of asset pricing models, investment performance in emerging markets and financial crisis and contagion effects in emerging markets.

Peter G. Szilagyi recently joined the Faculty of Economics and Business Administration at Tilburg University in the Netherlands, where he is undertaking doctoral studies at Tilburg University in the Netherlands, and is a member of the European Corporate Governance Institute. Previously, Peter worked as a freelance correspondent with the BBC World Service and as a financial markets consultant for the Asian Development Bank. He has published in the *International Journal of the Economics of Business* and the *Journal of Corporate Citizenship* and has co-edited a volume, *European Fixed Income Markets: Money, Bond and Interest Rate Derivatives*, as part of the Wiley Finance series.

David Tripe is the Director of the Centre for Banking Studies and a Senior Lecturer in the Department of Finance Banking & Property at Massey University, Palmerston North, New Zealand. His research interests include discussion of the special features of the New Zealand banking system (with particular emphases on bank performance, efficiency and measuring competition), retail payments systems and the residential mortgage market.

Yao-Chun Tsao is the instructor of Finance and Banking at Cheng-Shiu University and PhD student in finance management program at I-Shou University in Taiwan. He was an honor MBA at Soo-Chow University in Taiwan. Prior to his academic career, he used to be an officer in the Ministry of Finance and a portfolio risk controller in Oriented Securities for many years.

Xuan Vinh Vo is currently a PhD candidate at the School of Economics and Finance, University of Western Sydney. He is an associate lecturer at the

School of Economics and Finance and a research fellow of the Australasian Finance Research Group, University of Western Sydney. Prior to this he obtained the B.Bus from the National Economics University, Hanoi and B.E. from the University of Technology, Sydney. He also achieved the Master of Applied Finance at the University of Western Sydney as the top graduate. His PhD research topic is in the field of International Financial Integration.

Yun Wang is an analyst at the Commerce Commission of New Zealand. She graduated BMS (Honors) and MMS (Finance) from the University of Waikato, New Zealand.

Martin Young is currently an Associate Professor of Finance at the College of Business, Massey University. Prior to this he spent four years as a Senior Fellow at the Nanyang Business School in Singapore. Martin has wide experience working within financial markets and was a member of the New Zealand Stock Exchange for many years. Recent academic publications and research interests are in the areas of derivative usage, returns momentum and market structure.

Yang Zhang was a research student in the Department of Finance, Banking and Property, Massey University. She obtained the Bachelor of Business Studies with Honors in 2002 and Master Degree of Business Studies – (Finance) in 2003. Currently, she is working for Bank of New Zealand Cards as an Executive Risk Analyst.

Printed in the United States
118962LV00002B/13/A

9 780762 312580